THE BEST PLAYS OF 1927-28

THE
BEST PLAYS OF 1927-28

AND THE

YEAR BOOK OF THE DRAMA
IN AMERICA

Edited by
BURNS MANTLE

NEW YORK
DODD, MEAD AND COMPANY
1966

"Strange Interlude," copyright, 1927, by Eugene G. O'Neill.
Copyright and published, 1928, by Boni & Liveright, New York.

"The Royal Family," copyright, 1927, by Edna Ferber and George Kaufman.
Copyright and published, 1928, by Doubleday, Doran & Co., New York.

"Burlesque," copyright, 1927, by George Manker Watters and Arthur Hopkins.
Copyright and published, 1928, by Doubleday, Doran & Co.

"Coquette," copyright, 1927, by George Abbott and Ann Bridgers.
Copyright and published, 1928, by Longmans, Green & Co.,
New York, London, Toronto.

"Behold the Bridegroom," copyright, 1927, by George Kelly.
Copyright and published, 1928, by Little, Brown & Co., Boston, Mass.

"Porgy," copyright, 1926-27, by Du Bose Heyward.
Copyright and published, 1928, by George H. Doran Co.
and Doubleday, Doran & Co., New York.

"Paris Bound," copyright, 1927, by Philip Barry.

"Escape," copyright, 1927, by John Galsworthy.
Copyright and published, 1928, by Charles Scribner's Sons, New York.

"The Racket," copyright, 1927, by Bartlett Cormack.
Copyright and published, 1928, by Samuel French, Ltd., New York.

"The Plough and the Stars," copyright, 1926, by Sean O'Casey.
Copyright and published, 1926, by the Macmillan Company, New York.

COPYRIGHT, 1928,
By DODD, MEAD AND COMPANY, Inc.

PRINTED IN THE U. S.

INTRODUCTION

SELECTING the ten plays best calculated to represent fairly the theatre season of 1927-28 developed at least one interesting fact. Six of the ten were still playing in mid-June and no one of the six was popular because it was either a vulgar play or over-bold.

Of the four that had already called it a season, folded up their scenes and their scrapbooks and taken to what is still romantically referred to as the road, the same could be said.

From which situation it is satisfying again to draw attention to the fact that the drama has successfully weathered another twelve-month without going nearer to the dogs than what might be called a safe barking distance.

It is not contended that all ten of these plays are puritan pure in both speech and thought. I can count five of them in which words are used that still give the less calloused of us slightly unpleasant shocks when spoken, as we quaintly used to say, in the company of ladies and gentlemen.

There are character probings and exposed souls in "Strange Interlude" that stir a kind of resentment which common sense has a difficult time crying down with some of us. But "Strange Interlude" remains the most significant drama, by an American author, produced within the memory of living men.

You and I could go all our lives without knowing the intimate home thought of a burlesque queen and with nary a peek into her dressing room and still be content. But that fact does not belittle "Burlesque" as a human and holding comedy drama dealing with these curiously interesting commonplaces of stage life.

"The Racket" is a rough melodrama about rough people, as grimy as the wainscoting of a fly-specked police station and as sordid as a night court. But it still faithfully represents a modern trend in melodrama, and truthfully, I believe, exposes a situation linking crime and politics in one American city that reflects to some degree similar situations in a half dozen other American cities that the American citizenry should know about and think about.

No, the contention is not that the theatre has swung back to its older day when plays were pretty and pure and false. But that even in its newer day of freedom of speech and morals its most representative exhibits are intelligently and decently motivated.

The fact is worth mentioning, too, that eight of the ten plays are by native American authors and that all of these reflect some phase of the American scene. The ninth play is John Galsworthy's "Escape" and the tenth Sean O'Casey's "The Plough and the Stars."

The O'Casey play is the only one in the list that was not a popular box office success. Not only does its strong racial appeal limit its public but it also met a divided public of its own.

Irish Americans are growing increasingly resentful, they tell me, of seeing the Irish stage devoted exclusively to studies of tenement types in Dublin or the peasants of the countryside. "The Plough and the Stars" also has to do with the Easter riots of 1916 and therefore naturally arouses the opposition of those who feel that it casts the burden of its sympathies either too much for or too much against the protesting republicans.

I have included the play in this book because when I came to it I liked it as a play better than any of the others remaining on my tentative list, because it is worthily representative of its type of character comedy and because I feel its author is entitled to such encouragement as he may gain from having his work recognized in the American theatre.

The episodical "Escape" is typically Galsworthian in its faithful adherence to, and its many-sided discussion of definite human attributes and weaknesses. Herein but for the grace of God stand all of us faced with the problem of either aiding in the escape or the apprehension of a convicted prisoner. Sympathetically the prisoner carries all our hopes because we know him to have been scurvily treated by the fates. But to the people in the play he is no more than a man who has broken the law, been fairly tried in an English court, found guilty and sentenced to penal servitude. As a study in character reactions "Escape" offers provocative drama.

There are, it will be noted, few light plays in this year's list. Only a single comedy of the better class arose above a mean average and only one farce of first quality appeared. The comedy is George Kaufman and Edna Ferber's "The Royal Family." The farce was George Cohan's "Baby Cyclone," which did not quite make the grade in the matter of importance.

Philip Barry doubtless thinks of his "Paris Bound" as a comedy, and there are by actual count probably more laughs in it than there are in the average comedy. But it is essentially dramatic in seriousness of problem and theme. Mr. Barry has been bold enough to challenge those wives who theoretically extol marriage as a spiritual sacrament and yet are willing to wreck whole families to revenge its statutory violation with or without extenuating circumstances. As a result he has given the tea sippers and the bridge table post mortem addicts a change of subject that, I can attest, frequently becomes excessively heated.

"Coquette" is that most effective type of comedy drama that turns suddenly and quite unexpectedly into tragedy without unduly depressing its audience. Sympathetically played, as it is by Helen Hayes, it offers the world the luxury of a good cry and stimulates its love of good drama contrived with a skillfulness that is as deliberate as it is masterly.

George Kelly's "Behold the Bridegroom" is, to some of us, an important contribution to the American drama. And yet there is proof that the greater public does not so regard it. To those who see in it an epitomizing of the devastation certain aspects of the new freedom have wrought with America's young women it is thoughtful and moving drama. To those who accept it as no more than a romantic tale of a foolish heroine who died mysteriously of a love sickness, it is of no great importance. It happens that your editor is one of the first group. Hence "Behold the Bridegroom" as one of the ten.

"Porgy" lifts the drama of native Negro life to the highest point it has yet attained, and is therefore a significant feature of the year's work. Its telling performance by an all-Negro cast is probably also indicative of something or other, but means no more to this correspondent than that the Negro, like any other human with an exhibitionist urge, if given something to do that he can do and understand, is fully capable of acquitting himself with credit to his race.

The season as a whole will probably be longest remembered as that in which "Strange Interlude" was the Pulitzer prize winner, and introduced the first of a series of Eugene O'Neill dramas unlike any that previously had been written by an American playwright. This play carries Mr. O'Neill into the third phase of his development as a creative dramatist and establishes him even more firmly at home and over seas as the first of American playwrights.

The current, or ninth, volume of "The Best Plays" includes the familiar features of the series—a comprehensive review of the theatre in various western producing centers and a complete record of the season in New York. I trust it will be found a worthy addition to those that have gone before.

B. M.

Forest Hills, L. I., June 15, 1928.

CONTENTS

CONTENTS

THE BEST PLAYS OF 1927-28

THE BEST PLAYS OF 1927-28

THE SEASON IN NEW YORK

THE theatre season of 1927-28 will probably be remembered in New York, should occasion arise to remember it, as one that started promisingly and faded hopelessly. You can count its outstanding successes on the fingers of two hands. It would require the seeds of a watermelon to tally its failures.

And still any season that can produce a "Strange Interlude," a "Royal Family," a "Coquette" and a "Porgy" cannot be said to be completely lacking in distinction.

In many years of playgoing I have never known a season to break so completely shortly after the holidays. Nor do I remember any other season in which managers were forced to depend so desperately upon the revival of older successes and the all-starred circus affairs organized to prick the interests of bargain seekers and sentimentalists.

There were practically half a hundred old plays revived and old, but recent, successes returned to the competition. None of these did well, except the revival of "Our Betters" with Ina Claire. This was practically a new play in that it was played originally but a few weeks while the great war was in progress and withdrawn quickly once the unpopularity of its subject was proved. This subject is that of the rapacity of the female American vulgarian when title-hunting abroad. We were race conscious in 1917 and even an amusing satire did not sit well.

Once during the season there was an echo of our older censor agitations that promised some excitement. You may recall that a year ago our District Attorney, having been steamed into activity by this and that agency of protective reform, closed three plays of questionable morals, forced the withdrawal from the stage of one of them and sent the producers and chief actors of the other two to the workhouse.

As a result of that agitation, and following an unsuccessful attempt on the part of producers and playwrights to establish a protective censorship of their own, a bill was slipped through the

3

legislature known as the Wales padlock law. This gives the designated authorities power not only to arrest and bring to trial the producers and performers engaged in the presentation of a questionable play, but also, upon conviction, to padlock the theatre in which the play is given for a year.

The first play to attract the District Attorney this season was one called "Maya," a story of scarlet sisters operating close to the docks of Marseilles. Complaint being made that "Maya" "tended to corrupt the morals of youth," the District Attorney sent an assistant to see it. The assistant reported against it and it was ordered closed. Rather than stand the risk of having the theatre padlocked for a year the producers did not even appeal the case.

Complaint was also lodged against "Strange Interlude" and "Volpone," both Theatre Guild productions. But the District Attorney, after investigation, wisely refused to take any action against these plays and intimated that he did not intend that cranks or other social reform extremists should be permitted to belittle the law by overworking it.

Picking up the record where we left it in the previous volume of this series we find there were only a couple of summer stragglers the latter half of June, 1927. One was something colored called "Bottomland," which played the Princess for three weeks, and the other a "Bare Facts of 1927" revue which the indefatigable and not easily discouraged Kathleen Kirkwood, lessee of the Triangle Theatre in Greenwich Village, insists on doing each year.

Taking one July with another, that of 1927 was fairly active. The Messrs. Shubert could no longer restrain their producing urge and so came in with "Padlocks of 1927" the day after the country celebrated its independence by going swimming and automobiling. This revue brought Texas Guinan, the little girl with the great big hands, back to the stage after she had made several night clubs famous. Miss Guinan rode a horse, sang songs and jollied the audiences for nigh onto one hundred performances and then went back to her night clubs. She made the horse nervous, but the audiences soon got used to her.

Nothing very good followed for several weeks. A Miller and Lyles colored revue called "Rang Tang" played thirteen weeks at the Royale, and another at Daly's called "Africana" continued for seven weeks. "The Manhatters," semi-amateur and demi-clever, started in Greenwich Village and was moved uptown later for a run of ten or eleven weeks.

August's record did not amount to much, either. Eleven hopeful entertainments began the season that month, mostly the last two weeks. The best of them, as is frequently the case, was Mr. Ziegfeld's annual "Follies," with Eddie Cantor giving the major portion of the show. Four months later Mr. Cantor discovered that he was working much too hard and collapsed. Mr. Ziegfeld intimated that the collapse was at least partly commercial and due to Eddie's belief that, giving most of the show, he should also get most of the money. Charges were filed and suits threatened. Finally Mr. Cantor went to bed and the "Follies" with him. Equity investigated, there was a settlement in favor of Mr. Ziegfeld and then the comedian and the manager made it up.

A second summer revue was called "Allez-oop" and boasted a J. P. McEvoy base. There was an almost good melodrama called "Tenth Avenue" which started the fifteenth and ran for eleven weeks, coming to New York heavy with Chicago praise.

It was in August that Rosalie Stewart, for long the director of the George Kelly productions, thought she, too, would take a hand at producing a revue. She evolved one called "A la Carte." The Broadway smarties did not think much of it, which cost Miss Stewart considerable worry and a bankful of pennies.

By September the time was ripe for a hit and Arthur Hopkins furnished it with "Burlesque" the very first day of the month. This rowdy and human melodrama of the burlesque theatres, vividly enlivened by the performances of Barbara Stanwyck and Hal Skelly, ran the season through. It was never as big a success as "Broadway," the pacemaker of the year before, but it is, at this June writing, still popular and profitable.

The first musical comedy success, developing riotous tendencies, followed a week later when an impressively youthful affair called "Good News" danced into 46th Street. It was still dancing almost as riotously as this volume was headed for the printer's.

A loyal Dickensian, Frank Reilly by name, staged a rich and handsome version of "Pickwick" at the Empire on the 5th. At the end of a slightly forced run of nine weeks Mr. Reilly still had his handsome production and his faith in the immortal novelist. But that was about all.

The Shuberts brought in their patriotic operetta built around the Barbara Frietchie legend and called "My Maryland" on the 12th. It was a bigger hit out where America begins than it was in New York, but it managed to stay the season through.

Hits were frequent the last two weeks of September. Bayard Veiller's "The Trial of Mary Dugan" was the greatest of them, and is still running. Another was Lothar's audacious comedy, "The Command to Love," a third the Ed Wynn show "Manhattan Mary," a fourth George Cohan's musical comedy "The Merry Malones," and a fifth marked the return of the popular Gleason family to recite the small time adventures of "The Shannons of Broadway."

A tough, rough drama of the cheaper lodging houses called "Women Go On Forever" made a fight for recognition but could win over only the freer spirits, and John Golden barely missed a success with "Four Walls," in which the Yiddish actor, Muni Weisenfrend, scored a personal success.

This was the month Robert Milton flirted with a potential sensation. He thought a melodrama whittled from the Samuel Hopkins Adams' book, "Revelry," and supposed to reveal scandals of the Harding administration, would create a furore. But it didn't. The excitement created was slight and the play closed in six weeks.

Another disappointment to its promoters was Somerset Maugham's "The Letter," a close-knit murder drama with Katherine Cornell as the heroine. A fine performance but a drama of negative appeal. It was through as soon as the considerable Cornell public had been exhausted.

There had been thirty new plays and two important revivals in September. October, catching the season in its healthiest and most exciting stride, produced thirty-four plays that were new and three that were considered worth trying again. Thirty-seven major productions in a single month is a record of some kind or other. At least the figures have never previously been duplicated hereabouts.

Nothing startling came with the thirty-four new plays, unless we accept Dorothy and DuBose Heyward's picturesque colored drama "Porgy," with which the Theatre Guild began its season's work. This proved a venture in which the playgoers' interest builded consistently through the season.

Walter Hampden began with a revival of Ibsen's "An Enemy of the People," which he played for 127 performances. Arthur Hopkins suffered a failure with "The House of Women," dramatized from a popular Louis Bromfeld novel, and David Belasco went down by the pocketbook with a boldly psycho-analytical study written by William Hurlbut and called "Hidden." In this Beth Merrill played a sadly repressed spinster who finally stole her sister's husband.

Basil Sydney and Mary Ellis, starting bravely as a repertoire company at the Garrick, revived "The Taming of the Shrew" in modern clothes and built up so amusing a farce with it that they played on happily for twenty-three weeks. The other Hopkins, Charles, produced an A. A. Milne fantasy, "The Ivory Door," at his funny little theatre in 49th Street and, with the encouragement of the minor brokers, it ran through the season.

There was one fairly ordinary melodrama, "Interference," saved by an extraordinary cast, and a popular Galsworthy drama, "Escape," which Leslie Howard carried through till spring. There was a nice, human little comedy about golf for golfers called "The Nineteenth Hole," written by Frank Craven, and one musical comedy that made a run of it, "The Five O'Clock Girl." It was in October, too, that the first of the weird dramas started. This was "Dracula," the vampire piece, and it lasted all winter. It was in October, too, that Eva Le Gallienne called in the Civic Repertory company and began her season with a creditable revival of Heijerman's "The Good Hope."

Max Reinhardt did a lot for the November record. He had scored, as you remember, an impressive success in 1924 with "The Miracle." Now he came with a shipload of actors and tons of scenery direct from four or five of the principal German theatres. From the billing you gained the impression that whenever Mr. Reinhardt leaves Germany and takes his actors with him the theatre either goes completely into mourning or dolefully pegs along pending his return.

Whatever it did to Germany, the Reinhardt invasion of America on this occasion was impressively complete. He again took over the Century Theatre, refitted it back of the curtain with his patented circular platform stage and produced the German version of Shakespeare's "Midsummer Night's Dream." More gorgeously novel pictures and more funny sounds came out of this revival than had ever before been seen and heard in a Shakespearean revival in America and we were all wonderfully stirred. The scenes were Reinhardt's but the sounds were German.

The German stage master triumphed twice after that opening, once with "Everyman," the gifted Alexander Moissi playing the title rôle, and a second time with "Danton," with Paul Hartman in the name part. Then he moved down to the Cosmopolitan Theatre and staged a series of plays in the more intimate manner of the continental drama, permitting his actors to score, particularly with the German and German-American publics.

It was in November that Helen Hayes clinched the hold upon stardom that she had gained the year before with "What Every Woman Knows." She appeared in a new drama of the south called "Coquette." George Abbott wrote it, as more fully appears in other pages of this volume, from a story outlined by Ann Bridgers. "Coquette" ran the season through and was scheduled to continue right through the summer.

Arthur Hammerstein managed to complete the music temple he has built in memory of his father by the last of the month, and dedicated it with a production of "Golden Dawn," an operetta that missed wide popularity but ran nicely until spring. There were two other lighter weight musical pieces of the jazz school that were extremely popular, "A Connecticut Yankee" and one called "Funny Face" with the Astaires. "Take the Air," produced by Gene Buck, bringing a popular comedian named Will Mahoney over from vaudeville, also got better than two hundred performances.

The Irish Players came again with two Sean O'Casey plays, "The Plough and the Stars" and "Juno and the Paycock." Their artistic success was pronounced but the financial support vouchsafed them was nothing we can brag about.

Philip Barry suffered a failure that hurt both him and his defenders, a Biblical drama named "John," after the Baptist whom it concerned. A fine, honest work none too wisely cast. A bit of pearl-casting, as Ashton Stevens would say, before Broadway.

The Theatre Guild's acting company, headed by the increasingly popular Alfred Lunt and Lynn Fontanne, came home in November and brought its revival of Shaw's "The Doctor's Dilemma," setting the subscribers all a-titter. Billie Burke emerged from a periodic retirement to decorate a slight but amusing piece called "The Marquise" and a new playwright, Bartlett Cormack, came down from Chicago to score immediately with a cuss-and-crook melodrama about Chicago called "The Racket."

Around holiday time it seemed as though the producers of the town had gone slightly mad. New plays were coming in at the rate of six, eight and ten a week and going out almost as fast. During December there were, counting four revivals of importance, thirty-six attractions added to the one hundred and ten already produced since the opening of the season in August. And that was so much more than enough to satisfy everybody that the season practically began to curl up right there.

Interesting things happened in this December rush, however. For one thing three of what we are pleased to classify as the best plays of the season, and to include in this deathless volume, were produced that month—the George Kaufman-Edna Ferber "Royal Family," George Kelly's "Behold the Bridegroom" and Philip Barry's "Paris Bound."

"The Royal Family" had been touted from afar, but "Paris Bound" was a pleasant surprise, especially to young Barry, after the failure of his "John." "Behold the Bridegroom" divided the Kelly camp into two factions, one for and the other against the play. But it never went so very well with that portion of the general public that prefers to keep its caviare in Russia.

Christmas week there were seventeen new plays introduced to New York, eleven of them being offered Monday night. Which also is a record of sorts. One of the seventeen was the enormously successful "Show Boat."

Comparatively few of these plays lived to anything resembling their expectancy. One of the exceptions was another play about the theatre folk themselves, a vivid little piece called "Excess Baggage," written by John McGowan of the varieties and having to do with the adventures of the small timers in vaudeville. This one played the season out.

January tried to keep up the December record, but could do no better than twenty-seven new plays and five revivals. In this group I find but two hits of major proportions. One was the Pulitzer prize selection, Eugene O'Neill's "Strange Interlude," and the other a third Ziegfeld production, "Rosalie," with Marilyn Miller starred and Jack Donohue featured.

The Theatre Guild did fairly well with another O'Neill opus, "Marco's Millions," which was revealed on the 9th. Robert Sherwood's "The Queen's Husband," which everybody was hoping and rather expecting would duplicate the success of "The Road to Rome," did no better than fairly well and there were many expensive failures. Two seemed to me to be unfortunate. While "The Patriot," Alfred Neumann's vivid picture of the crash of Paul I of Russia, lacked popular appeal it was handsomely produced, splendidly acted and of a steadily mounting dramatic interest. It lasted but two weeks. And I thought Vincent Lawrence's "A Distant Drum" a much better drama than the buying public thought it. Eleven performances and it, too, was gone.

Beatrice Lillie's personal popularity stretched out the run of "She's My Baby" past nine weeks, and "A Free Soul" stayed on for a hundred performances when William A. Brady injected himself into the cast to play a slightly alcoholic lawyer.

It was in January that George Arliss played his long-promised Shylock in "The Merchant of Venice." His critics were respectfully polite, his friends a little disappointed, his business fair. And yet so genuinely fond of him is this fine actor's public that his road success seems assured.

The weakening quality of the new plays forced another five revivals in February, several of them played as return engagements. Joe Cook, the vaudeville comedian who has been definitely headed for stardom since first he left the short turns and encores entertainment and took up with Mr. Carroll's "Vanities," came to town the 9th with a piece called "Rain or Shine." It proved jazzy, noisy and common, but Joseph made it one of the most desired of the season's fun shows and can evidently continue with it another season at the same stand if he elects to do so.

Another mystery, "The Silent House," sent forth the shivering word that here was one that positively guaranteed a spinal massage, and played on prosperously for the next six months. George Cohan produced a comedy with characteristic touches called "Whispering Friends" which fell a trifle short of being the big success he had hoped and predicted for it.

The most successful of the revivals was that of "Our Betters," the Somerset Maugham exposé of American title hunters in London which was a failure here during the war. For the revival Ina Claire took over the rôle of the loose-moraled and scheming fascinator, Lady Grayson, and her personal success, coupled with that of Constance Collier, playing a caricatured American dowager, carried the play for sixteen prosperous weeks. It was in February that "Maya" was produced and closed by the district attorney, threatening another censor war that never quite came to a head.

At the end of the month David Belasco, who had been unduly quiescent for some weeks, stepped forth with a comedy written by Edward Childs Carpenter and called "The Bachelor Father." Being light and gay, touched with a slight boldness in speech and situation, and having June Walker to play its heroine, the comedy was a popular leader from its first performance.

Laurette Taylor came back to the theatre the first week in March. She had been on a quiet search for plays and had found one that she thought would do in a piece called "The Furies," written by Zoe Akins. Rather a fantastic melodrama, this one, and a little difficult for the crowd to accept. Miss Taylor's personal popularity helped greatly in carrying it for six weeks.

Mr. Ziegfeld again came dashing to the rescue of an already fading season with the musicalized version of "Three Musketeers." This, too, is set to continue through the summer and possibly next season, thanks partly to the personal success Dennis King has scored as D'Artagnan.

Walter Hampden made a production of "King Henry V" at his

home theatre and rallied the Shakespeareans with moderate success and the Mrs. Fiske-Otis Skinner-Henrietta Crosman revival of "The Merry Wives of Windsor" had three fair weeks at the Knickerbocker. The Sydney-Ellis players added an interesting bit in the production of Bruno Frank's "Twelve Thousand."

That the play list was fading, however, is proved by the fact that seven of the scanty twenty-one March shows were revivals of the classics or older successes.

The season, by April, had gone to pieces. The rush of new plays the early months had apparently not only exhausted the supply but had drawn so heavily upon the resources of the managers that they were forced in the cause of economy to fill in the open theatre spaces with more revivals and cheaply backed experiments.

The Guild brought forward a rowdy old Ben Jonson piece, "Volpone," as its spring production and that was interesting. George Tyler brought in his starred revivals of "She Stoops to Conquer" and "Diplomacy." The first was stupid entertainment and not well supported, but the second went much better and continued on for several weeks.

An incident of the month was a comedy of old Bowery days called "Diamond Lil." Mae West, the "Sex" lady of other years, was star and part author, and so amusing did that portion of society that takes its thrills vicariously find the old wasp-waist-and-bustle period drama that it made a fad of being seen in attendance. Billie Burke also came in from Hastings-on-Hudson to play the heroine of a comedy called "The Happy Husband" at the Empire.

At the end of April the first of the music shows intended for the summer trade were produced. Lew Fields, of Weberfields memories, having taken a lease on the Mansfield Theatre, offered there a kind of successor to "Hit the Deck" called "Present Arms," which pleased the crowds, and Aarons and Freedley brought in one called "Here's Howe" that had some, but not enough, snap.

Jane Cowl, having been touring since January, brought "The Road to Rome" back for additional weeks at the Playhouse. The Actor-Managers, organized by those who had had a hand in building up the Neighborhood playhouse productions, produced their annual "Grand Street Follies," spotted again with clever imitations and burlesques of the Broadway season, and the Guild's "Porgy," after several weeks in Boston, came back to continue at the Republic.

The Players' club revival of "The Beaux' Stratagem" at Hamp-

den's was the real event of the spring. For once there was a real
interest in this annual club celebration, an interest inspired this
time by the novelty of the revival and sustained by the quality
of the entertainment. The cast was of a familiar brilliance and,
being wisely chosen, seemed of something more than customary
competence. It included Lyn Harding, Fay Bainter, Helen Menken, Raymond Hitchcock, James T. Powers, Henrietta Crosman,
Wilfred Seagram, Dorothy Stickney, O. P. Heggie, William Courtleigh and other notables of the stage.

So another theatre season is brought arbitrarily to a June 15
close. It was nothing much to brag of, as seasons go, nor one of
which we are exactly ashamed. As we say of the comedies that
don't quite come off, it was fairly stupid, but it had its points.

Including the revivals, of which I count forty, there were two
hundred and seventy productions made during the season. It may
interest you to know that the statisticians also present figures to
prove that of two hundred plays classed as new and, in a manner
of speaking, original, one hundred and thirty-six were failures, and
only twenty-eight acknowledged box office successes.

This leaves thirty odd to be admitted as moderately successful,
and brings the season's average to what it usually offers—three
failures for each success.

THE SEASON IN CHICAGO

By Virginia Dale
Dramatic Critic, *Chicago Journal*

THE federal census bureau certifies Chicago's population at more than 3,100,000 at the middle of this year of grace 1928 and thus bulwarks what is known as civic pride and stimulates enthusiasm for the ornamental features of metropolitan life. The urge of beauty and business has set going a movement for a second world's fair, in 1933, on a necklace of shining islets off our curving south shore.

As the capital of the prairies, the dominant port at the headwaters of the St. Lawrence drainage system, the first railroad town, and the leading center of postal and commercial aviation in the western world, this considerable settlement, lifting its towers over what was, a century ago, the hunting ground of the bronze Potawatamies, adds nearly 100,000 to its population every twelve months at the expense of the cornlands and the villages near and far. In industry and commerce, in banking and butchering, in the building of museums, aquariums, zoos, race tracks, golf clubs, motor speedways, dance halls, parks and playgrounds, opera houses, de luxe hotels and whatever goes into the making of a seat of trade and culture, this city, backed by a great cluster of satellite towns, advances at a dizzy pace and envisions a dazzling future.

But where does the theatre come in? Less than a hundred plays, of both the tuneless and the lyric varieties, serve this capital's demands in a season. From Labor Day to Labor Day, Chicago, with all its vast population and its measureless wealth, and with the millions of people and billions of riches of the spreading American interior to draw upon, requires only a few more shows than are needed to fill the theatres of New York City on any night in the season.

So, it falls to the Island of Manhattan to lead in the provision of theatrical entertainment, while all the rest of the land within safe traveling distance of the premier seaport remains dependent upon it for such blessings as may be discovered with a ticket of admission. For a generation now other cities have talked of freeing themselves from the Knickerbocker dictatorship, and there's scarcely a town between Skowhegan and San Diego which has not had the daring to call itself a producing center, whatever that is. This tendency to rebellion has gone little farther than to propagate a lush crop of so-called Little theatres, *soi disant* keepers of the theatrical palladium. These do not go far, for the great majority of them are afflicted with an obsession for little plays, with inept direction, with intolerable acting. They rise, flourish a short time, then go into a slow decline. The necrology of Little theatres in America would overflow this volume; their tombstones dot the land. But like mushrooms which spring from decay, new Little theatres sprout from the bones of the old, and the eternal amateur finds a platform on which to hold his distorting mirror up to nature.

The irking domination of New York has led Chicago time and again to rattle its chains. All the actors of its Little theatres, living and dead, would require an hour to pass a given point, marching four abreast. But out of the puny playhouse has grown a movement which steadily gathers force, and out of many failures has come a close approach to success, and Chicago begins firmly to establish, in at least one temple, a stage sufficient unto itself. More of this anon.

The numerous and various independent enterprises in the commercial theatre in Chicago are mostly history. This manager or that one, a self-appointed St. George bent upon destroying the dragon of Manhattan, has broken his sword upon its impenetrable hide, and if he has remained in the show business, so-called, he is now paying commissions to the New York booking offices.

Meanwhile the number even of Chicago's standard playhouses decreases. Since the newest of the theatres in the central or loop district was set upon its foundation three others have abandoned the drama and musical comedy for the seductive silence of the acquisitive films, even though their darting and dancing snapshots do not always find many eyes to feed upon them

Though the number of theatres in Chicago devoted to the fine frenzies of the horizontal stage are scarcely five per cent. of the number allotted to the narrative pictures of the vertical screen, they have been unable in the season now closing to find a sufficient supply of shows to keep their lights burning. Most of them are closed at the end of June; many suffered costly periods of darkness at midseason.

So, the ills that afflict the theatre in Chicago are not all due to lack of interest and dull inattention on the part of the public, nor to the competition of the cinema, nor the rivalry of the opera, nor of the recitalists, nor of vaudeville. They are due, rather, to the failure of New York to justify its domination of the theatrical field. The fountain runs dry, whereas it should have a copious flow which would keep filled the basins around which gather the thirsty natives from Boston to San Francisco. New York is so preoccupied with keeping its own countless playhouses open that even by dint of great industry it cannot meet the demands made upon it by other cities.

Where producers of plays are huddled together they are inclined to follow closely in each other's footsteps and to produce plays and musical shows of such similarity of theme and incident that, in imitation of one another, they soon glut interest and ascribe declining patronage on the road to lack of appreciation of their efforts. Thus some plays which have proven highly profitable in the metropolis fail to thrive when they go roving. Some of New York's pet shows have found only a flash of favor in Chicago. It is an old story, this, of the darling of one town being scorned by another. This is less a matter of difference of taste than of faults of distribution. The recent Chicago season began on a note of crime melodrama and held this note too long, and though an occasional play of the gunmen or the light o' loves was embraced by the public, desire was soon jaded and other plays of this ilk, not much worse than those which succeeded, died in their tracks. The mystery plays, the shriekers and shockers, the night-club gimcracks and the trap-door and coffin dramas were fed to playgoers until they were weary of all but the best of them. A quail a day for thirty days will drive any man to fasting.

Perhaps not more than two worthy plays outside the shocker class fared badly in Chicago during the season. Inexplicably, "Saturday's Children" failed to win the general attention of the public. The failure of Patrick Kearney's photographic and phonographic tragi-comedy, "A Man's Man," the best play of the year on the score of truthful writing, was not difficult to understand, for its appeal was directed here at the very class whose lives it depicted and who go to the theatre not to gaze upon their own folly and misery, but to hear themselves extolled and to learn that life is full of sweetness and light.

The dozen or so plays which had no complaint to make of the Chicago seasons were about one-fifth of the total number. Almost without exception these dozen or so were the plays which should have succeeded. The perfect acting of Ethel Barrymore in Somerset Maugham's "The Constant Wife," in which she gave more to the dramatist than he to her, could not have failed to draw the town. Jeanne Eagels, demonstrating unsuspected qualities as a comediénne in "Her Cardboard Lover," scarcely could have been punished with neglect. Laura Hope Crews, acting with uncompromising truth in Sidney Howard's "The Silver Cord," was her own best advertisement. The Theatre Guild of New York, reviving Shaw's "Pygmalion" and submitting for the first time here that author's "The Doctor's Dilemma," Molnar's "The Guardsman" and Behrman's "The Second Man," gave performances so sharply marked by individual excellence and by perfection of ensemble that the abstention of the public would have been both inexplicable and unforgivable. "Broadway," with its amusing high-lighting of a night-club hoofer and its gusts of melodramatic excitement, was assured the prosperity it enjoyed. "Lulu Belle" rode into favor because of the popularity of Lenore Ulric and David Belasco's daring obeisance to the dusky god of jazz. The lamented Holbrook Blinn built his protracted engagement in "The Play's the Thing" on his sheer ability always to be interesting. Perhaps it was through its restrained daring, rather than through its measure of fun, that "The Road to Rome," lagging at first, found its way into the best seller class for Grace George. The Irish Players readily recaptured the public with "The Plough and the Stars."

Other new plays which worthily established themselves in the standard theatres were Patrick Kearney's footlighting of Theodore Dreiser's prolix novel, "An American Tragedy"; "Excess Baggage," with its racy argot of the vaudeville set; "The Nineteenth Hole," written and acted by the competent Frank Craven; George M. Cohan's diverting farce, "The Baby Cyclone," with Grant Mitchell starring and proving again that he knows what a serious business the acting of farce always must be; and Ring Lardner's "Elmer the Great," in which Walter Huston, arriving at the season's end to bridge the summer, evinces a talent for comedy which discounts even his fine flair for the serious drama.

Lardner has built his play on the stories of the bush league baseball player which he wrote several years ago. On the stage that egomaniac comes fully to life. He is a butt of ridicule and a laughing stock but he ploughs along, an irrepressible boob, until at last trouble of his own making overtakes him and uncovers his human side, yet leaves him at the finish the bounder and the fool into which nature fashioned him. The play has mechanical flaws, but it is so accurate a picture of a curious character and so alive with amusing speech that its success anywhere at any time is assured.

Revivals played an important part in the season. The Theatre Guild's restoration of "Pygmalion" was followed by the arrival of Mrs. Fiske, Otis Skinner and Henrietta Crosman in Shakespeare's "The Merry Wives of Windsor," and Shakespeare was further served by Fritz Leiber, who came with an extensive repertory. George C. Tyler's all-star restorations of "She Stoops to Conquer" and "Diplomacy" were extraordinarily popular, the Goldsmith comedy capturing the season's record for receipts. Tyler revived Tarkington and Wilson's "The Man from Home" under the new title of "Hoosiers Abroad" but it soon failed. "Rain," "Kongo" and "A Good Bad Woman" were restaged for bargain uses at a cut-rate theatre, and the first two served their purpose while the third quickly and deservedly succumbed. Mrs. Samuel Insull, in a second attempt to establish a repertory theatre, revived A. A. Milne's "Mr. Pim Passes By" with fair results, but made an unwise choice with Shaw's "Heartbreak House" and abandoned the venture while Shaw's "The Devil's Disciple" was in rehearsal.

Other essays in production in Chicago revealed a play by Edwin Stanley and Hugh Ford, titled "It Makes a Difference." It soon expired. Kenyon Nicholson and John Golden had a good idea for their "Fly-by-Night," a comedy of a wandering "Uncle Tom's Cabin" company, but they failed to support the idea with a serviceable story and the play was soon withdrawn. A play by Jean Archibald, wearing the alluring label, "A Companionate Marriage," was staged near the season's end after having had a week of test performances at the hands of an Evanston stock company. It tells, in a somewhat random manner, the story of a liberated daughter who assumes all the responsibilities of matrimony without taking pains to go to the altar, but the youth in the arrangement makes a good woman of her by tricking her into a legal ceremony.

Other plays wholly new to the stage were entrusted to the tender mercies of other stock companies, the recrudescence of which has been a phenomenon of the season. The total abandonment of the popular price circuit houses in the outer belt and the long confinement of neighborhood entertainment to the cinemas brought about a striking rebirth of interest in the stock company, and a half dozen of these industrious organizations sprang up in old outlying theatres and in converted film palaces, all of them staging royalty plays or works hitherto unacted, and some of them alternating drama and musical comedy.

A superstock or repertory company, the one surviving major development of the Little theatre idea in Chicago, is now soundly established at the Kenneth Sawyer Goodman Memorial Theater on the lake front. The Goodman has done admirable service and has won its way, step by step, into the confidence and esteem of Chicago playgoers. Its aim is gradual growth rather than quick arrival, with the attendant danger of a hurtful decline. To say that it plans to occupy in Chicago the position held by the Theatre Guild in New York is not to say it is imitative; it is indeed a pioneering institution. It offered an even dozen plays this last season, including three, Mrs. Mowatt's "Fashion," Shakespeare's "A Midsummer Night's Dream" and the younger Dumas' "The Tower of Nesle," which, in the rotation of the repertory system, were carried over from the previous season. The company produced with much credit Sean O'Casey's "Juno and the Paycock," revived. "She Stoops to Conquer," celebrated the Ibsen centenary with capital restorations of "The Wild Duck" and "The Vikings of Helgeland," adding interest to the latter by committing the lighting to Thomas Wilfred and his Clavilux, or color organ; gave L. W. Vedrenne's "Outbreak" its first test on any stage, with indifferent consequences; introduced Luigi Chiarelli's "The Mask and the Face" to Chicago; produced "Mixed Doubles," an inept and futile dramatization, by Louis E. Laflin, Jr., of Henry Kitchell Webster's novel, "Philopena"; presented the ancient Hindu drama, "The Little Clay Cart," and created, entirely within its own precincts, a happy burlesque, "Camille in Roaring Camp," arranged by Thomas Wood Stevens, the company's director, on Dumas' famous play of the tubercular coquette. "Camille" is given a Bret Harte atmosphere by setting it on a stage in a hall in a California mining camp before an audience of Forty-niners. This burlesque was a thoroughly original conception and was brought off with great spirit. The company had previously proven in its revival of "Fashion" its flexible comedic skill.

It was by chance rather than by design that the first Chicago performances of "Juno and the Paycock" were given by the resident repertory company instead of by the peripatetic one known as the Irish Players, who, because the Goodman organization had anticipated them, deferred this piece until they had tried the temper of the public, heavily Milesian, with O'Casey's "The

Plough and the Stars," which, with the acting bestowed upon it, afforded the season one of its high lights.

Theatrical fare available beside the sweet waters of Lake Michigan is usually almost equally divided between the drama and the song and dance diversions, but this last season the plays have outnumbered the musical shows more than two to one. The serial revues made their customary annual calls, the "Chauve-Souris" revisited the midlands, a number of singing and dancing stars whose orbits lead them here every year or two found refuge within our walls for terms long or short, usually according to their merit, and Winthrop Ames sent his Gilbert and Sullivan Comic Opera company on its first visit to the Great Central Basin. The Ames company sang "The Mikado," "The Pirates of Penzance" and "Iolanthe," giving charming performances of the delectable works to gratifying patronage and loud praise, and revealed as its chief glory a chorus that was as intelligent as it was attractive.

Of the other plays and musical shows a mere list of them would more than suffice. A considerable number of them paid dividends on their Chicago engagements. But neither these nor those which gave the season its greater interest left the stage of the midwestern metropolis in a healthier state than they found it, save in the case of the Goodman, whose third season was its best.

A survey of the year produces the conviction that the New York producers in control of the show business must increase the number and improve the average quality of their *divertimenti* and devote at least as much attention to supplying with attractions the theatres of Chicago and other major cities "on the road" as they do, both as a matter of business and of personal vanity, to keeping their home playhouses filled. It is not possible, apparently, to make this city independent of New York. It has been a source of abundant revenue to the eastern producers of ability who have played the game; it should become more and more important in their reckoning.

THE SEASON IN SAN FRANCISCO

By George C. Warren

Drama-Editor *San Francisco Chronicle*

THE theatre season in San Francisco and the bay region, beginning June 1, 1927, and ending May 30, 1928, had few real premières, three professional plays only having received their first performance, with half a dozen lesser "first times" among the amateur groups and the universities; these constituting the list.

However, the year was important in the development of Pacific Coast production; the expansion of Henry Duffy's stock-production houses, and two or three sensationally successful engagements in the local theatres.

The building of the Belasco and Mayan theatres in Los Angeles, twin playhouses lying side by side on Hill Street, brought about the joining of hands and finances of Edward Belasco, brother of New York's David, and Fred J. Butler, as a producing firm that is already cutting a wide path in Coast theatricals. They have made some interesting productions; have brought original casts, or nearly original—at least the principals—out from New York for such plays as "The Racket," "The Command to Love," "The Spider," and "The Road to Rome," for which Jane Cowl and Sir Guy Standing came West. These companies play both San Francisco and Los Angeles.

This firm produced Elmer Harris' farce, "The Great Necker," which had a thirteen weeks' run in their home theatre, the Belasco, and four fair weeks in San Francisco. They were interested, too, with Homer Curran in the production of John B. Colton's "The Devil's Plum Tree," a free adaptation from a Hungarian play that had to do with one of the saints of that nation. Ruth Chatterton was its star. It had its première in San Francisco at the Curran Theater, but despite the strong personal following of Miss Chatterton its run was limited to less than three weeks.

Colton worked on the play while it was here, getting it in fair shape for the Los Angeles run of seven weeks.

20

A. H. Woods was originally interested in the venture, but he seemingly withdrew, although it is possible the piece will yet be seen in the East. As in all of Colton's work for the stage, it is bizarre in theme and treatment, having to do with a fleshly wanton married to a saint and loving a bandit, and her development into sainthood through suffering and seeing suffering.

Lillian Albertson, another of the Coast producers, had a splendidly successful season, her production of "The Desert Song" getting gross receipts not far below $1,000,000, and "Hit the Deck," another of her ventures, totaling over half a million. Her dramatic productions were less triumphant, a production of Mae West's "Sex" lasting only a week in Los Angeles, and a good presentation of "Burlesque" holding for three weeks in San Francisco, the public here being unfamiliar with burlesque, as there is no circuit for these flashly musical things on the Coast.

Sam Salvin has just come into the producing field, he having taken a lease on the Mayan Theater, Los Angeles, where he has put on "Good News" and is having a glorious beginning of his California career with that sure fire hit.

Lou Wiswell, for so long chief lieutenant of Henry W. Savage, blossomed as a producer with two of his wife's plays, she being Zelda Sears. One of these had Aimee Semple McPherson for its heroine, and is called "Undertow." Miss Sears played the evangelist's mother in the Los Angeles production, which had Elise Bartlett (Mrs. Joseph Schildkraut) for the heroine. Plans are on foot for Pauline Frederick to take up the latter rôle.

The other Sears play is a farce called "The Scarlet Woman," written for Miss Frederick and produced in San Francisco, where it had a satisfactory run. Its story is of a young woman who goes away from the small town where she had been a sort of slave to an eminent father. She remains in a great city a year, and as she is lonely there, adopts a baby at an orphanage.

Her return with the child, the suspicions of the village ladies, and the search for a possible father for the infant, make up the body of the farce's action.

The other play produced here that may probably be seen in New York is "Madame Alias," a crook comedy by Florence Hopkins and Annette Westbay (Mrs. George Scarborough) produced at the Fulton Theater, Oakland, by George Ebey, for Marjorie Rambeau. The play has a rather ingenious plot; the efforts of detectives from various States to lure a beautiful crook into their territory in order to arrest her for crimes that are not extraditable.

She poses as a woman of wealth, and the men and women trying to trap her, are disguised as merchants, agents for big concerns, newspaper folk, waiters and hotel attendants.

In one of the scenes this motley crowd sit at dinner with the lady as her guests; each hoping to put her behind bars, and she laughing at them for fools to think they are deceiving her.

The Playmakers, body of Berkeley men and women interested in the theatre, gave four programs of one-act plays written by members of the organization, staged and acted by them. A number of them were taken for publication by firms that print such things.

The Duffy expansion goes on. At present this energetic and popular actor-producer has seven theatres in his chain, with two building for his use. His string includes the Alcazar and President here; the El Capitan in Hollywood; the President, formerly Morosco's, in Los Angeles, and one house each in Seattle, Wash., Portland, Ore., and Vancouver, B. C.

A large theatre, to be called the Duffwin, is nearly ready in Oakland, and another, also to be called the Duffwin—a combination of Duffy and Winter, Dale Winter being Mrs. Duffy—is started around the corner from the El Capitan in Hollywood.

The theatres in the Northwest are run as regular weekly-change stock houses, with a policy just now of guest stars, these including Berton Churchill, Leo Carillo, Sidney Toler, Marjorie Rambeau and Norman Hackett and Marion Lord.

In San Francisco and Los Angeles Duffy puts on the domestic comedies that have had runs in New York, and for nearly a year has pursued the plan of bringing the nucleus of the original cast to act in the plays on the Coast. He is able to give the actors from fifteen to thirty weeks through the various runs.

Interesting to watch has been the development and success of the Players Guild during the season just closed. It is the inheritor of the old Players Club, and has had a continued existence of nearly twenty years, many of them struggling years played in any old place that offered, part of the time in a remodeled church, which burned down two years ago.

At present the Guild is housed in a delightful small theatre in the Western Women's Club House, a theatre seating 750, with a well-equipped stage and a comfortable auditorium.

The season began with the Guild as a semi-professional organization, playing three nights a week, and changing its bill every three weeks, but the demands of time for rehearsals and the possibilities of performances every night, made it impossible for amateurs to remain, so the performances are almost wholly professional now, and continue through the week. There are something like 2,000 subscribers at present, but a well-planned drive is being made to increase this number, it is hoped, to 10,000.

Of the thirteen productions made during the season just ended, the most successful were Sem Benelli's "The Jest," which ran beyond its allotted time and was given extra performances; Franz Werfel's "Goat Song"; Professor Paul Green's Pulitzer prize play, "In Abraham's Bosom," and George Kelly's Pulitzer winner, "Craig's Wife."

The Playhouse Association in Berkeley, home of the University of California, did some fascinating things during the year. It is housed in a converted church. Sam J. Hume is the current president of the organization and Everett Glass its director.

Revival of three plays of varying age attracted attention during the season of a dozen productions. They were "Gammer Gurton's Needle," acted by a cast of men, as it was originally presented in one of the English universities; George Farquhar's "The Beaux' Stratagem," recently done with an all-star cast in New York, and Steele Mackaye's "Hazel Kirke," which still has power to stir the emotions, although it seemed more outmoded than Farquhar's Georgian comedy.

André Ferrier's French Theatre, La Gaite Française, continues to draw good sized audiences. It has just closed its eighth season, the most important production of the year being an elaborate presentation of Paul Claudel's "L'Annonce Faite a Marie." The tiny theatre, which seats 225 people, is ideal for the more intimate French plays and is filled during the season, one week each month being devoted to playing. There is a large French population in San Francisco.

One of the surprising engagements of the season was that of Nikita Balieff's "Chauve-Souris," which in three weeks played to more than $90,000, perhaps the largest receipts the Russians have ever had in that length of time.

THE SEASON IN SOUTHERN CALIFORNIA

By Monroe Lathrop

Drama-Editor *Los Angeles Express*

TO speak of the theatrical "season" in Southern California is a misnomer. The calendar has its seasons, but not the theatre.

Nature, with her cool nights the year around, is good to the custodians of the drama and the actors.

The arbitrary line drawn through the year's activities at June 20, for pause to check up, is as good as any, although it finds more prosperous hits overlapping and more good plays and actors cruising into this haven from the idle waters of the East than in midwinter.

But casting back from this mark one looks upon an eventful year, made so chiefly by the growth of the number of so-called legitimate theatres to sixteen in Los Angeles. A record of about 125 presentations, good and otherwise, composes a chronicle of achievement not hitherto matched.

After the primary importance of the scene that is connoted in these figures, come in importance for listing as the high lights:

The eclipse of the movie in mass favor, in the very citadel of the cinema.

The growth in the number of offerings in which most of the players stepped directly from metropolitan to local boards.

The expansion of Henry Duffy as the predominant single influence in the renaissance of the spoken drama.

The gain in prestige by the Pasadena Community Players through a single brilliant achievement; the rise of Edward Everett Horton as actor-producer, and failure of Joseph Schildkraut and Fritz Feld in a similar joint effort.

The expulsion of "The Captive," and its legal bearing on the stage.

Devotees of the older form of drama are in high fettle over the growing popularity of the stage as contrasted with an unprecedented decline in interest in the movie. For the first time the picture houses complain directly of the harmful competition of the stage and accredit it with being the cause of admitted financial injury.

The movie is plainly at a crisis, with congealed forms and lack of the variety that constantly induces fresh interest in the stage. But nothing is of more potential importance both to stage and screen than the advent in the past season of the vocal picture. Some shrewd students of its possibilities who are quite free of the bias of rivalry foresee a powerful commercial foe of the stage in the new medium. Complete reproductions of musical comedies, for example, with original casts, are visioned for the near future.

Henry Duffy, with two houses in Los Angeles and another soon to rise; three in San Francisco and Oakland, and one each in Portland, Seattle and Vancouver, has gained a power and prestige in his field and with the public that have made him the greatest theatrical force on the coast. He has successfully solved the problem of presenting original part-casts from the New York stage in tested plays at popular prices.

With a canny insight into the liking of the mass he has confined himself chiefly to comedies, and has had invariable success with such pieces as "New Brooms," "Tommy," "Two Girls Wanted," "The Patsy" and "Pigs" and similar light fare all over his circuit. His extension over the coast is believed to have just begun.

Mr. Horton, with "The Wild Westcotts," "The Queen's Husband," "A Single Man" (one of Hubert Henry Davies' comedies which served Cyril Maude in England but had not before been seen on this side) has proved by long runs that he has a large and devoted following at the Vine Street Theater in Hollywood.

Mr. Schildkraut and Mr. Feld essayed to establish at the Hollywood Play House something on the order of the New York Theatre Guild. They were unfortunate in their first venture. "From Hell Came a Lady," by George Scarborough, scenically pretentious but dramatically weak, was followed by "The Second Year" and a revival of Parker's archaic "Pomander Walk" with no better results, and the enterprise folded up.

Artistically the production by the Pasadena Community Players of Eugene O'Neill's "Lazarus Laughed" was one of the high achievements of the year. Scores of volunteer workers were aided by students of the University of Southern California in outfitting more than 100 players in O'Neill's masked drama on the order of the Greek classics.

So prodigious was the undertaking that no commercial theatre was found willing to risk the world première. The outcome was a veritable triumph for the director, Gilmor Brown. Public comment on O'Neill's part ran all the way from "profoundly moving" to "solemn absurdity," but the production was so sensationally fine that it packed the Pasadena Theater for a month and was then moved to the Music Box in Hollywood for a fortnight's stay, the volunteer cast from Pasadena's business and professional life being then forced to disband.

"The Captive's" expulsion, following a stubborn fight of the producers against private and newspaper assaults and repeated arrests of the actors by the public prosecutor, might have been a mere commotion of the moment but for one result. It brought about the adoption by the City Council of an ordinance with teeth, patterned after the New York Padlock Law.

Incidentally, another of Bourdet's plays, "The Rubicon" with a new title, also barred in New York, ran unmolested for several weeks at another house.

The year was notable for premières of plays either new to the native stage or to America. The best popular success attended Zelda Sears' "The Scarlet Woman," which belies its title and is a light comedy. After touring the coast it is still serving Pauline Frederick through the middle west as a fine vehicle.

"The Devil's Plum Tree" again brought forth John Colton, author of "The Shanghai Gesture" and "Rain." Its hectic story of a Croatian nymph whose pathological sorties ceased under the benign influence of a pious husband carried little conviction. The play disappeared after its Los Angeles run, which rallied the over-sexed women and curious girls.

That fine character actress, Lucille La Verne, almost put over a new melodrama, "Salt Chunk Mary," by Jack Black, a reformed ex-convict, and Bessie Beatty. Miss La Verne's drawing of a woman fence in a border town was a personal triumph, but couldn't overcome faults of the play and supporting company.

Lajos Biro's "Hotel Imperial," successful on the continental stage, had its first American showing at the Egan with the author present, but aroused small interest with its war story whose ground has been somewhat covered by our native pieces.

"Lilies of the Field," a comedy of manners by John Hastings Turner, the English dramatist, was another première to the credit of the Pasadena Players. The play bristled with the author's wit, had numerous sharply varied characters, and thumbs went up for it as a rarely fine specimen of high comedy.

"Undertow," by Zelda Sears and Garnet Weston, based upon commercialized evangelism, had pronounced merit but arrived tardily among a plethora of pieces on its theme.

Of other premières it is necessary to say only that they came and went speedily without rippling the waters: "That Funny Little Thing," by Agnes Christine Johnston, a movie scenarist; "His Blossom Bride," a dramaless drama of Hopi Indian life with which Richard Walton Tully, author of "The Bird of Paradise," failed utterly to reëstablish himself; "Tell Me Again" (musical), by Robert Woolsey, also its star; "The Ape," a mystery play by Adam Hull Shirk; "Who?" by John Reiwarts; "Two Fellows and a Girl" (musical); "The Hell Cat," by Guy Bragdon and Tom Burroughs.

The year's pronounced hits were "Lazarus Laughed" (as a production), "Good News," "Broadway," "The Trial of Mary Dugan," "A Night in Spain," "Appearances," "The Desert Song," "Hit the Deck," "Chauve-Souris," "Sunny," "Oh, Kay," "The Command to Love," "The Racket," "Excess Baggage," "Women Go On Forever" and "The Scarlet Woman."

Unexpected failures were "Saturday's Children," "Burlesque," "The Connecticut Yankee" and "Sex"—in two instances plainly owing to miscasting.

Many lovers of the best in the theatre look back with keenest pleasure to a visit from Eva Le Gallienne's company of players, who presented "The Cradle Song" for a week to charmed but limited audiences.

The closing days of the imaginary season here sketched brings the troupe of players from the Imperial Theater in Tokyo in "Ken Geki," an exhibition of the native swords-drama so unique and amazingly executed that leading citizens voluntarily sponsored its original and repeat engagements at Los Angeles and Hollywood theatres.

A pleasant event of the year was the celebration by the "Chauve-Souris" of the twenty-fifth anniversary of the birth of that Russian Bat troupe in a small Moscow cellar. Los Angeles' large actor colony entered into the felicities of the event, which the Muscovites carried off with characteristic ebullience.

"The Pilgrimage Play," California's night spectacle sub-named "The Life of Christ," had its customary summer run, and John Stephen McGroarty's pageant-play of the Franciscan founders of California, "The Mission Play," found its seventeenth year the most prosperous of its remarkable record, which is without a parallel.

Activities of the Little theatres are at rather low ebb. Aside from two mentioned, the Pasadena group did nothing notable. The Little Theater of Los Angeles after doing "The Great Catherine" and "The Jest" has seemingly become dormant. The Hollywood Community Players has recently done Shaw's "Cæsar and Cleopatra" and Strindberg's "The Dance of Death," and Reginald Pole revived Dostoievsky's "The Idiot."

STRANGE INTERLUDE

Drama in Nine Acts

By Eugene O'Neill

THERE was little surprise expressed in theatrical New York when this year's Pulitzer play prize was given to Eugene O'Neill for his "Strange Interlude." From the date of its production by the Theatre Guild (Jan. 30, 1928) this play was generally accepted not only as the outstanding novelty of the dramatic year, but as by far the most interesting and most significant contribution to the theatre made by an American playwright within the memory of living playgoers.

In form "Strange Interlude" is a violation of accepted stage conventions only in the matter of its extreme length and in so far as it restores to an honorable place in the technique of playwriting both the aside and the soliloquy commonly used in the old-time artificial drama. It is more than a restoration, however, for asides such as those employed in this unusual play have never before been used.

Herein Mr. O'Neill has expanded the idea he first worked with in "The Great God Brown," that of presenting two personalities, or of exposing two sides of the same personality, in the one character. In "The Great God Brown" he adapted the Greek mask to his purpose. In "Strange Interlude" he permits his characters to speak a part of their secret thought aloud, in addition to their normal speech.

To differentiate between the natural speech that is intended to be heard by the other characters on the stage and that which merely expresses the thought passing in the character's mind he has worked out the simple technical form of having the stage action remain static during the time any character is thinking aloud. Puzzling and a little mystifying at first, audiences soon adapt themselves to the change and, judging from frequent report, discover an added interest in following the expressed and hidden thoughts of the people of the play.

"Strange Interlude" is divided into nine short acts. While all nine could probably be played within four hours, or between

7.30 and 11.30, both Mr. O'Neill and the producers were convinced the strain would be too great upon both audience and actors. They decided, therefore, to begin the play at 5.15 in the afternoon, adjourn for an extended dinner recess at 7 and resume at 8.30.

This plan rather added to the novelty and popularity of the engagement in New York. "Strange Interlude" was an enormous success from its first performance and it is evident at this writing that it will continue playing so long as the actors are willing to continue. After which substitute casts will probably carry it through the summer and into next season.

The action of "Strange Interlude" opens in the library of Professor Leeds' home in a small university town in New England. "It is a small room with a low ceiling. The furniture has been selected with a love for old New England pieces. The walls are lined almost to the ceiling with glassed-in bookshelves. . . . The atmosphere of the room is that of a cosy, cultured retreat, sedulously built as a sanctuary where, secure with the culture of the past at his back, a fugitive from reality can view the present safely from a distance, as a superior with condescending disdain, pity, and even amusement.

"It is late afternoon of a day in August. Sunshine, cooled and dimmed in the shade of trees, fills the room with a soothing light."

A middle-aged maid shows Charles Marsden into the room. "He is a tall thin man of 35, meticulously well-dressed in tweeds of distinctly English tailoring, his appearance that of an Anglicized New England gentleman. . . . There is an indefinable feminine quality about him, but it is nothing apparent in either appearance or act. His manner is cool and poised.

Marsden, left to wait, stands just inside the door, "his tall, stooped figure leaning back against the books," and gazes appreciatively about the room. "He smiles affectionately and his amused voice recites the words with a rhetorical resonance."

"Sanctum sanctorum! (*His voice takes on a monotonous musing quality, his eyes stare idly at his drifting thoughts.*) How perfectly the professor's unique haven! (*He smiles.*) Primly classical . . . when New Englander meets Greek. . . . (*Looking at the books now.*) He hasn't added one book in years . . . how old was I when I first came here? . . . six . . . with my father . . . father . . . how dim his face has grown! . . . he wanted to speak to me just before he died . . . the hospital . . . smell of iodoform in the cool halls . . . hot summer . . . I bent down

. . . his voice had withdrawn so far away . . . always too near, too soon, too distant or too late! . . ."

Marsden's face saddens with the adolescent memories awakened and he goes on to other musings. Of the European tour from which he has just returned; of his inability to write over there; of his hope to recapture his muse in this quiet New England atmosphere.

He thinks of Professor Leeds, dominated so long by an aggressive wife; of Nina, the daughter, who is now the one who bosses him. But Nina's different—

". . . She has bossed me, too, ever since she was a baby . . . she's a woman now . . . known love and death. . . . Gordon brought down in flames . . . two days before the armistice . . . what fiendish irony! . . . his wonderful athlete's body . . . her lover . . . charred bones in a cage of twisted steel . . . no wonder she broke down . . . Mother said she's become quite queer lately . . . Mother seemed jealous of my concern . . . why have I never fallen in love with Nina? . . . could I? . . . that way . . . used to dance her on my knee . . . sit her on my lap . . . even now she'd never think anything about it . . . but sometimes the scent of her hair and skin . . . like a dreamy drug . . . dreamy! . . . there's the rub! . . . all dreams with me! . . . my sex life among the phantoms! . . ."

Professor Leeds' arrival interrupts Marsden's ruminations. The professor "is a small, slender man of 55, his hair gray, the top of his head bald. . . . Temperamentally timid, his defense is an assumption of his complacent, superior manner of the classroom toward the world at large."

The professor is glad to see Marsden, and surprised. They had not expected him back from Europe so soon, he says. Nina will be glad to see him too. But Nina has greatly changed. She can't forget Gordon. She dreams of Gordon. It has been so ever since news came of the aviator-lover's death.

The professor secretly resents the attitude of his daughter toward Gordon and the change it has made in her attitude toward him, her father. Gradually Nina is drawing away from her father, and thought of the loneliness for him that may follow is depressing. He hopes Marsden will not tell Nina anything that will remind her of the dead man.

"After all, Charlie, life must be lived, and Nina can't live with a corpse forever," he says, trying to control his irritation. "You see, I'm trying to see things through clearly and unsentimentally. If you'll remember, I was as broken up as any one over Gordon's death. I'd become so reconciled to Nina's love for him—although, as you know, I was opposed at first, and for fair reasons, I think, for the boy, for all his good looks and prowess in sport and his courses, really came of common people and had no money of his own except as he made a career for himself."

The men are not in agreement as to the possibilities of Gordon's chances for a career had he lived. Nor will Marsden credit the Professor's fears that his daughter is beginning to act as though she hated him—as though she blamed him for Gordon's death. That he had helped to influence Gordon's decision to put aside thoughts of marrying Nina until after the war he admits. But he had asked Gordon to keep the suggestion entirely confidential. And now Nina, in some strange way, seems to know.

The two men receive the indication of Nina's approach with mingled emotions, both a little pathetically self-analytical.

"My heart pounding!" mockingly thinks Marsden. "Seeing Nina again . . . how sentimental . . . how she'd laugh if she knew! . . . and quite rightly . . . absurd for me to react as if I loved . . . that way . . . her dear old Charlie . . . ha! . . . (*He smiles with bitter self-mockery.*)

"I hope she won't make a scene," the professor worriedly repeats to himself. "She's seemed on the verge all day . . . thank God, Charlie's like one of the family . . . but what a life for me! . . . with the opening of the new term only a few weeks off! . . . I can't do it . . . I'll have to call in a nerve specialist . . . but the last one did her no good . . . his outrageous fee . . . he can take it to court . . . I absolutely refuse . . . but if he should bring suit? . . . what a scandal . . . no, I'll have to pay . . . somehow . . . borrow . . . he has me in a corner, the robber! . . ."

Now Nina stands just inside the doorway "looking directly at her father with defiant eyes, her face set in an expression of stubborn resolve. She is twenty, tall with broad, square shoulders, slim, strong hips and long, beautifully developed legs—a fine athletic girl of the swimmer, tennis player, golfer type. Her straw-blond hair, framing her sunburned face, is bobbed. Her face is striking, handsome rather than pretty, the bone structure prominent, the forehead high, the lips of her rather large mouth clearly modelled above the firm jaw. Her eyes are beautiful and bewildering, extraordinarily large and a deep greenish blue. Since Gordon's death they have a quality of continually shuddering before some terrible enigma, of being wounded to their depths and made defiant and resentful by their pain. Her whole manner, the charged atmosphere she gives off, is totally at variance with her healthy outdoor physique. It is strained, nerve-racked, hectic, a terrible tension of will alone maintaining self-possession. She is dressed in smart sport clothes."

For the moment Nina does not even see Marsden. She is too intent upon the thing she has come to tell her father. And he, as one warding off the inevitable, seeks to reprove her for her seeming rudeness. When she does greet Marsden it is with a friendly perfunctoriness that is quite apparent, and which both try to cover.

What Nina wishes to tell her father is that she has decided to go away. Either she must get away or go crazy. Nor can his arguments alter her decision.

"I must keep calm," she mutters desperately to herself, when her father has finished. "I mustn't let go or I'll tell him everything . . . and I mustn't tell him . . . he's my father. . . ."

And then aloud she answers: "I've already had six months' training for a nurse. I will finish my training. There's a doctor I know at a sanitarium for crippled soldiers—a friend of Gordon's. I wrote to him and he answered that he'll gladly arrange it."

PROF. LEEDS (*thinking furiously*)—Gordon's friend . . . Gordon again! . . . (*Severely.*) You seriously mean to tell me you, in your condition, want to nurse in a soldiers' hospital! Absurd!

MARSDEN (*thinking with indignant revulsion*)—Quite right, Professor! . . . her beauty . . . all those men . . . in their beds . . . it's too revolting! . . . (*With a persuasive quizzing tone.*) Yes, I must say I can't see you as a peace-time Florence Nightingale, Nina!

Prof. Leeds furiously resents Nina's turning to Gordon's friend, and questions the wisdom of her intention. Marsden, too, is resentful as he visions Nina in a hospital full of men in bed. The professor is even ready to accuse her of being not quite herself.

But Nina is firm. They do not, cannot understand. "I must pay," she says, her voice uncannily flat as her thought breaks through. "It's my plain duty! Gordon is dead! What use is my life to me or any one? But I must make it of use by giving it. (*Fiercely.*) I must learn to give myself, do you hear—give and give until I can make that gift of myself for a man's happiness without scruple, without fear, without joy except in his joy! When I've accomplished this I'll have found myself, I'll know how to start living my own life over again. Don't you see? In the name of the commonest decency and honor, I owe it to Gordon!"

They cannot see, nor does her further statement that it is because she had denied herself to Gordon that last night before he had gone to the front when they were desperately in love with each other soften their assertions that she is behaving ridiculously.

NINA (*her eyes on her father's, intensely*)—Gordon wanted me! I wanted Gordon! I should have made him take me! I knew he would die and I would have no children, that there would be no big Gordon or little Gordon left to me, that happiness was calling me, never to call again if I refused! And yet I did refuse! I didn't make him! I lost him forever! And now I am lonely and not pregnant with anything at all, but—but loathing! (*She hurls this last at her father—fiercely.*) Why did I refuse? What was that cowardly something in me that cried, no, you mustn't, what would your father say?

PROF. LEEDS (*thinking furiously*)—What an animal! . . . and my daughter! . . . she doesn't get it from me! . . . was her mother like that? . . . (*Distracted.*) Nina! I can't really listen!

NINA (*savagely*)—And that's exactly what my father did say! Wait, he told Gordon! Wait for Nina until the war's over, and you've got a good job and can afford a marriage license!

Professor Leeds' defense crumbles. Pitifully he admits that her charges are true. He had been responsible for Gordon's decision. He had persuaded himself to think it was for the best. Now he knows that he was alone and that he wanted to keep his daughter's love. He was secretly glad when Gordon died!

Nina is forgiving. That her father has suffered, too, she understands. But he must know that she must find a way to give herself to Gordon still, that she may pay her debt and learn to forgive herself.

Marsden, confused and unhappy, tries to withdraw gracefully and get home to mother and tea. But Nina presses him into service to help her pack.

Soon the professor is at his books again. The new term will be on in three weeks and there is lots to do. . . . He's glad they had it out, he and Nina. . . . "His ghost will be gone now . . .

no more Gordon, Gordon, Gordon, love and praise and tears, all
for Gordon."

Probably Mary will do very well after all . . . and when Nina
is well she will come home again . . . little Nina. . . .

"Oh, God . . . I feel cold! . . . alone! . . . this home is
abandoned . . . the house is empty and full of death . . . there
is a pain about my heart!"

He calls to Nina and she answers cheerily. But he does not bid
her come to him. He just wanted to remind her to call a taxi.

Four hours and Nina will be gone . . . "and I'll die in here
some day . . . alone . . . gasp, cry out for help . . . the president will speak at the funeral. . . . Nina will be here again. . . .
Nina in black! Too late! . . ."

Again he calls. Nina does not answer. He turns again to his
books. The curtain falls.

ACT II

The scene is the same, the time a year later. But now the
shades of Professor Leeds' study are drawn down. They are "of
the color of pale flesh, giving the windows a suggestion of lifeless,
closed eyes and making the room seem more withdrawn from life
than before."

Charles Marsden, sunk wearily into a deep chair, his dark serge
suit strongly suggesting one in mourning, is casting up recent
events and his rather solemn reactions to them.

Professor Leeds is dead, he thinks aloud, even as he had proph-
esied. Will Nina feel deeply the grief of her father's passing?
Probably not. In the hospital Nina has seemed strangely detached. She has written occasionally to her father, but she never
has answered Marsden's letters! Probably Nina has had many
diverting experiences. Probably every male inmate in the hospital
has fallen in love with her. That last night he had seen her she
had talked quite brazenly about giving herself. . . .

"I wish I knew what she's been doing in that house full of
men," he mumbles; "particularly that self-important young ass
of a doctor—Gordon's friend! . . . Really, it's hardly a decent
time, is it, for that kind of speculation . . . with her father lying
dead upstairs?"

When Nina comes she is dressed in a nurse's uniform. "She
appears older than in the previous scene, her face is pale and

much thinner, her cheek bones stand out, her mouth is taut in
hard lines of a cynical scorn. Her eyes try to armor her wounded
spirit with a defensive stare of disillusionment. Her training has
also tended to coarsen her fiber a trifle, to make her insensitive
to suffering, to give her the nurse's professionally callous attitude.
. . . She remains strikingly handsome and her physical appeal is
enhanced by her pallor and the mysterious suggestion about her
of hidden experience."

Nina has been weeping. She greets Marsden perfunctorily.
Tells him that she has brought Dr. Darrell with her on the chance
that something still might be done.

The sight of her father's study reawakens childhood's memories.
Nina was never allowed to touch anything in the room, but it was
there that she used to sit in her father's lap and cuddle against
him "dreaming into the dark beyond the windows." Yet they
are meaningless memories.

"Yes, I hear you, little Nina," she says, "but I don't understand
one word of it. (*She smiles with a cynical self-contempt.*) I'm
sorry, father! . . . You see, you've been dead for me for a long
time. . . . When Gordon died, all men died. . . . What did you
feel for me then? . . . nothing . . . and now I feel nothing . . .
it's too bad. . . ."

Marsden, too, is sad. Secretly he had hoped Nina would throw
herself in his arms, cling to him, feel her dependence upon him.
Why did she have to bring that fellow Darrell with her?

Now Nina is speaking to him, explaining that she had had a
premonition that she would never see her father again. Her fault,
it is true. She had not tried to see him. Had not wanted her
father to see what he would have thought was her. . . .

Nina has gone upstairs to see her father and has taken Dr. Darrell with her. Marsden is alone with his thoughts again. "That
isn't Nina," he concludes. "They have killed her soul down there.
Poor old professor!"

Sam Evans has let himself in the front door. He introduces
himself to Marsden. Nina had told him to come. A shy young
man, Evans is embarrassed by the meeting.

"Evans is above the medium height, very blond, with guileless,
diffident blue eyes, his figure inclined to immature lumbering lines.
. . . There is a lack of self-confidence, a lost and strayed appealing air about him, yet with a hint of some unawakened obstinate
force beneath his apparent weakness. Although he is 25 and has

been out of college three years he still wears the latest in collegiate clothes."

The two men indulge a quick appraisal of each other. Evans, thinks Marsden, is no giant intellect; rather an overgrown boy with a likable quality. Marsden, decides Evans, seems like "a good egg."

Their only mutual interest is in Nina. Evans has not known her long—only since she has been in the hospital. But he had met her with Gordon. Evans was a classmate of Gordon's, and a worshipper of that hero-aviator.

Evans had been in the war, too, but only in the infantry. Never saw anything exciting. He had tried for the flying service, he reminds himself, but he couldn't make the physical exams. But he won't tell Marsden that. Might hurt his (Evans') chances with Nina. He's there now because Darrell had suggested that he come. Evans and Darrell are good friends, too. Roomed together at college. Darrell is another good egg.

"Don't want him to get the wrong idea of Ned," thinks Evans. "Ned's my best friend . . . doing all he can to help me with Nina . . . he thinks she'll marry me in the end . . . God, if she only would! . . . I wouldn't expect her to love me at first . . . be happy only to take care of her . . . cook her breakfast . . . bring it up to her in bed . . . tuck the pillows behind her . . . comb her hair for her . . . I'd be happy just to kiss her hair! . . ."

It is not Evans but Darrell who worries Marsden. What are Darrell's relations to Nina? Perhaps Evans knows.

"He's always trying to bully her into taking better care of herself," reports Evans, "but she only laughs at him . . . She isn't herself, Mr. Marsden. And I think nursing all those poor guys keeps the war before her when she ought to forget it. She ought to give up nursing and be nursed for a change, that's my idea."

They are agreed on this, and the fact of Marsden's understanding emboldens Evans to bring up a more personal interest. He is, he confesses, deeply in love with Nina and has asked her to marry him. She has not answered him. Only smiled.

Evans knows that Nina is still in love with Gordon and admires her for it. He is even willing that she should go on loving Gordon for a long time to come, if only she will give him the privilege of protecting and caring for her without expecting anything in re-

turn. He can live happily on the hope that she may come to love
him in time.
Marsden resents a little being thus accepted as a sort of
guardian for Nina, but Evans' suggestion of marriage is not entirely displeasing to him. It might offer a solution for Nina's immediate problems to be married to a simpleton. . . .
Dr. Darrell comes down stairs. "He is 27, short, dark, wiry,
his movements rapid and sure, his manner cool and observant,
his dark eyes analytical. His head is handsome and intelligent.
There is a quality about him, provoking and disturbing to women,
of intense passion which he has rigidly trained himself to control
and set free only for the objective satisfaction of studying his own
and their reactions; and so he has come to consider himself as
immune to love through his scientific understanding of its real sex-
ual nature."
Darrell writes a prescription, a sleeping powder for Nina.
Evans goes to have it filled. Darrell and Marsden turn to each
other, frankly curious.

"This Marsden doesn't like me," thinks Darrell; "that's evident . . . but he interests me . . . read his books . . . wanted
to know his bearing on Nina's case . . . his novels just well-
written surface . . . no depth, no digging underneath . . . why?
. . . has the talent but doesn't dare . . . afraid he'll meet himself somewhere . . . one of those poor devils who spend their
lives trying not to discover which sex they belong to! . . ."
"Giving me the fishy, diagnosing eye they practice at medical
school," concludes Marsden; "like freshmen from Ioway cultivating broad A's at Harvard! . . . what is his specialty? . . .
neurologist, I think . . . I hope not psychoanalyst . . . a lot to
account for, Herr Freud! . . . punishment to fit his crimes, be
forced to listen eternally during breakfast while innumerable plain
ones tell him dreams about snakes . . . pah, what an easy cure-
all! . . . sex the philosopher's stone . . . 'O Œdipus, O my
king! The world is adopting you! . . .'"
"Must pitch into him about Nina," continues Darrell, to himself; "have to have his help . . . Damn little time to convince
him . . . he's the kind you have to explode a bomb under to get
them to move . . . but not too big a bomb . . . they blow to
pieces easily. . . ."

And then he turns to Marsden, with brusque frankness.
"Nina's gone to pot again," he reports. "Not that her father's

death is a shock in the usual sense of grief. I wish to God it
were! No, it's a shock because it's finally convinced her she
can't feel anything any more. That's what she's doing upstairs
now—trying to goad herself into feeling something!"
Marsden thinks Dr. Darrell must be mistaken. But Darrell
knows. Nina is a corking girl, but the destructive experiences she
has been indulging of late are leading her straight down to where,
with a few more, "she'll dive for the gutter just to get the security
that comes from knowing she's touched bottom." And that's the
truth, whether Marsden wants to believe it or not.

"Nina has been giving way more and more to a morbid longing
for martyrdom," Darrell explains. "The reason for it is obvious.
Gordon went away without—well, let's say marrying her. The
war killed him. She was left suspended. Then she began to
blame herself and to want to sacrifice herself and at the same time
give happiness to various fellow war victims by pretending to
love them. It's a pretty idea, but it hasn't worked out. Nina's
a bad actress!"

Darrell's lying about Nina, Marsden tells himself. But he
realizes that she is in need of help and that he must work with
Darrell to help her.
It is Darrell's suggestion, somewhat to Marsden's astonishment,
that they combine their influence to get Nina married to Sam
Evans. Evans is unselfishly in love with her, he would give her
some one to mother and boss and also a chance to have children.
"She needs normal love objects for the emotional life Gordon's
death blocked up in her," Darrell explains.
He is convinced that, married to Sam, there is a chance for
Nina to snap out of her depression and he is sure such a marriage
will be the making of Evans, who is just starting in the advertising business. Evans comes from a family of good, solid upstate farmers and fruit growers and frequently, in a joking way,
Darrell has already suggested to Nina his suitability as a husband.
Marsden is half convinced that Darrell is really in love with
Nina himself, and is not above the suspicion that the doctor is
arranging a convenient triangle in which he may play a part,
but Darrell is vigorous in denial. To him Nina always belongs
to Gordon, and he couldn't share a woman—even with a ghost!
They are still in the midst of their discussion when Nina reappears at the hall door, "her face a pale, expressionless mask
drained of all emotional response to human contacts. It is as if

her eyes were acting on their own account as restless, prying, re-
cording instruments."

Before either of the men can speak to her she begins to talk in
a queer, flat voice. "Yes, he's dead—my father—whose passion
created me—who began me—he is ended. There is only his end
living—his death. It lives now to draw nearer me, to draw me
nearer, to become my end. . . . How we poor monkeys hide
from ourselves behind the sounds called words!"

She startles Marsden, but Darrell is interested in letting her
talk on until her mind is cleared. Now she is startled out of her
reverie and turns to Marsden.

"You look frightened, Charlie. Do I seem queer? It's because
I have suddenly seen the lies in the sounds called words. You
know—grief, sorrow, love, father—those sounds our lips make
and our hands write. You ought to know what I mean. You
work with them. Have you written another novel lately? But,
stop to think, you're just the one who couldn't know what I mean.
With you the lies have become the only truthful things. And I
suppose that's the logical conclusion to the whole evasive mess,
isn't it? Do you understand me, Charlie? Say lie—(*She says it,
drawing it out.*) L-i-i-e! Now say life. L-i-i-f-e! You see!
Life is just a long drawn out lie with a sniffling sigh at the end!"

She laughs and her laugh maddens Marsden, though he confines
his anger to his explosive thoughts. Nina turns to Darrell and
he, too, comes in for his rating. He is the kind of doctor, she
explains to Marsden, who couldn't be happy in heaven unless God
called him in because He'd caught something. Once, in a moment
of carnal weakness, Darrell had kissed her. She was as startled
as if a mummy had done it and then amused at the doctor's
discomfiture.

"Do you know what I was doing upstairs? I was trying to
pray. I tried hard to pray to the modern science God. I thought
of a million light years to a spiral nebula—one other universe
among innumerable others. But how could that God care about
our trifling misery of death-born-of-birth? I couldn't believe in
Him, and I wouldn't if I could! I'd rather imitate His indifference and prove I had that one trait at least in common! . . . I
wanted to believe in any God at any price—a heap of stones, a
mud image, a drawing on a wall, a bird, a fish, a snake, a baboon
—or even a good man preaching the simple platitudes of truth,

those Gospel words we love the sound of but whose meaning we pass on to spooks to live by!"

Again Marsden tries to stop her, tries to get her to lie down. Again Darrell seeks to make it easier for her to "talk this out of her system," by withdrawing and leaving Marsden and Nina alone, which is a little disconcerting to Marsden.

NINA (*suddenly, with pity yet with scorn*)—Why have you always been so timid, Charlie? Why are you always afraid? What are you afraid of?

MARSDEN (*thinking in a panic*)—She sneaked into my soul to spy! . . . (*Then boldly.*) Well then, a little truth for once in a way! (*Timidly.*) I'm afraid of—of life, Nina.

NINA (*nodding slowly*)—I know. (*After a pause—queerly.*) The mistake began when God was created in a male image. Of course, women would see Him that way, but men should have been gentlemen enough, remembering their mothers, to make God a woman! But the God of Gods—the Boss—has always been a man. That makes life so perverted, and death so unnatural. We should have imagined life as created in the birth-pain of God the Mother. Then we would understand why we, Her children, have inherited pain, for we would know that our life's rhythm beats from Her great heart, torn with the agony of love and birth. And we would feel that death meant reunion with Her, a passing back into Her substance, blood of Her blood again, peace of Her peace! (MARSDEN *has been listening to her fascinatedly. She gives a strange little laugh.*) Now wouldn't that be more logical and satisfying than having God a male whose chest thunders with egotism and is too hard for tired heads and thoroughly comfortless? Wouldn't it, Charlie?

MARSDEN (*with a strange passionate eagerness*)—Yes! It would, indeed! It would, Nina!

NINA (*suddenly jumping to her feet and going to him—with a horrible moaning desolation*)—Oh, God, Charlie, I want to believe in something! I want to believe so I can feel! I want to feel that he is dead—my father! And I can't feel anything, Charlie! I can't feel anything at all!

Now Nina has thrown herself on the floor at Marsden's feet and is sobbing. As he lifts her up she slips into his lap "like a little girl, and hides her face on his shoulder. His expression has become transported with a great happiness."

"As I dreamed," he mutters in an ecstatic whisper, kissing Nina's hair; "with a deeper sweetness. . . . There. . . . This is all my desire. . . . I am this kind of lover . . . this is my love . . . she is my girl . . . not woman . . . my little girl . . . and I am brave because of her little girl's pure love . . . and I am proud . . . no more afraid . . . no more ashamed of being pure! . . ."

He tries again to laugh and tease her out of her mood, and she is grateful. She has been homesick and eager to talk with him. She has wanted to run to him and confess her sins and be punished. She must be punished, out of mercy, so she can forgive herself. And, with her father gone, there is only Charlie to take the responsibility.

She must be punished, Nina repeats, for all that she has wildly done in the name of her love for Gordon. It has been in vain, all that bestial sacrifice of hers. She knows now. Gordon has come to her in a dream—"diving down out of the sky in flames."

"And he looked at me," she goes on, "with such sad, burning eyes, and all my poor, maimed men, too, seemed staring out of his eyes with a burning pain, and I woke up crying, my own eyes burning. Then I saw what a fool I'd been—a guilty fool! So be kind and punish me!"

The revelation is confusing to Marsden. He wishes Nina hadn't told him. He'd hate her for it if he could, but he can't, even though he is only "Dear Old Father Charlie" now. He manages finally to suggest, with an assumed parental authority, that by far the most desirable course for her to pursue would be to marry young Evans. He, a splendid, clean, boyish chap, needs a helpmeet to inspire him.

It might be a career, bringing a career to Evans, thinks Nina. And there is, as Marsden suggests, the thought of children. Nina wants children. . . . So it is agreed. She will marry Sam.

And then Nina falls asleep in Marsden's arms, as a tired child might do. Marsden is carrying her up to her room when Evans returns with the medicine.

MARSDEN (*smiling kindly at* EVANS)—Sssh! She's asleep. She cried and then she fell asleep—like a little girl. (*Then benignantly.*) But first we spoke a word about you, Evans, and I'm sure you have every reason to hope.

EVANS (*overcome*)—Thanks—I—I really don't know how to thank—

MARSDEN—I've got to go home. My mother is waiting up for

me. I'll just carry Nina upstairs and put her on her bed and throw something over her.

EVANS—Can't I help you, Mr. Marsden?

MARSDEN (*dully*)—No. I cannot help myself. (*As* EVANS *looks puzzled.*) You'd better call me just Charlie after this. (*He smiles bitterly to himself.*)

EVANS (*gleefully*)—Good egg! Good old Charlie! (*As if he had heard or guessed, Marsden's bitter laugh comes back from the end of the hallway.*)

The curtain falls.

ACT III

Seven months later Sam Evans, Nina and Charlie Marsden are at the Evans homestead in northern New York. It is a day in late spring. Nina is sitting at the table in "one of those misproportioned dining rooms that are found in the large jigsaw country houses scattered around the country as a result of the rural taste for grandeur in the eighties." She is reading to herself a letter she has been writing. "Her whole personality seems changed, her face has a contented expression, there is an inner calm about her."

The letter she has written is to Ned Darrell and is devoted largely to a description of the queer old Evans home. "There is something wrong with its psyche, I'm sure," she reads. "Therefore you'd simply adore it. It's a hideous old place, a faded gingerbread with orange fixin's and numerous lightning rods. Around it are acres and acres of apple trees in full bloom, all white and pinkish and beautiful, like brides just tripping out of church with the bridegroom, Spring, by the arm."

It is now six months since Nina and Sam were married, she reminds Darrell, and they have seen nothing of him. Is that a nice way for him to act? There is more about the strange old house, which seems some way to "have lost its soul and grown resigned to doing without it," and references to her failure to sleep well because of the weird suggestions her first experiences have given her. And yet she is no longer morbid. "I've never been more normal," she has written; "I feel contented and placid."

She pauses in her reading to debate with herself the question as to whether she should tell Darrell her secret—the secret of her pregnancy—and she decides not to. Not yet. Nor Sam, either. Nobody shall know until they have to. She wants to keep it her baby and only hers as long as she can. . . .

There is much in the letter about Sam's mother, too. A strange woman, Mrs. Evans, and very little like Sam. Nor is it easy for Nina to understand the attitude of this mother and son toward each other. Mrs. Evans has been desperately anxious that Sam should bring his wife to see her, but before these maternal commands began to arrive Sam had acted almost as though he had forgotten that he ever had a mother.

"And yet," she adds, "as soon as he saw her he was sweet enough. She seemed dreadfully upset to see Charlie with us, until we'd explained it was thanks to his kindness and in his car we were taking this deferred honeymoon. Charlie's like a fussy old woman about his car, he's afraid to let Sam or me drive it—"

Marsden is in. He, too, has been writing—to reassure his mother that they have not been murdered by rum bandits.

Marsden is afraid he detects a return of Nina's old morbid moods in her reports of not being able to sleep and her haunting impressions of the house without a soul, but she laughingly corrects him and runs away to "bum some more coffee."

Marsden is puzzled by the change in Nina, and still cruelly self-analytical as to his own stirrings of a vague jealousy at her seeming happiness. He suspects it may be that she is going to have a child, and when that happens it probably will be easier for him to accept the situation.

The sound of Evans' and his mother's voices in the garden turns his thoughts to them. He sees them now through the window.

"Sam with—his mother," he muses. "Peculiar woman . . . strong . . . good character for a novel . . . no, she's too somber . . . her eyes are the saddest . . . and, at the same time, the grimmest . . . they're coming in . . . I'll drive around the country a bit . . . give them a chance for a family conference . . . discuss Nina's pregnancy, I suppose . . . does Sam know? . . . he gives no indication . . . why do wives hide it from their husbands? . . . ancient shame . . . guilty of continuing life, of bringing fresh pain into the world. . . ."

Marsden passes Sam and Mrs. Evans on the porch. They come into the dining room.

"Sam looks timorously happy, as if he could not quite believe in his good fortune and had constantly to reassure himself about it, yet he is riding the crest of the wave, he radiates love and devotion and boyish adoration. He is a charming-looking fresh boy now. He wears a sweater and linen knickers, collegiate to the last degree. His mother is a tiny woman with a frail figure. . . . She is only about forty-five but she looks at least sixty. Her face with its delicate features must have once been of a romantic, tender, clinging-vine beauty, but what has happened to her has compressed its defenseless curves into planes, its mouth into the thin line around a locked door, its gentle chin has been forced out aggressively by a long reliance on clenched teeth. She is very pale. Her big dark eyes are grim with the prisoner-pain of a walled-in soul. Yet a sweet loving-kindness, the ghost of an old faith and trust in life's goodness, hovers girlishly, fleetingly, about the corners of her mouth and softens into deep sorrow the shadowy grimness of her eyes."

Sam is boasting good-naturedly of his success, and of what he will be able to do for his mother in a few years. She won't have to worry about the darned old apple crops much longer. He is making good, Sam reports, and it's his marriage to Nina that has helped. It's marriage that puts the right kind of ambition into a fellow. Marriage and children!

It was about the prospects of an addition to the family that Mrs. Evans had wanted to talk to her son. Is Nina going to have a baby? Sam doesn't know—he doesn't think so.

"He don't know," mutters his mother, "there's that much to be thankful for anyway—"

"If that'd only happen . . . soon!" muses Evans. "Nina's begun to love me . . . a little . . . I've felt it the last two months. . . . God, it's made me happy! . . . before that she didn't . . . only liked me . . . that was all I asked . . . never dared hope she'd come to love me . . . even a little . . . so soon . . . sometimes I feel it's too good to be true . . . don't deserve it . . . and now . . . if that'd happen . . . then I'd feel sure . . . it'd be there . . . half Nina, half me . . . living proof! . . . (*Then an apprehensive note creeping in.*) And I know she wants a baby so much . . . one reason why she married me . . . and I know she's felt right along that then she'd love me . . . really love me . . . (*Gloomily.*) I wonder why . . . ought to have happened before this . . . hope it's nothing wrong . . . with me! . . . (*He starts, flinging off this thought— then suddenly clutching at a straw, turns hopefully to his mother.*)

Why did you ask me that, mother? D'you think—?
"No, indeed!" Mrs. Evans says hastily, "I don't think she
is! I wouldn't say so at all!"

Mrs. Evans manages to send Sammy out to catch up with
Marsden and ride to town. She wants to have a talk with Nina.
Must have it. Nina must know—

Nina, back from the kitchen with a second cup of coffee, is
beaming. Shyly she greets Mrs. Evans with a "Good morning—
mother!" Suddenly she senses the seriousness of the older
woman's mood and an impending something assails her—"that
sick dead feeling when something is going to happen" that she felt
before she got the cable about Gordon!

Now Mrs. Evans is asking Nina if she is going to have a baby,
and Nina has answered quite simply that she is. Nor does she
think it is too soon, or that she should wait until Sam is making
more money. She is happy, she loves Sam and she wants a baby.

And then Mrs. Evans tells her that she *must* wait; she cannot
have a child. Because of Sammy, because they both must be
happy, there can be no children!

Nina will not listen, will not believe what she is hearing. She
cannot credit Mrs. Evans' story that she, too, had been told that
she should not bear an Evans child, even when she was carrying
Sammy; that she and Sammy's father had prayed, when there
was nothing else to do, that Sammy would be born dead; that
for Nina to bring Sam's baby into the world would be a crime
worse than murder.

Pitifully, hysterically, Nina protests that what she is hearing
cannot be true. She tries to put the thought from her. She
accuses the older woman of lying.

But Mrs. Evans goes on and on with the story of the family
secret; of the curse of the Evans family. There had been insanity
in that family. Sam's grandmother had died in an asylum and
her father before her. His aunt is even then living in a room on
the top floor she has not left for years.

Mrs. Evans did not know of the Evans curse until after she
had married Sam's father. Then she had tried to be, what he
had said she was, his "only hope of salvation." But Sammy
came. They had sworn never to have children, but there was
Sammy. And worry over what they had done, and of the future
of his son, had driven Sam's father crazy, too.

But Sammy never knew. All the years his mother has kept
the truth from him. Sent him away to school. Never had him

living at home, summer or winter. And Sammy must never know. Nina must see to that. If she loves him she will.

But how can she love Sam now? Nina demands. She hates him. She hates his mother. Why hadn't she told her son he could never marry? Because she could not without telling him everything, Mrs. Evans explains. She had not heard of Nina until after Nina and Sam were married. Then it was too late to do more than to send for them as soon as she could.

Nor can Nina leave Sam now that she knows, Mrs. Evans warns. He would go crazy sure then. Even if Nina doesn't love him. Even if she did only marry him because he needed her and she needed children, she can't tell him!

"You just said you married him because he needed you," the mother reminds her. "Don't he need you now—more'n ever? But I can't tell you not to leave him, not if you don't love him. But you oughtn't to have married him when you didn't love him. And it'll be your fault, what'll happen."

Slowly Nina comes to see the mother's point of view. She must play fair. Gordon would have expected that of her. She thinks she can hear Gordon speaking to her now, urging her to give Sam the life she did not give him. Sam was Gordon's friend, too. If they had a son, Sam had said, they should name it in Gordon's honor.

"All right, mother! I'll stay with Sam," she says. "There's nothing else I can do, is there, when it isn't his fault, poor boy." Suddenly Nina's nerves snap and she bursts out in a despairing cry. "But I'll be so lonely! I'll have lost my baby. Oh, mother, how can I keep on living?" She has sunk down on her knees at Mrs. Evans' feet and is crying piteously.

"Now she knows my suffering," thinks Mrs. Evans, miserably. "Now I got to help her. . . . She's got a right to have a baby . . . another baby . . . some time . . . somehow . . . she's giving her life to save my Sammy . . . I got to save her! . . ."

There may be a way. Sam's happiness must be considered, too. It is as important for him as it is for her, Nina says, that she should have a child. The mother knows that.

"There must be a way—somehow," gropingly mutters Mrs. Evans. "I remember when I was carrying Sam, sometimes I'd forget I was a wife, I'd only remember the child in me. And then I used to wish I'd gone out deliberate in our first year, without my husband knowing, and picked a man, a healthy male to breed by, same's we do with stock, to give the man I loved a healthy child. And if I didn't love that other man nor him me where would be the harm? Then God would whisper: It'd be a sin, adultery, the worst sin! But after He'd gone I'd argue back again to myself, then we'd have a healthy child, I needn't be afraid! And maybe my husband would feel without ever knowing how he felt it, that I wasn't afraid and that child wasn't cursed and so he needn't fear and I could save him. (*Then scornfully.*) But I was too afraid of God then to have ever done it! (*Very simply.*) He loved children so, my poor husband did, and the way they took to him, you never saw anything like it, he was a natural born father. And Sammy's the same."

NINA (*as from a distance—strangely*)—Yes, Sammy's the same. But I'm not the same as you. (*Defiantly.*) I don't believe in God the Father!

MRS. EVANS (*strangely*)—Then it'd be easy for you. (*With a grim smile.*) And I don't believe in Him, neither, not any more. I used to be a great one for worrying about what's God and what's devil, but I got richly over it living here with poor folks that was being punished for no sins of their own, and me being punished with them for no sin but loving much. (*With decision.*) Being happy, that's the nearest we can ever come to knowing what's good! Being happy, that's good! The rest is just talk! (*With a strange austere sternness.*) I love my boy, Sammy. I could see how much he wants you to have a baby. Sammy's got to feel sure you love him—to be happy. Whatever you can do to make him happy is good—is good, Nina! I don't care what! You've got to have a healthy baby—sometime—so's you can both be happy! It's your rightful duty!

NINA (*confusedly*)—Yes, mother. (*Thinking longingly.*) I want to be happy! . . . it's my right . . . and my duty! (*Then suddenly in guilty agony.*) Oh, my baby . . . my poor baby . . . I'm forgetting you . . . desiring another after you are dead! . . . I feel you beating against my heart for mercy . . . oh! . . . (*She weeps with bitter anguish.*)

MRS. EVANS (*with deep sympathy*)—I know what you're suffering. And I wouldn't say what I just said now only I know us two mustn't see each other ever again. You and Sammy have got to forget me. (*As NINA makes a motion of protest.*) Oh, yes, you will—easy. People forget everything. They got to, poor people! And I'm saying what I said about a healthy baby so's you will remember it when you need to, after you've forgotten—this one.

NINA (*sobbing pitifully*)—Don't!   Please, mother!

MRS. EVANS (*with sudden tenderness—gathering* NINA *up in her arms, brokenly*)—You poor child!   You're like the daughter of my sorrow!   You're closer to me now than ever Sammy could be!   I want you to be happy!   (*She begins to sob, too, kissing* NINA's *bowed head.*)

The curtain falls.

ACT IV

It is early evening.   Again seven months have elapsed.   Sam Evans, having moved his typewriter into Professor Leeds' study, is seeking rather disgustedly to type out satisfactory advertising copy.

The study has gone off a good deal in appearance and Evans has gone off a bit, too.   "His expression is dispirited, his eyes shift about, his shoulders are collapsed submissively.   He seems much thinner, his face drawn and sallow.   The collegiate clothes are no longer natty, they need pressing and look too big for him."

Evans is also troubled in his mind.   He finds it difficult to do his work at the office.   His boss has been disappointed with his work recently.   He can't, he agrees, deny that he has gone stale since that visit to his mother's!   Since Nina's been sick, too!   Five months, now!

He wonders, as he has often wondered before, what happened between his mother and Nina?   Why did Nina insist on leaving that day?   Why did his mother seem anxious for them to go?   Yet both insisted nothing was wrong.   And for weeks Nina seemed even more loving than ever before.   Then she crashed!   Disappointed because she didn't have a child, probably.   Could that be his fault?

Now Evans is pacing the floor distractedly.   "God, if we'd only have a kid! . . . then I'd show them all what I could do! . . . Cole always used to say I had the stuff, and Ned certainly thought so . . . (*With sudden relieved excitement.*)   By gosh, I was forgetting! . . . Ned's coming out to-night . . . forgot to tell Nina . . . mustn't let her get wise I got him to come to look her over . . . she'd hate me for swallowing my pride after he's never been to see us . . . but I had to . . . this has got my goat . . .   I've got to know what's wrong . . . and Ned's the only one I can trust . . ."

Evans is back at his typing when Nina comes silently through the door and stands looking at him, speaking thoughts inspired by an immediate reaction of contempt and dislike before she can stifle them.

How weak Sam is, thinks Nina. He'll never do anything; never give her her desire; why can't he fall in love with some one else and leave her free?

But immediately she is again contrite. Poor Sam! Trying so hard; loving her so much; she giving so little in return. Sam can't sleep now; he's worried; perhaps if she could overcome her revulsion— She must try to be good to Sam. "Oh, poor dead baby I dared not bear," she wails, "how I might have loved your father for your sake!"

Now Sam has noticed Nina and is worried for fear his typing has disturbed her.

"Why does he always cringe so?" thinks Nina. But that is like Sam. He'll always be a weakling of one sort or another.

She pities Sam, comforts him, tells him he is far too apprehensive. She kisses him and sits on the arm of his chair, pulling his head down onto her breast. She does want Sam to be happy.

Her thoughts are tinged with a bitter mockery as she remembers the operation and the ghost of Gordon following her reproachfully from room to room.

"Oh, Gordon," she muses, "I'm afraid this is a deeper point of honor than any that was ever shot down in flames! . . . what would your honor say now? . . . 'Stick to him! . . . play the game!' . . . oh, yes, I know . . . I'm sticking . . . but he isn't happy . . . I'm trying to play the game . . . then why do I keep myself from him? . . . but I was really sick . . . for a time after . . . since then, I couldn't . . . but . . . oh, I'll try . . . I'll try soon . . ."

Nina is determined the sacrifice shall be made for Sam's happiness. Their married life shall resume its normal ways. Thus will she keep Sam happy until the time he begins worrying again because there are to be no children.

"His mother said . . . You've got to have a healthy baby . . . sometime . . . it's your rightful duty . . . that seemed right then . . . but now . . . it seems cowardly . . . to betray poor Sam . . . and vile to give myself . . . without love or desire . . . and yet I've given myself to men before without a thought

just to give them a moment's happiness . . . can't I do that
again? . . . when it's a case of Sam's happiness? . . . and my
own? . . ."

Nina and Sam are expecting Marsden and Darrell. Charlie
is helping Nina with a biography of Gordon, but she did not
know about Darrell's coming. She is quite excited about it.
Immediately she plans that they will get rid of Charlie and get
the spare room ready for Ned.

Marsden, the first to arrive, is relieved rather than disappointed
to learn that Nina will not be able to give him any time. Mother
really needs him. Mother's not been feeling well. Charlie is
worried. . . .

The doorbell announces Darrell. What's he doing there?
Marsden wonders. Perhaps it was Darrell who had performed
Nina's operation! But why?

Now Evans, according to plan, has asked Marsden to take
him to the store in the car. Thus he will leave the way clear for
Darrell to have a good heart-to-heart talk with Nina.

Darrell, waiting for Nina, glances casually at the papers on
the disordered desk.

"Evidences of authorship," he notes. "Sam's ads? . . . isn't
making good, he said . . . was I wrong in thinking he had stuff
in him? . . . hope not . . . always liked Sam, don't know why
exactly . . . said Nina'd gotten into a bad state again . . .
what's happened to their marriage? . . . I felt a bit sorry for
myself at their wedding . . . not that I'd ever fallen . . . but I
did envy him in a way . . . she always had strong physical attraction for me . . . that time I kissed her . . . one reason I've
steered clear since . . . take no chances on emotional didos . . .
need all my mind on my work . . . got rid of even that slight
suspicion . . . I'd forgotten all about her . . . she's a strange
girl . . . interesting case . . . I should have kept in touch on
that account . . . hope she'll tell me about herself . . . can't
understand her not having child . . . it's so obviously the sensible thing . . . (*Cynically.*) Probably why . . . to expect
common sense of people proves you're lacking in it yourself! . . ."

When Nina comes in it is plain that she has been to some trouble to fix herself up. Her mood is also changed, "making her
appear a younger, prettier person for the moment." Darrell
greets her "with a smile of affectionate admiration."

"Wonderful-looking as ever," he thinks as he shakes hands
with her. "Sam's a lucky devil!"

"Strong hands like Gordon's," thinks Nina. "Take hold of
you . . . not like Sam's . . . yielding fingers that let you fall
back into yourself!"

Nina is reproachful because of the doctor's neglect of them.
Darrell is conventionally apologetic. Darrell is interested in
Nina's writing of Gordon's biography. Nina is curious as to why
Darrell is neither married nor thinking of marriage. She quotes
his own advice on marriage and the blessings of parenthood to
him and he admits she is right. Being right, why hasn't she
followed his advice? Where is her baby?

At first with bitterness in her heart, and then a little wearily,
Nina tells him the story of the visit to Sam's mother and of the
family revelations; of her love of her baby and of the operation
to which she submitted; of her own horror and finally of her
conclusion that there can be no happiness for either her or Sam
unless she bears another child.

"I've promised Sam's mother I'd make him happy," she reports, with a strange, monotonous insistence. "He's unhappy
now because he thinks he isn't able to give me a child. And
I'm unhappy because I've lost my child. So I must have another
baby—somehow—don't you think, doctor?" (*She looks up at
him pleadingly. For a moment they stare into each other's eyes—
then both turn away in guilty confusion.*)

Out of their confusion comes Darrell's demand for a frank
statement of all the facts and of the thought in Nina's mind.
And Nina's confession that, seeing the happiness of so many
depended on it, she had considered seeking a father for her
child; of picking out a healthy male about whom she cared nothing and having a child by him that Sam would believe was his
child; a child whose life would give him confidence in his own
living, who would be for him a living proof that his wife loved
him.

Darrell meets the confession "in his ultra-professional manner
—like an automaton of a doctor."

"I see," he says. "But this needs a lot of thinking over. It
isn't easy to prescribe—"

"I have a friend who has a wife," Darrell's thoughts run on.
"I was envious at his wedding . . . but what has that to do with
it? . . . damn it, my mind won't work! . . . it keeps running
away to her . . . it wants to mate with her mind . . . in the

interest of science? . . . what damned rot I'm thinking! . . ."

"This doctor is nothing to me but a healthy male," thinks Nina. "When he was Ned he once kissed me . . . but I cared nothing about him . . . so that's all right, isn't it, Sam's Mother?"

From his thought Darrell drifts into a consideration of himself in the laboratory studying the problem of Sam and Nina as two guinea pigs. He can also think of himself as a third guinea pig and observe his reactions to the problem.

Dispassionately he arrives at the conclusion that his duty is clear. He agrees with Sam's mother that Sam's wife should find a healthy father for Sam's child. "It is her sane duty to her husband."

In this they are in agreement, but now Nina finds herself frightened and timid as to her future course, and Darrell, assuming a professional detachment which his thoughts belie, seeks to encourage her in the cause of happiness, and of science. Concealment from Sam is necessary.

"To let Sam know would be insanely cruel of her," Darrell insists; "and stupid, for then no one could be the happier for her act!"

"Am I right to advise this?" he anxiously questions himself. "Yes, it is clearly the rational thing to do . . . but this advice betrays my friend! . . . no, it saves him! . . . it saves his wife . . . and if a third party should know a little happiness . . . is he any poorer, am I any the less his friend because I saved him? . . . no, my duty to him is plain . . . and my duty as an experimental searcher after truth . . . to observe these three guinea pigs, of which I am one . . ."

Again he seeks to strengthen Nina's determination and to belittle her fears of all "irrelevant moral ideas." If she has not great courage he will be obliged to give up the case.

But it is Darrell's courage and sympathy that she must have if she is to go on. It is he who must suggest the father. He is both her friend and Sam's friend.

The man must be some one who is not unattractive to her physically, Darrell agrees, and yet one with a mind—scientific mind "superior to the moral scruples that cause so much human blundering and unhappiness." Such a man should be her good friend and want to help her. He should not love her—"although he might, without harm, desire her."

NINA—Ned does not love her—but he used to like her and, I think, desire her. Does he now, doctor?

DARRELL (*thinking*)—Does he? . . . who is he? . . . he is Ned! . . . Ned is I! . . . I desire her! . . . I desire happiness! . . . (*Tremblingly now—gently.*) But, Madame, I must confess the Ned you are speaking of is I, and I am Ned.

NINA (*gently*)—And I am Nina, who wants her baby. (*Then she reaches out and turns his head until his face faces hers but he keeps his eyes down—she bends her head meekly and submissively—softly.*) I should be so grateful, Ned. (*He starts, looks up at her wildly, makes a motion as though to take her in his arms, then remains fixed for a moment in that attitude, staring at her bowed head as she repeats submissively*): I should be so humbly grateful.

DARRELL (*suddenly falling on his knees and taking her hand in both of his and kissing it humbly—with a sob*)—Yes—yes, Nina—yes—for your happiness—in that spirit! (*Thinking—fiercely triumphant*) I shall be happy for a while! . . .

NINA (*raising her head—thinking—proudly triumphant*)—I shall be happy! . . . I shall make my husband happy! . . .

The curtain falls.

ACT V

It is a bright morning in the following April. The Evanses have rented a small house in a seashore suburb of New York. "The room is a typical sitting-room of the quantity-production bungalow type," and all that Nina has been able to do in her effort "to take the curse of offensive, banal newness off the room with some of her own things" has not accomplished much.

Nina has been trying to read, but her book has dropped listlessly into her lap and she is deep in thought.

"A great change is noticeable in her face and bearing. She is again the pregnant woman of Act III but this time there is a triumphant strength about her expression, a ruthless self-confidence in her eyes. She has grown stouter, her face has filled out. One gets no impression of neurotic strain from her now, she seems nerveless and deeply calm."

Nina's thoughts are of the child stirring within her and of her love for Ned, the father—a great love that has come gradually to her, but which she has dutifully and calculatingly hidden from Darrell.

There are no more meetings with Ned now. For weeks after they had agreed to separate he had not even phoned, and no one knew where he was. And then he had come back.

"But I held him to his aloof doctor's pose and sent him away, proud of his will power . . . and sick of himself for desire of me," Nina recalls. "Every week since then he's been coming out here . . . as my doctor . . . we've talked about our child wisely, dispassionately . . . as if it were Sam's child . . . we've never given in to our desire . . . and I've watched love grow in him until I'm sure . . ."

Still, there are times when Nina doubts her own conclusions as to Darrell's love. But never for long nor ever during those moments in which she is conscious of her child.

"There . . . again . . . his child! . . . my child moving in my life . . . my life moving in my child . . . the world is whole and perfect . . . all things are each other's . . . life is . . . and the is is beyond reason . . . questions die in the silence of this peace. . . . I am living a dream within the great dream of the tide . . . breathing in the tide I dream and breathe back my dream into the tide . . . suspended in the movement of the tide, I feel life move in me, suspended in me . . . no whys matter . . . there is no why . . . I am a mother . . . God is a Mother . . ."

Evans is determined to face the truth. He will tell Nina his fears of his impotency and give her the chance for freedom for which he knows she hungers and to which he feels she is entitled. He faces Nina, "his eyes pitiably harried, his manner a distressingly obvious attempt to cover up a chronic state of nervous panic and guilty conscience."

He will agree to give Nina a divorce, Evans decides, even though he knows he cannot live without her. If she leaves him it at least will give him the courage to do away with himself.

But Nina, awaking, drives his intent from his mind. It is hard for Nina at first to think of Sam as her husband, hard for her to remember that people will think of him as the father of her child. She is entitled to be free of Sam. She is entitled to Ned's love . . . And yet, poor Sam is not to blame. . . .

After Darrell arrives Nina's attitude toward Evans is one of thinly veiled contempt, and this irritates Darrell. Makes him

feel like a swine to see Sam practically sent out of the room by
Nina and to think that Sam still trusts them!

"Why doesn't he take me in his arms," wonders Nina, frightenedly. "Oh, I feel he doesn't love me now! . . . he's so bitter!"

"Sometimes I almost hate her!" Darrell admits bitterly to himself. "If it wasn't for her I'd have kept my peace of mind . . .
no good for anything lately, damn it! . . . but it's idiotic to feel
guilty . . . if Sam only didn't trust me! . . . (*Then impatiently.*) Boch! . . . sentimental nonsense! . . . end justifies
means! . . . this will have a good end for Sam, I swear to that!
. . . why doesn't she tell him she's pregnant? . . . what's she
waiting for? . . ."

Despite the growing knowledge that Nina loves him; that she
has forgotten Gordon at last, Darrell tries stoutly to maintain
his professional detachment. But Nina's pleading finally masters
his resolution.

"Ned! I love you," she cries, passionately. "I can't hide it
any more! I won't! I love you, Ned!"

"Nina! Beautiful!" He has taken her in his arms and is
kissing her passionately.

"You love me, don't you?" she cries triumphantly, between
kisses. "Say you do, Ned?"

"Yes! Yes!"

"Thank God! At last you've told me! You've confessed it to
yourself! Oh, Ned, you've made me so happy!"

There is a ring at the doorbell. Guiltily the lovers separate.
Darrell's reaction is immediate and definite. Even as the maid
lets in Charlie Marsden, Darrell in self-torture is shouting to
Nina a denial of his confessed love.

Marsden is dressed immaculately in deep mourning, and "his
face is pale, drawn, haggard with loneliness and grief."

He is apologetic and miserable, and as Nina seeks to comfort
him he frankly gives way and is weeping upon her shoulder.
Yet he writhes inwardly beneath her sympathy and her "Dear
old Charlie" solicitude. It "shocks his pride to life."

Recovering his poise, Marsden senses something wrong in the
attitude of Nina and Darrell, something disgusting in that room,
something human and unnatural . . . "love and hate and passion and possession . . . cruelly indifferent to my loss . . .
mocking my loneliness! . . . no longer any love for me in any
room . . . lust in this room . . ."

Marsden would tell Sam of these suspicions if it were not that to do so would punish Nina, his little Nina, whom he wants so to be happy. To change his unhappy thoughts he begins telling them of his mother's passing. This burst of garrulity in turn throws him into a second state of semi-hysteria at thought of his grief and the cold indifference of his listeners. Finally in desperation he runs upstairs to look for Sam.

Nina and Darrell return again to the statement and denial of their lovers' confession. Darrell, again sane, as he keeps reminding himself, is determined that they shall stick to both the letter and the spirit of their agreement. Nina is equally determined that their love shall be acknowledged before the world. There is little use of their trying to go on as they planned. She is going to have her child, that's true. But her child wants its father. And she wants happiness—the happiness Sam's mother meant when she said that being happy was the nearest we could come to knowing what good is.

Stubbornly Darrell opposes the determination taking lodgment in Nina's mind. She must still remember Sam; must know what divorcing him, as she proposes, would mean to him.

Nina will not give up. Ned is her lover! Nothing else matters! Determinedly she takes his hands and as he looks deep in her eyes, forces a confession from him that all either of them can be sure of is their love.

They are standing with clasped hands when Evans comes in, but he attaches no more significance to that fact than that it is a part of Darrell's examination. He is eager to know of the patient's condition and to have the doctor's report. Nina is much better, Darrell assures him.

It is not until after Nina has gone to superintend the preparation of luncheon that Darrell is able to map his future course. That Nina has trapped him he is conscious. That Sam is his friend and trusts him he knows. That he (Darrell) would suffer such tortures of mind as would ruin his career if he were to be responsible for Sam's finish he is pitifully aware. He must stop it! But how? Suddenly the way is made clear to him.

". . . By God, I see," he mutters, in strange elation, "tell him about baby . . . that'll stop her! . . . when she knows I've told him that, she'll see it's hopeless! . . . she'll stick to him! . . . poor Nina! . . . I'm sorry! . . . she does love me! . . . hell! . . . she'll forget! . . . she'll have her child! . . . She'll be happy! . . . and Sam'll be happy! . . ."

Suddenly Darrell turns to Sam, who has been staring at him puzzledly, and excuses himself for running away. Fact is he is sailing for Europe in a few days and must make the most of his time. And as for the secret Nina had promised to tell him after luncheon—

"You're going to be a father, old scout! That's the secret!" he shouts. And as Evans "stares dumbly in a blissful satisfaction," Darrell continues: "And now I've got to run. See you again in a year or so. I've said good-by to Nina. Good-by, Sam. . . . And tell Nina I'll expect to find you both happy in your child—both of you, tell her—happy in your child! Tell her that, Sam!"

When Nina comes from the kitchen she finds Evans in a state of "happy stupefaction." He has fallen on his knees to thank God, and his thanks to her are equally fervent. Ned has told him her secret! He knows they are to have a child and oh, the happiness it will mean to him!

At first Nina will not, cannot credit the news. Wildly she protests it cannot be. She will run after Ned! She will call him up! She will go to him immediately! Frightenedly Evans seeks to calm her, to get her to lie down. Her condition, he concludes, is responsible for this attack.

In her anguish Nina is determined to be revenged upon Darrell, she prays for strength to hate him. She will tell Sam he lied. She will make Sam hate him, kill him! She will promise to love Sam if he kills him!

"He lied to you!" she shouts. "Ned lied to you!"

Desperately she tries to tell him of the deceit they have practiced upon him, but the hurt look in his eyes and his stammering demand for the truth halts her. He's her poor little boy, now, and—

"One gives birth to little boys," she tells herself. "One doesn't drive them mad and kill them!"

And so Nina comes to a decision. "I'll try to make you happy, Sammy," she agrees, pressing his head against her breast. And, as she stares out over his head, she murmurs as if she were repeating the words of some inner voice of life. "Not Ned's child! . . . not Sam's child! . . . mine! . . . there! . . . again! . . . I feel my child live . . . moving in my life . . . my life moving in my child . . . breathing in the tide I dream and breathe my dream back into the tide. . . . God is a Mother. . . . (*Then with sudden anguish*): Oh, afternoons . . . dear wonderful after-

noons of love with you, my lover . . . you are lost . . . gone
from me forever! . . ."

The curtain falls.

ACT VI

A year later the sitting room in the Evans house "has under-
gone a significant change. There is a comfortable, homey atmosphere as though now it definitely belonged to the type of person
it was built for."

At the moment it is peopled by Nina, Sam and Charlie Marsden. It is early evening. Sam is looking over the headlines of
his paper. Nina is knitting a tiny sweater. Marsden is on the
sofa glancing idly through a book he is pretending to read, though
his thought is largely centered on Sam and Nina.

Evans has changed. "He is stouter, the haggard look of worry
and self-conscious inferiority has gone from his face." He is solid
looking and self-confident.

"Nina looks noticeably older, the traces of former suffering are
marked on her face, but there is also an expression of present
contentment and calm."

"Marsden has aged greatly. His hair is gray, his expression
one of deep grief that is dying out into a resignation resentful of
itself."

As she knits Nina is thinking of her baby; of his likeness in
her imagination to Gordon, for whom he has been named; of Ned,
who has never written since he has been away; of the change
that has come over Sam in the past year; of Sam as the perfect
father who has, with her help, done so well; of her happiness in
making Sam happy; of how all things have worked out for the
best.

"I don't feel wicked. . . . I feel good." She smiles at her own
satisfaction.

Marsden is also deep in thoughts of the great change that has
come to his friends. He must have misjudged Darrell when he
suspected him of being Nina's lover. He recalls a recent meeting
with Darrell on the continent and his finding him dissipated and
unhappy.

The conversation of the three is desultory. Sam is confident a
great boom in business is coming. Secretly he is thinking of
Marsden as a possible backer when he wants to establish himself
in business. Marsden senses something of Sam's thought. A little success, he thinks, has made a great change in Sam.

Nina is inclined to tease Marsden about his selfish determination not to marry. This vow of perpetual bachelorhood is silly. Maybe she should pick out a wife for him? Marsden is only peeved at the suggestion.

Marsden tells them of meeting Darrell in Munich. Darrell was with a woman. Probably they were living together.

Nina resents that suggestion. She can't quite smother her instinctive jealousy at the thought of Ned with other women.

Is Ned coming back? Marsden doesn't think so. Ned had spoken of them and asked if Nina had had her baby?

Then, thinks Nina, he hadn't quite forgotten. She is secretly glad.

Nina, going to nurse the baby, seeks with some deliberation to reëstablish herself in Marsden's good graces. She must not risk losing Charlie's friendship! . . .

Evans is back from saying good night to little Gordon. A fine boy, Gordon. Sam is going to make an athlete of him. Another Gordon Shaw. Make him all the things he had wanted to be and couldn't. He'll train the boy's body. His mind will take care of itself, with Nina for a mother. All his father can do for him is to make money.

"I couldn't have said that two years ago and believed it," Evans admits. "I've changed a hell of a lot. Since the baby was born, I've felt as if I had a shot of dynamite in each arm. They can't pile on the work fast enough."

The thought gives Sam courage to hint at a partnership. But Marsden is not interested. Never mind. Sam will get his capital somewhere else.

Sam has gone for a walk. There is a knock at the door. Marsden opens it. It is Darrell!

Nina, from upstairs, greets the announcement with a glad cry. Darrell has come back "pale, thin, nervous, unhealthy looking." He had arrived that morning. The death of his father had brought him back unexpectedly. He is irritated by Marsden's somewhat searching questioning. He wishes Marsden would get out. He thinks of the waste he has made of his own life; of his unsuccessful effort to forget Nina or to deny the love of her that has completely conquered his pride.

Here is a new problem for Marsden. What will Evans' attitude be toward Darrell now? Marsden feels that he must protect Nina . . . and Sam!

Nina has put on a fresh dress, and is rouged and powdered for the meeting with Darrell. "She looks extremely pretty and this is heightened by the feverish state of mind she is in."

There is a suppressed joy in Nina's and Darrell's greeting, a joy tinged with both questioning doubt and the inner conviction that their love still lives, but must be hidden from Marsden. Mutually they confess that they have missed each other terribly.

Sam had missed Darrell, too, significantly reports Marsden. Which is proof of Sam's wonderful loyalty to Darrell. Darrell is going to be amazed at the change in Sam! So impressed is he (*Marsden*) with the new Sam that he is going to back him in business and become his silent partner.

"Yes, ever since the baby was born Sam's been another man—in fact, ever since he knew there was going to be a baby, isn't it, Nina?"

Nina agrees with him. Sam is a wonderful father. If anything should happen to little Gordon, Sam would probably lose his reason. She knows she would lose hers!

That they have named the baby Gordon is news to Darrell. Does that, he wonders, mean that Nina still loves Gordon? That he, the true father, has been forced out of this closed corporation?

"I couldn't find a better husband than Sam," thinks Nina, with a strange calculation. "And I couldn't find a better lover than Ned. . . . I need them both to be happy. . . ."

With despairing suddenness the suspicion strikes Marsden that little Gordon might be Darrell's child after all! Why has he never thought of that before? But if that's true, why should Nina go on living with Sam? He would have given her a divorce!

Marsden has gone to pick up Sam. Nina and Darrell face each other "guiltily and frightenedly. Then he comes to her and takes both of her hands uncertainly."

"Nina—I—I've come back to you—do you—do you still care —Nina?" he asks, stammeringly.

"I love you, Ned!" she says, "giving way to his love passionately as if to drown her fears."

DARRELL (*kissing her awkwardly—stammering*)—I—I didn't know—you seemed so cold—damn Marsden—he suspects, doesn't he?—but it makes no difference now, does it? (*Then in a flood of words.*) Oh, it's been hell, Nina! I couldn't forget you! Other women—they only made me love you more! I hated them and loved you even at the moment when—that's honest! It was always you in my arms—as you used to be—those afternoons— God, how I've thought of them—lying awake—recalling every word you said, each movement, each expression on your face, smelling your hair, feeling your soft body. (*Suddenly taking her*

in his arms and kissing her again and again—passionately.)
Nina! I love you so!

NINA—And I've longed for you so much! Do you think I've
forgotten those afternoons? (*Then in anguish.*) Oh, Ned, why
did you run away? I can never forgive that! I can never trust
you again!

DARRELL (*violently*)—I was a fool! I thought of Sam! And
that wasn't all! Oh, I wasn't all noble, I'll confess! I thought
of myself and my career! Damn my career! A lot of good that
did it! I didn't study! I didn't live! I longed for you—and
suffered! I paid in full, believe me, Nina! But I know better
now! I've come back. The time for lying is past! You've got
to come away with me! (*He kisses her.*)

NINA (*letting herself go, kissing him passionately*)—Yes! My
lover! (*Then suddenly resisting and pushing him away.*) No!
You're forgetting Sam—and Sam's baby!

DARRELL (*staring at her wildly*)—Sam's baby? Are you joking? Ours, you mean! We'll take him with us, of course!

NINA (*sadly*)—And Sam?

DARRELL—Damn Sam! He's got to give you a divorce! Let
him be generous for a change!

NINA (*sadly but determinedly*)—He would be. You must be
just to Sam. He'd give his life for my happiness. And this would
mean his life. Could we be happy then? You know we couldn't!
And I've changed, Ned. You've got to realize that. I'm not your
old mad Nina. I still love you. I will always love you. But
now I love my baby too. His happiness comes first with me!

DARRELL—But—he's mine, too!

NINA—No! You gave him to Sam to save Sam!

DARRELL—To hell with Sam! It was to make you happy!

NINA—So I could make Sam happy! That was in it too! I
was sincere in that, Ned! If I hadn't been I could never have
gone to you that first day—or if I had, I'd never have forgiven
myself. But as it is I don't feel guilty or wicked. I have made
Sam happy! And I'm proud! I love Sam's happiness! I love
the devoted husband and father in him! And I feel it's his baby
—that we've made it his baby!

Darrell is distracted. Can it be that Nina has come to love
Sam? If so he will go away and never come back. But Nina will
not have this. He is never to go away again! She doesn't love
Sam! She loves him! He will always have her love! He shall
be her lover again! That is the nearest they can come to making

every one happy and happiness is all that counts. Sam will never know. He is content with the happiness they have already given him. For all they have done for Sam he owes them their happiness.

Darrell is repulsed by the suggestion. No, he will go back to Europe. He could not endure staying on as Nina's lover, watching Sam with his (*Darrell's*) wife and child! She can go to hell! He will tell Sam everything!

Nina is not frightened. Ned could never do that to Sam!

The door opens. Marsden and Sam are back. With a bound Sam is at Darrell's side, shaking his hand, pounding his back, greeting him with effusive friendliness.

"Mercy, Sam, give Ned a chance to get a word in!" Nina interposes, affectionately. She looks at Ned pityingly but challengingly as she says to Sam, "Ned wants to tell you something."

"No—I mean yes—," Ned begins, crushed and stammering. "I want to tell you how damn glad I am—"

Nina, triumphantly calm, steps between them. They look around for Marsden. "Here, Nina, always here!" Marsden calls from the back of the room as he joins the group.

"Yes, you're here, Charlie—always! And you, Sam—and Ned!" Nina's gayety is strange. "Sit down, all of you! Make yourselves at home! You are my three men! This is your home with me!"

Then, in a half whisper she goes on. "Ssssh! I thought I heard the baby! You must all sit down and be very quiet! You must not wake our baby!"

Mechanically the three sit down, careful to make no noise. They sit staring before them in silence. Nina remains standing, dominating them.

"I couldn't," thinks Darrell, abjectly. "There are things one may not do and live with oneself afterwards . . . there are things one may not say . . . memory is too full of echoes! . . . there are secrets one must not reveal . . . memory is lined with mirrors! . . . he was too happy! . . . to kill happiness is a worse murder than taking life! . . . I gave him that happiness! . . . Sam deserves my happiness! . . . God bless you, Sam! . . . (*Then in a strange objective tone, thinking.*) My experimenting with the guinea pigs has been a success . . . the ailing ones, Sam, and the female, Nina, have been restored to health and normal function . . . only the other male, Ned, seems to have suffered deterioration."

"Sure good to see Ned again," thinks Evans, looking at Darrell affectionately. "A real friend if there ever was one . . . looks blue about something . . . oh, that's right, Charlie said his old man had kicked in . . . his old man was rich . . . that's an idea . . . I'll bet he'd put up that capital. . . . (*Then ashamed of himself.*) Aw, hell, what's the matter with me? . . . he's no sooner here than I start . . . he's done enough . . . forget it! . . . now anyway . . . he looks pretty dissipated . . . too many women . . . ought to get married and settle down . . . tell him that if I didn't think he'd laugh at me giving him advice . . . but he'll soon realize I'm not the old Sam he knew . . . I suppose Nina's been boasting about that already . . . she's proud . . . she's helped me . . . she's a wonderful wife and mother . . ."

"She's the old queer Nina now," broods Marsden; "the Nina I could never fathom . . . her three men! . . . and we are! . . . I? . . . yes, more deeply than either of the others since I serve for nothing . . . a queer kind of love, maybe . . . I am not ordinary! . . . our child . . . what could she mean by that? . . . child of us three? . . . on the surface, that's insane . . . but I felt when she said it there was something in it . . . she has strange devious intuitions that tap the hidden currents of life . . . dark intermingling currents that become the one stream of desire . . . I feel, with regard to Nina, my life queerly identified with Sam's and Darrell's . . . her child is the child of our three loves for her . . . I would like to believe that . . . I would like to be her husband in a sense . . . and the father of a child, after my fashion . . . I could forgive her everything . . . permit everything . . . (*Determinedly.*) And I do forgive! . . ."

"My three men!" Nina is more and more strangely triumphant. "I feel their desires converge in me! . . . to form one complete beautiful male desire which I absorb . . . and am whole . . . they dissolve in me, their life is my life . . . I am pregnant with the three! . . . husband! . . . lover! . . . father! . . . and the fourth man! . . . little man! . . . little Gordon! (*With an extravagant suppressed exultance.*) Why, I should be the proudest woman on earth! . . . I should be the happiest woman in the world! . . . (*Then suppressing an outbreak of hysterical triumphant laughter only by a tremendous effort.*) Ha-ha . . . only I better knock wood . . . (*she raps with both knuckles in a fierce tattoo on the table*) before God the Father hears my happiness! . . ."

All three men turn to her anxiously. But she quiets their anxiety. It is only her nerves.

Evans (*bullying her—with loving authority*)—Then you go right to bed, young lady! We'll excuse you.

Nina (*quietly and calmly now*)—All right, dear. I guess I do need to rest. (*She kisses him as she might kiss a big brother she loved—affectionately.*) Good night, you bossy old thing, you!

Evans (*with deep tenderness*)—Good night, darling.

Nina (*she goes and kisses* Charlie *dutifully on the cheek as she might her father—affectionately*)—Good night, Charlie.

Marsden (*with a touch of her father's manner*)—That's a good girl! Good night, dear.

Nina (*she goes and kisses* Darrell *lovingly on the lips as she would kiss her lover*)—Good night, Ned.

Darrell (*looks at her with grateful humility*)—Thank you. Good night. (*She turns and walks quietly out of the room. The eyes of the three men follow her.*)

The curtain falls.

ACT VII

Nearly eleven years have elapsed. Sam and Nina Evans are living on Park Avenue, New York, in an apartment that, judging by the living room, is a tribute to Nina's good taste.

Early in the afternoon of a fall day Nina, Darrell and the boy Gordon are sitting in this living room. Nina is thirty-five now and in the full bloom of her womanhood. But beneath her fine physical appearance "there is a sense of great mental strain."

Gordon, eleven, is a fine boy and already suggests the athlete. He is grave and "his eyes are full of a quick-tempered sensitiveness. . . . He seems to have sprung from a line distinct from any of the people we have seen. . . ."

Darrell has also aged noticeably, grown stout and puffy under the eyes. "He has the look of a man with no definite aim or ambition to which he can relate his living."

Gordon, at play, is thinking bitter thoughts. They are directed mostly at Darrell. Why is Darrell there? Why is he always hanging around Gordon's mother? "I'd think she'd get sick of the old fool and tell him to get out and never come back," thinks Gordon. "It's good for him he didn't bring me any birthday present or I'd smash it first chance I got!"

Nina's thoughts, as she watches her child, are sad and brooding. Already Gordon is growing away from her. At forty she will, like all her sex, she thinks, have finished living and be ready "to rot away in peace," sick of the fight for happiness.

She thinks of this as Gordon's birthday, of his likeness to the

Gordon for whom he is named, and of Ned, the father, who has suffered much at her hands the last several years. Her love and Ned's has bound them strangely together, but it has not brought them sustained happiness. Can it be that she has been the cause of Ned's weakened resolution? No, it was she who had induced him to take up biology. If Ned would only go away oftener and stay longer Nina would be pleased. "I always get a terrible feeling after he's been back awhile that he is waiting for Sam to die . . . or go insane! . . ." she confesses.

Darrell's thoughts also are bitter, and his mind puzzled. Often they will sit thus, silently brooding. "Our love has become the intimate thinking together of thoughts that are strangers," he concludes. Yet, whatever force it is that has bound them together, it is strong. Each has tried to break that bond and each has failed. Always they are drawn back to each other.

Darrell will be going back to the West Indies soon, he tells Nina, and young Gordon exults secretly at the news. Darrell takes no particular interest in his work these days. His real work, he intimates, significantly, has been finished for twelve years. Sam having made them all rich there is no incentive now for anything but play.

They talk of Gordon. The boy is not, Darrell insists, at all like the rah-rah boy for whom he has been named. He'd much rather Gordon should grow up in the image of the esteemed Samuel, now resting "so complacently on the proud assurance that he is self-made."

Gordon resents Darrell's tone; resents his making fun of his father. So worked up with resentment does the boy become that Nina is forced to send him from the room in punishment. Nor will Gordon 'pologize to his Uncle Ned. Not ever!

Darrell understands Gordon's antipathy. Natural that the child should hate him. They are to blame, not Gordon. They gave their son to Sam. Why shouldn't he act like Sam?

"Oh, Ned, do shut up!" Nina cries in exasperation. "I can't stand hearing the same old reproaches I've heard a thousand times before! I can't bear to hear myself making the same old bitter counter-accusations. And then there'll be the same old terrible scene of hate and you'll run away—it used to be to drink and women, now it's to the Station. Or I'll send you away. and then after a time I'll call you back, because I'll have gotten so lonely again living this lonely lie of my life, with no one to speak to except Sam's business friends and their deadly wives. (*She laughs helplessly.*) Or else you'll get lonely in your lie a little before I do and come back again of your own desire! And then we'll kiss and cry and love each other again!"

Darrell thinks he might consider marrying, but they both know neither could stand that experience. No, they seem fated to go on loving each other, they are agreed. So there must be some sort of compromise. Ned must go away now, before there can be another scene and while their love is still strong and they grateful for it.

Darrell is holding Nina in his arms, kissing her for this last good-by, when Gordon sees them from the doorway. "I mustn't see her," mutters the boy, in a passion of rage and grief; "pretend I didn't see her . . . mustn't ever let her know I saw her."

Gordon runs away and when he comes again he is careful to give warning of his approach. He has come now to tell his mother Uncle Charlie Marsden is downstairs, and so strained is his manner that Nina is convinced his attitude has strangely changed against her. Could Gordon have seen?

"To be on the safe side you'd better tell him you kissed me good-by to get rid of me," suggests Darrell.

Marsden is smiling and immaculately dressed, as usual. He is also much gayer than he has been. Darrell quite frankly has come to hate Marsden, partly for his constant and continued interest in the Evans affairs and not a little because of little Gordon's fondness for him.

The two men are soon covertly insulting each other and both seeking to avoid an open quarrel. Marsden is plainly hurt. In anguish of soul he seeks to account for changed and changing conditions. Darrell has become less and less to Nina, and her love for Sam cannot be anything more than perfunctory. Of late, thinks Marsden, Nina has been turning more and more to him as to one who understands and who can be implicitly trusted. "I've been playing the dear old Charlie of her girlhood again."

For her part Nina, looking at Marsden pityingly, can see him now only as "a perfect lover for one's old age." Then, with a sudden scornful revulsion, Nina is convinced that she hates all three of her men. Only little Gordon is her real man.

Darrell decides not to stay to lunch. No use his waiting for Sam, either. He has nothing to say to Sam. Sam is disgustingly healthy and sane, too. "Nina will soon be fighting Sam for my son's love!" he concludes, bitterly. "Oh, Christ, what a mess it all is!"

Gordon has found a sailboat that Darrell has brought for his birthday. He has deliberately broken it in front of its donor, because, as he admits, he hates Darrell, hates him more than ever since he saw that kissing. Nor is he content with Darrell's explanation that it was only a good-by kiss. He knows more than that. He knows Darrell is always hanging around his mother and he knows he is not his father's friend and sometime he is going to tell his father everything!

Darrell succeeds in convincing Gordon that there are some things men of honor never tell, and in that minute the boy and the man understand each other and accept each other as they never have before.

Sam Evans is in now, hearty and blustery. He has grown stouter and more executive and is expensively tailored. He greets his son with enthusiasm and is heartily glad to see Darrell.

Gordon is glad to tell his father about his birthday, but he is more anxious to have a few questions answered. Why, for instance, was he named Gordon? And was the Gordon for whom he was named ever his mother's beau? Being told that his mother and Gordon Shaw were very fond of each other young Gordon decides that that is the reason Darrell hates the name. Perhaps if he can grow up to be just like Gordon Shaw his mother will love him more than she does Darrell.

Then Gordon wants to know a lot about fighting. Could his father lick Darrell? Could Gordon Shaw have licked him? Nor is Nina very successful in getting Gordon and Sam away from the subject when she comes back into the room.

Finally she manages to say that she is glad Ned's gone; that he has of late made a good deal of a bore of himself, and that she finally had to exact a promise from him that he would get back to his work. When she had done that he had suddenly become silly and asked her to kiss him good-by for luck, she reports. Which, to get rid of him, she did.

Gordon is relieved by this news and climbs quickly into his mother's lap to kiss her as a reward.

Evans thinks perhaps Darrell is falling for Nina in his old age. But the real trouble probably is that Ned never married. A fellow needs a little feminine encouragement to help him keep his head up.

Nina, hugging her son to her, is conscience stricken for the moment. She is hardly fair to Ned, lying to his son against him. Is she worthy of Ned's love? It is her constant prayer that one day she may tell their son the truth.

Something of her thought young Gordon senses and pushes

himself promptly off her lap. He knows! Didn't he see them
kissing that time? She tries to make up with the boy but he
runs away.

She tries to baby Gordon too much, Sam insists. He wants his
son to grow up a regular he-man. Not another Charlie Marsden!

"Oh, Mother God, grant that I may some day tell this fool
the truth," Nina prays.

The curtain falls.

ACT VIII

An afternoon in late June, ten years later, the Evans' motor
cruiser is anchored in the Hudson at Poughkeepsie. Darrell,
Marsden and Nina are sitting grouped on the after deck in the
cool shade. At the rail Sam Evans and a young girl, Madeline
Arnold, are looking anxiously up the river, alternately sharing a
pair of binoculars.

"Nina's hair has turned completely white. She is desperately
trying to conceal the obvious inroads of time. . . . There is little
left of her face's charm except her eyes, which now seem larger
and more deeply mysterious than ever. But she has kept her
beautiful figure."

"Darrell has again the air of the cool, detached scientist regarding himself and the people around him as interesting phe-
nomena. . . . His skin is tanned almost black by his years in the
tropics. His thick hair is iron gray."

"Marsden has aged greatly. The stoop of his tall figure is ac-
centuated, his hair has grown whitish."

"Evans is simply Evans, his type logically developed by ten
years of continued success and accumulating wealth. . . . He has
grown very stout. His jowly broad face has a heavy, flushed,
apoplectic look."

"Madeline Arnold is a pretty girl of nineteen, with dark hair
and eyes. Her skin is deeply tanned, her figure tall and athletic.
Her personality is direct and frank . . . a good sport who is
popular with her own sex as well as sought after by men."

It is about time for the race to start, and the radio has gone
dead. Sam Evans is nervous and excited.

Gordon is in that boat upstream in which the Evans party is
most interested, and Gordon, they fear, is not having a very happy
time of it just now.

Nina is frankly troubled by this Madeline Arnold, who evidently is intent on possessing herself of Gordon's love. Nina doesn't purpose letting any one take her son away from her—not as long as she lives.

Madeline senses Mrs. Evans' enmity and wonders at it. She has tried to be as nice as she could be to Gordon's mother for Gordon's sake.

Sam is conscious of it, too. Just Nina's crazy jealousy, that's what it is. And he doesn't intend that because of it Nina shall separate Gordon and Madeline.

Darrell knows of the contest Nina is waging; knows she will smash her son's engagement if she can. Which makes him glad that he had managed finally to break the chains with which Nina at one time had held him.

Evans' excitement distresses Nina, and the kill-joy attitude of the guests exasperates Evans. He probably will have to take Madeline and Gordon and stage a real celebration party for them in town.

There the others sit, Darrell congratulating himself secretly on the fact that he has broken the Nina charm; Charlie Marsden wondering why he ever agreed to come to the stupid old race; Nina miserably unhappy over her son's new interests.

The talk now has turned to Gordon. He is a better man than Gordon Shaw ever was, Sam insists. All the experts admit that much. Neither Darrell nor Nina is annoyed by the suggestion. Yet, Gordon is more like Sam than any one else, Nina thinks. So much like Sam that Darrell will hardly recognize him. Anyway, excitement is very bad for Sam's high blood pressure and he must be careful.

Now Sam has taken Charlie Marsden and Madeline into the cabin to "shoot a drink" and left Darrell and Nina together.

A little sadly these two review their secret thought.

"I can look into her eyes," confesses Darrell with melancholy interest, "without desire or jealousy or bitterness . . . was she ever my mistress? . . . can she be the mother of my child? . . . is there such a person as my son? . . . I can't think of these things as real any more . . . they must have happened in another life. . . ."

"My old lover," ruminates Nina, sadly. "How well and young he looks . . . now we no longer love each other at all . . . our account with God the Father is settled . . . afternoons of happiness paid for with years of pain . . . love, passion, ecstasy . . .

in what a far-off life were they alive! . . . the only living life is
in the past and future . . . the present is an interlude . . .
strange interlude in which we call on past and future to bear
witness we are living! . . ."

Nina feels that she needs Darrell's confidence. Else how can
she hope to gain his help in holding Gordon?

Madeline Arnold rushes in to report that the race has started
and that Gordon's boat is third in line! Madeline's enthusiasm
enrages Nina. To think a young thing like that could take Gordon away from her!

Darrell, on the other hand, is pleased. In Gordon's shoes he
would feel the same. Nina must come to realize that they are
getting old. That Gordon and Madeline are young. As for helping her, Darrell has sworn never again to meddle in human lives.
. . . Nina is persistent. With or without support she will not
give Gordon up.

Sam Evans reappears from the cabin, his excitement at fever
pitch. Gordon is still third! Navy and Washington are leading
him! Sam can't understand Darrell's and Nina's lack of interest,
sitting there like dead clams! He rushes back to the radio.

Nina, in desperation, tries again to reawaken Darrell's interest
in her and her problems. To do so she is even prepared to tell
Sam the whole truth. It is time Sam gave their son, hers and
Ned's, back to them! Ned must take a hand! He must tell
Sam! He must help her reclaim their son!

Under the influence of her pleading Darrell sways toward her,
but the return of Sam and Madeline, wildly excited because Gordon's crew is forging ahead, saves the situation. Evans has grown
apoplectic in his excitement.

Now Marsden has joined the group. He, too, is in a state of
excitement, helped by the liquor he has drunk. But he is praying
that Gordon will lose! He tries to comfort Nina. Let Gordon
be beaten! What does it matter?

The excitement of the race grows hectic. Marsden, slightly
maudlin, insists that all is for the best. He can vision the time
when he and Nina will be married. Then he can write his best
novel. Then he can bare the whole truth of all their lives.

"Now I am going to give an honest healthy yell," he shouts;
"turn on the sun into the shadows of lies about 'This is life and
this is sex, and here are passion and hatred and regret and joy
and pain and ecstasy, and these are men and women and sons and

daughters whose hearts are weak and strong, whose blood is blood and not a soothing syrup!' Oh, I can do it, Nina! I can write the truth! I've seen it in you, your father, my mother, sister, Gordon, Sam, Darrell and myself. I'll write the book of us! But here I am talking while my last chapters are in the making—right here and now—"

The excitement of the finish of the race stops him. He has rushed off to hear the latest from the radio.

Nina, left alone, has a lingering hope of triumph. She can find some pretext to tell Madeline Sam Evans' family history! In that way she will get Gordon back.

Deliberately Nina tries to draw Madeline away from her excited interest in the race. Craftily, excitedly, she maneuvers until she has Madeline's attention. There is something, she tells the girl, something about Gordon that will prevent their marriage, Madeline should know—

Darrell has sensed what is happening. Quickly he interposes an explanation and a protest. Madeline must not listen to Nina, he explains. Nina, having passed through a crucial time in a woman's life, is not quite responsible for anything she says. Madeline had better run back to the race.

Nina goes on. She is in a sort of trance now, staring ahead of her. Only Marsden is listening. The rest are at the rail excitedly watching the onsweep of the boats. Like a young girl Nina repeats what she has decided to tell.

"Because all of Sam's father's family have been insane. His mother told me that time so I wouldn't have his baby. I was going to tell Madeline that so she wouldn't marry Gordon. But it would have been a lie because Gordon isn't really Sam's child at all, he's Ned's. Ned gave him to me and I gave him to Sam so Sam could have a healthy child and be well and happy. And Sam is well and happy, don't you think? (*Childishly.*) So I haven't been such an awfully wicked girl, have I, Father?"

No one has heard. Sam Evans, beside himself with excitement, is still trying to get them to the rail to watch the finish. Only Marsden stays with Nina. Only Marsden hears her.

"Oh, Nina," he tries to comfort her. "Poor little Nina—how you must have suffered! I forgive you! I forgive you everything! I forgive even your trying to tell Madeline—you wanted to keep Gordon—oh, I understand that—and I forgive you!"

At the rail the others are cheering for Gordon! Only Darrell is a discordant note. He is yelling for Navy! "We've got to beat these Gordons, Sam— We've got to beat—"

Furiously Sam turns to Darrell. He is ready to strike his old friend. Ironically, with a bitter, hopeless laugh, Darrell admits his yelling for Navy must have been a slip of the tongue!

Now there is a wild yelling from the crowds nearer the race. Hysterically Nina is praying!

"I hear the Father laughing," she cries, in a strange, strident, wild passion. "Oh, Mother God, protect my son! . . . let Gordon fly to you in heaven! . . . quick, Gordon! . . . love is the Father's lightning! . . . Madeline will bring you down in flames! . . . I hear His screaming laughter! . . . fly back to me! . . ."

EVANS (*holding on to a stanchion and leaning far out at the imminent risk of falling in*)—One spurt more will do it! Come on, boy, come on! It took death to beat Gordon Shaw! You can't be beaten either, Gordon! Lift her out of the water, son! Stroke! Stroke! He's gaining! Now! Over the line, boy! Over with her! Stroke! That's done it! He's won! He's won!

MADELINE (*has been shrieking at the same time*)—Gordon! Gordon! He's won! Oh, he's fainted! Poor dear darling! (*She remains standing at the rail, leaning down longingly toward his shell.*)

EVANS (*bounding back to the deck, his face congested and purple with a frenzy of joy, dancing about*)—He's won! By God, it was close! Greatest race in the history of rowing! He's the greatest oarsmen God ever made! (*Embracing* NINA *and kissing her frantically.*) Aren't you happy, Nina? Our Gordon! The greatest ever!

NINA (*torturedly—trying incoherently to force out a last despairing protest*)—No!—not yours!—mine!—and Gordon's!— Gordon is Gordon's!—he was my Gordon! -his Gordon is mine!

EVANS (*soothingly, humoring her—kissing her again*)—Of course he's yours, dear—and a dead ringer for Gordon Shaw, too! Gordon's body! Gordon's spirit! Your body and spirit, too, Nina! He's not like me, lucky for him! I'm a poor boob! I never could row worth a damn!

Evans suddenly staggers, gives a gasp and collapses inertly to the deck. Marsden stares stupidly. He knew something like that would happen. He calls Nina's attention. She, too, bewildered at first, sinks on her knees beside the stricken man.

They call Dr. Darrell. Even as he pronounces the attack only a stroke Darrell is forced to assure himself that an old hope of his is not being revived.

Nina, dully, loyally, swears to give her happiness to help Sam. Marsden, ashamed of the thought that he will not have long to wait for Nina now, protests his love and admiration for the stricken man. Darrell, his human grief for an old chum conquering other thought, pledges his life to save his friend.

And Madeline, staring after Gordon's shell, calls comfortingly: "Gordon! . . . dear lover . . . how tired . . . but you'll rest in my arms . . . your head will lie on my breast . . . soon!" The curtain falls.

ACT IX

Several months later, on the terrace of Sam Evans' Long Island estate, Gordon Evans is sitting on a stone bench bowed in grief. Madeline Arnold, her arm about his shoulders, is standing over him comfortingly.

"Gordon is over six feet tall, with the figure of a trained athlete. His sun-bronzed face is extremely handsome after the fashion of the magazine cover American collegian. It is a strong face but of a strength wholly material in quality.

"Madeline is much the same as in the previous act except that there is now a distinct maternal older feeling in her attitude toward Gordon as she endeavors to console him."

Sam Evans has just been buried. Gordon, in his grief, is inclined to reproach his mother. He has never felt that she really loved his father. Her love was dutiful rather than real. Gordon has always had the feeling, since he was a little boy, that Nina really had been in love with Darrell. That she has been wonderful through his father's illness he admits, but still there was always something— Yet he does not blame Darrell. Whatever attachment there may have been Darrell always had done his best to fight it down.

Gordon is grateful for Madeline's sympathy. He takes her in his arms and kisses her with rising passion.

Charlie Marsden comes upon them as they are embraced. For a moment he is scandalized, and then he understands.

"What has their loving to do with me?" he questions himself. "My life is cool green shade wherein comes no scorching zenith sun of passion and possession to wither the heart with bitter poisons . . . my life gathers roses, coolly crimson, in sheltered gardens, on late afternoons in love with evening . . . roses heavy with after-blooming of the long day, desiring evening . . . my life is an evening. . . . Nina is a rose, my rose, exhausted by the long, hot day, leaning wearily toward peace. . . . (*He kisses one of the roses with a simple sentimental smile—then still smiling, makes a gesture toward the two lovers.*) That is on another planet, called the world. . . . Nina and I have moved on to the moon. . . ."

Gordon and Madeline become aware of Marsden's presence. He has brought them flowers. Flowers, he has found, are comforting. He advises Gordon to go to his mother. She will want to see him before he flies back to New York.

It seems rotten and selfish to be happy, Gordon admits, when they have left him, and yet he knows his father understands.

"It's funny how I got to care more for dad than for mother," he soliloquizes. "I suppose it was finding out that she loved Darrell . . . I can remember that day seeing her kiss him . . . it did something to me I never got over . . . but she made dad happy . . . she gave up her own happiness for his sake . . . that was certainly damn fine . . . that was playing the game . . . I'm a hell of a one to criticize . . . my own mother! . . ."

Nina and Darrell come from the house. "Nina looks much older. . . . Resignation has come into her face, a resignation that uses no make-up, that has given up the struggle to be sexually attractive and look younger. She is dressed in deep black. Darrell's deep sunburn of the tropics has faded, leaving his skin a Mongolian yellow."

"Your message was a godsend, Gordon," Nina tells him. "Those stupid people with their social condolences were killing me. Perhaps I'm morbid but I always have the feeling that they're secretly glad some one is dead—that it flatters their vanity and makes them feel superior because they're living."

"They were all good friends of dad's. Why shouldn't they be sincerely sorry? His death ought to be a loss to every one who knew him."

Nina feels that Gordon is reproaching her because she is not weeping. But she does not feel guilty. She had done her duty by Sam. She is conscious of her freedom—freedom to rot away in peace. She will turn to Charlie now. He will understand.

Darrell feels the lack of sympathy between Gordon and Nina. He resents Gordon's tears for Sam the father. If Gordon knew the truth! Darrell is tempted to tell him. . . .

Now Gordon has gained control of himself. Quite calmly he speaks of his father's will. It leaves everything to him and to Nina, except half a million dollars that is to go to Dr. Darrell's biological work.

Darrell resents Sam's gift. He will accept nothing. Either for himself or for the station. But both Nina and Gordon insist that the bequest shall go to science, through the station. Darrell is obdurate. He takes Gordon's insistence as an insult, and Gordon is angered by the older man's attitude. He is ready to strike Darrell.

Nina steps between them. She is almost hysterical. Now the men are mutually apologetic. Perfunctorily they shake hands.

"Mother, stop laughing," commands Gordon of the hysterical Nina. "Please! It's all right—all right between us—I've apologized! (*As she has grown calmer.*) And now I want to say what I was going to say. It wasn't anything bad. It was just that I want you to know how fine I think you've both acted. I've known ever since I was a kid that you and Darrell were in love with each other. I hated the idea on father's account—that's only natural, isn't it?—but I knew it was unfair, that people can't help loving each other any more than Madeline and I could have helped ourselves. And I saw how fair you both were to dad— what a good wife you were, mother—what a true friend you were, Darrell—and how damn much he loved you both! So all I wanted to say is, now he's dead, I hope you'll get married and I hope you'll be as happy as you both deserve— (*Here he breaks down, kissing her and then breaking away.*) I've got to say good-by—got to fly back before dark—Madeline's waiting. (*He takes* DARRELL's *hand and shakes it again. They have both been staring at him stupidly.*) Good-by, Darrell! Good luck!"

"Listen, son. It's my turn. I've got to tell you something—"

Again Nina interrupts. She gets Gordon away, his repeated apologies trailing back of him.

With an ironical smile Darrell repeats the proposal that Gordon had suggested. Will Nina marry him?

"No! Certainly not," she is quick to reply. "Our ghosts would torture us to death. But I wish I did love you, Ned," she adds, forlornly. "Those were wonderful afternoons long ago!

The Nina of those afternoons will always live in me, will always love her lover, Ned, the father of her baby!"

Tenderly Darrell lifts her hand to his lips. He will always adore her. But she had better marry Marsden if she wants peace.

Marsden has returned from the house. He senses that Nina and Darrell have been talking about him, a thought that Nina confirms by telling him of Darrell's proposal, and of her refusal.

"I suspected as much," admits Marsden. "Then whom do you love, Nina, Cara Nina?"

"You, Charlie," Nina replies, with a sad smile. "I have always loved your love for me." She kisses him wistfully. "Will you let me rot away in peace?"

"All my life I've waited to bring you peace," he replies.

From under the cliff the hum of an airplane is heard. Gordon is flying away from them without a backward look. And then the plane rises, circles and comes back. From the cockpit Gordon waves to them! Nina waves frantically after him, but he does not see nor hear her tortured good-by!

"Fly up to heaven, Gordon!" she cries. "Fly with your love to heaven! Fly always! Never crash to earth like my old Gordon! Be happy, dear! You've got to be happy!"

DARRELL (*sardonically*)—I've heard that cry for happiness before, Nina! I remember hearing myself cry it—once—it must have been long ago! I'll get back to my cells—sensible unicellular life that floats in the sea and has never learned the cry for happiness! I'm going, Nina. (*As she remains oblivious, staring after the plane—thinking fatalistically.*) She doesn't hear, either. . . . (*He laughs up at the sky.*) Oh, God, so deaf and dumb and blind! . . . teach me to be resigned to be an atom! . . . (*He enters the house.*)

NINA (*finally lowering her eyes—confusedly*)—Gone. My eyes are growing dim. Where is Ned? Gone, too. And Sam is gone. They're all dead. Where are father and Charlie? (*With a shiver of fear she hurries over and sits on the bench beside* MARSDEN, *huddling against him.*) Gordon is dead, father. I've just had a cable. What I mean is, he flew away to another life—my son, Gordon, Charlie. So we're alone again—just as we used to be.

MARSDEN (*putting his arm around her—affectionately*)—Just as we used to be, dear Nina Cara Nina, before Gordon came.

NINA (*looking up at the sky—strangely*)—My having a son was a failure, wasn't it? He couldn't give me happiness. Sons are always their fathers. They pass through the mother to become their father again. The Sons of the Father have all been failures! Failing they died for us, they flew away to other lives, they could not stay with us, they could not give us happiness!

MARSDEN (*paternally—in her father's tone*)—You had best forget the whole affair of your association with the Gordons. After all, dear Nina, there was something unreal in all that has happened since you first met Gordon Shaw, something extravagant and fantastic, the sort of thing that isn't done, really, in our afternoons. So let's you and me forget the whole distressing episode, regard it as an interlude, of trial and preparation, say, in which our souls have been scraped clean of impure flesh and made worthy to bleach in peace.

NINA (*with a strange smile*)—Strange interlude! Yes, our lives are merely strange dark interludes in the electrical display of God the Father! (*Resting her head on his shoulder.*) You're so restful, Charlie. I feel as if I were a girl again and you were my father and the Charlie of those days made into one. I wonder is our old garden the same? We'll pick flowers together in the aging afternoons of spring and summer, won't we? It will be a comfort to get home—to be old and to be home again at last— to be in love with peace together—to love each other's peace— to sleep with peace together—! (*she kisses him—then shuts her eyes with a deep sigh of requited weariness*)—to die in peace! I'm so contentedly weary with life!

MARSDEN (*with a serene peace*)—Rest, dear Nina. (*Then tenderly.*) It has been a long day. Why don't you sleep now—as you used to, remember?—for a little while?

NINA (*murmurs with drowsy gratitude*)—Thank you, Father —have I been wicked?—you're so good—dear old Charlie!

MARSDEN (*reacting automatically and wincing with pain— thinking mechanically*)—God damn dear old . . . ! (*Then with a glance down at* NINA's *face, with a happy smile.*) No, God bless dear old Charlie . . . who, passed beyond desire, has all the luck at last! . . . (*NINA has fallen asleep. He watches with contented eyes the evening shadows closing in around them.*)

The curtain falls.

THE ROYAL FAMILY
A Comedy in Three Acts

By George Kaufman and Edna Ferber

IT was natural for any one even superficially conversant with stage affairs in America to jump to the conclusion that George Kaufman and Edna Ferber had deliberately taken the Barrymores as their models when they wrote "The Royal Family."

The authors, however, were at pains to deny the charge, and the general content of their comedy bears them out. I think it is reasonable to assume that if there had been no Barrymores associated with the American theatre there is little likelihood that "The Royal Family" ever would have been written. But so far as stage history records the facts, the adventures of the Barrymores we know and the Cavendishes Mr. Kaufman and Miss Ferber have put in their play are in no way identical. Nor has there been conscious effort to reproduce individual characteristics.

Let us say, then, that "The Royal Family" tells an entirely imaginary story of an American stage family that might easily have been the Barrymores had the Barrymores been exactly that kind of a stage family.

The authors, and the producer, Jed Harris, had some difficulty in finding a proper cast for the play, and kept it touring for some weeks previous to the New York première, which occurred at the Selwyn Theatre the night of December 28, 1927. It was, as it turned out, one of the big first nights of the year, and the sophisticated Broadway public was happily enthusiastic about the play. So were the critical reviews that followed. As a result "The Royal Family" continued at the head of the list of popular dramatic offerings the season through.

The scene of the play is the spacious and high-ceilinged living room of the Cavendish apartment indefinitely placed in the East Fifties of New York.

Parts of two floors can be seen, the balcony off which the bedrooms open above and the main room below. This room, as the authors reveal, "has about it nothing of the commonplace. At a glance one sees that it is lived in by an unusual family. It is rich, careless, crowded, comfortable. Almost cluttering it are deep-cushioned chairs, little corner clusters of couch, table, lamp; photographs in silver frames are all about; magazines, cushions. A profusion of flowers." . . . "All sorts of periods and styles have gone into the making of the room. Prominently placed is a portrait in oils of the late Aubrey Cavendish in his most celebrated rôle, all bristling mustachios, high stick, romantic cape, glittering orders, gold braid, silk and boots and swagger."

It is about 1 o'clock of a November afternoon and this family of actors is barely astir. Phones and doorbells have begun to ring, however, both in the front of the house and the rear, and, between trying to answer the bells and get the breakfast trays to her slowly awaking sleepers Della, the maid, is about run to death. She is able to impress Jo, the houseman, into service, but Jo is no great bargain as a helper, demanding a considerable amount of direction himself.

Despite the developing confusion we are able to gather, from the receiving end of the phone conversations that Mr. Wolfe, the manager, wants to talk with Fanny Cavendish; that Miss Julie Cavendish is expected not to forget a dinner engagement at Mrs. Sherwin's, in Park Avenue, and that it will be quite impossible for Miss Julie to see any one until after she has finished her morning's boxing lesson, now in progress, with young McDermott, her trainer.

Early callers include two other members of the family group—Herbert Dean, Fanny Cavendish's brother, and Kitty LeMoyne Dean, his wife. Herbert "is about fifty-seven, very dressy, an excellent actor, beginning to show his age. The flower of the Lamb's Club. Necktie, shirt and handkerchief always blend. Massage has been his most active form of exercise. His appearance inevitably brings to mind the adjective 'well-preserved.'"

This morning Dean is jaunty and hopeful, until Mrs. Dean follows too closely upon his heels. Kitty Dean "is about forty-eight but doesn't believe it. An actress for many years, never more than mediocre."

Kitty is also quite evidently in a temper with Mr. Dean and barely able to restrain herself in the presence of the servants. At the first opportunity she is up and at Herbert with the charge that he has tried deliberately to elude her and sneak off for another conference with his blessed family.

Furthermore it is Kitty's fixed determination, if he does the certain play about which he has come to consult his sister, that she shall play the feminine lead. Nor do his repeated declarations that it is not at all her type of part mollify her in the least. That the Cavendish women should be consulted about a script that she, Kitty Dean, is not even allowed to discuss irritates her beyond expression. And, so far as Dean can see, for no good reason at all.

DEAN—. . . I have never done a play without consulting Fanny and Julie.

KITTY—Maybe that's why you never have a hit.

DEAN—I'll have one this time! I can see myself in every line of it, every gesture! Take the Nero scene! (*A pose.*) The Abraham Lincoln scene! As Frederick the Great! But you, my dear Kitty—the woman who plays this part must be— You see, your technique is more—uh—mellow—

KITTY—Are you by any chance telling me that I'm too old?

DEAN—Oh, my dear Kitty!

KITTY—Then I suppose I'm not a good enough actress! I was good enough to support Mansfield, though, wasn't I?

DEAN—Plenty!

KITTY—I'm as good an actress as your precious Julie, even if she is a Cavendish. And I'm better than that sister of yours ever was.

DEAN—My dear Kitty, please do not embarrass me by comparing yourself with Julie Cavendish, or with her mother, the greatest Lady Macbeth of her day.

KITTY—Oh, for— Listen! There are a few actresses whose name isn't Cavendish. Cavendish! Cavendish! I've had the royal family Cavendished up to me for twelve years. God, but I'm sick of them!

DEAN—You are sick of the Cavendishes! You are—the most distinguished. . . . And who are you, I'd like to know, to be sick of the Cavendishes! What were you when I married you?

KITTY—I was understudying Mannering in "The Garden of Allah."

DEAN—You were an off-stage noise!

The battle might have grown in volume if Gwen Cavendish had not broken in just then. Gwen represents the latest generation of the family. "She is in riding clothes; a slim, lovely young thing of nineteen. She is, perhaps, less a Cavendish than any of the others of the family."

With Gwen is young Perry Stewart, "a personable young fellow of about twenty-eight. Piping Rock, Long Island, bonds." He takes the introductions to the Deans gracefully and then retires with the promise that he will be back for Gwen at 2.30. His mother, who is a bit fussy, is giving a tea for Gwen in Scarsdale and he is eager that the guest of honor shall be on time. This, her Uncle Herbert reminds Gwen, is her last week of play. No more morning rides once rehearsals have started. And next week they will be on full blast. Gwen seems considerably less excited by the prospect than Dean. To him the chance she is about to be given represents her greatest opportunity.

"You ought to be very proud, my dear," he declares, with a modest actorial flourish. "At your age, to be appearing with your mother. Quite an event! Quite an event in the theatre!" Toast and napkin in hand, he gives the effect of a speech as his mood gains in warmth and splendor. "Yes, sir! About to enter into your great inheritance! To come before the public as the descendant of a distinguished family! It is not a trust to be taken lightly, my dear. Remember that not only will all of us be watching you, but your gifted ancestors as well."

The heavy "Ahem!" with which Dean closes would have been more impressive if just at that moment Fanny Cavendish had not opened her door on the balcony and called down:

"I think that speech needs cutting, Bertie."

"Fanny Cavendish is seventy-two. Managerial, pungent, rather magnificent. Given to domineering and to reminiscence. Her clothes are rich, but careless and somewhat out-dated."

She is downstairs now, prepared to take charge of any situation that may arise. She is interested in Kitty Dean's report that Herbert is about to call another of his family conclaves; amused to find that Julie has not yet put in an appearance. Probably because the prize-fighter is with her.

"Time I was Julie's age I didn't have to box to keep my figger," Fanny boasts. "You could span my waist with your two hands."

KITTY—I like a nice womanly figure myself.

FANNY—You ought to be very happy.

DEAN (*a pat on the shoulder*)—Well, Fanny, you certainly don't seem an invalid. You're looking splendid.

FANNY—Invalid? Well as I ever was. I'm going into rehearsal as soon as Wolfe can pick a cast.

DEAN—Now, now, Fanny. You've had a long siege of it. After a year's illness—

KITTY—Nearer two, isn't it?

FANNY—And what if it is! Two years out of a life-time! I played fifty-three years without missing a performance, except when Tony was born.

KITTY—And surely when Julie was born!

FANNY—Not Julie! She knows her business better than that. Julie was born during Holy Week.

DEAN—But look here now, Fanny. What are you going to do? You haven't a new play, have you?

FANNY—Who said anything about a new play! I'm reviving "Mrs. Castlemaine."

DEAN—But that's rather old-fashioned, Fanny. New York won't come to see that, even with you in it.

FANNY—New York! You talk like a Follies girl! I'm going to take it on the road.

DEAN—The road? You're mad.

FANNY—I know your views, Bertie. You think Albany is somewhere in the Antipodes.

DEAN—I don't belittle the road. It's quite all right in its way. But my public is in New York.

KITTY—Or was, when last heard from.

FANNY—Well, I'm not like you, Bertie. I've been a trouper all my life, and I'm going to keep on trouping. I'd rather pack 'em into a tent in Texas than play highbrow matinées every Tuesday and Friday at the Teacup Theatre in New York.

DEAN—But you've been ill, Fanny. You can't stand what you used to. Those dreadful small town hotels! Sleeping in Pullmans!

FANNY—I did it when there weren't any Pullmans! When many a time I had to sit up all night—yes, with Julie asleep on one side, and Tony generally yelling his head off on the other.

DEAN—But that belongs to the past, Fanny. You're too important a figure to-day.

FANNY (*in spite of her infirmity rises to her feet*)—I was Fanny Cavendish then, just as I am now. When the bills said Aubrey and Fanny Cavendish people knew what they were going to see. You had to know how to act—(*a slow turn toward Kitty*) —when you went on the stage in those days.

KITTY—You had your method. We of the younger school have ours.

FANNY—Ah, youth, youth!

DEAN (*in the manner of a formal announcement*)—If you do go back this season, Fanny, that's going to mean the whole family on the boards.

FANNY—The whole family?

DEAN—Except Tony, of course. You can't call pictures acting. But with you in "Castlemaine," Julie and Gwen in their play, and—(*a triumphant reach for the manuscript on the table. The doorbell rings*)—your humble servant as the star of—

FANNY (*in a surprising shout*)—Della! Della! (*Turns to DEAN again.*) What's that about your being the bright particular star?

DEAN—I sent the manuscript of my next play over to Julie last night.

FANNY—I know it. (DELLA *enters. Goes to outer door.*)

DEAN—Have you read it?

FANNY—Only the first ten scenes. (Jo *enters with* KITTY's *tray.*)

DEAN—Well?

FANNY—I was afraid to read the second act for fear you played two parts at once.

Oscar Wolfe is calling. Oscar "is a figure of authority: dark, stocky, slightly gray, dressed with a picturesque richness. A rakish velour hat. Altogether the entrepreneur."

He has come at this surprising hour, this "first pale crack of dawn," as Gwen puts it, to see Julie. But he discovers that there are others who want to see him. Dean, for one. And Fanny, for another. Dean has at last found the play for which he has been searching, and Fanny, well and strong again as ever she was, according to Fanny, is determined to get back to acting immediately.

The manager puts Dean off a little impatiently and tries to joke Fanny into forgetting her revived ambitions. He even tries to divert them by playing strains of this and that popular composition while they nibble at the food Jo has brought them.

And then Julie appears on the balcony. "Julie is thirty-nine, beautiful, slim, mature. She is wearing a smart, rather tailored afternoon gown. Is evidently dressed for the day. She comes out slowly, curious to know who is playing. She crosses the width of the balcony, stands at the railing, looking down. Her first glance is toward the piano. She sees Wolfe there. Her gaze encompasses the rest of the room. Four of its occupants are busily eating. One at a time, she takes them in."

"Have you a table for one, Jo, not too near the music?" she calls.

"A very good entrance, Julie," smiles Fanny.

"Dear little mother! Wouldn't you like to go up and come down again?" answers her actress daughter.

It happens that Julie brings news. She is carrying a telegram and, save for a necessary pause while she borrows thirty-nine dol-

lars from Wolfe to pay for a C. O. D. package that has quite
slipped her mind, and another slight delay caused by her inability to set an hour during the next two or three busy days
when she can take another boxing lesson from McDermott, she
finally manages to read it.

The telegram is from Tony—"dear little brother Tony." So
far Julie has not been quite able to make it out, seeing that it is
rather sketchy, but as nearly as she can come to it Tony has evidently killed somebody.

"Any one we know?" demands Fanny.

Then Julie reads the telegram: "Pay no attention to possible
accounts of Deming incident injuries not fatal takes more than
that to kill a lousy movie director I arrive New York Saturday
California police have no authority outside state on no condition
talk to reporters Zeta Zaydak on this train but no trouble so far
as am locked in drawing room love to all of you he was dirty
hound anyhow. Tony."

KITTY—What did I tell you!

JULIE—It lacks a certain clarity, doesn't it?

FANNY—California police!

DEAN—What's this, what's this!

(*There now ensues a babel of sound—exclamations, conjec-
tures, questions. What's it mean? You know* TONY. *What's it
all about? Who's Zeta Zaydak? Read that again.*)

WOLFE (*comes over to* JULIE)—Let me have that, Julie. Now,
just a minute, people. Let's get at this. This may not be so
funny.

FANNY—Do you think it's serious?

JULIE—Of course not, Mother. It never is.

WOLFE (*re-reading fragments of the telegram to himself, but
aloud*)—Possible accounts of Deming incident—

GWEN—Deming is his director.

WOLFE—Arrive New York Saturday.

DEAN—That's to-morrow.

WOLFE— . . . Zeta Zaydak on this train. . . .

KITTY—She's that Polish hussy.

WOLFE—A fine business.

FANNY—What's she on the train for?

WOLFE—On no condition talk to reporters. . . .

JULIE—Have there been any reporters?

DEAN—Before you were down. The *Graphic!*

JULIE—The *Graphic!* Whatever we've done, we've always kept out of the tabloids.

WOLFE—Who's kept you out, I'd like to know! Wolfe! If it wasn't for me they'd have been running long ago a contest Which Is the Craziest Cavendish.

JULIE—Here's another chance for you. What are we going to do?

WOLFE—Now, wait a minute. Let's look this over. Maybe it's not as bad as it seems.

FANNY—No.

GWEN—Of course not, Grandma. Such a fuss because Tony's punched some director. I'm sure to be late. (*On her way up the stairs. Escapes.*)

WOLFE (*still concentrating on the telegram*)—Now the way I figure it, it was like this. The fella says something Tony doesn't like. Tony knocks him down, of course. And to keep from having to answer a lot of questions about it, he gets on this train.

JULIE—With the picture half finished, naturally.

WOLFE—Omaha he sent this from. Omaha last night. That means he got to Chicago this morning. Naturally he got on the Century. To-morrow morning you'll be just one happy family.

JULIE—We've got to keep the newspapers off him. You know Tony and the papers. They've been laying for him ever since that Mauretania thing.

KITTY—I must say I don't blame them.

DEAN—Yes, he never should have thrown that reporter overboard.

WOLFE—A big mistake.

JULIE—We mustn't let them get at him this time. They're sure to know he's on the Century. They'll swarm on him at the station. He'll start to smash cameras. (*A gesture that says "Whoop!"*)

FANNY—That poor boy.

WOLFE—(*snaps his fingers*)—I tell you how I fix it. He don't come into Grand Central. He gets off at 125th Street.

JULIE—It doesn't stop there.

WOLFE—To-morrow it will—for one second. (*Points wisely to himself.*) I get him off the train, I bring him here before the newspapers know it, he stays quiet a couple of weeks. If they find it out, he's having a nervous collapse—and nobody can see him.

JULIE—Oh, Oscar! That'll be wonderful! There you are, Mrs. C. Everything's grand.

FANNY—Everything grand! Who's this Zany woman! What's she doing on the train?

JULIE—Well—uh—Oscar, tell mother the facts of life.

WOLFE (*pats* FANNY'S *shoulder*)—Satisfied, Fanny? Huh? Your boy ain't in danger?

FANNY—You're the manager.

WOLFE—Good! Now! If nobody else has got anything to do, that you would like to have me wait until you do it—Julie, you don't want to take a massage first, or something? . . . No? . . . Well, then, do you mind if I waste just a minute of your time on my business?

Wolfe's business is an appointment he has made for Julie and Gwen to meet St. John Throckmorton, the English author of their new play, at his office at 3 that afternoon and hear him read the play.

With Wolfe it is very serious and he cannot take lightly Julie's indifference to any one who is "only an author," nor her flat refusal to break her other appointments just to hear one read a play.

Pleadingly Oscar demands that they help him out. A great deal depends upon St. John's first impression of theatrical America. He is naturally a sensitive person and expectant. They can't afford, no one of them can afford, to offend him. And there is no chance of postponing the meeting. All the other days are taken up—Saturdays with a matinée; Sunday St. John will be out at Otto Kahn's; Monday rehearsals start. It just has to be to-day.

Finally Julie gives in. "You win, Oscar," she agrees. "At 3 o'clock— Enter Julie Cavendish, laughing."

There is still the matter of the play Dean has discovered for himself, which Oscar continues to evade. And again the question of whether or not Herbert is going to succeed in sidetracking Kitty, just because, as Kitty believes, he knows she is good and is afraid to surround himself with anything but incompetent actors. Oscar manages finally to get away and Julie effectively squelches the quarreling Deans by pushing them into the library.

Which leaves only a few minor Cavendish misunderstandings to be ironed out. For one thing Fanny would like to know exactly what is troubling Julie. Why the "big renunciation scene" over not being able to break an engagement to hear her play read?

It happens, Julie explains, that Gil Marshall is back—and she was planning rather enthusiastically on having the afternoon clear.

Gil Marshall! After nineteen years he has come back! It's a wonder, Fanny insists, the newspapers haven't been full of him— the great South American diamond king! It's emeralds, Julie corrects her.

FANNY—Emeralds or diamonds! When I think that if it hadn't been for me you'd have gone off to South America—given up your career—everything.

JULIE—I wonder what he's like now. He may have grown very charming. South America, and millions, and perhaps a little grey here. (*Touches her temple.*) Sounds rather romantic.

FANNY—No more romantic now than he was nineteen years ago! Ah! What a siege that was!

JULIE—And what a demon you were!

FANNY—I had to be. You thought because he looked serious and didn't say much that he was doing a lot of deep thinking. I knew it was because he couldn't think of anything to say.

JULIE—You certainly acted like a mother in a melodrama.

FANNY—I told him. I showed him that he couldn't hope to make you happy. A home and a husband for a girl like you! I said: "Here's a girl that's going to have fame and fortune—the world spread before her. Do you think that you can make up to her for all the things you'd rob her of! You and your South America! You and your engineering! . . ."

JULIE—Yes, yes, I know, Mother. He went away, and we both lived happy ever after.

FANNY—How I ever got you where you are to-day is more than I know. You were always at the point of running off with some young squirt.

JULIE—But I never did. So it couldn't have been so serious.

FANNY—Serious enough for them! That young Earl of Pembroke who went off to Africa, and that Philadelphia fellow that shot himself—

JULIE—He was cleaning his gun.

FANNY—They were always cleaning their guns. And when you finally married Rex Talbot! . . . I'll never forget the goings-on then.

JULIE—Mother, out of the whole crowd of them, why did I marry Rex?

FANNY—He was the weakest, I guess.

JULIE—I always said I wouldn't marry an actor. And Rex wasn't even a good actor. What was there about him, Mother?

FANNY—Rex Talbot was a brilliant young loafer! And he had the most beautiful manners. He was the kind of man who could kiss your hand without looking silly.

JULIE—I guess that was what he was always doing when I needed him. That's one thing you will admit about Gil, Mother. He would have been dependable.

FANNY—When you're eighteen you don't marry a man because he's dependable.

JULIE—But when you're a little older, you begin to think that maybe—

FANNY (*quickly*)—What's that?

JULIE—Don't be alarmed. But I am curious to see him again. That's natural, isn't it? Only it can't be this afternoon—that's sure. I had it all staged so beautifully, too. I was going to wear my rose beige, and a hat with a brim, and be dignified and wistful, yet girlish withal.

FANNY—You can put on that act for him just as well after the show to-night. It's been nineteen years. What's a couple of hours more!

JULIE—No. Midnight isn't as kind to me as it used to be. I'm just vain enough to want to look my best.

FANNY—You are, eh?

JULIE—I want to look fresh and young and radiant.

FANNY—Is that all?

Now it is Gwen's turn. Blithely, happily she comes downstairs in search of her tan bag. She is ready, and Perry Stewart is due. Then she hears of the play reading and is crushed. She simply *can't* break her engagement with the Stewarts! She's to be the guest of honor—and she never has met Perry's mother. She probably will never be asked again.

"And I couldn't go if she did ask me," Gwen wails. "I'll be rehearsing all the time, and then I'll be acting, and it'll just go on like that forever. First thing you know I'll be an old woman—"

Suddenly there are two long rings at the doorbell followed by a terrific hammering. They are all startled into an excited wondering. The servants rush for the doors. The Deans come back from the library, their quarreling over "The Conqueror" for the moment stopped. And then the excited exclamations in the hall herald the arrival of Anthony Cavendish.

The chorus of greeting and hysterical demands for explanations rises to a perfect babel until Tony is able to quiet them. Breaking through the family crowd, he finally is able to enter the room, shushing them into silence as he comes.

"He is wearing an all-enveloping fur coat, the collar of which is turned up so that his face is concealed. The brim of his soft felt hat is pulled down over his eyes. He comes down swiftly, almost in the manner of one who is backing away from something he fears."

They follow him, bewilderment in their expressions. They in turn are followed by a retinue of helpers loaded down with Tony's belongings—"a violin case, half a dozen bags and suitcases, very smart and glittering; an overcoat, a rug, golf sticks, hat-box, tennis racquet, fencing foils in a case, a pillow envelope."

Again the barrage of questioning is resumed, and finally, with the luggage disposed of, the help from outside paid and dismissed, Tony is able to get out of his fur coat. His left arm is in a sling, but he is able quickly to allay their first fears as to the seriousness of his hurt.

TONY—It doesn't amount to anything. I hit him too hard, that's all. (FANNY *makes a pitying sound between tongue and teeth.*)

JULIE—How did it start in the first place?

DEAN—Let's hear about it.

TONY—Della, I'm starved. I haven't had a bite for twelve hours. Bring me everything you've got. (DELLA *goes.*) First I've got to have a hot bath. Come on upstairs, everybody, while I take a bath. (*With* KITTY *and* DEAN *in the lead,* KITTY *having one foot on the stairway, they all go up toward the stairs.* FANNY *is last.*)

JULIE—Tony, will you listen to me! How did you get here to-day? You were in Omaha yesterday.

TONY—I flew, of course. Came by aeroplane from Chicago.

DEAN—Aeroplane!

KITTY—Flew!

JULIE—Tony Cavendish!

TONY—I couldn't come on a train. They're watching the trains. I've got to lay low in this apartment till I sail.

FANNY—Sail!

JULIE—Sail where?

TONY—Europe, of course. To-morrow on the *Aquitania.* . . . God, I hate pictures. . . . I've got to have a bath. If you want to hear the rest of it come on up!

(TONY *starts again for the stairway, and* KITTY *and* DEAN

mount quickly ahead of him. JULIE *follows just behind, with*
FANNY *bringing up the rear.* GWEN *remains on stage. As they*
ascend the stairs, TONY, JULIE, DEAN *and* KITTY *are talking*
constantly and simultaneously.)

DEAN—What happened out there, Tony? How did you get
into this fight?

TONY—He had it coming to him ever since we started to shoot.
He put his girl into the picture and when she got stuck on me
he got sore. The blow off came when we were out on location.
Doing a desert scene and Deming picked out the worst camel in
the pack and said to me, "You ride that one." I took one look
at it and said, "The hell I will!" He said, "Who's directing this
picture, you or me?" I said, "You're directing the picture, but
you're not directing me. I'm through with it, and you can take
this to remember me by."

JULIE—Unless you've killed him, Tony, I don't see why they're
making all this fuss. And as for your going to Europe, I think
it's the most ridiculous thing I've ever heard of. And you walked
out in the middle of a picture, of course. They'll probably sue
you for a million dollars, and you'll never get another picture job.
(*Over balcony railing, just exiting.*) Get your things on, Gwen
—I'll be right down.

It is while the family is upstairs and Tony is completing the
cleansing processes of which he stands in such need, that Perry
Stewart calls for Gwen, learns that she cannot go, and is properly
shocked and incensed.

Nothing that he can think of will excuse Gwen to his mother,
and there is a growing conviction in his own mind that Gwen's
interest in him is completely discounted by her interest in the
theatre.

If that is true, what is there for them to build their hope of a
happy home life upon? What are they headed for? How is it
all going to work out?

GWEN—Why—I don't know. What is there to work out?

PERRY—After all, you marry the person that you'd rather be
with than any one else in the world. But where'll you be half the
time? Rehearsing, or something.

GWEN—Now don't be fantastic! Rehearsals last three weeks.

PERRY—All right. And then what! You're at the theatre
every night. Your work will just begin when mine is all over.
You'll have dinner at six. I'll probably not even be home. By
midnight you're all keyed up and ready to start out, but I've got

to be at work in the morning. We'll be living in two different
worlds!

GWEN—But those things adjust themselves. Lots of other people have got around it.

PERRY—I'd do anything in the world for you, Gwen. I'd die
for you! But I can't be one of those husbands. Hanging around
dressing rooms! Side-stepping scenery. Calling up the costumer.
What am I going to do every night? See the show?

GWEN—But you wouldn't want me to be one of those wives,
would you? Bridge and household and babies?

PERRY—Well, why not? What's the matter with that?

GWEN—Because I can't do that sort of thing any more than
you can do the other. I'm an actress, Perry. An actress!

PERRY—Oh, what does that mean? Suppose you turn out to
be as good as your mother—or better! What is there to it when
it's all over? Get your name up in electric lights, and a fuse
blows out—and where are you?

GWEN—I won't let you belittle my work. It's just as important as yours. I suppose the world would go to pieces if you
didn't sell a hundred shares of Consolidated Whatnot for ten
cents more than somebody paid for it!

PERRY—You can't compare business with acting.

GWEN—Is that so! I can give you the names of actors and
actresses of three hundred years ago—dozens of them! Name me
two Seventeenth Century stockbrokers.

PERRY—All right, I'll give up my work. That'll be dandy!
And trail along behind you carrying your Pekinese, huh? . . .
Not me!

GWEN—It's not a Pekinese! . . . Oh, Perry, what are we talking like this for! It's horrible. (*Goes to him.*) Forgive me!
How could I talk like that to you!

PERRY—It's my fault. I didn't know what I was saying.

GWEN—Perry—dear! (*He takes her in his arms.*)

PERRY—Oh, what does anything matter?

GWEN—Weren't we a couple of idiots! We've never quarreled
before.

PERRY—And we won't again. There isn't anything that matters to me except you. Business and acting— We must have
been crazy!

GWEN—And you're all that matters to me.

Now that that is settled Perry is for starting off again. But
Gwen didn't mean that it has been settled that way. She just

can't go. So Perry, hurt and angry, makes an embarrassed exit, slamming the door behind him.

Slowly Gwen realizes what has happened, and the thought of it does not put her in any too good a mood to follow her mother's instructions—get herself ready for the journey to Wolfe's office.

In fact as the family regathers and resumes its normal confusions Gwen's voice can be heard declaring with evident determination that she is not going. She is not going now—or ever. She is not going to be in this play, or any other play. She is through. She is never going to act again.

GWEN—Please! I've made up my mind, and all of you put together can't stop me. I'm through with the stage, and I'll tell you why, if you want to know. I'm not going to have it mess up my whole life!

(*An hysterical jumble of attempted explanation. Her talk is pierced from time to time by exclamations from the others of the family.*) . . . do you know what he did! He walked right out of the room. . . . If you think I'm going to give him up for a miserable little stage career just because we've always done it . . . we'd never see each other . . . he'd get up in the morning and I wouldn't go to work till night. . . . Look at this afternoon with his mother waiting out there . . . it'll be like that for years and years . . . only it's not going to be! You're not going to ruin my life! I'm going to quit now, while there's time! I'm going to marry Perry Stewart and be a regular person! And nothing you can say is going to stop me!

JULIE—I never heard such silly rot in all my life!

(*From* DEAN, FANNY, TONY, KITTY *such lines as:* "Why, it's preposterous! Quit and get married!" (TONY.) "Who's Perry Stewart?" (FANNY.) "Never thought I'd live to see this day. I don't know what you're talking about."

GWEN—Well, *I* know what I'm talking about. I'm sick of all this. I'm sick of being a Cavendish! I want to be a human being! (*From the others a shocked murmur.*)

FANNY—What's that!

DEAN—But you *are* a Cavendish!

JULIE—Of course you are.

GWEN—But I don't want to be!

JULIE—You've got to be! What do you think we've worked for all these years?

FANNY—You can't do this to us!

JULIE—My God! What any one else would give for your chance!

DEAN—Yes!

FANNY—It's absurd!

JULIE—You can be the greatest of us all. Aubrey and Fanny Cavendish have just been stepping stones for you!

FANNY (*rises. She is all dignity*)—What's that! What's that!

JULIE—Oh, Mother, please!

FANNY—I'll be a stepping stone for nobody! And as for Aubrey Cavendish, there's nobody since his day that can touch him!

DEAN—One minute, please!

GWEN (*taut, defiant*)—Listen to them! *That's* what I mean.

DEAN—I believe my Macbeth still takes rank as the finest interpretation of its day and age.

JULIE (*cutting in on* DEAN's *speech and topping it*)—For heaven's sake, you two! Telling how good you are! I'm pretty good myself, but you don't hear me talking about it!

KITTY (*very haughtily*)—Well, if you want *my* opinion—

JULIE—Well, we don't want your opinion.

(*From this spot on,* KITTY *and* JULIE *are talking together at each other; and* DEAN *and* FANNY *are talking together, combating each other. All this time* TONY, *on the stairs, has been viewing this family scene with a good deal of interest and enjoyment.*)

KITTY—No, I suppose not. Just because I'm not one of your precious Cavendishes I haven't the right to speak. But I want to tell you that Kitty LeMoyne can hold her head up with the best of them when it comes to acting. I may not have reached my present position by stepping on the heads of other people. I've won out by talent and hard work. It isn't always the people who have their names up in electric lights that are the best actors. I may not be a tradition in the theatre but just the same—

JULIE (*at the same time*)—This is purely a family matter and it seems to me that you'll save yourself a good deal of trouble if you'll just keep out of it. (*Turns her attention to* FANNY *and* DEAN, *who, by now, have resumed their argument.*) Oh, who cares which of you was the best actor! If it comes to a showdown probably neither of you was so dog-goned good! And while you're about it, Herbert Dean, will you tell that wife of yours to stop talking. This is no concern of hers. Why doesn't she keep out of it! And why shouldn't Gwen be a greater actress than any of us! At least she's got intelligence on her side, and that's more than I can say of any of the rest of you. (*Turning again to* KITTY.) Oh, all right! You're Bernhardt! You're Modjeska! You're Duse!

DEAN—Rôle for rôle, my dear Fanny, I am a better actor than Aubrey Cavendish ever dreamed of being. You must remember that his was the day of the provinces, and while I have no doubt that he was a great favourite in the hamlets, it is quite another thing to win critical acclaim in London and New York. You may recall that on three successive nights I played Othello, Iago, and Petruchio, and that never under the historic roof of Wallack's Theatre have there been three such ovations. And a year later, at the old Vic I—

FANNY—You miserable upstart! Do you expect me to stand here and allow you to mention yourself and Aubrey Cavendish in the same breath? Aubrey Cavendish was an artist. He wouldn't have had you as his dresser! The greatest actors of his generation have sat at the feet of Aubrey Cavendish. Henry Irving, Beerbohm Tree, Richard Mansfield! And you have the presumption to fancy that your absurd struttings are comparable in any way with the histrionism of Aubrey Cavendish, the greatest actor that the English-speaking stage has ever seen! You can stand there and tell me—

(*As the four voices approach a climax the telephone starts ringing. Simultaneously* DELLA *and* JO *enter, each with a laden tray.* TONY *greets the trays.*)

TONY—Ah! Food! Right over here, Jo!

(GWEN *is standing a little apart from the others, intense.* DELLA *deposits her tray hurriedly. Goes to telephone.*)

DELLA (*in phone*)—Hello! . . . She's on her way down, Mr. Wolfe! . . . Quite a while ago. . . .

The argument is still raging as the curtain falls.

ACT II

It is six o'clock the following Saturday afternoon. The Cavendish living-room lies lightly in the evening shadows. Only two of the lamps have been lighted. The room is empty of people, but from above stairs there come sounds of what is apparently a wild combat with swords, including a variety of exclamations employed in attack and defense, a variety that swings excitingly from a medieval "Have at thee, varlet!" to a modern, "Heh, go easy there!"

Julie Cavendish is not yet home from the matinée. Fanny Cavendish, having dozed off in the library, awakes to find the crowd of curious citizenry outside the house larger than ever. In fact the maid believes it to be a record crowd in size—much larger than that which gathered when Mr. Tony got his first divorce. Now Tony, pressing young McDermott fiercely in their battle with the foils, emerges from his room upstairs and continues the wild fighting across the balcony and finally down the stairway, Tony calling out his victory with gusto.

"Ha! He gives ground! Black Fennifer knows now the dark fate that soon is to o'ertake him! . . . Came the dawn, and yet they battled grimly upon the ancient parapet!" . . . "Ha, ha, varlet! Thou didst not know, what time thou didst dash a flagon of Burgundy from this hand, that thou hadst run smack up against the niftiest little swordsman in all Gascony!"

The battle is ended, the fair Fanny elaborately claimed as bride by Anthony the Elegant and McDermott is dismissed. And now it occurs suddenly to Tony that it is time for him to be getting excited about the non-arrival of his sister with his passport. The boat sails at midnight and he must positively sail with it. Fanny is not so sure. At least she can see no cause for his extreme anxiety. Suppose Julie fails to get the passport? Who says he has got to get on that particular boat? And what for?

Tony—A million reasons! I feel like it! I want to get so far from Hollywood and sunshine—I never want to hear camera again! Or stage either, for that matter! You can have it! I'm through!

Fanny—Through! You've been saying that ever since "Fauntleroy."

Tony—I mean it this time! That's why I'm going abroad! Give me two years in Munich with my violin—under Ascher—and I'll show you what the stage means to me! I can be a great musician! . . . Or I may go away into India with Krishnamurti and study Hindu philosophy! It's the only real thing in the world! You wear just one garment—a long white robe—and you eat just one food! Rice!

Fanny—That'll be restful!

Tony—The stage! I'd rather spend ten minutes in the Cathedral at Chartres—I don't give a damn if I nev— (*In the course of making a sweeping gesture he encounters the huge pile of letters on the table.*) What the hell is all this stuff? They've been here all day! What are they?

FANNY (*shouting at him*)—They're for you! We've told you a dozen times! It's your mail we've been saving!

TONY—Well, why didn't you say so? (*A second's calm while he picks up a handful of letters. Then he dumps them all into the waste basket. Turns away a few steps.*)

FANNY (*advancing on him*)—Don't think you're fooling me about why you're going to Europe. Cathedrals, and violins, and rice! It's this Dago woman you're running away from. Else why was she on the train with you?

TONY—Oh, I'm not afraid of her. I gave her the slip at Chicago.

FANNY—Just the same, that's why you're going to Europe! Don't lie to me, Tony Cavendish!

TONY (*reluctantly giving ground*)—Well, suppose I am! (*Flares up again.*) Only I'm not afraid of her!

FANNY—Then what is it?

TONY (*paces a bit first*)—It's that God damned process server she's got after me!

FANNY—What God damned process server?

TONY (*it is being torn out of him*)—The breach of promise suit.

FANNY—Breach of promise?

TONY (*scornfully*)—Two hundred thousand dollars! She wants two hun— (*On fire again.*) That's why I've got to stay cooped up here! You don't think I'm afraid of reporters, do you? But if they ever clap that paper on me I can't sail!

FANNY—Two hundred thousand for breach of promise. Assault and battery on this director—probably another hundred thousand. And breaking your contract with the picture company —I guess half a million will cover it.

TONY—It's worth it, I tell you! God, that sunshine!

FANNY (*fiercely*)—What did you ever promise this movie actress that's worth two hundred thousand dollars?

TONY—Oh, she claims to have some letters—I didn't want her in the first place! She was Deming's girl! That's why he got sore!

FANNY—Who is she, anyhow? Where'd she come from?

TONY—Zeta Zaydak! She's a Pole.

FANNY—Look out for Poles!

Julie arrives a little ruffled from her contact with Tony's dear public in front of the house. Memories of her own matinée, at which the audience had arrived late and wet and barked like so many sea lions all through the performance, account in part for her agitation. "Lincoln couldn't have held them with the Gettysburg address!" That's the kind of an audience it was.

With some deliberation Julie keeps Tony waiting for news of his passport and then she can only tell him that Wolfe is to bring it later and to bring him the money he will need. She has already paid for his reservation and she is far from pleased to discover that he is "roughing it across in the royal suite."

"I can't travel like a stowaway."

"Hire a battleship for all I care! But remember I'm a working girl. What do you do with all your money, anyway? You go out to Hollywood with a billion dollar contract and you buy a pink plaster palace for one hundred and fifty thousand, an Isotta Fraschini for twenty thousand, an Hispano Suiza for twenty-five, a camp in the Sierras for another fifty—good God, you were sunk a quarter of a million before they ever turned a crank on you! . . . And as soon as they start to take a picture you knock out the director and quit."

Tony's optimism is unshakable. Everything will blow over in a month. During which time he will be bathing himself in the pure beauty of Athens or, it may be, losing himself in the dark depths of the Black Forest—any place will do so long as it rains all the time and he never sees the sun.

There is some one at the door. It may be a process server or it may be Wolfe. They must be prepared for anything. But it turns out to be nobody but Herbert Dean.

A state of mind Dean is in, too. Oscar Wolfe hasn't made any sort of a report on the play he is reading for Herbert and a play just now would be a godsend to him. He isn't getting any younger, he realizes that, although he has managed to keep his figure. With the pink lights on no one would ever think he was over thirty.

But even if Oscar approves the play there is the problem of Kitty. Kitty simply cannot be permitted to play the heroine. If she does she will ruin practically everything. So Julie has got to agree to take Kitty off Herbert's hands by giving her a part in her own new play. Even if she has to dismiss the woman already engaged. It's the only way the situation can be handled tactfully.

If Julie will do this for Herbert—and loan him another five hundred—his faith in the world and in their fine family loyalty will be in a measure restored. Julie agrees to do what she can.

When he arrives, Oscar Wolfe also finds it difficult getting through the mob outside. Nor does he like that kind of publicity.

Neither is Wolfe at all excited about the prospects of Herbert Dean's play. He has read it—but—it will take a lot of doing—a lot of money—

Dean is not in the least discouraged. They can do the whole thing with drapes and start rehearsals as soon as he lines up a cast! Herbert is away to the Lambs Club to plan things out almost before they know it.

But if Wolfe is stunned and perplexed by the Cavendishes in general there is always understanding in Fanny's sympathy for him.

"I think Bertie has retired and doesn't know it," she ventures as Dean disappears.

WOLFE—I wish they were all like you, Fanny. (*Comes over and pats her shoulder.*) What d'you think? Going to be able to troupe again after the holidays?

FANNY—Tried to tell you yesterday, but you were so busy with your English playwrights.

WOLFE—Say, if I had to pick one actress out of the whole caboodle of 'em you know who it'd be. Come on, tell me. Think you can start out again? Sure enough?

FANNY—You can dust off the "Castlemaine" scenery, and I'd just as soon you'd route me to the coast.

WOLFE—'At a girl! You're worth a dozen of these New-York-run actresses. No foolishness about you. No private cars, and maids in the contract, and telegrams from the company manager you won't go on because the theatre's cold. No, sir! You're the girl that does twenty-eight hundred in Boise City, Idaho, and catches the six-fourteen next morning for Pocatello.

FANNY—I did twenty-nine hundred in Boise City.

WOLFE—Chairs in the aisle, h'm? I tell you——(*a gesture toward the departed figure.*)—if Bert had taken his hits out on the road he wouldn't be in this jam to-day. But by nature Bertie is a Lamb's Club actor, and look what happens! In a couple more years he'll own six toupees, and be playing Baron Stein in an all-star revival of "Diplomacy."

FANNY (*getting to her feet to take the oath*)—May God strike me dead if I ever appear in an all-star revival! (*She sits again.*) (JULIE *appears on the balcony. Starts downstairs.*)

JULIE—Well, she's promised to dress and come out of that room, anyhow. That's more than she's done all day.

WOLFE—Say, what kind of a show are you going to give to-night, with all this hullabaloo!

JULIE—Once Tony goes, things will be a little better. It's so restful to think that at midnight he'll be rounding Sandy Hook.

WOLFE—M-m—that's what I came to talk about.

JULIE (*alarmed*)—What!

WOLFE—It don't go so quick. These fellows—

JULIE—You mean you can't get a passport! Oh!

WOLFE—Well, now, hold on. I don't say I can't yet exactly. There seems to be some sort of monkey business going on. Maybe they got wind of something and don't want him to get away.

JULIE—Oscar, another twenty-four hours with this caged lunatic and you can order strait-jackets for two. He's impossible to live with—and those terrible people on the street! If you think I gave a rotten matinée just wait till you see the night show!

WOLFE—Now, now, now! Did Oscar ever fail you? We'll get it all right—I hope. Anyhow, here's his money. That's that much.

FANNY—*How* much?

JULIE—What's the difference, Mother? He has to have it. (*To* WOLFE. *Her hand on his arm.*) Oscar, I owe you a ghastly lot of money, don't I? How much?

WOLFE—The money you're welcome to, Julie. But it oughtn't to be that you got to come to me like this. You make as much money as any woman in the business. Forty-one weeks you've had in this show alone—ten per cent. of the gross—over fifteen hundred a week you've averaged. What the devil do you do with all your money, anyhow?

JULIE—Why—I don't know. What do you mean—do with it?

FANNY—What does anybody do with it?

WOLFE—Well, just for argument's sake, let me ask you once. Forty-one weeks, you've made sixty thousand since you opened in this play, and that says nothing about all the other ones. In the past twenty years I bet you made a million dollars. Now how much of it have you actually got?

JULIE—Let's see—where's my bag? I've got over three dollars in that, and Della owes me seventy-five cents— (*Jo enters on balcony; starts to descend stairs.*) Oh, I don't know, Oscar. It just goes.

Julie orders caviar for Gwen's dinner, thinking to tempt her appetite. All day Gwen has been "moping in her room like Elsie

Dinsmore," according to her grandmother, and her mother is anxious to get her out. So far as Fanny can see Gwen's young man, being quite average, is no one to mope about.

"They're all average young men, except to the girl who thinks they're wonderful," Julie reminds her.

When Gwen does get downstairs she is quite plainly miserable. Perry Stewart hasn't even telephoned. The fact that Tony has had the receiver off the wire most of the day probably explains that, Fanny suggests. That possibility is so cheering to Gwen she weeps a little. She does love Perry so!

FANNY—You can love him and marry him too, can't you?

JULIE—Of course you can marry him, Gwen, and live happy ever after.

FANNY—Only why you think you have to quit the stage to do it is more than I can figure out.

JULIE—It's hard for us to realize that you wouldn't want to keep on, Gwen.

FANNY—Your mother and I both got married. But we didn't drop more important things to do it.

GWEN—There isn't anything more important.

FANNY—Fiddlesticks! Marriage isn't a career—it's an incident. Aubrey Cavendish and I were married in the Church of St. Mary Redcliffe, in Bristol, England, just before the matinée. The wedding supper was served on the stage of the Theatre Royale between the matinée and the night performance—we played "She Stoops to Conquer" in the afternoon, and "A Scrap of Paper" was the night bill. They sent the supper in from the George and Lion next door, and very nice it was, too, but I remember they'd gone and put nutmeg in the gooseberry tarts, and Aubrey never could abide nutmeg. It must have been that that upset him, for he gave the only bad performance that night that I ever saw him give.

GWEN—I know, Grandma. But that's got nothing to do with me. You married an actor and—(turning to her mother, swiftly) —so did you. You lived the same sort of lives. Don't you see that this is different!

JULIE—Oh, I knew some rather nice men who weren't actors— didn't I, Fanny? (A gesture from FANNY of utter dismissal of this subject as being too vast and agonizing to go into.) There were lots of times when I thought that being a wife and mother was all that mattered in the world. And then each time I'd learn all over again that that wasn't enough for me.

FANNY—I should say not.

JULIE—Earthquakes, and cyclones, and fire and flood, and somehow you still give the show. I know it says in the contract that you stop for acts of God, but I can't remember that I ever did.

FANNY—Nor I. Nor your grandfather. Nobody ever knew what a sick man Aubrey Cavendish was, those last months. But he played a full season of thirty-five weeks. Dropped dead on the stage of Macauley's in Louisville two minutes after the curtain fell on Saturday night, the week we closed. Not only that, but he waited to take four calls.

GWEN—I know, I know. (*Rises.*) But—I'm not like that, that's all.

JULIE (*rises*)—You think you're not, but you are! Marry him if you love him, Gwen, but don't give up everything to do it! The day might come when you'd hate him for it.

GWEN—Hate Perry! (*A little bitter scornful laugh.*) You just don't know what you're talking about.

JULIE—Gwen, do you think it's going to be any fun for me to have them see you step out—acting with me in my play, and for all I know, walking away with it! You'll be so fresh, and such a surprise! And it'll be your night. I'll be proud and happy, of course. (*A very little pause, and then, almost as though to convince herself.*) . . . of course. They'll say, "That's her daughter." But ten years from now it'll be, "That's her mother."

GWEN—I'll never be half the actress you are.

JULIE—Gwen, if I could only make you realize that the thrill you get out of doing your work is bigger than any other single thing in the world! (*A little gesture of protest from* GWEN.) Oh, I know! There's love. But you can be the most fortunate person in the world, Gwen. You can have both. But for God's sake don't make the mistake of giving up one for the other.

FANNY—No, child!

GWEN—Work! Acting isn't anything. What's acting compared to—

FANNY—It's everything! They'll tell you it isn't—your fancy friends—but it's a lie! And they know it's a lie! They'd give their ears to be in your place! Don't make any mistake about that!

JULIE—They'll say, "Come on and play," and you'll say, "I have to work," and they'll say, "Oh, work!" There'll be plenty of things that you'll have to give up—gay things and amusing things— (DELLA *appears in the doorway, evidently meaning to get* JULIE's *attention*.) I've missed parties and dinners and rides and walks! All my life I've had to get up just before dessert was served and just when conversation was most entertaining.

FANNY—What is it, Della?

DELLA—How about dinner?

FANNY—Don't bother us! (DELLA *goes, puzzled*.) (*Stealing* JULIE's *thunder*.) You've got to leave, and go down to a stuffy dressing room and smear paint on your face and go out on the stage and speak a lot of fool lines, and you love it! You couldn't live without it! Do you suppose I could have stood these two years, hobbling around with this thing—(*brandishing her cane*) —if I hadn't known I was going back to it!

JULIE—Long as I've been on the stage there isn't a night when I stand in the wings waiting for my cue that I don't get that sick feeling at the pit of my stomach! And my hands are cold and my cheeks are hot, and you'd think I'd never seen a stage before!

FANNY—Yes, yes! That's it! (*Struggling to her feet in her excitement*.) Every night when I'm sitting here alone I'm really down there at the theatre! Seven-thirty, and they're going in at the stage door! Good evening to the door man. Taking down their keys and looking in the mail rack. Eight o'clock. The stage hands are setting up. (*Raps with her cane*.) Half hour, Miss Cavendish! Grease paint, rouge, máscara! Fifteen minutes, Miss Cavendish! My costume! . . . More rouge! . . . Where's the rabbit's foot! . . . Overture! . . . How's the house to-night? . . . The curtain's up! . . . Props! . . . Cue! . . . Enter! . . . That's all that's kept me alive these two years. If you weren't down there for me, I wouldn't want to live. . . . I couldn't live. You . . . down there . . . for me . . . going on . . . going on . . . going on . . .

The excitement and the strain are too much for Fanny. "Suddenly she goes limp, topples, crumples. Julie and Gwen, standing near her, catch her as she is about to fall, and place her in the chair from which she has risen. She is briefly unconscious."

Excitement is intense as Julie and Gwen try to rouse the house, and above the calling for assistance Gwen can be heard protesting remorsefully: "It's all right, Grandma! I'll do it. I will! I will! Grandma! I'll do it!"

Now Tony comes, and McDermott. And finally Della and Jo. And everybody rushes around a little aimlessly trying to do something without knowing what to do. Jo brings a flask of whisky.

Julie moistens Fanny's lips with that and bathes her forehead with cold water.

Slowly Fanny opens her eyes. She is bewildered and weakened. Feebly she tries to rise, "to assert her independence. Her voice is little more than a whisper."

"I'm all right," she insists. "There's nothing the matter. But I think I'll go up and lie down."

They all gather around to assist her. With Tony on one side and McDermott on the other, with Della and Jo going on ahead to prepare the room and with Julie and Gwen following anxiously after, they make their way slowly up the stairs. About half-way up Fanny Cavendish pauses.

"No use," she sighs. "No use fooling myself. . . . I'm through. . . . I'll never go back again. . . . It's finished!"

"Oh, Mother, what nonsense," protests Julie.

"You'll be as good as new to-morrow," echoes Tony. And the march is continued.

It is in the middle of the excitement of getting Fanny settled in her room that Gilbert Marshall appears. "He is forty-seven, quiet, dominant, successful. He gives the effect of power and control."

He senses from the confusion that there is something wrong and suggests that it probably would be better if he did not wait. Jo, however, insists that Mrs. Cavendish has suffered no more than a fainting fit and he is sure Miss Julie will be right down.

Marshall is still half decided about going when Julie appears on the balcony and stops him. She is far from the composed and beautiful actress she had hoped to be at this meeting. In fact when he puts his hand on her shoulder reassuringly she sinks weakly into his arms and clings to him as one who has found a refuge.

"Oh, Gil. . . . It's been such a hellish day," she explains. "Everything in the world that could happen—Gil, you're still sane, aren't you?—and solid, and reliable and sure?"

"I hope so."

"How nice—"

For a hurried few minutes they indulge the usual explanations of why neither has even heard from the other for so long a time, interrupted by Della warning Julie that the hour of the evening performance is nearing, and by telephone calls and reports from Fanny's room.

Now there is real trouble over the phone. With all his influence Wolfe has been unable to get Tony a passport!

When Tony finally worms that information out of Julie he is an hysterically excited young man! Also he refuses to be calmed. What kind of a jam do they think he's in, anyway? What do they think he's trying to get away from? A crazy woman, that's all! There's no telling what that Polecat will do! She's a killer —that's what she is—

And Julie! Julie's a hell of a sister! But let her wait until this story breaks! Let her wait until she and Gwen and the whole damned family are on the front page and see how she likes that!

With which gentle sally he smashes to the floor one of the minor objets d'art he has inadvertently lifted from its resting place and turns sweetly, though still intensely, to acknowledge his sister's slightly flustered introduction to Mr. Marshall.

"Pleased to have met you, Mr. Gilson!" he calls and dashes wildly up the stairs.

"Is he always like that?" queries Marshall.

"Oh, no," Julie reassures him. "That's the brighter side."

Then it transpires that Gil Marshall is probably the one person in the world who can manage an emergency passport for Tony. This he proceeds to do over the telephone, to the intense delight and gratitude of Julie and, a moment later, the excited amazement of Tony.

Now the house is again a bedlam as Tony prepares to pack, dress and be ready to be out of the house in five minutes on his way to be smuggled aboard the *Aquitania*. His sister is a swell girl now, and her friend a fine fellow. The ways of the Cavendishes are an incredible mystery to Gil Marshall.

"Why do you stand for all this?" he demands of Julie, the moment there is even a faint suggestion of quiet.

"Oh, Tony doesn't mean anything," she answers. "He's always like that."

GIL—What do you mean! That you have this kind of thing all the time, and that you go ahead and put up with it?

JULIE—Oh, sometimes families are. . . . It just happens to-day that blood is thicker than usual.

GIL—But these other things that you were talking about. You oughtn't to allow them to do that! You're a successful actress. Head of your profession. You ought to be the one they're running around for. And look! Everybody dumping their troubles on you.

JULIE—Oh, it isn't always like this.

GIL—You know, Julie, the reason I went away was so that you could go ahead and be an actress. All that stuff about Cavendish, and the stage being your real life, and the only way you could be happy. Well, here you are. You've got everything you went after. And how about it? Are you happy?

JULIE—Happy! I don't know.

GIL—Of course you're not. Julie, I've stayed away all these years because I thought at least you were living the life you wanted most. And then I come back and find this. You ought to have everything in the world. You ought to have everything done for you—done for you by some one who loves you . . . and I do love you, Julie, still.

JULIE—Oh, don't, Gil—don't say things that will make us both—

GIL—Don't you know what you ought to be doing instead of this! The way you ought to be living! Why, you ought to be in a country house somewhere, with a garden around it, and trees. Julie, if you could see the place I've got in England. Wyckhamshire. An old stone house, and the river's right down here, and a rose garden that's famous. People come from miles around. It's a beautiful place, Julie; and there it stands, empty.

JULIE—Oh, Gil!

GIL—And I've got a villa at Como—with the lake! (*A gesture.*) I don't know why I bought all these places—it must have been for you. Or we can go any place else you want—Cairo, St. Moritz—anywhere you say. Don't you know that's the way you ought to be living! Don't you? Don't you! Don't you!

JULIE—I don't know! I don't know!

GIL—Julie! (*Takes her in his arms.*) What fools we've been! What fools!

JULIE—Gil—wait! Let me think a minute. Let me get my breath.

GIL—You've had too long to think. It's settled. (*Again he takes her in his arms.*)

JULIE (*as she gently frees herself*)—No—please! I'm not quite sure what's happened. I can't think very clearly—

GIL—I'll tell you what's happened. Something that should have happened twenty years ago. That's what's happened.

JULIE—Well, perhaps if—maybe—Gil, you'd better go now. I think you'd better go. It's late.

GIL—All right. . . . Must I?

JULIE—Please.

GIL—I—I can't take you to the theatre?

JULIE—No—please. I must get Tony away, and—I couldn't give a performance if—just a minute alone—

GIL (*going up into alcove; getting hat and coat*)—It'll only be for a few hours—this time.

JULIE—You'll call for me at the theatre?

GIL—At eleven? Is that all right?

JULIE—At eleven.

GIL—I'll be waiting.

JULIE—That'll be wonderful.

GIL—Good-by.

JULIE (*gayly*)—Good-by!

Now Tony is at it again. Wildly he dashes down the stairs. He is in his b. v. d.'s and a silk bathrobe is billowing behind him. He also is yelling profanely for Jo and demanding that he hurry. . . . Now Tony has found Jo, and a hall-boy, in uniform, for whom he has sent. . . . Now Della has tried to force Julie to eat a little something hot—to take at least a little hot broth— before she leaves for the theatre. No one can give a performance on an empty stomach.

And now, in the midst of all the hullabaloo, Fanny Cavendish appears in the door of her room and demands that the clatter cease.

Nor will she let any of them send her back. Finally Tony and Julie are forced to stop their rushing about long enough to help Fanny downstairs. She will not go to bed until she has seen Tony off. Nor does all Julie's urging alter her determination. There's nothing to do then but leave Fanny in Gwen's care while Julie goes to the theatre and Tony is put finally on the boat for Europe.

Then there comes a strange procession down the stairs. "It consists of Jo and Mac laden with all the luggage that Tony arrived with on the preceding day. Then comes the hall-boy disguised in Tony's hat and coat—the upturned fur collar, the pulled-down slouch hat, just as Tony entered in the first act. His face is concealed almost entirely by the coat collar and the hat."

The women do not recognize the disguise. They call their good-bys to Tony and their final instructions for his greater care of himself until suddenly they realize he is not going to bid them good-by. They can't believe their eyes.

"Tony, my boy! Don't let him go!" Fanny Cavendish calls

pathetically. "He's never gone like that! . . . He didn't even talk to me! He didn't look at me! Tony. . . ."

Julie would run after Tony, but realizes that her mother needs her most and comes back.

And then the Deans appear to add to the confusion, with Kitty Dean bristling for an answer as to whether or not Julie—

At which moment Tony, gay in the hall-boy's uniform, darts out on the balcony. He is rather pleased with himself, in this, his farewell appearance. He struts a little as he comes into the group.

"They'll make a dash for the taxi—the crowd will all swarm after them—give 'em a nice run up Fifth Avenue. Then I go down, cab at the door, ten minutes I'm on the dock. Voilà!" Tony is proud of that plan.

He has made a swift leap across the room, scattering a general good-by. Then he takes Fanny's head in his two hands and kisses her.

"Good-by, Mother!" he cries, assuming a dramatic pose. "The open sea! The salt spray! The Arctic wind! . . . I'm on my way! . . . Remember the Guaranty Trust!"

Tony is gone. Fanny has sunk back weakly into her chair and the Deans are closing in. Kitty is still demanding her answer.

"Did you offer me that part of your own accord?" she demands of Julie. "Or did Bert put you up to it?"

Before Julie answers she seems slowly to uncoil from the position into which she has slumped in a chair. "Her whole attitude is so sinister and desperate that Kitty shrinks back a little."

JULIE—No! No, it isn't possible! You! You come to me with your miserable little—Your part! Bert's. . . . (*A little high hysterical laugh.*) After all that I've . . . it's too . . . I can't. . . .

GWEN—Mother! Don't! (PERRY *enters.*) Perry!

PERRY—What's the matter! What's going on?

JULIE—Well—what else! What else! Come on! What else! Perry! for God's sake take her out of this! Take her away before it's too late. Take her where she'll never hear stage again! Take her away! Take her away! Take her away!

FANNY—Julie! Julie!

GWEN—No! No! I won't do it! I'm not going to marry him!

JULIE (*pushes her hair back from her forehead with her open palm—a gesture of desperation*)—Not going to marry him! Not going to ma— You mean because we said to you—(*A finger pointing to the spot where* JULIE, GWEN *and* FANNY *have talked earlier.*)

GWEN—I'm not going to marry him and spoil his life! I love him too much for that!

PERRY—Gwen!

GWEN—No, no!

JULIE—Oh, no, you won't! If you think I'm going to let you throw away your whole life! . . . And for what! . . . *This!* . . . So that nineteen years from now you can be standing here as I am, a mad woman in a family of maniacs! Money for this one, jobs for that one, rehearsals and readings and *Graphics* and tickets for God knows where! I'm damned if you're going to! You're going to get out of it now! You're going to marry Perry Stewart—

GWEN—No, no!

JULIE—Oh, yes, you are! You're going to do what I didn't do. They told me I had to be a Cavendish. (*A movement from her mother.*) Oh, yes, you did! (*Wheeling to* GWEN *again.*) Well, you're not going to be one! You're going to marry him now—to-night—to-morrow. And I'm going to be there with you, and stand up beside you, and cry for happiness, and wish to God it was me! (*Her voice suddenly low, thoughtful.*) Of course. . . . Of course. . . . There isn't any reason why not. . . . I'm not dead yet. I've got some of my life left. And I'm going to live it to suit *me!* You've all had your turn. Who's crazy *now!* I can walk out of this, and nobody can stop me. I can still have peace and serenity and beauty for the rest of my life. And I'm going to have it. (*Exclamations from the others.*) You don't believe it, h'm? I'll show you! I'm going to marry Gil Marshall and go to Egypt and Venice and Constantinople—and what do you know about that! As far as the stage is concerned—I make you a present of it. It's yours! I'm through with it! It doesn't exist! The whole silly business doesn't exist! From this time on I'm going to live life, and leave imitation behind me! I'm through! Cavendish! To hell with Cavendish! I'm never going to act again! I'm never going to set foot on another stage as long as I live! I'm never going inside a theatre! I'm ne—

DELLA (*rushing on*)—Miss Julie! It's eight o'clock!

JULIE (*grabs her coat. Rushes, in a panic, toward the outer door*)—Oh, my God!

The curtain falls.

ACT III

It is November, a year later.   As usual the Cavendish living-room is filled with flowers.   And, also as usual, Della, the maid, is serving, or preparing to serve, some member of the Cavendish family with refreshment.   She is arranging the tea things when Julie, "wearing a costume slip of gold or silver, with only straps over the shoulder" (over which a tea coat is presently to be slipped), appears on the balcony and suggests that tea be served in the library.

Six are expected to tea, according to Della's count, so she warns Jo that they had better prepare for twelve.   Della has also taken the precaution to have a fire laid in the library, seeing she heard Miss Gwen was bringing over the baby.

Gil Marshall is also expected.   Which is one reason Della has spread his American Beauty roses all around the living-room.   She thinks he probably will like to see them.   Marshall has been in South America the better part of the year and every day he has been away he has sent the roses.

With Gwen married and settled, Julie expecting to marry Mr. Marshall, and Mrs. Cavendish planning to go touring again, it looks to Della as though the Cavendish family is breaking up. But Julie advises her not to worry about that.   For one thing Julie knows that Fanny Cavendish will never travel again.

No such dire foreboding is worrying Fanny, however.   She is out of her room, wearing her plum silk gown and posed gayly on the balcony at this moment.

"And purple her habiliments and scarlet was her soul," she quotes.   Leaning over the balcony she calls tremulously for her love.   "Romeo, wherefore art thou, Romeo?"

It is Marshall's coming that has put Fanny in this gay mood. He will come, she opines, bringing another quart of emeralds, of which there is already one stack in the cellar.   Fanny likes Gil, at least as well as she ever did, and understands him, too, however much Julie may doubt her.   But she does not entirely approve of his being different.

"If there's one way to take the romance out of roses it's know-ing that you are going to get them every day."   That's Fanny's idea.   "We've been wading through rose petals ever since he went away.   There was a whole week when you couldn't see the rug. . . . I'll bet he's worked out your honeymoon by algebra. Arrive Constantinople January twelfth, arrive Cairo February twenty-fourth.   He'll tell you that the next Sahara sunset is at

6.49, and it had better be. And while you're sitting on the hill
at Fiesole he'll know to the minute when you'll be in Copen-
hagen."
    "Even that'll be restful. After twenty years of checking my
own trunk."
    Julie is permitting her wedding plans to wait on Gil's return.
Much will depend on him. As for herself, she has decided that
she does not want to go far away. She had thought she did, but
now she had rather be within reach—if anything should happen—
if Gwen or her mother should need her.
    "What for?" bristles Fanny. "Gwen certainly doesn't need
you—settled and through with the stage. . . . And as for me,
while you're drifting down the Nile I'll be playing Ogden, Utah,
and doing pretty well. I sold out there in 1894."
    Let them all talk as much as they like, Fanny Cavendish does
not purpose giving up her career just to keep the house open
and comfortable for them whenever they may decide to return
to it.
    The Deans are calling. Kitty is sporting a new fur coat and
Herbert, "who has been quite gray and nearly bald in the preceding acts, displays, when he removes his hat, a fine and unexpected
crop of coal black hair."
    The Deans are chatty and a little excited. It has occurred to
them that there will not be many more chances for family gath-
erings. "You won't be keeping this great big place when the
family breaks up," says Kitty.
    "I was not aware that the Cavendish family is breaking up,"
snaps Fanny.

    KITTY—Well, after all, with you on the road, and Julie God
knows where, and Gwen married—I don't see that you'll have
any use for it. You can't count on Tony. It looks as if he's
going to stay in Europe forever.
    DEAN (intercepting DELLA as she passes him with her laden
tray, he gathers up a rich and crumbly piece of cake, which he
negotiates with some difficulty through the following lines)—Just
what are your plans, Fanny? (Pauses, cake in hand, ready for a
bite.) How about all this stuff? (A huge bite.) What are you
going to do with everything? (A gesture that indicates the room
about him, but which does not disturb the precarious business in
hand. DELLA takes the tea into the library.)
    FANNY—It'll all go to the storehouse, I suppose. And Aubrey

there along with it. . . . But we're held together by something
more than tables and chairs.

KITTY—It occurred to me this morning—remember I was saying to you, Bert—that aside from Fanny on the road, it will be
Bert and I who'll be carrying on the family tradition.

FANNY—Thanks for including me, anyhow.

KITTY—Has Bert told you what we're planning to do?

FANNY—Why, no.

JULIE—No.

DEAN (*as all eyes go to him*)—Well, I was keeping it as a sort
of surprise, but—ah—I have become more and more impressed,
in recent months, with the opportunities offered by the so-called
vaudeville field.

FANNY—Vaudeville?

DEAN—Why not? Why not? They don't want good plays
any more—they proved that in the way they received "The Conqueror." Finest play of my career, and what happened?

FANNY—It closed.

DEAN—Now here comes this opportunity to reach a wide public, to create an audience for the finer things.

KITTY—We're getting eighteen hundred dollars a week, together.

DEAN—Ah—yes, and twenty weeks right in New York, and
around it. They've got up a very neat little act for us. Amusing.
Human. Now here's the plot.

JULIE—Oh, yes. Tell us.

FANNY—I'm all of a twitter.

DEAN—Well, I'm supposed to be a sort of bachelor chap—
thirty-five or thereabouts—very rich, and have had an unhappy
love affair that I tell the butler about.

KITTY—Ever since then he's been a woman hater.

DEAN—Yes. Then comes this letter from Australia. It seems
that an old college friend has died out there, and it was his last
wish that I should take care of his little girl—be her guardian.

JULIE—The letter is delayed in transit, so that it happens to
arrive just before the little girl herself.

DEAN—You've read it!

JULIE—Oh, no. No.

DEAN--All events, presently there's a lot of noise outside—
automobile horn, so on—the door opens, and instead of the little
child they were expecting, there stands an ex-quisite young girl
of eighteen.

FANNY—Kitty. (*She rises and starts for the library.*)

DEAN—Hold on, Fanny—I'm not through. (*Doorbell rings.*)

FANNY—Oh, yes, you are. Besides, that's probably Marshall. Why don't you two come in there with me for a while? (DELLA *enters from library. Goes toward front door.*)

DELLA—Tea's all ready, Mrs. Cavendish.

FANNY—Come on. Have some tea. (*A step or two toward library door. A feeling of general movement of the group.*)

KITTY—I come in with my little dog Rags, that my father gave me—(*as she talks she is walking in what evidently is meant to be the way in which* BERT'S *ward will walk. Toes in, and is pretty cute*)—and I'm sort of a pathetic figure.

FANNY—You don't say!

Oscar Wolfe drops in to chide them. They've all deserted Oscar. All except Fanny.

There's a trouper for you! He has come now to see if she can open a.week earlier in Toledo and split the week with Columbus. But as soon as Julie can get a private word with him the manager learns that Fanny Cavendish is through touring.

"I went to see Randall yesterday," says Julie. "She's through, Oscar. She can't go on this tour. She can't do anything. . . . She's got to have absolute quiet and rest. The least strain or exertion, and she's likely to go—like that." A snapping of the fingers emphasizes the point.

It is hard for Oscar to believe that Fanny Cavendish has made her last tour. Hard for him to realize the change that must have taken place in the last year, even while she was planning so far ahead. But when he does realize it he promises to coöperate with Julie in keeping Fanny away from the road without ever letting her know the truth.

"First I'll tell her on account of booking troubles we can't open just yet—make it March, say, instead of January. Then when March comes along it's late in the season, the road ain't so good any more—maybe we ought to wait until next year. And I guarantee you, the way I do it, she won't suspect a thing."

"Oscar, what a grand person you are."

"I wish I could really do something. Thirty-five years we been together. They don't make them like her any more. . . . I wish you could have seen her the first time I did, Julie. Her face. Young, and gay, and beautiful—but so much more than beautiful. And how she treated me that first meeting. Me—a beginner, a nobody. I went in there, I tried not to show how I was shaking. I came out, I could have been Sir Charles Wyndham."

Julie's plans, she admits, are uncertain. She cannot, with any peace of mind, go far from home under the circumstances, and yet she knows that Gil has set his heart on a trip to the very ends of the earth.

Perhaps, if she is diplomatic Gil will be willing to let her take a house in town for awhile, where she would be near her mother.

And if she does that, Oscar is quick to suggest, why couldn't she go on—

Julie anticipates his suggestion. "No, no! I'm through with it, Oscar," she announces, flatly. "Through with it forever."

WOLFE—So. You—Gwen—Fanny—that ends it, huh? And for you there's no excuse.

JULIE—I'm going to be married, Oscar. That's a pretty good excuse.

WOLFE—Tell me, what do you talk about when you're with this fellow? The theatre he says he don't care about. Imagine!

JULIE—There are other things in the world beside the theatre.

WOLFE—Sure! But not for you.

JULIE—I want to relax, and play around, and have some fun.

WOLFE—Fun! Fun is work! It's work that's fun. You've had more fun in the last twenty years than any woman in America. And let me tell you, Julie, the theatre is just beginning in this country. It used to be London—Paris—Berlin. Now it's New York. I tell you, a fine actress to-day—there's nothing she can't do. And the finest one of them all, that could do the biggest things of them all, she says she wants to have fun.

JULIE—Oh, Oscar, there are lots of actresses, and so many good ones.

WOLFE—Yes, good, but not for this play.

JULIE—What play?

WOLFE—Not even any of these smart young ones that are coming up. Gwen, maybe. A little young, but she could do this play. Only—(a gesture of hopelessness)—she's gone, too.

JULIE—Oscar, what play? What are you talking about?

WOLFE—Julie, I've never been one of these artistic producers —you know—The Theatre of the Future. Way back when I was a call boy at Daly's Theatre for two dollars a week I made up my mind show business was a good place to make money in, and so I went into it, and I been in it forty years, and I haven't got a nickel. Mind you, I've done a few good plays too, but always I had an idea they would also make a few dollars. But this time

it's different. I have got, I tell you, a play I am so crazy to produce it I don't care how much I lose on it.

JULIE—Really, Oscar! What is it? Who wrote it?

WOLFE—A new fellow you never heard of. Gunther his name
is—a college professor out in Idaho. You wouldn't believe a college professor could know so much. He sits out there in that
desert, mind you, and he writes this play and he doesn't know
himself how good it is.

JULIE—What's it about?

WOLFE—That doesn't matter—it's how he does it. It's going
to revolutionize the theatre—bring in a whole new kind of playwriting. They've never seen anything like this! God, what a
play!

JULIE—Oscar! How exciting!

WOLFE—Exciting, yes. If I can do it right. But how am I
going to do it? You gone. Gwen gone.

JULIE—You'll find some one. You're sure to.

WOLFE—All right. Never mind. Go ahead and relax, when
you could be making history. I do the play anyhow. Not so
perfect maybe—but I do it. I do it because I want to be known
as the man who produced this play.

JULIE—But if it's as good as that it would run years and
years, wouldn't it?

WOLFE—No. A month—two months—I don't give it more
than that. The first ones like this—they got to get used to
them.

JULIE—I couldn't, Oscar. I couldn't.

WOLFE—All right. Get married and be a bazaar patroness.
Mark my words, you'll come back again.

JULIE—They don't always come back. Look at Gwen. And
Tony. He's been away a year.

Gwen and Perry are in. Following them the nurse is bringing
the baby, who must be allowed his rest either before his bottle
or after, Gwen can't quite remember which.

There is a suggestion of repressed excitement in the Stewart
family. Perry's obviously detached attitude shows it. When
finally it is told it seems that Gwen has had an offer from the
Theatre Guild to play the sort of part in a piece from the Hungarian that she has always been simply dying to play.

It isn't a play that is likely to run more than four or five
weeks at the most, and Gwen thinks, so long as the baby is two
months old, and won't really get so he even kind of knows her for

weeks, and Perry is going away on a business trip—Gwen doesn't see why she shouldn't go back to the theatre—just, of course, for this one subscription engagement. As for Perry—of course he's for anything that will make Gwen as happy as that.

The Cavendishes are variously excited by Gwen's news. To Fanny it is about time some such thing was happening. To Julie the news is a little disturbing. There is something about it that makes her own decision to leave the stage a little less agreeable. Kitty and Bert are quite normally thrilled. And Oscar Wolfe— well, Oscar figures hurriedly that if the Theatre Guild gets five weeks out of the new play that should mean that Gwen will be available early in January!

There is great excitement at the door when Gil Marshall arrives. He is modestly pleased when they tell him that the family has gathered all in honor of his coming. He's been eighteen and a half days on the steamer and it is good to be ashore—although he had a very pleasant voyage. Met a lot of interesting people— big South American planters.

"Oh, here's something that'll interest you folks," he suddenly recollects. "There was a theatrical troupe on board. American. They'd been down in Buenos Aires trying to play in English. Ridiculous, of course! Poor devils! Didn't even have money enough to pay their passage. There they all were, on the dock. Of course we couldn't see them stranded. So we got together enough to see them home. I guess I felt a little sentimental about them on account of you people."

"Oh!" ejaculates Julie. There is a second's rather terrible pause.

"Really!" remarks Fanny, significantly.

"Seems the manager had skipped out with the money," continues Gil, innocently; "you know how those fellows are. You'd think they'd be down-hearted, but they were care-free enough, once they got on the boat. I talked to some of them; turned out to be a very decent lot. Couple of them were married—uh— lived in Jersey some place—had—uh—"

Led by Fanny Cavendish the family arises, almost as one, and moves into the library, Gwen bravely trying to cover the exit with chatter about her baby and her plans.

The warmth has some way gone out of Julie's greeting, too. She can't quite understand how Gil could have talked about the troopers' misfortunes the way he did.

GIL—What do you mean! What did I do?

JULIE—You— Oh, never mind. It doesn't matter.

Gil—But, Julie, if you'd just tell me. What was it?

Julie—No. . . . Tell me about your . . . trip, Gil. Did you have a nice time?

Gil—The trip didn't matter. It just meant reaching you.

Julie—Oh, that's so nice—I—

Gil—You're looking just lovely, Julie. I've never seen you so beautiful. Kiss me, dear. (*She turns a cheek to him, coldly. There is nothing else she can do.*) It's been the longest six months of my life. When you finally wired that the end was in sight—that the play was actually closing—do you know what I did? I gave everybody on the place a holiday with double pay. It took them all next day to sober up enough to come back to work.

Julie—I'm very—honoured.

Gil—They're like a lot of children down there. It's a great country, Julie.

Julie—It must be.

Gil—It's as different from the life up here as you can imagine. At Córdoba I was in bed every night at ten o'clock, for four months. Up at six, in the saddle eight hours a day.

Julie—Oh! Yes?

Gil—You'll love it there, Julie. It's so beautiful—and peaceful—and big! And you'll meet real people. None of your . . . Solid! Substantial! The kind that make a country what it is. This man Zamaco who was on the boat. He's my nearest neighbour, you know. Has the next estancia.

Julie—Oh, yes. You told me.

Gil—Yes, indeed. You'll see a lot of the Zamacos. He's a Spaniard of the highest type—very big cattle man. She was a Kansas City girl—Krantz—you know—daughter of Julius Krantz —packer.

Julie—Oh! Julius Krantz.

Gil—Very fine woman, and most entertaining.

Julie—I'm sure.

Gil—They're stopping at the Ritz. I thought we'd dine together Sunday night—the four of us—they're getting tickets for a concert some place—she used to be a harpist, you know.

Julie—No, I didn't.

Gil—Of course it'll be wonderful for you down at Córdoba— having her only thirty miles from us. She'll be company for you while I'm off at the mines.

Julie—Mines?

Gil—Though for that matter you'd be perfectly safe alone.

There are fifteen house servants and most of them have been there
for years. Old Sebastian, for example. Do you know what he'll
do, if necessary? He'll sleep on the floor outside your door all
night.

JULIE—Oh, no—really, I'd rather he didn't. You see, I'd start
getting sorry for him, and I'd give him one of my pillows, and
then a blanket, and pretty soon I'd be out there and he'd be in
the bed.

A ring at the doorbell is supposed to signalize the arrival of the
infant Stewart in the company of his nurse. In place of which
there is such a bedlam of voices and the barking of dogs that the
family trails excitedly back from the library.

The arrival is Tony Cavendish, preceded this time by the "tall,
sinister figure of Gunga. Gunga is an East Indian, wearing his
native costume with turban. In one hand he carries a cage in
which there is a brilliant-hued bird as large as a parrot. On his
shoulder is a monkey. He stands silent after his entrance."

Now Tony is in. "Ahead of him, straining at the leash, are two
huge police dogs. Tony wears a dashing top coat of camel's hair,
and a light felt hat with a brush or feather in it, of the sort one
sees in the Austrian Tyrol."

Tony's reception is as wild as it can well be, and for minutes
the room is a tangled mess of animals, human and domesticated,
and the air is shivering with excited greetings. Gradually out of
it emerges Tony's explanation. He had been forced, as it were,
to burst in upon them in this fashion. He was afraid to let them
know that he was coming. That's why he came by way of
Canada.

FANNY—Canada!

JULIE—Why?

TONY—Because Albania and Schlesingen were going to declare
war on each other. I knew if I got out she'd marry him and
everything would be all right.

JULIE—Who'd marry whom!

FANNY—What's that?!

DEAN—What's he talking about?

GWEN—He's making it up!

TONY—It's been in the papers! Natalia broke off her engagement with Rupert of Schlesingen. Then the Albanians—

JULIE—Wait a minute!

GWEN—Hold on!

WOLFE—Natalia! Natalia!

FANNY—Who's Natalia?

TONY (*patiently*)—Natalia's the Princess of Albania. She's a nice kid, but God! I didn't mean anything serious. That's the trouble with those princesses. Sheltered lives. Dance with 'em a couple of times and they want to elope with you. Of course when she broke off with Rupert, and the Prime Minister sent for me—

JULIE—Oh! I'm beginning to understand. You've started a European war.

TONY—Oh, I don't think they'll fight. I'm gone. She'll get over it. . . . Anyhow, that isn't why I came home. Oscar, listen! I was cruising around the Bayerstrasse in Koenigsberg one night, and I happened to pass a little theatre. Stuck away in a court-yard. There was a poster of this thing outside. I started to read it—I don't know, I got a hunch about it, and went in. (GIL *and* PERRY *find their interest in this narrative flagging. They stand a little apart from the group, hands in pockets, thoughtful.*) Well, say!

WOLFE—Good, huh?

TONY—Good? It's the God-damnedest play I ever saw in my life, and I bought it. You're to wire 'em three thousand dollars to-morrow. American money.

Now Tony has launched into an extravagantly dramatic story of the new play and a description of its employment of the new constructivist scenery which groups the actors first on one level and then on another, with their entrances and exits negotiated sometimes by chute and sometimes by wires from which they are suspended and lowered from the flies.

During this recital Perry Stewart and Gil Marshall have drawn apart from the group and are earnestly engaged in a good solid business man's conversation, snatches of which occasionally break through the turmoil around Tony.

". . . and by shipping through the canal, of course," Marshall is heard explaining, "we cut our overhead fourteen per cent."

"That swings the whole thing around," Tony is assuring his wide-eyed listeners; "the audience become the actors and the actors become the audience."

"Serve 'em right!" mutters Julie.

"I tell you it's a knockout," explodes Tony. "It's been running a year in this hole, mind you, and nobody ever heard of it. Then all of a sudden—you know the way those things are—I looked around one night and there was Hopkins in the second row. I knew what that meant, so I streaked it up the aisle, found Meyerhoff, and settled it then and there. Of course the great thing about this play is it takes two nights to do it."

Now Tony has moved over to the piano to illustrate the incidental music of this "modern passion play" in which he expects to play the lead. Gil and Perry politely ask to be excused, pleading previous engagements, and Tony's piano work proceeds boomingly.

It is during the briefest of interludes that Julie manages to attract Wolfe's attention.

"Why don't you let me read the play?" she asks.

"What?"

"That play by your college professor. Why don't you let me read it?"

"What do you mean, read it? What for?"

"Why, I just thought I'd like to, that's all. To sort of get an idea of the part."

"I'll send you up the manuscript this evening."

Tony has just moved on to the music of the fire-worship scene, which, he assures them, is the biggest kick of all, when the doorbell again announces an arrival and Miss Peake, proudly bearing the infant Stewart, is ushered in.

The show moves over from Tony to the baby, and for the next few minutes the air is filled with baby talk, mingling admiration and advice. Fanny Cavendish manages finally to rescue the child and, standing proudly before the portrait of his great grandfather gently admonishes him.

"Do you know who that is, young man? You were named for him, Aubrey Cavendish Stewart, and see that you live up to it. . . ."

KITTY—Do you think he'll be an actor?

WOLFE—Say, *he* shouldn't be an actor! Look at him! (*A sudden thought. A snap of the fingers.*) Here's an idea!

GWEN (*who is fluffing the baby's hair a little after removing his hood*)—Yes? What?

WOLFE—Listen, show folks! I got a great new play I'm going to produce—(*a side look at Julie*)—and in it they talk all the time about a baby. Why shouldn't we have a scene where the baby is carried on, and— (*A gesture toward the baby.*)

GWEN—You're crazy, Wolfey! Perry wouldn't hear of it.

JULIE—Gwen, he'll have to start *some* time.

FANNY—Certainly will!

DEAN (*holding up his cocktail glass, and signalling the others to join him*)—Here's to Aubrey Cavendish Stewart! (*A chorus of assent from the others. A little rush for the cocktails.*)

ALL—Yes! Yes! Aubrey!

TONY (*gives a glass to* FANNY)—Here you are, Fanny! (*Holds aloft his glass.*) To the kid!

FANNY (*the child in her arm. Takes the glass in her hand. Holds it aloft*)—To Aubrey Cavendish!

GWEN—Stewart!

FANNY—That won't stop him! He's a Cavendish, and he's going to carry on. We always have, and we always will. When one drops out there's always another one to take his place. (*A pause. She drops to repeat the last phrase, but in a different tone.*) When one drops out, there's always another—

JULIE (*a hand on* FANNY's *arm*)—Now, Mother—

FANNY (*gathering herself together with a great effort. . . . Raises her glass*)—To the future greatest actor of his day! Aubrey Cavendish Second! (*They all drink.*)

MISS PEAKE—I really think, Mrs. Stewart—

GWEN (*takes the child from* FANNY)—Yes. All right, Miss Peake. Come on, everybody. He's got to go in where it's warm. (*A general movement toward the library door. More clucking and hubbub over the child. "Look! He's laughing! . . . Here we go! . . . He knows what it's all about. . . . Can't fool this bimbo!"*)

TONY—Wait till you hear the ballet music, you people! How's this piano?

JULIE—Come on, Mother dear. (*All except* FANNY *go into the library. The noise goes on from there, fainter, of course, but still heard, very merry.* TONY *is playing some gay strains on library piano.* FANNY *has remained in her chair. As the others have passed into the next room she has slowly and unobtrusively sunk back in the deep chair so that she is almost entirely lost to the audience. Now her hand holding the glass with which she has drunk the toast, is seen groping rather aimlessly for the table at the side of the chair. The hand reaches, wavers, the glass drops from the fingers, the hand drops to the side.* DELLA *comes on carrying the ginger bread; crosses to library door. She speaks as she crosses, scarcely looking at the figure in the chair.*)

DELLA—Isn't he the cute one, though? (*Goes into the library. There is a moment's pause. The voices from the next room come up, high and gay, and there is laughter, and chirping to the baby.*)

GWEN (*voice from the library*)—Where's Fanny?

JULIE—Where's Mother? . . . Mother, come on in! See what he's doing now! Mother, where are you? (*Appears in library doorway.*) Mother, come on in! He just did the cutest . . . (*Stops, startled, at something queer in the figure huddled in the chair. Comes quickly, fearfully, goes to the chair, one hand outstretched. Comes around in front of chair. Touches* FANNY. *Calls.*) Gwen! Tony! Quick! Quick!

GWEN (*rather gayly*)—What? What is it?

JULIE—Come! Quick! Oscar! (*At the note in her voice they come, streaming in slowly, talking a little, perhaps, in a subdued tone, and rather apprehensive. At the look in* JULIE's *face they are warned. Their faces take on a stricken look. Awed, fearful, they tiptoe toward the still form in the chair.*)

The curtain falls.

BURLESQUE

A Comedy in Three Acts

BY GEORGE MANKER WATTERS AND ARTHUR HOPKINS

THE production histories of "Burlesque" and "Broadway" run curiously parallel. Both plays were written by men of the theatre about people of the theatre. Both were peddled extensively before a buyer could be found for either. Both were notably successful during preliminary road trials and both were what the profession knows as overnight hits in New York.

The impression was general at the time of "Burlesque's" appearance that the success of "Broadway" the previous season had inspired George Manker Watters to write the newer play, but Mr. Watters explains that he had the first draft of his comedy well under way before the Dunning-Abbott play was produced.

Watters, having spent his life in the theatre, was particularly insistent that "Burlesque" should present the burlesque actors as he knows them. And though he was eager to dispose of his play he refused the offers of several producers who were willing to buy if he would permit them to make what he considered drastic changes of character and mood in the story.

The play finally reached the offices of Arthur Hopkins and that producer took it home to read it over the week-end. He read it Saturday night and spent Sunday rewriting the second act. Monday he took the play back to town, called Mr. Watters in and gave him the new act to read without telling him who wrote it.

The playwright, although he had sworn not to let any one touch his script, admitted the new act was an improvement and agreed to work with the collaborator who had written it. Mr. Hopkins thereupon figuratively stepped out from behind his whiskers and became a playwright.

After a spring tour that caused more or less excitement among the early summer resorters "Burlesque" was brought into the Plymouth Theatre Thursday night, September 1, 1927, and began a run that was continuing popularly as this record was written. Its first night reception was enthusiastic, the news of its success was mysteriously wirelessed from end to end of the town, as fre-

quently happens in such cases, the press reviews were confirma-
tory and seats were at a premium for months thereafter.

"Burlesque" is rough drama in the sense that it cross-sections
life among the lowly and uncultured performers of the burlesque
theatres, revealing them on good authority as they live and as
they are, refining no more than their mental reactions and only
occasionally softening the common speech of their kind.

One of the cheaper burlesque troupes is touring the middle
west. In a dressing room under the stage of a theatre located in
St. Paul, or it might be Milwaukee, Skid and Bonny Johnson are
introduced during the progress of the entertainment. When the
door of the room is open the music of the theatre orchestra can be
faintly heard, and later, during any given lull in the conversation
the tapping of the dancers on the floor above is audible. It is
just before the overture and the voice of the callboy can be heard
urging the girls to hurry stageward.

Bonny is beading her eyelashes and worrying about Skid. It
is 8.20. Jimmy, the callboy, has toured the speakeasies and still
there is no sign of Skid. Being the leading comedian of the
troupe his tardiness is of considerable importance, and his known
weaknesses inspire Bonny with apprehension.

Her worry, however, is for nothing. Skid hustles in a minute
later, sober and prepared to do a lightning dressing act. "Skid,
the fireman's child," he reminds them, can dress sliding down a
pole, so why the worry? Why the worry, anyway? What if he
didn't show up for dinner? He wasn't hungry, and he needed
air. So he got to playin' a little pool, and— That was that!

Bonny just naturally can't help worrying about Skid. Here
he's workin' without any dinner, and goin' to an Elks' smoker
after the show, still without any regular food. Not if she knows
it! He's simply gotta eat!

And there is something else that does not set well with Bonny.
There's a certain dame in this show that's been a little too friendly
with Skid. Especially that time when Bonny was in the hospital. Her name's Sylvia Marco, and it has been one of the minor
ambitions of Bonny's life since she has heard about Marco's win-
ning ways to lam her one, as they say in the profession.

The opportunity and the excuse are soon presented. Miss
Marco is leaving that night to join the "Manhattan Follies"
troupe in New York. Charlie Dillingham has sent for her. And
she is visiting the dressing rooms now to "gurgle her farewells."

Bonny opens the door to Marco and insists upon her coming
in, even if Skid isn't there—he having gone on for one of his

dance numbers. Then Bonny proceeds to tell her visitor what's what and what may happen if ever she (Marco) attempts to try her fascinations upon the susceptible Skid again. And then, with the eager assistance of a pugnacious little party named Mazie, Bonny throws Sylvia out.

"What's the big idea of bein' so sweet to her?" demands Mazie. "I'd a lammed her once."

"Oh, what's the good," queries Bonny. "I been thinkin' for weeks what a pleasure it would be to burn her up good and now that I've done it I don't feel so good myself."

If it isn't one worry it's another with Bonny. Now Skid has gone into his dance upstairs and whenever he does a funny fall it shakes the stage. It also shakes Bonny. "Every time Skid takes one o' those falls it hurts me spine," she says. "The dam fool's too good a comic to be doin' that stuff."

Now Skid is back to make his next change and Bonny is still worrying about him. Skid, however, is quite content. Only worried a little because Bonny worries so much.

Skid—What's wrong, kid, you ain't looking so cheerful.

Bonny—Say, if you had to sit in this room and listen to those falls you take, you wouldn't be so merry neither.

Skid—They're in the plot, ain't they?

Bonny—Yeah, but why do you have to worry so much about the plot? Nobody else cares a dam' about it. Not even the guy that stole it.

Skid—You gotta make up your mind, Bonny, that I'm a hoak comic. Don't waste no time tryin' to clean me up because I'd be a flop. When I was a baby the first thing I reached for was a custard pie. My grandma said I was goin' to be a baker. Grandma was a smart old lady, but she never went to shows, so she didn't know nothin' at all about the real meanin' of custard pies. If it happened to-day, she'd know dam' well I was goin' to be a movie actor.

Bonny—What's the use of kiddin' all your life. Ain't you ever goin' to be serious? Don't you want to ever get ahead in this game? Don't it make you sick to see the success of those ham comics in New York they call stars, and think of yourself draggin' your tail through these bum tanks?

Skid—Whaddya mean draggin' my tail? We're workin' all the time, ain't we? I ain't hangin' around Broadway makin' touches, am I? There ain't no landlady threatenin' to throw us out, is there? Whaddya want me to be—a big mafeffer? Well, I ain't nuts about all that stuff. I've been around the Friars and the Lambs and seen a lotta big actors. Well, I'd rather work. Those guys spend their lives turnin' down offers and when offers don't come no more, they still tell how they're turnin' 'em down.

BONNY—Well, who asked you to be a Friar or a Lamb? I'm talkin' about you're gettin' where you belong. Have I gotta have all the ambition for this family? Ain't you got none? Boy, if I had your talent! Why, there ain't nothin' could stop you if you decided to step out. No, you must stick to the same old routine. You're doin' the same stuff now you wuz five years ago and you'll do it till you die, if your haunches don't wear out.

SKID—Say, how d'ye know I'd be so good? I could be a big flop, too, in a real show. There ain't nobody that can't flop no matter how good they look to the family.

BONNY—There's the tip-off. You're scared. All the rest of this gab is apple-sauce. You ain't got the guts.

SKID—Say, how many times are you goin' to pull that on me?

BONNY—How many times are you goin' to make me?

Lefty, the company manager, stops in and agrees with Bonny, when he is drawn into the argument, that Skid is wasting his talent and his youth where he is. The "old man," who is the proprietor of the show, has come to take him for granted and has lost interest in him. Furthermore Lefty happens to know that Skid's chance may come sooner than he expects. There have been certain scouts around watching the burlesquers and Lefty knows that at least one of these has turned in a favorable report to Dillingham on Skid's possibilities as a big time comedian. If that offer comes Lefty, as Skid's friend rather than his boss, thinks the comedian should grab it. But Skid refuses to take the suggestion and shuffles stageward again.

"You know, there's the only actor I ever met that don't give a dam' about New York," Lefty tells Bonny.

"Yeah, and if he ever lands there they'll have to chloroform him to get him on the road again," wisely observes Bonny.

Lefty also has a bit of news for Bonny. The cattle king who never fails them in this town has shown up again. Came in Sunday morning and bought the same seat for fourteen shows. Has done that every year for four years. And yet he never has even met Bonny, who appears to be his passion. Lefty thinks perhaps if he were to bring this loyalist back stage he'd know there was a heaven. To which Bonny agrees.

Bozo, one of the minor comics, is in with a telegram for Skid.

Telegrams always mean touches to Bonny and Skid. "We never get none except from station S O S," says she, as she puts this one on Skid's dressing table.

Her big boy is back now, limping a little. One of his falls did not go so well. He sees the telegram and is for tearing it up. But Bonny insists he open it. When he does so he has the shock of his life.

"Have a chance to place you with new Dillingham show 'Manhattan Follies' opening next week," it reads. "Is there any way you can get out of present engagement (*stop*). Can get you five hundred maybe more (*stop*). Leave salary to me (*stop*). Great chance. No comedy in show at present. You would have to be here Sunday for rehearsal. Wire Max Levy."

Levy they know to be one of the big agents in New York, but it sounds to Skid like some one is trying to kid him. Bonny knows. Knows that it is Skid's opportunity come at last. And knows, too, that she is not even mentioned.

Furthermore she knows that the "Marco dame" is going to be with that same "Manhattan Follies"—that'll be Skid's chance, too. It may be only a coincidence but Bonny is painfully suspicious of its being a conspiracy as well. It's a frame-up, that's what it is, and neither Skid nor Marco had the courage to come clean and admit it.

Bonny is in a passion now, fighting tears and riding Skid. "I've been a dam' fool, nursin' you along and tryin' to pound some sense into that thick dome o' yours, tryin' to get you somewhere, for what? I been just readyin' you up for some cheap jane to grab you off."

Yet Bonny insists she isn't jealous. Jealous, indeed! "Of what? A bum comedian who ain't got a laugh above his hips? Say, if you was to fall for a girl that meant anything I'd wish you luck, but that empty-headed little tart! . . . I ain't jealous. I'm insulted."

"Well, you can stop blowin' off steam and cool out, cause I ain't goin'."

"Who said you wasn't goin'?"

"I said it and that settles it."

"Oh, it does? Since when does what you say settle things?"

"It settles this one. . . . I gotta go on for my race track bit."

As he is closing the door Bonny calls after him:

"Ha! You're sore, ain't you?"

Lefty brings the cattleman back. He is a big fellow, this Mr. Howell—big and wholesome after the commoner notion of western ranchmen. And there is nothing of the stage door John about him. He is a little embarrassed to meet Bonny, after feeling that he has known her so long, from the other side of the footlights, but his divinity soon puts him at his ease with the help of the old routine.

BONNY—Well, Mr. Howell, how do you like our fair city?

HARVEY—I never liked this city much.

BONNY—Well, you sure like burlesque. I'm goin' to enter you in a Customer's contest.

HARVEY (*laughs*)—Your show's the only one I ever see.

BONNY—Of course we've all been wonderin' about you. The company started talkin' about you two weeks ago wonderin' whether you'd be here again this year.

HARVEY (*laughs*)—They ought to be able to depend on me by now.

BONNY—This is the fourth year, ain't it?

HARVEY—It's the fourth year I been comin' regular. I saw one performance five years ago on a Saturday night and I made up my mind the next year I'd see the show right.

BONNY—I can't figure it out.

HARVEY—Well, it's easy enough. It's the only chance I have of seein' you.

BONNY—You ain't goin' to start kiddin' me, are you, Mr. Howell?

HARVEY—I wouldn't know how to do that.

BONNY—I guess I was only kiddin' myself.

HARVEY—But even if I don't see you, I keep track of you.

BONNY—Yeah? How?

HARVEY—I always know where you're playin'. I take two theatre papers, *Variety* and *Billboard*, so I know where your company is all the time. Of course, I lose track of you in the summer, but I pick up your trail again in the fall.

BONNY—Ain't it funny to have some one thinkin' about you that you don't know nothin' about?

HARVEY—I saw a squib about you in *Variety* that time you were in the hospital in Des Moines. Of course, by the time I read it you were probably well and out, but I sent you some flowers anyway.

BONNY—I got them.

HARVEY—No!

BONNY—I did—and I always wondered who sent them. Thought they must have been meant for some one else.

HARVEY—Well, ain't that great? I'd like to send that paper a present. (*Laughs.*) My sister makes a lot of fun of me for takin' those papers. Says I'm stage-struck and am goin' to take Bill Rogers' place.

BONNY—Your ranch is in Wyoming, ain't it?

HARVEY—Yes, Pedmond.

BONNY—Have you got any family?

HARVEY—Only my sister. We're all that's left.

BONNY—Ain't you never married?

HARVEY (*pause*)—No. (*Pause.*)   But I'm hopin' awful hard I'm goin' to be, soon.

BONNY (*pause*)—I been married six years.

HARVEY (*pause*)—You are married?

BONNY—Yeah, I'm draggin' the old ball and chain around.

HARVEY—I'm sorry. But I'm glad you told me. I was just gettin' ready to put my foot in it.

BONNY—I knew you wuz; that's why I stopped you. (*Rises.*) Come on, we'll have a drink. (*Gets out bottle and glasses, pours two drinks.*)   Here's to you, Mr. Howell, and may you never marry.

HARVEY—I wouldn't like to drink to that.

BONNY—Then may you marry some one as decent as yourself, that'll keep you single. (*Unfastens dress, drops it off, then places it over the back of her chair.*)

HARVEY—Do you want me to think you're wild?

BONNY—No, I want to show you something about marriage. Here you are, and if I know anything about men, you're as fine as they come—and if I wuz free, without knowin' a dam' thing about me, you'd be willin' to marry me. Well, that ain't an experience a girl has every day. If I wuzn't cuckoo it'd mean something to me, but Mr. Howell, it don't mean a dam' thing. All I can think of is a bum comic upstairs slidin' around on his tail. He's a stew. He runs out on me; sometimes I think he don't give a dam' about me. But he's all I can think of— And do you know what I'm doin' now? I'm usin' you to see if I can make him jealous when he comes in. That's what marriage does to you.

HARVEY—Maybe it's not marriage. Maybe it's love.

BONNY—Well, whatever it is, pray that it never hits you. And now, Mr. Howell, you can see I ain't what you dreamed I wuz at all. Come on and we'll drink to the dream that's out. (*Both drink. She takes his glass to refill it.*)

HARVEY—I wish you were free.

BONNY—What, yet?

HARVEY—I've got a feeling love don't have to be the way you say it is.

BONNY—It's gotta be that way with me because I've only loved one man—and I've got a hunch I ain't ever goin' to feel any other kind o' love. (*Commotion at outside is heard.*) That's the intermission. Well, Mr. Howell, it's been great to meet you and I hope I'm goin' to see you again before we leave.

HARVEY—I'll come back again to-morrow afternoon if it's all right.

BONNY—Sure, it's all right any time. Now have your drink. (*Hands him drink.*)

HARVEY (*rises*)—Thanks, I will. We'll drink to you.

BONNY (*getting her own drink*)—Yeah, to me the sap.

They are raising their glasses when Skid comes in. The scene does not startle him. He accepts Howell, when Bonny introduces him, quite as a matter of course, even when he recognizes the cattleman as the devoted admirer who has been sitting out front for four years.

"What wuz it, a sentence?" he asks.

"No," Howell explains, "I just found something I like and I stuck to it."

"It ain't a bad idea at that. Why don't you have supper with us some night?"

"Sure, I'd be glad to."

And so it is arranged. That, Bonny concludes, is the last touch! Again she is furious. A fine piece of bologny, Skid! So wrapped up in that Marco dame he can't even see his wife any more.

"It don't mean a thing to you to find your wife undressed, drinkin' with a strange man, does it?"

"Well, as far as that goes, Bonny, I've seen you more undressed than that on the stage, and God knows drinkin' with a strange man ain't goin' to hurt you unless the hooch is bad."

It is all a lot of foolishness, this whole business, to Skid. He knows Bonny's all right and able to take care of herself any time, anywhere. He's perfectly satisfied with his job and his chances. And he ain't goin' to New York.

How can he? Walk out on Lefty? They're all a lot of simps, if you asked Skid.

"Well, you don't know it yet, big boy, but you're goin' to New

York and you're goin' to knock 'em dead," prophesies Bonny,
with a glow of her old enthusiasm. "Yes, sir, they're goin' to see
my Skid! And they ain't seen nothin' yet! Boy, how I'd like
to be there for that opening!"
But Skid can't see it yet. It's all a joke. Even when Lefty
comes back to order him out of the theatre so he can catch a New
York train in twenty minutes Skid is doubtful. Is he bein'
canned?
Sure he is. That's the only excuse Lefty will have to offer the
old man for losing his pet comedian. He's being canned for being
late and holding the curtain three times the same week. And his
tickets will be at the railroad station waitin' for him.

BONNY—Lefty, I'll never forget you for this.
LEFTY—That's all right, kid. It's all for the sake of art.
(*Goes, closes door.*)
BONNY (*putting* SKID'S *costume, wig and shoes in old suit-
case.*) Wire me as soon as you get in, darling.
SKID (*going.*)—Sure.
BONNY—And write me often. I'll be awful lonesome without
you.
SKID—Jeez. I'll be an awful sap without you, Bonny. We
ain't never been apart before.
BONNY—As soon as the season's over, darling, I'll come
right on.
SKID—Mebbe the show'll be a flop and I can come back soon.
BONNY—You can't come back, you're fired.
SKID—Hey, I didn't think of that. That ain't so good.
BONNY—Forget it, honey, it's sink or swim now.
SKID—I don't like the way you say sink.
BONNY—Well, how do you like the way I say swim. (BONNY
*reaches inside of bodice and unpins a chamois pouch which she
hands to* SKID.) Here's our bank-roll, Skid.
SKID—I can't take that. We've saved it together. It's yours
as much as mine.
BONNY—I don't need it. What can I use money for workin'
with this trick? Take it, honey. (SKID *comes down to her.*) I
don't want you to be short in the big town. If they don't treat
you right you can walk out.
SKID (*takes it*)—All right, kid. I'm always goin' to keep this
boodle bag. It was the first one we ever had, wasn't it?
BONNY—Yeah. We had that long before we had anything to
put in it.

SKID (*taking* BONNY)—Don't think I'm scared, darling, 'cause I ain't, but I wish I wasn't goin'. I have a feelin' we're makin' a mistake.

BONNY—Mistake to grab a leading part in the biggest show o' the year on Broadway? Why, honey, it's the greatest break we ever had.

SKID—Well, maybe you're right. But what the hell if you ain't? We can always go back to the old tent show, can't we, honey?

BONNY—That's the idea. If New York don't like you, that's their loss.

SKID (*looks around*)—Well, I guess that's all. I don't know how to say good-by, darling. I ain't never said good-by to you. (*She embraces him. He kisses her.*)

BONNY (*crying softly*)—I'll miss you, Skid. I love you, Skid. I'll miss you, Skid.

SKID—I'm lost already without you, Bonny. (MAZIE, BOZO, GUSSIE *and* JIMMY *come in.*)

MAZIE—Hey, Skid, we heard the news. Atta boy, Skid.

BOZO—Poison 'em, Skid. (*Members of chorus begin crowding back of others, some of them crying.*)

1ST GIRL—He's ready to leave.

2ND GIRL—He's going.

3RD GIRL—Oh, gee! I hate to see him go.

SKID—Jeez, look at the kids, crying. Whatsmatter, girls? I ain't dead yet. (*Turns quickly, grabs* BONNY *again.*) Good-by, honey. I'll wire and write you.

BONNY—Good-by, Skid. (SKID *hurries to door and is at once surrounded by the Company who drag him down the hall amid a confusion of congratulations and farewells.* BONNY *goes to the door and looks off after them. She remains looking after all is silent.*)

The curtain falls.

ACT II

Four months later Bonny picks up the phone in the drawing room of her New York hotel suite and discovers that Mazie, the pugnacious little friend of her trouping days, is at the other end of the wire, downstairs.

Having been trying to get in touch with Mazie for three days, Bonny is delighted to have a chance to talk with her and to explain at least a few of the things that have happened since their show closed.

First there is the report about Skid. The expected has happened so far as he is concerned. Skid is not only a great Broadway success but he has taken up with Sylvia Marco, just as Bonny had feared he would do.

Bonny, hearing of this and having had the news confirmed by letter from Skid, has filed her papers in Chicago and is promised a final decree of divorce in the fall. As soon as she is divorced Bonny has promised to marry Harvey Howell and go to live with him and his sister on their Wyoming ranch.

"They'll never be another Skid for me," she admits to Mazie. "But what's the use? He'll always be a bum. He just wants one long drunken party and any dame that'll stay up with him. I kept him kind of straight in the sticks but I'd never get away with it in this town. I used to think if he landed right in this game he'd take a tumble to himself but since his big hit here he's worse than ever."

"Yeah, he's gettin' in bad. He's been goin' on stewed regular, and there's plenty o' hammers out for him."

Bonny—Harvey and me went to see his show last night. He came on fried. Some of his falls were a surprise to him, but the audience laughed at all of 'em. My God, he is funny, the poor sap. (*Cries a little.*) I sent a note over to the Friars askin' him to come around and see me. I'm going to try to talk a little sense to him. I guess it ain't any use.

Mazie—That ain't why you're sendin' for him, Bonny. You're still cuckoo about that bird.

Bonny—Maybe I am but I'm goin' to forget it and he did used to listen to me sometimes.

Mazie—I ain't seen the show yet. I hear he's a riot.

Bonny—He's sure a hit. I got a big kick outa watchin' him last night. It ain't often you have a dream come out, Mazie. For years I been dreamin' of Skid landin' on Broadway and knockin' the soup-an-fish for a goal and there it all was—happenin' right in front o' me. It still seemed like a dream. I had to pinch myself. It'll be a dam' shame if he tosses it all off.

It is at Howell's suggestion that Bonny is in New York. He thought she should come on and put in a few days buying some new clothes. He drops in now to see how she is getting along. Also to tell her that she has made a little extra money. Some of the stock he had put away for her has gone up twenty points.

Life is so simple for Bonny now that she doesn't really know what to do with her profits, a condition of mind that Mazie would simply adore rescuing her from, if that were possible. In fact if Mr. Howell has a little brother, or even a little cousin, Mazie has an idea she could use him to great advantage.

Now Mazie has disappeared and Howell is trying again to make Bonny understand exactly how he feels about everything. He has brought her a beautiful jewelled bracelet and he slips it over her wrist while her eyes are closed. When she opens them and begins to cry a little he is greatly distressed.

He is just trying to show her that his love is very deep and very genuine, he explains, and he is hoping that not only will she understand but that she will be ready to go home with him very, very soon, and leave all her old troubles behind her.

She will go, Bonny says, any time he is ready. She is through with New York, excepting that she does want to see Skid and try to talk a little sense to him before they go. She has sent word to Skid and he has promised to come.

"I can't figure it out," Bonny explains to Mazie, after Howell has gone. "Harvey's the finest guy I ever met. When I'm away from him I think how wonderful he is and how lucky I am, but somehow when I'm with him I want to cry. It's like I was ashamed of myself, but I ain't. I ain't ever done nothin' I'm ashamed of. And then I can't help feeling that Harvey's gettin' the worst of it somehow and I'd rather die than give a guy like that the worst of it. I'd always rather take the worst of it myself. Maybe I'm a sap, but I've been that way since I was a kid.

MAZIE—I'll tell you the trouble with you, Bonny, you ain't used to bein' treated well, but that's somethin' you don't have to take no college course to get on to. You'll learn.

BONNY—Maybe some of us are only happy when we ain't treated well. God knows I never knew where I was at with Skid. Always wondering where he was and who he was with and was he cock-eyed, and could he go on, and was he coming home. Never a day's peace for six years but I gotta say I was happy with him.

MAZIE—What'd you give him up for?

BONNY—Because I made up my mind I wasn't goin' to be a mug all my life. Because I made up my mind it was time for me to find some one who'd do a little worryin' about me.

MAZIE—Well, you've found him. Now look here, Bonny, you're right to give Skid the gate. I didn't think you'd have the guts to do it, but you did. Howell's a real man, not a plastered comic with a rubber spine. He loves you. You've been a great

kid all your life and at last you're gettin' a break. Now for
God's sake don't get it into your head that you're the kind of jane
that can't bear to be treated nice. They ain't no such jane.

It is Skid's ring on the phone that interrupts them. Suddenly
Bonny is trembling at the thought of seeing him again and Mazie
is a little disgusted with her. This, Mazie hopes, is the last time
Bonny will ever play mamma to Skid. See him once and get it
over with, that's Mazie's idea.

Skid arrives, joyful and free, bringing a party with him.
There's Lefty, for one, and Jerry Evans, a song writer, for another. They have been going all night and the others can't do
a thing to discourage Skid. He wants to keep on going.

Skid is glad to see Bonny. A little sore that she has been in
town a week and hasn't let him know. A little worried because
she has been crying—and she can't fool him about that, because
he has seen her cry too often. He is worried because he fears,
maybe, the new guy ain't treatin' Bonny right. Which isn't true,
snaps Mazie—and none of his business if it were.

"Say, I suppose what happens to you is none of my business,"
Skid protests to Bonny with what passes for hurt feelings. "I
suppose I'm goin' to forget that you're the only girl in the world
that I ever gave a dam' about."

"Yeah! Me and how many others?" answers Bonny. "I got
tired o' bein' a mob scene. Are you still with that Marco dame,
or is she cold turkey?"

SKID—Jeez, it's just like old times. I come here when you ask
me to, I'm tickled to death to see you. I try to tell you you're
the whole works and you start ridin' me.

BONNY—And I suppose you couldn't come alone. What was
you afraid I'd do to you?

SKID—Well, you wouldn't have me shake these guys, would
you? They been with me all night.

BONNY—Yeah. I suppose you're the King of the night clubs
now.

SKID—Yeah. That's me. I'm givin' all the little girlies a great
big hand.

BONNY—Yeah. You look fine with that black eye. When
your nose gets a little redder they'll think you're the flag of Rou-
mania. Who hung that on you?

SKID—A friend o' mine.

BONNY—I never knew Marco packed as good a wallop as that.

SKID—Oh, lay off Marco. She ain't a bad skate. She always speaks well of you. (*There is a knock on the door.* SKID *rises and strolls to door.*) Well, there's the little boy with the white rock. (*Goes to door, admits* WAITER, *who puts tray on table.*) Open 'em up, will you? (JERRY *plays "Something."*)

WAITER—Certainly, sir. Both of them?

SKID—Yes.

WAITER (*opening bottles*)—If you need any Scotch or gin, sir.

SKID—Yeah, I know.

WAITER—My number is Eighty-six.

SKID—That's just Lefty's age.

LEFTY (*stirring in his doze*)—Ah, you big bum, why don't you go to bed?

SKID (*pays* WAITER)—Keep the change.

WAITER—Thank you, sir. Thank you very much, and my number is . . .

SKID (*up at table*)—Yeah. Eighty-six. I know. (WAITER *exits.* SKID *draws enormous flask from pocket.*) Do you want yours straight or highball, Mazie?

MAZIE—Plenty o' Scotch and just a little water. Who stepped on your eye, Skid?

SKID (*who is fixing highballs*)—I bumped me knee takin' bows. (*Takes highball and lowball to* BONNY *and* MAZIE.) Say, Bonny. Have you caught our show yet?

BONNY—Yeah. I saw it last night.

SKID—I wasn't so good last night. I wish you'd been in Tuesday.

BONNY—I'll bet you'll be good to-night.

SKID (*shaking* LEFTY)—Hey, you dirty-out-all-night, have a drink. (*Gives* LEFTY *highball.*)

LEFTY—Jeez, another? I wish somebody'd treat me to a bed. (SKID *goes to table and gets* BONNY'S *and his own drink.*)

SKID (*going down to couch*)—Here, Bonny. You and me'll have a quiet one together.

BONNY—No. I don't want any.

SKID—Come on, don't be a crab. Take your drink. Gee, it's great to see you, Bonn. (*Rises.*) Come on, let's all drink to Bonn, the best little girl that ever frisked a husband's clothes for evidence. (JERRY *and* MAZIE *laugh.* JERRY *stops playing.*)

LEFTY—Here's to Bonn!

BONNY—Yeah. I suppose an alley cat thinks now and then that he's a husband. (JERRY *begins playing "Sunny Disposis."*)

SKID (*sits again*)—Yeah, that's what makes him howl. Aw,

come on, Bonn, let's stop crackin' at each other and have some fun.

BONNY (*starting to cry*)—I didn't start it.

SKID (*putting his arms about her*)—I know you didn't. It's my fault. I was only kiddin', you never would stand bein' kidded. I oughta know better.

BONNY—Don't bother, Skid. I guess I'm a damn fool.

SKID—Come on, finish your drink and I'll shake up a fresh one.

BONNY—I don't want any more, Skid.

SKID—Yes, you do, now go on, finish that, go on . . . atta baby! (*She does, he takes glass and goes to table, gets* MAZIE'S *and* JERRY'S *glasses.* JERRY *begins to play "Just Around the Corner."*) Why, old Ted Lewis! . . . Yes, sir. (SKID *sings the song while mixing and serving drinks.*)

Just around the corner may be sunshine for you,
Just around the corner skies above may be blue,
Keep a little smile on, that's the right thing to do,
In a little while your troubles,
They will disappear like bubbles,
Just around the corner, there's a bluebird on high,
Waiting on a rainbow in the sky, why
Even tho' it's dark and cloudy,
Sun may peep through and say "Howdy"
Just around the corner from you.

(*At end of song he wakes up* LEFTY, *handing him a highball.*) Wake up, Mr. Moore, it's time for your medicine.

LEFTY (*drowsily*)—Are you up yet? Say, who does your sleepin' for you? (*Takes drink, is caught by rhythm of tune* JERRY *is playing, and rather solemnly tries to execute a dance.*)

SKID—Say, Bonn, when are you goin' to marry this jazzbo you wrote about?

BONNY—I can't get married till fall. (JERRY *plays "Lucky Day."*)

SKID—What are you goin' to do till then?

BONNY—Goin' out to live on the ranch with him and his sister.

SKID—His sister?

BONNY—Yeah.

SKID (*up at table*)—That'll be nice. I know those dames. They always want to know all the inside dirt of show business. She'll probably ask you if Klaw and Erlanger wuz ever married.

LEFTY (*stirring drowsily*)—Well, what's the difference as long as they love each other?

The party goes on, gaining momentum with the circulation of the drinks. At the piano Mazie is recalling an old love to Jerry, who is a loving man but forgetful.

Now they have Bonny dancing and soon Skid has joined her and they fall naturally into their old steps, singing huskily the song Jerry pounds out spiritedly on the piano. When they finish dancing Skid takes Bonny in his arms.

"Oh, boy, that's like old times," he puffs. "None o' these high-priced janes can dance like Bonny."

"You wouldn't kid me, would you, Mister?"

"I would if I could, Lady, I would if I could."

It's a damn shame, Lefty insists, that Bonny is quitting the show business. And he has a little scheme. Next season he is going to buy the show from the old man if he can find a sugar daddy, and he thinks he can. If he does, nothing would be sweeter than to have Bonny back with the show. Would her big breath of fresh air from Wyoming object to that?

Object or not, Bonny is through. When she washed up with Skid she quit show business and that's that. Skid will have to struggle on alone and from the looks of things she does not think it will be a very long struggle. "Your two weeks' notice is printed on every bottle of Scotch in the city," she warns him.

But Skid can't see that. Charlie Dillingham is crazy about him. Ziegfeld's been flirting with him for weeks. "They always need comics, dearie," he reminds her, "and as long as contented cows give us bladders I'll be alright."

"Yeah? Well, if you wuz a smart little fella you'd go out to Youngstown and have Bonesetter Reese take a look at your head. Mebbe he could snap it back."

"Just a jolly little girl! Will somebody say something pleasant? I will! Have a drink? Well, thank you so much."

Now the party is under way again. Skid grows more and more reminiscent. Remembers the time he and Bonny were stranded up in Michigan and joined up with a tent show. Remembers the old waltz clog they used to do, with funny sayings. Bonny knows the old routine as well as Skid, and now they are giving an exhibition of the dance and patter they used to do, to the great delight of their giggling audience.

But the reminiscence is a little too much for Bonny. She would run away if Skid would let her. For a minute or two he is serious. It is when Lefty recalls the night the year before that he fired Skid so he could make a train and get his chance with Dillingham in New York.

SKID (*laughing*)—Will you ever forget that, Bonn?

BONNY—No. That seemed like the greatest kindness anybody ever did for us.

SKID—It sure was. But you're lucky at that, Lefty. All the guys that fire me get rich.

LEFTY—That's me, hoofer, that's me. I'm goin' to get a bundle doin' a little glorifyin' of my own.

SKID—Well, speaking of law and order, let's have a little drink. (*Goes to table, starts pouring.*)

BONNY—I wish you wouldn't, Skid.

SKID—No? (*Hesitates.*) Alright. Will you have one, honey?

BONNY—No, I don't want any more.

SKID—I ain't goin' to ask you, Mazie. I'm just goin' to hand it to you. (*Hands* MAZIE *a drink.*)

MAZIE—Smott Beby!

SKID—Say, Bonny, you ain't told me whether I'm good or rotten in the show.

BONNY—The jury was in long before I got here, Skid.

SKID (*going down to couch*)—This is funny, ain't it? You tellin' me for years what a riot I'd be if I got a chance. You push me into my chance and I click. All the time I'm wishin' you're here to see me get away with it. You finally get here and see me and we don't even talk about it.

BONNY (*on couch*)—Skid, I could never tell you all the different feelings I had watchin' you last night.

JERRY—Say, Mazie . . . (*He stops playing.*)

BONNY—I don't think anybody could stand that more than a couple times in their lives.

SKID (*sitting on couch*)—No, but what I'm gettin' at is how can people plan for something so long and when it happens just let it go at that. I ain't kickin' because you didn't tell me I was good. I know you'd stage a battle with anybody that said I wasn't, but I'm wonderin' if plannin' for things so long don't take all the kick out of them. I suppose nothin' can be as good as you think it's goin' to be.

BONNY—You see, I saw so much last night, Skid. I saw us at so many different times and in so many different places—some of the things I saw were silly, some grand; some ugly, but it was as though you was dancing against a screen of moving places and

people, with you and me among them. I didn't see you very well,
last night, Skid, but somehow I knew all the time you was goin'
great, and I was awful proud.

Jerry breaks into a fast number and soon they are all dancing
a little, or trying to. Then the suggestion grows that they should
continue the party. Skid wants to give a grand little blowout in
Bonny's honor, burn up the old Boston Post Road and all that.
Everybody's for it except Bonny. She expects to be leaving for
the West next day and will have to pack.

They are still urging her to reconsider, and Skid is growing
both confidential and serious, when Harvey Howell returns. He
is plainly surprised, but quite pleasant about it. Bonny, he decides, is giving a party and that is quite all right.

Harvey meets the strangers, greets Skid affably, compliments
him on his performance of the night before and even accepts the
drink that Skid pours for him. He wants them to go right on
with their music. But when they ask him to suggest a song he is
a little embarrassed. He can't remember any newer than "In
the Gloaming." Bonny sang that for him once. Bonny will sing
it again, she agrees after a little urging. Her voice is shaky and
a little tearful when she tries it. Only Harvey seems much
cheered by the song. "That's beautiful, Bonny," he insists as she
finishes.

"Yeah!" explodes Skid, with the suggestion of a sneer. "It's
so nice and gay. What're we celebratin', anyway? A weddin' or
a funeral? Shouldn't we be toastin' the bride and singin' gay
ditties with the groom?"

Harvey—I wouldn't have spoken about it if you hadn't, Mister. I don't know whether it makes you uncomfortable to have
me here. I admit I feel a little awkward. In a way of speaking
I am your successor but I don't want to flaunt it in your face.
By what misfortune you lost Bonny I don't know and under the
circumstances I don't want to dwell on my good fortune except
to assure you that it will be my aim to make life happy for Bonny,
and I'm sure that you, bein' her husband, will be glad to know
that.

Skid—Sure, I'm glad to know it. Why wouldn't I be glad to
know that Bonny's goin' to get along all right without me? But
what I'm sayin' is why can't we be gay about it? Why can't we
have the weddin' march played with pep and ginger, and why
can't I be givin' the bride away?

Bonny—Stop it, Skid.

Skid—Why? Who has a better right to be givin' the bride away? It shows there's no hard feelin's. Why do people get sore and crab when they lose out in marriage? Why don't they join in the festivities? Come on, Jerry, play the weddin' march and play it fast. It's a dancin' weddin'. Here comes the Minister . . . and here comes the bride! (*He dances with imaginary prayer book in hand.*)

Here comes the groom!

(*He dances.*) (Jerry *plays patter.*)

Do you take this man? Do you take this man?

(*As the bride.*)

I do! I do! I do!

(*As the minister.*)

Do you take this gal? Do you take this gal?

(*As the groom.*)

I do! I do! I do!

(*As minister.*)

To love, and obey?

(*As man.*)

I do! I do! I do!

(*As minister.*)

Till death do you part? Till death do you part?

(*As bride and groom.*)

We do! We do! We do!

(*As minister.*)

I now pronounce you man and wife!

(*Still dancing grotesquely and violently. Sings.*)

Man and wife—Man and wife. Come on, sing everybody! Here comes the bride! Here comes the bride!

Bonny—Stop him! Stop him! Stop all of you!

Skid—Here comes the bride! Here comes the bride!

Harvey (*going to him a little threateningly*)—I think you'd better go!

Skid (*still dancing*)—I'm goin', Mister. I'm goin'! (*Dancing toward halldoor.*) Good-by, Bonny! (*Dances out and is gone.*)

The curtain falls.

ACT III

By September Lefty Moore had found his "sugar daddy," organized his show and was ready to open in Paterson, N. J., on Labor Day. But the chances of opening look pretty dim on this, the day before the date set.

Skid, who is the principal comic of the organization, has been missing for days, after having rehearsed no more than half his stuff. Lefty, having called the company together for a final dress rehearsal, is half crazed with the uncertainty, and in no fit condition even to watch the performance. He finally sends the company and the stage crew out at 5 o'clock to wait until 7 in the hope that Jimmy, his helper, may by that time have found Skid.

That hope proves false, too. Jimmy is back. He had come upon Skid in a joint on Tenth Avenue in New York and got him as far as the Pennsylvania station. But there the comic dodged him and now he is lost again, nobody knows where. Which does not seem so terrifically important to Jimmy since seeing Skid. That hoofer is in no condition to open anyway, and will not be for days. "He couldn't last through his first dance," is Jimmy's belief. "You'd have to carry him off."

This last bender, it seems, is the worst one Skid has been on. He has acquired a passion for invading speak-easies and regaling the guests with comic renditions of the wedding march.

And then, out of the off-stage darkness, a thrill of hope carries across the bare stage to Lefty. He hears the voice of Bonny, and it is the sweetest sound that has smote his ears for months.

Lefty, in his distress, had wired Bonny to come on, but not having heard from her he had given her up. It never had occurred to Bonny that he would not know that she was on her way. Otherwise she would have wired.

She has a pretty clear idea, too, of what the trouble is. Skid, of course. She has not heard a word from Skid since that day, nearly three months before, when he danced out of her room in the hotel. Now it seems that when he danced out of that room he also danced right out of show business.

"He went on a grand bust and he ain't played since," Lefty reports.

Bonny—That's terrible. (*Pause.*) He scared me that day. How's he been livin'?

Lefty—Touchin' anybody he can. They're all duckin' him now. I staked him for as long as I could, but he's too swift for me. I trailed for a while, about all I was doin' was puttin' him to bed, but as soon as I'd leave him I'd meet him somewhere, all dressed up and goin' strong again. Everybody said he was through, but I could never smoke that so when I dug up a bankroll for this show I made up my mind that Skid'd be a great bet and I signed him. He's been givin' me a dizzy ride. I'm openin'

to-morrow night and up to now he ain't rehearsed half his stuff.
I could have canned him. I made up my mind once to do it, then
I felt I'd rather have the show flop than have that on me mind,
so bein' a big brave guy, Bonny, I wired for you to come and
help me.

BONNY—Where is he?

LEFTY—In New York. Jimmy got him as far as the station
awhile ago and then lost him.

BONNY (*after a pause*)—Of course, Lefty, I know what's in
your mind and what you want me to do. So I'm goin' to save
you the trouble of askin' me. I'll do what I can. How's your
show?

LEFTY—It's a bear. They never seen a show on the wheel before. I've copped everything good that the big 5.50 producers
have put on. Those boys don't know it, but they've been workin'
for me.

BONNY—Maybe you oughtn't to do that, Lefty.

LEFTY—What the hell! Those guys cop all their stuff. Either
from Paris or each other. I should be a Quaker and sing "Broth-
erly Love."

BONNY—Have you got any of the old people?

LEFTY—Yeah! Bozo and Gussie and Mazie and Jimmy and
some of the chorus.

BONNY—That's great.

LEFTY—How about yourself, Bonny? Did Howell come with
you?

BONNY—No. I only expected to be here a few days. I'm to
meet him in Chicago next week and get my final papers. Have
you got any costumes I can wear?

LEFTY—Jeez, Bonny, you're an ace. I ain't goin' to try to tell
you what you're doin' for me, but I'm even right now no matter
what happens to this show. How long will you stay?

BONNY—Until you get your show right and Skid gets straightened out. There he is now!

Skid staggers across the stage. He is in a pitiable condition.
When he first sees Bonny he is afraid to trust his eyes, and when
he touches her and finds her real, and feels her in his arms again
he sobs violently.

He soon recovers himself and pretends to be angered at the
trick he suspects Lefty has played on them. To get his lousy
show open Lefty'd even called Bonny outa the grave! But she
doesn't have to stay! Skid, the fireman's child, will be there!

He'll be all right in a jiffy—if they'll slip him a drink. Lefty can't see that.

"You gotta stop being Joe Morgan and snap out of it," he warns.

BONNY—Never mind, Skid. You'll get whatever you need, but you gotta begin taperin' off now.

SKID (*going to* BONNY)—You're the only one I ever knew that had any sense. (*Puts his arm around her.*) Are you ashamed of me, Bonny?

BONNY—No, Skid.

SKID—I been an awful sap, but don't ride me, will you, Bonny? Don't ride me.

BONNY—I won't ride you, Skid.

SKID—That's right, honey. I've listened to so many lectures that I carry me own slides.

BONNY—Don't you think you better get some sleep, Skid?

SKID—Naw, I never bother about sleep, honey. (*Goes to her, takes her arms.*) Jeez, Bonny. It's great to see you. I told you I'd be an awful sap without you.

BONNY—You never was a sap, Skid. You got more brains than all the comics put together. You make mistakes, but who don't? But, after all, Skid, fun's fun. Lefty's openin' his first show to-morrow night. Without you, he'll be sunk. He's been too good a friend of ours for you to throw him.

SKID—Jeez, Bonn, I don't think I could ever make it.

BONNY—Sure you can make it.

SKID—I'm all shot, honey.

BONNY—You can come out of it.

SKID—You think I can?

BONNY—I know it.

SKID—You wouldn't kid me, would you, Lady?

BONNY—I would if I could, Mister, I would if I could.

SKID—Where's your cattle rustler? Say, he got sore at me that day, didn't he?

BONNY—I don't know.

SKID—Sure, he did. For singing "Here Comes the Bride." (*Tries to sing and dance "Here Comes the Bride" and crumples into a faint.*)

BONNY (*at his side*)—Get some cold water, Lefty. (*She sits on floor, lifts his head onto her lap, unfastens necktie and collar. LEFTY returns with water.*) Give me your handkerchief. (LEFTY does so. She begins bathing his forehead.) Get a room at the hotel here for Skid and one for me.　Later I'll want you to send some one over to the Waldorf for my things.

LEFTY—Do you think I'd better postpone the opening, Bonny?

BONNY—Let's try not to, Lefty.　I'd hate to see you muff your first opening and it wouldn't look so good for Skid either.

LEFTY—I ain't goin' to try to tell you what you're doin' for me, Bonny.　I'll never forget you for this.

BONNY—That's what I said to you the night you fixed it for Skid to get away from the show.

LEFTY—Yeah, I remember.

BONNY—Poor Skid.　(*She breaks down.*)

LEFTY—There, there, Bonny.　There, there.

BONNY—I'm alright, Lefty.　You go along.

LEFTY—Don't you think we better get him over to the hotel?

BONNY—No, let him rest here awhile.

LEFTY—I'll go and see about the rooms and come back.

BONNY—Alright . . . (*He goes.　Speaking to the unconscious* SKID)—You'll be alright, honey.　Nothin' can stop you.　You'll be alright.　You'll knock 'em dead!　You ain't started yet! You'll be alright!　You'll be alright, honey.　You gotta be alright! You'll be alright.　You'll be . . . (*Breaks down, puts her head on* SKID *and cries.*)

The curtain falls.

. . . .

They open the show next night in Paterson.　Skid is a little wobbly on his pins.　He barely gets through a burlesque bit in a divorce sketch, and when he finishes Jimmy's voice can be heard telling some one to catch him as he falls.

Fortunately there are a couple of chorus numbers between the skit and Bonny's and Skid's dance.　Skid is pretty good by that time.

They dance in now, Skid from the right and Bonny from the left, and go into their soft shoe dance to the tune of "Suwannee River."　Just once does Skid seem to be a little uncertain, and then you can hear Bonny encouraging him gently.　It doesn't much matter to either of them whether the audience hears or not.

BONNY—How are you comin', honey?

SKID—I'm alright.

BONNY—Do you think you can make it?

SKID—I can if you stick.

BONNY—I'll stick.

SKID—For good?

BONNY—Yes. (SKID *stops dancing and is about to start toward her.*) Keep dancing, honey, keep dancing! (*He resumes. After a pause.*) I guess it's like the guy that spliced us said. For better or for worse.

SKID—Yeah. Better for me and worse for you.

BONNY—It's alright with me, darling. (*The music swells and the dance continues as—*

The curtain falls.

COQUETTE

A Drama in Three Acts

By George Abbott and Ann Preston Bridgers

IT was during the run of "Broadway" at the Broadhurst Theatre that George Abbott, who served that success as both co-author and stage director, was putting the finishing touches on a new drama called "Coquette."

The story had been told him by an actress in the company, Ann Bridgers by name, who was also in the cast of "Dulcy" when Abbott was an actor. She had come not so long ago from her native South and she had long thought this play story was worth using.

Mr. Abbott thought so, too, and his next spare moments he devoted to writing it out, Miss Bridgers serving as expert adviser in assigning the personal characteristics of the people she had in mind and their probable reactions to the drama Mr. Abbott was constructing.

"Coquette" was the result of these joint efforts. Helen Hayes was selected to play the name part. Miss Hayes had been starring for two years in a revival of J. M. Barrie's "What Every Woman Knows" and had added generously to that expanding public that has delighted in her playing the last several seasons. Her success in "Coquette" (Maxine Elliott's Theatre, November 8, 1927), was immediate and pronounced. Her first performance was generously cheered by her audience. The reviewers echoed the cheers and "Coquette" promptly became the best seller of the early season dramas.

It is September in the South, and early evening. The family of Dr. Besant, just finishing its dinner, is gravitating toward the living room. Dr. Besant is there with Stanley Wentworth, a dinner guest, and young Jimmie Besant.

"Dr. Besant is a gentleman of the old South, dignified and formally courteous. Although his manner is gentle we detect in him an impatient restraint," report the authors, "an intolerance of things outside his own strict code of conduct. There is a rela-

146

tionship of intimacy and affection between him and his children which is sufficient proof that the young people have never questioned the chivalrous tradition in which they have been brought up.

"Stanley Wentworth is of the same tradition, a clean-cut, well-bred young man, dependable, likable and romantic."

Stanley also is one of numerous suitors for Norma Besant's favors, and is kept pretty constantly in an uncertain state of mind by that young woman's refusal to take his advances seriously. If he sends her sweet peas to wear to a dance she is quite likely to appear, as she did the last time, with a bouquet of orchids—and a sweet excuse.

Dr. Besant is quite in sympathy with Stanley's reasonable protests. He, too, is given to worrying a little about Norma. He does not, naturally, keep unduly close watch of his daughter, but he does most sincerely hope that she does not follow the prevalent custom of smoking cigarettes and he certainly refuses even to listen to such reports as one he heard recently that Norma really did have a glass too much punch at a recent Country Club dance. That, sir, is a malicious insinuation.

Young Jimmie also has opinions concerning his sister's method of conduct in general. For one thing he does not at all approve of her custom of curtailing his helpings of fried chicken at dinner so she will have more to feed her beaux at 11 o'clock at night.

For another he is convinced that Norma is all wrong in her selection and treatment of those same beaux. Duke Gaston, for one, is a cheese. What kind of cheese Jimmie politely refrains from saying. But a cheese none the less. Which is not as important as it was, seeing that, according to Jimmie, Norma is already through with young Mr. Gaston.

"She's going to give him the air, anyway," reports Jimmie. "It's always the latest one with Norma, and she makes such a fuss over each new one, you'd think he was the Prince of Wales—and the way she gets over it! Did you hear about who she's got a crush on now? Michael Jeffery! You know that fellow, a roughneck. That's a good one, after all these fancy buys."

The question of Norma's developing interest in Michael Jeffery is a source of considerable worry, both to Dr. Besant and to Stanley Wentworth, and the fact that the box of flowers that has just arrived is from young Jeffery threatens to bring the matter quickly to an issue. It takes a good deal of quick thinking on Norma's part to allay, first, the suspicions, and then the resentment of her father and her friend.

Dr. Besant—Norma, do I understand that you are—ah—cultivating the society of this Michael Jeffery?

Norma—Now, darling, I can tell without your saying a word, that you don't think well of Michael. (*She goes over to him and sits in a chair by his smoking table.*)

Dr. Besant—But I've gathered that he's just an ordinary loafer, Norma—

Norma (*persuasively*)—Now, daddy, you really don't know a thing about him.

Dr. Besant—No, I don't. I've simply heard him spoken of as a quarrelsome young fellow, who does a good deal of drinking and gambling.

Norma—Well, maybe he has a quick temper. I mean he was shell-shocked in the war and—but he really has a wonderful lot of sterling qualities, hasn't he, Stanley? (*She signals "yes" to* Stanley *sitting over by the windows.*)

Stanley—Oh, yes—yes, indeed—yes, sir.

Norma (*being very innocent*)—Why, only the other night, but of course I hardly know him anyhow. I mean any more than I know everybody else. Of course he tips his hat to me and two weeks ago I met him at Susie's and of course I couldn't help talking to him, could I? That's when I said the foolish thing about the flowers. I wish I hadn't, of course.

Dr. Besant—You mustn't give him any false impression.

Norma—Why, no, silly, of course not.

Dr. Besant—Stanley, wasn't he one of the boys that was mixed up in the shooting down at the garage last winter?

Norma (*indignantly*)—No, he wasn't! (*Recovering quickly.*) No. He—he told me all about that—he didn't have anything to do with it. Anyhow, I don't know why we should be so uppish about a shooting in our family—you thought it was splendid when Uncle Avery shot Mr. Mortimer.

Dr. Besant—Well, Norma, you certainly realize the difference between—

Norma—Oh, yes. I know—whenever a relation of ours kills somebody he's a wonderful man defending the honor of pure womanhood. (*She has heard it all a hundred times.*)

Dr. Besant—I don't think that's a nice way to talk. Norma.

Norma (*fearing she has betrayed her serious interest in* Michael)—Well, what's it all about, anyhow—this fuss about Michael, just because I say a kind word about him.

Dr. Besant—Young men sometimes take things for granted, that's all, Norma. (*Feeling his pockets for his glasses.*) Where the dickens did I— A friendly word is liable to be misinterpreted— (*He goes through the door leading into his office, taking his paper with him.*)

Now it is Stanley's turn. Something has happened that Norma thinks Stanley should know about. First, she wants him to promise that he will be nice about it and let her out of her engagement to go to the Country Club dance with him that night.

It just happens that one day when she was calling on a friend Michael Jeffery was there and she had asked him, quite casually, why he never came to any of the dances and Michael had said that he didn't know any of the girls in that crowd. What could Norma say then, knowing that Michael had been shell-shocked in the war and everything and was desperately lonesome? Before she knew it she had said she would be glad to go with him—and then she remembered her engagement with Stanley.

Stanley is pretty well used to playing Norma's game Norma's way, and he gracefully accepts his dismissal. He is none too well pleased, however, to discover a moment later that not only has Norma broken her own engagement, but she has fixed up another for him.

He is to be a good boy and take Betty Lee Reynolds to the dance in Norma's place. Betty being only eighteen, and young for her years, according to Stanley, the prospect is not pleasing.

"You not only ditch me, but you plan to hand me over to an infant in swaddling clothes," he explodes, with some fervor.

But after Norma has pleaded prettily and agreed not only to give him every other dance but also to break a date she has with Richard Wells for another party the next week and go with him instead, Stanley gives up. He will do whatever she suggests. That puts him right back in the "darling" class so far as Norma is concerned.

Dr. Besant is neither as easily nor as completely won over. He does not like the idea of Norma's having anything to do with young Jeffery, no matter how generous her motives. The report is that he is lazy and lets his sisters support him, that he gambles and is just generally no good.

Norma's defense is passionately sustained. Michael Jeffery is "awfully nice when you know him—so serious and sort of sensitive." He works, too, now and then; takes surveying parties up in the hills. And in South America he made a lot of money. People who say he lost it gambling talk too much.

Betty Lee is in and arrangements are made for her to stay

with Norma, for all her Aunt Martha is opposed to her going to parties at her age. And Stanley Wentworth's father, "a friendly, genial man, more practical than the doctor," has called.

He, too, it shortly appears, is worried about Norma's interest in Michael Jeffery. And after much serious cogitation he has come to feel that he should speak to Dr. Besant about it. He loves Norma and he had hoped Stanley would put enough ginger in his courtship to bring her into the Wentworth family. Now he wants to talk to Dr. Besant alone.

It appears that there has been some sort of fight down town and that Norma's name was mixed up in it. Michael Jeffery and Duke Gaston were the fighters. It had started, it seems, at the florist's, and then the boys had drifted out into the street and finished in a sort of rough and tumble.

Dr. Besant is greatly disturbed by this news. These young hot-heads have no right to be dragging his daughter's name into a street brawl, even if they do think they love her. He is of a mind to take some kind of definite action until the elder Wentworth, as his friend and his lawyer, induces him to see the boys in a kindly spirit and get it all straightened out without further trouble and more gossip. The doctor goes at once in search of the young men.

Norma is puzzled, but she does not suspect what is going on in her father's mind. Probably worried about one of his patients. She is too intent the next few minutes getting Betty Lee fixed up with one of her sister Jane's dresses for the party to think much about it. And then Michael calls.

"He is handsome, insolent, hot tempered and passionate." He has come early to tell Norma that he cannot go with her to the party after all because—because—well, because he doesn't own a dress suit and can't afford to buy one.

Norma refuses to admit that the lack of a dress suit is anything like as important as Michael seems to think—even without one, she assures him—if he goes just as he is now—he will still be the best-looking man there. But even that compliment does not melt Michael. Nor is he particularly impressed when she becomes serious and dignified and blames him for having led her on practically to throw herself at his head, asking him to take her to the dance, and then refusing to go. It's quite clear he does not want to be seen with her.

MICHAEL (*bluntly*)—You know that isn't so.

NORMA (*turning away from him, a lady very much aggrieved*)

—Excuse me. That's just the only way I can see it. And I'm mighty sorry, Mr. Jeffery, that I've forgotten my pride so far as to throw myself at a man who doesn't— What are you laughing at?

MICHAEL—You're just carrying on now, aren't you?

NORMA—Carrying on!

MICHAEL—You know you don't mean a word of that.

NORMA—I think, Mr. Jeffery, it's about time for you to say good-night.

MICHAEL—I will in a minute. I don't belong with that crowd up at the Country Club. They sort of look down on me. I know.

NORMA (*immediately compassionate again*)—Oh—

MICHAEL—That doesn't worry me any, if I could go there and show them I can behave as well as any of the rest of them. This way I'd feel out of place. (*With a short laugh.*) I know it's damned foolish to feel that way, but— If you'd like to go somewhere else with me sometime— (*He gets no answer.*) Well, I guess I'd better say good-night. (*He goes on out into the hallway.* NORMA *stands a second, then runs after him.*)

NORMA—Michael! Come back here. (*He comes.*) You needn't rush away like that just because you're turning me down. It's the first time that's ever happened to me, and I don't know but that it's sort of interesting. But you are an awful stubborn, just the same. You're sure you won't come?

MICHAEL—I told you I can't. (NORMA *accepts defeat this time and changes the subject.*)

NORMA (*quite seriously*)—What did you and Duke fight about this afternoon?

MICHAEL (*reluctantly*)—He said something I didn't take a fancy to.

NORMA—About me?

MICHAEL (*after a moment*)—Yes.

NORMA—What was it?

MICHAEL—I— If it's all the same to you, I'd just as soon not talk about it.

NORMA—I know. May Brandon called me up and told me. Duke said I was nothing but a silly little coquette, didn't he? (*He makes no answer.*) And you thrashed him for it. . . . Thank you, Michael. . . . Since I heard it, I've been sort of wondering if it isn't true. Part of it. (*The horn of a car is heard, then voices.*) Oh, bother! They're back. (MICHAEL *turns to go.*) Don't go yet, Michael . . . Please . . . There's something else I want to . . . Oh, shucks!

The party is gathering for the ride to the Country Club and Jimmie Besant is sporting his first dress suit, much to the amusement of the others. Michael has withdrawn as much as he can to the corner of the room, and is with some difficulty dragged out for the introductions.

Now the crowd has gone on and Norma and Michael are alone, a little embarrassed, it may be, but rapidly feeling that there is a curious feeling of understanding between them.

"Shall I play for you?" Norma asks.

"I'd just like to have you sit here and talk to me," Michael answers.

NORMA (*sitting beside him*)—You talk. I'll listen.

MICHAEL—I don't talk much. I guess you know that by this time. But I think a good deal. (*Laughing at himself.*) That sounds sort of silly, doesn't it? It's easier to talk to you than anybody else. You kind of go out of your way to make me feel comfortable.

NORMA—I guess we just naturally have a lot of things to say to each other, that's all. I always did think you were interesting.

MICHAEL—You haven't known me but about two weeks. I've been around town for a year or so but I never got a chance to talk to you till—till that afternoon.

NORMA—Maybe I knew you even before a year ago.

MICHAEL—What do you mean?

NORMA—Oh, when you used to be around here just after the war.

MICHAEL (*surprised*)—You can't remember me then.

NORMA—One day in the post office you came rushing past and nearly knocked me down.

MICHAEL (*his slightly hysterical laugh betrays his happiness*) —Honestly! You can remember that? I can remember you, of course. I thought you were an awfully pretty little thing.

NORMA—I thought you were terribly rude.

MICHAEL—I guess I was. I reckon I still am. I don't mean to be rude. I just naturally say the wrong things. That time I bumped into you I would have begged your pardon, only I didn't want you to think I was kow-towing to you. I thought you were stuck up.

NORMA—Aren't you funny?

MICHAEL—And sitting here with you right now, I'm not sure

it's actually so. This house and you always seemed so far away.

NORMA (*her voice is small and intimate*)—But I'm not far away—I'm right close.

MICHAEL—Do you mind if I put a straight question to you?

NORMA—No, I like straight questions.

MICHAEL—Why have you been going out of your way to be nice to me?

NORMA—I imagined you'd like to have me.

MICHAEL—I do.

NORMA—If I tell you something that is really so, you won't think I—I'm—

MICHAEL—What?

NORMA—You won't think I'm—well, never mind. I'll tell you anyway. I passed you in the street maybe dozens and dozens of times and every time I've had the strangest feeling that you were turning around to look at me. As a matter of fact, I caught you doing it. Of course I can't say that is a particularly strange thing to have happen to a girl, but I've had the strangest feeling about it with you.

MICHAEL—What do you mean?

NORMA—That you weren't just trying to flirt, but that you . . . that you . . . that you really wanted to know me and be my friend and . . . I may be all wrong.

MICHAEL—No. You're dead right.

NORMA—Oh, am I? (*She rises quickly and walks over by the window.*) Well, I felt the same way about you.

Outside the door Dr. Besant's footsteps can be heard coming along the porch. Norma rises and stands waiting apprehensively for her father to come in. The room is almost dark. When Dr. Besant switches on the lights, and he sees Michael standing before the couch, his face takes on a set expression and his manner becomes frigidly courteous. The next moment he has sent Norma away. He has something he would like to say to Michael alone.

Norma protests and Michael suggests that so far as he knows they have nothing private to talk over. But Dr. Besant is firm. Norma finally starts toward the stairs, but "when she hears her father's first words to Michael she steals back down again and hovers in the hallway."

"I shall have to ask you to discontinue seeing my daughter," Dr. Besant begins.

"Why?"

"In the first place, Mr. Jeffery, you're not the kind of young man I want my daughter to associate with."

"You don't know so very much about me."

"I'll come to that presently. This afternoon you engaged in a street brawl, in which my daughter's name was mentioned."

"Did you find out why?" Michael's tone is one that might suggest prideful defiance and justification for his own actions.

"Yes, sir, I did," tartly answers Dr. Besant. "I have just been getting some first-hand information. Duke has made me a public apology. I have his word that he will never see or speak to Norma again. I appreciate your motive, sir, but I also want you to understand that if my daughter's name needs defending, she has men in her family who are fully capable of attending to it."

"I suppose in the future you'd like me first to . . ."

"In the future you can attend strictly to your own affairs, sir."

It then transpires that among the other indiscretions with which Michael is charged is that he had the presumption to boast openly that he would marry Norma Besant.

He might have said that, Michael admits. He was pretty angry. But there is an explanation. He had meant that he would not permit Norma nor any other girl to make a fool of him; that if she accepted his attentions it would be because she cared for him. And if she cared for him he would marry her. If the doctor demands an apology for that Michael is willing to say that he is sorry. Apologizing is an awkward business for him.

With that settled Dr. Besant repeats his ultimatum. He does not want Michael to see Norma again. Not because he is not a member of the Country Club set, as Michael charges, but because he is wild and unsteady in his habits and because he apparently cannot hold a steady job and has no prospects.

"What are you looking for? A meal ticket?" shouts Michael, angrily.

"In the first place, sir, I'm looking for a gentleman."

They are advancing toward each other threateningly when Norma runs between them, gently reproving Michael and trying to mollify her father.

"Daddy, I almost forgot. Mrs. Carey called up to say that her baby is much worse. She wants you to go right away."

And that he may have faith that Michael also is going she reaches for the latter's hat and carries it to him.

The Mrs. Carey story is a fib, but it gets the doctor out of the house and that, as Norma sees it, just had to be done some way.

"I don't suppose he'll ever trust me again," she ruminates, sadly, as her father disappears.

MICHAEL—I reckon you think that was a damned rotten thing for me to say.

NORMA—What?

MICHAEL—About—about my going to marry you. I said that because—I—love you.

NORMA—Oh. . . .

MICHAEL—I've been in love with you for months. I thought I was crazy to feel that way about you, because I didn't think I'd ever get to know you well enough to tell you about it. When I got into that row with Duke, I guess I must have begun blabbing out all the things I'd been thinking and hoping without— Well . . . You've given your word to your father not to see me again. So I guess I'd better—move on.

NORMA—Michael . . . Michael, I . . . Don't—don't go yet.

MICHAEL—What's there to keep me here? (*She tries to say something, she does not know quite what. She casts a beseeching look at him and turns away. He comes to her swiftly.*)

MICHAEL—Do you care at all about me, Norma? Because if I thought you cared about me, Norma, I could settle down and go to work and make something of myself. I could show your father that I could qualify as your husband as well as any other man. Only I mean, Norma, really care for me. Really love me. Not play around with me. That's what I mean. . . . Why don't you say something, Norma? If you don't care for me, why just say so and I'll beat it and you'll never see me around this town again.

NORMA—Oh, don't say that. (*She goes to the sofa.*) Michael, sit here. . . . The way I feel about you, Michael, it's so different from what I've felt about anybody else. I've felt that way from the very first minute I knew you. It's something very deep, I guess, and that's why it scares me so. You want me to say I love you and that I'm willing to marry you?

MICHAEL—Yes.

NORMA (*simply*)—Oh, I do love you, Michael, I do. (*Putting her hand over his.*) More than anybody in the world. Oh, why did this terrible fight have to happen? And why did daddy have to get so set against you?

MICHAEL—I'll wait until he gets back and tell him.

NORMA—No, no! You mustn't do that. You don't know my

daddy. He's so set. Oh, no—no. We mustn't do anything. I'll tell him myself. I'll tell him exactly how I feel about you, Michael. And, Michael, you go away for awhile so's daddy can get a chance to calm down about you. You go away and show him that you really can settle down and be steady and make a living. Only, don't go too far away.

MICHAEL—You do love me, Norma?

NORMA—Yes.

MICHAEL—That's all I want to know. I'll show your father. People think I'm too lazy to work. It's just that I can't breathe when I'm shut up.

NORMA—Oh.

MICHAEL—It wasn't that way before the war. But I could stand anything for you, Norma. I'd go to hell and back for you. I love you so much. I can get a job surveying up in the hills. I'm going up there to-morrow. And, Norma, this is what I'll do. I'll stay up there for six months.

NORMA (*protesting*)—Oh—

MICHAEL—You tell him that, Norma. And tell him that I'm coming back at the end of six months to marry you.

NORMA—Six months!

MICHAEL—It will seem like six hundred years. Good-by, Norma.

NORMA (*coming very close to him*)—Michael. . . .

MICHAEL—I'm not going to kiss you, Norma. I've seen all those others doing it. I'll kiss you when I come back to marry you. That will be worth waiting for. Good-by. (*He stands irresolutely a second.*) Well—this isn't getting us anywhere, is it? Good-by. (*He goes out through the window. NORMA stands gazing after him.*)

The curtain falls.

ACT II

Three months later, one bright morning, Stanley Wentworth is calling to see Norma Besant and is having no luck at all. He has sent Betty Lee to intercede for him, but still Norma refuses a favorable answer. She is dressing, Betty Lee reports, and she may be crying a little. It is plain to Stanley that something has happened.

It has! Michael is back! Came back the night before, Betty Lee reports excitedly and a little fearfully. Came right to the dance.

"At first he didn't say much," says Betty Lee. "Just stood

around and scowled. It's the first time he's been back in three months—and I think he'd been drinking. I don't know—I mean I ought not to say that because I couldn't be sure—but anyhow he started dancing with Norma, and she just began to cut dances right and left and just dance practically every one with him, and then they went out and got into that old Ford of his and drove off and just never did come back. Now for heaven's sake don't go and say I told you all this, will you?"

Stanley promises. He isn't jealous any more. He is also greatly relieved to learn that Dr. Besant doesn't know anything about Michael's return. But there is more to it. Betty Lee doesn't think she should tell, seeing it is a secret—but—anyway, there it is.

"I don't know if I ought," admits Betty Lee, "but somebody should know—and Norma's acting awful funny, and of course I don't know what it's all about."

She is greatly relieved now that she has made up her mind to tell all she knows, and hurries on.

"Anyhow, I talked to Susie this morning. She was sitting on the porch late last night—she's engaged, so it's all right—well, she was sitting there till after three o'clock—and who should she see going by, but Michael and Norma. So wherever they were after they left the dance, they wouldn't have got home till goodness knows when. Not that I think that means so much except that—well, you know what people would say."

Jimmie Besant is in, greatly excited because he has been elected treasurer of the baseball team. This is a position not only of trust but one of great responsibility as well, seeing that he not only has to keep an account for all the club monies, but first he has to raise the money. That will take a bit of doing, but with the help of the family and his friends Jimmie thinks he can look forward to a successful administration.

A moment later he is considerably upset. Dr. Besant, taking advantage of a cleared room, would like to know of James, how he happened to be so late arriving home the night before.

This is news to Jim. He wasn't late! Four o'clock? Some one heard him coming in at 4 o'clock? They're sil—

And then "a sudden apprehension flashed across Jimmie's face. He settles back into his chair, his mouth fixed into a determined line." And thereafter he makes no further denial. He guesses it must have been pretty late when he came in, but he wasn't doing anything much—only fooling around with the boys. He can't remember exactly what he was doing, and his father is not

too pressing. Dr. Besant wants to be fair. He is very proud of
his children. "Don't do anything that will make me ashamed
of you, Jim," he pleads. "Or—anything that will make you
ashamed of yourself."

"No, sir. Honest, Dad, I haven't."

Now Norma is down and Dr. Besant takes up the matter of
late hours with her. Norma, it appears, had left her key in
the door when she came home from the dance. She doesn't remember it, but—as Jimmie reminds her, quickly—if she hadn't
how else could he have got in at 4? What time *did* she come in?
It must have been about 12.30, she thinks. At which point Dr.
Besant is fortunately called to the office.

Norma is grateful to Jimmie for covering her late arrival, and
Jimmie, though the hero rôle is irksome to him, thinks perhaps
that as a man and a brother he ought to speak to Norma about
certain things.

NORMA (*relieved*)—Oh, Jimmie, you're a darling!

JIMMIE (*embarrassed*)—Oh, can it!

NORMA—Well, I appreciate it just the same.

JIMMIE—He doesn't know about Michael coming back, does
he?

NORMA—No.

JIMMIE—Well, wait till he finds that out.

NORMA—It was sweet of you, Jimmie. I'll do something for
you some time.

JIMMIE—Well, you better be careful, that's all. If father ever
found out the way you acted, he'd raise Cain. He hasn't got the
slightest idea of the kind of things that go on here. Gosh, he's
innocent tho'. Father thinks all women are noble and pure.
But they ain't, except mother. I guess she was, all right.

NORMA—Yes.

JIMMIE—See here, Norma, what do you think mother would
think about the way you're acting, anyway? Course *I* don't think
you've ever done anything bad, but you got sense enough to
know you oughtn't to be staying out till three o'clock with *any*
man.

NORMA—I'll stay out as late as I please. You and daddy make
me sick with all your preaching. He thinks I'm a little doll with
no feelings at all. And I'm not. If I was as good as you and
daddy think I ought to be, I'd be nothing but a dummy.

JIMMIE—Well—I like a girl that can be serious sometimes
and sometimes silly. I like a girl that can go to a dance and

laugh and raise the dickens but on a moonlight night out in a canoe, I like a girl that can discuss life seriously.

NORMA (*earnestly*)—I'm going to be serious from now on, Jimmie.

JIMMIE—Aw, you just think you're in love again.

NORMA—Yes.

JIMMIE—Then I'll give you some advice, young woman. Don't stay out necking with him till 3 o'clock.

NORMA—Don't be disgusting.

JIMMIE—I ain't going to marry any necking girl, I can tell you that.

NORMA—But, Jimmie, I don't think every man wants a woman up on a pedestal like you and daddy.

JIMMIE—I tell you—a man wants a girl down where he can grab her, but he doesn't want every other man in sight grabbing her.

NORMA—That must be how it is.

JIMMIE—You see, if a fellow doesn't get too fresh I reckon it's all right, it doesn't do any harm to have a little fun.

The younger people rush in. They are roughhousing the place so far as a miniature prom dance can do that, when Dr. Besant returns and plants a further fear of possible consequences in Norma's mind. He wants to take Betty Lee with him for a little walk and talk. Seems quite determined about it, and Norma sees them go with a frightened look in her eyes. Can dad be planning to pump Betty Lee?

The dance is continuing when the doorbell rings and Michael Jeffery appears. Stanley, who is dancing with Norma, permits her to break from his arms. For a moment she stands staring at Michael and then, with forced gayety, greets him as casually as she is able.

Stanley, sensing the seriousness of the meeting, clears the young folks out of the room.

"Dad's coming back pretty soon," warns Jimmie, turning off the victrola.

"That's fine," answers Michael, firmly. "I want to see him."

For a moment after they are left alone there is silence and Michael and Norma stand looking at each other intently. Then she turns away embarrassedly and he speaks to her.

MICHAEL—I suppose you must hate the sight of me. I don't blame you much. I ought to have come here sooner. Norma, I hate myself. I could kill myself.

NORMA—It wasn't your fault.

MICHAEL—I feel like a skunk.

NORMA—It wasn't your fault any more than mine.

MICHAEL—Somebody ought to take me out and shoot me.

NORMA—But, Michael, if you love me, I don't care.

MICHAEL—That's the trouble. I love you till I'm crazy.

NORMA—Then I don't care about anything else.

MICHAEL—I've been saying to myself all these months, I've been saying, I won't see her and I'll work hard, and I won't see her. But yesterday, up in the hills, I got so desperately lonesome, I thought I'd have just one look at you, darling, and then I'd go back. But when I saw you in there with all those fellows .. . . putting their arms around you, holding you close, I just couldn't stay outside, that's all. I was, honest to God, like I was going crazy. And then afterwards, when I found you still loved me, loved me more than ever . . .

NORMA—Michael, I don't care.

MICHAEL—You say that so I won't feel so rotten, but—

NORMA—Michael, I'm glad!

MICHAEL (*taking her face in his hands*)—God bless you, Norma. I don't know what to say—you don't know what I've been through since last night, hating myself for acting that way. (*Kneeling beside her, their arms around each other.*) I ought to have been shot in the war, that's what ought to have happened instead of left around hurting the people that I love so much.

NORMA—Michael, I'm not sorry. You're the only man I ever loved like that—and I'm glad—because now we're just bound together forever, aren't we?

MICHAEL—Yes.

NORMA—It was my fault as much as yours. Maybe we're not perfect, but I don't care if you don't.

MICHAEL—I care on account of you, that's all, but anyhow I've been thinking about it. We'll get married.

NORMA—Right away.

MICHAEL—Suppose you—should be— We don't want to take any chances having people saying things about you later on. And we don't want to have a child that folks would say things about either. (*He rises.*) I'll just tell your dad we're going to be married and he can kick up a fuss or not, just as he pleases.

NORMA (*immediately alarmed*)—Michael, I know how to get around daddy better than you do.

MICHAEL—I've thought it all out, Norma. I've thought the whole thing out.

NORMA—I realize you know more about dealing with most people, but I know how to handle daddy. He's awfully stubborn if you stand straight against him, but it's easy to get round him if you just go at it right, see?

MICHAEL (*reassuringly*)—I'm not going to lose my temper. But it's my job to tell him and I might as well get it over. (*Darkly.*) I've been skunk enough as it is, without doing any running away.

NORMA—Suppose he won't give in?

MICHAEL—Well, we'll go over to Watertown and get married whether he likes it or not. You can come live with my sisters or you can stay at the hotel till I get money enough to buy a place I know of. I'm going to cutting timber. I've been figuring it out. You'll never regret throwing your lot with mine. Because I'm going to show you, I'm going to show everybody what I amount to. I'm going to be well-to-do in five years.

NORMA—I know you will, Michael!

MICHAEL—I will—or I won't be here to tell about it.

NORMA—And, Michael, I'm going to be nice—I'm going to be so good to you. (*He pulls her down on his lap.*) I'll keep house for you—and I'll scrub and I'll take care of you. And if things don't go so well, I won't mind, because I'll have you. You won't know me, I'll be so good. And, Michael— (*She stops abruptly. Crossing to the window, she looks out.*) It's father.

Dr. Besant does not come in immediately. He evidently is looking for Jimmie, probably to question him further, Norma thinks. And she tries again to induce Michael to be careful and not to oppose her father. She is so fearfully afraid of trouble.

But Michael is both firm and hopeful. She'll see. He will eat mud if he has to. There's something more important than just his feelings for him to think about now.

Norma must be content with this. She will go now and send in her father, but first he must hold her tight for just a minute.

"I love you more than all the men and women and houses and everything—can't you feel how much I love you?" she is saying when Dr. Besant opens the door and sees them.

He regards them coldly and calmly walks over and hangs his hat in the hall. Then he politely orders Norma out of the room. She tries at first to make light of his seriousness and to explain that Michael had just that minute asked her to send for him. But there is no lightness in either Dr. Besant's tone or manner.

His daughter has broken her word to him, has told him a deliberate untruth and involved her brother in another. As for Michael, he must have known the consequences, the false and malicious gossip, that would naturally follow actions such as his.

Michael is ready to take all the blame for the late hour, but he is not willing to admit that any one would dare say anything about Norma. Nor is he ready, at the doctor's angry invitation, to leave the house—not before he has said what he has come to say.

MICHAEL—It seems to me with all this chivalry that's always being paraded around here, I might at least explain my side of the story. I never stood for so much abuse from anybody.

DR. BESANT—If I didn't think it unbecoming to my years, you'd stand abuse of a different kind.

MICHAEL—No, sir, I wouldn't—if it wasn't for your years, you wouldn't have said what you've already said.

NORMA—Michael, you go now and let me talk to him—

DR. BESANT—If he doesn't go, I'll put him out. I'm not holding you blameless, Norma, but you haven't the slightest idea what's in the mind of a man like this fellow. And you can thank God that you've a father who'll protect you.

MICHAEL—When she's married to me, you won't need to protect her.

NORMA—Michael—!

DR. BESANT—My daughter will never marry you, not any *trash* like you! The sooner you get that through your head and take yourself away from here, the better for all concerned. . . .

NORMA—Daddy, please don't, why won't you let me say something—

MICHAEL (*lost to all caution*)—She understands more than you think she does. She understands more than you do. We both do. And we're going to be married so you might as well understand that.

DR. BESANT—Hold your tongue. Hold your tongue, sir.

NORMA—Daddy. . . .

DR. BESANT (*pushing her aside*)—Get away from me. (*Advancing to* MICHAEL.) Now, you impudent scoundrel. You get out of here.

MICHAEL—Sure, I will, but I'll marry her just the same.

DR. BESANT—And you'll get out of this town, too.

MICHAEL—Oh, you own the town, too. I'll get out of town if

I want to, and I'll take her with me. I'll go pack my things, Norma, and come back for you. We'll go to my sisters'.

DR. BESANT—If you were anything of a gentleman, sir—

MICHAEL—Oh, shut up, you God-damned old hypocrite!

DR. BESANT—Sir!

NORMA—Michael—

MICHAEL—I'll kill him. I've stood enough. Stand around bleating your head off while I'm trying to do what's right.

DR. BESANT—Get out, sir, get out!

MICHAEL—Listen! If you'd shut up for a while and find out what's happened you wouldn't be so damned afraid I'd marry her—

NORMA—Michael, please, please.

MICHAEL—I'm going to marry her. Get that through your head. And you can't stop me. If you had any sense you'd be begging me to marry her, because we've lived together already, because we're just as good as man and wife now. Oh, hell. Now I reckon you'll shut your mouth for a while. (*To* NORMA.) I'll come back this afternoon and get you. (*He rushes out*—DR. BESANT *stands transfixed*.)

NORMA—Daddy, he didn't know. He lost his temper. Sometimes he gets like that.

DR. BESANT—Be still. Julia! Of course I don't have to be told that the things he said about you aren't true— (*No answer.*) Norma?

NORMA (*in terror of her father*)—No, daddy, no.

With ominous dignity Dr. Besant sends for Julia to take her young mistress into the other room. Jimmie he orders to look after his sister. And when Stanley Wentworth ventures in he is asked to stay there and see that Norma stays. Then he walks to the desk, opens the drawer and takes out a pistol. With this in his pocket he leaves the house, despite Stanley's effort to stay him.

There is confusion aplenty for a moment. Now Norma has brushed Jimmie aside and is demanding to know what has happened. Nothing has happened—except Dr. Besant has rushed out threatening to go to law about his trouble with Michael and to see his lawyer about it, Stanley explains. And rushes out himself to see if he can't do something to pacify the doctor.

The thought is a little reassuring to Norma. The law! That's silly, but— She is leaning against the sofa when suddenly a slight dizziness overcomes her and she staggers, just as though, she says,—as though she had been shot. Funny!

Now she has noticed the open drawer of the desk and that one of the pistols is missing! Her heart is again clutched with fear, but Jimmie insists there has been only one pistol there for a long time.

And now Stanley is back, white and eager to talk with Norma alone.

NORMA—Stanley, there is something.

STANLEY—Norma, dear—

NORMA—Stanley!

STANLEY—Norma, honey, let's sit down.

NORMA—What in the world is going on?

STANLEY—Norma dear, you know I wouldn't act any way that wasn't the very best I knew. Now come on, dear, can't you just sit here with me and let me talk to you for a moment? (NORMA *sits beside him on the sofa.*) I might as well be frank and tell you that there's been a little something wrong.

NORMA—He did take that pistol.

STANLEY—All it is, dear, all there is to it, you've got to be very brave and not lose control of yourself—

NORMA—Stop it, Stanley. What's happened?

STANLEY—Your father and Michael had a quarrel.

NORMA—Oh, my God! He did shoot him. He did shoot him. I knew it.

STANLEY—Norma, Norma, now, honey.

NORMA—Stanley, you're driving me crazy. You've got to tell me.

STANLEY—Norma, some one's been hurt.

NORMA—Michael!

STANLEY—Yes.

NORMA (*controlling herself*)—Well—is it bad?

STANLEY—I reckon it is, dear.

NORMA—Well?

STANLEY—You promised me that—

NORMA—Please tell me everything.

STANLEY—Michael was shot—and—I'm afraid—

NORMA—Stanley—? Oh, my God—he didn't kill him? Michael's not dead?

STANLEY—Yes, dear, I'm awfully sorry. I'm terribly sorry. Somebody had to tell you. (NORMA's *throat clutches breathlessly through her moans— She clings to* STANLEY's *hands, in desperate need of help.*) Norma, darling.

NORMA—Oh, my God! Oh, my God, Stanley, I can't stand it! Stanley, it can't be true. He's just hurt, Stanley.

STANLEY—Norma, honey—

NORMA—He was right here, Stanley—he said he was coming back for me!

STANLEY—Poor darling.

NORMA—Please—tell me—where is he? I must go to him! I told him I wouldn't be shallow and silly! I must find him—he needs me so!

STANLEY—No, darling, there is nothing you can do.

NORMA—Stanley, we've got to do something! We've got to do something! Stanley, please, for God's sake, don't stand there that way! Please—please take me where he is!

STANLEY—Michael is dead, Norma.

NORMA (*hysterically*)—You mustn't keep saying that! Do you hear, Stanley? You mustn't say that again! If you won't help me I'll find him myself. (*She tries to get away.*)

STANLEY (*holding her*)—No—no—you must stay here.

NORMA—No, I won't, I tell you. Let me go!

STANLEY (*sternly, holding her as she tries to get past him*)—Do you want to go out where a curious crowd will watch you? What good will it do you? If you could help Michael I would take you to him, but you can't. He was shot twice through the heart—and he died instantly.

Pathetically Norma tries to accept the news. Blindly she continues to grope for a suggestion of something she can do to ward off this tragedy that must not happen. She is hysterical as she demands her right to go to Michael to protect him from the crowd —the staring crowd he hated so!

But none can help, and only her old Julia can comfort her.

Then Stanley's father comes and attempts to establish order by sending them all away. Dr. Besant, he reports, has gone to give himself up and the affair is in the hands of the authorities. But there is something they must do, that Norma must do. Kindly but firmly he lifts her limp form from Julia's lap.

"Norma, you've got to listen to me," he says, and the note of his voice is both anxious and imperative.

NORMA (*exhausted*)—What do you want of me? What more do they want of me?

WENTWORTH—I want you to listen to me, Norma.

NORMA—Oh, God!

WENTWORTH—I've got to talk to you.

NORMA—What's the difference what I do? Oh, Michael—
Michael—

WENTWORTH—Now listen to me. Michael's gone, Norma, you
can't get him back no matter what you do. But I'm asking you
to control yourself now, and do what you can to save your father
from prison—or even worse—yes, dear, it's possible. It's going
to be a hard fight to save him, and you've got to help.

NORMA—Why don't you leave me alone? I wish I'd run away
with Michael, that's what I wish.

WENTWORTH—Our chance to save your father is based on the
plea that he was defending your good name. You've got to say
that you resented Michael's attentions; that your father protected
you from insult, and you're proud of him.

NORMA (*with sullen vehemence*)—No, I won't! I hate him!
I wish I'd never seen him!

WENTWORTH—Norma!

NORMA—I hate him! He killed the one thing in the world that
I loved! He did that to me, and I don't care what happens to
him now. Let them put him in prison, I don't care!

WENTWORTH—You don't realize what you're saying, dear.

NORMA (*her voice rising hysterically*)—I could see him in
prison for the rest of his life and not care! I could see him hung
—I don't care what they do—I don't want to help—

WENTWORTH—Norma!

NORMA (*spent and pleading*)—Leave me alone—leave me
alone!

The curtain falls.

ACT III

It is a sunless, cold spring day in March. Norma and Jimmie
are back from the trial of Dr. Besant. Norma is weary and de-
jected, Jimmie resentful because of the things the district attorney
has been saying and implying about dad. He's a rotten guy, that
district attorney, if you ask Jimmie.

And these school teachers that expect a fellow to keep his mind
on Latin and things like that at a time like this—they aren't so
good, either. Giving him a D minus!

Norma is sorry for Jimmie, but it's a lot more important at the
moment that they stand by their father than that they should
worry about class marks. It is all her fault, she realizes that, and
says so. If she had not broken her promise to her father, if she
had just refused to see Michael all would be as it was before.

Betty Lee's brother Joe is in to see Jimmie—and to report, a little embarrassedly, that everything isn't sounding as good as it might the way they talk about the courtroom. Some fellows were saying that they were going to raise a row if Dr. Besant was given any more special privileges, like being brought home by the sheriff.

Lawyer Wentworth has come from court to see Norma, and he is plainly worried. They can't any of them be too careful. Nothing should be done, like playing the radio, for instance, that is likely to alienate public sentiment. He amplifies the suggestion to Norma.

NORMA—Has anything gone wrong?

WENTWORTH—No, my dear—not wrong exactly—but things tremble in the balance at a time like this. There is some very high feeling in certain quarters. The way the Press and Dispatch has gone after us is a disgrace. But I'm not discouraged—I don't mean that—I just meant that—we mustn't do anything that—I hope we'll have the whole thing cleared up in a short time and everything just as it used to be. Now, I think your sister and I better have a little talk, Jimmie.

JIMMIE—Yes, sir. (JIMMIE *leaves with his book.*)

NORMA—There really is some trouble.

WENTWORTH—Not exactly.

NORMA—Oh, please tell me. I want you to tell me the truth.

WENTWORTH—It just seems that sentiment is—not as favorable as it should be—the Legion is making a little trouble—and the so-called law and order crowd—but I think we'll come out all right. Has the prosecution subpœnaed you, Norma?

NORMA—No. (*Fearfully.*) Are they going to?

WENTWORTH—Graham intimated that he'd call you if the defense didn't.

NORMA (*in a panic*)—I don't want to get up there on the stand.

WENTWORTH—It's all very simple, dear, I don't know why it should frighten you so, just to get up there and answer a few questions.

NORMA—But they aren't trying me.

WENTWORTH—Well, yes, in a sense.

NORMA—How do you mean?

WENTWORTH—I want to quash all this backstairs talk, all this gossip—people have begun to say things.

NORMA—What kind of things?

WENTWORTH—Things that it distresses me to repeat, Norma—because I know that you are as pure and sweet as any girl that ever lived. They say we're afraid to put you on the stand.

NORMA—It's bad enough to have everybody staring at me where I sit now, but to be asked questions—

WENTWORTH—It shouldn't be so difficult.

NORMA—I loved Michael, that's all—I loved him—I love him still—and if they keep asking me—to—to deny him—and to—to get up on the stand and tell lies about him—no—I—won't. (*With a distracted movement.*) No—

WENTWORTH—You've got to pull yourself together. Just one final effort, dear, and then perhaps we can put this all behind us and just forget the whole business.

NORMA—Oh, yes, of course, it's so easy to forget.

WENTWORTH—If the jury gets the impression that you're not a pure girl, Norma—

NORMA—What do you mean?

WENTWORTH—I mean that that's what the prosecution is trying to imply and that—

NORMA—What difference does it make about me? I'd do anything to save my father's life of course. But why do they keep picking on me? Suppose I weren't pure, what's that got to do with it?

WENTWORTH—My dear, it makes all the difference between justice and murder. The fact that you are a virgin gives your father the right to defend your name. The prosecution is trying by innuendo to create the impression that you are not. They don't dare say it out. But some of my colleagues have even gone so far as to suggest that a committee of reputable physicians be called into the case.

NORMA (*startled*)—What for?

WENTWORTH—To establish beyond any question that you are a chaste girl.

NORMA (*after a pause, with deadly calm*)—But I'm not.

WENTWORTH (*dazed*)—My dear.

NORMA (*yielding to hysteria*)—So you may as well know. Now don't talk to me about it, because I don't want to talk. And don't let them humiliate me. I guess if I were dead, then the dear old chivalry wouldn't let them—

WENTWORTH—What do you mean?

NORMA (*with sudden control of her emotion*)—Dear Mr. Wentworth, don't pay any attention to me. I don't know what I'm saying. I'm just raving on. You come back after supper, will you? And I'll go over all the testimony with you. And don't look so upset, because no matter how I feel I'm going to save daddy's life, don't you worry.

Both Stanley Wentworth, who has followed his father, and Jimmie try to make little of Norma's going on the stand. There is nothing much she will have to fear. They're a lot of roughnecks, those lawyers and jurymen, anyway, says Stanley.

"Every man on it, if he's got an instinct of a gentleman, would have done the same thing to defend the sanctity of his daughter," echoes Jimmie.

But Norma is irritated rather than cheered. Getting rid of Jimmie, she is eager to change the subject with Stanley, and jokingly takes him to task for having gone over completely to her rivals since she has left the social whirl.

It isn't a joking subject with Stanley. No one else has or ever can take her place with him, and she knows it.

Norma admits that perhaps she does. She has always felt that she owned him. Which is probably why she has always been so mean and selfish and indifferent toward him. But she has always felt that there couldn't be any better friends than they have been.

Now it doesn't seem as though there were very many friends left. Strange, too. "It isn't the first family that has had a nice, polite shooting scandal," says Norma, "so it can't be that that scares them away. No, it must be something about me."

Stanley is ready to laugh at that idea. She could have half the town paying court to her with the crook of a finger, and she knows it.

"You, too?" she asks.

"You don't have to ask about me," he answers, seriously.

NORMA—You are an awfully good boy, aren't you? Stanley, I'm going to have a baby.

STANLEY—What?

NORMA—There! I've said it! I didn't mean to!

STANLEY—Norma!

NORMA—It's been fluttering in my mind so long that I reckon it was bound to pop out sometime.

STANLEY—I don't understand.

NORMA—It's quite simple. I'm carrying Michael's child, that's all. Makes it all quite complicated, doesn't it? Of course, I'd rather you didn't tell any of your friends about it.

STANLEY—Norma.

Norma—I didn't mean to mention it. It's one of those things —naturally I haven't any one to go to. I haven't any one to talk to.

Stanley—You could have come to me, dear, you know that. You could always come to me.

Norma—Well, that's what I did. I mean that's what I seem to have done, haven't I—in a very crude way. You won't misunderstand me of course. I didn't mean to say anything—my secret just got away from me, that's all. But I feel much better now I've said it, even though I didn't intend to— (*With a smile.*) Well, let's talk about something else—like Jimmie's baseball team for instance. Do you hate me?

Stanley—No, dear.

Norma—But you didn't think I was that kind of a girl, I suppose. Well, I'm not.

Stanley—Norma, would you do me the very great honor to marry me?

Norma (*almost in tears*)—Oh, that's sweet of you. You are a good friend, Stanley, and a brave one, too. You said that just as if you meant it.

Stanley—I do mean it, dear.

Norma—Oh, you dear boy, I know what you meant.

Stanley—But, Norma, you don't think I'd have kept asking you to marry me all these years if I hadn't meant it.

Norma—You used to, I know that—but now you love Eloise. And it very nearly killed you to say those words to me. I reckon of all the times you've asked me I'm proudest of this last one when you didn't mean it. That's about the sweetest thing that ever happened to me, Stanley. I can never forget that. That's the kind of love, I guess, that's even nicer than regular love.

Stanley—But, Norma, dear, I tell you—

Norma—But you don't need to keep arguing about it—because I don't love you either. I couldn't marry anybody but Michael. I love him.

Stanley—What can I do?

Norma—Don't ever tell anybody as long as you live.

Stanley (*gently*)—But, Norma, honey, some one's got to be told.

Norma (*alarmed*)—What do you mean?

Stanley—I mean—father ought to know this—if the jury ever—

Norma (*with panic*)—Stanley, if you dare say a word of this to your father or anybody I'll—

STANLEY—You can trust father.

NORMA—No, no. Listen to me. Everything's going to come out all right. I am absolutely sure of it. Just don't tell any one. You see, when your father finally got it through my head that daddy's life hinged on my maidenly virtue, I was a little—flabbergasted, because I do love daddy—I love him next to Michael—

It isn't easy to make Stanley understand that there is nothing much that can be done about anything, now. But there is some little relief in knowing that Norma is happier, that she feels someway as though she "was coming out of the fog" at last—and that he had had a part in that.

When he has gone Norma, her eyes fixed on the drawer from which Dr. Besant had taken one pistol, strolls slowly toward it. At first she passes by the desk, trying to control her emotion. Then she turns, deliberately opens the drawer, looks in and with a tremor quickly closes it shut and walks away. She hears Julia coming.

Now Julia has finished what she had come to do and has gone on with her cleaning upstairs. "Norma waits until she is out of sight, then walks to the desk and takes the pistol out. She hears Betty Lee's voice calling her. Looking frantically around for something to hide the pistol, she sees her pocketbook on the table. She stuffs the pistol in it, and stands trying to look self-possessed, the pocketbook under her arm, as Betty Lee comes in.

Betty Lee is mildly excited by the fact that she has been named as class poet, but also a little worried as to whether she should make up funny rhymes about everybody or do it differently and write nice things. Norma is of the opinion that the parents would probably like the nice rhymes best, but they couldn't possibly be so much fun.

Jimmie bursts in to remind Betty Lee that she had something important to tell Norma about. This turns out to be an invitation for the summer. They are all to have Aunt Martha's cottage, and Norma and Jimmie are to come up for July, unless Norma'd rather come when Stanley can be there, now that—

"I don't want him," Norma assures them, quickly. "If I'd wanted Stanley I could have had him any time."

"Lordy, I know that. You could have anybody you wanted, I reckon."

"I wanted Michael."

"Are you terribly unhappy, Norma?"

Norma sadly smiles an answer, and Jimmie squelches Betty

Lee. The dumbness of some people is appalling to Jimmie, always asking people about their feelings, which are private! Gosh!

Dr. Besant is in the hall. Ed Forsythe is with him, but not at all an obnoxious guardian of the law. Ed thinks it will be all right if he waits outside in the car, and the doctor is grateful.

Dr. Besant is pleasantly dignified in his greetings to them, though not over cordial toward Norma. They have not been very friendly since the tragedy.

But now Norma deliberately puts herself in her father's way. "Daddy, be nice to me," she pleads. Let him stay and talk a little with her, even though he has dozens and dozens of things to do. He can do them to-morrow.

"I'm not sure but that I'll be confined for the balance of the time," calmly answers Dr. Besant, "so I haven't a moment to lose."

NORMA (*vehemently*)—Daddy! If I ask you just one favor—
DR. BESANT—What is it, my dear?
NORMA—Daddy, you don't think unkindly of me, do you?
DR. BESANT—No, daughter, no, daughter—of course I don't.
NORMA—Then don't be so methodical about it!
DR. BESANT—What do you want me to do?
NORMA—Just for one minute I want you to be as you used to. Let's just pretend we're like we used to be before any of this happened—that's all. (*Still holding the bag with the pistol under one arm, she puts the other around her father's neck. His arms go tenderly around her and he holds her close.*) Good-by, darling. . . . Now I'll let you go. (DR. BESANT, *very much affected, goes to his office.*)
JIMMIE—Well, I think it's a good thing you made it up with him. (NORMA *walks into the dining room without looking at him.*)
STANLEY (*entering*)—Jimmie, do you know if your father's busy now?
JIMMIE—Well, I suppose he is. (*A shot is heard.*) If you— what the dickens?
STANLEY (*vaguely*)—What was that?
JIMMIE—That's what I'd like to know!
JULIA (*running down the stairway*)—What was that?
JIMMIE—Sounded like a gun going off!
JULIA—Whar's Miss Norma?
JIMMIE—She's in there. (*He and* JULIA *go to dining room.*) Norma! (MR. WENTWORTH *comes in.*)

STANLEY—Hello, father, I'm afraid I've kept you—   (JULIA *screams and moans.*) For God's sake!

WENTWORTH—Stanley, what is it?

JIMMIE—Hey, come in here, some of you, come in here! What'll we do, what'll we do! (*He sees his father come into the living room as* STANLEY *and* WENTWORTH *go to* NORMA.)

DR. BESANT—James—

JIMMIE—Don't come out, father. You stay in there!

DR. BESANT—What's happened?

JIMMIE (*holding his father*)—Father, you wait here.

DR. BESANT—What is it? What's the matter?

JIMMIE—Wait a minute!

DR. BESANT—James, let me go. What is the matter?

JIMMIE (*forcing his father down into a chair he holds him*)— No, I won't do it. You've got to stay here. Listen to me. Now, listen, father, will you? (*Crying.*) Oh, gee whiz—oh, gee whiz— (WENTWORTH *comes in.*)

DR. BESANT—Bob, what's happened?

WENTWORTH—There's nothing you can do, Will.

DR. BESANT—For Christ's sake, tell me what's happened. . . . Norma?

WENTWORTH—She's done it!   (DR. BESANT *collapses in a chair.*) You mustn't feel like that, old man! Norma didn't kill herself for love of Michael. Don't you understand? Don't you see? She did it for you. James—   (*He motions for* JAMES *to take his father into the office.*)

JIMMIE (*lifting his father with the tenderness and strength of a boy now grown into a man*)—Come on, father. Come on, daddy. Let's you and me go into the other room.

The curtain falls.

BEHOLD THE BRIDEGROOM

A Drama in Three Acts

By George Kelly

THE night after Christmas, December 26, 1927, eleven new plays were produced in New York. It was a record list of openings and a record week for first nights. Eighteen new productions were offered between Monday and Saturday, which the statisticians are eager to point out is equal to three a day.

Of the eleven plays presented on this historical Monday night George Kelly's "Behold the Bridegroom" appealed to the professional reviewers as being the most important. Kelly is by way of being a favorite with these gentlemen, and always a dramatist of promise. His "Show Off," "Craig's Wife" and "Daisy Mayme" have given him a definite standing in the theatre and placed him well up among the native dramatists upon whom the American theatre of the future seems safest in depending.

His "Behold the Bridegroom," however, proved a bit puzzling to the public, and was none too simple of classification to its critics. Its success for a time was moderate, it grew in popularity with discussion, enjoyed a month or two of excellent business and then sloped away again to only moderate returns.

It seems fair, therefore, to accept it as a drama the theme and treatment of which automatically limit its public. Those who like it like it very much indeed, and those who do not cannot abide even a discussion of it.

In writing "Behold the Bridegroom," Mr. Kelly reverts to that type of character analysis which inspired "Craig's Wife." Opposed to his study of the all-possessive wife in that drama he offers another of a young woman who, entering freely into the life and liberties inspired by modern tendencies of sophistication, comes upon days of disillusionment that prove rather tragically devastating.

She is Antoinette Lyle, daughter of Robert Lyle, widower, and living, when not roaming Europe, with her father at Shadow Brook, which is just beyond the city line of an American metropolis. At the play's opening Antoinette is discovered just returned unheralded and unexpected from Europe.

In "a kind of lounge conservatory, outside the drawing room," she is "sitting slouched on a luxurious divan reading a novel "

"Her dress is a rather daring Paris creation in scarlet velvet that shows every line of her lovely figure. And her slippers and stockings are honey-colored. She is wearing a necklace of twenty fine gold chains caught with clasps of jade, and the bracelet on her right arm and her two rings are of jade. The bracelet on her left arm is three inches wide and is set solidly with alternating rows of diamonds, sapphires, emeralds and rubies. Personally, Miss Lyle is the color of her dress, bold and bizarre—a hussy of the high world."

Although restless, Antoinette is irritated by the discovery that certain of her friends already know that she is at home. Connie Peyton, for one, telephones, and being informed that Miss Lyle is still in Europe, demands the privilege of speaking with her anyway. She knows where she is.

And a few moments later who should be reported driving into the grounds but Eleanor Ridgway, accompanied by a strange man. As it transpires Mrs. Ridgway does not know that Miss Lyle is home. She has only brought a friend to look at the Lyle rose garden this first week of June. But when she steps into the house to use the telephone she finds Antoinette and the possibility of the returned traveller's enjoying a quietly secretive homecoming is practically ruined.

The greeting of these two is friendly and emotional, and charged with the usual exchange of explanations and current comment. Mr. Ridgway is well; Mrs. Ridgway is domestically content; no, there is nothing even remotely significant in her appearance to-day with Spencer Train in tow, and she thinks Antoinette's new Paris gown is horrible.

For her part, Miss Lyle is still suspicious of Mrs. Ridgway's domestic contentment, mildly curious about Mr. Train, and willing to admit that the gown is rather terrible—one of those gowns, in fact, made of "that damned stuff that pulls up every move you make. If you only draw your breath it's up around your neck," she admits. As for her reason for wanting to keep her homecoming secret, that is because she does not expect to stay. Her father is in the Argentine, and Antoinette thought perhaps she would run down to White Sulphur Springs and see Connie Peyton.

Now, it seems, Miss Peyton is home again and—of all unexpected things—engaged to be married! Antoinette can barely credit that news. To a brain specialist, too!

Something should be done about that, insists Antoinette, and she purposes doing it. She will simply have to stop that marriage. "I mean," she explains, "it wouldn't be fair—to the unborn. I mean, it just wouldn't."

"It's love, my darling," cautions Mrs. Ridgway.

"It's inactivity, Eleanor. She simply had nothing to do and she got nervous."

For the moment Connie Peyton's matrimonial prospects and problems are put aside while the gossips make some decision about dinner. Mrs. Ridgway has invited Mr. Train to her house, but it is Miss Lyle's idea that they should both stay at Shadow Brook with her. She is, she admits, curious to see this Mr. Train. She has heard something about him. One of their mutual friends fairly raves about him.

That Train is charming Mrs. Ridgway is willing to admit. He is in his early thirties, good looking and unmarried. But it is Fenton Ridgway, her husband, who invites him to the Ridgway home all the time.

"Is he really Fenton's boss?"

"My dear, he is *everybody's* boss. Lansing's been abroad, you know, for nearly a year; and he's practically had entire charge down there. And Fenton says he's a positive wizard. And he's entirely self-educated you know—at least, as far as that business is concerned; for he came in there first simply as Mr. Lansing's secretary. Of course, he's worked like a dog."

"He should give some lessons to a few friends of mine."

The mention of their idle men friends reminds Mrs. Ridgway of Gehring Fitler. Where is he? Antoinette doesn't know and, evidently, doesn't care a great deal.

MRS. RIDGWAY—He probably doesn't know where you are.

MISS LYLE—Oh, I'll hear from him, sooner or later; he always manages to locate me.

MRS. RIDGWAY—When are you going to marry him, Tony?

MISS LYLE—Now, how should *I* know *when* I'm going to marry him, Eleanor?

MRS. RIDGWAY—Well, I think it's time you *did* know *something* about it, dear; you've been stringing the man along for nearly three years.

MISS LYLE—Well, I think a girl should be naturally a bit hesitant about becoming the wife of a drunkard.

Mrs. Ridgway—Well, I think that's largely your fault, Tony. (Miss Lyle *makes a sound of amusement.*)   Yes, I do.

Miss Lyle—I expected you'd say that.

Mrs. Ridgway—Because I think it's true.

Miss Lyle—Now, why do you say such a thing, Eleanor?

Mrs. Ridgway—Because he never drank till he met you. (Miss Lyle *shrieks.*)   No, he didn't.

Miss Lyle—That's delicious.

Mrs. Ridgway—For I've known him for years.

Miss Lyle—And I suppose I taught him to drink?

Mrs. Ridgway—No, but I think you've unsettled his life, Tony.

Miss Lyle—Oh, rot, Eleanor. (*She turns away.*)

Mrs. Ridgway—Well, I think you have, nevertheless.—He's perfectly mad about you, and has been from the first day he met you.

Miss Lyle—Well, I don't think my marrying him would re-settle his life.

Mrs. Ridgway—Well, I think it *would*, Antoinette; I think that's just what's the matter with him.   He's wandering around from post to pillar, drinking his head off, just to try to get you off his mind.—And I think it might settle *your* life a bit, too, Tony, as well as his.

Miss Lyle (*rising and going up to the stand for another cigarette*)—Now, please don't start to lecture me, Eleanor—

Mrs. Ridgway—I'm not lecturing you at all.

Miss Lyle—I've just come back from Europe to avoid that.

Mrs. Ridgway—But Gehring Fitler is a friend of mine—and a very charming boy.   And all you've done for the past three years is sit back and ridicule his sincere regard—just as you've ridiculed everybody else that was ever fond of you.—And that's rather a horrid thing to do, Antoinette—*I* think.   But Gehring is so *desperately* fond of you that his feeling has survived even that.

Miss Lyle (*sauntering across at the back towards the left door*)—Has he sent you here to plead his cause?

Mrs. Ridgway—No, he hasn't done anything of the kind; I haven't seen him since the Horse Show.—But, I *do* think you've given him a rather shabby deal.—And so do a great many other people; for everybody in the world knows that he's asked you to marry him at least a dozen times.

Miss Lyle (*coming forward at the left, and looking straight out*)—I think that's something of a habit with him, Eleanor.

Mrs. Ridgway—Well, if it is, I don't think it's a habit that your ridicule will cure.

Miss Lyle (*turning upon her*)—I've never ridiculed Gehring Fitler in my life.

Mrs. Ridgway—You've made him *look* ridiculous a thousand times.

Miss Lyle—Because I wouldn't marry him?

Mrs. Ridgway—Exactly.

Miss Lyle—And, must I marry a man simply because he asks me?

Mrs. Ridgway—Well, what good reason have you, Tony, for *not* marrying him?

Miss Lyle (*with a gesture of annoyance*)—Because I don't *want* to marry him. (*She moves across in front of* Mrs. Ridgway *to the divan again. And there is a pause.*)

Mrs. Ridgway—He's quite as eligible as anybody we know.— And *certainly* you'll marry somebody sometime.

Miss Lyle (*sinking into the divan*)—Sometimes I think I won't.

Mrs. Ridgway—Oh, every girl says that, Antoinette.

Miss Lyle—Some women don't.

Mrs. Ridgway (*rising*)—Well, you're not the kind that won't, you can take that from me. (*She circles down and towards the left, to the bench.*)

Miss Lyle—I might surprise you, darling.

Mrs. Ridgway—Maybe you will; but I don't think so.

It is Mrs. Ridgway's idea, too, that Antoinette owes it to her father to marry. Undoubtedly he would like to marry again himself, and probably would, if it were not for his reluctance to put a stepmother over his daughter.

Miss Lyle is vastly amused at Mrs. Ridgway's deductions, and interested as well in her justification for them. Particularly is she interested in Mrs. Ridgway's statement that she knows exactly why she has not married.

"It's because you are so profoundly romantic, Antoinette. And you're waiting for the kind of love experience that you think will satisfy you. But I think you're waiting in vain, dear, for even if it were to come, I think you'd find you weren't ready for the occasion—by any means."

Miss Lyle—You know, I think you're just a little bit rough on me, Eleanor.

MRS. RIDGWAY (*drifting away from the chair and moving towards her*)—No—I'm not at all, Antoinette; I'm simply telling you what I honestly believe. (*She stops a few paces from her and looks at her narrowly.*) I think I *know* you just a little bit better than anybody else; and I'd like to see you happy. Because, to be perfectly frank, dear, I think life is beginning to play out with you. You've *been* everywhere, you've *seen* everything, and you've *had* everything. And it isn't enough—for *your particular* kind of nature.

MISS LYLE—So you think I should get married.

MRS. RIDGWAY—I think *you* should, yes.

MISS LYLE—Even though I don't love the man.

MRS. RIDGWAY—Everybody isn't capable of love, Tony. It's a thing one's got to be prepared for. And I don't think *you* have been. (MISS LYLE *is amused, and faintly embarrassed.*)

MISS LYLE (*raising her arms and letting them fall over the back of the divan*)—Then, you think that for me the heavens are empty, Eleanor, as far as love is concerned?

MRS. RIDGWAY—As far as any knight in armor is concerned, yes—decidedly. (EDWARDS *appears in the left door.*) That's the reason I think you're foolish to wait for it.

EDWARDS—Mr. Train is at the front door, Mrs. Ridgway.

MRS. RIDGWAY (*turning and crossing in front of the center chair*)—Thanks, Edwards.

EDWARDS—He told me to tell you he'd brought the car up.

MRS. RIDGWAY (*going up to the telephone at the back, and speaking over her left shoulder to* MISS LYLE)—He's probably gotten tired waiting. (*To* EDWARDS.) Tell him I'll be out in two minutes.

MISS LYLE—Ask Mr. Train to come in, Edwards.

EDWARDS (*withdrawing*)—Very good, Miss.

MRS. RIDGWAY—Now, I've told you I've got to go in a minute, Tony.

MISS LYLE—You haven't got your call yet.

MRS. RIDGWAY (*coming forward to the bench for her pocketbook*)—I know you just want me to object, so that you can accuse me (MISS LYLE *laughs*) but I won't please you. (*She opens her pocketbook and powders her nose.*)

MISS LYLE—Don't be alarmed, darling, I'll be very nice to him.

MRS. RIDGWAY—Oh, Hell—

MISS LYLE—Why, Eleanor!—How self-conscious you are about him.

Mrs. Ridgway—He probably won't know you're on the boat.

Miss Lyle—You *almost* make me suspect that you're—

Mrs. Ridgway (*closing her pocketbook, and moving towards* Miss Lyle)—Now, stop being obvious, Tony.

When Spencer Train arrives, tall, handsome, conventionally garbed in a dark suit and wearing the first rose of summer proudly as a boutonnière, Miss Lyle responds to the introduction by hailing him smilingly with:

"Behold the Bridegroom cometh!"

Which starts their acquaintanceship with laughter.

"He does look rather like a bridegroom, doesn't he?" comments Mrs. Ridgway.

"All but the nervousness," agrees Antoinette.

Train refuses to be talked or laughed out of the perfect poise that appears to be characteristic with him. He is frank to say that he is happy at having had an opportunity to see the gardens and that he is not very particular where he dines. If it turns out that Mr. Ridgway is not coming home, which Mrs. Ridgway is trying to find out by phone, he will be happy to stay and have dinner with Miss Lyle and Mrs. Ridgway at Shadow Brook.

Miss Lyle—You'll be doing an act of charity, really, if you will; for otherwise I shall dine in solitary grandeur. There isn't a soul out here, you know; my father's away.

Train—This is rather a big place to be alone in.

Miss Lyle—It's much too big, *I* think; I don't know why Daddy keeps it up. He's away a great deal of the time; and I'm scarcely ever here.

Train (*getting up and moving forward, looking straight out*)— That's too bad; it's a very beautiful place.

Miss Lyle (*observing him narrowly*)—Yes, the gardens are pretty—I don't know much about the rest of it. But, I think you're a bit early to *see* the rose gardens, really.

Train (*turning to her*)—Yes, I think they *are* a bit late this year. This was the only one that was out.

Miss Lyle—Oh, really?

Train—I suppose we should have left it—

Miss Lyle—Not at all—

Train—But—

Miss Lyle—Why should you?

Train—Mrs. Ridgway insisted that I wear it.

Miss Lyle—Well, I'm very glad she did; it looks very well on you.

Train—A bit fancy, don't you think?

Miss Lyle (*smiling*)—I should say daring—(*he breaks into a little laugh*)—with those clothes you're wearing.

Train—Why?

Miss Lyle—Why—I think you're in very grave danger of being captured and led directly to the altar.

Train (*laughing*)—No, I'm hardly so alluring as that.

Miss Lyle—Well, this is the month for that kind of thing, you know.

Train (*taking the flower from his coat as he moves closer to her*)—Wouldn't you like to have this rose, Miss Lyle?

Miss Lyle—No, really, Mr. Train, I much prefer that she should have it.

Train (*offering the flower*)—It's the first rose of summer, you know. (*She laughs faintly.*) And blooming quite as much alone as the last one.

Miss Lyle—That's the reason I think you should keep it.

Train—But I'm sure it'll look much better on you than it does on me. (*She looks up into his eyes and smiles.*) Do take it— please.

Miss Lyle (*taking the flower*)—Is it good luck or something?

Train—It should be. (*She makes a faint sound of amusement.*)

Miss Lyle—Thanks so much.

Train—Don't mention it. (*He turns away, and, taking a cigarette from his case, strolls towards the left; and* Miss Lyle, *sliding her right arm out to full length across the lower arm of the divan, looks meditatively at the flower.*) I hope I haven't broken it, taking it off.

Miss Lyle (*abstractedly*)—No, it's quite perfect.

Train (*turning and coming back to the little table at the right of the center chair to dispose of the burnt match*)—It *is* rather a perfect rose, isn't it?

Miss Lyle—Too perfect, for this world, I'm afraid, Mr. Train. I suppose that's the reason they don't survive.

Train—A great many people don't care for white roses.

Miss Lyle—I don't myself, particularly; there's something rather deathly about them. So I think I'll press this. (*She reaches for the book beside her.*)

Train—In the book, you mean?

Miss Lyle—Yes; my mother used to do that all the time.

TRAIN—Really?

MISS LYLE—Yes; there's an enormous book of hers upstairs, and it's quite filled with pressed flowers. (*She settles the rose in the book.*)

TRAIN—How long has your mother been dead, Miss Lyle?

MISS LYLE—She died the year I was born. And I'm twenty-seven—(*she looks at him*)—if you won't tell anybody.

During the pressing of the flower Miss Lyle's diplomatic investigations reveal the fact that Mr. Train is, though the honor is largely technical, the executive in charge of the business which employs Mr. Ridgway; that in that business there are incidentally some seven hundred women employés, and that it never occurred to Mr. Train that these women are at all frightened of him. He is not, he is sure, a very formidable person, as Antoinette seems to believe.

"You're not afraid of me, are you?" he counters.

"You're not my boss," she answers.

Mrs. Ridgway is back with the news that Mr. Ridgway will not be able to get home for dinner, and Miss Lyle is modestly triumphant at having snared a dinner guest.

"I appealed to his sense of chivalry," she explains, over Mrs. Ridgway's protest; "so please sit down, darling, and don't be difficult, or Mr. Train will think we're fighting over him."

The pre-dinner cocktails and dinner for four are ordered with the expectation that Connie Peyton will drop in and stay. She usually does stay, according to Miss Lyle. She does not even have to be asked. Connie also can be depended upon to help out with the cocktails, which neither Mr. Train nor Mrs. Ridgway will drink—he because he doesn't drink anything and she because it is the doctor's orders.

Now the conversation has turned half laughingly to the pressing of the rose and such romantic significance as it *might* suggest. Nor will Mrs. Ridgway admit that such suggestions are impossible to Miss Lyle.

"She's been trying to persuade everybody for years, Spencer, that she's simply an emotional negative," explains Mrs. Ridgway, "and I assure you she's the most romantic person I know."

MISS LYLE—Eleanor thinks that because *she* is capable of high romance, Mr. Train, that everybody else is. (*She sits on the arm of the divan and leans back, luxuriously.*)

MRS. RIDGWAY—No, I don't think anything of the kind, now,

Tony. And I don't think that what I did had anything high or romantic about it.

Miss Lyle—Don't you think it was rather romantic, Mr. Train, for the daughter of a very rich man to marry a man who had absolutely no money whatever?

Mrs. Ridgway—I simply fell in love with a man and I married him.

Miss Lyle—What do you think about it, Mr. Train? (*He laughs.*)

Train (*between two fires*)—Why—*I'm* rather inclined to think that it was more romantic of the man than the woman.

Miss Lyle—Of the man?

Train—I mean, if he loved her.

Miss Lyle—But, my dear Mr. Train, the *man* wasn't giving up anything.

Train—It seems to me he was running the risk of having to give *her* up.

Miss Lyle—How do you mean?

Train—By losing her, to her own people again; if he weren't able to provide satisfactorily for her.

Miss Lyle—But, it seems to me that he was *inviting* dissatisfaction on her part, Mr. Train, for his first commandment was—that for the first five years she was to accept absolutely nothing in the way of material assistance from her people.

Mrs. Ridgway—Which was perfectly right, wasn't it, Spencer?

Miss Lyle—Now, *please* don't agree with her, Mr. Train—(*he laughs again*)—for we've argued this thing till we're both black in the face.

Train—Well, really, I don't see how he could have very well done anything else, under the circumstances. (Miss Lyle *despairs.*)

Mrs. Ridgway—Of course he couldn't.

Miss Lyle—Oh, now, Mr. Train.

Train—I mean, after all, a man should want to feel that he is at least capable of being responsible for his wife.

Mrs. Ridgway—And if his wife is willing to *be* his wife, then she should be willing to live within his income.

Miss Lyle—She'll quote that to me now, Mr. Train, every time we discuss it.

Mrs. Ridgway—That's been the point of our entire argument, Spencer. She said when I told her I was going to marry Fenton that I was mad; and that it wouldn't last two weeks; and it's lasted two years. And it's going to go on lasting.

Miss Lyle—But, things have improved for you since then, my dear.

Mrs. Ridgway—But, we've improved them, darling. And the last two years have been the most thrilling of my life; for they've not only given me something to do, but they've given me an enormous amount of self-respect. For they've shown me that I *could* deprive myself of practically everything I'd been accustomed to, out of consideration for somebody else.

Miss Lyle—But, why *deprive* oneself of anything.

Mrs. Ridgway—I'm not making any virtue of it, Tony—

Miss Lyle—I mean, unnecessarily.

Mrs. Ridgway—After all, I wanted to do it. And even if I hadn't, my sense of sportsmanship would have held me to it.

Miss Lyle (*dragging herself up from the arm of the divan*)—Well—I suppose it's all very noble—(*she moves towards the center of the room pulling down her dress*)—but I'm afraid there isn't much danger of my letting myself in for anything of the kind.

Mrs. Ridgway—You're just the kind that would, my dear.

Miss Lyle—I don't see the necessity of it, Eleanor.

Mrs. Ridgway—It isn't a question of necessity, Tony; it's a question of meeting the *man*. (Miss Lyle *gives a little toot of amusement*.) And if you ever *do* meet him, you'll find yourself quite as sacrificial as any other woman.

Miss Lyle—Maybe so, darling; but I think you overestimate my quality.

Mrs. Ridgway—Well, *I* don't think I do at all. (Miss Lyle *looks at* Train.)

Miss Lyle—Joy was never duty to *me*, Mr. Train. (*He looks steadily at her, curiously; and she holds his eye for a dead pause. The smile dies gradually from her face. Slowly she raises her left arm and hand and flicks her fingers at him: then turns away and moves down towards the extreme right.*) But you mustn't look at me so disapprovingly.

Train (*without altering his position or expression*)—I'm sorry to give you that impression, Miss Lyle.

Miss Lyle—Unconsciously, perhaps; but there's a rebuke—in your eyes—(*she turns and looks at him, then moves up towards the back of the room*)—that with my present state of conscience may induce a moral reform—which would vindicate Eleanor, and I couldn't bear that. (*She stands looking off to the right.*)

Mrs. Ridgway—I'll be vindicated, my dear, if I live long enough.

Miss Lyle—Why should you wish to be vindicated, Eleanor?

Mrs. Ridgway—For your own happiness, Tony.

Miss Lyle (*raising her right arm with a yearning gesture*)— Ah—but that road to—conscious worth—is so frightfully long and rutty. And after I'd traveled it, I should probably be more dissatisfied than I am now. (*She tilts her head and looks over her left shoulder, rather whimsically, at* Train, *who is watching her. And he laughs; and looks at* Mrs. Ridgway. Mr. Train *is amused. She looks off to the right again.*)

Train—Don't you like to be amusing, Miss Lyle?

Miss Lyle (*with sudden and bitter fury*)—I hate it—intensely. (*There is a rather astonished pause.* Train *turns slowly and meets* Mrs. Ridgway's *eyes; and* Miss Lyle *comes forward smolderingly at the right.*) But I suppose it's the only impression I'm capable of making.

Connie Peyton is of the super-flapper type, attractive but flighty, irresponsible and irrepressible. She arrives now "with glass in hand to welcome the prodigal," and for the next fifteen minutes rather dominates the chatter, particularly after the cocktails have been served.

Miss Peyton has been having tea, "with variations," with a feminine emancipator. She is happy to meet Mr. Train and free to admit at first glance that he is very good looking. She is quite ready to stay to dinner, though she has been warned by the dietitians to be most strict about her foods.

The best place for her, Connie feels, in the selection of seating accommodations, is near the cocktails, because that will save her the bother of moving. And, speaking of cocktails, she is quite surprised to find her friend Antoinette sober.

"I said to Marcella Travers, immediately she told me you were back, I said: 'She probably went out on a tear over there and never came to until she found herself *home*,'" laughs Connie.

Miss Lyle (*very coldly*)—I thought you were at White Sulphur.

Miss Peyton (*flipping her hand at her*)—Now, never mind about me—I want to know why they *chased* you out of France; for I know you've been deported or something, or you'd never have come back at this time of year.

Miss Lyle—I went away with the wrong people.

Miss Peyton (*with a complete change in manner and dropping her voice to a level key*)—My dear—*anybody* is the wrong people to go away with—as I have found from *bitter* experience. (*She turns to* TRAIN, *who is regarding her curiously, and becomes very gracious.*) I have been in the West Indies all winter, Mr. Train, with my aunt—(*with another change to level bitterness*)— and if ever there was a living *devil* it's that woman. (MRS. RIDGWAY *bursts out laughing.*) Oh, I'm telling you, my dear, there should be something *done* about these white-haired old *women;* they've been getting away with *murder* for *years.*

MRS. RIDGWAY—What did she do, Connie?

MISS PEYTON—Why, my dear, the woman is *simply out* of her mind, that's all. She fights with everybody in the hotels; accuses every maid of stealing from her. (*To* MISS LYLE.) She's had five since February. (*Then to* TRAIN.) And she's gotten the idea *lately* that every bit of paper money she gets is *counterfeit.* (TRAIN *and* MRS. RIDGWAY *laugh.*) Did you ever hear of such a thing? It's no wonder I'm the way I am. (*She opens her purse and starts to rummage for her cigarettes.*) She wakened me one morning at White Sulphur at *six o'clock*—to examine some dollar bills that the desk had sent up the night before. Now, I *ask* you—(*she returns to her purse*)—as ladies in the rough.

It is while Mrs. Ridgway and Spencer Train are brushing up for dinner that Connie Peyton further unburdens her mind of its gossip content. She thinks Spencer Train is nice and she knows she knows some one who knows him well and is more or less mad about him.

She suspects, as well, that Antoinette has been trying to impress Mr. Train, and that in itself is a new idea, seeing that Antoinette previously has specialized in married men.

This charge Miss Lyle is quick to resent. Further than that she is also far from pleased with the impression Miss Peyton has sought to give Train of her (Antoinette's) manner of living and the character of her friends. Is Connie trying to give this stranger the impression that Antoinette is *fast?*

Miss Peyton hadn't thought much about what impression she was giving any one. She was just talking, and she could go on talking and say a lot more, if Antoinette would like to hear her. Among other things she could tell her what she had really come over to tell her—that her (Miss Lyle's) father is going to be married. Yes, ma'am, going to marry a widow named Gibson, just as soon as Antoinette makes up her mind about her own marriage to Gehring Fitler.

Connie doesn't know what she is talking about, Miss Lyle suggests with some spirit. The idea of Mr. Lyle marrying is preposterous. Why doesn't Miss Peyton talk about her own marriage if she wants to talk about something? Why is she keeping that so secret?

Miss Peyton replies that, in the first place, it isn't true, and, in the second place, if it is true, it isn't anybody's business.

The return of Spencer Train is all that saves the old friends from a further exchange of acerbities. Soon Mrs. Ridgway is down and dinner is announced.

Mr. Train has just finished telling Connie Peyton that he may have to go back to Russia the end of the year on a business trip, which is a perfectly terrifying suggestion to Connie. She just knows they would put her to death or something in that terrible Russia.

Now Miss Peyton and Mrs. Ridgway have disappeared down the hall toward the dining room and Mr. Train and Antoinette are about to follow.

Miss Lyle—I've gotten so lately that I absolutely *hate* to travel; and yet I simply *cannot* content myself in any one place. (*She attempts to get up, and sinks back, laughing.*)

Train (*stepping over to her and offering her his hand*)—Can't you get up, Miss Lyle?

Miss Lyle (*taking his hand*)—Thanks. This divan is so low. (*He draws her up; but as she puts her right foot on the floor it gives under her and she makes a slight exclamation, laughs, and sinks against him. He catches her in his arms. She becomes suddenly still; and the laughter dies on her lips. And there is a curious pause. She gradually raises her eyes to his, then detaches herself slowly and moves away a step or two to the right, where she stands looking straight out—very still.*)

Train—Are you ill, Miss Lyle?

Miss Lyle (*tonelessly*)—No, I'm all right.

Train—Can't I get you something?

Miss Lyle—No, it's nothing. (*She gives a faint little sound of amusement.*) I suppose I'm not over my little spell of seasickness yet.

Train—Shall I send Mrs. Ridgway out?

Miss Lyle—No, don't, please; I don't want them to know; or they'll swear I've been running wild in Europe. Just go in yourself, Mr. Train, and tell them I'll be in in a moment. (*He starts across towards the left, but stops in the middle of the room and looks back at her.*)

TRAIN—I really don't like to leave you this way.
MISS LYLE—I'm quite all right, I assure you.

"He continues, rather reluctantly, across and up to the left door. And she remains perfectly still over at the divan, looking straight out. He climbs the three steps leading up to the door, then turns again, with a slightly troubled expression, and looks back at her. And there is a physical stillness. Then he turns away slowly and goes down the hallway. She waits quietly for a moment, then gradually lets her eyes follow his pathway—along the floor; and presently she moves in a dream to the middle of the room, her eyes still fastened on the door. At the middle of the room she stops, and beholds the mystery.

"The curtain commences to descend slowly as she wanders towards the left door."

ACT II

Four weeks later Gehring Fitler calls at Shadow Brook. He has been in Canada for three weeks and had no idea that Antoinette Lyle was home. Would not know it now if he had not happened to bump into Fenton Ridgway at the club.

Mary McGrath, Antoinette's maid, tries to clarify the situation somewhat for Mr. Fitler by explaining that Miss Lyle has not been at all well these last four weeks. A strange sort of illness hers appears to be. Not once has she stepped outside the grounds of Shadow Brook during the whole four weeks nor has any one stepped inside. All her friends have been kept in as complete ignorance of Tony Lyle's whereabouts as he.

Eleanor Ridgway, having been told that Antoinette planned to return to White Sulphur Springs with Connie Peyton, had not thought of inquiring further until a letter addressed to Miss Lyle at the Springs had been returned. Then she called Miss McGrath and learned the truth.

"I thought it was time to tell somebody something," explains McGrath, "because things can't go on this way."

FITLER—Is Mrs. Ridgway coming out?
McGRATH—She said she'd be out right away; so I've been expecting her all day. I knew Mr. Lyle'd blame *me* if anything happened, and Miss Lyle wouldn't let me send him word of any kind.
FITLER—When is Mr. Lyle coming back?
McGRATH—He's due here to-day; the secretary called up from

his office to have one of the chauffeurs meet him at the station this afternoon.

FITLER—Well, Miss Lyle isn't really *ill,* is she, Mary?

McGRATH—There's something the matter with her, Mr. Fitler, whatever it is. She won't come to her meals, and when she does come she just sits there and picks like a child that'd be half sick. There were two days last week that I don't think she broke her fast once.

FITLER—And you say she doesn't go out at all?

McGRATH—She hardly ever comes out of her room, Mr. Fitler —(FITLER *turns away slowly, with a troubled expression*) except maybe once and a while in the afternoon she'll take a walk down to the rose gardens and sit there. . . . I guess that's where she is now. . . . And I went down there the other evening to try and coax her to come to her dinner; and I'm telling you the truth, Mr. Fitler, I could hear her crying before I saw her. (FITLER *turns sharply and looks at her quizzically.*) I don't think I ever heard anybody cry so hard in *my* life. So I wish you'd talk to her, Mr. Fitler, if you get the chance while you're here, and try to find out what's the matter with her, for she has me worried sick. And she gets into such tempers if you say anything to her, that for peace sake you keep quiet. She has that poor French maid of hers nearly out of her mind. (*She starts for the door.*)

FITLER—She's probably out here by herself too much.

When Antoinette comes from the garden a moment later she is seen to be greatly changed. "She is pale, and the cold, almost meditative blue of her dress seems to fit, or probably reflect, her personal tone. She is wearing a full-length coat of the same material as the dress, heavily trimmed with summer ermine."

A little irritably Antoinette gives such account of her movements since Gehring lost track of her as she is pleased to give. She has kept herself in seclusion, she says, because she is tired of seeing people. She is grateful for his interest, and conscious of his devoted love for her. But that she can feel any differently about it than she does she is at no pains to deny.

Also Mary McGrath's report that she eats little and is apparently ill are greatly exaggerated. That there is, as Gehring insists, something wrong with her she is willing to admit provisionally. And yet what it is she does not herself know, and is therefore quite unable to tell him.

FITLER—Haven't you anything to say to me, Tony?

MISS LYLE—What about?

FITLER—About the only thing that's of any interest to me. (*She looks straight ahead, and he looks at her steadily, under his brows.*) I had rather expected that you would have, when you'd get back.

MISS LYLE (*in a level tone*)—Yes, I have something to say to you about that, Gehring; perhaps that's what I've been evading; for I don't think it'll be very agreeable news to you. (*He remains very still.*) But I hope you won't mind too much. I suppose we've all got to hear certain bits of bad news in a lifetime. I heard one particularly bad bit when I got back. And it's really more or less on account of that that I feel obliged to give you this news now. (*She looks at him.*) I heard that my father was thinking about getting married again; and, naturally, it was quite a shock to me. Not at first, particularly, because I simply dismissed it as an absurdity; but since then I've had time to think it over more reasonably, and I'm amazed that the probability hadn't occurred to me before. But somehow or another I'd never thought of my father in that connection. I don't know why I didn't particularly,—he's a comparatively young man,—but I just didn't. But, evidently, from what I hear, *he* did; and has been thinking that way for some time. And, according to report, he's simply waiting now for me to think the same way about myself;—so that he'll be spared the necessity of putting a stepmother over me, I suppose. So we expect him back to-day, and he and I'll very likely discuss it; and I want to be able to tell him definitely not to wait; that I have no idea of getting married.— That's the bit of disagreeable news that I have to give you, Gehring. (*There is a pause.*)

FITLER—Well, you mean that you have no idea of getting married right away; (*she shakes her head negatively*) that's what you mean, isn't it, Tony?

MISS LYLE—No, it isn't; I mean that I have no idea of getting married at all. (*He gets up, with a stunned expression, and, keeping his eyes on her, moves across nearer to her.*)

FITLER—You can't mean that, Tony?

MISS LYLE—That is exactly what I mean, Gehring.

FITLER—But, my dear girl, everybody is waiting for the announcement of our engagement.

MISS LYLE—I know they are; that's what my father's waiting for, too.

FITLER—Well, naturally, Tony, why shouldn't he?

MISS LYLE—But, we were never definitely engaged.

FITLER—My dear, what difference does that make; we could

have been engaged long ago if you'd been willing; but, naturally, people assumed that that would follow whenever you were ready.

MISS LYLE (*rising, with a touch of desperation, and moving towards the right*)—I did myself; but I've changed my mind.

FITLER (*following her*)—Well, what has *made* you change your mind, Tony?

MISS LYLE (*stopping at the right*)—Many things.

FITLER—Well, why don't you tell me what they are?

MISS LYLE—Because I don't know what they are myself.

FITLER—You must know what they are, Tony!

MISS LYLE (*raising her left hand to silence him*)—Listen, Gehring, it isn't only my mind that's changed, it's everything about me.

FITLER—Well, what has caused the change, Tony? There must be some reason for it.

MISS LYLE—There is; but that reason is not enough in itself to have made the change that has come about in me.

Gehring, still unsatisfied, is insistent upon a further explanation and gradually Antoinette tells him what she can.

It is true, as she said, that she had not met any one in Europe who had been responsible for the change in her. But it is also true that she has met some one since she returned home.

"I met him the day after I got back," Antoinette confesses, "and he was the first man that ever held me cheap."

Since that adventure she has come to know many things. Among others that she never had been in love before. She may have thought she loved Gehring, now she knows she did not even know the meaning of the word.

"What did he do that you say he held you cheap?" demands Fitler.

"He simply looked at me. And listened to my inane chatter. . . . He looked at me in a way that made me see myself through his eyes."

"But why should you regard his estimate of you as so important?"

"Because it was the true one!—the one that I've been gravitating toward myself for a long time. The estimate of a sane and decent and worthy man."

No one of his arguments can change her fixed estimate of her own unworthiness. Nothing can alter her conviction that they, she and Gehring, can never be anything to each other. She is desperately sorry for him, for herself, for all of them. But there they are—and nothing can be done to change that.

Gehring pleads earnestly for that other chance to which he feels entitled. Given that he is certain of his ability to make life take on a new hope for her, and give him back not only the self-respect that perfect devotion to a new ideal would inspire, but perfect happiness in the achievement as well. If she denies him now what is to become of him? He will probably drink himself to death!

Miss Lyle—It's that quality in you, Gehring, that's part of the hopelessness of all this.

Fitler (*coming forward at the right*)—I can't *help* it, Tony; I am what I am. (*Moving towards her.*) One of those men that simply *must* have some woman to devote his life to. And what woman *could* I devote my life to after you?

Miss Lyle—You have no idea how funny that sounds to me.

Fitler—That's because you're depreciating yourself, dear, (*she shakes her head slowly from side to side*) just as everybody does when he's first in love.

Miss Lyle—I'm simply not deceiving myself any longer.

Fitler—Why, what have you *done*, Tony, that you should have such an idea?

Miss Lyle (*vehemently*)—I've done nothing at all! That's precisely the point. With every advantage that a girl could possibly have, I've done absolutely nothing.

Fitler—Well, what *could* you have done in your position?

Miss Lyle (*rising, and violently*)—I could have been *civil* to people, at least; (*she passes in front of him and continues towards the right*) and I haven't been. *You* should know *that*, if anybody should.

Fitler (*moving to the center of the room*)—I haven't minded that, Tony.

Miss Lyle—Well, I should have minded it, for I knew better. (*She turns and comes forward.*) But I had a rôle to play. The Notorious Tony Lyle—that ridiculed every sincerity and thought it smart to say and do the meanest and most embarrassing thing to everybody on every occasion.

Fitler—You haven't done anything of the kind.

Miss Lyle (*raising her hand to him*)—I know *exactly* what I've done, Gehring. (*She moves down to the right.*) You can't tell me anything about it. (*She comes to a stop and stands looking straight out. And there is a pause. He stands looking at her.*) I've been a law unto myself ever since I can remember; and people have been stupid enough to put up with it,—and develop in me an arrogance of attitude, and sense of self-importance, that seems so cheap and ridiculous to me now (*she moves across towards the left again*) that I want to run away somewhere, and hide myself for the rest of my life.

FITLER—I can't see that you've done very differently from any other girl in your set.

MISS LYLE (*passing below the bench and up towards the back of the room at the left*)—Well, that set has become intolerable to me. (*She turns at the back of the room and comes forward again, at the right of the bench.*) I haven't one single accomplishment.

FITLER—That isn't true, Antoinette.

MISS LYLE—Not a solitary one; for I've never done anything that required the slightest exertion or caused me the least inconvenience.

FITLER—You have many accomplishments.

MISS LYLE—Well, tell me what they are.

FITLER—I can't enumerate them offhand.

MISS LYLE (*turning away, and moving forward to the lower corner of the bench*)—Because they're not there to enumerate.— I can sputter a few French phrases, and I've read the latest dirty novel; and that's the extent of my accomplishments. (*She sits on the bench and taps her foot on the floor. Suddenly she turns and looks at him.*) I've never even been to school; did you know that? For I refused to go; and when instructors were brought here they refused to stay; because I laughed at the idea of correction or discipline of any kind. (*She turns away again, and makes a little sound of bitter amusement.*) I don't believe I could add up a single column of figures, and do it correctly.

FITLER—A girl in your position has no particular need of accomplishments of that kind.

MISS LYLE (*turning to him with a touch of anguish*)—It isn't the *lack* of accomplishment that I'm deploring; it's the lack of the quality in *me*—that goes into the making of accomplishment. —I seem to have absolutely nothing—(*she looks away out, searchingly*) but the ability to see that nothingness. I suppose that's rather an unfortunate ability in a girl situated and brought up as I've been; for sooner or later it's bound to bring her face to face with herself.

FITLER (*turning away, and half-sitting on the arm of the center chair*)—I don't think you'd have come to any such conclusion if you hadn't met this man.

Miss Lyle—Oh, yes, I would; this has been growing on me for a long time. I think it began rather definitely about three years ago, when a girl had to come out here from my father's office to go over some things with me in my mother's estate.—I remember it was about three o'clock in the afternoon when she came, and I wasn't up yet. I had danced till nearly six that morning, and I was dead. So I had them send her upstairs. And when she came into my room—and I listened to her for a while—I found myself thinking—what a *nice* girl she was—so clear and intelligent. And I thought she'd probably been up since seven in the morning,—going over my *undistributed* income. (*She gives a hard little laugh.*) And it appealed to my sense of humor. And I got the impression that it appealed to hers. I felt so messy, and stupid, and common, by comparison. And that's exactly the way I felt when this man looked at me here a month ago. (Fitler *is annoyed.*) I was a product that he didn't approve. A kind of —social curiosity, that he didn't quite think should be publicly exhibited.

Fitler—He probably didn't think anything of the kind.

Miss Lyle—It was in his eyes; I could see it. I resented it terribly at first, of course; I'd been accustomed to a different attitude from men. But after I'd listened to him at dinner, and then afterwards, the few times he was here, I found myself thinking, why not?—Why shouldn't he regard me in that way?

Fitler (*rising impatiently*)—You might feel very different about him and his impressions if you knew him better.

Miss Lyle—I wouldn't feel different about my own.

Still Gehring pleads for another chance, and still Antoinette stands firm. That he will give her his word does not interest her. Whenever has his word amounted to anything? That he will try to be different she admits as likely, but he has been drinking and idling ever since she has known him, and that is indicative of their kind.

"Listen, Gehring—eleven out of the fourteen girls that came out the year I came out have been married since and divorced. And some of them married again and divorced. . . . I can't afford the risk. . . . I will not become one of those caricatures of women that I am running into all over the world. Disillusioned and divorced, and married and divorced again—like a lot of horrible monkeys. My life is sufficiently ridiculous, without making it any more so."

Nor is Eleanor Ridgway, who passes Gehring in the hall as he is leaving, any more successful in trying to extract reasonable explanations from Antoinette. Gehring, she reports, looks a good deal like a dead man to her, and she thinks that demands at least some explaining. She is really alarmed for Gehring.

Antoinette has done nothing to the young man, she insists. Nothing more than to tell him that any idea of a marriage between them is quite out of the question. That may be, as Eleanor fears, the finish of Gehring, Antoinette agrees, but it also may be the finish of her. There is nothing that Antoinette can do about it.

"Gehring Fitler and I are the only ones who could do anything in this case and we haven't done it. And now we've got to face the result."

"What is it, Tony? Things are never nearly so hopeless after they have been talked over with some one, and I think you ought to be able to talk it over with me. What is it, dear?"

Miss Lyle—I'm simply what you call—in love, I suppose. And it's done something to me. It's given me an entirely different point of view—about myself, and my life; and the lives of everybody that's made up my life. It's sort of crystallized—and clarified—everything. (*She makes a little sound of bitter amusement.*) That must sound rather ironic to you, Eleanor.

Mrs. Ridgway—It doesn't at all, my dear.

Miss Lyle—After all the fun I've made of people who were in love. And of you, particularly.

Mrs. Ridgway—You simply didn't understand it then, Tony.

Miss Lyle—I do now. And I understand how you were able to go through all you did. I believe you said something about that—that day you two were out here.

Mrs. Ridgway—I don't remember, dear.

Miss Lyle—Something about it simply being a question with me of meeting the man.

Mrs. Ridgway—I knew that's all it was, Tony.

Miss Lyle—Well,—I've met him, Eleanor; and I agree with you. (*There is a shrewd pause, during which* Mrs. Ridgway *thinks narrowly; then looks directly at* Miss Lyle.)

Mrs. Ridgway (*in a level tone*)—Who is it, Tony,—Spencer Train? (Miss Lyle *is very still. Then she turns her head slowly and meets* Mrs. Ridgway's *eyes. She inclines her head.*)

Miss Lyle—Yes—that's who it is. (*Her eyes travel down and along the floor.*) I suppose women don't usually mention names in cases of unrequited love,—but I don't mind *your* knowing it.

I've set him up as a kind of standard, Eleanor; and the men of my acquaintance have suffered so horribly by comparison that the thought of marrying any one of them is simply beyond my powers of imagination.

MRS. RIDGWAY—Have you seen him at all lately?

MISS LYLE—Where would I see him?

MRS. RIDGWAY—I thought he might have called you up or something.

MISS LYLE—*He* doesn't want to see *me*, Eleanor.

MRS. RIDGWAY (*coming forward at the right*)—You don't know whether he does or not.

MISS LYLE—The eyes of love are keen, my dear.

MRS. RIDGWAY—Mr. Train might be very much interested in you if he knew you better.

MISS LYLE—Why *should* he be, Eleanor?

MRS. RIDGWAY—Because you have many qualities that are worthy of his interest. (MISS LYLE *makes a movement of deprecation.*) But he certainly can't know about them, Antoinette, if you sit out here brooding like a recluse, and refusing to let anybody know that you're even out here.

MISS LYLE—I haven't been brooding, I've been thinking.

MRS. RIDGWAY—Well, whatever you've been doing, it's been very bad for you (*she moves forward, down to the right*) for you've no idea how you look. I got a positive shock when I saw you. And if I'd known about it before, you may be sure I'd have done something.

MISS LYLE—Well, you mustn't throw me at Mr. Train, either, Eleanor, now that you do know about it—

MRS. RIDGWAY—I can't throw you at him—

MISS LYLE—I won't allow it.

MRS. RIDGWAY—He isn't here. (MISS LYLE *becomes suddenly still.*)

MISS LYLE—Where is he?

MRS. RIDGWAY—He's in Mexico on business; he won't be back before the middle of September. (MISS LYLE *gets up wearily, and moves away.* MRS. RIDGWAY *goes to her.*) But, as soon as he comes back, Tony, we've got to do something in the way of meeting him.

MISS LYLE—To what end, Eleanor?

MRS. RIDGWAY—Why, to interest him, of course.

MISS LYLE—So that he'd ask me to marry him, I suppose.

MRS. RIDGWAY—Well, why not, Tony?

MISS LYLE—Because it wouldn't be fair, Eleanor. (MRS.

RIDGWAY *is annoyed.*) Mr. Train is a good man; and what have *I* left to give him?

MRS. RIDGWAY—Why, you have ycurself, Tony. (MISS LYLE *makes a sound of vast amusement.*)

MISS LYLE (*moving back to the center chair*)—After all the rest, I suppose?

MRS. RIDGWAY—Why, what do you mean, Antoinette?

MISS LYLE (*speaking low and direct*)—After Lennie Rooks— that I lived with for four months at San Sebastian the summer before last. And Harvey Price—that I separated from his wife, and paid *her* a hundred thousand dollars to keep my name out of it. And the string of others that I've taken and used when I've wanted them, and then flung them aside—when I didn't want them any longer.

MRS. RIDGWAY (*aghast*)—I won't believe a word you're saying, Antoinette!

MISS LYLE—It's the truth—whether you believe it or not!

MRS. RIDGWAY—You're simply lovesick, Tony, and you're exaggerating things.

MISS LYLE—Maybe I am; but that hasn't prevented me from thinking clearly. And one of the things that I've been thinking is—that we can only do—what we are ready to do.

Robert Lyle, home from his latest South American pilgrimage, bursts in upon them. He is a breezy, confident, enthusiastic sort of person and he seems genuinely pleased at being with his daughter again. But he, too, is seriously exercised at Antoinette's appearance. Surely something is wrong with her. Probably lack of exercise. If not that, lack of interest. She should open the seashore place. She should go somewhere, do something, to lift her out of the depression that has evidently settled upon her.

Now Mrs. Ridgway has gone on to visit her mother and Antoinette and her father are alone. There is the natural exchange of news regarding their respective trips, the confession of Antoinette that she could not stand traveling with the Farnsworths, and, finally, with some urging on his daughter's part, the confession of Mr. Lyle that it is true, as she has heard, that he has given some little thought to marrying again. Still, he points out, "it is rather a long way between thinking about a thing and actually doing it."

The thought of marrying has occurred to him, just as it has occurred to many others—just as it has occurred no doubt to Antoinette herself. But he has no intention of making any such move until after she is herself married. Then, perhaps, if he finds existence too lonesome—

But Antoinette has no intention of marrying, she tells him. She is particularly anxious that he should not wait for her. No, she has had no misunderstanding with Gehring Fitler. Even if she should marry, it would not be Gehring. She neither loves Gehring nor respects him very much. And she has been frank enough to tell him so.

Now that Gehring understands, continues Antoinette, and she has, even belatedly, come to realize how she has been standing in the way of her father's possible happiness—just because he did not want to bring a stepmother into their home—she is eager that he should go ahead with his plans.

But Mr. Lyle is not sure that he wants to marry again. He has been content. True, they have not seen any too much of each other, he and his daughter, but that has been largely his fault. He has travelled too much.

Antoinette will not accept this explanation. Their separations have been largely due to her own selfishness, she insists. She could have been more with her father, if she had wanted to. But she has consulted her own pleasures. She did not think about that, just as she did not think about his ever wanting to marry again. Now she is not only reconciled to the thought of yielding the scepter, but eager that he should first of all consider his own happiness.

MR. LYLE (*smiling as he slips down beside her on the divan*)— You're such a sudden old lady.

MISS LYLE—I suppose that's the way one grows old,—very suddenly.

MR. LYLE (*taking her hand, leaning his cheek against hers, and putting his right arm around her shoulders*)—Well, can't we spend our declining years together, darling? Just you and I, sitting here in the sunset of life, talking about old times. (*He kisses her, looks at her, and laughs.*)

MISS LYLE—I don't like the prospect, Father.

MR. LYLE—But, if I am satisfied.

MISS LYLE—But, you're not.

MR. LYLE—I am with *you*.

MISS LYLE—But, I may not always be here.

MR. LYLE—Where will you be?

MISS LYLE (*wistfully*)—Oh,—a thousand places.

MR. LYLE—You know what I think, Tony?—I think you're in

love. (*He pats her hand and rises.*) Yes, sir, by George, if I don't. I think you like Gehring a great deal more than you think you do. (*She looks out and away.*) And he's been your beau for a long time. And when you don't see him coming around any more, you're going to miss him. Now, you see if you don't. Blessings brighten as they take their flight, you know, Tony. And that beau thing is a habit that it isn't so easy to get out of. (*He turns and strolls towards her again.*) Yes, sir, I'll bet you two'll have it all made up again before the month is out. You'll never be able to keep Gehring away from here; remember what I'm telling you. And after you've seen him a few times, you won't *want* to keep him away. (*He leans over ana pats her hands.*) Now, you see if I'm not right. (*He turns towards the left again.*) I know a little something about that business. Only, in the meantime, we'll have to see what we can do about finding you *another* beau—(*he turns and looks at her, with a twinkle in his eye*) unless you want to let *me* be your beau. (*She doesn't smile; and he moves towards her.*) I've had a lot of experience. And I can start in rather impressively, too; for I brought you something *ver-ry* nice from Buenos Aires. (*He plays a little tattoo on her hands again.*) I have it out here in my satchel. I'll go right now and get it for you. And when you see it, you'll be sorry you ever had any other beau. (*He dashes out of sight. She breaks suddenly and weeps bitterly. The telephone bell rings out at the left. She straightens up and tries to look composed.* EDWARDS' *voice can be indistinctly heard on the telephone.*)

EDWARDS—Hello— Why, no, she isn't; I'm sorry; she left here a few minutes ago.—I'm sorry, I don't.—Well, will you wait just one moment, please; I'll ask her cousin, Miss Lyle; she may know.—Not at all. Just wait one moment. (*There is a slight pause, then* EDWARDS *appears in the left door.*) There's a gentleman on the telephone, Miss Lyle, that would like to speak to Mrs. Ridgway.

MISS LYLE—Mrs. Ridgway has gone.

EDWARDS—Yes, Miss, I told him that, and he asked me if I knew where he might get in touch with her right away; he says it's very important.

MISS LYLE—Who is it, *Mr.* Ridgway?

EDWARDS—No, Miss, it's a gentleman calling from the Bachelors' Club.

MISS LYLE (*rising*)—Hang up out there, Edwards. (*She goes up and across at the back, to the telephone.*)

EDWARDS (*withdrawing*)—Yes, Miss.

MISS LYLE (*at the telephone*)—Hello— No, this is Mrs. Ridg-way's cousin, Miss Lyle— Oh, how do you do, Mr. Sloane.—Why, I'm sorry, Mr. Sloane, she just left here about ten minutes ago.—Yes, she said she was going over to her mother's place.—Yes, it's Beechwood, three, four, eight. But, I don't think she's reached there yet, Mr. Sloane; she's only been gone from here a few minutes.—Yes, it's too bad. But, she'll probably stop back here again on her way into town, so if you want to leave any message, in case you don't get in touch with her.—Yes, I shall, Mr. Sloane.—What sort of an accident, Mr. Sloane; anything serious?—Oh, my God, how dreadful—I hope it isn't anybody *I* know—(*She listens acutely, then suddenly utters a short, breathless moan and sinks upon the telephone table, dropping the telephone and receiver from her hands. The receiver falls clear of the table and swings back and forth. After a black moment, she drags herself into a standing position.*) Oh, my God—(*She staggers uncertainly and slowly backwards from the telephone, looking at it curiously, and reaching out blindly with her right hand, for support. As she nears the center chair, she turns slowly and looks straight out, hollow-eyed.*) Ah, Gehring, you poor boy—(*She moves a step or two forward, then lifts her left hand towards the door and says faintly*) Father—(*She falls in a dead faint. The telephone receiver swings back and forth.*)

The curtain falls.

ACT III

About the middle of September, Antoinette's condition having steadily grown worse, Mr. Lyle has called in Dr. Loebell, a specialist in mental diseases, to consult with Dr. Huntington, the Lyle family physician.

Dr. Loebell has just come from Antoinette's room and in the library is making his report to Mr. Lyle. There are certain prescriptions he would like to have filled, and certain minor changes he would like to see made in the general attitude of the nurses and the family toward Antoinette.

The specialist finds the case extremely interesting, and, in one particular at least, rather encouraging. Antoinette can still laugh. In the quite long talk he has just had with her she had broken into a peal of laughter that was healthy and indicative.

MR. LYLE—What was she laughing about, Doctor? (LOEBELL *makes a gesture of significance.*)

LOEBELL—That's a very important point, Mr. Lyle,—very important indeed. If I could be sure of that, I think I could be sure of a great many other points in the case. But there's a factor of feminine reservation there; and your daughter is very shrewd. She let me know only as much as she wished me to know.

HUNTINGTON—I daresay you were able to discover certain things for yourself, though, weren't you, Doctor?

LOEBELL—Oh, yes, yes—experience counts for something, I suppose.

MR. LYLE—Have you had similar cases to this one in your experience, Doctor?

LOEBELL—I have had about five, I should say, Mr. Lyle, in my time. Not recently; but years ago they were not at all uncommon—especially among women. They used to be known in those days as cases of repining,—lack of the will to live. But they've become rather rare these late years; due, I have no doubt, to the many compensating factors in modern life—people are not apt to take any one experience too seriously nowadays. But, they *do* occur occasionally.

MR. LYLE—Is there any way of accounting for them, Doctor?

LOEBELL—Yes, there are a great many ways, Mr. Lyle; but, unfortunately, they lead us into considerations of psychology; and the medical profession has probably thought it wiser to avoid those considerations. But, nevertheless, we are being constantly confronted with them. I daresay you've encountered something of the kind from time to time in your practice, haven't you, Doctor?

HUNTINGTON—Yes, indeed I have, Doctor—

LOEBELL—Yes.

HUNTINGTON—Many times.

LOEBELL—I'm sure of it.

HUNTINGTON—It's rather disquieting, too, (LOEBELL *makes a little sound of amusement*) to an orthodox medical practitioner.

LOEBELL—Yes, very disquieting, indeed. We've probably been hugging certain of our present theories too closely.

HUNTINGTON—I'm afraid so, Doctor.

LOEBELL—Yes, I'm afraid we have. Particularly, the theory that the physical condition is simply the chorus of its atoms.

HUNTINGTON—Yes, I think we've been holding that one much too closely.

LOEBELL—Much too closely, I agree with you. I think we need hardly go beyond the present case for a contradiction of it.

HUNTINGTON—I was just thinking that myself.

MR. LYLE—You mean that my daughter's physical condition seems pretty good, Doctor?

LOEBELL—Surprisingly good, Mr. Lyle. In fact, in that respect I can't do any more than confirm the diagnosis of Doctor Huntington here.

MR. LYLE—How do you account for these sinking spells she's been having, Doctor?

LOEBELL—Well, I think they can be accounted for very largely on the basis of malnutrition, Mr. Lyle; I understand that she eats practically nothing.

MR. LYLE—Nothing at all.

LOEBELL—Well—that—with certain emotional reaction, would very easily bring about a condition of that kind. But, in my opinion, it is chiefly with that emotional reaction that we have to deal—to discover the *cause* of it. Because it is my conviction, Mr. Lyle, that your daughter is simply—lovesick. (MR. LYLE *keeps his eyes on him steadily; and there is a shrewd pause.* HUNTINGTON *shifts his eyes from* LOEBELL *to* MR. LYLE.) I asked her very bluntly if she were in love; and that was when she laughed. But she laughed a bit too long, I thought; and I got the impression that the laughter was something in the nature of a *disguised* reaction—that I had put my finger on the point. (MR. LYLE *smiles wryly, and with a glance at* HUNTINGTON, *moves towards the back of the room, where he turns and starts forward again.*) So I am going to ask *you*, Mr. Lyle, if *you* can be of any assistance to us in this case.

MR. LYLE—How do you mean, Doctor?

LOEBELL—I mean in the matter of information; for I'm convinced that there's a *man* here.

Mr. Lyle admits that there is a man, though he has never met him. And this man, by all reports, is most desirable, though that fact does not appear to have influenced Antoinette at all, "except as a sort of standard of comparison for the other men of her acquaintance."

"That's the most unfortunate part of it," continues Mr. Lyle; "for the result of the comparison is the fixed idea in her mind that she's unworthy of this man's attention—or of anybody's attention, for that matter."

"It's part of the idealism of feminine love," ventures Dr. Loebell.

Nor is Antoinette's reaction either uncommon or at all extreme, according to the specialist. The fact that because of it she promptly broke her engagement to the young man to whom she had been engaged for three years, and that he had gone straight to the Bachelors' Club after leaving her and shot himself, undoubtedly has affected Antoinette deeply: certainly she was in no condition for so severe a shock.

Now, Dr. Loebell is convinced, there is but one thing to do. They must send for the man.

Mr. Lyle, fortunately, has already done so. Train is just back from Mexico, having arrived the night before, and Eleanor Ridgway is to bring him to Shadow Brook as soon as she can get in touch with him, which will probably be some time during the day.

As for the results that may reasonably be expected to follow this meeting Dr. Loebell is hopeful but none too sanguine.

"You don't think I've possibly let it go too long?" anxiously inquires Mr. Lyle.

"Well, of course, that remains to be seen. I have seen patients that were worse get better, and patients that were better, get worse. However, I would suggest that when this man comes here, your daughter does not see him alone—for the first time, at least. I think it would be better if some one else were present, yourself, or your niece, or some other member of the family."

"I see."

"Because I don't think your daughter is quite in the condition at the present time to withstand any very serious emotional reaction."

It is the specialist's idea, too, that Mr. Lyle should meet Train, when he comes, and quite freely explain the situation to him. "It seems to me that it would be better to present the situation on the basis of a romantic attachment rather than a medical necessity," he explains.

In taking his departure Dr. Loebell again seeks, with professional optimism, to strengthen the hope of a cure. He remembers that in a similar case he was called to attend a young lady who had quarreled with her fiancé and immediately fallen into a serious decline. She was in a dying condition, but four days after the young man was brought back to her she was well enough to elope with him.

Eleanor Ridgway and Spencer Train have been waiting until the doctors have left. Now they are shown in and are anxious to know Antoinette's condition and what they can do to help.

Mr. Lyle is apologetic for having had to send for Mr. Train, but Mr. Train is not only glad that he was sent for, but is most eager to do anything he can to be of assistance. Mrs. Ridgway has told him something of Antoinette's condition and of the part he unknowingly has played in it.

"Dr. Loebell assures me that there are factors of feminine psychology in the case," explains Mr. Lyle, "that are quite beyond his reach. He says that my daughter has evidently been impressed, in a rather extreme degree, by some *man:* and while she has never discussed anything of the kind with me, she appears to have done so with my niece, Mrs. Ridgway; and *she* tells me, Mr. Train, that *you* are that man. (*There is a second's stillness.*) As a matter of fact, she told me this some time ago, and suggested that I write you,—or allow her to do so; but, as I say, the whole thing seemed so vague and incredible to me, that I didn't think it quite fair to annoy you with it. But, when she told me you were coming back, I thought at least it wouldn't do any harm to ask you to come out. And Professor Loebell here to-day seemed to think that that was really the only thing that could be done."

"In what way does he suggest that I can be of assistance, Mr. Lyle?"

"In the way of—mental stimulation, I think." Mr. Lyle smiles pathetically, and a little helplessly, at his inability to explain further. "At least that is what I gathered from the way he talked. He says that that is what he has been obliged to do in other cases of the kind, and the results have usually justified it.—But,—for some reason or other, Mr. Train,—at least, so Mrs. Ridgway tells me,—my daughter has the impression that you don't *want* to meet her—that you didn't like her when you met her here last summer."

Mr. Train is very sorry that Miss Lyle should feel as she does and quite at a loss to understand. He has met her but a few times, does not know her well at all and has never been conscious that either of them had ever created any sort of definite impression upon the other. Certainly he has not been attracted to Antoinette by considerations of her social position, he replies to Mr. Lyle's queries, nor would he have been influenced by that or any similar considerations if he had been so attracted.

TRAIN—Your daughter and I have been derived from such very different settings, Mr. Lyle, that I'm afraid nothing very satisfactory could come of an interest in each other. (*He looks at* MR. LYLE; *and* MR. LYLE *holds his eye for a second and smiles.*)

MR. LYLE—You mean that you wouldn't care to *allow* yourself to become interested?

TRAIN—It would involve a risk—that I shouldn't care to take —unnecessarily.

MR. LYLE—In what way, Mr. Train?

TRAIN—Our points of view are too dissimilar—particularly, our points of view in the matter of any ultimate relationship.

MR. LYLE—Do you feel that you know my daughter well enough to be sure of that?

TRAIN—I've heard something of an expression of her views on the subject.

MR. LYLE—On the subject of marriage, you mean?

TRAIN (*with a shade of apology*)—Yes. And I'm afraid we were very far from agreement. I think probably that may have been the reason she thought I didn't like her; she may have sensed something of that lack of agreement.

MR. LYLE—But, don't you think, Mr. Train, that many of these young people simply wish to give an impression of extreme sophistication?

TRAIN—I have no doubt that that is so, in a great many instances; but you'll pardon me, Mr. Lyle, if I say that I do *not* think it applies in the present one. (MR. LYLE *tilts his head, and looks at him curiously.*)

MR. LYLE—Why not, Mr. Train?

TRAIN—Because I think the kind of life that girls in your daughter's set are permitted to live rather tends to make that sophistication very real.

What he has believed of others in her set Train has come to believe of Antoinette through what he has heard of her and read of her activities in the society columns. Much of it no doubt has been idle and often untrue gossip. But all of it does imply an idea of personal liberty that is frightening to him, though, naturally, he does not wish to suggest that he is considering himself too much in the matter.

"But, as I say," he concludes, "I scarcely *know* your daughter—I didn't flatter myself that she even remembered me."

"Yes, she seems to have remembered you very well, Mr. Train. I think you must have come into her life at a particular psychological time. I've heard her say several times during the past

weeks that life had played out with her. And I blame myself
very largely for that, Mr. Train; she's probably been allowed to
live too intensively; and it's exhausted her life interest. (*Turning towards the back of the room.*) It's a great mistake; for it
leaves them absolutely nothing in the way of resource, when
they are confronted with something like this—something that *we*
cannot *buy* for them. (*He shakes his head ruefully.*) Life has a
strange way, Mr. Train, of stepping in and punishing us for
our idolatries— We through them, and they through us; and so
it goes—on out and around the world, I suppose,—until the
balance is adjusted."

As he is talking, one of the doors at back opens noiselessly,
"and the wraith of Miss Lyle, in a pale velvet negligee, leans
helplessly against the door jamb. She has the little book in her
hand that she was reading the day she met Train. There is a
physical stillness, broken suddenly by Antoinette's greeting."

"How do you do, Mr. Train?"

The men turn to greet her. Deeply concerned at her appearance Mr. Lyle rushes to his daughter's support and would urge
her back to her room. But Antoinette has eluded the nurse and
has no intention of returning until she has talked with Mr. Train.

They help her into a chair, and hover a little anxiously and
helplessly over her. Antoinette, however, is quite composed,
though plainly laboring under an emotional strain.

It seems an age, she confesses significantly, since she has seen
Mr. Train. She has been waiting for the middle of September.
Eleanor Ridgway had told her he was coming then. Probably
Eleanor has told him many things, too, about her being ill. And
her father? He, too, has been telling Mr. Train things. They
are all very, very subtle! But she has developed the cunning of
the invalid, and she knows—many things.

"It's a lost cause, I'm afraid," she smiles.

"You mustn't say that, my dear," protests Mr. Lyle.

"Yes, the bridegroom has tarried too long—in Mexico—even
if he were interested—which I'm sure he isn't."

"I wish I could make you understand how interested I am,
Miss Lyle."

"That's very chivalrous of you, Mr. Train, but how could you
be? It would be against the logic of things. And that is one
appreciation I have developed in these last few months." She
shakes her head wisely.

"What, Tony dear?"

"The stark beauty of the fact. I haven't an illusion left,—even about myself. And what is there after that?—For one only comes to that, I suppose, by way of one heartbreak or another."

Now she has sent her father away and insisted that she be permitted to say what she has to say to Mr. Train alone. It tires her to see him standing. She would have him sit near her. He draws up a stool and sits facing her.

Mr. Lyle is reluctant to leave them; fearful lest Antoinette will tire herself; pleading with anxious eyes that Spencer Train will understand all that he may hear. Assured by Antoinette that she is quite as comfortable as she possibly could be in her room, he kisses his daughter's hair tenderly and is gone.

"I hope they haven't been appealing to your chivalry here," she says to Train, when they are alone.

"No, they haven't been, Miss Lyle."

Miss Lyle—It occurred to me that they might be; and I didn't know how sentimental you were. I didn't want this affair to be made to appear in any way a tragedy of yours.

Train—It's quite tragedy enough for me, Miss Lyle, to see you so ill.

Miss Lyle—I'm sorry if it depresses you. But I'm really not so ill as I am—life-wearied. And no wonder, after all the madness of the past ten years. It exhausts me even to think of it. For it seemed that the days weren't long enough for all the frenzy that I wanted to crowd into them. And there was nobody to restrain me. And this is the result.

Train—I don't think you should blame yourself entirely for the result.

Miss Lyle—I don't, entirely—

Train—Considering what you say, I mean.

Miss Lyle—No,—up to a certain point, I daresay I was the victim of circumstances. But, after that I knew better. I've known better for several years. And yet it was during those years that I was particularly unrestrained. The recklessness of despair, probably. For something in my nature *told me* that I had blundered fatally; and that some day I would realize it. And I did. I realized it—the day I met *you*, Mr. Train. You seemed to symbolize something for me that in my madness I'd lost sight of. It was very curious. And as I've thought it over during these past few months, I've concluded that *you* were the first man that ever appealed to the maternal in me. For as I watched you that first day,—you were a strange mingling of the man and the little boy. One moment I saw only the man,—who attracted me; and immediately I decided upon my usual campaign—that had been so successful with many a man before you. —And then I'd see the little boy. And it suggested what a little boy of yours might look like. And that *did* something to me— A kind of casting out of the seven devils, I suppose. For at that point I decided to withdraw—in favor of a woman who could go to you—as a woman *should* go to her husband. I said to myself, "This man deserves a better fate. And that—little boy of his—deserves a better mother." (TRAIN *reaches slowly and takes one of her hands; and bows his head.*) You see, I can be very impersonal with you, Mr. Train; for, as I told you, I knew from the first,—that my cause was lost.

TRAIN—You make me feel very unworthy, Miss Lyle.

MISS LYLE—But you're not, I'm sure. And I realize that my telling you these things imposes upon you something of a rather solemn responsibility. For, after all, it may be that *I* am more or less the victim of the idealism with which I have invested *you:* so you must maintain my cause. (TRAIN *raises his head and looks into her eyes.*)

TRAIN—I think I could maintain it better with your honesty to help me.

MISS LYLE (*with a regretful smile*)—Too late for that, my dear Mr. Train. Besides, it wouldn't be just. My lamp was not trimmed and burning when the cry was raised; and so I mustn't whine—if I am not permitted to go in—to the marriage supper.

TRAIN—What can I say to you, my dear girl—

MISS LYLE—There's nothing to be said; and you mustn't reproach yourself. You couldn't be expected to know that I was capable of this; I didn't know it myself. And by the time I *did* know it,—it was too late. And, after all, perhaps it's unimportant.

TRAIN (*rising*)—I'm afraid it'll be very important to me.

MISS LYLE—No, I told you that this must not be in any way a tragedy for you.

TRAIN (*looking toward the back of the room*)—I've had my part in it. (*He moves up to the window and stands looking out.*)

MISS LYLE—The better part it was, though, Mr. Train,—remember that. And as for me—(*she fixes her eyes beyond time*) I've grown so old these past few months,—that already I find myself looking back on this,—as though it happened to some other girl—I knew when I was young. (*There is a silence, during which* TRAIN *moves slowly across towards the left, above the table.*) But, I'm indebted to you for a new experience, Mr. Train.

TRAIN—What is that, Miss Lyle?

MISS LYLE—You've made me sentimental.

TRAIN (*moving forward at the left of the table*)—Have I?

MISS LYLE—Yes.—I've had an unconquerable desire, these past few weeks, to see you once again—exactly as I saw you that first day I met you—when I said you looked like a bridegroom.

TRAIN—Yes, I remember.

MISS LYLE—You had a dark coat on; and a white rose—that Eleanor had given you down in the garden.

TRAIN—This is the coat.

MISS LYLE (*smiling wanly*)—And I have the rose.

TRAIN—Have you, really?

MISS LYLE (*opening the little book in her hand*)—Yes, you remember you pressed it for me in this book here.

TRAIN (*reaching for the book*)—Oh, yes, I remember.

MISS LYLE—I brought it down with me.

TRAIN (*lifting the pressed flower carefully out of the book*)—It's kept very well, hasn't it?

MISS LYLE—You see how sentimental I've become. (TRAIN *tries to smile, and puts the book down on the table.*) But a friend of mine told me that if I were to see you again, I should be disillusioned—that you'd suffer from—familiarity. And while I don't want to be disillusioned, so far as *you* are concerned, my love of *the fact* is even greaten than my fear of that disillusionment. So I'm going to ask you to put that rose in your coat again.

TRAIN—I'm afraid I can't, Miss Lyle; it'll break.

MISS LYLE—Then, just *hold* it—against your coat. I want to see if you really *are* the bridegroom I remember; for I feel somewhat better prepared to meet him now. (TRAIN *lifts the flower slowly to his lapel, and looks at her tenderly. She beholds the bridegroom again; and, raising her hand haltingly, in a gesture of unbearable sorrow, droops heavily across the arm of the chair, weeping bitterly.* TRAIN *puts the rose on to the table and steps to her side, kneeling on one knee.*)

TRAIN—Miss Lyle—you mustn't cry.—Miss Lyle, you mustn't cry that way. (*She gradually stops, from weakness.*) Antoinette

—(*she hears him say her name; then raises herself slowly and looks at him. He takes her in his arms*) don't cry. (*She weakly lifts her right hand and smooths his hair.*)

MISS LYLE (*sinking slowly back into the chair*)—My Beloved.

There is a note of alarm in Train's voice as he calls to Antoinette and she does not respond. He puts her gently back in the chair and summons the nurse. Miss Lyle has fainted, he thinks. The nurse quickly takes Antoinette's pulse. The look of concern deepens upon her face.

"Do you think I'd better carry her upstairs?" Train asks.

"I think so, yes, if you will, please. She shouldn't have come down at all."

The nurse leads the way and Train follows with the unconscious Antoinette in his arms.

For a moment the room is empty. Then Lyle is seen hurrying past the door into the hall at back. Shortly after the butler follows.

Mrs. Ridgway has returned to the library. Now she calls Sheppard, the maid, in from the hall to learn the details of Antoinette's collapse.

A moment later Train is back, plainly shocked by the experience he has been through. Tonelessly he tells Mrs. Ridgway what has happened.

MRS. RIDGWAY—I was looking at a book out there in the lounge, and I suddenly *felt* that something had happened. *I* thought that you and Uncle Robert were still in here.

TRAIN (*slowly picking up the rose and the book from the table*) —She said she wanted to talk to me alone for a few minutes.

MRS. RIDGWAY—What did she want to say to you, Spencer?

TRAIN (*mournfully*)—Oh—

MRS. RIDGWAY—Was it anything important?

TRAIN—She said a great many things to me, Eleanor.—She said she wasn't *ready* when the *bridegroom* came. (MRS. RIDGWAY *turns away slowly and moves across to the sofa at the right, where, covering her face with her hand, she sits down and weeps softly to herself. TRAIN looks out and away off.*) I'm wondering if *I* was ready, Eleanor.

MRS. RIDGWAY—But you *were* the bridegroom, Spencer. (TRAIN *shakes his head slowly.*)

TRAIN—No, I think perhaps the bridegroom, Eleanor, is the kind of thing that she had to give; and I think if I'd been ready,

I might have recognized it sooner than I did.—And it may not *come* my way again. (*The curtain commences to descend very slowly. He looks at the rose, then reverently places it in the book.*)

The curtain is down.

PORGY

A Drama in Four Acts

BY DOROTHY AND DU BOSE HEYWARD

THE Theatre Guild, grown now to an organization of 25,000 interested and apparently contented subscribers, began its new season on October 10, with a production of "Porgy," a folk play of the Charleston, S. C., negroes dramatized by Dorothy and Du Bose Heyward, from Mr. Heyward's novel of the same name, written two years before.

The leadership of the Guild in American theatricals has not been successfully challenged since its achievement some years back. The fact that it has of recent seasons devoted its outstanding talents to the production of several fine samples of American drama has notably strengthened its position. Dramas of the calibre of Sidney Howard's "The Silver Cord" and the same author's "Ned McCobb's Daughter," and that of S. N. Behrman's "The Second Man" the previous season not only added lustre to the Guild record but also did much to combat the formerly growing conviction that its directors were interested principally in the foreign drama, and held the efforts of native dramatists in slight esteem.

"Usually novels are verbose and diffuse in comparison with the slender architecture of a play," wrote J. Brooks Atkinson, the critic of the *Times*, in commenting upon the stage version of "Porgy." "But Mr. Heyward wrote his novel so economically—employing the neatly woven style typical of a poet dabbling in prose—that the play seems this time to be the looser medium. Instead of dominating the story, Porgy becomes one aspect of it in a Negro hippodrome on the Guild stage where fifty-three Harlem actors communicate the flavor of life in Catfish Alley. 'Porgy' as a play rarely dwindles to vivid acting between two or three characters. Usually the background teems with scrambling children and neighbors."

The action of the early scenes in "Porgy" occurs in "the court of Catfish Row, now a negro tenement in a fallen quarter of Charleston, but in Colonial days one of the finest buildings of the

212

aristocracy. The walls rise around a court, except a part of the rear wall of the old house, which breaks to leave a section of lower wall pierced at its centre by a massive wrought-iron gate of great beauty which hangs unsteadily between brick pillars surmounted by pineapples carved of Italian marble.

"By day, the walls of the entire structure present a mottled colour effect of varying pastel shades, caused by the atmospheric action on many layers of colour wash. A brilliant note is added by rows of blooming flame-coloured geraniums in old vegetable tins on narrow shelves attached to each window sill. All of the windows are equipped with dilapidated slat shutters, some of which are open, others closed, but with the slats turned so that any one inside could look out without being seen. The floor of the spacious court is paved with large flagstones, and these gleam in faintly varying colours under their accumulated grime.

"Beyond the gate and above the wall, one sees a littered cobbled street, an old gas street lamp, and, beyond that again, the blue expanse of the bay with Fort Sumter showing on the horizon. Over the wall can be seen masts and spars of fishing boats lying on the beach.

"By night, the court depends for its illumination upon the wheezing gas lamp, and the kerosene lamps and lanterns that come and go in the hands of the occupants of the Row."

The principal activity of the opening scene is the Saturday night crap game indulged by the men of the Row. Jake, a captain of the fishing fleet, is "rolling the bones" with characteristic pleas to the gods of the game. Mingo and Sporting Life are his opponents. The latter, "bootlegger to Catfish Row, a slender, overdressed, high-yellow Negro," would prefer to roll his own dice. But inasmuch as Jake is suspicious of the "cock-eyed dice" that Sporting Life carries, they are promptly ruled out of the game.

Now Robbins, "a well set up Negro of about 30," slightly in liquor, would join the game, and does join it, despite the pleading protests of Serena, his wife, "a self-respecting white folks' Negress."

The men play, the women look on, their comments acidly critical or amiable and friendly as their personal interests dictate. From down the street old Peter, the honey man, can be heard approaching, singing his wares. "Here comes de honey man. Yo' gots honey?—Yes, ma'am, I gots honey in de comb.—Yo gots honey cheap?—Yes, ma'am, my honey cheap."

Soon Porgy "drives up to the gate in his soap-box chariot. He is a crippled beggar of the Charleston streets, who has done much to overcome his handicap of almost powerless legs by supplying himself with a cart made of an upturned soap box, on two lopsided wheels, which bears the inscription, 'Wild Rose Soap, Pure and Fragrant.'

"Porgy is no longer young, and yet not old. There is a suggestion of the mystic in his thoughtful, sensitive face. He is black, with the almost purple blackness of unadulterated Congo blood."

Porgy is a crap-shooter, too, and eager to play. "I gots a pocketful ob de buckra money, an' he goin' to any man whut gots de guts fo' shoot 'em off me!"

There is talk of waiting for another player, Crown by name, and evidently a person to be reckoned with in the social life of the Row.

"I seen him comin'," reports Jim, "takin' de whole sidewalk, an' he look like he ain't goin' stan' no foolin'."

PORGY—Is Bess wid um?

JAKE—Listen to Porgy! I t'ink he sof' on Crown's Bess! (*All the men laugh.*)

PORGY—Gawd make cripple to be lonely. 'Taint no use for um to be sof' on a 'oman.

MARIA—Porgy gots too good sense to look twice at dat licker-guzzlin' slut.

LILY—Licker-guzzlin'! It takes mor'n licker fo' sati'fy Crown's Bess.

SERENA—Happy dus'! Dat's what it take! Dat gal Bess ain't fit for Gawd-fearin' ladies to 'sociate wid!

PORGY—Can't yo' keep yo' mout' off Bess! Between de Gawd-fearin' ladies an' de Gawd-damnin' men, dat gal ain't gots no chance.

JAKE—Ain't I tells yo' Porgy sof' on um? (*More laughter.*)

PORGY—I ain't neber swap one word wid she.

Now Crown and Bess arrive. "Crown is a huge Negro of magnificent physique, a stevedore on the cotton wharfs. He is wearing blue denim pants and tan shirt with a bright bandanna about his neck. From his belt hangs a long gleaming cotton hook.

"Bess is slender, but sinewy; very black, wide nostrils, and large, but well-formed mouth. She flaunts a typical, but debased, Negro beauty."

Fortified by the better part of a pint of liquor which he buys from Sporting Life and for which Bess pays, Crown is soon actively engaged in the crap game. He is ugly and suspicious, frequently accusing the others of grabbing up the dice before he is able to read them. If it is true that he is too cock-eyed to read the dice, Crown insists it is because he isn't drunk enough. A pinch of "happy dus' " is what he needs. Bess begs Sporting Life not to give Crown any of that stuff, but the ugly one insists and nervously inhales the powder.

"Frien' an' dice an' happy dus' ain't meant to 'sociate. Yo' mens bes' go slow," warns old Peter.

The game goes on. Now Porgy has the dice, apostrophizing them in a sort of sing song chant.

"Oh, little stars, roll me some light. (*Shoots.*) 'Leben little stars come home. (*Pulls in pot. All ante.*) Roll dis poor beggar a sun an' moon!" (*Shoots.*)

"Snake eyes!" reports Mingo, bending over the dice.

"Dem ain't no snake eyes," exults the optimistic Porgy. "Dey is a flock ob mornin' an' ebenin' stars. An' jus' yo' watch um rise for dis po' beggar." (*Shoots.*)

"Made um!" "Dat's he point," yell the others.

"Roll up dat nigger sleeve," protests the suspicious Crown. Porgy complies. "Well, yo' gots dem damn dice conjer den," growls Crown.

Now Robbins has the dice, with a nine to make. He "whistles, shoots, snaps his fingers, makes his point, sweeps up the dice and reaches for the money." But Crown seizes his wrist.

"Tech dat money an' meet yo' Gawd!" the bad man threatens.

"Take yo' han' off me, yo' lousy houn'!" warns Robbins, turning to Jake. "Han' me dat brick behin' yo'."

"Jake reaches brickbat and puts it in his free hand. Crown jerks his cotton hook out of his belt and lunges forward, bowling Robbins over, and knocking brick from his hand. Crown then steps back and kicks over lamp, extinguishing it."

In the dark the fight continues. Shafts of light thrown from the windows at which the excited onlookers have thrown open the shutters, reveal the fighters as they flash momentarily into view and are then lost in the darkness.

"Suddenly, out of the dark, Crown swings Robbins into a shaft of light, holding him by the throat at arm's length. With a triumphant snarl, he swings the hook downward."

"There is a dead silence now. In it Crown looks down at his hands, opening and closing them. Then he draws his arm across his eyes. . . ."

Out of the darkness Bess appears beside Crown. She shakes him violently by the arm.

BESS—Wake up an' hit it out. Yo' ain't got no time to lose.

CROWN (*looking stupidly into the gloom at* SERENA *and the body of her man*)—Whut de matter?

BESS (*hysterically*)—Yo' done kill Robbins, an' de police'll be comin'. (*She starts to pull him toward the gate.*)

CROWN—Whar yo' goin' hide? Dey knows you an' me pulls togedder.

(*In the half light, it can now be seen that the court has been deserted, except for* SERENA, *who sits beside the body with her head bowed, and sways from side to side with a low moaning. A match is scratched and held in* PORGY'S *hand. He is crouched on his doorstep. He looks toward* ROBBINS'S *body, and his face shows horror and fear. He gives a whimpering moan, and as the match burns out, he drags himself over his threshold and closes the door.*)

BESS—Dey wouldn't look fuh me here. I'll stay here an' hide. Somebody always willin' to take care ob Bess.

CROWN (*now at gate*)—Well, git dis: he's temporary. I'se comin' back when de hell dies down.

BESS—All right. Only git out now. Here, take dis.

(*Thrusts the money into his hand. She pushes him out of the gate. He disappears into the shadows. She turns around and faces the court. It is silent and empty except for the body and* SERENA. SPORTING LIFE *steps out of the shadows under* SERENA'S *steps, startling her.*) Dat yo', Sportin' Life? Fo' Gawd's sake, gib me a little touch happy dus'. I shakin' so I can hardly stan'. (*Suddenly remembering.*) Oh, I done gib all de money to Crown. I can't pay fo' um. But, for Gawd's sake, gib me jus' a touch!

SPORTING LIFE—Yo' ain't needs to pay fo' um, Bess. (*Pours powder into her hand.*) Sportin' Life ain't go back on a frien' in trouble like dese odder low-life nigger'. (BESS *inhales powder.*) Listen! I'll be goin' back up to Noo Yo'k soon. All yo' gots to do is to come wid me now. I'll hide yo' out an' take yo' on wid me when I go. Why, yo' an' me'll be a swell team! Wid yo' looks an' all de frien' I gots dere, it'll be ebery night an' all night —licker, dus', bright lights, an' de sky de limit! (*He looks apprehensively toward gate. Takes her arm.*) Come 'long! We gots to beat it while de beatin's good. (BESS *draws away sharply from his grasp.*) Nobody 'round here's goin' to take in Crown's Bess. Yo' bes' go wid yo' only frien'.

BESS—I ain't come to dat yet.

SPORTING LIFE—Well, de cops ain't goin' find me here fo' *no* 'oman! (*Slinks out gate.*)

(BESS *looks desperately about for shelter. She advances timidly and takes up lamp from the wash bench. She starts at rear left, and tries all of the doors as she goes. They are either locked, or slammed in her face as she reaches out to them. She comes to* MARIA'S *shop door, and as she reaches it, it is jerked open and* MARIA *confronts her.*)

MARIA (*in a tense voice*)—Yo' done bring trouble 'nough. Git out 'fore de police comes.

BESS—Yo' wouldn't hab a heart, an' let me in?

MARIA—Not till hell freeze! (*A light is lit in* PORGY'S *room, showing at window and crack in door.*)

BESS (*indicating* PORGY'S *room*)—Who lib ober dere?

MARIA—He ain't no use to yo' kin'. Dat's Porgy. He a cripple an' a begger.

(BESS *seems to agree with* MARIA *that* PORGY *is of no use to her. Crosses to gate, hesitates. Then she turns slowly toward* PORGY'S *room and crosses, shuddering away from* SERENA *and the body, which she must pass on the way. She reaches the door, puts her hand on the knob, hesitates, then slowly she opens it, enters, and closes it behind her.*)

It is seven o'clock the following evening. In Serena's room, a room "which still bears traces of its ancient beauty in its high panelled walls and tall, slender mantel with Grecian frieze and intricate scroll work," the body of the dead man, Robbins, lies on the bed. On its chest is a large blue saucer, half filled with coins. "Standing about the bed or seated on the floor are Negroes, all singing and swaying and patting with their large feet." There are a few kerosene lamps and these throw huge and fantastic shadows upon the yellowing walls.

The singing has been going on for hours and the monotony and steady beat of it has lulled several into a state of coma.

The spiritual of the moment is "Deat', ain't yuh gots no shame," with its recurring lines of accusation, "Take dis man an' gone, gone—Leabe dis 'oman, lone, lone—Deat', ain't yuh gots no shame?"

Peter, the honey man, slides modestly past the door, adds his coin to the saucer collection and joins the swayers.

Serena, the widow, seated at the foot of the bed, pauses in her dismal swaying long enough to reach for the saucer and count the coins. The result is disappointing. There is only fourteen dolluh and thirty-six cent in dat saucer. It cost more'n dat to bury Robbins, more'n twice dat, an' de Boa'd of Healt' demands that the dead man shall be buried the next day.

SERENA—What I goin' to do ef I ain't gots de money?

PETER (*understanding that they refer to saucer*)—Gawd gots plenty coin' fo' de saucer.

SERENA—Bless de Lo'd.

PETER—An' He goin' soften dese nigger heart' fo' fill de saucer till he spill ober.

SERENA—Amen, my Jedus!

PETER—De Lord will provide a grabe fo' He chillun.

CLARA—Bless de Lo'd! (*The swaying gradually changes to the rhythm of* PETER's *prayer.*)

PETER—An' he gots comfort fo' de widder.

SERENA—Oh, my Jedus!

PETER—An' food fo' de fadderless.

SERENA—Yes, Lo'd!

PETER—An' he goin' raise dis poor nigger out de grabe.

JAKE—Allelujah!

PETER—An' set him in de seat ob de righteous. Amen.

SERENA—Amen, my brudder. (*They all sway in silence.*)

ANNIE (*looking toward door*)—What dat?

CLARA—I hear somebody comin' up de steps now bringing much penny fo' de saucer. (MARIA *opens the door and looks out.*)

SERENA—Who dat?

MARIA—It's Porgy comin' up de steps.

JAKE (*starting to rise*)—Somebody bes' go help um.

MARIA—He gots help. Crown's Bess is a-helpin' um.

SERENA (*springing to her feet*)—What's she a-comin' here fo'? (*They are all silent, looking toward door.* PORGY *and* BESS *enter.* PORGY *looks about; makes a movement toward corpse.* BESS *starts to lead him across room.* SERENA *stands defiant, silent, till they have gone half the way.*) What yo' bring dat 'oman here fo'?

Bess, Porgy explains, has come to sing. She's a good shouter. But Serena is not mollified. Nor will she let Bess add her contribution to the saucer until Porgy assures her that it is not Crown's money Bess is offering, but some he has himself given

her. Then Serena accepts the money and permits Bess to help
Porgy to a seat on the floor. She draws the line at Bess' singing,
however. "She can sit ober dere in de corner, ef she want to.
But she can't sing."

The singing and swaying go on, Bess a silent participant. But
though she can control her voice she cannot keep her body from
following the rhythm of the others.

Suddenly the door is burst open and a detective strides into the
room, leaving police guards at the door. Abruptly the singing
stops. "All the Negroes' eyes are riveted on the white man and
filled with fear."

The detective recognizes the scene. Another "saucer-buried
nigger." Threateningly he bids Serena be sure that her man is
buried by the next day as he circles the room, gazing fixedly into
each fear-tortured face. Before Peter he pauses, fixes him with a
piercing gaze and shouts:

"You killed Robbins, and I'm going to hang you for it!"

Poor Peter is in a panic of fear. He can't hear. He can't
understand more than that he is being accused of something of
which he is innocent. Wailingly he protests his innocence, and
the others raise the protest to a chorus. But the detective, revolver drawn, drags Peter to his feet.

"Who did it, then? You heard me! Who did it?"

"Crown done um, boss. I done see him do um."

The detective is satisfied with this, but wants confirmation.
Quickly he wheels on Porgy and points the pistol in his face.

"You saw it, too!— Come! Out with it! I don't want to
have to put the law on you! Look at me, you damned nigger!"

"I ain't know nuttin' about um, boss," answers Porgy, gazing
calmly back into his accuser's eyes. Nor can further questioning
shake this testimony. He was asleep on his bed with his door
closed and he "ain't know nuttin' 'bout um." That's all the detective gets from Porgy.

They drag old Peter out as a material witness and promise that
they will lock him up until they hang Crown.

"I can't puzzle dis t'ing out," muses Porgy, when they have
gone. "Peter war a good man. And dat nigger Crown war a
killer an' fo'ever gettin' into trouble. But dere go Peter fo' be
lock up like t'ief, an' here lie Robbins wid he wife an' fadderless
chillun. An' Crown done lone he was fo' do de same t'ing ober
again somewheres else."

Gradually the singing and swaying are resumed. "What de
matter, Chillun?" is the next spiritual, with its wailing explana-

tion: "Pain gots de body an' I can't stan' still." "What's de mattuh, sistuh? What's de mattuh, sistuh?" "Jedus gots our brudder, an' I can't stan' still."

Now the undertaker, "a short yellow Negro with a low, oily voice, and dressed entirely in black," is in for a second conference with Serena. Heavy is his disappointment, too, when the widow is obliged to report but fifteen dollah in the saucer. Can't bury anybody for fifteen dollah.

"He gots to git buried tomorruh or de Boa'd ob Healt'll take um an' gib um to de students," explains Jake.

"Oh, fo' Gawd's sake, bury um in de grabeyahd," implores Serena, seizing the undertaker's hand in both of hers. "Don't let de students hab um! I goin' to work Monday, an' I swear to God I goin' to pay you ebery cent."

Tensely the mourners wait on the undertaker's answer. And he, affected, permits his professional manner to slip from him for the moment.

"All right, sistuh," he says, simply. "Wid de box an' one carriage it'll cost me more'n twenty-five, but I'll see yo' through."

Serena silently relaxes across the foot of the bed, her head between her outstretched arms, and an expression of vast relief sweeps into every face.

"You can all be ready at eight tomorruh. It's a long trip to de cemetery," the undertaker adds, and the Negroes' eyes, pathetic with gratitude, follow him to the door. Even Bess forgets the ban that has been placed upon her singing and lifts a strong, beautiful voice in triumphant chant.

BESS—"Oh, I gots a little brudder in de new grabeyahd
          What outshine de sun,
          Outshine de sun,"

(PORGY'S *voice joins hers*):

"Outshine de sun."

(*By the fourth line, many of the Negro voices have joined in, and the song grows steadily in volume and fervour.*)

"Oh, I gots a little brudder in de new grabeyahd
          What outshine de sun,
          An' I'll meet um in de Primus Lan'.""

(BESS'S *voice is heard again for one brief moment alone as it rises high and clear on the first line of the chorus*):

"I will meet um in de Primus Lan'!"

(*Then a full chorus, with deep basses predominating, crashes in on the second line of the refrain.* SERENA, *last of all, joins enthusiastically in the chorus.*)

"Oh, I'll meet um in de Primus Lan'!
I will meet um, meet um, meet um,
I will meet um, meet um, meet um,
I will meet um in de Primus Lan'!

"Oh, I gots a mansion up on high
What ain't make wid' han',
Ain't make wid han',
Ain't make wid han',
Oh, I gots a mansion up on high
What ain't make wid' han',
An' I'll meet um in de Primus Lan'!"

"The beautiful old spiritual beats triumphantly through the narrow room, steadily gaining in speed. Serena is the first to leap to her feet and begin to 'shout.' One by one, as the spirit moves them, the Negroes follow her example till they are all on their feet, swaying, shuffling, clapping their hands.

"Bess leads the 'shouting' as she has the singing, throwing her whole soul into an intricate shuffle and complete turn. Each Negro 'shouts' in his own individual way, some dancing in place, others merely swaying and patting their hands.

" 'Allelujahs' and cries of 'Yes, Lord,' are interjected into the singing. And the rhythm swells till the old walls seem to rock and surge with the sweep of it."

The curtain falls.

ACT II

A month later there is considerable excitement in the court of Catfish Row. This is the day of the picnic of "The Sons and Daughters of Repent Ye Saith the Lord," and everybody is going. Everybody, at least, except Porgy and Bess. Porgy wants Bess to go, and Jake, who is to be the marshal of the parade, insists that she is welcome. But Bess hasn't heard any invitations from the women of Catfish Row, and she thinks she'll stay home. She'd rather be with Porgy, anyway.

Serena, back from her white folk's job, brings news for Porgy. She has been talking to her white friends about Peter and they tell her a lawyer gentleman friend of theirs, a Mistah Archdale, will stop in the court to see Porgy about getting the old honey man out of jail. Serena has suggested Porgy as the proper one to talk to, despite her prejudice against his relations with Bess. She hates that "murderin' she-debil, dat Crown's Bess," and she is at no pains to hide her hate. Nor will she agree with Maria and Jake that Bess has made a big difference in Porgy's life.

"Go 'long wid yo'. Dat 'oman ain't de kin' fo' make cripple happy," sneers Serena. "It takes a killer like Crown fo' hol' she down."

"Dat may be so," admits Maria, "but Porgy don't know dat yet. An' 'sides, ef a man is de kin' what need a 'oman, he goin' be happy regahdless."

To which sentiment Jake also subscribes. "Dat's de trut', sistuh. Him dress she up in he own eye, till she stan' like de Queen ob Sheba to he."

Good or bad, Crown's Bess appears to have been good for Porgy. The cripple has softened noticeably the last month. He even brings candy to the chillun ob de court these days, and he used to hate 'em all.

Now Maria has another problem on her hands. She has been giving Sporting Life a late breakfast outside her cook shop, and she returns to the table just in time to catch him helping himself to a pinch of the happy dus' in which he deals. Before he can sniff it she has managed to open his hand and blow the powder away.

SPORTING LIFE (*furiously*)—What you t'ink yo' doin'! Dat stuff cos' money. (MARIA *stands back, arms akimbo, staring down at him for a moment in silence.* SPORTING LIFE *shifts uneasily in his chair.*)

MARIA (*in stentorian tones*)—Nigger! I jus' tryin' to figger out wedder I better kill yuh decent now, wid yo' frien' about yo' —or leabe yo' fuh de white folks to hang atter a while. I ain't say nuttin' no matter how drunk yo' gets dese boys on yo' rot-gut whisky. But nobody ain't goin' peddle happy dus' roun' my shop. Yo' heah what I say?

SPORTING LIFE—Come now, ole lady, don't talk like dese ole-fashioned, lamp-oil niggers. Why, up in Noo Yo'k, where I been waitin' in a-hotel—

MARIA—Hotel, eh? I suppose dese gal' yo' tryin' to get to go back to Noo Yo'k wid yo' is goin' to be bordahs! (*Shouting*): Don't yo' try any ob yo' Noo Yo'kin' roun' dis town. Ef I had my way, I'd go down to dat Noo Yo'k boat an' take ebery Gawd's nigger what come up de gangplank wid a Joseph coat on he back an' a glass headlight on he bussum an' drap um to de catfish 'fore he foot hit decent groun'. Yes! my belly fair ache wid dis Noo Yo'k talk. (*Bangs table so violently with her fist that* SPORTING LIFE *leaps from his chair and extends a propitiating hand toward her.*)

SPORTING LIFE—Dat's all right, Auntie. Le's you an' me be frien'.

MARIA—Frien' wid yo'! One ob dese day I might lie down wid rattlesnake, an' when dat time come, yo' kin come right 'long an' git in de bed. But till den, keep yo' shiny carcass in Noo Yo'k 'til de debble ready to take ch'ge ob um.

Simon Frazier, an elderly Negro, impressive in black frock coat, is a visitor. He, too, is looking for Porgy and he brings a message from the same Mistah Archdale, the lawyer. Porgy, it appears, has been in the habit of hitching his goat just outside the building in which Mistah Archdale has his law offices, and the latter has commissioned his friend, Lawyer Frazier, to inform Porgy that he should hereafter "Mobe on." The order is a bit puzzling both to Porgy and to Lawyer Frazier.

"I been hitch on dat corner mos' a mont' now," protests the cripple. "Why he don't want me 'roun?"

"I ain't quite make dat out," admits Frazier. "He say sompen 'bout de goat an' de commodity advertise on de chariot. (*Pointing to cart*): "Pure an' fragrant. Dat's soap, ain't it? I gather dat he t'ink yo' goat need soap."

Lawyer Frazier's more important business, it now appears, is with Crown's Bess. And if she is no longer Crown's Bess, but Porgy's Bess, then his business is with her just the same, because she will probably be wanting a divorce. Porgy doesn't quite understand.

FRAZIER—Ef de 'oman goin' stay wid' yo', she gots to hab divorce from Crown or else it ain't legal. (*Takes legal-looking document from pocket. Shows it to* PORGY. PORGY *looks at it, much impressed. Passes it to* BESS.)

PORGY—How much it cos'?

FRAZIER—One dollah, ef dere ain't no complications. (PORGY *looks dubious. Frazier quickly takes huge seal from his coat-tail pocket. Shows it to* PORGY.) When yo' gits divorce, I puts dis seal on de paper to show you has paid cash.

PORGY—Bess, yo' likes to hab divorce?

BESS (*with longing*)—Whut yo' t'ink, Porgy? (*The other Negroes are gradually edging nearer to listen.*)

Porgy—I goin' buy yo' divorce. Bring me my pocketbook. (Bess *goes into room and returns immediately with a number of small coins tied up in a rag, hands it to* Porgy. *He laboriously counts out a dollar in nickels and pennies. In the meantime,* Frazier *is filling in document with fountain pen. Group of Negroes now listening frankly.*)

Frazier (*pocketing coins*)—Wait a minute. 'Tain't legal yet. (*Holding paper in hands, lowers glasses on his nose. Begins in solemn tones*): Yo' name?

Bess—Bess. (Frazier *makes note.*)

Frazier—Yo' age?

Bess—Twenty-six yeah.

Frazier—Yo' desire to be divorce from dis man Crown?

Bess—Yas, boss.

Frazier—Address de co't as Yo' Honour.

Bess—Yas, Yo' Honour.

Frazier—When was yo' an' Crown marry? (Bess *hesitates.*)

Bess—I don' rightly 'member, boss— Yo' Honour.

Frazier—One yeah? Ten yeah?

Bess—Ain't I done tell yo' I don' remember?

Lily—She ain't neber been marry.

Frazier (*to* Bess)—Dat de trut'?

Bess—Yas, Yo' Honour.

Frazier (*triumphantly*)—Ah, dat's a complication.

Bess—I ain't know dat mattered.

Porgy—Yo' can't gib she divorce? Gib me back my dollah.

Frazier—Who say I can't gib she divorce? But, under circumstances, dis divorce cos' two dollah. It take expert fuh divorce 'oman whut ain't marry.

Bess—Don't yuh pay um no two dollah, Porgy. It ain't wuth it.

Frazier—Berry well, den, ef yo' wants to go on libbin' in sin. (*Takes coins from pocket and begins to count. Seeing that they do not weaken, he pauses abruptly in his counting.*) Seein' that we is ole frien', I goin' make dis divo'ce dollah an' er half.

With the official seal attached and the paper in his pocket, Porgy is quite happy. Frazier, too, takes pride in the knowledge that for a comparatively small sum he has made a lady out of a woman. But there is still one other complication that should be taken care of. Now that they have gone this far, the lawyer advises, Porgy and Bess should be stylish like the white folk and follow up divorce with a marriage license. But the thought of further complications is rather depressing to the contracting parties.

Catfish Row is continuing with its preparations for the parade and picnic and Porgy has gone to his room to rest when Alan Archdale, "a tall kindly man in early middle age, whose bearing at once stamps him the aristocrat," makes his visit. He inquires for Porgy, but curiously none of those he addresses ever heard the name—until Serena identifies Mistah Archdale as "folks." Then everybody remembers Porgy and is eager to fetch him out.

Archdale has come to see what can be done about Peter. Getting the facts from Porgy he thinks he can arrange bail for the old man. Which is good news to the Row, despite the fact that even as the kindly lawyer is arranging matters a buzzard flies overhead and threatens to light and there is a great commotion among the Negroes until he is driven off.

"Boss, dat bird mean trouble," Porgy explains. "Once de buzzard fol' he wing an' light ober yo' do', yo' know all yo' happiness done dead."

Only Serena is proof against the superstition. "It sho makes me 'shamed to see all dese superstitious nigger makin' spectacle ob demself befo' de w'ite gentlemans," she protests. "Ain't we all see dat buzzard sit smack on Maria's table day fo' yesterday? An' whut happen? Nuttin'! No bad luck 'tall."

"Bad luck!" answers Maria, indignantly. "What dat 'oman call bad luck? Ain't I had more drunk customer yesterday dan any day dis mont'? Day fair bus' up my shop."

Mistah Archdale also takes occasion to speak to Porgy about his use of the parking space directly in front of the Archdale offices. True, the lawyer admits, he has no objection to Porgy's taking his stand there; he has a place in his heart for the cripple, he admits, but none for the goat.

Still Porgy can't understand. It is a very nice goat. And he can't need soap, as Lawyer Frazier has intimated, because he has done eat up Serena's washin' soap for two weeks han' runnin'.

"He doesn't need it inside," Archdale admits.

Then the light breaks and Porgy agrees to scrub that goat until "you can't tell um from one ob dose rose bush in de park."

Lawyer Frazier, emerging from Maria's cook shop, is just in time to come in for an Archdale lecture, too. When the white lawyer hears of the promising business Frazier has been doing in selling divorces, with and without complications, he is of a mind to report the matter to the judge. Frazier has been warned before that if he does not cease being what the reformers call a "menace to morals" that he will be indicted.

Porgy (*suspiciously; handing paper to* Archdale)—Ain't dis no good as he stan', boss? 'Cause I ain't goin' to pay um fo' no more complications. (*As* Archdale *glances over the paper,* Porgy *glares vindictively at* Frazier.) Dat nigger come 'round heah in he By-God coat, an' fo' yo' can crack yo' teet', he gone wid yo' las' cent.

Archdale (*reading*)—"I, Simon Frazier, hereby divorce Bess and Crown for a charge of one dollar and fifty cents cash. Signed, Simon Frazier." Well, that's simple enough. (*Examines seal.*) "Sealed—Charleston Steamboat Company." Where did you get this seal?

Frazier—I done buy um from de junk-shop Jew, boss.

Archdale—Don't you know that there is no such thing as divorce in this state?

Frazier—I heah tell dere ain't no such er t'ing fuh de w'ite folks; but de nigger need um so bad, I ain't see no reason why I can't make one up whut sattify de nigger. (*His voice breaks.*) Dem divo'ce is keepin' me alibe, boss, an' whut mo', he is keepin' de nigger straight.

Archdale—How's that?

Frazier—Dat jedge say de gots to lib togedder anyhow till dey done dead. Dat's de law, he say. But nigger ain't make dat way. I done get my black folks all properly moralize, an' now he say he goin' jail me. Ef I stops now de nigger leabe each odder anyway. Ef it don't cos' de nigger nuttin' to leabe he wife, he ain't goin' keep she er mont'. But when he gots fuh pay dolluh to get 'way, he goin' t'ink twice 'fore he trabble. (Archdale *keeps from laughing with difficulty.*)

Bess—Ain't mah divo'ce no good, boss? Porgy done pay one dolluh an' er half fuh it.

Archdale (*looking at paper*)—I could hardly say that it is legal.

Bess—Legal! Dat wo'd mean good?

Archdale—Well, sometimes.

Porgy—Plenty ob our frien' is divo'ce', boss.

Archdale (*with accusing look at* Frazier, *who cringes*)—So I hear. (*Again consults paper.*) You've left this man, Crown, and intend to stay with Porgy.

Bess—Yes, suh.

ARCHDALE—I suppose this makes a respectable woman of you. Um—on the whole—I'd keep it. I imagine that respectability at one-fifty would be a bargain anywhere. (*Hands paper to* BESS. *Turns back to* FRAZIER.) But remember, Frazier: *No more divorces!* Or to jail you go. I won't report you this time.

There is much happiness for the moment. Frazier is cheered because of his promised immunity, and Porgy because, having heard the Archdale laughter he knows that he is not going to be made to move on from his beggar's stand.

Gradually the excitement incident to the departure for the picnic renews itself in the court. There is much scurrying back and forth, much adjustment of the gorgeously colored dresses of the women, the "Repent Ye Saith the Lord" sashes, and a general rounding up of all the excited young folk.

Porgy has gone back to his room and Bess sits on the steps outside wistfully watching the excitement. Sporting Life saunters in and tries to cheer her. First he urges her to go to the picnic. Then he tries to stimulate her enthusiasm by slipping her a bit of the happy dus' she is trying to quit.

Bess's resolution is slipping, and Sporting Life is just about to pour a pinch of the powder into her hand when Porgy's arm reaches out through the door and grabs the bootlegger's wrist in a grip that makes him drop the powder and cry out in pain. Then the hand is as quietly withdrawn.

"Go 'long, now," warns Bess.

"All right," agrees Sporting Life. "Yo' men frien' come and dey go. But 'membuh, ole Sporting Life an' de happy dus' here all along."

From a distance a band is heard playing "Ain't It Hard to Be a Nigger." One by one the excited picnickers pick up the words of the chorus, in no way discouraged by the discords of the musicians.

Porgy and Bess are sitting on their doorstep watching, and Porgy is again urging Bess to go. Jake, boat captain and marshal, adds his pleas to those of Porgy.

PORGY (*triumphantly*)—Dere! Don' yo' hear Jake ask yo' fo' go? Go 'long!

BESS—Plenty ob de mens ask me. Yo' ain't hear none ob de ladies sayin' nuttin'.

PORGY—Bess, yo' can put on my lodge sash an' be just as good as any 'oman in dat crowd.

BESS (*with a little laugh*)—Yo' an' me know it take more'n sash. (*The confusion grows. Picnickers once started on their way come scurrying back for forgotten bundles.* SCIPIO *runs in at gate in high excitement.*)

SCIPIO (*breathless; to* SERENA)—Ma, I gots good news fo' yo'.

SERENA—What dat?

SCIPIO—De bandmaster say I can be a orphan! (*The song breaks out in greater volume.*)

> "Ain't it hahd to be a nigger!
> Ain't it hahd to be a nigger!
> Ain't it hahd to be a nigger!
> 'Cause yo' can't git yo' rights when yo' do.
> I was sleepin' on a pile ob lumbah
> Jus' as happy as a man could be
> When a w'ite man woke me from my slumbah
> An' he say, 'Yo' gots fo' work now cause yo' free.' "

(*Other voices are calling back and forth: "How dem little nigger' can play!" "Ain't yo' ready! Time fo' go!" "We off fo' Kittiwah!" The band plays with more abandon.* BESS *wears the expression of a dreamer who sees herself in the midst of the merrymakers. Her feet begin to shuffle in time to the music.* PORGY *does not look up, but his eyes watch the shuffling feet.*)

PORGY (*mournfully*)—Yo' can't tell me yo' ain't wants to go. (*The Negroes troop across the court all carrying their baskets. In twos and threes they go out at the gate. Among the last to go,* MARIA *comes hurrying from her shop carrying a gigantic basket. Turns to follow the others. Sees* PORGY *and* BESS. *Hesitates. As though afraid of being left behind, turns again toward gate. Then resolutely sets down her basket.*)

MARIA—What de mattuh wid yo', sistuh? Ain't yo' know yo' late fo' de picnic? (*A sudden wave of happiness breaks over* BESS's *face. She is too surprised to answer.*)

PORGY—Bess says she ain't figgerin' to go.

MARIA (*crosses rapidly to them*)—Sho she goin'! Eberybody goin'. She gots to help me wid my basket. I gots 'nough fo' six. Where yo' hat? (*Reaches hat just inside door and puts it on* BESS's *head.*)

PORGY (*taking sash from pocket and holding it out to* BESS)— Here my sash, Bess.

(MARIA *unties* BESS's *apron. Throws it through door. Takes sash from* PORGY, *pins it across* BESS's *breast, jerking her peremptorily about to save time. Then starts for her basket.*)

MARIA—Come 'long now!

BESS (*hesitating*)—I hates fo' leabe yo', Porgy.

PORGY (*happily*)—I too happy fo' hab yo' go.

MARIA—Ain't yo' goin' help me wid dis basket? (BESS *hurries to her and takes one handle of basket.*) See yo' some mo', Porgy! (MARIA *crosses rapidly to gate. To keep her hold on the basket,* BESS *is forced to hurry.*)

BESS (*looking back*)—Good-bye, Porgy!

(MARIA, *apparently seeing the others far ahead and anxious not to be left behind, breaks into a lumbering run, dragging* BESS *after her.* BESS *is waving to* PORGY *as she goes. The voices of the Negroes grow fainter. Then the last distant crashes of the band are heard, and the court is quiet.* PORGY *sits on his doorstep dreaming, gazing happily into space, rocking a little. Takes pipe from his pocket, knocks out ashes; lights it. Across the sunlit walls falls the shadow of the buzzard flying lazily over the court.* PORGY *remains in happy abstraction, oblivious of the bird. Puffs leisurely at his pipe. The shadow hovers over his door; then falls across his face. He looks up suddenly and sees the bird. Swift terror sweeps into his face.*)

PORGY (*frantically*)—Get out ob here! Don' yo' light! Lef' it! Yo' hear me! Lef' it! (*He waves futile arms at it. The bird continues to hover above him.*) Get out! Somebody bring broom! Don' yo' light on my door, yo' debil! Help! Somebody help me! Oh, Gawd! (*He struggles down the steps and at last reaches the brick. The shadow wings of the bird close as it comes to rest directly over* PORGY's *door. Grasping the brick, he again looks up to take aim. His fingers slowly relax, and the brick falls to the ground.*) 'Tain't no use now. 'Tain't no use. He done lit. (PORGY *regains his seat on step and sits looking up at the bird with an expression of hopelessness as the curtain falls.*)

That night, on Kittiwah island, the picnic is about to break up. Down by the boat landing the band is playing, still loyal to its star piece, "Ain't It Hahd to Be a Nigger?" Frequent toots of the steamer whistle indicate that its navigating officers are impatient to be off.

At the edge of a palmetto thicket Maria and Serena have stopped to look for Maria's pipe. Maria remembers leaving it there earlier in the evening when she was scared away by a "ha'nt"—"a Plat-eye ha'nt"—a-peerin' at her through the bushes.

Serena is skeptical of "ha'nts!" particularly of the Plat-eye variety. She can't remember ever having seen any reference to them in the Bible. But Maria needs no other evidence than her own eyesight—and she done see that ha'nt!

Bess and Lily join the searchers and, when the whistle tooting becomes more and more imperative, they urge Maria to move on toward the boat while they, being the faster walkers, stay behind and continue the search.

The others have wandered up the stretch of moonlight that fringes the thicket and Serena is alone when she, too, suddenly sees Maria's "ha'nt"—two great burning eyes staring at her from the blackness of the thicket. One long look is enough for Serena, and she follows Maria down the boat trail as fast as she can run.

Now Bess is back, and alone, still searching for the glasses, when a great black hand reaches out and opens a pathway in the thicket. Bess, scared rigid, knows instinctively that it is Crown who is approaching.

The fugitive has been hidden on the island since his escape. "He is naked to the waist, his cotton trousers frayed away to the knees.

"I seen yo' land, an' I been waitin' all day fo' yo'. I mos' dead on dis damn' island," explains Crown.

But Bess is not impressed. "Yo' ain't look mos' dead," she counters. "Yo' bigger'n eber."

Crown admits that he has managed to find enough to eat. There are plenty of birds' eggs and oysters. But he has been most dead of lonesomeness. A condition, he assumes, that will be corrected, now that Bess has come.

But Bess has no intention of staying. And, besides, she has something to tell him.

She is living with the cripple Porgy, and she done change her ways. "I—I libin' wid Porgy now—an' I libin' decent."

The arrangement carries its humorous aspects to Crown, but he is content—so long as Bess realizes that it is purely temporary; that he will be returning for her in a couple of weeks and that she will come to him at his bidding.

Otherwise it will be just as well for her to prepare to meet her God! To emphasize his feelings in the matter Crown seizes the resisting Bess savagely by the arm and draws her toward him. Nor will he release her when the steamboat whistles its last warning. She doesn't have to get that boat! There'll be another the day after to-morrow!

BESS—Take yo' hot han' off me. I tells yo' I stayin' wid Porgy for keeps.

CROWN—Yo' is tellin' me yo' radder hab dat crawlin' cripple dan Crown?

BESS (*taking a propitiatory tone*)—It like dis, Crown—I de only 'oman Porgy eber hab. An' I thinkin' how it goin' be if all dese odder nigger' goes back to Catfish Row to-night, an' I ain't come home to um. He be like a little chil' dat los' its ma. (CROWN, *still holding her, throws back his head and laughs.* BESS *begins to be frightened.*) Yo' can laugh, but I tells yo' I change'!

CROWN—Yo' change' all right. Yo' ain't neber been so funny. (*The boat whistles. She tries to pull away. He stops laughing and holds her tighter with lowering look. Draws her nearer.*)

BESS—Lemme go, Crown! Yo' can get plenty odder women.

CROWN—What I wants wid odder women? I gots a 'oman. An' dat's yo'. See?

BESS (*trying flattery*)—Yo' know how it always been wid yo', Crown—yo' ain't neber want for a 'oman. Look at dis chest, an' look at dese arm' yo' got! Dere's plenty better-lookin' gal dan me. Yo' know how it always been wid yo'. Dese five year' now I been yo' 'oman—yo' could kick me in de street, an' den, when yo' ready fo' me back, yo' could whistle fo' me, an' dere I was again a-lickin' yo' han'. What yo' wants wid Bess? She gettin' ole now. (*She sees that her flattery has failed and is terrified.*) Dat boat goin' widout me! Lemme go! Crown, I'll come back fo' see yo'. I swear to Gawd I'll come on de Friday boat. Jus' lemme go *now!* I can't stop out here all night. I 'fraid! Dere's t'ings movin' in de t'icket—rattlesnake, an' such! Lemme go, I tells yo'. Take yo' han' off me!

CROWN (*holding her and looking steadily at her*)—No man ever take my 'oman from me. It goin' to be good joke on Crown ef he lose um to one wid no leg' an' no gizzard. (*Draws her closer.*) So yo' is change, is yo'? (*Grips her more tightly. Looks straight into her eyes.*) Whut yo' say now?

BESS (*summoning the last of her resolution*)—I stayin' wid Porgy fo' good. (*His jaw shoots forward, and his huge shoulder muscles bulge and set. Slowly his giant hands close round her throat. He brings his eyes still closer to hers. The boat whistles long and loud, but neither gives signs of hearing it. After a moment, CROWN laughs with satisfaction at what he sees in BESS's eyes. His hands leave her throat and clasp her savagely by the shoulders. BESS throws back her head with a wild hysterical laugh.*)

CROWN—I knows yo' ain't change'! Wid yo' an' me, it always

goin' be de same. See? (*He swings her about and hurls her face
forward through an opening in the thicket. Then, with a low
laugh, he follows her. She regains her balance and goes on ahead
of him. The band is still playing, but growing faint in the distance.*)
The curtain falls.

ACT III

It is just before dawn a week later. Jake and the fishermen are
getting their early breakfasts and preparing for the start to the
fishing banks. Luck has been running with them the last several
days and they are eager to make the most of their chances for
another big catch before the threatening storms arrive.

From Porgy's room in the court comes the moaning voice of
Bess in droning delirium. "Eighteen mile to Kittiwah—eighteen
mile—palmetto bush by de sho'—rattlesnakes and such!"

Old Peter, the honey man, is out of jail and his welcome at the
court rises enthusiastically for a moment above the repeated droning of Bess, whose voice is now joined by that of Porgy, evidently
sitting by the sick woman's bed and trying to comfort her.

"Yo' right here wid Porgy an' nuttin' can hurt yo'," Porgy's
voice can be heard assuring Bess. "Soon de cool wedder comin'
an' chill off dese febers. . . . Ain't yo' remembuh how de cool
win' come to town wid de smell ob pine tree, an' how de stars is
all polishin' up like w'ite folks silber? Den eberybody git well.
Ain't yo' know? Yo' jus' keep still an' watch what Porgy say."

For nearly two weeks Bess has been ill of a fever—ever since
the picnic. It was there, Serena explains, that she wandered off by
herself and was lost in the palmetto thicket for two days.

Now Porgy has come wearily from his room. Out of their sympathy his neighbors would advise him what to do for Bess. Old
Peter is of the opinion that the ailing sister should be sent to the
hospital, but Maria is strongly against that. In the w'ite folks
hospital they let niggers die so they can give the bodies to the
students, insists Maria. Porgy is sadly distressed by the thought,
moaning a prayer that God will keep Bess from the hospital.

Serena, too, believes in prayer. Hasn't she prayed Clara's baby
out of convulsions before this? She knows she can help Bess.
With encouragement she gives voice to an earnest supplication.

"Oh, Jedus who done trouble de watah in de Sea of Gallerie—
an' likewise who don' cas' de debil out ob de afflicted time an'
time again—what make yo' ain't lay yo' han' on dis sistuh head

—an' send de debil out o' she, down a steep place into de sea, like
yo' used to do, time an' time again."

Serena is joined in the prayer with many an earnest "Amen!"
And when she is finished there is a new peace in the hearts of
most of them.

Maria, however, has more faith in conjurin'. If Porgy wants
Bess cured, let him lose no time sending Mingo with two dollars
to Lody "to make conjur' fo' cast de debil out o' Bess."

Mingo is not eager to take so long a journey with a stomach
as empty as his, but with the promise of a free breakfast when
he returns and an extra quarter added to Porgy's bid for his
services he agrees to go.

"Yo' t'ink dat cure she?" eagerly Porgy demands of Maria.

"I ain't t'ink. I know. Yo' watch what I say, my brudder.
Bess good as cure right now. Yo' gots jus' a quartuh hour to wait.
Come five o'clock, dat 'oman well."

It is an ominous hour in Catfish Row. Outside the waters of
the bay seem unusually deep and black. Jake's wife, Clara,
watching fearfully at the gate, never did see the water so black
before. Nor can Maria remember when everything looked so still
like.

"He too still," ventures Clara. "An' somet'ing in my head keep
a-listenin' fo' dat hurricane bell."

There is an effort to change the subject. Maria would gossip
a bit about Porgy's Bess and where she was stayin' that two
nights on Kittiwah islan'. It is Maria's opinion that Bess was
with that nigger Crown. Bess loves Porgy, all right, and wants
to stay with him. Maria admits that. But she knows the kind
that Crown nigger is, too.

"Ef dat nigger come after she," Maria predicts, solemnly, "dey
ain't goin' be nobody around here but Porgy an' de goat!"

Now Peter, the honey man, has started again on his rounds,
singing his old song: "I gots honey. Has yo' gots honey? Yes,
ma'am, I gots honey—I gots honey cheap?"

Porgy comes disconsolately from his room. It is nearing 5
o'clock and that is the hour for Bess's cure, if Lody's conjurin' is
going to help.

Now St. Michael's is chiming the hour and Maria, almost as
anxious as Porgy, has come from her cook shop to listen. "She
and Porgy gaze at each other across the court with tense, expectant faces. The chimes cease."

"Now de time! Oh, Gawd!" mutters Porgy.

And then, as it might be in answer to his prayer, Bess's voice is heard calling from her sick room.

"Porgy!" And again: "Porgy! Dat yo' dere, ain't it? Why yo' ain't talk to me?"

PORGY (*with a half-laugh that breaks in a sob*)—T'ank Gawd! T'ank Gawd! (BESS *appears in the doorway in her white nightgown. She is very weak.*)

BESS—I lonesome here all by myself. (MARIA *crosses to her quickly. Gently assists her as she lowers herself to seat beside* PORGY.) It hot in dere. Let me sit here awhile in de cool.

MARIA—I'll get yo' blanket.

PORGY—Maria, ain't she ought to go back to bed?

MARIA (*going past them into room*)—Let she be. What I done tell yo'? Ain't dat conjur' cured she?

BESS—I been sick, ain't it?

PORGY—Oh, Bess! Bess!

BESS—What de mattuh?

PORGY (*almost sobbing with relief*)—Yo' been berry sick! T'ank Gawd de conjur' cure yo'! (MARIA *reappears with blanket, which she wraps about* BESS.)

MARIA—I ain't goin' let yo' set here berry long. (*Returns to her shop.*)

PORGY—I got yo' back, Bess!

BESS—How long I been sick, Porgy?

PORGY—Jus' a week. Yo' come back from Kittiwah wid yo' eye like fireball, an' Maria git yo' in de bed. An' yo' ain't know me! (BESS *suddenly catches her breath in a stifled sob.*) What de mattuh, Bess?

BESS—I guess I ain't know nuttin' wid de feber—or I ain't come back at all!

PORGY—Yo' ain't come back to Porgy? (*She begins to moan hysterically.*)

BESS—No, I ain't ought to come back!

PORGY (*soothingly*)—Dat all right. Don' yo' worry none, Bess. I knows yo' been wid Crown. (BESS *draws in her breath sharply, then speaks in a whisper.*)

BESS—How yo' know?

PORGY—Yo' been talk 'bout um while yo' out ob yo' head.

BESS—What I say?

PORGY—Yo' ain't say nuttin' 'cept crazy stuff, but Gawd gib cripple to know many t'ing' he ain't gib strong men.

BESS—Yo' ain't want me go away?

PORGY—No, I ain't want yo' go, Bess. (*Looks at her keenly.
A moment of silence.*) Yo' neber lie to me, Bess.

BESS—No, I neber lie to yo'. Yo' gots to gib me dat. (*Another silence.*)

PORGY—How t'ings stan' 'tween yo' an' Crown?

BESS (*after a pause*)—He comin' fo' me when de cotton come
to town.

PORGY—Yo' goin'?

BESS—I tell um—yes.

(PORGY *turns his head from her and sits looking straight before
him. After a moment,* BESS *reaches out timidly and lays her hand
on his arm. Then she tries to encircle it with her fingers.*)
Porgy! Gawd! Yo' gots de arm like stebedore! Why yo'
muscle pull up like dat? (*He looks at her, his face set and stern.
She cowers, her hand still on his arm.*) It makes me 'fraid! (*A
pause.*)

PORGY—Yo' ain't gots nuttin' fo' be 'fraid of. I ain't try to
keep no 'oman what don' want to stay. Ef yo' wants to go wid
Crown, dat fo' yo' to say.

BESS—I ain't wants to go, Porgy. (PORGY *looks at her with
hope.*) But I ain't yo' kin'. When Crown put he hand on me
dat day, I run to he like watuh. Some day again he goin' put he
han' on my throat. It goin' be like dyin', den. But I gots to
talk de trut' to yo'. When dem time come, I goin' to go.
(*Silence.*)

PORGY (*in a whisper*)—Ef dey wa'n't no Crown, Bess! Ef
dey was only jus' yo' an' Porgy, what den? (*She looks into his
face with an expression of yearning. Then, suddenly, the weakness of her illness sweeps down upon her and she breaks out hysterically, trembling with fear.*)

BESS—Oh, fo' Gawd's sake, Porgy! Don' let dat man come
an' handle me! Ef yo' is willin' to keep me, den lemme stay!
(*Her voice rises hysterically, broken by sobs.*) Ef he jus' don'
put dem hot han' on me, I can be good! I can 'membuh! I can
be happy! (*The sobs overcome her.*)

PORGY—Dere, dere, Bess. (*Pats her arm soothingly, waiting
for the storm to spend itself. She grows suddenly quiet, except
for occasional silent, rending sighs.*) Yo' ain't need to be afraid.
Ain't yo' gots yo' man? Ain't yo' gots Porgy fo' take care ob
yo'? What kin' ob nigger yo' t'inks yo' gots anyway, fo' let
anudder nigger carry he 'oman? No, suh! Yo' gots yo' man
now! Yo' gots Porgy! (BESS *has become quiet. A pause.*)
Dere, now. Yo' been set up too long. Let Porgy help yo' back

to bed. (*He draws himself up by the door frame.* BESS *rises unsteadily and, with a hand on his arm, they make their way into the room.* PORGY *closes the door behind them.*)

Mingo is back, and Mingo is drunk. He hasn't seen the conjurin' Lody at all. Maria discovers this much after a vigorous cross-examination. Mingo's spent Porgy's money for cheap liquor and Maria is at his throat as though she would shake the confession out of him. Having gained that she warns him awesomely that she is going to lock him up until he is sober enough to keep his mouth shut. After that if he ever mentions to any living person that he failed to deliver Porgy's message to Lody he will answer to her, and she will have nigger blood on her soul when she stands at the judgment seat.

Even after she has shoved the shivering Mingo into her room and shut the door on him Maria is still troubled in her mind. "Mus' hab been Jedus done cure Bess after all," she mutters. But this is no more than a fleeting doubt with Maria. She pauses half way to Porgy's room and declares herself with decision. "No, I be damn' ef he did. He ain't gots it in um!" And she bangs the door of her room behind her as she enters.

"For a moment the court is empty and silent. Suddenly, the silence is broken by the deep, ominous clang of a bell, very different from the silver tone of St. Michael's."

Now every resident of Catfish Row, except Mingo and Bess, comes piling into the court or is leaping from windows flung suddenly open. An apprehensive fear grips them as they count the strokes of the bell. Twelve strokes will mean a hot wave, and nothing more terrible. But more than twelve—

At the stroke of twelve there is a tightening of breath—and a wild gasp of horror as the strokes continue—on and on until twenty are counted!

"Dat bell mus' be mistake," Serena insists, trying to comfort the distraught Clara. "Ain't yo' 'membuh de las' hurricane? How he take two day fo' blow up?"

But there is little comfort in Serena's words. And none in Porgy's advice to watch the flag on the Custom House, or Maria's confirmation.

"Ain't yo' know long as de American flag wabin' ober de Custom House dat mean eberyt'ing all right, jus' like—"

But before Maria can finish her prophecy the flag is down and "a new wave of horror sweeps simultaneously over every face."

CLARA (*her terror giving way to dull hopelessness*)—Dey don' hab to run up no hurricane signal to tell me nuttin'. My head stop listenin' fo' um now.

PORGY—Dε mens goin' see de signal an' come home quick.

CLARA—Dey can't see dat signal from de Blackfish Banks, an' dey dere by dis time.

ANNIE (*hysterically*)—How dey goin' come back wid no win' fo' de sail?

MARIA (*sternly silencing her*)—Dey can row in 'fo' dis storm come. He ain't here yet, is he?

PORGY—No, he ain't here yet.

LILY—I ain't fo' worryin' 'bout t'ing dat mightn't happen 'tall. (*There is a general babble of voices: "Time 'nough fo' worry when de storm come!" "Mebby by to-morruh we habe li'l' storm!" etc. While they reassure themselves, the sea is darkening. The shutters of Catfish Row begin to flap back and forth in a sudden wind. CLARA stands watching the swinging shutters.*)

There is the sound of the wind and the waves outside Catfish Row. Just before morning, in Serena's room, "dim and shadowy in the light of guttering kerosene lamps, the Negroes are huddled together in groups. A few have found seats on the chairs and bed. Others sit on the floor."

They are all singing "The Judgment Day Spiritual," their voices rising with the howl of the storm. At the window Clara, her baby in her arms, continues to search the darkness for signs of an abating hurricane.

All day they have been singing, but Clara can find no comfort in the spirituals. She has "mos' lose her min' " at the monotony of the chant. But, as Serena points out, they all want to be ready when "de grabe gib up de dead an' Gabriel sound de trumpet." And this isn't any time to be taking chances.

When sudden gusts of wind and rain set the shutters flapping and the singers cower and draw closer to each other, Bess and Porgy sit calmly together through the disturbance.

"Yo' ain't afraid, Bess?" Porgy asks. And as Bess shakes her head he adds. "What make yo' ain't say nuttin'?"

"I jus' t'inkin'. . . . You know what I t'inkin' 'bout?"

"Yo' t'inkin' whut storm like dis mus' be like out on de sea islan's," ventures Porgy.

"Wabe like dese mus' wash clean across Kittiwah."

"Yo' sorry?"

"I sorry for any man lef' out in storm like dis. But I can stop a-listenin' now fo' his step a-comin'," adds Bess, putting her hand in Porgy's. "I guess yo' gots me fo' keeps, Porgy."

"Ain't I tells yo' dat all 'long?"

Outside a great roar is heard, coming steadily nearer. Trembling fear grips the singers and there is barely strength left them to carry on the singing of the next spiritual: ,

> "Dere's somebody knockin' at de do',
> Dere's somebody knockin' at de do',
> Oh, Mary, oh, Mart'a,
> Somebody knockin' at de do'."

Now the spiritual swells and gains in tempo, and the swaying bodies and patting is followed by hysterical shouting. Old Peter is certain death is knockin' at de do', but the others are more skeptical—until there is, indeed, a great knocking.

In their hysteria the watchers pile furniture before the door to bar the unwelcome presence, but it is no use. "With a sucking sound of the wind the door slowly opens, pushing away the flimsy furniture. Shrieks of terror and prayers fill the room!"

Then Crown enters, "bent double against the wind." There are relieved cries of "Gawd, it's Crown!"

"Yo' is a nice pa'cel of nigger! Shut a frien' out in a storm like dis!" is the fugitive's greeting.

There are doubts in several minds as to whose friend Crown is. He is no friend of Serena's, she assures him. And Porgy and Bess sit rigid and fearful of the intruder's next move.

They are not kept waiting long. Crown is in both a defiant and rebellious mood. He has come for Bess and he is of no mind to wait long for her to come to him.

"Yo' ain't done much fo' yo'self while I been gone," he sneers, looking down at the unhappy Porgy. "Ain't dere no whole ones left?"

BESS (*rising and facing him*)—Keep yo' mout' off Porgy!

CROWN—Well, fo' Gawd's sake! Dem humn-whiners got yo' too?

BESS—I tol' yo' I ain't goin' wid yo' no more. I stayin' wid Porgy fo' good.

CROWN—'Oman! Do yo' want to meet yo' Gawd? Come here!

BESS (*holding her ground*)—Porgy my man now.

CROWN (*laughing*)—Yo' call dat a man! Don' yo' min'. I
gots de forgivin' nature, an' I goin' take yo' back. (*Reaches for
her.* BESS *violently repulses him.*)

BESS—Keep yo' han' off me!

SERENA (*to* CROWN)—Ef yo' stick 'round here, yo' sure to get
killed sooner or later. Den de w'ite folks goin' figger I done um.
Dey gots it in de writin' now dat I been Robbins' wife. An' dey
goin' lock me up fo' um anyway. So I might as well do um.
(BESS *returns to her seat by* PORGY.)

CROWN (*laughing*)—What makes yo' t'ink I goin' get killed?
Ef Gawd want to kill me, he got plenty ob chance 'tween here an'
Kittiwah Islan'. Me an' Him been havin' it out all de way from
Kittiwah; first Him on top, den me. Dere ain't nuttin' He likes
better'n a scrap wid a man! Gawd an' me frien'! (*A terrific
roar of wind.*)

SERENA (*terror-stricken*)—Yo' fool! Ain't yo' gots more sense
dan talk 'bout Gawd like dat in a storm like dis! (*Another sudden gust.*)

CROWN—Gawd's laughin' at yo'!

PETER—It berry dangerous fo' we all to hab dat blasphemin'
nigger 'mong us. Le's we sing unto de Lord! (*A woman's voice
leads the spiritual, "Got to Meet de Jedgment."*)

THE WOMEN—"All I know—

SEVERAL MEN—I got to meet de Jedgment.

THE WOMEN—"All I know—

THE MEN—Got to meet de Jedgment.

THE WOMEN—"All I know—

THE MEN—Got to meet de Jedgment.

TOGETHER—"All I know, All I know, All I know—

THE WOMEN—"All I moan—

THE MEN—I got to meet de Jedgment.

(*As the wind subsides, the spiritual rises strong and clear. The
Negroes sing and sway for a moment uninterrupted.*)

CROWN (*his voice rising above the singing*)—Yo' folk mus'
t'ink de Lord bery easy pleased ef yo' t'ink he like to listen to
dat. (*They sing on.*) Ef it affec' Him de way it do me, yo' is
gibin' um de lonesome blues. (CROWN *shouts above the singing.*)
Here, here! Cut dat! I didn't come all de way from Kittiwah
to sit up wid no corpses! Dem as is in such a hurry fo' de
Jedgment, all dey gots fo' do is to kiss demselves good-bye an'
step out dat door. Yo', Uncle Peter, here's yo' chance. The Jim
Crow's leabin' an' yo' don' need no ticket. (*Turning to* SERENA.)

How 'bout yo', sistuh? All abo'd! What, dey ain't no trabbelers? (*A roar of wind.*)

CROWN—Dere go de train! An' yo' miss yo' chance! (*The wind rises above the singing.* CROWN *shouts up at ceiling.*) Dat's right, drown um out! Don' yo' listen to um sing! Dey don' gib yo' credit fo' no taste in music. How 'bout dis one, Big Frien'? (*Sings*):

> "Rock in de mountain,
> Fish in de sea,
> Dere neber was a nigger
> Take an 'oman from me."

LILY—Jedus! He goin' call down Gawd' wrath on we all! (*The wind rises to its highest pitch. The Negroes huddle together in terror. They begin to sway and moan.* CROWN *stands in middle of room, his arms thrown wide. His voice rises above the wind.*)

CROWN—Don' yo' hear Gawd A'mighty—laughing up dere? Dat's right, Ole Frien'! Gawd laugh, an' Crown laugh back! (*Throws back his head and laughs. The wind shrieks above his laugh.*) Dat's right! Yo' like um, Gawd? I'll gib yo' anudder verse! (*Sings*):

> "I ain't no doctor,
> No doctor' son,
> But I can cool yo' feber
> Till de doctor come."

(*While he is singing, the wind suddenly ceases. The Negroes look at one another, appalled by the suddenness of the change.*)

BESS—Mus' be de storm ober.

PORGY—He jus' takin' a res'. When de wind lull like dis, he come back soon, worse'n eber.

CROWN—Ain't I tell yo' Gawd like um? He quiet now fo' listen. (*He bursts again into song*):

> "I laugh in de country,
> I laugh in de town,
> 'Cause a cripple t'ink he goin'
> Take an 'oman from Crown."

(*Then begins to shuffle.*) Come on, Bess! Yo' ain't one ob dese spiritual-whimperin' niggers. What, ain't yo' got no guts! Come 'long! Yo' used to be de bes' dancer in Charleston. Ef yo' don' want to dance wid Crown, mebby yo' new man'll dance wid yo'! (*Roars with laughter.* BESS *is silent. He dances a few more steps.*) Come 'long, Maria! Yo' can't tell me dese Gawd-f'arin' whiners has got yo'! (MARIA *hesitates,* CROWN *dances on. Laughs.*) Dis ole lady too fat fo' dance!

MARIA (*indignantly*)—Who say I'm too fat! (*Gets lumberingly to her feet and begins to shuffle.* MINGO *begins to clap for them.*)

CROWN (*dancing*)—How 'bout ole Sportin' Life? (SPORTING LIFE *joins in the dancing.* PETER *begins to clap.*)

LILY—Stop dat, yo' ole fool!

CROWN (*dancing near* PETER *and shouting in his ear*)—Dis nigger too ole fo' dance!

PETER (*indignant, puffing out his chest*)—Who say I too ole! (*Gets laboriously to his feet and begins a feeble shuffle.*)

Half the Negroes are dancing now, forgetting their terror. Only Serena and her friends are left to pray and disapprove. Porgy and Bess, as though clinging each to the other, sit by. There is a wild kind of grace in Crown's dancing. Now he laughingly stops before Bess and cuts one of his showiest pigeon wings, but she ignores him and her gaze returns to Porgy.

Now there is a wild shriek from the window. Clara, still peering into the darkness, has caught sight of an overturned boat beating against the shore. A fishing boat with red gunnels, like Jake's *Sea Gull!*

Fearfully they wait for the hull to turn over in the waves that they may be sure of the identification—and then they know!

"Gawd! It de *Sea Gull* fo' sure!"

With a wild shriek Clara breaks for the door, pushing Serena aside and old Peter. At the door she turns to come back and put her baby in Bess's arms.

"Yo' keep my baby until I comes back," she says, and is out the door before any one can stop her.

The storm has quieted but they know it will return in fury and there is a wild call for some one to go after Clara—a wild call with none to answer.

"Dere ain't nobody in here got de guts ob a chicken," sneers Maria, and Bess, looking scornfully over the room, demands accusingly: "Ain't dere no man 'round here?"

"Yes! Where all dem nigger been wantin' to meet de jedgment?" cries Crown. "Go 'long! Yo' been askin' fo' somet'ing, an' yo' ain't got de gizzards to go an' get um. Now's yo' chance. (*Laughs. Goes and stands before* BESS, *looking sideways to see effect on her.*) Porgy, what yo' sittin' dere fo'? Ain't yo' hear yo' 'oman calling fo' a *man?* Yes, looks to me like only *one man* 'round here! (*Again glances toward* BESS; *then runs to door, throwing up his arms and calling. Calls the men by name*): "Go 'long, Sam!" etc. All right, Ole Frien' up dere! We's on fo' anudder bout!"

He jerks open the door and runs out. At the window the Negroes crowd to watch him. It is lighter outside now. They see Clara reach the edge of the wharf. The water is up to her waist now. Behind her Crown is splashing through the crashing waves.

Suddenly there is a great roar of wind and water. Darkness follows. The storm has come back with redoubled fury. It is God answerin' Crown, agrees Serena, falling to her knees in prayer. Now the others are praying around her, moaning in terror.

Suddenly at the window Mingo's voice rises high in terror. "De wharf goin'! Gawd A'mighty!"

Outside there is a terrific roar, followed by a crashing of timbers. An awed silence overcomes the group of watchers. Now they huddle together again in the middle of the room, around Serena's praying group. Bess is sitting beside Porgy, Clara's baby in her arms. With one accord they take up the chant of the "Jedgment Day Spiritual."

> "We will all pray togedduh on dat day,
> We will all pray togedduh on dat day,
> An' I'll fall upon my knees and face de risin' sun.
> Oh, Lord, hab mercy on me!"

"Allelujah! Gawd hab mercy on de souls ob Clara an' Crown!" wails old Peter.

"Bess turns and looks directly at Porgy. With an expression of awe in his face he reaches out a timid hand and touches the baby's cheek.

"The roar increases. The shutters fly back and forth. With fear-stricken eyes, the Negroes sway and pat and sing, their voices sometimes rising above the roar of the wind and sometimes drowned by it.

"Bess continues silent, looking straight ahead of her, tenderness, yearning and awe in her face. Porgy sits watching her.

"The shutters crash more violently. The roar of wind and water increases. The Negroes huddle closer and sing on."

The curtain falls.

ACT IV

The following night, after the storm had passed, there were mourning songs sung for those who had been killed. But some were not at the singing. Maria, for one, was obliged to give some attention to straightening up her cook shop, seeing her stove had been washed clean across the street.

"An' sides," explains Maria, "it break my heart to hear dese 'omans mourning fo' de mens dat provide um wid bread and what was dey lover' too. All dem fine, strong mens, dead in de storm! (*In lower voice*): It gib me de creeps, Serena, to t'ink how many ghost' must be listenin' 'round dis court to-night."

At the window of his room, the shutters half closed so he is screened from the court, sits Porgy. He has been there all day— waiting for something. If Crown's dead, as they all believe, it may be Porgy thinks his ghost may be coming back to worry Bess.

"Gawd gib dat cripple to see many t'ing yo' an' me can't see," ventures Maria when Serena questions Porgy's actions; "an' ef he is watch for sompen, den dere is sompen for watch for."

Bess, still carrying Clara's baby, has also quit the singing. She couldn't stay when they started praying for Jake and Clara. She is clear in her mind about one thing, though. She certainly is going to keep Clara's baby, just as its mother done ask her to do. And Serena may rail all she wants to about that child's getting a proper Christian raising.

"Can't yo' see I ain't de same 'oman what used to run wid Crown," Bess impulsively demands of the doubter. "Gawd wouldn't ha' let Clara gib me dis baby if He hadn't seen I was different inside. He wouldn't ha' gib me Porgy if he didn't want to gib me my chance. (*Looking down at baby*): See! He t'ink already dat I he ma. I gots de big brightness all inside me to-day. I can't stan' not to hab eberybody kind to me to-day! (*Holds baby out to* SERENA.) Look at um now, Serena—hold um a minute. Tell um he gots a good ma what goin' stan' by um!"

"Yas—I reckon yo' gots a good ma now," admits Serena. "She gots Gawd in she heart at las'. Yo' ain't no cause fo' fret."

In the funeral room where the mourners are holding forth the singers have reached the soul of Crown and are lifting up supplications that even he be saved. Suddenly from under the stairs leading to Serena's room a raucous laugh is heard.

Investigation reveals Sporting Life, and his joy is great at the thought of the singers "stowin'" his old friend Crown. It may be Crown is dead for sure, as the watchers who saw the wharf washed away under him believe. In which case it must be Crown's ghost that he has seen hanging around there.

Sporting Life's shiftiness convinces Maria that he has seen Crown, but she is still at a loss to understand that as a cause for his exultant mood.

"Ef Bess gots two mens, dat sho count yo' out," she ventures.

"Dat jus' where I comes in," replies Sporting Life, and there is a movement of the shutter at Porgy's window. "When a 'oman gots jus' one man, mebbe she gots um for keep. But when she gots two mens—dere's mighty apt to be carvin'!—An' de cops takes de leabin's."

Maria has driven the swaggering Sporting Life from the court, though Sporting Life has sneaked back to his hidden position under the stairs, and is putting up the shutters of her shop. Now she sees that everything is apparently clear for the night, goes in her shop and locks the door.

From Porgy's room there comes the whimper of a child, followed by the crooning of a lullaby. Bess is singing in the darkness, "Hush, little baby, don' yo' cry, mother an' father born to die."

"Her voice trails off sleepily and is silent. During her lullaby, the last singers have come from the funeral room and crossed to their own rooms or gone out at gate. The light in the funeral room goes out. Maria's light goes out.

"A moment of complete darkness and silence in Catfish Row; then the sudden flash of a match in the darkness reveals Sporting Life about to light a cigarette. He hears something at gate and hurriedly extinguishes match, with cigarette unlit.

Against the gray background beyond the gate a gigantic figure can be seen. The gate opens very slowly and noiselessly. Crown comes stealthily into court; very gently closes gate behind him. Picks his way slowly and silently across court. Stops to listen. Silence. Goes on to Porgy's door. Again listens. Puts his hand on knob and softly tries door. Opens it very cautiously, inch by inch. When it is wide enough, he stealthily slips through. Inch by inch, the door closes.

"A full minute of absolute silence. Maria is in her wrapper; opens her door and stands listening. Satisfied, she is turning back.

"A muffled thud sounds from Porgy's room. Maria stops short. Stands motionless. Suddenly Porgy's laugh is heard, deep, swelling, lustful. The baby cries out."

BESS (*within room. Horror in her voice*)—Fo' Gawd's sake,
Porgy! What yo' laughin' 'bout?

PORGY (*triumphantly*)—Dat all right, honey. Don' yo' be
worryin'. Yo' gots Porgy now, an' he look atter he 'oman. Ain't
I don' tell yo'? Yo' gots a *man* now! (MARIA *crosses the court
swiftly. Opens* PORGY'S *door, goes in, and closes it behind her.
Again the flash of a match in the shadows.* SPORTING LIFE *lights
his cigarette and continues his vigil.*)

It is early next morning. Catfish Row is silent and apparently
deserted. When the detective who arrested Peter arrives with
the coroner there is no one in sight, nor any sound to be heard.
But to the detective this means nothing.

Catfish Row, to him, is always "alive with crooked niggers."

"If you was on the force 'stead of sitting down in the coroner's
office, you'd know we don't make a move that isn't watched by a
hundred pair of eyes," he explains.

The coroner is there to get a witness to identify Crown's body
at the inquest. Even that is not likely to prove as simple as it
sounds, the detective warns him, and seeks to strengthen the
statement by kicking open the door to Serena's room and bellow-
ing an order for her to come down.

For a moment there is no answer. Then the shutters of
Serena's window slowly open and the Negress Annie looks out.

"Serena been sick in she bed three day, an' I been here wid she
all dat time," Annie reports.

Nor can threats of sending for the wagon and taking the sick
Serena and all her friends to jail change Annie's story. When
the detective becomes more threatening Annie opens the window
that he may hear the painful moaning of the patient, and finally,
with the aid of another witness, Annie produces Serena herself,
her head bandaged in a towel. Serena weakly collapses across
the window sill. She has, she repeats between gasps, been sick in
bed for three days, and this, according to the others, is "de
Gawd's trut'."

"There you are—an airtight alibi." The detective is scornful,
but helpless, and after another vain attempt at cross-examination
he gives up.

"Oh, hell! You might as well argue with a parrot cage, but
you'll never break them without your own witnesses, and you'll
never get 'em."

They try next with Lily, who is old Peter's wife. The coroner
recognizes Lily as a girl who had worked for his family. Lily

Holmes she was then, but she left to get married. She is still
Lily Holmes, Lily assures them. She has taken old Peter as a
husband but not his name.

"You ain't t'ink I goin' be responsible for no ole nigger name?"
she demands, indignantly. "No, suh! An' I ain't gib um my
name, nedder."

Furthermore it is little use for them to try to question
Peter. Lily insists, seeing that the old man is not only deaf but
"ain't got good sense, nohow." Yet Peter is of a perfectly suitable
age for husbands, she insists, being just 82.

"An old man like that is apt to linger on your hands," suggests
the friendly coroner.

"No, boss," promptly answers Lily, while Peter, not hearing,
smiles in affable agreement; "ef I is marry to young man an' he
took sick, mebbe *he* linger on my han'. But," and she points to
Peter, who smiles even more amiably, "he ain't linger on my han'.
He took sick—he gone!"

"What did you marry him for?"

"Why, yo' see, boss, he like dis," explains Lily. "Ain't yo'
membuh how I used to hab dem crazy fits of misery in my
stomach? I wake up in de night wid 'em. De doctor say to me,
'Lily Holmes, one ob dese nights yo' goin' dead in yo' bed all by
yo'self.' So I t'ink I bes' marry dat nigger so as I won't go dead
all by myself. But since I marry um, I gets well ob my misery,
an' I ain't got no furder use for 'um."

With some show of impatience the detective suggests that he
is not there to pay a social call, and insists on returning to the
case. Let them try to get something from the cripple and his
woman. Porgy is also hard to handle, but he may come through.

In response to the detective's call, after he has followed his
custom of kicking open their door, Bess helps Porgy to a seat on
the doorstep.

There is, however, little more gained in questioning these two
than there was with the others. Porgy and Bess both knew
Crown, they admit, and Porgy would know him if he were to see
him again, though he doesn't care anything about seeing him.

As for the detective's discovery that Bess's room is freshly
scrubbed and that she has overlooked a stain of blood under the
bed—that is foolish, too. She always scrubs her room every
week—ask anybody—and there ain't no blood there because no
one has killed Crown in her room.

The coroner, making a note in his book, has his witness, he

says, and is ready to go. The detective is forced reluctantly to
follow.

Now the court is again silent and apparently deserted. Then
in one room a voice is heard singing "Ain't It Hard to Be a
Nigger!"

"Another voice joins, then another. In a moment the empty
court is ringing with the song, sung mockingly, triumphantly."

Now the windows begin to open and the Negroes to come, by
ones and twos, into the court again, all singing. Serena has her
washing to hang out. Old Peter is ready to start forth with his
tray of honey, which Lily helps to balance on his head. Scipio,
Serena's young son, is driving Porgy's goat cart through the
archway. There is a great relief and happiness in the air.
The song is changed to a wilder tune.

> "Sit down! I can't sit down!
> Sit down! I can't sit down!
> My soul's so happy dat I can't sit down!"

Suddenly a Negro near the gate gives a warning hiss and waves
his arms. The singing stops. Back into their rooms steal the
Negroes. Stealthily the doors and windows are closed. Again
the court is silent and empty.

Only Porgy, whom Bess had no time to get back into his room,
is visible, and he is pretending to doze on his doorstep.

A policeman strides through the archway, notes the empty
court and sees Porgy. Sleepily the cripple opens his eyes and
accepts the paper shoved at him. It is, the policeman assures
him, nothing to be frightened about. Only a summons to appear
as a witness at the coroner's inquest, view the body and tell the
coroner who it is. The thought strikes terror to Porgy's soul.

PORGY—I gots to go an' look on Crown's face?

POLICEMAN—Yes, that's all.

PORGY—Wid all dem w'ite folks lookin' at me?

POLICEMAN—Oh, cheer up! I reckon you've seen a dead
nigger before. It'll be all over in a few minutes. (BESS *appears
in doorway, her eyes wide with horror.*)

PORGY—Dere ain't goin' be no nigger in dat room 'cept me?

POLICEMAN—Just you and Crown— If you still call him one.
(*Turns away.*)

PORGY (*scarcely able to speak for terror*)—Boss—I couldn'
jus' bring a 'oman wid me? I couldn't eben carry my—my
'oman?

POLICEMAN (*slightly impatient*)—No, you can't bring any one. Say, you're the cripple, aren't you? I'll get the wagon and carry you down. And as soon as you've seen Crown, you can come home. (*Starts for gate.*)

PORGY (*desperately*)—Boss—

POLICEMAN—Now, listen, I've summoned you, and you've got to go, or it's contempt of court. I'll call the wagon for you.

(*As soon as he has gone, doors open stealthily. The Negroes come out and gather about* PORGY, *speaking in low, frightened tones.*)

PORGY—Oh, Gawd! Whut I goin' to do?

BESS—Yo' gots to go, Porgy. Mebby yo' can jus' make like to look at um an' keep yo' eye' shut.

MARIA—Yo' goin' be all right, Porgy. Yo' jus' goin' to be a witness.

SPORTING LIFE—I ain't so sure ob dat. (*They all look at him in alarm.*) I don' know who done de killin'. All I knows is, when de man what done um goes in dat room, Crown' wounds begin to bleed.

PORGY (*terror-stricken*)—Oh, Jedus!

SPORTING LIFE—Dat's one way de cops got ob tellin' who done um.

PORGY (*in a panic; moaning*)—I can't look on he face! Oh, Gawd! What I goin' to do!

SPORTING LIFE (*taking command of the situation*)—Listen to me! Yo' do jus' as I say an' yo' won't hab to look on he face.

PORGY—What I do, Sporting Life?

SPORTING LIFE—Get busy, yo' niggers. We gots to get Porgy out ob here! Get de goat, Scipio. Here, Mingo! Yo' stan' by to gib me a han' wid Porgy.

BESS—Don' yo' go, Porgy! He can't get away!

SPORTING LIFE—He gots to get away or dey'll hang um sure.

PORGY—Oh, Gawd!

Scipio brings the goat cart and, Sporting Life directing, they load the moaning Porgy in. But before they can get him away the clang of the patrol wagon bell tells them the police are upon them.

They still have a chance, Sporting Life thinks. Quickly they get Porgy and the goat under the archway and mass in front of them so the police cannot see. When the officers are well in the court and searching the rooms Porgy twists the tail of his goat and dashes off down the street.

The officers, taken by surprise, are still so amused at the sight of the disappearing goat cart and Porgy's attempt to beat them in a race, that they are convulsed with laughter. They are sporting enough, too, to give Porgy and the goat a start. Then they dash for their wagon and soon the clanging bell indicates that the race is on. Massed in the archway all Catfish Row tensely and silently prays that Porgy may make the corner and outwit the officers, but their hope is slight.

Now they turn back sadly into the court. "Dey got um!" reports Lily. "Dey putting him an' de goat all two in de wagon," Serena adds.

Slowly they disappear in their several rooms. Bess is sitting hopelessly on her doorstep, and Sporting Life saunters carelessly across the court to sit beside her.

BESS—Oh, Gawd! Dey goin' carry um to look on Crown' face!

SPORTING LIFE (*laughing*)—Don' yo' worry none 'bout dat, sistuh. Dat nigger ain't a witness now. Dey goin' lock um up in de jail.

MINGO (*at gate*)—Dat's de trut'. Dey done turn de wagon 'round toward de jail.

BESS—Well, dat better'n makin' um look on Crown. (*Fearfully*): Not for long, Sportin' Life?

SPORTING LIFE (*sympathetically*)—No, not for long. Jus' a yeah, mebby.

BESS—A yeah.

SPORTING LIFE—Contempt ob court—dat's a serious offence. (BESS *drops her face into her hands.*) Jus' like I tol' yo'. Nobody home now but Bess an' ole Sportin' Life.

BESS—I ain't gots no time fo' yo'.

SPORTING LIFE (*laughing*)—Fo' sho yo' has. Yo' jus' gots nice little vacation now fo' play 'round wid yo' ole frien'. Contempt ob court—dat serious offence. Dat nigger ain't be back heah fo' a yeah.

BESS (*alarmed*)—Sportin' Life, yo' ain't t'ink dey puts Porgy up fo' a yeah?

SPORTING LIFE—A yeah for sho. Cheer up, sistuh! Gib me yo' han'. (*He takes her hand. She is too preoccupied to resist.*) Ole Sportin' Life got de stuff fo' scare away de lonesome blues. (*Pours powder into her hand.* BESS *looks down at it.*)

BESS—Happy dus'! (*Gazes at the powder with fascinated horror.*) I ain't want none ob dat stuff, I tells yo'.

SPORTING LIFE—Ain't nuff ter hurt er flea.

BESS—Take dat stuff away, nigger! (*But she continues to hold it in her hand.*)

SPORTING LIFE—Jus' a little touch fo' ole time' sake. (BESS *suddenly claps her hand over her face. When she takes it away, it is empty.* SPORTING LIFE *smiles with satisfaction.*) Dat de t'ing, ain't it? An' membuh, dere's plenty more where dat come from. Dere's a boat to Noo Yo'k to-morruh an' I'm goin'. (*Pauses significantly.* BESS *says nothing.*) Why yo' such a fool, Bess? What yo' goin' to do a whole yeah here by yo'self? Now's yo' chance. (BESS *leaps to her feet, her eyes blazing. She glares at* SPORTING LIFE *with contempt and hatred.*)

BESS—Yo' low, crawlin' houn'! Git 'way from my door, I tells yo'! Lef' it, yo'! Rattlesnake! Dat's whut yo' is! Rattlesnake! (*While she berates him,* SPORTING LIFE *lights a cigarette, continues to sit on step.*)

SPORTING LIFE—Rave on, sistuh! But I'll be right here when yo' is wantin' dat second shot. (BESS *runs suddenly past him into her room. Slams door behind her.* SPORTING LIFE *sits smiling to himself and leisurely blowing smoke rings.* MARIA *comes to her doorway. Sees him. Crosses to him.*)

MARIA (*contemptuously*)—What yo' waitin' 'round here for?

SPORTING LIFE—Jus' waitin'. (*Smokes contentedly.*)

MARIA—What yo' t'ink yo' goin' to get?

SPORTING LIFE (*with shrug of shoulders*)—Uummmmmmm—jus' waitin'.

MARIA (*turning scornfully away*)—Yo' don' know Bess. (*Recrosses to her shop.* SPORTING LIFE *watches her till she has reached her doorstep.*)

SPORTING LIFE (*in a low voice, not intended for* MARIA *to hear*)—You don' know happy dus'. (MARIA *does not hear. Goes into shop; closes door.* SPORTING LIFE *continues to wait. St. Michael's chimes the half hour.*)

Five days later, one bright afternoon, while all the Negroes are moving about their accustomed tasks in the court of Catfish Row Porgy drives up to the gate. Serena is sitting near her door crooning a lullaby to the baby in her arms, and Maria is moving in and out of her shop, but neither sees him.

Scipio, playing near the gate, lets Porgy in. Now all the Negroes see him, but none greets him. Silently they fade away into their rooms. Porgy doesn't notice. He is too happy with the thought that he is back and with a surprise for all of them, and particularly for Bess, to notice. There is a new harmonica for Scipio, and a new bonnet for Lily, and a bright new dress for Bess, which he shakes out and lays on the table.

"Now, dat's de style for Bess," he announces, exultantly, as he produces a hat to go with the dress. "She is one gal what always look good in red. I reckon I is de fus' nigger anybody roun' here ebber see what go to jail po', an' leabe dere rich. But Porgy' luck ridin' high now. Ain't nuttin' can stop um. When de buckra search me in de jail, I all de time gots my lucky bones in my mout'—see! an' time I get settle' in my new boardin' house, I start to go right t'rough dem odder crap-shootin' nigger' like Glory Hallelujah. (*He takes a package from the cart, opens it, and holds up a baby dress.*) Now, ain't dis de t'ing! Course, de baby ain't really big 'nough for wear dress yet, but he goin' grow fas'. You watch, he goin' be in dat dress by de fus' frost. (*Continues his story.*) Yas, suh! dere warn't no stoppin' dem bones. Dey jus' gone whoopin' right t'rough dat jail, a-pullin' me after 'em. And den, on de las' day, de big buckra guard hear 'bout it, an' he come an' say I gots to gib up de bones. But I been seein' um roll wid de jailer in de watch house, an' I know he weakness. I ask dat buckra if he ain't likes me to teach um how to sing lucky to de bones 'fore I gib dem up, an' 'fore he git 'way I done gone t'rough um for t'ree dollar an' seben cent an' dis shirt. (*He proudly exhibits shirt that he is wearing. His purchases are now all spread out on the table, and he looks from them to the faces of the Negroes.*) Now it time to call Bess. Oh, Bess. Here Porgy come home. (*There is a moment of absolute silence.* LILY *gets to her feet, buries her face in her hands, and runs to her room.* PETER *starts to follow.* MINGO *rises and goes toward* MARIA'S *door.*) Here, Lily, Peter, Mingo, where you all goin'? What de hell kin' ob a welcome dis for a man what been in jail for a week, an' for de contemp' ob court at dat. Oh, now I see. Well, yo' ain't gots to min' Bess an' me. All de time we wants to hab we frien' wid us. Eben now, we ain't wants to be jus' by weself. (*They continue to withdraw. He looks about him in growing surprise, and discovers* SERENA *hunched up silently over the baby.*) Why, hello! Dere's Serena. Yo' sho' work fas', sistuh. I ain't been gone a week, an' yo' done gots a new baby. (SERENA *rises hurriedly, exposing baby for first time.*) Here, hold on. Let me see dat chile. Dat's Bess's baby, ain't it? Where yo' get um? Where Bess, anyhow? She ain't answer me.

SERENA (*calling*)—Maria, come out dat cookshop. Here Porgy

come home. *You* gots to talk wid um. (PORGY *drives to his own door.*)

PORGY—Bess! Ain't yo' dere, Bess? (MARIA *comes to her doorway.* PORGY *turns to her, his eyes wide with alarm.*) Where's Bess? (MARIA *sits on her doorstep.* PORGY *turns his goat and drives over to her.*) Tell me quick. Where's Bess? (MARIA *does not answer.*) Where? Where?

Bravely Maria tries to tell him. Didn't they all say Bess wasn't fit for him? An' that dirty dog, Sportin' Life, made them all think Porgy was to be locked up for a year.

Naturally Bess was very low in her mind and she just went back to the happy dus' and the red eye and was drunk for two days.

That doesn't matter, Porgy keeps insisting. What Bess has done doesn't matter. Where is she now? That's all Porgy wants to know. Where is she?

SERENA—She gone, Porgy. An' I done take dis chile to gib um a Christian raisin'—

PORGY—*Where* she gone?

SERENA—Dat gal ain't neber had Gawd in she heart, an' de debil get um at last.

MARIA—'Tain't de debil. De happy dus' done for um.

PORGY (*wildly*)—You—Bess?— Yo' ain't means Bess dead?

SERENA—She worse dan dead.

LILY—Sportin' Life carry she away on de Noo Yo'k boat. (*They are all silent, gazing at* PORGY. *He, too, is silent for a moment.*)

PORGY—Where dat dey take she?

MINGO—Noo Yo'k.

MARIA—Dat's way up Nort'.

PORGY (*pointing*)—It dat way?

MARIA—It take two days by de boat. Yo' can't find um.

PORGY—I ain't say I can find um. I say, where it is?

MARIA—Yo' can't go after she. Ain't yo' hear we say yo' can't find um?

ANNIE—Ain't yo' know Noo Yo'k mos' a t'ousand mile' from here?

PORGY—Which way dat?

LILY (*pointing*)—Up Nort'—past de Custom House. (PORGY *turns his goat and drives slowly with bowed head toward the gate.*)

MARIA—Porgy, I tells yo' it ain't no use!

LILY—Dat great big city. Yo' can't find um dere!

SERENA—Ain't we tells yo'— (*But* PORGY *is going on toward gate as if he did not hear, and they cease to protest and stand motionless watching him. As* PORGY *reaches the gate,* SCIPIO *silently opens it.* PORGY *drives through and turns to left, as* LILY *pointed. St. Michael's chimes the quarter hour. The gate clangs shut.*)

The curtain falls.

PARIS BOUND

A Comedy in Three Acts

By Philip Barry

PHILIP BARRY won a Harvard prize in his playwriting youth with a comedy called "You and I." He followed that with a moderately successful second play, "The Youngest," and then slipped gracefully down among the playwrights who were merely present and accounted for the last two seasons.

His "In a Garden" was no more than what a drama critic might call a *succes d'estime,* although both Arthur Hopkins as producer and Laurette Taylor as chief actress labored earnestly the season of 1925-26 to save it. His "White Wings," a sparkling but unpopular satire, could not be sold, even by Winthrop Ames, the season of 1926-27. Last November Barry offered "John," a dignified and dramatic study of the Baptist who was the forerunner, but it, too, suffered a quick defeat.

It happens, however, that Mr. Barry is a hard and persistent worker. The trucks bearing the scenic remains of "John" had barely reached the storehouse when two additional Barry plays were announced—a comedy first named "The Wedding" and finally called "Paris Bound," and a mystery piece frankly labelled "Cock Robin," that Barry had written in a spirit of fun with Elmer Rice.

"Paris Bound," which came in Christmas week with the popular Madge Kennedy as a star, was an overnight success. Of the seventeen new plays offered that week only four lasted until Lent, and of the four the Barry play was the outstanding comedy favorite.

This is a story of a youthful adventure with love and marriage related by those moderately exclusive humans of the upper middle class about whom this author writes so intimately and so understandingly. It is lightly touched with a marital problem sufficiently common to give it universal significance and sufficiently serious to bring its audiences to quick attention.

At the play's outset the month is July, the year 1922, the scene the upstairs sitting room of a house in the country near New

254

York—an attractively furnished room shielded from a hot summer sun by awnings that shade a stretch of windows on the west.

Mary and Jim Hutton have been married less than two hours. The marriage breakfast is just over and from below stairs the sounds of revelry, the music and the laughter, would indicate that the party has reached or is about to reach its peak with the planned departure of the bride and groom.

Jim and Mary Hutton are, as they enter the room for a minute's respite from the almost too affectionate attentions of their friends, a good-looking, happy pair—Jim a stalwart twenty-six, Mary a sweet and modest twenty-two. They are still in their bridal finery and there is time for only a word—Mary's whispered assurance to Jim that she never has enjoyed a wedding so much in her life, and Jim's enthusiastic admission that he feels the same; Mary's sober little confession that she's a fool about him, and his echoing assurance, sealed with a kiss, that she has nothing on him.

Then Jim is away to change his clothes and collect his bags and Mary has found Julia, the maid, and gone to her room to be put into her going-away things. A valuable aid is Julia. "Aunt Grace asked me if there was anything in this house that I wanted to take with me for my house, and I said you," admits Mary. And that makes Julia happy, too.

It is while Jim and Mary are dressing that Helen White and James Hutton, Sr., Jim's divorced mother and father, meet in this same dressing room.

Mrs. White, who now lives in Europe, has come many miles only to feel a good deal like a stranger at her own son's wedding. Two of Mary's wedding attendants, Nora Cope and Fanny Shippan, have left these somewhat embarrassed parents there and slipped with as much grace as circumstances permit into Mary's room to help with the dressing.

It is fifteen years since Jim's parents have seen each other and the meeting is not without its emotional reactions. James, Sr., never could quite understand why the former Mrs. Hutton had married White, an "exceptionally dull man," if there ever was one, and Mrs. White would like to be as indifferent as possible to anything he may think about her or her actions.

James, Sr., however, is of a mind to discuss many things. For one thing he is not at all averse to reopening the question of their own separation. He feels that young Jim and Mary have an excellent chance of happiness and success in their married life, but no better chance than he and she had.

From what she has heard, Mrs. White admits, the young people are as completely fortified against failure in marriage as it ever is possible for young people to be.

"Youth, health, love, money and an occupation—they seem to have the odds on their side, at any rate," says she.

James—So did we.

Helen—So "More shame to us?"

James—More shame to you, Helen. (*A brief pause.*)

Helen—The years haven't put wrinkles in your cheek, have they, James?

James—Cheek?

Helen—Cheek.

James—Still bitter. It's amazing.

Helen—Poor dear, life is such a constant surprise to you.—As I remember, you were amazed when I divorced you.

James—That was an act of resentment on the part of a raw young girl. You're past forty now, and should know better.

Helen—You still don't accept the impossibility of my living with you after what you did—

James—I shan't ever accept it.

Helen—Well, I give up. In fact I gave up, some time ago, didn't I?

James—I know: that's one of your troubles.

Helen—I'm afraid I must—

James—Duck—dodge again—get out from under. All right, my dear. (*She turns on him.*)

Helen—Jim, I—! Which of us was in the wrong, you or me!

James—You were. I may have committed adultery, Helen, but I never committed divorce.

Helen—When you had your affair with—with that woman—

James (*amused*)—Mrs. Bliss, her name was—Kitty Bliss— pretty name.

Helen—And a pretty affair. By means of it you destroyed our marriage.

James—I think it was you who did the destroying, Helen.

Helen—How do you figure that?

James—Through what you made of it. All that *we* had—you and I—*our* province was never touched by it.

Helen—That's easy enough to say.

James—It's gospel, my dear.

Helen—I'm afraid I don't understand these separate provinces of yours.

JAMES—Mine?—Every one's!

HELEN—I don't understand them.

JAMES—Well, here's your son Jim: he is attractive to women. His wife Mary is attractive to men. He's twenty-six, she is twenty-two. Is he never to know another woman, or she another man?

HELEN—Know them? But of course!

JAMES—Well, love them, then.

HELEN—Even love them—in a way.

JAMES—Provided they "behave."

HELEN—Naturally. (*He smiles.*)

JAMES—Provided they behave naturally—

HELEN (*indignant*)—I didn't say—

JAMES—Well, I don't think it's very important whether they do or not.

HELEN—In fact, why any marriage at all?

JAMES—Simply because marriage of one woman to one man for a life-time is the most civilized and beautiful idea poor humanity has ever conceived of.

HELEN—Imagine your thinking so.

JAMES—I've never thought otherwise. And any two people, I don't care who they are, who marry for love as we did—as most do—and live before the world as man and wife create between them something they can never get away from and never hope to duplicate.

HELEN—I wonder if they can't.

JAMES—You know they can't. It's an entity as real as any child is and it's born without them knowing it, simply of the fact that a man and woman in love have elected to face *all* the facts of life together, from under one roof.

HELEN—So I denied our spiritual child, is that it?

JAMES—That will do, yes.

HELEN—It was for that that I left *you*, Jim.

JAMES—You left me because you found out that I had gone with another woman.—*Found it out.*

HELEN (*sharply*)—And wasn't that almost enough?

JAMES—No. It didn't begin to be.—For following a physical impulse which I share with the rest of the animal kingdom, you destroyed a spiritual relationship which belonged only to us. For an act which in reality was of little or no importance to you, you did me out of my marriage and my home, of the daughter I've always longed for—very nearly out of the son I already had. You did a good, thorough job, my dear.

But where, Mr. Hutton would like to know, has this achievement in divorce led the former Mrs. Hutton? Even her refusal to discuss the matter further is proof that she has not changed. She is still unable to stand very much; soft where she should be hard and hard as nails where she should be soft.

"I think you might have struck a better balance if you had weathered that one rough stretch, as you should have done," he firmly insists. "You might still be the wronged wife, but you'd be ten times the person you are now."

Now young Jim is in, dressed and ready for the flight and eagerly fit. He finds it good to see his parents together. He is grateful to both of them for coming. They are a great pair, even if they did not hit it off together. Why, he wonders, didn't they?

"It happened," explains his father, with a calm but defiant frankness, "that I was once what your mother calls 'unfaithful' to her."

"You mean you wanted to quit mother, and—?"

"Oh, no—no, never for a minute. But I—"

Young Jim understands and, faced with the necessity of seeming to, in a way, take sides, he is free to admit that he thinks his mother was at least hasty.

"It strikes me as damned short-sighted and pretty damned unjust," he tells her.

He also is convinced that Mary would feel the same. "Marriage is a pretty big job, of course," he concludes. "But it seems to me that if both people use their heads they can manage it."

"You may be sure they can," insists James, Sr.

"I think you would do well, however, to learn to profit by your father's mistake," warns the mother.

"Aren't you being a little rough on him, mother?" Jim demands, smilingly. "I tell you what: I'll do that if you'll teach Mary to profit by yours."

Now Mary is ready, and equally radiant in her going-away things, a bride most enthusiastically, even wildly, approved by her new husband and all the relatives.

Peter, having a perfect timing sense, is in with a tray and a bottle of champagne that the proper healths may be drunk before the grand but secret departure.

Their plan, as Jim explains, is to drive to town, where Peter has engaged rooms at a hotel. They will dine (*in their sitting room, if they have one, at* MARY's *suggestion*) and see a revue. Then they will go aboard their ship, which sails at midnight.

Later, in London, they hope to have more of a visit with Jim's mother, and thereafter Jim is quite likely to see her periodically, because his firm is talking about his making an annual crossing for the good of the business.

Now Jim's father and mother have gone back to the dance— to dance together, as the senior Hutton suggests, and scandalize the guests. The sight of them, leaving the room arm in arm, is a little sad to Mary, and to Jim, too. At the door James, Sr., turns.

"I've only one thing to say to both of you," he offers as a parting word of advice; "if at first you don't succeed—don't try again."

Mrs. White refuses to sanction the sentiment, but she is forced to drag him away to cover her irritation.

As Mary looks after them she pulls Jim down on the couch beside her. For a moment she clings to his arm, and then she speaks.

MARY—Oh, Jim—how awful—

JIM—I know, dear—but don't you worry.

MARY (suddenly)—You know, it occurs to me I've married you under fairly false pretences.

JIM (amused)—Oh? Such as—?

MARY—I've got a lot of bum theories about marriage. You've never heard them.

JIM (grinning)—Let's save 'em for the long winter evenings, shall we?

MARY—I'm afraid I'll forget them.

JIM—How do they go?

MARY—Well, for one thing, I don't believe much in monopolies.

JIM—No?

MARY—Not for us, anyhow. We're too fond of—people.

JIM—You and me and the great throbbing heart of America— that'll be all right.

MARY—Not quite so general as that, maybe.

JIM—I'll like you best, Mary.

MARY—So will I you.—But the point is, I don't expect never to see another man, and I don't expect you never to see another girl.—We've simply got to make ourselves see them! Then there won't even be the danger of them getting to be—to be—

JIM—Novelties to us?

MARY (gratefully)—Exactly—and I like to be alone a lot. I may seem sullen, but it won't mean anything, really it won't.

JIM—I'll look the other way.

MARY—"Respect each other's privacy." Oh, that sounds terrible. Like hints to the love-lorn.

JIM—All theories are terrible.

MARY—Of course they are. But what are you going to do?

JIM—Dunno. (*A brief pause.*) One thing, we're being nice and sensible and modern, aren't we?

MARY—Oh, Jim, we've got to be! (JIM's *smile fades.*) I mean it. We've simply got to be a success. All my life, I've seen nothing but—

JIM—But how can we help but be? *You*—? *Me*—?

MARY—It isn't as easy as that, Jim. There's where people make the mistake. It takes work, and they won't work. *I know it takes work.*

JIM—Mary—

MARY—What? (*His smile reasserts itself.*)

JIM—Beads of sweat'll be standing out on my forehead. (*She laughs, and holds her hand out to him in quick gesture. He takes it.*)

MARY—I'm a fool.

JIM—Nope. Not a bit. (*Kisses hand.*) But I think we'll be all right.

MARY—I know we shall.

Peter has lowered the baggage down from the window, and Tom, the chauffeur, has carried it to the car the runaways are to use. At the proper moment Peter will signal the orchestra to crash into the wedding march, Mary and Jim will join hands and scurry down the stairs, dodging the rice and rose petals, and dive for the car they are supposed to take.

"You'll recognize it by its decorations and wall mottos, mostly very obscene," Peter explains. "I printed them myself last night."

Then they are to rush across the tennis court and out to the south drive, where Tom will be waiting with Peter's own high-powered Pope-Toledo.

But the getting away is not the only problem. Another has arisen of which Noel Farley is the set but slightly unsteady pivot. Fanny Shippan has found Noel "laughing and carrying on in a generally outrageous manner"; and she is fearfully afraid this young woman will end up by making some sort of wretched scene.

There is only one thing to do, Mary decides. Noel's actions, as every one knows, are induced by her frankly expressed love of Jim. They had, at one time, been better than good friends, and

although that was years ago, and Mary had indicated her understanding of the situation, and thought she would put an end to
all the talk, by asking Noel to be one of her attendants, it is quite
evident that Noel still harbors unhappy memories. Therefore
the only thing likely to pull her up now is for Jim to talk with
her. Jim doesn't want to, but he will do it if Mary thinks best.
And Mary does.

Mary knows that Noel loved Jim and thinks she probably still
loves him—terribly. Of Jim's feelings she is not so sure, but she
doesn't think she would care very much if he still cared for Noel
—a little. Nor can she agree with Nora that after a month or
two she will acquire the usual wifely sense of proprietorship and
be furious at every woman Jim even so much as looks at sideways.
Certainly she expects to keep her men friends!

A fine, big-hearted Mary she is, Nora admits. But her ideas
won't work. Try them and she and Jim will be just "another
once-loving pair—bound for Paris."

Mary has left the room when Noel Farley arrives, and Nora
follows shortly on the pretext that she must look for Peter. Jim
is at the other side of the room, and Noel, without moving, is
staring directly at him.

Jim, plainly worried, asks that as a favor Noel will quit the
party after she sees Mary and go home. Noel is willing. She
might even go out the back way, so as not to be seen, or perhaps
she could be hidden somewhere. Her tone is sarcastic. What
does it matter? And then, after they have stared at each other
for a long minute, she adds:

"Do you enjoy it, Jim?"

"Do I enjoy what?"

NOEL—Standing there, kissing me.

JIM—My God, Noel.

NOEL—Mine, too, Jim. It's what you've been doing for a long
while now—each time we've been together. What's it matter that
you've never been much closer to me than this—so long as you've
thought it and wished it?

JIM—You've—had a good deal to drink, haven't you?

NOEL—Yes.—But I've been drunker than this before on no
wine at all. And so have you, my dear, dear, dear—

JIM—Oh, quit it, quit it, will you?

NOEL—I love you, Jim, and I die hard. There should have
been two of you, you know—one for me.

JIM—Listen: have I ever said or done the slightest—

NOEL—I think there *are* two of you—and one *is*.—No, you haven't. But you want me, and I want you and if it keeps up, some day there'll be hell to pay. I'm telling you.

JIM—Noel—

NOEL—I know. You've always behaved with the most praiseworthy restraint. That's been splendid of you, I suppose, though I rather wish you hadn't. But you can't fool any one as Irish as me, about love. I couldn't have felt as I do about you, if you didn't feel much the same about me. It doesn't happen that way. It takes two.

JIM—I'm sorry, but I don't agree with you.

NOEL—You don't have to. Nor need you think for a minute that I'm not aware how terribly you love your Mary, and how utterly different it is to what you feel for me. I envy her, but she need never envy me. Not if she's wise.

JIM—How do you mean wise?

NOEL—*She* knows.

JIM—Noel, I haven't the remotest idea of what you're driving at, I really haven't.

NOEL—Well, great intelligence never was your long-suit, was it? (*A brief pause. She adds*): And *I've* done a tall lot of thinking, these last few weeks. I've damn well had to.

JIM—I can't see you've got very far.

NOEL—I've gone a tremendous ways. I'll tell you where I've arrived if you like.

JIM—You needn't mind.

NOEL—I'd rather—if *you* don't. (*She waits. He is silent.*) It's my little pleasure to acknowledge, now, that I'm yours, heart and soul—

JIM—Noel—

NOEL—But you needn't let it upset you: I'm inclined to glory in it. A day like to-day is fairly rough-going, of course, but I imagine I'll survive it. Because you see, I'm just as sure as I am of my name, that part of you is mine. I can't make head or tail of it—I'm still frightfully balled-up in every direction, but of what's between us, I'm quite sure. I wish we'd been something—important to each other. I wish something actual had happened. Our chances for pulling out of it would be better, then But we weren't—and nothing has. So here we are, and here we'll be—and you'd better shun me as you would the devil!

JIM—When you see me running from some one, you'll know it.

NOEL—That's the boy!—Spoken like a Yale man.

JIM (*turns—faces up-stage*)—Oh, shut up.

NOEL—You can't be indifferent to me, Jimmy Hut—so don't try. (*She softens in an instant.*) Oh, come here a minute—let me look at you. Never mind—I'll come there. (*She moves toward him.*) Jim—Jim— (*Takes hold of his left arm.*)

JIM (*turns face to her*)—Quit it, Noel.

NOEL—What a handsome groom you were, Jim—I was proud of you, truly I was. I could feel my heart swell to see you, really I could—so straight, and so well turned-out, and so damned cocksure of yourself, and so much in need of a beating. I didn't kiss you when the others did, did I? Here—I shall— (*She puts her hands behind his shoulders, and leans up to him.*)

JIM (*grasps her by elbows, trying to shake her into a realization of the situation*)—Noel—God damn it, Noel—this is my wedding-day!

NOEL—Stupid—stupid—we'd have had a much better chance, if you'd let that go— (*A pause. She turns up toward table.*) Well— (*She tries to compose herself.*) Is this some one's wine? (*She lifts a full glass from the tray.*) Here's to your great happiness—and may I share in it. (*She drains the glass.*) Damn.

Noel dashes the empty glass against a stone vase on the table. There is a knock at the door. It is Mary come to collect her husband and say good-by to her friend.

Noel is faintly apologetic. Jim, she explains, has been taking her over the coals for enjoying the party too much, and she has promised to be a good girl.

Now Noel has gone and Jim is relieved. That, at least, is over with. Mary is relieved, too, but she can't resist one little inquiry. "Is it still me, Jim?"

She stops him before he can answer her with becoming and darkly significant protestations of loyalty.

They're ready for Peter now. But they will give him only three minutes. If he is not ready by that time they will make a run for it.

"In the meantime," suggests Mary, "let's form a group called 'Alone at last,' shall we?"

They are standing by the table holding hands when Jim answers, with great conviction:

JIM—Lord knows I'm willing. (MARY *closes her eyes.*)

MARY—I'm just so damn tired—happy—

JIM—So am I.

MARY—It's like a warm bath.

JIM—It's better.

MARY—I don't expect to have another serious thought for months on end, now.

JIM—If you feel one stealing up on you, fight like hell.

MARY—All that silly talk of mine about theories and stratagems and what-nots generally—don't mind it. It's just that when I think anything awful might happen to you and me, my heart slides right down to my toes in a panic. It's just—wanting desperately to guard the most precious thing I've ever had or shall have.

JIM—I know, Darling. That goes for me, too.

MARY—Then it's on—

JIM—You bet it is.—Let's make just one blanket agreement, shall we?

MARY—What is it?

JIM—Whatever happens, never quit each other. (*She presses her cheek against his.*)

MARY—Never, never.

JIM—Never in this world.

MARY—In any world.

The orchestra has swung into the "Dardanella" which is the first signal and the wedding-march impends. Julie has had the last good-by and the last word of instruction from her mistress. And now the orchestra pauses for the change of tune.

MARY—Sh!

JIM—What?

MARY—It's *it!*

JIM—Is it?

MARY—Yes! Listen!

JIM—You're right.

MARY—Come on, sweet!

JIM—Where's my hat?

MARY—Oh, never mind your hat.

JIM—All right, the hell with it.

MARY—Give me your hand!

JIM—Give me yours. I'm the man. (*Their hands fumble for each other.*)

MARY—Quit fooling, stupid. Hurry up, or they'll murder us.

JIM—What's the rush? We've got fifty years.—To Mary from Jim, with love. (*He kisses her.*) Here we go! (*He takes her hand and rushes for the hall. Curtain starts to fall. From downstairs, rising above the wedding-march, comes the sound of shouts*

and laughter and cheers. From outside the house, the sound of a motor horn.)
The curtain falls.

ACT II

Five years have passed. It is May, 1927. Jim and Mary are living in New York, over near the East River. The scene is the music room on the top floor of the Hutton house, added on for them by Jim's father as a wedding gift.

There is a large fireplace in it, and a studio window at back. "The furniture is rather dark and includes an ebony grand piano. The walls are of smooth gray plaster."

At the moment Richard Parrish, a young composer, is playing a theme from his newest ballet and Mary is listening. "Richard is about twenty-seven or eight, he is not handsome nor particularly well dressed. He has no gift for pretty speeches, has only natural manners and natural grace."

There are parts of the ballet that do not please Mary, and she is not at all backward about telling Richard so. Sometimes he agrees with her and sometimes he does not.

Mary is convinced that Richard has a great gift, and she is glad to have offered the studio to him. He can use it every morning and all morning, until his ballet is finished, and she will never bother him—unless she should be expressly invited.

She is not only invited, Richard is quick to insist, but he would be very grateful if she would help him. He thinks perhaps he can finish the composition in two months, or less, with her aid. Mary is pleased with that plan. It will give her something to think about while Jim is making his annual trip abroad. Jim is about to start on that trip and will be gone six weeks. He was going to-day—but he could not get a reservation.

"Why don't you go with him?"

"I don't know," explains Mary. "I just never do. Once I did, the first year. Then the next year I was about to have a baby, and the next year Aunt Grace was about to have an appendix, and the next year I'd just had another baby, and last year both of them had whooping cough and this year, when I could go, I won't."

Of course Mary is crazy to go. And yet she has a feeling that married people need holidays from each other.

RICHARD—You're a funny pair.
MARY—We're a nice pair, don't you think?

RICHARD—Sure; very nice— Terribly in love, too, aren't you?

MARY—Oh, yes, terribly.

RICHARD—How long is it?

MARY—Six years the tenth of July.

RICHARD—Pretty good.

MARY—It keeps getting better.

RICHARD—I suppose you aren't likely ever to crash now unless one of you falls in love with some one else.

MARY—I don't think Jim and I could crash even on that.

RICHARD—No?

MARY—No.

RICHARD—Well! There's not much chance it'll happen, is there?

MARY—It might. To Jim it might.

RICHARD—And if it did?

MARY—My one fear in the world is that he wouldn't quite understand how little it meant to me. (*A silence.*)

RICHARD—I guess there's nothing to be said to that.

MARY—There it is!

RICHARD (*after a pause*)—D'you know, I can't tell you how much I grant you two. And it is a funny thing, because you're the kind of people I've resented all my life. I never expected to believe that you could be so—so damned valuable. I used to curse into my beard whenever I passed a house like this. I used to spit on the pavement whenever a decent-looking motor passed me. I don't any more, because I've found two among you whom I know to be of absolutely first importance in all the ways I value. You're hard in the right places, you're wise with a most beautiful wisdom and for your life as you live it, I've nothing but salutes and cheers.

MARY (*overcome*)—Why, Richard—

RICHARD—Why, your grandmother. It's true, and I mean it. What about this bollicking ballet? Do you really want to help me get it down?

MARY—I ask for nothing better. The babies are in the country with Aunt Grace. They're thriving. I'll spend four days a week in town and you can come out for week-ends. She's got a Knabe. It's old, and the lacquer's cracked, but it's sweet as a nut.

RICHARD—When does Jim sail?

MARY—Saturday. He was to have gone on the *Paris* to-day but he couldn't get a cabin. Now it's not until the *France,* May fifteenth. I can go to work on the sixteenth.

RICHARD—Lord, it'd be wonderful. You know you *have* got a pretty good ear.

MARY—I've got a first-rate ear, and I can write the stuff down like a house on fire.

RICHARD—Imagine finishing it! (*Plays few chords.*)

MARY (*after a pause*)—How many things *have* you finished, Richard? (RICHARD *stops playing.*)

RICHARD—Oh, be still. (*Starts playing.*)

(JULIE *enters with a tray containing glass of milk and a plate of sandwiches.* RICHARD *frowns at it.*)

RICHARD (*stops playing*)—Speaking of babies, I think I can live without this milk every morning.

MARY—It builds you up. See what a big girl I am.

Richard's ballet is a bit fantastical, completely cock-eyed he calls it, but he has great hopes that it may prove amusing, if it is ever produced. Probably it never will be. It would cost too much for one thing. But if it ever is done he would like an American to do it.

"Not the Metropolitan—or any of the Art boys, either," he stipulates. "I'd like some good, hard-boiled revue-manager. Then they'd dance, by God, and not waddle around picking dream-flowers off the ground-cloth. And I'd have an orchestra for whom the world didn't end with Debussy."

The idea of the ballet is ever so modernistic and mechanistic, with "a lot of religion in it, and a lot of test-tubes and micro-scopes and down-town at lunch hour, and Madison Square Garden with a hockey-match and that joint in Harlem where I've got a new job playing the piano from twelve to two—it's a swell place, really, and, oh, God, there's a lot in it, really."

Richard is deep in a recital of the ballet's plot to Mary when Jim comes rushing home, bringing news.

He is off to London on the afternoon boat. The cancelled res-ervation has been unexpectedly recovered, and as it is desirable that he be in London as soon as possible he is sailing at 1. Mary is none too happy about this sudden change of plans. Nor is Jim. But there it is.

"Come with me, darling," suggests Jim, when Richard has said his good-by—and left. "It's a big cabin."

MARY—No. I can't.

JIM—We'd have fun.

MARY—Shut up! Shut up!

JIM—I think this is all rot, you know. This enforced-holiday business.

MARY—Maybe it is.—When will you be back?

JIM—By July—the tenth surely, now. Where's your party for the anniversary to be—here or in the country?

MARY—Here. I'm going to keep the house open until the fifteenth anyway. Do make it in time, Jim. It's important to me. I'm a fool about Christmas and birthdays and things like that.

JIM—You leave it to me. I'll be here. (MARY *smiles*.)

MARY—I've always said if we got safely past the sixth—

JIM—It's been a good go, hasn't it, darling?

MARY—Hasn't it, though?

JIM—I'd do it again, wouldn't you?

MARY—Oh, maybe I wouldn't!

JIM—Kiss me, please. (MARY *starts to put arms about his neck*.) Very small: I've got a boat to catch. (*Kiss*)— Thanks.

There are all the hurried arrangements for Jim's departure. There is telephoning to the country that Jim may say good-by to his young son and promise him ever and ever so many things from the other side. There is the matter of Mary's private account at the bank, which, fortunately, is bursting; and the decision about putting gravel on the roof so they may have a garden. There is the question of the possible defection of the newest maid; and the question of the baby's legs being properly massaged, not because they are any different from any other baby's legs, but because her father suffers a mighty fear that she may grow up with fat legs.

JIM—Don't have any vaccinations or anything till I get back, will you?

MARY—I wasn't planning any.

JIM—Just keep cool with Coolidge.

MARY—You betcha.

JIM—What'll you be doing all the time?

MARY—Music with Richard, mostly. He's got a grand idea for a ballet.

JIM—Where'd you find him, Mary?

MARY—Richard? He was at the Rosalskys' that night. Don't you remember?

JIM—Oh, yes. (*A moment*)— He's not the kind that makes passes, is he?

MARY—Richard?—Not in the least.

JIM—If any one does, haul off and paste him one for me.

MARY—No one will.

JIM—*I* would.

MARY—Most men have more manners.

JIM—Mary.

MARY—What?

JIM—I'm in love with you.

MARY—But what about my children?

JIM—Forget 'em. Come with me in my death-car.

MARY—When do we leave?

JIM—How would, say, twelve-thirty do? We could—

Before Mary can answer, the phone breaks up their bantering, which has been a little desperately sustained to fight off the tears that are near.

Now Jim has come to the final checking up of his list of last-minute things not to be overlooked.

JIM—Oh, would you tell Peter I can't play golf with him Wednesday.

MARY (*a mental note*)— Peter—golf—Wednesday.

JIM—Let's see, now: (*He reads the list.*) "Telephone Father" —check. "Telephone the country"—check. "Kiss Mary." (*He kisses her*)—check. "Don't forget passport." (*He feels for it.*) "Tell Julie plenty underwear"—check. "Tell Mary love her." (*He turns to her.*) Love you.

MARY—You are good, and kind.

JIM—Check. "About liquor supply"—if you need anything, telephone Trotter at the Club.

MARY—Trotter?

JIM—Trotter.

MARY—Liquor—Trotter—club. (JIM *looks at the list.*)

JIM—Keep out of drafts, don't eat starchy foods, pump up bicycle-tires and be at foot of West 14th Street at ten minutes to one. (*Puts list in pocket.*)

MARY—Ten minutes to one. Six weeks. (*To him.*) Jim, Jim, Jim, Jim!

JIM—Aw, Mary—

MARY—I'm going to weep.

JIM—Blink your eyes. (*She blinks.*) Swallow— (*She swallows.*) That's the girl.

MARY—Write me all the time. Cable me every minute.

JIM—You bet I will.

MARY—Don't have a French doctor even for a cold.

JIM—No.

MARY—If the ship starts to sink, kick all the women and children out of the way and grab the biggest life-belt and—

JIM—You bet I will.

MARY—Say your prayers night and morning—and— (*Suddenly she clings to him.*) Oh, Jim—Jim!—

JIM—Oh, cut it out, will you? (*He kisses her. She strains
against him. A moment, then* JAMES HUTTON'S *voice is heard
from the hall.*)

The elder Hutton is shortly followed by Fanny Shippan, herself just back from two years abroad, and Fanny's bubbling spirits
and eager gossip saves the domestic scene. Fanny has had all
she wants of travel for the present. Britain for the British is
perfectly all right with her. New York is a perfectly wonderful
place to get back to, and she is going to stay for years and years.
She brings them gorgeous presents, earrings for Mary and hand-
painted braces for Jim, and her love, and she is, as she confesses
to Mary when Jim has gone to see that Julie has left nothing out
of his bags, happily surprised to find that nothing has happened
to spoil the sweet serenity of their married lives.

FANNY—Honestly, Mary, I never saw two happier looking
people in my life.

MARY—We're pretty sunk over this trip, just at present.

FANNY—Most people I know would be cheering. You're in
luck. You don't realize it.

MARY—Oh, yes, we do!

FANNY (*to* JAMES)—It isn't just put on, is it?

JAMES (*smiling*)—I don't think so.

FANNY—I've got a little skeptical about marriage—me, who
had such faith. Paris is simply alive with people you know, getting divorces.

MARY—Well, I think it's sickening.

FANNY—So do I. What I hate most, is what it does to their
what-do-you-call-it, souls, characters. Honestly, just listening to
their tales, I felt like Bad Fanny, the wickedest woman in Bridge-
port. I claim it shows in their faces. You wouldn't know Susie
Price.

MARY—*She* isn't too!

FANNY—Indeed she is!—Her precious little individuality was
being stifled.

MARY—*Her what!?* I didn't know she had one.

FANNY—Home-life developed it.—But of course as soon as the

decree is handed down, she's going to try again with some fifth-rate Englishman. She's living with him now in the South-of-France somewhere.

MARY—It *is* vile.

FANNY—Just thank your stars, Girlie. Because there's something awfully wrong with marriage.

MARY—There's something awfully wrong with the people who *get* married.

FANNY—How are Peter and Nora? Are they all right?

MARY—Now don't go *looking* for trouble, Fanny.

FANNY—Catch me! These days I spread oil wherever I go. You have to.

JAMES—Did you get to the South at all, Fanny?

FANNY—Of France? No, worse luck. (*To* MARY.) Oh, but I must tell you. Zoe Evans was at Cannes—

MARY—I don't know her.

FANNY—I know you don't. But she knows Jim and she said she saw you and him two or three times at—what's the name of that little place up in the mountains back of Antibes? St. Paul du—something—St. Paul de Var! And she was going to speak to you, only—

MARY—When was that?

FANNY—Last May.

MARY—Oh, yes.

FANNY—Only she couldn't get Jim's eye and you both looked so devoted she concluded you were there to escape Americans. They thought at the Inn you were a run-away couple living in— Well, it isn't sin to the French, is it? Zoe said the patron told her you'd taken the sweetest little studio-place with actually a bathroom. I didn't even know you were over. Why didn't you look me up?

MARY—Well, it was—

FANNY—You *were* trying to avoid Americans! (*A moment.*)

MARY—It was the shortest kind of a trip.

FANNY—You didn't run into Noel, did you? Some one told me she was down there somewhere on the Riviera—or maybe it was Rome.

MARY—No, we didn't.

FANNY—Apparently she's got an idea that she can write or paint or something—

MARY—And can she?

FANNY—I doubt it. There's a girl I never could make out.

MARY—Couldn't you, Fanny? I don't think Noel's hard.

Fanny is gaily on her way in another moment or two, calling her good-bys to Jim as she passes his room on the floor below.

Mary, a little stunned by what she has heard, turns to the window and is staring thoughtfully into space when Jim's father seeks to reassure her.

For one thing he would not, if he were Mary, jump too quickly to conclusions. Nor would Mary. To prove which she goes calmly to the phone and calls up Mrs. Farley to make sure of Noel's address. And there it is, repeated to her over the phone: "Villa May. St. Paul-du-Var. Alpes Maritimes."

"You know, this isn't fair at all," protests James Hutton. "This is—"

"I know Jim, father, and I know Noel. And if they were there together—"

She can't finish. She feels that the charge is true, and the thought is horrible to her. If it is true, if it is Noel and not her that Jim wants, Mary knows what she will do.

JAMES—Jim loves you as few women are loved.

MARY—He could hardly love me—and go with her, could he?

JAMES—Couldn't he, Mary?

MARY—No!

JAMES—It's not conceivable, is it?

MARY—If it were, I shouldn't let it be!

JAMES—Ah—I see.

MARY—I'm not doing any sharing—I'm not going any halves with—with—oh, I can't say her name, now.

JAMES—You'll never be called upon to share what you and Jim have.

MARY—What Jim and I have—what is it we have? What's left of it now? He's taken the whole beautiful thing in his hands and done that with it. (*With a gesture of breaking it in two.*)

JAMES—If what you suppose has happened *has* happened, one good crass fact explains it.

MARY—It might have once. Not now.

JAMES—But, Mary, you must know—

MARY—I know that six years ago Jim and I were married.

JIM (*from the hall below*)—Oh, Mary! (*She does not answer.*) Darling—! (*She starts to the doorway and calls faintly*):

MARY—Yes? (JIM *not hearing her calls again.*) Darling—! (*at doorway*)—Yes?

JIM—Where are those shiny new studs of mine?

MARY—They're on the dressing-table in my room.

Jim—Right!—You're all ready, aren't you?

Mary—Yes, I'm ready.—We ought to leave in two minutes! (*She presses the button on the door.*)

Jim—Oh, damn it! Let's make it three— (*Pause.*)

James (*softly*)— Don't you see, my dear, that *that's* the real thing—and the other just a—? (*Her gesture cuts him short. A moment, then*): May I ask what you intend to do?

Mary—I don't know yet. I'll have a month to myself to think in. When he comes back, I'll know.

James—Surely you'll say nothing now.

Mary—I'll say nothing now. (*She closes her eyes in pain, and averts her head.*) I'll say less than nothing.

James—If you're wise, my dear, you'll say nothing ever.

Jim is in, with a box of flowers. He has found time to send one of the maids to the corner for them. That was sweet of him, Mary admits. No, there is nothing—nothing the matter with her! Of course she wants to go to the dock with him!

Jim promises his father that he will not work too hard on the trip. In fact, after he gets through the worst of the job in London, he thinks perhaps he will run over to Cannes or Antibes for a few days before sailing.

"I thought you hated the Riviera," suggests Mary, catching her breath as she hides her face in the flowers.

"That was in season," blandly replies Jim.

Mary—I didn't know you'd ever been there out of season.

Jim—They say it's another place after the crowds go. Father, would you tell the bank to cable a couple of thou. to my credit in London?

James—Have you got enough now?

Jim—Plenty, thanks.

Mary—Here you are— (*She sets in* Jim's *buttonhole a flower from her bouquet.*)

Jim (*takes her in arms—not an embrace*)—Oh, thanks, darling.

James—If you see your mother, give her my love.

Jim—I'll do that. (*Crosses to father, shakes hands.*) Goodby, sir. You're a grand guy.

James—Thanks, so are you—but hurry.

Jim (*crosses above to* Mary)—Come on, Angel—

Mary—Here I am.

Jim—Just take Jimmy's hand— (*He holds his hand out to her. She puts her hand in it.*) And away we go!

MARY—Away we go— (*They start for door.*)

JIM (*stops*)—Wait a minute—I must have one good last look. (*He takes her other hand, faces her about and looks at her. She returns his gaze smiling.*)

MARY—Is that all right?

JIM—Father—am I in luck, or am I not?

JAMES—I think you're in great luck, Son.

JIM—And don't I know it! (*To* MARY.) Listen, Sweet, I've got a great idea—

MARY—What is it, dear?

JIM—This stupid enforced holiday—why not make it four weeks, instead of six? You could take a fast boat, and we'd have ten days in Paris, and then come back together. (*Start exiting as curtain starts falling.*) No, but seriously I don't see any reason why we shouldn't have at least a week there, and a *little* holiday together after this idiotic month of— (*His voice has faded out until it is no longer heard.* JAMES *stands alone, looking after them—*)

The curtain falls.

ACT III

Six weeks later, on an early July night, the windows of the Hutton studio are open wide to catch such cooling breezes as may blow up from the river.

Mary is at the piano, playing idly, when James Hutton calls. It is late, sometime around 11, but his visit has apparently been planned. Mary has written him and he has given up a fishing trip to respond. The fact that there may be matters of serious import to discuss keeps them fencing conventionally for several minutes.

Thus it is duly reported by Mary that the children are simply thriving in the country; that she has been working like mad with her music and staying in town a lot, practically alone in the house, but that by putting an electric attachment on the front door she has been able to turn the studio into a small apartment and answer only those bells the signal rings of which she recognizes.

In trade for which she learns that Mr. Hutton has been finding some relief for his neuritis by sunning himself on the beach at Newport, that he was glad to give up his fishing trip and that he is hoping for the best from what he has come to learn—which is Mary's decision respecting Jim.

The only word that Mary has had from Jim is a radio reading:

"Giant liner battered by storms. Floating palace twelve hours late. Much love."

Indications are that the ship will not reach her berth before early morning and that Jim will not be out there before breakfast time.

As for Mary's decision—it is against Jim. She has found out that the reports about his having been with Noel Farley in Italy were definitely true. She has not written Jim, nor told a soul. She will tell him on his arrival. To-morrow is the date of their wedding anniversary. Six years! It probably is a very fair average as marriages go nowadays. Perhaps the average is even less than that. Mary has decided to divorce Jim.

MARY—It's too bad, I know. But you see it's all gone, now.

JAMES—What is? Your love for him?

MARY—I don't know about that. I can't tell about that, yet awhile. But my life with him—that's gone, all right.

JAMES—Only if you let it go.

MARY—I'm afraid I'm not much good at hanging on to things, once they've begun to slip from me. I'm afraid I don't want them much after that.

JAMES—What a fine, deep love it must have been, eh? (*She looks at him. He explains.*) To chuck the whole thing overboard so lightly, so easily.

MARY—I haven't had much ease these last weeks, Father. And I don't feel light, precisely. But if I mean no more to him than that—

JAMES—Than what?

MARY—If his love for me wasn't strong enough to—

JAMES—Listen to me, Mary: If you're going to quit Jim, quit him. But in heaven's name don't let it do this to you.

MARY—Do what to me?

JAMES—Fog your intellect, fog your reason—make an honest, fearless, first-rate woman into a softy.

MARY—I beg your pardon.

JAMES—"If I mean no more to him—" "If his love for me wasn't strong enough—" Really, for you, of all people to talk that kind of second-rate trash, is about the limit.

MARY—That's going it pretty stiff, don't you think?

JAMES—Yes, I do. And I'm amazed to think you need it.— What on earth has one misstep of Jim's to do with you?

MARY—It has a great deal to do with me.

JAMES—Nonsense!— If your hatred of the Farley girl, or

your jealousy of Jim is stronger than anything else you feel, all right, but this sense of grievance—personal injury—good heavens, Mary, what can Noel Farley do to *you?* If Jim has been anything to her—*he* may lose by it, but what *you* lose I can't see.

MARY—I neither hate Noel nor am I jealous of Jim nor do I feel that I've been injured. But I've lost about everything I had, I think.

JAMES—How so?

MARY—Jim belonged to me. Jim was all my own.

JAMES—Don't glory in your sense of possession, Mary. It's the lowest instinct you've got.

MARY—I'm glorying in very little, now. It's—rather awful, to know you're not loved. You miss it terribly.

JAMES—Jim loves you as he always has. I'm as sure of that as I am of my name.

MARY—In any event, I don't feel called upon to share him.

JAMES—I doubt if you've shared anything. If you have, it's the least important element in your whole relationship.

MARY—It seems not to be.

JAMES—I don't mean to belittle sex, my dear. I acknowledge quite cheerfully its power and its delights. Sex holds a high and dishonored place among other forms of intoxication. But love is something else again, and marriage is still another thing—

MARY (*bitterly*)—Yes, and a great thing, isn't it?—Man's most divine conception—pure poetry—religion—sacrament—

JAMES—By God, it ought to be!

MARY—I was rather for it myself, if you'll remember. It was church to me, all right. But now, you see, I'm left with all the candles out, and rosy windows smashed and rotten ragtime playing through my church, where there was nothing but plain chant and Palestrina all the whole day long. I think I *have* lost something—

Calmly and earnestly the elder Hutton pleads with Mary. Nothing has gone, nothing will go out of her life unless she permits it to go. Where now are all her fine boasts that nothing could ever separate her and Jim?

Theories, Mary admits, are fine things until something happens. Then you find, then a woman finds, at least, that she cannot think straight—she can only feel straight. Many things Mary believes she could have stood. Even mistresses, someway, seem a possible, though hateful sort of compromise. But with her and Jim and Noel Farley— That's different.

Nor can her father-in-law's arguments change her. The thought that physical attraction is not limited to one man or one woman may be true, but there must have been something more than mere physical attraction between Jim and Noel. True, when Jim came back from that particular trip she neither sensed any change in him nor felt anything in her bones as she says, to indicate that anything that might have happened had in any way encroached upon her province.

True, also, her decision will mean that she will probably join the rest of the defeated sisterhood in Paris, ready to bribe her way to freedom through the French courts. But—

MARY—If that's the way it's done. How else?

JAMES—Are you asking me? Then I say not only put divorce completely out of mind, but never by so much as one word let him know what you know. Refuse to admit it, Mary. Refuse even to yourself, to admit it. Above all, don't speak of it. If there's one destructive thing in this world, it's words—spoken—

MARY—I shall tell him the first moment that I see him.

JAMES—Well, it's quite beyond me. I counted on great things for you and Jim. When I stood there beside that boy in that hot little country church six years ago, and saw you coming up to him, I can't tell you what I felt about you both. It seemed to me that you had everything; strength, beauty, youth and wisdom—minds as open as any ever I've encountered—enormous gayety—a great joy in each other, and in life. Such a wedding-garment as you two brought to your marriage, I've never known.

MARY—Well, it's in rags now, all right.

JAMES—And why?—If you and Jim had spent the last six years rowing with each other that would be one thing. Actual, hopeless incompatibility I can understand. Drunkenness—cruelty —insanity— But this, *this*.

MARY—About the best reason there is, I think.

JAMES—Mary, not three months ago all of you came to me for Easter. Jim arrived late. You hadn't seen him in three days— three whole days. I heard your voices from the next room. You chattered on about nothing until morning. You laughed a great deal. It was great music, Mary. There was more love in it than in all the sighs and picked-up roses in the world.

MARY—It's no use, Father.

JAMES—No?—Then all that's left for me to say is that a most uncommon marriage is about to go to smash because a once wise woman has become vain and selfish, because a good, hard mind has nicked it's edge off on as rotten and false a conception as ever yet existed. You're going to quit Jim because he had an affair with another woman—well, suppose he did, what of it? How big a part does that play in *your* life? Do you describe your marriage in those terms alone? I'm appalled you set so slight a value on yourself. I'm appalled that you accept defeat so easily, and on such a count.

MARY—I hoped you would understand me. Evidently you don't. If ours had been just any ordinary, halfway-happy marriage, perhaps it might survive this. But it was so perfect for so long, it can't. It goes from all to nothing.

JAMES—Talk. Don't blind yourself with any such glamorous mist as that, my dear. Everything you've told me to-night confirms my first suspicion; that it's the physical fact alone you can't escape. All you've said has been just one repeated statement that to you the most important thing in your whole marriage has been your physical relation to your husband.

MARY—You think so!

JAMES—Over and over you've said it. And now, because you insist on a monopoly of that particular thing, and find you haven't it—you take the lowest possible advantage of your ample means to indulge yourself in a luxury the lucky poor cannot afford. Bid up vanity! Bid up revenge!—Well, do it, and you're a failure, Mary—a complete failure—not only in your marriage—but in every last department of your life.

MARY—That's enough, I think.

JAMES—I am ashamed of you. I cannot believe—

MARY—Quite enough. (*He looks at her intently. There is a silence.*)

JAMES—Very well. Good-night, my dear.

MARY—Good-night. (*A brief pause.*)

JAMES (*a last appeal*)—Mary—

MARY—Good-night.

Richard Parrish and Mr. Hutton pass each other at the door. The composer has come on ahead of Nora and Peter Copes and Fanny Shippan, who are also expected.

Richard is visibly restless. He has had his dinner, and he doesn't care to drink. In fact he is very plainly in a mood to resent her attempt to cheer him or to probe the reason for his state of mind.

There is still a little work to do on the last movement of the ballet, Mary reminds him, but Richard will not work on it; will

not even give it another half hour, after all the work they have
done together on it the last several weeks!

He is disgusted with the ballet, he snaps. It hasn't a snow-
ball's chance, anyway. It never had!

Hurt and mystified, Mary asks Richard to leave her, and then
calls him back again for some explanation of his actions. He
tells her that the time has come when she must know how he
feels toward her. He must have a long talk with her—alone.
When the bell rings to announce Peter and Nora let her refuse
to answer. Let him stay on. Unless she is afraid?

MARY (*a small step backward*)—Good-by, Richard.—And
some time, if you can manage it, I wish you'd finish *something*.

RICHARD (*softly*)—Oh, damn you—

MARY (*in a burst*)—And damn you! Go and tune pianos,
that's where *you* belong! A fine artist *you* are—lazy, dabbling,
worthless— (*He rises quickly and seizes her by the shoulders.*)

RICHARD—I can't finish that ballet, because that ballet's you
and me, and we aren't finished and never shall be. So *it* won't.

MARY—You can let go my shoulders now.

RICHARD—I won't though.

MARY—What's it all about, Richard?

RICHARD—I love you, Mary.

MARY—I think you love music, my dear.

RICHARD—You and it—you're one to me.

MARY—Thanks. That's very sweet.

RICHARD—Oh, don't talk like such a fool.

MARY—I don't know what to say to you. What do you want
me to say?

RICHARD—Something I'll— Anything you want to.

MARY—I like you very much—so much, so much. And I shall
miss you horribly.

RICHARD—We've been together all the time, for five weeks—
so will I you.

MARY—I shan't know what to do with myself.

RICHARD—But you'll find something, won't you?

MARY—I'll try awfully hard.

RICHARD—Oh, don't you feel a thing for me—not anything at
all? (*She looks at him, a little startled.*)

MARY—I never thought—

RICHARD—Mary— I think you do, Mary.

MARY—Do you suppose?

RICHARD—Yes.—Don't *you?*

MARY—It would be very funny if I did.

RICHARD—And would you laugh a great deal?

MARY—I think I'd cry my eyes out.

RICHARD—Then never mind. (*She turns to him again, swiftly.*)

MARY—Oh, you dear person, you—

RICHARD—Mary—come here to me a moment—

MARY—I can't.

RICHARD—You don't want to—

MARY—I—didn't say that—

RICHARD—Then why?

MARY—I don't know. It just seems to me I can't.

RICHARD—All right.—Good-by. Thanks ever so much for—ever so many things.

MARY—Oh, *don't* say that! It's I, who—

RICHARD—I expect when you take me all in all, I'm just a bum.

MARY—You're a pretty important bum, I think. To me you are, anyhow.

RICHARD—That'll do nicely. Good-by. (*He holds out his right hand to her. She hesitates one instant, then moves directly and kisses him, then puts head down on his shoulder.*) Look up at me!

MARY—No, no—

RICHARD—Look up! (*They have long kiss—breaking on* MARY's *next line.*)

MARY (*trying to push him away—he holds her*)—Oh, this isn't me!

RICHARD—It *is* you.

MARY—No, no.

RICHARD—For the first time, it's you.

MARY—It's—just something raging inside me. It isn't me—it isn't.

RICHARD—It's *my* you.—It's the you *I* know.

Richard, however, refuses to leave. He is going to stay on, with her. Weakly she pleads with him to leave her, and yet realizes that she wants him to stay. The Mary in his arms is not the Mary she always has known. She senses the difference, yet feels she is powerless.

"You think it will be just the beginning of something," Richard's voice is whispering to her. "It won't. It'll be the end. You're always saying things must be finished. So must this, Mary. It must be finished. Sweet, really it must, or we'll haunt each other our whole lives long. We'd never get away from it

then, never, never, never. Oh, why won't you see that, Mary?
. . . We aren't three people, you and he and I. We're four
people: you and he and you and I. *His* you can't ever in this
world be mine, any more than *my* you can be his. Don't you
know that it has nothing to do with any one or anything but us
and *our* life? Don't you, Mary? . . . It won't be taking anything from any one. You have enough love in you to give me—
you keep making it, making it all the time—love and more love.
And this is *our* life, it really is—there is no one else in it but you
and me—there's no one could come into it. Haven't you always
said?—"

"I've said lots of things!"

The buzzer rings and she does not answer. Her last defense is
crumbling.

"I shouldn't think you'd want me this way," she protests. "It
won't be me at all—it will be—just any woman—"

Her face is contorted and her eyes imploring as Richard holds
her away from him and looks at her intently. "That's true, you
know. It *is* true!" she adds.

In answer he plans the next few minutes. He will leave shortly
after the others arrive and wait a half hour. That will be about
as long as they will stay. Then he will come back. However
she may plead with him he *will* come back—and then she may let
him in or not, as she pleases. She will have had time to decide.

Now Mary has let the callers in and gone to the stair and
called gaily down to them. Richard is at the piano playing a little
wildly. It was probably because of the music, Mary explains,
that they did not hear the bell.

The Copes and Miss Shippan had stopped in at a cellar on
Forty-ninth Street after the show, which explains their being late.
They've been drinking white wine and seltzer, and they are all
pleasantly gay. They're going on some place to dance. They
want Mary to come with them. But Mary wouldn't think of it.

It'll be good to have Jim back, they decide, if only to get Mary
out of her doldrums. For weeks now she hasn't been herself.

"Six weeks without him is just too much to bear, it's too much
to bear," twits Fanny, in melodramatic mockery.

"Never mind," adds Nora; "to-morrow we'll have our old Mary
back again."

"She had charm, that girl," sighs the foolish Peter. "Always a
smile for every one."

"And now it's a curse or a blow," wails Fanny.

"Love is like that," moans Peter.

But their gay spirits and their fooling leave Mary cold. They cannot understand what has happened. And why, among other things, is she determined not to give the usual anniversary party to-morrow? Her excuse that she hasn't any servants in town is foolish. They will loan her all she needs. If she doesn't want that, Fanny will give the party.

Still, Mary stands firmly against it. They are all very kind— but she simply can't face a party. And that, as Peter is free to observe, is quite unmistakably that!

The buzzer rings. A telegram most likely. No one else is expected.

And then Jim walks in!

"Mary stands frozen. Richard's head bends lower over the piano and his hands drop once more upon the keys, which he fingers without sound."

With something resembling a restrained bound Jim is by Mary's side and has gathered her into his arms with a catch of joy in his breath. Still a little stunned she submits to the embrace.

Now the news of most importance has been told: Jim's explanation of how he managed to get himself aboard the mail boat and Mary's report that his children are blooming. And now the party is breaking up, with Peter still joking outrageously and Fanny playing up to him with great success.

Talk of the anniversary party is also put back on the calendar. Jim wants a party, too. Of course they can all come—all except Richard. He is going away, it develops; going south on a United Fruit boat on which he has a purser friend. He'll be gone for four or five months.

"I know a fellow did that once," warns Peter. "It was years after before he could even take orange juice."

Jim is a little puzzled at Richard's and Mary's seriousness. It may be he is a trifle suspicious.

"But how about this ballad you and Mary have been writing?"

"Ballet, you idiot," Fanny corrects him.

"Well, ballet, then. Is it finished?"

"I've just been playing the end of it," says Richard. "I'll bat it out on paper to-night and send it to you in the morning, Mary."

"That would be perfect."

At the finish of the ballet, as Richard sees it now, the hero and heroine are followed across the roof of an apartment by the police. They go over the edge and their bodies are found in the courtyard below.

"I see," mumbles Mary.

"It's a nice practical little ballet," Richard explains to the still wondering Jim. "It wouldn't cost more than a hundred thousand or so to put it on."

"Well, good luck with it, anyhow."

"Thanks. I had that already. Good-by."

With her permission Richard kisses Mary, and promises to write.

Now the others are going, having been somewhat forcefully reminded that that is what is expected of them by Jim. And though Mary is still insistent that there shall be no party they cling to the hope that she will change her mind in time to telephone them next day.

The moment they are alone Mary tries to tell Jim all that is on her mind, but he will not listen. He just wants to ask questions. About his father. And the children. And the help. And all the things she was planning to do while he was gone.

He wants to tell her of his trip, of his visit with his mother in London, of the marvellous success he had with his business errands.

"Did you get down to Cannes?" she asks.

JIM—I hadn't time. Oh, listen—all the presents, yours and the children's too—they're in my bag—I'll have to send to the dock for it, I'll— Oh, Mary, *do* you?

MARY (*lowly*)—What, Jim?

JIM—Love me, Mary? (*She turns away with a cry, half sob of pain.*) Why, what's the matter, dear?

MARY—I don't know—

JIM—Nothin's—really troubling you?

MARY—Jim, you've got to listen to me. I—

JIM—Stop it! (*Then.*) Look here, darling—I don't ever want to hear any bad news, do you understand? (*She nods, dumbly.*) There's nothing ever can affect *us,* you know—nothing in this world— Is there?

MARY (*after a long moment*)—No. I expect there's not.

JIM—Then—there'll never be anything but good news, will there? (*She looks at him and shakes her head.*) That's right! Mary from Jim—much love. (*He kisses her.*)

MARY—Much love. (*His arm goes around her.*)

Now Jim is all for reviving the party. What if there hasn't been anything done about it? There's plenty of time. Plenty of time for a small party. Small parties are more fun anyway. And she can get out her wedding dress, and take a hitch in it. And all the men of the wedding party can get their cutaway coats out of the camphor.

"We'll give a camphor ball," chortles Jim, and Mary laughs happily at his foolishness.

"I'll feel a thousand," she protests.

JIM—You'll look six. I wish we could bring the babies in for it.

MARY—They might come out of a pie and turn handsprings.

JIM—Are they really blooming?

MARY—Wait till you see them!

JIM—Let's go see them now. Where's the motor?

MARY—In the garage. (JIM *goes to the telephone.*) What are you doing?

JIM (*to the telephone*)—Rhinelander 0890.

MARY—You're a madman! It's two o'clock!

JIM—What's the difference?

MARY—It'd be four by the time we got there.

JIM (*puts arm around her*)—Four's early.

MARY—It certainly is.

JIM (*to the telephone*)—Hello, is this the garage? Is that you, Sam? Hello, Sam, this is Mr. Hutton—

MARY—Wait a minute! Wait a *minute!*

JIM (*to the telephone*)—Just to-night. Half an hour ago. You bet your life I'm glad. Look here, Sam, it's hot in this attic and we think we need some air—

MARY—Will you *listen* to me!

JIM—Shhh! How can I talk with all this jabber-jabber? (*To the telephone*)—That's right. Send the roadster right over, will you? Thanks, Sam. See you soon. Make it quick. That's the boy! Good-by! (*He replaces the telephone and smiles at* MARY.)

MARY (*backs a step*)—Jim—really—I'm a woman of thirty.

JIM—Not quite. Come to your children, they need us.

MARY—But they don't wake up until six.

JIM—While we wait we'll pick flowers and match pennies. (MARY *laughs.*)

MARY—I'm not dressed.

JIM—Where's your wrap?

MARY—It's downstairs.

JIM—I love to see them when they're asleep.

MARY—Honestly, Jim, this is ridiculous.

JIM—Tie something round your head and come on. (*Crosses to chair and gets scarf.*)

MARY—Jim, I *tell* you, I—!

JIM (*severely*)—You will do as I say.

MARY—It *would* be fun, you know.

JIM—Fun—? My dear girl, it's our duty! (*He ties scarf around her head.*) There! All you need is the dress now. Come on, sweet. (*They start to go, he has arm about her.*)

MARY (*stops*)—The lights!

JIM—Never mind the lights.

MARY—All right, I won't. (*Starts to go again.*)

JIM (*stopping*)—You haven't forgotten anything, have you?

MARY—Not a thing. Just my dignity.

JIM (*they start toward door*)—That's not serious.

MARY—Who said it was? Give me your hand.

JIM—Give me yours.

(*Their hands fumble for each other. They begin to laugh and move toward the hall.*)

JIM—Here we go, then!

(*Auto horn as they are almost in the doorway and—*
The curtain falls.

ESCAPE

Drama in Prologue and Two Parts

By John Galsworthy

A REPORT was quite generally circulated, following the appearance of "Escape" in London, that John Galsworthy had said this was to be his last play.

As it turned out, some months later, he had said nothing of the kind. Or, having said something of the kind, did not mean it in the way in which it was quoted by the interested press person to whom it was said.

Mr. Galsworthy was quite sure that if he felt another play coming on, so to speak, he would do nothing to discourage the inspiration. "To avoid shock to the Public when I write my next play, I may say at once that it is just as probable that this 'vanishing playwright' (as I am now called) will write more plays if and when the spirit moves him, as it was before he wrote 'Escape' or any other of his 'last plays,' or 'farewells to the theatre.'"

"Escape" is, by the author's confession, "an episodic play." The more particular experts of the drama are suspicious of episodic plays. They find in them a frequent breaking of continuity which is often irritating. The story hops along when properly it should glide from scene to scene, and the frequent interjection of new characters and detached bits of narrative seldom serve to keep audiences contented.

The Galsworthy drama, however, took the handicap in its stride and never faltered. Produced in August, 1926, in London, it ran for nearly a year. Brought to America by Winthrop Ames in October, 1927, it played through the season at the Booth Theatre in New York. Some part of its popularity may reasonably be traced to the appearance of Leslie Howard in the chief rôle, but there is no questioning the appeal of the play itself or the human sympathies inspired by the characteristically honest Galsworthian text.

The prologue of "Escape" is laid in Hyde Park, London, on a summer night. A woman, or girl (you can't tell, warns the author) is sitting alone on a park bench that stands against a low iron railing guarding the grass. A dim radiance is cast by unseen lamps revealing her "painted mask" as not unattractive. And yet any passing plain clothes man would have no difficulty in seeing what she is. One passes now, in fact, and glances knowingly, if not a little threateningly, at her.

Presently, just as the girl has powdered her nose and is about to move on to other fields, Matt Denant appears. "He is a young man, tallish and athletic, dressed as if he has been racing in hot weather; he has a pair of race glasses and a cigar."

The girl speaks to him, guardedly. Catching his attention for a moment, she begs a light for her cigarette. Soon they are in the midst of a bantering conversation comparing women and horses and the beauty and vice of them.

Denant finds himself momentarily interested in the girl's viewpoint, and she, forgetting the profession that she adorns, plainly enjoys the novelty of being talked to as one human to another.

"You don't like women, that's clear," she is saying to him.
"Not too much."

GIRL (*smiling*)—You speak your mind, anyway.

MATT—If you ask me, they've got such a lot of vice about 'em compared with horses.

GIRL—And who puts vice into them?

MATT—I know—you all say men, but d'you believe it?

GIRL (*with a laugh*)—Well, I don't know. Don't men put vice into horses?

MATT (*struck*)—M'yes! (*Sitting down.*) All the same, there's nothing wilder than a wild horse—I've seen 'em out West.

GIRL—There's nothing *so* wild as a wild woman. (*A momentary silence while they stare at each other.*)

MATT—Women haven't the excuse of horses—they've been tame since Eve gave Adam his tea.

GIRL—Um! Garden of Eden! Must have been something like Hyde Park—there was a prize cop there, anyway.

MATT—D'you come here often?

GIRL (*nodding*)—Where else *can* one go? They're so particular now.

MATT—They do seem to keep you on the run.

GIRL—What are you—soldier?

MATT—Once upon a time.

GIRL—What now?

MATT—Thinking of being a parson.

GIRL (*laughs*)—You've got money of your own, then?

MATT—A little.

GIRL (*with a sigh*)—If I had money of my own, d'you know what I'd do?

MATT—Get rid of it.

GIRL—Just what I wouldn't. If ever I got myself dependent on you men again, (*very grimly*) shut my lights off.

MATT—Not like the lady under laughing gas.

GIRL—What was the matter with her?

MATT—Kept shouting, "I don't want to be a free, independent, economic agent! I want to be loved."

GIRL—She was wrong— No, *Sir!* Get my head under a second time? Not much! But we can't save—don't make enough. So there you are! It's a good bit worse than it used to be, they say—

MATT—The ordinary girl more free and easy now, you mean?

GIRL (*grimly*)—The *ordinary* girl?

MATT—Well, you don't call yourself ordinary, do you? (*The* GIRL *sits quite still and doesn't answer.*) Sorry! Didn't mean to hurt you.

GIRL—Give me the fellow that does: he doesn't hurt half so much. But you're quite right. (*Bitterly.*) There isn't much excuse for us, now.

MATT—Aren't we getting a bit solemn?

GIRL—The gay girl—eh? They say you get used to anything: but I'll tell you—you never get used to playing the canary when you don't feel like it.

MATT—Ah! I always sympathised with canaries—expected to sing, and so permanently yellow.

GIRL—It was nice of you to sit down and talk.

MATT—Thanks; it's all secondary education.

Politely but kindly Denant refuses her invitation to inspect her apartment. She would, if she could, have him believe that there is at least a little difference between her and the common run of those ladies of the pave who follow her profession. And he is not without a sympathetic understanding. But he must be on his way.

Denant has barely left when the plain clothes man reappears, grabs the girl roughly by the arm, and would place her under arrest.

The girl protests that she has been doing nothing for which she can be held liable to the law, but the officer is firm and a little rough. Before he can get her started toward the station, however, Denant reappears and the girl appeals to him for support of her behavior.

The officer is of no mind to accept calmly Denant's interference. In fact it will become his bounden duty, and evidently an added pleasure to take Matt along, too, if he does not immediately cease interfering with the law. And to substantiate his authority he places his whistle in his mouth and blows lustily for assistance.

At this Matt shows fight and the plain clothes man, dropping the girl's arm, grabs him. While they are circling and charging each other Matt calls to the girl to run, but she will not. She stays to plead that they stop fighting and that he should not do this thing for her. The police are bound to win.

Suddenly, as the policeman is charging in, Denant catches him with a stiff right-hand blow to the point of the jaw and the officer falls. As he does so he strikes his head on the iron railing and rolls over as lifeless as a log.

GIRL—Oh! Oh!

MATT—Run, you little idiot; run!

GIRL (*aghast*)—Oh! he hit his head—on the rail! I heard the crack. See, he don't move.

MATT—Well, of course. I knocked him out. (*He goes a step nearer, looking down.*) The rail—did he—?

GIRL (*kneeling and feeling the Plain Clothes Man's head*)— Feel!

MATT—My God! That was a wump. I say!

GIRL—I told you not to fight. What did you want to fight for?

MATT (*pulling open the Plain Clothes Man's coat, and diving for his heart*)—I can't feel it. Curse! Now we can't leave him. (*Feeling for the heart.*) Good God!

GIRL (*bending and snatching at his arm*)—Quick! Before anybody comes. Across the grass back there. Who'd know?

MATT (*listening*)—I can't leave the poor devil like this. (*Looking round.*) Take his hat; go and get some water in it from the Serpentine. (*The* GIRL *picks up the hat and stands undecided.*)

GIRL (*agonised*)—No, no! Come away! It's awful, this! Suppose—suppose he's dead! (*She pulls at him.*)

MATT (*shaking her off*)—Don't be a little fool! Go and get some water. Go on! (*The* GIRL *wrings her hands, then turns and runs off Left, with the hat.* MATT *continues to kneel, rub-*

bing the Plain Clothes Man's temples, feeling his pulse, listening at heart.) I don't see how it's possible! (*With a gesture of despair he resumes his efforts to revive the body. Suddenly he looks up. Two Policemen have come from the Right.*)

POLICEMAN—What's this?

MATT—I don't know. I'm a little afraid he—

POLICEMAN—What! Who is he? (*Looking at the face.*) Phew! One of ours! (*Bending, kneeling, putting the back of his hand to the mouth.*) Not a breath! How did this happen?

MATT (*pointing to the rail*)—He knocked his head on that.

POLICEMAN—Where's his hat?

MATT—It fell off. Some one's gone to get water in it.

POLICEMAN—Who?

MATT—A girl—

POLICEMAN—He blew his whistle. Did you hit him?

MATT—There was a row. He seized me. I smote him on the jaw. He fell back and hit his head on the rail.

POLICEMAN—What was the row about?

MATT (*putting his hands to his head*)—Oh! God knows! Original sin.

POLICEMAN (*to the other Policeman*)—Mate, stay with him. I'll get an ambulance. (*To MATT*) And you—come with me!

The curtain falls.

EPISODE I

Something more than a year later Matt Denant is serving his sentence on the prison farm at Dartmoor. It is a dark, foggy morning and with a fellow prisoner he is picking up potatoes the two have previously dug and throwing them into baskets. As they work they manage a little guarded conversation in low voices.

Matt is telling his companion of his conviction and sentence; of how they gave him five years for manslaughter, three of which he still has to serve, and of how the only thing that saved him from hanging was the testimony of the girl, who came bravely to his defense at the trial.

Matt is in a rebellious state of mind. He is, he admits when charged, some kind of gentleman; at least he is possessed of an Oxford education and he instinctively resents being spoken to like a dog.

He'd have a try at escape if everybody wasn't agreed that it never had been done and probably could not be done. The moors is an 'ell of a place, the fellow convict insists, and they (the guards) are certain to get you. A fellow'd have to have money and clothes and a car even to have a dog's chance of escape from that place.

Still it might be done, Matt thinks. And the more he thinks of it the more fascinated does he become. The gruff command of the warder that these two finish their row and prepare to return to the prison finally brings the hope to crystallization in Matt's mind.

There'll be a chance while the guards are rounding up the men. If he goes now he will have a ten-minute start of them before they discover he is missing. Then they will have to march the other prisoners back to the prison before they can begin the search. By that time, with the help of the map his fellow convict has drawn in the sand for him, he should be well away.

Now his mind is made up. For a moment he studies the chart in the soil intently. Then the warder calls again.

WARDER'S VOICE (*off*)—Hurry up with that last row—you two men! (*The fog grows thicker.*)

MATT (*smearing out the chart with his foot*)—It's real thick now. Gosh! I'll have a shot! (*They move back, beginning the last row.*)

FELLOW CONVICT (*jerking his thumb Left*)—There's another blighter thirty yards out on the wall there. 'E'll shoot.

MATT—I know. I'm going over that wall in the corner, and then along under his nose on the near side. Ten to one he'll be looking out on the off side in this fog. If that chap there (*jerking his head, Right*) doesn't spot me, I'll get by.

FELLOW CONVICT—You're mad, Guv'nor. They'll shoot at sight. And if they don' see you—in ten minutes I'll have finished this row, an' they're bound to know you're gone. You 'aven't the chance of a cock-louse.

MATT—All right, friend, don't worry! A bullet'd be a nice change for me. If I don't get one—I'll give 'em a run for their money.

FELLOW CONVICT—Well, if you must go, mate—strike the main road and run that way. (*Pointing.*) In this fog they'll 'ave to take us back before they dare start after you. You'll find a scrap of a wood a bit beyond the river on the left side. Get into it and cover yourself with leaves till it's dead dark. Then you'll still be close to the road and you can myke shift in a stack or something till morning. If you go wandering about the moor all night in this fog, you won't get nowhere, and you'll be done in stiff before dawn.

Matt—Thanks. Sooner the better, now— Never stop to look at a fence. Next time the steam's full on. (*Puts some potatoes in his pocket.*) Pommes crus—sauce Dartmoor. Can one eat these raw? I ate turnips in Germany.

Fellow Convict—Never tried, Guv'nor. Tyke this. (*He holds out a slice of bread.*)

Matt—Thanks awfully. You're a good chap.

Fellow Convict—Wish you luck. Wish I was comin' too, but I 'aven't got the pluck, an' that's a fact.

Matt—Now! Turn your head the other way and keep it there. Remember me to Blighty. So long. (*He moves three steps away from his fellow convict, pauses a few seconds, then suddenly, stooping low, runs to the wall, Left, and is over it like a cat. In the minute of silence that follows, one can see the* Convict *listening.*)

Fellow Convict (*counting the seconds to himself, up to twenty, in an excited murmur*)—Gawd! 'E's past that blighter! (*Listens again.*) Gawd! 'E's orf! (*With realisation of his fellow's escape comes an itch to attempt it himself.*) Shall I 'ave a shoot meself? Shall I? Gawd! I must! (*He has just turned to sneak off, when the* Warder's *voice is heard off right.*)

Warder—You, man, there! Where's your mate?

Fellow Convict—'Ad a call, Sir. (*He stands still.*)

Voice of Warder (*nearing*)—What d'you mean?

Fellow Convict—Went over to that wall, Sir.

Warder (*appearing*)—He's not there. Now then! Where is he?

Fellow Convict—No use arstin' me. I don' know where he is.

Warder—Come with me. (*He marches sharply along the wall back, towards the Left. Halting.*) Convict! Out there! Answer! Warder! You, Williams! Any one passed you? Lost a man here!

Voice of Second Warder—No one's passed.

First Warder—Sharp, then! There's a man gone! (Second Warder *appears on the top of the wall.*)

Second Warder—He must ha' got past *you*, then.

First Warder—Curse this fog! Fire a shot for warning. No, don't, or we'll have others running for it. Muster sharp and get off home and report—that's the only thing. (*To* Convict.) Here, you! Keep your mouth shut. You know all about it, I bet.

Fellow Convict—Not me, Sir. 'E just said 'e 'ad a call to 'ave tea with the Duchess; an' I went on pickin' up, knowin' you was in an 'urry.

FIRST WARDER—Mind your lip!   Come on, Williams.   March, you!

The curtain falls.

EPISODE II

Seven hours later, the fog still thick, two warders from the prison are guarding a main road near the prison.   A disgusting job it is to them, too.   Cold and wet and stayin' out all night is tryin' on any nature.   Even the liquor they take from time to time doesn't warm them overmuch.   A great circus, this.   Fit only for the movies.   For one of those "duggie" pictures, if you ask the warders.

Across the road they have stretched a rope.   It will strike any one running that way just below the knee and over he'll go. Before he can get to his feet one of them, probably both of them, will be on top of him.

And then what they will do to this inconsiderate fellow who has the brass to try a run for it a night like this!   Perhaps they had better draw lots to see which of them shall have the first go at him!   Which they do.

Now they hear footsteps and whisper their final plans.

SECOND WARDER (*in a whisper*)—Look here, mate!   Just before he gets to the rope, I'll throw the light into his face, then dowse it sharp.   He'll start to run forward and go head foremost.   Stand by!   (*They listen.*)

FIRST WARDER—He's comin' on!   Suppose it isn't him?

SECOND WARDER—Must chance that.   I'll throw the light as I say— (*A moment of utter black tenseness, during which the footsteps are heard clearer and clearer.*)   Now!   Stand by!   (*He flashes the light on the figure of* MATT *advancing along the road. The light is dowsed, the* WARDERS *rush forward.   Darkness and the sound of a scramble.*)

SECOND WARDER'S VOICE—I've got him!

FIRST WARDER'S VOICE (*half strangled*)—No, you ruddy fool —you've got me!

The curtain falls.

EPISODE III

Thirty-two hours later, in the bedroom of an inn on the moor, a shingled lady is asleep in a bed that juts out into the room from between curtained windows at back.   It is still fairly dark, with streaks of the new day coming through the windows.   On a chair at the foot of the bed the lady's undergarments have been tossed and her dressing-gown lies across the footrail.

The lady's maid is in to announce the arrival of the day and likewise the drawing of the bath. Out of bed the lady, in her pyjamas, proves as attractive as ladies getting out of bed in pyjamas can be. Sleepily she listens to the maid's recital of the more important news. It is still foggy, and after two days of it, too. And they haven't yet caught the escaped convict—the young man who killed the detective in Hyde Park.

The lady remembers the case. Remembers Captain Denant's name. Interesting case, but she is not particularly concerned, even though the maid insists the prison officials are sure to catch him. They never get away from Dartmoor. They need clothes, and they have to eat, and that's what traps them.

The lady is up and gone to the bathroom when Matt Denant edges his way into the room from back of the window curtains nearest the bed. "He looks haggard, sodden and crumpled, and has his boots in his hand. He goes to the window, looks cautiously out, then recoils."

He is making for the door when the lady returns suddenly from the bath. The water is not yet warm. Matt squeezes himself against the wall back of the door as she enters the room and is not discovered until a moment later. He is again trying to get out when she sees him in the mirror.

Her impulse is to scream aloud, but Matt's attitude reassures her. A moment later she has recognized him as the hunted man and, despite an evident doubt that she is doing the right thing, is inspired by curiosity and human interest to let him explain his position.

He had, he confesses, been under her bed for hours—not knowing, of course, that a lady was sleeping above him. He is even afraid he fell asleep. Of course, if he'd known— He is perfectly willing to relieve her of his embarrassing presence, but he can't quite see how it can be done. His appearance is so terribly against him. His clothes, and the fact that he is frightfully hungry. Perhaps she could manage something to eat for him? For forty hours he has had nothing but a piece of bread and two raw potatoes.

Protesting that she really should ring and hand him over, the lady does find a bar of chocolate in her dresser for him and lets him help himself to the drinking water on the stand. She manages, when his back is turned, to slip her underclothes under the bedcovers and is a bit more at her ease.

MATT—Ever had the hunted feeling? (*She shakes her head.*) Well, don't! A coursed hare is nothing to it. Oh! I am so jolly stiff!

LADY (*thrilled in spite of herself*)—Do you know you're only three miles from the Prison?

MATT—I do. The first night I meant to get near Exeter by morning, and where d'you think I was? A mile from where I started. I'd been ringing. That's what you do in fog. Is that a razor?

LADY (*on stilts*)—My husband's. Why? (*As* MATT *takes it up.*) No! There's a limit, Captain Denant. You can't have a weapon.

MATT—No, of course! But would you mind awfully if I shaved? You see, like this (*passes his hand over his chin*) I haven't an earthly, even if I could get clothes. There's nothing more attractive than a three days' beard. (*While speaking he has lathered himself without a brush.*) I'm a very quick shaver. It takes me three minutes. I can do it in thirty-two and a half strokes.

LADY (*gasping*)—Well, I never— It takes me (*hand to her neck*) that is—I mean— Have you nearly been caught?

MATT (*between scraping motions of the razor*)—Twice I've been within twenty feet of the hounds—

LADY—Hounds!

MATT—Human! Just out of their jaws. (*Groans.*) D'you know anything so frightful as a shave like this?

LADY—Well, really—

MATT—I mean except, of course, not having it.

LADY—How did you get in here?

MATT—You see, I *did* so want a dry night, so I hid up and waited till every light was out. I tried to get in below, and couldn't; then I made a boss shot at the corner of the balcony and fell on my back— Did you feel a sort of earthquake? No? I did. When I got over that, I had another shot at a pillar and made it that time. I chose your window because it was open— hooked it up again and slid straight under the bed. I meant to sneak some clothes, and be off before daylight, but I only woke up when the maid came in. (*She indicates a towel; he steeps it in water and wipes his face.*) D'you mind if I put on my boots? (*He stoops and puts them on.*)

LADY—So you actually slept under there?

MATT—Alas! I did.

LADY—Well! It's about the limit.

MATT—Will be if I get clear—no one ever has.

LADY—Tell me, Captain Denant, weren't you at Harcheston with my brother—he used to talk of a Matt Denant, who was an awfully good runner.

MATT—Quite likely. I was at school with an awful lot of brothers. What was his name?

LADY—No. That won't do.

MATT—You're right. Never tell a convict anything he can tell anybody else.

LADY—I really don't see how I can help you.

MATT—Nor do I, worse luck!

LADY—I read your trial.

MATT (*standing up*)—And you think me a bad lot, of course. (*Bitterly.*) D'you know how I spend most of my time in prison? Holding imaginary conversations with the respectable.

LADY (*with a smile*)—Respectable! D'you think you're holding a real one now?

MATT—I certainly don't . . . I . . . I beg your pardon. . . . You know what I mean. But I bet most people have put me down a rotter.

LADY—Was all you said true?

MATT—Gospel.

LADY—I suppose they do hunt those girls rather.

MATT—Yes, but you know, I didn't even really see red. I've been sorry enough for that poor chap.

LADY—Well, Captain Denant, what now?

MATT—You've been most awfully kind and I don't want to impose on you; but I shall never get out of here as I am.

LADY—Why not?

MATT (*jerking his head towards the window*)—They're too thoughtful. There's a picket out there. (*The* LADY *turns to the window and looks out; then she turns to* MATT *and finds him smiling.*) Oh! No, I wasn't scared. One doesn't give one's own kind away.

LADY—I don't know that. Go and try some of those other rooms. Try the couple next door to me.

They are both startled by the knock of the maid to announce that the lady's bath water is hot at last, and worried for fear they may have been overheard. Evidently everything is all right so far. And now Matt, apologetic for the trouble he has caused, must make another try at getting away. He plans to sneak down the balcony when the picket's back is turned, drop off the end and make a run for it. But the lady has a better plan.

LADY (*after a long look at him*)—No! Look here! When I
go to my bath I'll make sure there's no one. If I don't come
back, slip down the stairs, they're almost opposite. In the hall,
hanging, you'll find my husband's old Burberry and fishing basket,
rod and fishing hat; a long brown Burberry, with stains, and
flies in the hat. Put them on and go out of the front door; the
river's down to the left. Can you fish? (*At his nod.*) You'd
better, then. The bathroom's not that side, so I shan't see you.
But—whistle "Lady, Be Good," if you know it.

MATT—Rather! It's the only tune that's got into prison.
Well, I can't thank you—you're just a brick! (*He holds out his
hand.*)

LADY (*taking it*)—Good luck! (*She passes him to the door.*)
Wait a second! (*Getting a flask from drawer.*) Take this. If
you see any one looking at you—drink! Nothing gives one more
confidence in a man than to see him drinking.

MATT—Splendid! What are you going to say to your husband?

LADY—Um! Yes! He comes to-night. Well, if he doesn't
like it, he'll have to lump it. Oh! And these two pounds. It's
all I've got here. (*She has taken two pounds out of her bag
lying on the dressing-table.*)

MATT (*moved*)—By George! I think you're sublime!

LADY—I'm afraid I doubt it.

MATT—If I'm caught, I shall say I pinched everything, of
course; and if I get clear, I'll—

LADY—Oh! Don't bother about that! Get behind the door
now. (MATT *gets behind the door, and she opens it and goes out.
After a moment she returns.*) All clear!

The maid, still a little suspicious of something, opens the door
again and peers in. Matt barely has time to get behind the door.
Now the lady calls to the maid to bring her a suit that has been
drying. With the maid away, the lady returns long enough to
hurry Matt down the stairs.

She has pushed back the curtains and is standing at the window
when she hears, a half minute later, the faint strains of "Lady,
Be Good."

EPISODE IV

For the better part of a day Matt Denant has fished the river
toward Dartmeet. He is resting now in an open space "above
the river and away from the trippers." Beside him is his catch,

eight smallish trout. He is eating the last of his chocolate and has already drained his flask.

An old gentleman in Lovat tweeds strays idly in the fisherman's direction. Matt pretends to be busily engaged in taking his rod to pieces. The old gentleman stops and is pleasantly conversational. Occasionally there would seem to be a suspicious emphasis placed upon certain of his observations. He keeps Denant anxious without making him unduly apprehensive.

The old gentleman recalls the morning fog and the fact that fogs aren't any good to any one—unless it be to convicts. True, none of these, even with the help of the fog, ever get away—but they try.

"I've often wondered what I should do if I blundered into an escaped convict?" the old gentleman wonders.

Matt agrees that such an experience would present a problem. Although, he insists, a chap who tries to escape is at least a sportsman. He takes a pretty long chance. But, the old gentleman points out, the English are a law-abiding people.

"I remember being very much struck with the difference in America last year," says he. "Vital race, that—sublime disregard of the law themselves, and a strong sense of moral turpitude in others."

Personally, Matt admits a complex. He, himself, escaped from Germany during the war. He knows what it is like.

Soon they are discussing the case of this Captain Denant who is even now being hunted over the moors. The old gentleman remembers the Denant trial very well. He had found it quite interesting.

"I suppose one might run across that convict fellow any moment," he continues. "It would be a little like meeting an adder. The poor thing only wants to get away from you. And yet, if you don't break it's back ten to one it'll bite a dog. I had two dogs die of snakebite. It's a duty, perhaps. What do you say?"

"Probably. But I don't always do mine."

"Oh! Don't you? I'm so glad of that. Neither do I."

Matt has taken a proffered cigar and found that smoking on an empty stomach has made him a little sick. The old gentleman, kindly sympathetic, provides another that the fisherman may try again after tea. Now Matt has his fishing things together and, a little nervously, is trying to take his departure.

OLD GENTLEMAN—Well (*getting up*) I must be getting on too. It's been very pleasant. I've enjoyed our little talk. At my time of life one doesn't often get new sensations.

MATT (*nonplussed*)—Good Lord, Sir! Have I given you any?

OLD GENTLEMAN—Well, I don't remember ever having talked before to a prisoner who'd escaped from—Germany.

MATT—Good-by, Sir.

OLD GENTLEMAN—Good-by, Captain Denant— (MATT *starts.*) I hope you'll have a pleasant journey, especially as no one seems to have noticed our little chat.

MATT (*staring at him*)—D'you mind frightfully telling me how you spotted me?

OLD GENTLEMAN—Not at all! First, the way you looked at your trout—shall I say—er—wolfishly? And then—forgive me—your legs.

MATT (*drawing up his Burberry and contemplating his legs*)—Yes. I hoped you'd think I was a leader of fashion.

OLD GENTLEMAN—And there was another thing—your obvious sympathy with yourself.

MATT—That's a prison habit, Sir. You're not allowed to sympathise with other people, for fear of contaminating them. Before I got into quod I don't remember ever feeling sorry for myself. But I doubt if I shall ever again feel sorry for any one else.

OLD GENTLEMAN—That must be very natural. Well, it's been most interesting, because now you see I know what I should do—

MATT (*intently*)—Is it indiscreet to ask, Sir?

OLD GENTLEMAN—Well, Captain Denant, this time—I say *this* time—wink the other eye. Good-day to you!

MATT—Good-day, Sir. It's most frightfully sporting of you. For the moment I feel quite human.

OLD GENTLEMAN—Do you know, that's been rather the effect on me. Original sin, I suppose. Good-day! (*He goes off, watching the smoke of his cigar and smiling faintly to himself. On* MATT, *affected by kindness*

The curtain falls.

EPISODE V

An hour later Denant has come upon a picnic party taking lunch on a high spot of the moor. There are four of these trippers—two men and two women—recently disgorged from a Ford car. "One of the men, about fifty, in blue clothes, has a Merchant Service look and a concertina; the other looks more like a shopkeeper, and is perhaps fifty-five. His wife is a stout woman, about forty, of mellow appearance. The other woman is the shopkeeper's sister, dried-up and spinsterish. Their clothes are of a suitable nature—some feathers. They are all eating heavily."

Coming into the group, his Burberry buttoned tightly about the throat, Matt casually inquires the way to Bovey, and being assured that the town is a good twelve miles away, extracts rather precise directions from the one of the group they call the Captain.

He makes friends with the women by giving them his catch of fish, and during the conversation incidental to the transfer he tries to maneuver himself into a position from which it will not be too hard to annex a loaf of bread.

Now the Captain's wife has discovered, in the copy of the *Daily Mail* with which she was planning to wrap the remains of the lunch, the continuing story of the escaped convict—"the man that killed the poor detective in 'Yde Park." Matt is interested in that story, too.

SHOPKEEPER—I 'ope everybody's helping to catch him. He must be a regular desperado. That was a bad case. I never believed the girl.

SISTER—I should think not, indeed!

SHOPKEEPER—Nor the young man neither. They were up to no good there. They tell me those London parks are in a proper state.

CAPTAIN—They ain't a Sunday School, that's certain.

WIFE—Fie, Captain!

SISTER (*acidly*)—I believe some people quite sympathised with him. Fancy!

MATT—Well, if you won't think it too eccentric, I did, for one.

SHOPKEEPER—You!—Why?

MATT—I thought he had devilish hard luck.

SHOPKEEPER—Ah! There's always a fuss made about the Law. You can't even 'ang a woman for murderin' her 'usband without a lot of 'ysterical nonsense. Look at that case not long ago—there was a petition as long as your arm.

CAPTAIN—I remember. The young chap was a steward. I don't recall this Hyde Park case.

WIFE—Why! The detective arrested one o' those women this young man had been sittin' with—a gentleman he was too—and if he didn't 'it him an' break 'is 'ead, an' kill 'im, poor man!

CAPTAIN—Then why didn't they string him up?

MATT—The jury found it was a quarrel, not an attempt to evade arrest. Besides, in falling the detective hit his head on the iron railing of the Row, and the doctors said he died of the concussion.

SHOPKEEPER—That didn't ought to have got 'im off. He hit the man. If 'e 'adn't 'it him, 'e wouldn't have fallen.

MATT—Exactly! Brilliant! But if the detective hadn't seized him, he wouldn't have hit him.

SHOPKEEPER—Well! *I'd* 'ave hung 'im.

WIFE—Don't be so bloodthirsty, Father!

SHOPKEEPER—Well, I would. Hitting an officer for doing his duty. Sitting with a woman in the Park, too! He only got off because he was quality.

MATT—Don't you think that's a superstition? (*The* SHOPKEEPER *glares at him, but decides that he is a gentleman, and therefore prejudiced, and only snorts slightly.*)

SISTER—Did they punish the woman?

MATT—What for, ma'am?

SISTER—*I'd* keep them shut up; then they wouldn't tempt young men—the 'arpies!

MATT (*unexpectedly*)—Oh, God! (*They all stare at him.*)

The conversation turns to the Ford. A good car, the Shopkeeper allows, particularly in that hilly country. "I'd engage to catch any convict in my car," declares the Ford owner boastfully.

Which gives Matt an idea. He manages, in taking his leave, to pocket a few scraps of food and then he sidles out of the picture. A moment later they are measurably excited to note that he is fooling with their car, and before they can do more than yell shrilly in protest both car and Matt are flying down the road.

Now they know him for the villain he is, this seeming gentleman. The escaped convict, sure! Come to think of it he didn't have the leggins of a gentleman and Sister had distinctly seen him, with her own eyes, take the scraps of food.

Well, there isn't anything to do about it. The Captain is the least worried. It is his opinion their auto thief will leave the car in a ditch whenever he gets as far as he thinks he can go with it. There's nothing for them to do but pick up their gear and tote it until they get a lift.

They are off down the road, with the Captain playing his concertina, as the curtain falls.

EPISODE VI

A little later, at a point where a man and his wife returning from a walk have stopped in an open space in the moor, Matt

Denant leaves the Ford on the near-by road and approaches them to ask his way to Bovey.

The wife is a bit flustered because, having picked up a pebble in her shoe which has worked through her stocking, she has taken off the stocking and barely has time to slip on her shoe and hold the stocking behind her when Matt appears.

The man knows little more about the location of Bovey than Matt himself, which doesn't help. He is rather anxious to reach Bovey, too. He has some aunts there. Good place for aunts, Bovey. Awfully good knitting there, too.

They giggle at that. The wife is quite plainly pleased with the young man. It is plain to be seen that he has quality, she tells her husband after Matt has gone on.

"He saw my leg and kept his eyes off it. I thought that was charming of him," says she.

"Fellow-feelin'. He had some shocking leg gear on himself."

Now a second traveller appears. A constable this time. A very hot constable with a bicycle. He is looking for an escaped convict.

They haven't seen any convict, they report. Only a gentleman riding in a Ford car and inquiring his way to Bovey where he had aunts. But from their description the constable knows the gentleman to have been 'im, the convict.

"But, really, he was a gentleman," protests the wife.

"Volk 'e stole that car from 'alf an hour gone don't think so," dryly observes the constable.

He's quite disgusted with them for not stopping their visitor on suspicion. "Stop first—suspect arterwards," that's the constable's motto.

After he has wheeled his bicycle back to the road there is further discussion. The man is sorry he had not recognized the convict and stopped him. The wife is frankly glad he didn't.

"A convict's a convict. You can't play about with the law," protests the husband.

"Well, we have, that's one comfort," answers the wife. "That constable didn't keep *his* eye off my leg."

They are still arguing a little wildly when they see Matt returning. That does present a problem to the man. Whatever shall he do now?

Run out and stop him and warn him about the constable, says the wife. If he doesn't she will. Even over his most earnest protests.

Matt saves them the trouble of a decision by coming to them.

His car is not acting so well and he thinks he had better try and make Widecombe after all.

No, he had better go on, warns the wife. There's a constable in Widecombe.

There are two constables in the other direction, reports Matt. So that way's closed.

It is the man's idea that Matt should be a sport and give himself up, seeing they now know him for what he is. But that isn't Matt's idea. He has a much better idea. Why can't they all three ride into Widecombe together?

MATT—You see, if you're with me, I shall get through Widecombe all right, and I'll drop you just on the far side.

MAN—But—! What? No—that won't—

MATT—It's all right. You take me in custody into Widecombe—you can't help it if I whizz through and shoot you out. I want to make it easy for you, and I hope you want to make it easy for me.

MAN—Why should I? An escaped convict!

MATT—What do you call *yourself?*

MAN—What! Just an average man.

MATT—D'you mean to say the average man isn't a sportsman?

MAN—Yes. But I've had warning. I'm up against it.

WIFE—*I'll* come in the car. If you're with a lady, you'll get through without being spotted.

MATT—Splendid! Thanks ever so! Will you get in?

MAN—Joan!

MATT—Put yourself in my position, Sir—

MAN—Look here! I ought to be knocking you down and sitting on your head, if you know what I mean.

MATT (*squaring up*)—Well, any little thing you've got to do, please do it quickly.

MAN—Well, I mean—that's very crude.

WIFE (*ironically*)—Oh! no, Philip! Oh, no!

MAN—Well, suppose you let me drive.

MATT—Why should I? I stole the car. Now, Madam, shall we start?

WIFE (*winding her scarf round her face*)—Right-o!

MAN—This is monstrous! Look here, Sir, you seem to think—

MATT—I'll tell you what I think— (*Grimly.*) I've been in purgatory too long, and I'm going to get out, and you're not going to stop me, if you know what I mean.

MAN—I jolly well am!

WIFE—Philip!

MAN—I'm not going to have it. If you won't surrender, I shall tackle you.

MATT (*dangerously*)—Oh! (*He takes a spanner out of his pocket.*)

WIFE (*stepping between them—to* MATT)—D'you know, I think you'd better go on.

MATT—I think so, too. Sorry to be a boor and bring out a thing like this. (*Tapping the spanner.*) But I'm not playing, you see. (*Sombrely.*) The life we live spoils our sense of humour! Good-by, Ma'am, I'm very grateful to *you*. (*He turns and vanishes.*)

MAN—Look here! You're not going like that—I'm damned if you are! Stop!

WIFE—Masterly, Philip! Masterly! (*Sound of a car starting.*) Run! My dear! Run! It's all right. You'll be too late.

MAN—You really are— (*They stand looking at each other as the sound of the car fails slowly, and*

The curtain falls.

EPISODE VII

The day wears on. Denant, having ditched the car, is feigning sleep in the hollow of a gravel pit at the edge of the moor waiting for the dark when he is rather rudely aroused by a pair of rather burly laborers carrying their shovels and bearing themselves with every indication of suspicion.

They are, they frankly confess, in search of an escaped convict and they have a thought that perhaps they may have found him. Matt would laugh off their suspicion. Does he talk like a convict? As to that the country fellow does not know, never having heard a convict talk. "They'm town folk, I rackon—mosly." That's his opinion of convicts.

The laborers refuse to be turned from their investigation. One stands guard over Matt while the other goes to bring their employer, Farmer Browning. Matt is just about to tackle his lone guard and make another run for it when the Farmer, accompanied by his 13-year-old daughter and the second laborer, walks into the picture.

FARMER—Now then, now then! That'll du, Jim. Yu there, on my land, kindly give me yure name, and account for yureself.

There's a rough customer about, with a fishin'-rod, same as yu.

MATT—Mr. Browning.

FARMER—Ay! That's my name.

MATT—Mine's Matthew. Captain Matthew. I'm staying at the Inn at Lustleigh. There's some very absurd mistake. This good trusty dog thinks he's treed a convict.

FARMER (*impressed by* MATT's *accent and air, and the flask in his hand*)—Well, Sir, when there's these escapes on the moor, we 'ave to be careful. Miss 'Lizabeth, yu run along. (*The* LITTLE GIRL *does not move, but remains spellbound.*) Constable's just been in wi' nues from Widecombe of the car yonder, and the man that pinched it 'ad a long brown coat, a fishin'-rod, and an 'at like yurn.

MATT—If the constable's here still, you'd better take me to him.

FARMER—No, rackon I'll ask 'im to step over 'ere. George, run and fetch constable, he'm down along by thiccy car. (*The* SECOND LABORER *departs. The* LITTLE GIRL *still lurks breathless.*)

MATT—Now, Mr. Browning—dash it all!—you ought to know better than this!

FARMER—Oh! I daresay yu'm a gentleman, but so's this convict, seemin'ly. Leastways he'm a captain. Perhaps yu'll tell me the name o' the innkeeper where yu'm stayin' at Lustleigh?

MATT—Has he got a name? I hadn't noticed.

FARMER—No; nor the name of the Inn neither, maybe?

MATT—The Red Lion.

FARMER—Ha!

MATT—Well, it ought to be.

FARMER—And per'aps yu'll show me the clothes yu've got on.

MATT (*taking a resolution*)—Well, I own up.

LITTLE GIRL—Oh!

FARMER—I thowt yu'd come to it.

MATT (*lowering his voice*)—Be sporting. Give me a show!

FARMER—Now yu know I can't du that; what's the yuse of askin'?

MATT—Well, I've had forty-eight hours' freedom, and given them a good run. You haven't a cigarette?

FARMER—I don't smoke them things. Jim, got a fag for this gentleman? (FIRST LABORER *brings out a packet of cigarettes which he holds out.*)

MATT—Thanks very much!

Apparently relieved at having finally given himself up Matt

sits at the edge of the wheelbarrow talking more or less casually with the Brownings.

He signs his name in the little girl's autograph album, and, being unsuccessful in inducing Farmer Browning to give him a chance, he resigns himself to capture. He hopes the good farmer will see to it that the first laborer collects the reward for his apprehension.

" 'E can 'ave it," agrees the Farmer; "I don't want no reward for duin' my duty."

"That's lucky," says Matt. "I appreciate your excellent intentions, Mr. Browning. Glad to have met you! Good-by!"

With which surprising farewell Matt jumps to his feet, bolts directly at the Farmer, "and with a twist like a footballer evading a tackle, is past him and away."

The laborers and the amazed Browning lumber after him, and the little girl claps her hands. They are around the corner of the gravel pit when the second laborer returns with the constable.

"Which way, missy?" they shout.

"I don't know," she replies. And adds, prayerfully, as they take up the chase: "Oh! I do hope he gets off! Oh!"

The curtain falls.

EPISODE VIII

In the parlor of a "cottage of gentility" two maiden ladies—"Miss Grace, about 47," is brewing tea, and "Miss Dora, much younger, still dressed in hunting togs, is standing at the open French window at back."

Miss Dora, back from the hunt, reports a kill and that everybody was looking out for the escaped convict. It is Miss Dora's hope that he will escape, and Miss Grace thinks it extremely inconsistent that her sister should find sport in hunting foxes and still feel so kindly toward other hunted things.

"Foxes hunt and expect to be hunted."

"So do convicts. Sympathy's wasted on them."

They are far from agreement, these sisters. And this argument of theirs, like many others, trails off into a statement of familiar and long debated conclusions.

"I wish to God, Dora, you'd give up free thought," expostulates Miss Grace.

"I wish to God, Grace, you'd give up religion," replies Miss Dora.

They are at tea when suddenly Matt Denant rushes through

their French windows, "makes a sudden revealing gesture of appeal, and blots himself out behind a window curtain."

There is a hue and cry from the yard, and then the Farmer appears a little breathless at the window to demand the direction taken by their fleeing quarry. They had seen him come over the wall and around the corner.

"Oh! Yes! I thought I saw," quickly speaks up Miss Dora; "across the lawn and over the wall at the far end, Mr. Browning. Quick!"

Miss Grace does not dispute Miss Dora, but her face and figure are studies in an expression of protest.

Now the hue and cry of the pack has passed through the yard and Matt, still breathless, stands apologetically forward. He is most grateful to them.

It is Miss Dora who suggests that he take a cup of tea, which he drinks straight off, and Miss Grace who continues silently but vigorously protestant. When she does speak it is to object most earnestly to any man who would place her sister in the position she is now in.

"When you're hunted all you think of is the next move," Matt tries to explain.

"I'm afraid you're awfully done," sympathizes Miss Dora.

MATT—Thanks, I'm getting my wind back. I feel like kissing the hem of your garment.

MISS DORA—It hasn't got one. Wasn't it rather mad to escape?

MATT—I don't think so. It's shown me how decent people can be.

MISS DORA—Did they ill-treat you?

MATT—Oh! no, the treatment's all right—a trifle monotonous.

MISS DORA—Listen! (*They listen. Faint shouting.*) Where are you making for?

MATT—No plan. They're no good. It's like a battle—you change 'em before you use 'em.

MISS DORA—I read who you were in the papers.

MATT—Oh! yes. I'm in big print? Thank you most awfully. I'll clear out now.

MISS DORA—No, wait! (*At the curtains.*) I'll be back in a minute. (*She slips out.*)

MISS GRACE (*turning round to him*)—I suppose you call yourself a gentleman?

MATT—I really don't know. Depends on who I'm with. I might be contradicted.

MISS GRACE—You see the sort of woman my sister is—impulsive, humanitarian. I'm—I'm very fond of her.

MATT—Naturally. She's splendid.

MISS GRACE—If you don't want to involve her—

MISS DORA (*reappearing through the curtains*)—I think I can hide you.

MISS GRACE—Dora!

MATT—No, no! It's not good enough. I can't let you—

MISS DORA (*turning on her sister*)—I'm going to, Grace. (*They speak together in rapid tones.*)

MISS GRACE—Not in this house.

MISS DORA—It's as much my house as yours. You need have nothing to do with it.

MISS GRACE (*drawing her from the window*)—At least you haven't broken the law yet. And you're not going to now.

MISS DORA—I can't bear to see a soldier and a gentleman chased by a lot of chawbacons.

MISS GRACE (*with a glance at* MATT)—Dora, you mustn't. It's wrong and it's absurd.

MISS DORA (*heated*)—Go up-stairs. If I have to refer to you, I'll say you've seen nothing. And so can you.

MISS GRACE (*her voice rising*)—You expect *me* to tell lies! (MATT, *unseen in the heat of this discussion, makes a motion of despair and slips out of the window.*)

MISS DORA—I'm going to hide him, I tell you. Captain— (*Suddenly turning to* MATT, *she sees that he is no longer there.*) Where is he? (*The two sisters stand silent, blankly gazing about them.*)

The test of their decision comes a moment later when the Farmer, unable to find the convict in the yard or beyond, is back for further inquiry. There is still a lurking suspicion in his manner, as he announces an intention of searching the house.

Again Miss Dora is determined to do something to save the hunted man and equally positive is Miss Grace that she shall not permit her to do anything that will break the law.

With the searchers out of the room the sisters become almost hysterical in their excitement and are threatening to come to blows when the Farmer returns.

Again he puts the question flatly to them. Has either of them seen the man since he disappeared over the wall?

Miss Dora is prompt and firm in her denial. Miss Grace hesitates but finally manages a rather resounding "No!" She is crushed by the thought of that lie even after the Farmer has gone. But Miss Dora is triumphant, and proud of her sister.

"You'd make me do it again!" almost wails Miss Grace.

"I would," Miss Dora answers, simply. "Poor fellow!"

The curtain falls.

EPISODE IX

The vestry of the village church is lighted by an oil lamp. At the back of the room there is a curtained rack where the surplices and cassocks are hung on pegs. It is a bare room, with only a table pushed against the wall and a chair or two to furnish it.

From a door leading to the church the Parson enters. "He is a slim, grizzle-haired, brown, active, middle-aged man with a good, lined, clean-shaven face, and a black Norfolk jacket; obviously a little 'High' in his doctrine. He pours water from a jug into two large vases, humming: 'O for the wings—for the wings of a dove!' "

The Parson has carried the vases into the church when the hunted and hatless Denant slips into the room and, hearing the Parson returning, hides behind the cassocks. It is not a good hiding place. The first thing the returning Parson does is to reach for his cassock and, taking it down, reveal Matt standing in its place.

The hunted man pleads for sanctuary in the name of the church, a plea the Parson is hesitant to extend. The church, he reminds the fugitive, is not in the same position it held formerly.

"In the old days the church was a thing apart; now it belongs to the state."

But he has read the case of Captain Denant and it is evident his sympathies have been strongly attacked. The Parson, too, went through the war as a Padre and he knows the records of men of the Denant type. But there is sympathy and there is a man's duty to himself and to his calling!

MATT (*suddenly*)—Well, Padre, how does it look to you? Giving me up?

PARSON (*moved*)—Padre! (*He takes a turn and comes to a sudden halt in front of* MATT's *chair*.) As man to man—who am I to give you up? One poor fellow to another? (*Shaking his head*.) I can't help you to escape, but if you want rest, take it.

MATT (*suddenly*)—Wonder what Christ would have done!

PARSON (*gravely*)—That, Captain Denant, is the hardest question in the world. Nobody ever knows. You may answer this or that, but nobody ever knows. The more you read those writings, the more you realise that He was incalculable. You see— He was a genius! It makes it hard for us who try to follow Him. (*Gazing at* MATT, *who is sitting forward with his elbows on his knees and his head on his hands.*)   Very tired?

MATT—Gosh!   I didn't think one could feel so tired.   My joints have gone on strike.   I was a three-mile runner, too.

PARSON—Were you?   Good man!

MATT—It's the strain here. (*Touching his head.*)   If they get me and I have to go back!   Odd!   I didn't feel it half as much when I was escaping from Germany.

PARSON—Did any one see you come in here?

MATT—Can't have—they'd have been in on my heels.

PARSON—Who's after you?

MATT—Villagers—and a constable.

PARSON—My villagers—and here am I—

MATT (*standing up*)—By George, yes, Padre!   It's too bad. I'll clear out.

PARSON (*putting his hand on his shoulder and pressing him back into the chair*)—No, no!   Rest while you can.   You've asked for sanctuary.   I don't know that I've the right to turn you out of here.   I don't know—anyway I can't.   Take your time.   I have a little brandy here.   Sometimes we get a faint in church— (*He takes a bottle and a little glass from the corner cupboard.*)   Drink it down.

MATT (*drinking it off.   Pulling out the flask*)—I say—I wonder if you'd return *this* for me; it's empty—to that name and address. (*He takes a tailor-sewn label out of his pocket.*)   I ripped it off this Burberry.   You might say "with unending gratitude." But please don't give that name away.

PARSON—No, no; I'll see to it. (*Pockets it.*)   Tell me!   What made you escape?

MATT—Stick a bob-cat in a cage and open the door by mistake; and see what happens. (*Looking at the* PARSON'S *face.*)   Oh! Yes, I know what you mean—but I've paid my scot long ago.

PARSON—Didn't you have a fair trial?

MATT—You can't "try" bad luck.

PARSON—All bad luck?

MATT—Well, I oughtn't to have hit him, of course; original sin, you know; but for an ordinary knockout six weeks is about all you'd get; and I got four years more for that Rotten Row rail. Yes, I think I was perfectly entitled to have a shot.

PARSON—If you're quiet in your own mind—that's the only thing.

Again the troubling thought of duty and conscience recurs to the Parson. What should he tell his parishioners when Matt is gone? Should he keep silent and still not confess his silence? If he does and they should find him out, would he have a right to expect to hold what little influence he exerts over them in the light of his own failure to help the law?

There is some one at the door! It is only Thomas, the old bellringer, and he is sent around to the other door.

There is to be service at half-past six. The Parson suggests that Matt might stay for that. There will be only two or three gathered together and Matt could rest through the service.

"You're a trump," Matt agrees. "But I'd rather go and take my chance again. It's dark now. I don't like to give in. I'll bolt and be caught in the open. You might give me your blessing."

The Parson shakes his head.

"Not certain enough of myself," he answers. "It takes a bishop at least to give a blessing."

Now there is a very loud knocking at the door and Matt knows that he has been trapped. Again he springs to the cassocks and blots himself out, as the Parson delays the entrance of the constable and his followers at the door by demanding the cause of their intrusion.

Now the pack has bulged into the room. It is the old bellringer who is responsible for their insistence. He is sure he has seen a man enter the church, and the constable considers it his duty to make a search.

Has the Parson been there long? About an hour. Is he sure there is no one in the church?

"I don't know that you have the right to search a holy place," the Parson replies, as he moves toward the church door; "but look for yourselves, as quietly as you can, please."

The searchers, led by the constable, and followed, reluctantly, by the bellringer, pass into the church.

It is the instant that Matt must use to get away. "Now, quick!" mutters the Parson, barely moving his lips.

But before the hunted man can step from in back of the cassocks the Farmer is back from the church convinced there is no one there, but still suspicious.

" 'E can run and twist like a rabbit," he reports of the escaped one. "He'm a desperate foxy chap! What's behind they cassocks?"

"I'll look, Browning," quickly answers the Parson.

His search is thorough—from the middle to the left side—and he finds nothing.

Now the constable and the others are back. It is time for service, and the Parson suggests that they had better all be going, unless they would like to stay. At the mere suggestion the constable prepares to move on.

CONSTABLE (*opening the door and beckoning the men out*)— My juty, Zurr, ef yu'll excuse us.

PARSON—That's all right, Constable.

FARMER (*suddenly*)—Jest a minute, Vicar. Yu'll pardon me askin', but are yo zartun zure as yu'm not zeen this joker?

PARSON (*drawing himself up*)—What is it you are asking me?

FARMER—I'm askin' yu on yure honour as a Christian gentleman, whether or no yu've zeen the escaped convict? (*After a moment's intense silence.*) Parson—I—

MATT (*stepping out without the Burberry*)—Certainly he's not. Sorry, Sir, I was hidden there. (*Holding up his hands.*) I surrender, Constable.

FARMER—Woi! The varmint! Got un! Worry, worry, worry!

PARSON—Be quiet in this place; and go out— You shame God! (*Astonished at this outburst, they slink out, leaving* MATT *in the grip of the* CONSTABLE.)

MATT (*to the* PARSON)—Forgive me, Sir! Oughtn't to have come in here. It wasn't playing cricket.

PARSON—No, no! That you *have* done—that you *have* done.

MATT—It's one's decent *self* one can't escape.

PARSON—Ah! that's it! (*Very low.*) God keep you! (*He watches the* CONSTABLE *and* MATT *go out. The bell begins to ring.*)

The curtain falls.

THE RACKET

Melodrama in Three Acts

By Bartlett Cormack

IT was late in November, 1927 (the 22nd day, to be exact), when "The Racket" was produced in New York. That happened to be a busy week for play reviewers and none of those known to the profession as "first string critics" attended the premier. These gentry were mostly busy that evening with a musical comedy frankly, though obscurely, entitled "Funny Face," which was to bring Fred and Adele Astaire, a popular dancing duo, back to Broadway following a season's success in London.

The reviewers of the "second string," however, were genuinely enthusiastic about "The Racket." So was the first audience. And in time most of the other reviewers and as many as a hundred and nineteen other audiences endorsed this enthusiasm.

"The Racket," I think, wins favor as a play by the forthrightness of its writing and the honesty of its drama. It is not a pretty piece, and it may, as has been charged, exaggerate the then current picture of Chicago's struggle with crooks, in office and out. But it bears unmistakably the stamp of authenticity in character, scene and speech and reflects vividly a phase of civic life in America that is more likely to be corrected by exposure than by concealment.

Bartlett Cormack, the Chicago newspaperman who wrote "The Racket" the year following the season Maurine Watkins, Chicago newspaper woman, wrote the equally illuminating "Chicago," is at definite pains to deny that he has lifted either the story or the people of his play directly from the Chicago scene. What was happening, what has been happening, in Chicago during the period of the playwright's observations merely stimulated his creative urge, he says, to set down in terms of drama such human actions and reactions as he found both interesting and exciting.

So far as playgoers in general are concerned the matter of Chicago's actual contribution to Mr. Cormack's play is unimportant. The drama is sufficiently alive and sufficiently credible to stand on its own acts. Those auditors who are reasonably bright and fairly regular as newspaper readers will draw their own conclusions as to Chicago's responsibility, and not all the king's Cormacks nor all the mayor's men can prevent them from doing so.

The scene of "The Racket" is the central room of an outlying police station on the southwest side of Chicago. The time is early November, just before a mayoralty election.

"The station is an old, remodeled Victorian house, and so this room is large, with a high ceiling, smoky old wainscoting, and soiled kalsomined walls in one of which there is a streak of fresh plaster that has lately repaired a crack." The street entrance is at back. Doors to the Captain's office, to the interior of the station and to the lieutenant's office let out of the side walls, and there is a wooden partition, breast-high, around the sergeant's desk.

It is nearing midnight. Two reporters, Pratt of the *Tribune* and Miller of the *Herald-Examiner,* are playing rummy at an ancient kitchen table.

"Miller is thirty-two, robust, unkempt, and now, as usual, slightly drunk. He is wearing the old topcoat he never is without, and in its pocket a copy of the *American Mercury.* A pint bottle of whiskey, a third full, is at his elbow. Pratt is twenty-nine, and debonair. His overcoat is folded on the bench, and his hat is at the correctly cocky angle on his head. They are cynical fellows—Pratt lightly, amusedly; Miller heavily, bored."

It has been a dull night for these reporters. Sent out to this lonesome district in the hope that they will be able to get an interview with the new captain, one McQuigg, recently transferred, they find it dull business putting in the time and waiting for something, anything, to happen. At the moment they are about ready to quit. And yet they have a sneaky feeling that, with McQuigg on the job, something big may happen any minute.

"You got a policeman in your new captain," Miller of the *Herald-Examiner* assures Sergeant Sullivan. "There's plenty of sand in his spinach."

But Pratt of the *Tribune* is not so optimistic.

"Don't let him get your hopes raised, Sarge," he warns. "He's worked on that sheet of his so long his imagination runs in purple headlines across a yellow sky."

Still Miller persists and his prophecies are at least exciting. Any district is likely to be a hot district with McQuigg in it and Nick Scarsi anywhere within reaching distance. The captain and Scarsi "are itchin' to have each other's eyes for grapes," says he.

It was Scarsi's influence that got the captain transferred, and if that situation isn't loaded with possibilities nothing is.

For the present, however, everything's dead. A few pre-election raids and that's all. The station basement is full of befuddled girls taken from the more notorious "cat houses" in the district. And the ward is lively with campaign meetings. But nothing like real news is happening. Pratt and Miller will hang around until the City Press fellow arrives to cover the station and then they'll blow.

Assistant State's Attorney Welch, "forty-two, pale and tight," drops in. He's been attending one of the campaign meetings—the one the Old Man spoke at—and he has also brought Sergeant Turck from his office to have a hand in the raids.

There is little, if any, love lost between the press boys and Welch. Particularly between Welch and Pratt. "Welch is nothing but a frightened little yes-man," according to Pratt. But, as for that, "Who ain't?" Miller wants to know.

Miller is unusually grouchy at the moment. He has just received an assignment from his office to be in Speeders' court early next morning to help get a friend of a friend of God, the city editor, off "for tryin' to beat a moonbeam across the Michigan Avenue bridge." As he drains his flask to assuage the hurt, he tosses the empty bottle through the window. A second later Captain McQuigg walks in with the bottle in his hand.

"That's a fine thing to come sailing out of a police station in this God-Almighty respectable ward. Whose is it?" he demands.

"You can have it, Captain," offers Miller.

"I thought it'd be you boys. No policeman'd drink that class o' goods."

McQuigg, in uniform, "is a man of burly virility, smooth-shaven, ruddy, with close-cropped, iron-gray hair and steady eyes. He is fifty-three."

McQuigg is also friendly but preoccupied. He will not talk. He has nothing to say. Policemen have been transferred before? What of it?

"I know what you'd like, knowin' the papers," he tells them. "You'd like me to let out a bray that'd make an election issue for you and a jack-ass out o' me. . . ."

PRATT—Captain, suppose one of our leading gangsters—?

McQuigg (*sharply*)—Who?

PRATT (*smiling*)—Well, perhaps I should say one of our leading big-business men, a nice, new model big-business man with all

the latest Republican improvements and accessories—a punk with
about nine murders and no convictions against him—with a liquor
and blackmail and graft racket that's a gold mine, and a lot of
protection for helping the boys out at elections—a cocky, all
wrapped-up-in-cotton-batting big-business man—like Nick Scarsi,
say—?

McQuigg—What about him?

Pratt—Suppose the policeman in command of the District
that Scarsi's richest liquor territory was in had been fighting his
lordship over who'd run that District, Mr. Scarsi, or the police?

McQuigg (*his eyes pinching*)—Well?

Pratt—And then one of Scarsi's important men got in a jam
on a charge that wasn't bailable, like rape? And that in view of
this approaching election, the powers-that-be thought the charge
ought to be changed to contributing to the delinquency of a
minor, because that charge is bailable, and probational, and in
every way a much nicer charge than rape? But that the policeman who'd caught Scarsi's man, and knew he could make the rape
charge stick, got his back up, and swore he'd send him down if it
was the last thing—

McQuigg—That's strong, for a policeman, these days.

Pratt—Suppose he was a Captain, and that he worked so fast
he yanked Nick's man up before a reform judge and did send him
down? And then he got exiled to the sticks. Wouldn't that be
a story?

McQuigg—For the movies. (*He goes into his office and slams
the door.*)

Miller—Flop.

Pratt—He's got something in the back of his head.

Miller—You knew he wouldn't talk. You think he's crazy?
They can't transfer him any farther away. But, no, you make
speeches till I'll never get home to-night.

With the reporters out of the room McQuigg is somewhat more
talkative. He has the report of Detective Sergeant Delaney on
an old brewery that recently has been reopened in the district and
is running full blast on near-beer permits with a detail of "mugs
from the Prohibition Department to give it a legal air." And he
is startled a bit to learn that none other than Nick Scarsi himself
is in charge of this beer running. It does not take the Captain
long to react positively to that information.

McQuigg (*to* Gill)—General order for all shifts—watch that
brewery.

GILL (*staring*)—At Ninety-first and Western there.

McQUIGG—I'm glad you know where it is, anyway.

GILL—Why, that brewery's been abandoned! The Federal authorities padlocked it.

McQUIGG—Well Mr. Nick Scarsi's opened it up again.

GILL (*worriedly*)—He oughtn't to come into this District.

McQUIGG—He is in.

GILL—What'll we do about that brewery?

McQUIGG—Nothin'. I'm after Nick. And if he thinks he can lick me again, in this District— (*To* DELANEY): Get back to that brewery, Jim, and find if Nick's staying here. He may be for awhile, till he gets his truck routes set. Buzz one o' that Prohibition detail about what he's goin' to do.

DELANEY—Give one o' those babies a dollar and he'd make a confession against himself. (*He goes out to the street.*)

McQUIGG (*starting for his office*)—You don't know Nick Scarsi, do you, Lieutenant?

GILL—Not me!

McQUIGG—You may. He don't like me. And when he's around me he usually drops in to tell me so. So long as he's in the neighborhood keep the men inside the station awake, as well as those out on beats. It'd be a shame, havin' your station all mussed up.

When Dave Ames, the City Press man, arrives he proves to be a boy of twenty-three, "eager with young enthusiasm and full of an inexperienced, romantic capacity for surprise."

The older press men are inclined to kid Ames lightly, but their greeting is fraternal and characteristic. Ames, too, has been told to get an interview with McQuigg on the subject of his transfer and he can't understand why it can't be done.

AMES (*to* PRATT)—Don't you think the Captain might say something?

PRATT—He can't. Lèse-majesté. You're new to the newspaper business, aren't you?

AMES—Yes, but I've studied it a lot, so— (*As* PRATT *smiles.*) In school, I mean. I took Journalism.

PRATT—Illinois?

AMES—No, Nebraska—where I live. When I graduated, my Dean told me Chicago was the best newspaper town in the world, so I stopped off for experience. Of course, from here I'm going on to New York.

PRATT (*drily*)—Of course. Well, we're still salty here. But you'd better forget everything you learned in Journalism school. They have Journalism in New York, I guess, but not here.

AMES (*grinning*)—I'm finding that out. But what I don't understand, is—

PRATT—You'll catch on.

AMES—I mean about the Captain's transfer? If what they say downtown's true— How do Municipal Authorities get away with that stuff?

PRATT—It's all regular.

AMES—It's wrong, isn't it?

PRATT (*startled*)—What?

AMES—I mean— (*Embarrassedly.*) Well—

PRATT—Where they erred with McQuigg was trying to make a goat of a mule, that's all. This Captain's no reformer, Kid. He's taken his "legitimate," like every one else. It's just that— You know who Nick Scarsi is, don't you?

AMES—I've read about him.

PRATT—Well, Nick's so cocky he gets on these old-fashioned policemen's nerves. McQuigg's pretty cocky, himself.

AMES—I know, but— How does Scarsi control voters? You'd think a criminal—

PRATT—He gives them their daily beer, so hallowed be his name. Anyway, weren't you always fascinated by pirates rather than saints? (*To* SULLIVAN): Come on, Sarge, give the Press the gossip, and we'll trek.

Ames stays on after Miller and Pratt have gone and at the first opportunity introduces himself to Captain McQuigg. The Captain is again friendly but frozen so far as the interview is concerned. He listens with a touch of paternal interest to the young man's argument favoring the right of the people to know what their servants are up to, and the determination of the papers to stand up and speak out for the people's rights. But he is not impressed.

"This standin' up for things an' fightin' other people's battles'll only get you a smack on the nose," the Captain warns Ames.

"You're pretty cynical," replies the boy reporter. "Well, I'm not."

"Yet!" laconically concludes McQuigg.

In the street outside there is the rumble and crash of a heavy truck tearing past. Suddenly the sound of a shot, followed by a crash of glass in the entry way. McQuigg jumps to the door and pulls it open in time to hear a shout from raised, tough voices: "Hi-i-i, McQuigg!"

"Must have been some of those campaign meeting drunks," ventures Ames. "There were some shots fired up there."

"Yeh," agrees McQuigg, drily. "That's it! Let it go!"

But Ames is no sooner out of the room than the Captain completes his thought for the benefit of Sergeant Sullivan.

"Campaign drunks, hell!" says he, digging a bullet out of the door and bouncing it in his hand. "Some of the Scarsi mob leaving Nick's calling card! Sweep it up!"

Assistant State's Attorney Welch is back, and this time fortunate in finding Captain McQuigg on the job. He has come, it develops, to extend a friendly hand and suggest a course of action on the Captain's part, that will straighten everything out in no time. He would like to have the talk a little more privately, but so long as McQuigg prefers the open office he can't do much about it.

What Welch has come to say is that McQuigg is to get his old station back IF he behaves himself where he is. To behave himself, the Captain discovers, is to promise to let Nick Scarsi alone and forget about the brewery that has just been turned over to him through Washington. Those are practically the Old Man's orders. Above all McQuigg's got to lay off until after election, because the party needs the river wards Scarsi controls.

"Welch," McQuigg says, finally, "you've always been decenter than most of that crowd of yours. Why do you stick to Scarsi?"

WELCH—I'm not sticking to Scarsi. I'm sticking to the Old Man. (*His voice rising.*) Why shouldn't I? He's helped me— put me on the ticket for County Judge. This is for him. And the quieter things are till after Tuesday— Nick's too influential to fuss with, that's all. And how he knows it! Last month he damn near kicked over the traces when they wouldn't let him be one of the official welcoming committee and ride down the boulevard in a silk hat with Queen Marie. Yes! And socially ambitious, too—changing that gold tooth of his for a white one! Sending that young brother of his to that snob college, East. Nick's got so big—

McQUIGG (*interrupting*)—By usin' politics that are crazier than he is, and a public that takes the performance as a hell of a funny show and don't know enough to come in out o' the rain. (*As* WELCH *starts to speak.*) But that's all right! That's the game.

WELCH (*rather wretchedly*)—Yes.

McQuigg—But Nick Scarsi's personal with me.

WELCH—Oh, it's all in the—

McQuigg (*cutting him short*)—I'd been runnin' that District o' mine for nine years when Scarsi moved in and made a monkey o' me by protectin' his rackets and his mob so close I couldn't even get murders to trial. (*Rising.*) I fought that. That District was mine! But I got shot at from closed cars. A bomb blew off the porch o' my house. My wife's still gettin' phone calls tellin' her I'm goin' to be killed. (*After pacing a moment.*) One day Mr. Scarsi strolled into my station tellin' me to lay off one o' his men I had, and I threw him out. Then my good men got transferred. And when I got one o' his vice-presidents for rape—

WELCH (*interrupting*)—We know that.

McQuigg—I got transferred.

WELCH (*rising*)—You'll go back. If you forget Nick, that's all.

McQuigg—With him spitting on my doorstep here? I will not.

WELCH—You've got to.

McQuigg—If I get my hands on him—

WELCH—They'll break you.

McQuigg—Who?

WELCH—The Organization. And what else can you work at? Think of your family. Do you want them hit—hard—by this? (SULLIVAN *returns.*) And here's another tip—when you can't lick an Organization, join it. Use your head. You can't just jam things through any more.

McQuigg—What?

WELCH—Nowadays, things operate—(*tapping his forehead significantly*)—upstairs. (*After a moment.*) Glad I saw you. Good-night.

A moment later there is again the grinding whir of a high-powered motor car turning into the alley alongside the station. Now Patrolman Johnson has kicked open the door and pushed an arrested man through, giving him another push that brings him up against the sergeant's desk with a crash.

The arrest is a "young, a bit too flashily dressed Americanized second generation Italian, nasty in his arrogance, flushed with drink. One side of his face is scratched and swollen." Patrolman Johnson, an ideal copper type, is panting happily.

The arrest refuses to answer the sergeant's questions. He has been caught, according to Johnson, driving a "hot" car, a stolen Rolls-Royce reported over the ticker that afternoon. He had another fellow and a girl with him, who had gotten away while Johnson was subduing the arrest.

Again the Italian refuses to answer the sergeant's questions. He's even defiant about it, and threatening as to what will happen to them for what they're doing to him. He would spring at Lieutenant Gill, but Johnson holds him back and slaps him into a condition of comparative subjection.

His name, he says finally, is Camino and he knows nothing about the stolen car. His memory practically fails him after that and the officers take him into the lieutenant's room to see if they can't help him recover it.

McQuigg, summoned by Lieutenant Gill, takes charge of the situation. He is interested to learn that the arrest had seemingly suffered a slight shock when he heard that he (McQuigg) was the new captain of that district. For the present he forbids the reporters sending in their stories. He wants to learn more of this arrest. "Any one who's afraid o' me's got lots of friends down town," says he. "And *I'm* handlin' this station myself!"

From Lieutenant Gill's offices there come repeated demands for answers, followed by a defiant "I won't!" and the thud of a blow

That, concludes young Ames, must be third degree stuff, but no one will let him telephone what he thinks to his office.

They have all gone into the lieutenant's office except Sergeant Sullivan and Ames when Irene Hayes comes through the door. "She is twenty-eight, beautifully bodied, sophisticated, hard, wearing a large solitaire diamond ring and carrying an expensive purse and silver fox."

Irene has come to inquire about a boy friend. They may have picked him up for a parking violation. But he had told her he would not be in long, and she was to come and meet him. The sergeant can do nothing for her. So Ames tries.

Ames has recognized Irene. Seen her at Weinberg's, where she sings. Liked her singing, too. Thought she was great. Nearly got up the nerve to ask her to dance with him once. But there were a lot of men at her table, and—

"They're part of the job. From ten to two," explains Irene.

AMES—Then I will come in. Some night next week.
IRENE—Yes? (*Coldly.*) What for?
AMES—Why, I'd like to see you again, that's all.
IRENE—I was waiting for that one.

AMES—What do you mean?

IRENE—And all you want's a nice, sweet friendship, eh?

AMES—With you?

IRENE—That's how they usually start. But, of course, you're not after anything more?

AMES (*backing away*)—No! That's the trouble with you women. I say hello to you or something, and you think I want to— (*He stops embarrassedly.*)

IRENE—Excuse me!

AMES (*jerking on his hat*)—I'd like to know somebody in this town, that's all!

IRENE—Heavens! Why?

AMES—I'm tired of being on the outside of things.

IRENE—So am I. That's why I'm engaged to Joe Scarsi—to get on the inside quick.

AMES—Joe—who? (*After a startled look at* GILL's *office.*) Are you engaged—?

IRENE (*interrupting*)—Well, of course, darling, that was before I met you.

AMES—Is he—in there—some relation to Nick?

IRENE—His baby brother. Didn't he tell them who he was? (McQUIGG *comes in,* PRATT *after him.*)

McQUIGG—No, I'm tellin' you—Camino's the name. Full confession, and voluntary. He says he was out ridin' so's he could make some girl.

IRENE—He didn't. (McQUIGG *turns.*) Where is he?

McQUIGG—If you mean this Camino—

IRENE (*after a laugh*)—Don't you think I know who's my fiancé?

McQUIGG—Maybe he gave you a phoney name. They do that regular now.

IRENE—Not with me. No, he told me to meet him here. He said he'd only be a minute.

McQUIGG—He's goin' to stay.

IRENE—Oh. (*After a moment.*) Then I won't wait. (*She starts quickly for the street.*)

AMES—Tell him.

IRENE (*stopping.*) Keep quiet!

McQUIGG—Tell me what?

AMES—She's engaged to that fellow in there. He's Nick Scarsi's brother. (PRATT *grabs the phone.*)

McQUIGG (*to* PRATT)—Stop that! (PRATT *replaces the phone.*

To IRENE.) So you're the girl in the car, uh? Then you can tell me somethin' about that boy.

IRENE—No, Policeman. I'm tongue-tied.

McQUIGG (*going to her*)—You'd better talk to me.

IRENE (*backing away*)—I'm liable to. Maybe you're framing him, but you'll not me. Listen! You get off base with Joe Scarsi and you'll get tagged out, like the last one who tried to take one of Nick's friends for a ride. Don't make any errors—

The next minute McQuigg has called in two officers and sent Irene below stairs to mingle with the other guests. Orders concerning her will come from him and he'll listen to no one, not even Reporter Ames, who is rather concerned about Miss Hayes' situation, though he gets no thanks from her for it. Ames, says Irene, is a fool.

Quickly McQuigg states his position. Camino may and may not be Nick Scarsi's brother. If he is the only way for him to hold him until he can put him over for the theft of the auto is to keep him sealed up in the station. Therefore the newspaper boys are to lay off the story until the case is set. To see that they do Captain McQuigg is going to keep them in the station.

A moment later Miller of the *Herald-Examiner* drifts back. He had disappeared about the time they brought Camino in.

"Hi, Captain," Miller calls, cheerily. "How's young Scarsi takin' it? Je's, he's all Nick cares about—that kid! And him droppin' into your hands! We're playin' it big, too, believe—"

PRATT—Did you know who he was?

MILLER—Say, I made that "Camino" for Nick's brother the minute I came in. We'll be on the street downtown with the story in less than a half an—

PRATT (*to* McQUIGG)—You'll never hold him now!

McQUIGG (*to* MILLER)—Get out of here!

MILLER—What's the ma—?

McQUIGG (*going to the desk*)—All o' you!

PRATT (*grabbing* AMES' *overcoat, throwing it to him, and starting for the street*)—Come on. There's a phone at the Greek's. (*He goes out,* MILLER, *then* AMES, *after him.*)

McQUIGG (*to* SULLIVAN)—Keep two squads on station duty. Throw another one around that brewery.

SULLIVAN—Yes, sir. (*He goes out right.* McQUIGG *starts for his office again.* WELCH *comes in from the street, breathing hard.*)

WELCH—Mac! (McQUIGG *turns*.) I just called downtown. The *Herald-Examiner's* got a story that you've got Joe Scarsi here.

McQUIGG—I have.

WELCH—Better let him go before Nick hears—

McQUIGG—I want Nick to hear.

WELCH—Mac, he's Nick's one soft spot—this boy.

McQUIGG—Then this ought to make him squirm.

WELCH (*excitedly*)—You'll get yourself a suspension—

McQUIGG (*sharply*)—What?

WELCH—I— (*He stops*.)

McQUIGG—You cracked about me gettin' suspended.

WELCH—I cracked too fast. But you are greased for a suspension, and— Now the order WILL go to the Trial Board.

McQUIGG—What's the charge?

WELCH—What's the difference?

McQUIGG—Who fixed it?

WELCH—Nick. (*Hastily*.) But I'll quash it, if you'll let Joe Scarsi go.

McQUIGG—I'll mix with Nick to the finish now. Tell that to the PEOPLE'S Trial Board.

WELCH—Now, Mac!

McQUIGG—Tell it to the Old Man.

WELCH—Wait a min—

McQUIGG—Tell it to Scarsi! (SULLIVAN *comes in and returns to the desk*.) Sullivan!

WELCH—What are you going to do?

McQUIGG (*tapping his forehead*)—"Operate upstairs." (*To* SULLIVAN): Put that girl in a crowded cell. That'll make her mad enough to talk. And book that boy—grand larceny, and carryin' concealed weapons, too.

WELCH—Nick will start something now!

McQUIGG (*striding to his office*)—I'm starting somethin' myself. I'm ripe to fight. (*Turning*.) It's this country air! (*He goes out*.)

The curtain falls.

ACT II

It is the next day. The blackboard of the station house dismally prescribe raincoats for the outgoing squads. But inside the station everything is moving brightly. There has not been more excitement in years, according to Sergeant Sullivan. Well, anyway, not since they picked up that body thrown out of a car on Western Avenue a year before.

The disorderly house raids are still on, and nicely organized as to time so the routine of those establishments may be disturbed as little as possible, and the stories still make the early editions.

McQuigg is working as fast as he can on the Joe Scarsi case. The trial is set for Wednesday, by which time McQuigg hopes to have all the necessary evidence in hand.

Meantime news has come that Nick Scarsi is at the old brewery recently reopened and is attending personally to the establishment of his beer routes. Nick has brought his chauffeur and his personal barber with him and five or six of his "guns." The boys have been doing a few odd jobs, stickin' up a delicatessen dealer here and there, but nothing big.

Detective Delaney is not so sure McQuigg can make the auto theft case against Joe Scarsi stick, even before an honest judge. Even if Irene Hayes swears Joe stole the car Nick Scarsi is sure to get to her! But McQuigg's confidence holds. There's the witness Johnson, the patrolman who made the arrest— (*Which reminds the Captain that they had better keep* JOHNSON *inside for the present.*) "Bein' a witness against a Scarsi," says he, "if he's on a beat to-night he might be on a slab by mornin', with those guns out here."

But Johnson, being young and enthusiastic, is hard to handle. Sergeant Sullivan can't do anything with the bantam.

The newspaper men, Pratt and Miller, are out on their daily hope, Miller disgustedly sure the trip will get them nothing, Pratt not so sure.

The new alderman of the ward, Kublacek, "a heavy-set politician of the servile sort, exuding an air of excessive good fellowship and sweat," is in. "He is neither well dressed nor well washed, but carries plenty of cigars."

Kublacek, having promised the people of the ward "a clean home neighborhood," has come to congratulate Captain McQuigg and thank Patrolman Johnson, for the start the new régime has made.

He has his chance at Johnson shortly, that young patrolman having arrived late but happy. Johnson has been working on a case of his own. Also he sees no reason why he should be thanked by the alderman for what he had done in the Scarsi case—makin' arrests is a policeman's job—or why he should, as the alderman suggests, go easy on the Scarsi boy or the girl, either. But Kublacek can't see it.

"I mean," protests the alderman, "if it'd been anythin' *serious*, like murder—"

"I'm tickled to death it wasn't murder," agrees Johnson. "There's some chance o' him gettin' a couple o' years for stealin' a car. Listen, Alderman, I know what you're up against—all you C. O. D. boys who have to do the dirty work for the Organization. So I won't ask you to come out with your proposition to see I get slipped somethin' good if I throw Joe Scarsi's case. One o' Nick Scarsi's own men tried that last night, and instead of him gettin' me, I got him. (KUBLACEK *hurriedly gestures* "Quiet.") Joe ain't a drop in the bucket to the case I'm finishin' up to-night, so you just tell that big brother o' his to go to hell, will you? And tell him I told you!"

Johnson starts for the street, but Kublacek stops him. "Officer," he pleads, "I want to tell y'—if I don't put this over with you, they'll knife me, next election. And if this Scarsi kid even gets fined, I got to pay it out o' my own pocket. They told me. (*He drops to a chair at the table, the ash from his cigar spilling over his vest.*) JOHNSON (*after eyeing him a moment*): Christ! (*He starts for the street.*)

"You can't bribe the young ones. They get insulted," suggests Sergeant Sullivan, returning to the room and sensing what has been happening.

Assistant State's Attorney Welch calls to leave another warning with Captain McQuigg, but the Captain is not impressed. He'll have Joe Scarsi up for trial Wednesday, organization or no organization, and that's that!

Sam Meyer, from Reilly, Platka & Cohn, is another caller. Mr. Meyer brings a bond to effect the release of Joe Scarsi. And he is in a bit of a rush. He has to get back down to detective headquarters in an hour with another bond. Some days, when he's busy as a deputy sheriff, too, serving habeas corpus writs, Mr. Meyer thinks business is almost too good.

"A hell o' a lot o' good it does us, haulin' *in* crooks," remarks Sergeant Sullivan.

"You shouldn't go monkeyin' with the big ones," explains Meyer.

"In the old days crooks were hard, all right," admits Sullivan; "but they were dumb and you liked 'em. Now they're smart an' you don't like 'em."

Lieutenant Gill, having accepted the bond, has Joe Scarsi and Irene Hayes up from the cell room. But it soon appears that Mr. Meyer hasn't any bond for Irene, which does not serve in the least to mollify her rising disgust with young Scarsi. And when he, as she charges, refuses to ask Meyer, or brother Nick, to get her out she is good and sore.

"I had you cured of being afraid of him (Nick) so there was something to you," she tells Joe. "But you get in a jam and cry for him, and leave me in with a lot of tarts."

"Maybe they'll teach you not to be so touchy, so next time you're out with somebody you'll play."

"Not me, you cocky fool!"

And with Scarsi's further suggestion that he certainly never had any intention of marrying her, Irene strips his ring from her finger and throws it at him. She is also about to tell the world what Scarsi told her when he was tight—about what Nick did to—

She gets no further. "The other fellow I told you about," shouts Joe to the lieutenant; "he stole that car. But she was with him, so that makes her an accessory, don't it?"

"You dirty rat!" Irene yells after him, as he dodges out the door.

Dave Ames of the City Press finds her there, sitting glumly at the table, and far from talkative. Ames is wearing a yellow slicker "with the Greek letters of his college fraternity painted large on its back." And he is glad Irene is there because he wants to tell her how sorry he is that he was even partly responsible for getting her in bad by telling who Joe Scarsi was. Naturally, he did it because he thought it was right, but—

"Listen, Boy Scout," warns Irene, "if you keep on trying to do what's right . . . you're in for a lot of headaches trying to figure out why everything you've been taught is right is wrong."

AMES—Oh, if you go by what other people say—

IRENE (*rising*)—I go by myself.

AMES—But just because this went wrong—

IRENE—"Just!" Nick Scarsi will frame me with that car, to protect this brother of his, he's so wild to make a *gentleman* of Joe.

AMES—Frame you?

IRENE—Yes, Joe threw that at me when they took him out, among the rest of his bouquets.

AMES—They took him. (*At* SULLIVAN): Then why don't you let her go? (*To* IRENE): They can't hang this on you! I'll see the Captain. (*He starts for* McQUIGG'S *office.*) He'll have to let you go. It's my fault.

IRENE—Oh— (*Wearily.*) Shut up. (AMES *stops confusedly.*)
AMES (*after a moment*)—Well—it's stopped raining, anyway.
IRENE—Doesn't it rain in Nebraska?
AMES—Sure. But not this dishwater. Now in New York—
(*enthusiastically*)—I always get a kick when I see the skyline, or
Fifth Avenue in the sunshine, in a newsreel. It'll be different
there.
IRENE (*looking up at him*)—Marvellous!
AMES—It will be! When I get to be what I want to be, I
mean.
IRENE—Darling, I don't know what will happen to you if you
ever have a baby and no one's tipped you off about storks.

They have taken Irene back to the cell room and Ames has
stormed out determined to do something about it. Pratt and
Miller have another try at getting Captain McQuigg to talk.
What's the Captain going to do to put through his case against
Joe Scarsi if Taylor, the owner of the stolen auto, refuses to
prosecute, Pratt wants to know? And Taylor's a big paving con-
tractor! Let him think that over!
Although McQuigg refuses to be moved to words for publication, he knows there is truth in Pratt's predictions, and danger
of Taylor's drawing out of the case. McQuigg's best chance is to
get Irene Hayes to come clean with the story and then get that
story in print. Then Taylor will have to prosecute!
The captain has Irene in to discover the state of her mind, and
Dave Ames follows after. Irene is sore. There is no doubt about
that. And so is young Ames. He reintroduces himself to the
Captain as the representative of the City Press and confesses that
he darned near got fired because he had not turned in the stuff
from McQuigg the city editor expected, and was late with the
Scarsi arrest.
McQuigg is inclined to bark at Ames and Irene feels called on
to take the boy's part. The kid's all right. Let him alone. Let
him have feelings.
"Let these Big Thinkers have the Ideas," she says to Dave.
"You keep the heart stuff. And if no one else wants it, give it to
me. I can use it this season."

McQuigg—Seems to me if anybody gave you any more feelin'
right now, you'd bust.
AMES (*patiently*)—Do you have to talk to her like that?
McQuigg—Run along, Son. Run along. I've got to—ah—

interview this young lady. (AMES *sighs and goes out right.*)
Well, Miss Hayes?

IRENE—Why put me in with those hookers? Even if you are
McQuigg? Oh, I know who you are, now. (*After a moment.*)
One of those girls down there cried all night for her mother.

McQUIGG—I know who you are, too, now, Miss Hayes. You
used to stall—tease along the come-ons—for Beauty Parker's
mob. And since Beauty went down you've been singin' at Weinberg's, and seein' Joe Scarsi after the show. You weren't there
last night—told one o' the girls you were goin' to marry Joe.
Tryin' to cop off a rich guy for yourself.

IRENE—Why not?

McQUIGG—But you didn't marry him, did you?

IRENE—I'll get what I wanted without having to take on Joe
Scarsi now.

McQUIGG—You can get out o' here if you tell me about that
auto theft.

IRENE—I'll tell that to Nick.

McQUIGG—Tell it to me.

IRENE—I'm not stooling for policemen, yet.

McQUIGG—Goin' back to last night—what made the noise that
caused the complaint about that Rolls?

IRENE—Joe, the little—(*contemptuously*)—gentleman, tried to
—beat the wedding bells, and when he discovered he'd have to
wait he threw a fit. None of these foreigners can keep their temper. God, they drive you mad! If that big brother of his had
seen me—

McQUIGG (*interrupting*)—Women talk too much for Nick.

IRENE—Nick! I've heard "Nick—Nick" from Joe, till I wanted
to scream. You'd think Nick Scarsi was God and the Devil both,
listening to Joe brag about what he pulls off.

McQUIGG—It usually takes a woman to beat a combination o'
the Devil and God, Miss Hayes. But you haven't, have you?

IRENE (*angrily*)—I'll—

McQUIGG (*cutting her short*)—Nick's got you cold! And
your Joe'll be home in a minute, dressin' for dinner in that exclusive North Side apartment o' theirs, laughin' with Nick at you—

IRENE—Nick's out here, at some brewery he bought. Joe
told me.

McQUIGG—And you're here, too, aren't you? In a dirty cell.
Why, the Scarsis 've shaken you, made a monkey o' you. You'll
be laughed at—

IRENE (*seething*)—Yeh?

McQuigg—Nick's laughin' at you now.

Irene—Women talk too much for him. Ha!

McQuigg—But you're afraid to, when it comes to him.

Irene—I'm not.

McQuigg—Even with him turnin' this job on you, you're afraid—yellow, for fear of a braggin' wop.

Irene—You're a liar.

McQuigg (*quickly*)—Then who else was with you in that car last night?

Irene—Nobody! Joe Scarsi stole it himself.

McQuigg—Sullivan! Get that City Press. (Sullivan *goes out right.*)

Irene—Tell that to Nick, and tell him I'll tell it to a judge.

McQuigg—Not so afraid o' him now, uh?

Irene—No! No! Not after what Joe's told me about him. "Women talk too much for him." (*She laughs sharply.* Ames *comes in, followed by* Sullivan, *who returns to the desk.*) It's Nick Scarsi's own brother who's talked too much for him. Tell him I know what happened to the Secretary of this Old Man they talk about—Higgins!—who—(*sarcastically*)—"disappeared" last week, and then see if he'll try to frame *me* with this car his beloved brother stole.

McQuigg (*sharply*)—What? (*Stepping quickly to her, seizing her arm and pulling her around.*) What do you know about that?

Irene—Enough to make Joe come through if you can find him again.

McQuigg (*to* Sullivan)—Is there a squad in?

Sullivan—Yes, sir. Anderson's.

McQuigg—Jump 'em out. Tell 'em to pick up Joe Scarsi and bring him back. (Sullivan *goes out right.*) Now let's go into detail about this, Miss Hayes, inside. (*He goes to* Gill's *office, and opens the door.*)

Irene—Charmed. (*She picks up her things and goes to* Gill's *office.*)

McQuigg—Take a statement from Hayes, Lieutenant, about young Scarsi stealin' that car. Make carbons, and get 'em all witnessed and signed, this business is gettin' so damn legal now'-days. (Irene *goes into* Gill's *office. To* Ames): Turn that in about Joe Scarsi stealin' that car. But not the rest of it till I tell you. Hear?"

Feverishly Ames grabs a telephone, and tries to tell his editor

about the story. But no one will listen to him. Let him go on
chasing the little stuff—the births and deaths! That's his assignment.

With the station staff taking Miss Hayes' confession in Lieutenant Gill's room and the reporters gone, Assistant State's Attorney Welch finds a chance to telephone a little private business.
He gets Nick Scarsi on the wire and passes along word to him
of the most recent happenings. Tells him about the Hayes girl's
talking, and about her spilling to McQuigg something about the
Higgins case. It is no time for such rumors to gain ground, and—

Interruptions prevent this finishing. Pratt and Miller are back
and Ames follows them. There is something for the reporters
this time. McQuigg gives them Irene Hayes' statement on young
Scarsi's stealing the Taylor car and he'd love to see it spread all
all over their first pages.

With the Hayes statements on their way there is a lull in the
activities of the station. Pratt and Miller think they will go in
search of food. Detective Delaney is to take Miss Hayes to a
neighboring restaurant, feed her and bring her back. Young
Ames takes advantage of the quiet to do a little telephoning on
his own account. Now he bursts jubilantly from the booth.

"Nebraska has beaten Harvard!" he shouts.

"Who hasn't?" demands Miller the cynic. And that's all any
one cares.

Life is certainly stuffed with disillusions to Dave Ames. "It's
all like a can of angleworms to me," he admits. "What I don't
understand is—"

IRENE (*smiling*)—You don't understand anything.

AMES—I don't?

IRENE—That's why you get such a kick out of everything.

AMES—I'll get to understand it.

IRENE—No, you should have stayed in college longer.

AMES—I'm glad I didn't. I wouldn't have known anything.
But I'll get *this* dope.

IRENE—Don't get too much. Just go on having Nebraska beat
Harvard like that, all over the place. And don't let these other
reporters shame you into being "wise"—crammed full of important, inside dirt. Or you won't.

AMES—Won't what?

IRENE—Be so full of breeze. Now, you're like a ride in an
airplane. See?

AMES—Well, I have to—

IRENE—Be like every one else, and know so much you can't believe in anything any more?

AMES—You don't believe in much, do you?

IRENE—Oh, I did, darling. Till I got black and blue inside. And damn tired.

AMES (*exasperatedly*)—Of what?

IRENE—Men. And their— (*Wrenching irritably.*) Why shouldn't I have used Joe Scarsi to get on the inside, safe? And when he was going to get me for that auto theft why shouldn't I get him first? Men live by this dog-eat-dog stuff. And when you're stuck in the middle of things that are run by men, you have to play their game. Or—(*dropping to the bench*)—try like the devil. And then take a kick in the face because you can't. (*Lightly.*) Said she!

AMES—Oh, you're not as hard-boiled as you think.

IRENE—Do tell! Give me a cigarette.

AMES (*getting out his cigarettes*)—Can you smoke these?

IRENE—If they're cheap enough.

AMES—They are. (IRENE *takes a cigarette.* AMES *lights it for her.*)

IRENE—Listen. I'm sorry I took you so for granted last night.

AMES—That's all right.

IRENE (*amusedly*)—Thank you.

AMES—You're welcome. (*Sitting beside her.*) I suppose you would think I was after you.

IRENE—Yes, I would. But don't you get so every one can identify the kind you are by a glance. Just keep on being natural, Youngster. (*With mock gaiety.*) Be yourself!

AMES—I can be, with you.

IRENE—Go on.

AMES—I don't believe in much, either, except—well, standing up for what you do believe in, and getting some place with what you want to do.

IRENE (*smiling*)—That *is* a little, anyway.

AMES—Yes. (*Rising.*) But that's what they kid me for. What do *you* think?

IRENE (*rising*)—I think you—affect me like a mammy song! I— (*Laughing derisively.*) My God! (DELANEY *comes in.*)

DELANEY (*to* IRENE)—All right, Kid. Food. (SULLIVAN *comes from* GILL'S *office and returns to the desk.*) Come on.

IRENE (*eyeing* AMES *reflectively*)—It's a shame they have to grow up. (*She turns for the street.*)

AMES—Coming back?

IRENE—Will you be here?

AMES—Sure.

IRENE—I'll be back.

The station isn't quiet for long. Johnson, the late patrolman, is back keyed to a fever pitch with excitement and in no mood to argue with the sergeant as to whether or not he has any right to be late. Johnson has been working on a case that, when the Captain hears what he's done, he'll be that anxious about him he will want to put him in a safe.

But stayin' inside on orders isn't to Johnson's liking. Makes it look like he's yellow, hidin' inside—

"Get in there," the sergeant orders. "You bantam, you got a lot o' gall, but no brains—like all you young ones."

"No brains, uh?" retorts Johnson. "It took brains to grab off what I did last night and this afternoon. And then tellin' me to hide! That Scarsi mob ain't got any bullets that'll fit a hole in me! It's me that'll knock them, with this case I got. That ain't so dumb, is it?"

Outside there is the sound of a high-powered car driving up and coming to a stop. It's Schmidt's squad, thinks the sergeant, as he goes into Lieutenant Gill's office, leaving Johnson to look after things.

Through the street door a man enters. "He is a muscular, hard-bodied, Americanized Italian of thirty-eight, in a slightly form-fitted brown topcoat and soft hat. He is smartly dressed, but under the knot of his necktie his soft, colored shirt-collar is fastened with a diamond barpin."

"You the Johnson that picked up Joe Scarsi last night?" the man demands, edging his way into the room.

"What of it?"

THE MAN—Wait a second. (JOHNSON *turns*.) I came to see a witness you got—girl by the name o' Hayes.

JOHNSON—See the sergeant.

THE MAN—But I might as well see you, too. I'm a friend o' that Scarsi kid's.

JOHNSON—I just told his last friend to—

THE MAN—Choke it. We don't want any trouble with you. You did your duty, but—

JOHNSON—That's a lot o' manure about "duty," too. I get paid for my job. I like it, and so I do it. If I didn't like it, I wouldn't be doin' it. I don't like crooks for the same reasons I don't like a lot o' other people, and because they banged my old man, and because, generally speakin', I'm a better man than they are.

THE MAN—Don't take it so personal.

JOHNSON—There ain't much that amounts to anythin' that ain't personal.

THE MAN—You must be kind o' young, talkin' like that.

JOHNSON—I ain't used to it yet, that's all.

THE MAN—Joe Scarsi's not used to it yet, either. That's why he's got to be looked after for a while. That girl you got kissed him into sellin' his own car to buy her a ring, and then— Playin' him for his brother's jack, that's all.

JOHNSON—Why doesn't that big brother o' his look after him?

THE MAN—He tried to.

JOHNSON—Do you know him?

THE MAN—Nick? Yeh.

JOHNSON—Everybody knows him. But nobody meets him. (jerking up his belt.) I'd like to meet the yellow—

THE MAN (cutting him short)—I thought Nick had a lot o' guts.

JOHNSON—Guts, my can! These newspaper bad-men don't take the air without half a dozen armed guards stickin' to 'em. Catch one—two—three of them alone and you could slap 'em to sleep.

THE MAN—Yeh?

JOHNSON—Yeh.

THE MAN—Yeh?

JOHNSON—Yeh!

THE MAN—If Scarsi's so yellow, how do you happen to be hidin' inside?

JOHNSON (curtly)—Orders.

THE MAN—Afraid the witness'd get banged, uh?

JOHNSON—I ain't afraid—

THE MAN—You're cocky, for a kindergarten cop.

JOHNSON (his fists clenching)—I ain't afraid o' Scarsi. Or any of his mob. And as for Joe Scarsi, no little wop's goin' to tell me who I can pinch, and grand-stand around about what he's goin' to do to me, and get away with it.

THE MAN—No?

JOHNSON—No! And that goes for that big brother o' his, too.

THE MAN—Yeh?

JOHNSON—And if you're from Nick Scarsi, tell him I told you.

And tell him to quit his bragging, too, because I know how Higgins—this political Old Man's private secretary—disappeared.

The Man—What? Where'd you get that?

Johnson—From one o' Nick's own men who tried to scare me into layin' off Joe Scarsi's case.

The Man (*quickly*)—Who?

Johnson—And after I gave him the treatment he spilled all the dope—how Higgins got his head blown off, because he knew too much. (*The man turns slightly away, his right hand slipping into his left overcoat sleeve.*) Yeh! And in another hour we'll have the evidence—(*turning away*)—because I know—

The next instant The Man has turned sharply, whipped a blue steel revolver from his pocket, and shot Johnson in the back.

As the patrolman falls forward to the floor Ames comes panting in from the street. Johnson's shoulders wrench convulsively as he pitches on his face against the desk. The Man jams the revolver into his pocket and jumps for the street door. Ames tries to tackle him and is knocked down, and kicked in the head. The Man is away and his shouted order to the chauffeur to "Step on it!" comes floating back above the grumbling of grinding gears.

Sullivan and Gill rush from Gill's office; orders are shouted for Schmidt's squad to follow the car; Ames, wiping his pale face, sways a little and sinks into a chair as Delaney and Irene Hayes, followed by Captain McQuigg, arrive.

Haltingly Ames tries to tell the Captain what he saw, but his information is distressingly meagre. An unidentified man—that's all they have to work on! McQuigg orders the roads blocked and phones the chief!

Ames, recovering enough to remember his job, makes a grab for the telephone. He gets his office, but gets no farther than "This is Ames—" before they hang up on him. Before he can call again Sergeant Sullivan stops him. The story isn't to go in yet.

When Delaney reports that Johnson is dead, Dave Ames threatens to cave in. Hysterically he is ready to fight the system that can take murder so calmly.

"He oughtn't to be out there—just lying there—like that," he cries, his voice rising shrilly. "How do you know he's dead? Maybe he's bleeding to— Isn't there even a doctor out there? God *damn* this town!"

"What the hell's the matter with you?" demands Officer Glick, pushing Ames back into his chair.

"Growing pains!" answers Irene, as she pushes Glick aside and takes charge of Ames. She would take the boy out and get him some coffee even though they try to stop her, but at that moment Sergeant Schmidt rushes in with news of the chase. They've got one of the men! Schmidt and Clark got him when the car he was tryin' to make his getaway in got stalled by a freight at 86th and Halstead streets! He's the one that dashed out of the station after the shooting and jumped the running board of the car! The other flipped the freight and Patrolman Ross is after him! Clark's bringing in the guy they got!

Clark's in a minute later with the man who shot Johnson. Clark is also carrying a couple of sawed-off shotguns he had taken from the car. The man's hat is pulled down over his eyes.

Captain McQuigg takes a narrow-eyed look at the man, orders the search continued, warns Gill and Sullivan to give nothing to headquarters until he gives the word, and then walks over and knocks up the arrest's hat.

"Hello, Nick!" he says.

"Good evening, Mac," replies Scarsi. "You like it out here?"

McQuigg—I'm beginnin' to. Thanks for not asking me why I'm here.

Scarsi—You're not a gover'ment cop—dumb. What's the matter? That driver o' mine pull somethin' off in here?

McQuigg—Somebody did.

Scarsi—What'd he do?

McQuigg—Who?

Scarsi—"Breeze" Enright. My driver I sent in here.

McQuigg—I thought Enright was down for some bank job.

Scarsi—He must've got paroled.

McQuigg—Yeh. A lot do, since they equipped that penitentiary with revolvin' doors. What brought Enright in here?

Scarsi—I sent him to see that girl you got about how much she wants to lay off that brother o' mine. And— Yeh, I told him to see that copper—Johnson—o' yours, too, since I heard you were keepin' him in.

McQuigg—I wanted him in, knowin' what he was up against. But we haven't got this protection business down as efficient as you—big-business men!

Scarsi—Big-business runs this country. I'd get wise if I were you.

McQuigg—I am.

Scarsi—What do you want him for?

McQuigg—Who?

Scarsi—Enright.

McQuigg—I don't want him.

Scarsi—Then if he didn't pull something—?

McQuigg—Somebody did, and, by God, I got you!

Scarsi—Are you so sore about your transfer you're thinkin' o' hangin' somethin' on to me? (Ames *comes in from the street.* Clark *tries to stop him.*)

Ames (*pushing* Clark *aside*)—Let me in! Captain, I know. That man who came in— (*Seeing* Scarsi, *he stiffens.*) That's him. He did it.

Scarsi—What?

McQuigg—Now, Nick! How'll you alibi this?

Ames—Is he—?

McQuigg (*to* Delaney)—Lock him up.

Scarsi—What's the charge?

McQuigg—Same old thing for you. Murder.

Scarsi (*after a moment*)—All right. I'll call my lawyer. (*He starts for the phone on the partition.* McQuigg *motions to* De-laney. Delaney *blocks* Scarsi.)

McQuigg—Forget who he is. (Sam Meyer *comes wearily in from the street.*)

Meyer—Back again.

Scarsi—Where the hell've you been?

Meyer—I couldn't help it, Mr. Scarsi.

McQuigg (*to* Meyer)—Who're you?

Meyer—Sam Meyer, Captain, from Reilly, Platka and Cohn. But I'm a deputy sheriff now. (*Taking a paper from his pocket.*) I got a writ o' habeas corpus to take him out.

Ames (*to* McQuigg)—I tried to tell you. My office phoned me—

Scarsi (*to* McQuigg)—"Efficiency." Do you imagine for God's sake, I don't leave word where I'll be? They know what to do when I'm late reportin' in.

Meyer (*handing the writ summons to* McQuigg)—All legal. Just issued by Judge—

McQuigg (*to* Delaney)—Take (*indicating* Scarsi) him down!

Scarsi—McQuigg!

McQuigg (*unheeding*)—Hang onto (*indicating* Ames) that boy.

SCARSI (*shoving* DELANEY *aside*)—Didn't you hear him about that writ?

McQUIGG—Try and serve it.

SCARSI—Are you trying to trick me?

McQUIGG—No, that's your way—in the dark, so's you can hide, and frame and fix, and grab, till everybody's rotten with fear and don't-give-a-damn, and a man can't call his soul his own. It's the racket o' this whole damn town. But I'm through.

SCARSI—Not yet. (*Snatching the writ from* MEYER, *he extends it to* McQUIGG.) You got to recognize a writ. That's the law.

McQUIGG (*after a moment*)—I'm licked again by due process o' law, uh? Well—(*seizing and tearing up the writ*) I'm sick o' the law. We'll fight this out here.

SCARSI—You'll get contempt o' court for that. (*To* MEYER.) Go phone that to the Judge. (MEYER *turns for the door.*)

McQUIGG—Jim!

DELANEY (*to* CLARK)—Hi! (*He trips up* MEYER *and, as he falls, pushes him to* CLARK, *who mixes with him and shoves him back to* DELANEY.)

SCARSI—Look out! They're framin' you!

DELANEY (*jerking* MEYER *up by the collar*)—Pickin' a fight, uh? Drunk, uh?

McQUIGG—Lock him up till he sobers up!

DELANEY (*getting* MEYER *to the door, right*)—Reilly, Platka and Cohn resistin' arrest, uh? The Department's been wantin' a crack at that outfit. (*He gets him out.*)

The curtain falls.

ACT III

It is a few minutes later. Captain McQuigg has gone directly to his private office, followed by Delaney. The room is old-fashioned and high-ceilinged, like the other rooms of the station, and is lighted principally from a high arched window at one end. At the moment the window is obscured by a slightly cracked green shade which is pulled down. It is, by the calendar on Captain McQuigg's desk, Saturday, the 3rd of November.

It is Delaney's opinion that Nick Scarsi has put the whole organization in a trap with this particular job, and McQuigg finds satisfaction in the thought that for once the organization will have to treat with him if it treats with anybody. He is of a mood, too, to defy them to ride him down. He'll get Scarsi to trial if he has to use the machine to do it. Being only a policeman that is as far as he can take him.

Then he sends for Scarsi. The talk between the two is personal
and free. Scarsi regrets that Enright, his chauffeur, had killed
Johnson, and McQuigg wonders that Scarsi persists in clinging to
that particular stall. Scarsi admits that the costs of buying
crooks out of jail are increasing and McQuigg resents the system
that empties the jails of crooks as fast as the police can fill them.
Scarsi suspects it is because it has become difficult to depend on
juries and McQuigg knows that the Scarsis of the town have
specialized in arranging for the disappearance of any juror found
heroic enough to vote for a conviction in particular cases.

"Times've changed," declared Scarsi. "You can get by with it
(*murder*) better now."

"Yeh," agrees McQuigg, sarcastically. "We've got to do
thinkin' to keep up with you."

SCARSI—I'll take anythin' you four-thousand-dollar-a-year
harps can think up for me.

McQUIGG—Shut up, you peacock, and get this! I've got a lot
o' bones to pick with you. (SCARSI *laughs*.) Oh, I know you're
powerful. You've got a lot o' political sluts on their backs.

SCARSI—And takin' candy.

McQUIGG—And they've got a lot of our leadin' business-men
on *their* backs, takin' candy from them. But I don't like that
kind o' candy.

SCARSI—No?

McQUIGG—And when my job makes me swallow it, I'm sick
till I get it up again. This time I'm goin' to get it up with such
a commotion that hereafter it'll leave me alone.

SCARSI—Yeh?

McQUIGG—And I'm gettin' you out o' my system at the same
time.

SCARSI (*rising*)—Gettin' *me* out o' your system. You got any
idea they'll let you lock me up?

McQUIGG—Why, with you out o' the way I'll feel like a kid
again.

SCARSI—You don't imagine I'm goin' to hang or anythin', do
you?

McQUIGG—No.

SCARSI—Not these days.

McQUIGG—No, the (*contemptuously*) law wouldn't let you.
But there just might be even a chance o' that once this election's
out o' the way and the powers-that-be quit shaking at mention o'
your name. Yeh, and prosecuted by Welch! (*He laughs*.)

That'd give the whole Department a laugh, and we could use some laughin' in this business now.

SCARSI—Don't make me laugh. Where is Welch? I know he's here, for raids.

McQUIGG—They can't fix this.

SCARSI—He'll have to.

McQUIGG (*after a moment*)—H'm. They couldn't take the chance! (*He abruptly rises and opens the center door.*) Sullivan! (*To* SCARSI.) All right. You asked for Welch. (SULLIVAN *comes to the door.*) Send around to the restaurant at the corner o' Western and get Mr. Assistant State's Attorney Welch. (*His eyes on* SCARSI.) We'll see what he can do.

SULLIVAN—Yes, sir. (*He goes out.*)

SCARSI—He'll take care o' me.

McQUIGG (*going to door, right*)—He'll take care o' himself. He'll take care o' me! (SCARSI *laughs.*) Go on. You'll laugh yourself to death. (*Opening the door. To the patrolman there*): Put him in the bullpen where he'll be handy.

SCARSI—You ought to be in the Marines.

Pratt and Miller, back from supper, are still after the details of the Scarsi arrest and Captain McQuigg still unwilling to give them out. The story of an arrest is already on the streets but "no one has spilled the pinch's name."

"Captain," explodes Pratt, "if you can nail Scarsi for this, the organization won't sleep to-night. And if they try to spring him, the stuff we'll print may rouse a few of the last of the Anglo-Saxons into voting, anyway."

McQuigg is rid of the press men with a promise to give them the story after he has talked with Welch. Now he will talk with Irene Hayes.

Miss Hayes is worried about Dave Ames. She doesn't want McQuigg to use the boy as a witness. If Ames goes on the stand and identifies Scarsi it means the gang'll get him sure.

"Can't you think of any one but yourselves?" she demands. "You and Nick Scarsi both. So cocky you kill a policeman trying to get at each other's throats, and show this boy so much—"

She hasn't a chance to finish before Ames is there to defend himself. He doesn't need any one to look after him, he tells Irene. But there are a lot of other things around there that need some one to look after them.

"Nobody seems to realize that somebody's been killed. And the one that did it giggling over it, and every one calling him by his first name!" His voice rises again, and trembles with excitement.

"Havin' a tough time of it, aren't you?" ventures McQuigg.

AMES—Aren't you—with the public hiring you to protect them and then not giving a damn whether you do or not?

McQuigg—Yeh.

IRENE—They can't do anything. Not to Scarsi.

AMES—Maybe you can't do anything—the way things are, I mean. I don't know anything, any more. But somebody's got to try, haven't they?

IRENE—Not you.

AMES—Yes, me.

IRENE—Because of your pride, or your honor, or whatever it is you men call your lack of sense? (*To* McQUIGG.) You're in this. Tangling (*indicating* AMES) him in these manly principles of yours until he's afraid to run away from even being killed. Make him go! (*To* AMES.) Tell him you won't testify.

AMES—I've got to. I'll identify him, Captain. I'll testify.

McQuigg (*rising*)—Good boy.

AMES (*to* IRENE)—Oh, I have to!

IRENE—All right. (*After a shrug. To* McQUIGG)—Count me in, too, then. I'll try fighting again, myself. And (*her eyes on* AMES) if Scarsi tries anything, I'll do some testifying that'll put Dunn and Bradstreet themselves up on the stand.

Ames thinks perhaps he had better call his office and see how he stands, and Irene approves the idea.

The office answers back, apparently, that Mr. Ames does not stand very well, nor will listen to any explanations. Which emboldens the Nebraska journalist to tell the gentleman to whom he is talking that so far as he (Ames) is concerned they can take their old City Press and stick it in the lake. He's through!

He's not through with reporting, however. He will go to New York. They'll print his stories there—

IRENE—I'd print anything you'd say, to me.

AMES (*after a moment*)—I wonder if I will be able to get a job in New York?

IRENE—If you can keep your mind on it longer than you can on—this.

AMES—This what?

IRENE—You and Me.

AMES—What—?

IRENE—We could talk to each other—couldn't we—if you'd be satisfied with this "experience" for awhile, and not have to make a flying tackle at New York? If you'd just tie to— (*She stops.*)

AMES—The only thing you can tie to is yourself.

IRENE—And the girl-friend?

AMES—Girls? What do I care about gi— Oh. You. Sure, I can talk to you. (*He sits down beside her.*)

IRENE—I'm listening.

AMES—Well, a fellow can't just keep on talking to himself!

IRENE—Don't.

AMES—I mean, there's none o' this love-making stuff with you.

IRENE—Oh! (*After a moment.*) No?

AMES—No. That's a lot of bunk.

IRENE—What's the idea?

AMES—I'm getting a lot of ideas. (*After a moment.*) Everything you believe in and try to do—you can't! Nobody gives a damn. You learn to hold your head up for a lot of bunk.

IRENE (*laughing a little*)—You're so "experienced" now I suppose you wouldn't let yourself fall in love, even if you could.

AMES—What?

IRENE (*rising*)—I mean, if I wasn't so intimate with inside dirt, there wouldn't be such a ditch between you and me, would there?

AMES (*impatiently*)—There's nothing between you and me!

IRENE—No?

AMES—What's the matter with you?

IRENE—"A lot o' bunk." I—like you, you damn fool.

AMES—Well, I like you, too.

IRENE—Yes? (*She shrugs.*) We'll let it go at that.

Welch is worried when he meets McQuigg. And more worried the longer he talks with McQuigg. That they are all—Welch, the Old Man, the Chief, and the Organization—all in a tough spot is McQuigg's firmest conviction. They can't "spring" Scarsi without putting deadly campaign material in the hands of the reformers and they can't refuse to spring him without risking the loss of the river wards Scarsi controls.

Nor is Mr. Welch's interview with the prisoner Scarsi any pleasanter or more illuminating. Scarsi demands instant action. Whatever he (Scarsi) has done, whether he has obeyed the Old Man's orders to keep away from McQuigg or not, he wants out!

They'll not keep *him* locked up until after election! Not Nick
Scarsi! Let them get him out and he'll fix it with "B*r*eeze" Enright, the chauffeur, to plead guilty, take a second degree sentence and go back to the penitentiary until he (Scarsi) can buy
him out again. But this plan is slightly weakened when McQuigg
returns.

"A break for justice, Welch!" announces the Captain. "Such
an influential citizen might force whoever was with him to take
this rap, if that gent' was handy at all. But I just heard from
my man who was after Mr. Scarsi's chauffeur, and he's not handy.
He's gone, got away, dropped off that freight in the dark. And
we're not lookin' for him. So don't let (*indicating* Scarsi) him
worry the prosecution with that."

The Captain invites in Ames and Irene that Ames may make
his identification of Scarsi to the State's Attorney.

Scarsi (*rising*)—I been wantin' to hear if this loud-speaker o'
yours was positive about that.

Ames—Yes. You—

Welch—You're a minor, aren't you? Your testimony (*running down weakly*) might not—be any good.

Ames—I'm twenty-three. And right now I feel about fifty. So
what do you think of that? He shot Johnson.

Scarsi (*jerking him around*)—Take a look at me.

Ames—Just as I came in—

Scarsi—Maybe you'll change your mind.

Ames (*knocking* Scarsi's *hand away*)—I'm not afraid of you.

Scarsi—With what I got on a couple of fancy doctors downtown, they'll tend to you.

Irene—Leave him alone, you hero.

Scarsi (*after a moment*)—You're Hayes, uh?

Irene—Yes. And you're Scarsi, the Awful—afraid of women,
but death on kids. I've known enough men to realize that you
couldn't be anything but just another one, so vain you have to
play only with men because women would laugh, and you can't
stand being laughed at, can you?

Scarsi—Nobody laughs at me.

Irene—I thought you might be heroic, you're so damn bad.
But you were scared stiff when I got in your brother's way.

Scarsi—You won't get in his way again.

Irene—No, now I'm getting in yours. (Scarsi *laughs.*) I'll
play you off the board. Anybody can trick you.

SCARSI—No woman has yet.

IRENE—Then why were you so afraid to see me when Joe wanted you to?

SCARSI—Now cut this stuff! Do you imagine I'd stand for you with Joe after what I made o' him? I educated him, East, didn't I? Yeh. He's a college man. He can go any place—mix with the high-class people—in this town. He's not in the racket, and he won't be, because I'm keepin' him out, d'you hear? And with the jack he'll have he can marry right—on the Drive—high class—and not you, you common—

(IRENE *quickly slaps him across the mouth.*)

SCARSI (*rigid with fury*)—I'll— (*He starts for her.*)

McQUIGG—Get back! (*He seizes and spins* SCARSI *back.*)

IRENE—Nobody ought to be afraid of you.

SCARSI (*seething*)—No?

IRENE—No. Not when you had to kick this (*indicating* AMES) baby in the face.

SCARSI—What the hell'd he get in my way for?

IRENE (*to* McQUIGG)—There's your confession. (SCARSI *stiffens.* WELCH *drops to the chair.*) If he was the one who kicked Ames, he was the one who shot Johnson, wasn't he?

McQUIGG (*at* SCARSI)—Ha! Women are still poison to you. (*To* IRENE *and* AMES.) Wait outside. (*To* AMES.) You'll be all right, with her.

SCARSI (*to* AMES)—I'll see you later.

Scarsi's defiance of the Ames identification takes the form of a last warning to McQuigg that if he gives the story out he (McQuigg) will suffer most. The public will want to know how it happens that anybody can stroll into a police station and shoot a policeman under the noses of the whole staff? They'll be demandin' somebody's head for that!

"All right," replies McQuigg, going to call the reporters. "Any head in a storm, Nick! Boys! *Tribune!* (To SCARSI.) I'm givin' 'em yours first, Nick!"

"Do we shoot now?" Pratt wants to know.

"Fast, and quote me," answers McQuigg. "Mr. Scarsi swaggered in here a half hour ago to scare Johnson and Hayes here into layin' off his brother's case. Johnson started to throw him out, and Scarsi killed him—'a public servant'—without even givin' him a chance to draw. Ames came in and saw him, and when I got him, made the identification, cold. And Miss Hayes just tricked him into admittin' the killin', himself. . . . I got Scarsi ten minutes after the shooting. Get that part of it from Sergeant Schmidt, and give him and his squad the credit. And here's Mr. Assistant State's Attorney Welch, already on the job for the people o' the State of Illinois! What the State's goin' to do about it, you can get from him."

"I'll see you after I talk to the accused," replies Welch.

Scarsi's anger and defiance grow with the delay. He'll fix 'em yet! There's still time for him to swing the river wards, and they'll be swung. "You're all lice, whichever side you're on, so it don't matter to me who I'm with," he shouts. "What do you suppose I gave fifty grand to both factions' campaign funds for? You didn't know I play both ends against the middle, uh? Whoever's in's got to be with me."

There is a call for Welch on the phone. The Old Man has been reached at last. Word comes, too, that the coroner has been notified, more or less mysteriously, and is on his way. And probably a squad of Homicide dicks from the Detective Bureau. Not so promising for Scarsi, these Homicide detectives, thinks McQuigg. They're often fairly rough with a fellow who kills a policeman. If Scarsi is forced to spend three days at detective headquarters he is not likely to come out looking very tidy.

Delaney is in with Scarsi's revolver. Found it down near the corner where the gangman had been picked up. One chamber empty and the others loaded with dum-dum bullets. They don't even allow them in war!

Welch, from the other room, calls Turck, his assistant, for a conference. A moment later they are back in McQuigg's office. Delaney has been sent out to wait for the coroner and Gill returns to the main room.

"So that's what the Old Man told you to do?" mumbles Turck, knowingly.

Turck and Welch fix the window shade with a weight to hold it down with the spring released. Then they call in Scarsi.

He has talked with the Old Man, Welch reports, and he thinks Scarsi ought to stay in jail until after election. Scarsi will see them all in hell first. Either he gets out or he sinks the ticket, and Welch's campaign for County Judge with it.

"Then where'll you be with the jack you owe?" he demands, sneeringly. "You know you haven't got a dime. . . . Your wife's such a shopper she even runs through your graft!"

McQuigg steps in to report the Detective Bureau car, with the Homicide squad aboard, just passing Seventy-ninth Street. And again he warns Scarsi of what is likely to happen to him.

"They'll have to carry you to the scaffold—you'll still be too weak to climb," prophesies the Captain. "And you know it takes about twenty minutes to hang by the neck till dead unless the knot o' the rope's just right."

SCARSI (*to* WELCH)—If anybody touches me I'll drown your whole ticket. You'll lose—

WELCH—We'll lose either way, with you.

SCARSI—I'll get the papers in here, and— Yeh, I'll give 'em a story! With names, and dates, and figures, that'll raise such a stink there won't be any prominent people left to hand-shake Queens. (*Starting for the door.*) *Examiner! Tribune!* (McQUIGG *seizes him by the neck and flings him back.*)

McQUIGG—I'll take care o' them. (*He goes out.*)

SCARSI (*in cornered fury*)—I'll give 'em one o' their exposés of politics and business and crime that'll rip this town wide open! (*He jerks open the door. The* PATROLMAN *there starts for him.*)

PATROLMAN—Keep in there! (SCARSI *slams the door in his face.*)

WELCH—You won't get the chance.

SCARSI—All right then. All right! The facts'll spill easy after I been beat up by dicks. Who that Organization o' yours paid to get its names first on the ballot this time—

WELCH—Who'd believe you?

SCARSI—I got it on paper. Yeh, I got everythin' up my sleeve —ready for a double-cross by you. How you made that special investigatin' grand jury o' prominent high-hats fold up last month by condemnin' the elevators in a couple o' million dollar department stores! Yeh! And by remindin' some o' our leadin' citizens o' the extra apartments they keep!

WELCH—Stop!

SCARSI—How the Old Man had that kid in that treasurer's office accidentally killed by a train because his wife made him promise to squeal about the public funds grabbed there!

WELCH—You'll get—

SCARSI—How you framed the Civics Board, to get your own hogs in there, because *that* Board's got seventy-five million to spend next year!

WELCH—Keep qui—

SCARSI—I won't stop at blowin' up this town! I'll talk some o' your State politicians into court—makin' me pay ten grand a head for pardons and paroles. I'll talk some o' your Republicans in the Federal Building into committin' suicide over the liquor dope I got. Who do you suppose I pay for the breweries I own? Who do you suppose I pay for the alcohol I get? I'll knock your whole Organization cuckoo!

WELCH—Shut up! The Old Man thought you'd try that.

SCARSI—He did, uh?

WELCH—But you won't.

SCARSI—I won't, uh? I'll talk him into flyin' the country if I even whisper about what happened to that friend o' yours, Higgins, last week.

WELCH (*struck, horribly*)—What?

SCARSI—Who do you suppose ordered him out o' the way, so that my guns had to do the job? (WELCH *stares.*) The Old Man!

WELCH—You're lying! The Old Man wouldn't—

SCARSI—Higgins had been collectin' for him for years! Yeh! He was gettin' too big to carry, too. Christ, *you'll* be next!

WELCH (*waving a limp hand at the window*)—Go on. The window. It's fixed, for a getaway.

SCARSI—I thought you'd crawl when I spoke that piece. (*He springs to the chair against the window, pulls the shade aside, sees that the window is open, then jumps down. To* TURCK.) Here. Give me your rod.

WELCH (*coming to, and hurriedly pushing* SCARSI *on the window*)—Hurry up! There's an Elevated two blocks north—that railroad— Hide in a basement, till you can get to your men!

SCARSI—Give me— (MCQUIGG *comes in center.*)

WELCH (*grabbing* SCARSI's *arm*)—Wait!

SCARSI (*jerking away*)—No!

MCQUIGG—What're you up to?

SCARSI—Tell him.

WELCH—Wait!

SCARSI—Not me. (*He backs to the window, his eyes on* MCQUIGG.) Did you imagine I'd let any lousy politicians who'd knock their own mothers over the head for a vote tell *me* what to do? (*At* WELCH.) I'm off you worms! You haven't got a prayer for Tuesday now. I'm goin' to deliver the River Wards to the Reform gang, for a laugh. And if you think you can steal this Primary, fight it out with the mob I'll have Tuesday at the polls. To lick you, we'll have an election for a change that's square! (*He notices the revolver* DELANEY *left on the desk, snatches it up, holds it on* MCQUIGG, *and puts one foot on the chair to spring to the window.*)

MCQUIGG (*hunching*)—Give me that gun!

SCARSI—In the belly if you don't get back. (McQUIGG *starts for him.* SCARSI *fires. The pin only clicks. He fires frantically again. Realizing that the gun is empty.*) You bastards! (*He flings the gun at* McQUIGG, *who ducks and jumps to the window sill.*)

WELCH—Turck! (TURCK *draws a revolver and fires at* SCARSI, *then again.* SCARSI *pitches to the floor. The patrolmen burst in, right.* McQUIGG *after a look at* TURCK, *then at* WELCH, *goes to* SCARSI, *bends, examines him, and rises.*)

McQUIGG—Out.

TURCK—It was the second one that got him. (McQUIGG *motions the patrolmen out, picks up the gun* SCARSI *threw, and breaks it, inspecting the chambers.*) He didn't know it wasn't loaded! (*He goes out right.* McQUIGG *tosses the gun to the desk.*)

McQUIGG (*eyeing the body*)—Well—uh—Judge, that issue's out o' the way. (WELCH *hands him* SCARSI'S *overcoat.* McQUIGG *covers the body with the coat, then sits at the desk.*) The Grand Old Party here'll probably run you for Mayor, for that. (*There is a commotion outside the center door.* MILLER *and* PRATT *push in past the patrolman there. To* MILLER *and* PRATT.) Mr. Scarsi tried a getaway. Sergeant Turck o' the State's Attorney office got him.

MILLER (*starting out*)—Jeez, what a break for the Sunday papers! (*Indicating the body.*) Is he—?

McQUIGG—He is.

PRATT (*innocently*)—Why, Mr. Welch?

MILLER (*going out*)—So that gover'ment o' the professionals, by the professionals, and for the professionals, shall not perish from the earth.

PRATT (*to* WELCH)—What were the events leading up to the tragedy?

WELCH—He— (*He cannot go on.*)

PRATT—That will do. An inquest's hardly legal any more without a little perjury. (*Eyeing the body.*) Well, that blows this election exposé of mine to hell. The long-delayed rising of the upper classes will have to be postponed. (*He goes out.*)

WELCH—I'm going to—get—some—coffee. (*He goes out right.*)

McQUIGG *to the* PATROLMAN *outside the center door*)—Send those two in. (AMES *and* IRENE *come in.*) You can go now.

AMES—Thanks. (*They shake hands.*)

McQUIGG—Good luck. Keep your feet.

AMES—Sure. (DELANEY *comes in right.*)

DELANEY—Where you goin', Kid?

AMES—New York. (*Eagerly.*) Were you ever there?

DELANEY—Yeh. A hick town.

AMES (*grinning*)—Aw-w—! (*To* IRENE.) Going downtown, Irene? Come on.

IRENE—Not your way, darling. Run along.

AMES—Well— Good-by then. (*He goes out.*)

IRENE (*after a glance at the body*)—Dog eat dog to the last ditch, Policeman, eh?

McQUIGG—"Old dogs—," Miss Hayes!

IRENE—Yes. You and me both. (*She goes slowly out.*)

McQUIGG (*gazing at the body*)—I thought they might have to do that.

DELANEY—I thought you did, when he sent for Welch. (*After a moment.*) What now, Captain?

McQUIGG—I'd like some sleep. (DELANEY *goes out.*) But (*rising and snapping on his cap*) by the time I get through with the Coroner, and the papers, and headquarters, and the rest o' the public servants that'll be out here, it'll be time to go to mass. (*He pushes off the light, and goes out, closing the door.*)

"The room is still, and dark except for the night blue coming in through the open window and making Scarsi's body faintly visible. Outside there is again the careening rumble of a passing truck and a raucous shout of 'Yah-h-h, McQuigg!'"

The curtain falls.

THE PLOUGH AND THE STARS

A Tragedy in Four Acts

By Sean O'Casey

SEAN O'CASEY arose suddenly to playwriting prominence at home with the production of his "Juno and the Paycock" two years ago. This play won for him the Hawthorndon prize "for the best work of imaginative literature produced during the year by a writer under forty" and gave him his place in the theatre. He followed "Juno" with "The Plough and the Stars," with which play he again invades the Irish tenements from which he, himself, has sprung. This time his observations are made during the days of the abortive rebellions of 1915-16 in Dublin.

Both plays have been produced in New York, "Juno and the Paycock" by Augustin Duncan in March, 1926, and "The Plough and the Stars" by the Irish players, directed by George C. Tyler and headed by Arthur Sinclair and Sara Allgood in November, 1927.

Neither engagement proved successful in a popular sense, and yet both the O'Casey dramas were generously praised as being forthright and honest in their interpretations of Irish character and were credited with presenting illuminating pictures of Irish tenement life. They also were accepted as evidence that a new literary figure of promise had arisen in Ireland.

Mr. O'Casey has his most talented countrymen's gift of a sure dramatic sense touched with poetic imagery. His love of abrupt contrasts is likewise strong, and lurking back of his recital of a tragedy is the ironical laughter of a man who has studied life seriously and accepted precious little of it as being inspired by God.

"The Plough and the Stars" gets under way in the home of the Clitheroes, Jack, a commandant in the Irish Citizen army, and Nora, his wife, a timid protestor against fighting in general and any kind of war that is likely to involve her beloved man.

The home "consists of the front and back drawing-rooms in a fine old Georgian house struggling for its life against the assaults

of time and the more savage assaults of the tenants." . . . "The
room directly in front of the audience is furnished in a way that
suggests an attempt towards a finer expression of domestic life.
The large fireplace on right is of wood, painted to look like
marble (the original has been taken away by the landlord). On
the mantelshelf are two candlesticks of dark carved wood. Between them is a small clock. Over the clock is hanging a calendar which displays a picture of 'The Sleeping Venus.' In the
centre of the breast of the chimney hangs a picture of Robert
Emmett. On the right of the entrance to the front drawing-
room is a copy of 'The Gleaners,' on the opposite side a copy of
'The Angelus.' "

At the moment there are workmen repairing the street outside
by the light of a flaring gasoline lamp. Inside Fluther Good is
fixing the lock of the door. "A clawhammer is on a chair beside
him, and a screwdriver is in his hand. He is a man of forty
years of age, rarely surrendering to thoughts of anxiety, fond
of his 'oil' but determined to conquer the habit before he dies.
He is square-jawed and harshly featured; under the left eye is
a scar, and his nose is bent from a smashing blow received in a
fistic battle long ago. He is bald, save for a few peeping tufts
of reddish hair around his ears; and his upper lip is hidden by a
scrubby red moustache, embroidered here and there with a grey
hair. He is dressed in a seedy black suit, cotton shirt with a soft
collar, and wears a very respectable little black bow. On his
head is a faded jerry hat, which, when he is excited, he has a
habit of knocking farther back on his head, in a series of taps. In
an argument he usually fills with sound and fury generally sig-
nifying a row. He is in his shirt sleeves at present, and wears
a soiled white apron, from a pocket in which sticks a carpenter's two-foot rule. He has just finished the job of putting on a
new lock, and, filled with satisfaction, he is opening and shutting
the door, enjoying the completion of a work well done. Sitting at
the fire, airing a white shirt, is Peter Flynn. He is a little,
thin bit of a man, with a face shaped like a lozenge; on his
cheeks and under his chin is a straggling wiry beard of dirty-
white and lemon hue. His face invariably wears a look of ani-
mated anguish, mixed with irritated defiance, as if everybody was
at war with him, and he at war with everybody."

Mrs. Gogan, in the hall outside, having intercepted the delivery of a parcel addressed to Mrs. Clitheroe, takes upon herself the completion of that delivery for the satisfaction of her
curiosity concerning it. Mrs. Gogan "is a doleful looking little

woman of forty, insinuating manner and sallow complexion. She is fidgety and nervous, terribly talkative, has a habit of taking up things that may be near her and fiddling with them while she is speaking. Her heart is aflame with curiosity, and a fly could not come into nor go out of the house without her knowing."

It is a woman's hat that Mrs. Gogan has taken the trouble to deliver, a discovery she makes when she unties the package and tries on the hat. Moreover it is a hat that, she is convinced, cost something more than a penny and is rather indicative of those notions of "upperosity" she feels Nora Clitheroe is acquiring.

"She's a pretty little Judy all the same," Fluther insists.

MRS. GOGAN—Ah, she is, an' she isn't. There's prettiness an' prettiness in it. I'm always sayin' that her skirts are a little too short for a married woman. An' to see her sometimes of an evenin', in her glad-neck gown would make a body's blood run cold. I do be ashamed of me life before her husband. An' th' way she thries to be polite, with "Good mornin', Mrs. Gogan," when she's goin' down, an' her "Good evenin', Mrs. Gogan," when she's comin' up. But there's politeness an' politeness in it.

FLUTHER—They seem to get on well together, all the same.

MRS. GOGAN—Ah, they do, an' they don't. The pair o' them used to be like two turtle doves always billin' an' cooin'. You couldn't come into th' room but you'd feel, instinctively like, that they'd just been after kissin' an' cuddlin' each other. . . . It often made me shiver, for, after all, there's kissin' an' cuddlin' in it. But I'm thinkin' he's beginnin' to take things more quietly; the mysthery of havin' a woman's a mysthery no longer . . . She dhresses herself to keep him with her, but it's no use—after a month or two, th' wondher of a woman wears off.

FLUTHER—I dunno, I dunno. Not wishin' to say anything derogatory, I think it's all a question of location: when a man finds th' wondher of one woman beginnin' to die, it's usually beginnin' to live in another.

MRS. GOGAN—She's always grumblin' about havin' to live in a tenement house. "I wouldn't like to spend me last hour in one, let alone live me life in a tenement," says she. "Vaults," says she, "that are hidin' th' dead, instead of homes that are sheltherin' th' livin'." "Many a good one," says I, "was reared in a tenement house." Oh, you know, she's a well-up little lassie, too; able to make a shillin' go where another would have to spend a pound. She's wipin' the eyes of th' Covey an' poor oul' Pether—everybody knows that—screwin' every penny she can out o'

them, in ordher to turn th' place into a babby-house. An' she
has th' life frightened out o' them; washin' their face, combin'
their hair, wipin' their feet, brushin' their clothes, thrimmin' their
nails, cleanin' their teeth—God Almighty, you'd think th' poor
men were undhergoin' penal servitude.

FLUTHER (*with an exclamation of disgust*)—A-a-ah, that's
goin' beyond th' beyonds in a tenement house. That's a little bit
too derogatory.

Not all the affairs of the neighborhood can be settled by Mrs.
Gogan and Fluther at one meeting, but it is still their accepted
belief that Peter Flynn, who is even now fixin' himself up for
a meeting of Irish patriots that evening, is a funny little man
who, dressed up in his "canonicals" looks a good deal like something you'd pick off a Christmas tree, and that Jack Clitheroe
himself has suffered a bitter disappointment in not being elected
a captain or something in the Citizen army, for all Nora's objection to his having anything to do with it.

Now the workmen outside have thrown down their tools with
a clang, as well as a cheer, and the Covey, a Clitheroe boarder,
arriving home, is able to explain that the men have been mobil-
ized to march in the night's demonstration under the banner of
the Plough and the Stars.

The Covey "is about twenty-five, tall, thin, with lines on his
face that form a perpetual protest against life as he conceives it
to be. Heavy seams fall from each side of his nose down around
his lips, as if they were suspenders keeping his mouth from
falling."

Nor is the Covey at all satisfied with things as they are. The
attitude of the mob irritates him excessively, but not more than
his attitude irritates the Fluther.

"Didn't you hear them cheerrin', the mugs!" shouts the Covey.
"They have to renew their political baptismal vows to be faithful
in seculo seculorum."

FLUTHER (*forgetting his fear in his indignation*)—There's no
reason to bring religion into it. I think we ought to have as great
a regard for religion as we can, so as to keep it out of as many
things as possible.

THE COVEY (*pausing in the taking off of his dungarees*)—Oh,
you're one of the boys that climb into religion as high as a short
Mass on Sunday mornin's? I suppose you'll be singin' songs o'
Sion an' songs o' Tara at the meetin' too.

FLUTHER—We're all Irishmen, anyhow, aren't we?

THE COVEY (*with hand outstretched, and in a professional tone*)—Look here, comrade, there's no such thing as an Irishman, or an Englishman, or a German or a Turk; we're all only human bein's. Scientifically speakin', it's all a question of the accidental gatherin' together of mollycewels an' atoms. (PETER *comes in with a collar in his hand. He goes over to mirror, Left, and proceeds to try to put it on.*)

FLUTHER—Mollycewels an' atoms! D'ye think I'm goin' to listen to you thryin' to juggle Fluther's mind with complicated cunundhrums of mollycewels an' atoms?

THE COVEY (*rather loudly*)—There's nothing complicated in it. There's no fear o' the Church tellin' you that mollycewels is a stickin' together of millions of atoms o' sodium, carbon, potassium o' iodide, etcetera, that accordin' to th' way they're mixed, make a flower, a fish, a star that you see shinin' in th' sky, or a man with a big brain like me, or a man with a little brain like you!

FLUTHER (*more loudly still*)—There's no necessity to be raisin' your voice; shoutin's no manifestin' forth of a growin' mind.

THE COVEY (*loudly*)—There's no use o' arguin' with you; it's education you want, comrade.

FLUTHER—The Covey an' God made th' world, I suppose, wha'?

THE COVEY—When I hear some men talkin' I'm inclined to disbelieve that th' world's eight-hundhred million years old, for it's not long since th' fathers o' some o' them crawled out o' th' sheltherin' slime o' the sea.

MRS. GOGAN (*from room at back*)—There, they're afther formin' fours, an' now they're goin' to march away.

FLUTHER (*scornfully*)—Mollycewels! (*He begins to untie his apron*)—What about Adam an' Eve?

THE COVEY—Well, what about them?

FLUTHER (*fiercely*)—What about them, you?

THE COVEY—Adam an' Eve! Is that as far as you've got? Are you still thinkin' there was nobody in th' world before Adam an' Eve? (*Loudly.*) Did you ever hear, man, of th' skeleton of th' man o' Java?

FLUTHER (*viciously folding his apron*)—Ah, you're not goin' to be let tap your rubbidge o' thoughts into th' mind o' Fluther.

THE COVEY—You're afraid to listen to th' thruth!

FLUTHER—Who's afraid?

THE COVEY—You are.

FLUTHER—G'way, you wurum!

THE COVEY—Who's a worum?

FLUTHER—You are, or you wouldn't talk th' way you're talkin'.

THE COVEY—Th' oul', ignorant savage leppin' up in you, when science shows you that th' head of your god is an empty one. Well, I hope you're enjoyin' th' blessin' o' havin' to live be th' sweat of your brow.

FLUTHER—You'll be kickin' an' yellin' for th' priest yet, me boyo. I'm not goin' to stand silent an' simple listenin' to a thick like you makin' a maddenin' mockery o' God Almighty. It 'ud be a nice derogatory thing on me conscience, an' me dyin' to look back in rememberin' shame of talkin' to a word-weavin' little ignorant yahoo of a red flag Socialist!

It is Mrs. Gogan who stops the row. At least she diverts it. But the Covey and Fluther have no sooner let up on each other than the Covey and Peter Flynn are at it, threatenin' to come to blows if Fluther wasn't there to stop them. Fluther has managed to get the Covey locked up in the next room and to keep Peter from yellin' insults through the keyhole when Nora Clitheroe arrives. Nora "is a young woman of twenty-two, alert, swift, full of nervous energy, and a little anxious to get on in the world. The firm lines of her face are considerably opposed by a soft, amorous mouth, and gentle eyes. When her firmness fails her, she persuades with her feminine charm. She is dressed in a tailor-made costume, and wears around her neck a silver fox fur."

Nora is sick and tired of the battling lodgers. She has threatened before and she threatens again to turn them out if they can't learn to behave. But Nora's trouble does not end with that settlement. She is harmlessly and a little pridefully examining the lock on the door that Fluther has fixed when Bessie Burgess appears on the landing outside. Bessie "is a woman of forty, vigorously built. Her face is a dogged one, hardened by toil and a little coarsened by drink." And it is Bessie Burgess' opinion that Nora is putting a lock on the door to insult her poor neighbors. Which is a second insult, seein' that Nora already has complained against Miss Burgess's singing hymns at night "when she has a few up." And it is Bessie's intention, which she would like to emphasize with a paste in Nora's face, that she'll sing her hymns whenever she damn well likes.

Again it is Fluther, helped presently by young Jack Clitheroe, who comes to the rescue. Between them they are able to push the obstreperous Bessie out the door.

Clitheroe "is a tall, well-made fellow of twenty-five. His face has none of the strength of Nora's. It is a face in which is the desire for authority without the power to attain it."

The four of them—Nora and Jack, the Covey and Peter Flynn, are at tea when the night's meeting is again mentioned. It's certain to be a great meeting, Jack thinks. But Nora will have none of it. He can go if he likes.

CLITHEROE—To-night is the first chance that Brennan has got of showing himself off since they made a Captain of him—why, God only knows. It'll be a treat to see him swankin' it at th' head of the Citizen Army carryin' th' flag of the Plough an' th' Stars. . . . (*Looking roguishly at* NORA.) He was sweet on you, once, Nora?

NORA—He may have been . . . I never liked him. I always thought he was a bit of a thick.

THE COVEY—They're bringin' nice disgrace on that banner now.

CLITHEROE (*remonstratively*)—How are they bringin' disgrace on it?

THE COVEY (*snappily*)—Because it's a Labour flag, an' was never meant for politics. What does th' design of th' plough, bearin' on it th' stars of th' heavenly plough, mean, if it's not Communism? It's a flag that should only be used when we're buildin' th' barricades to fight for a Workers' Republic!

PETER (*with a puff of derision*)—P-phuh!

THE COVEY (*angrily*)—What are you phuhin' out o' you for? Your mind is the mind of a mummy. (*Rising.*) I betther go an' get a good place to have a look at Ireland's warriors passin' by. (*He goes into room, Left, and returns with his cap.*)

NORA (*to the* COVEY)—Oh, Willie, brush your clothes before you go.

THE COVEY—Oh, they'll do well enough.

NORA—Go an' brush them; th' brush is in th' drawer there. (*The* COVEY *goes to the drawer, muttering, gets the brush, and starts to brush his clothes.*)

THE COVEY (*singing at* PETER, *as he does so*):

> Oh, where's th' slave so lowly,
> Condemn'd to chains unholy,
> Who, could he burst his bonds at first,
> Would pine beneath them slowly?

We tread th' land that . . . bore us,
Th' green flag glitters . . . o'er us,
Th' friends we've tried are by our side,
An' th' foe we hate . . . before us!

PETER (*leaping to his feet in a whirl of rage*)—Now, I'm tellin' you, me young Covey, once for all, that I'll not stick any longer these tittherin' taunts of yours, rovin' around to sing your slights an' slandhers, reddenin' th' mind of a man to th' thinkin' an' sayin' of things that sicken his soul with sin! (*Hysterically; lifting up a cup to fling at the* COVEY)—Be God, I'll—

CLITHEROE (*catching his arm*)—Now then, none o' that, none o' that!

NORA—Uncle Pether, Uncle Pether, Uncle Pether!

THE COVEY (*at the door about to go out*)—Isn't that th' malignant oul' varmint! Lookin' like th' illegitimate son of an illegitimate child of a corporal in th' Mexican army! (*He goes out.*)

PETER (*plaintively*)—He's afther leavin' me now in such a state of agitation that I won't be able to do meself justice when I'm marchin' to th' meetin'.

NORA (*jumping up*)—Oh, for God's sake, here, buckle your sword on, and go to your meetin' so that we'll have at least one hour of peace! (*She proceeds to belt on the sword.*)

CLITHEROE (*irritably*)—For God's sake hurry him up ou' o' this, Nora.

PETER—Are yous all goin' to thry to start to twart me now?

NORA (*putting on his plumed hat*)—S-s-sh. Now your hat's on, your house is thatched; off you pop! (*She gently pushes him from her.*)

PETER (*going and turning as he reaches the door*)—Now, if that young Covey—

NORA—Go on, go on.

For a moment there's peace in the house, but not for long. The meeting's the cause of further disagreement. Clitheroe has given up going, but he is not very happy about it. And yet he'd like a little wifely appreciation. He is not altogether neglectful. He has remembered Nora's birthday for one thing, and she has the new hat to prove it. His little red-lipped Nora should be givin' him a kiss for that.

Nora is still resenting the lure of the meeting, and not inclined to be openly forgiving. In fact she's a little snotty about it, according to Jack. But they're made up again presently and

Jack takes Nora on his lap and sings one of the old honeymoon songs to her—the one called "When You Said You Loved Me," to the tune of "When You and I Were Young, Maggie"—

"Th' violets were scenting the woods, Nora,
Displaying their charm to th' bee,
When I first said I loved only you, Nora,
And you said you loved only me!"

Clitheroe has just finished the last verse of the song when there is a quick, imperative sort of knock at the door. Nervously Nora clings to her husband, nor would let him answer the summons at all if she could hold him. A voice follows the knock.

"Commandant Clitheroe! Commandant Clitheroe! Are you there? A messenger from General Jim Connolly!"

Pleadingly, a little wildly, Nora tries to hold Jack back. But he insists on going to the door. It is Captain Brennan, a young man in the full uniform of the Irish Citizen Army—"green suit; slouch green hat caught up at one side by a small red hand badge; Sam Browne belt with a revolver in the holster."

Captain Brennan brings an order. "Commandant Clitheroe is to take command of the eighth battalion of the I. C. A. which will assemble to proceed to the meeting at nine o'clock. He is to see that all units are provided with full equipment: two days' rations and fifty rounds of ammunition. At two o'clock A.M. the army will leave Liberty Hall for a reconnaissance attack on Dublin Castle.—Com.-Gen. Connolly."

Clitheroe is puzzled by the "Commandant." Why should he be addressed by that title?

Because, Brennan explains, the staff had appointed him a fortnight ago and the General had confirmed the appointment. Word was sent him at the time. Brennan himself had brought it and given it to Mrs. Clitheroe.

Nora will not admit that she got the letter nor answer Clitheroe's charge that she withheld it. Pleadingly again she puts her arms about her husband's neck and begs that he forget the Army and stay with her. But Clitheroe is insistent.

CLITHEROE (*angrily*)—Why didn't you give me th' letter? What did you do with it? . . . (*He shakes her by the shoulder.*) What did you do with the letter?

NORA (*flaming up*)—I burned it, I burned it! That's what I did with it! Is General Connolly an' th' Citizen Army goin' to be your only care? Is your home goin' to be only a place to rest in? Am I goin' to be only somethin' to provide merry-makin' at night for you? Your vanity'll be th' ruin of you an' me yet. . . . That's what's movin' you: because they've made an officer of you, you'll make a glorious cause of what you're doin', while your little red-lipped Nora can go on sittin' here, makin' a companion of th' loneliness of th' night!

CLITHEROE (*fiercely*)—You burned it, did you? (*He grips her arm.*)—Well, me good lady—

NORA—Let go—you're hurtin' me!

CLITHEROE—You deserve to be hurt. . . . Any letther that comes to me for th' future, take care that I get it. . . . D'ye hear—take care that I get it! (*He goes to the chest of drawers and takes out a Sam Browne belt, which he puts on, and then puts a revolver in the holster. He puts on his hat, and looks towards* NORA.) You needn't wait up for me; if I'm in at all, it won't be before six in th' morning.

NORA (*bitterly*)—I don't care if you never come back!

CLITHEROE (*to* CAPT. BRENNAN)—Come along, Ned. (*They go out.*)

With a bitter movement Nora grabs her new hat from her head and flings it to the end of the room. There is a light knock at the door, followed by the appearance of Mollser Gogan. "She is about fifteen, but looks to be only about ten, for the ravages of consumption have shrivelled her up. She is pitifully worn, walks feebly and frequently coughs."

Mrs. Gogan, too, has gone to the meeting and left Mollser alone. Seeking company, she thought she would come and sit with Mrs. Clitheroe. She's envious of Nora, of the health she has and the lovely home—

From outside the music of a brass band is faintly heard. It is playing "It's a Long Way to Tipperary." Now marching men have taken up the words of the chorus and are singing as they swing past the house. Suddenly Bessie Burgess appears at the door Mollser Gogan has left open.

"There's the men marchin' out into the dhread dimness o' danger," shouts Bessie, "while th' lice is crawlin' about feedin' on th' fatness o' the land! But yous'll not escape from th' arrow that flieth be night, or th' sickness that wasteth be day . . . An' ladyship an' all, as some o' them may be, they'll be scatthered abroad, like the dust in the darkness!"

Bessie has gone away and Nora, closing the door, has flung herself down on the couch beside Mollser.

"Is there anybody goin', Mrs. Clitheroe, with a titther o' sense?" asks Mollser as the curtain falls.

ACT II

An hour later, in the south corner of a public house just outside the window of which Platform No. 1 is placed for the speakers who will address the meeting in the square, Rosie Redmond is standing at the counter discussing the situation in general with the Barman.

There are beer-pulls and glasses on the counter, and on shelves at back rows of bottles can be seen. There is a cushioned seat under the window at back, and swinging doors letting into the street are at the left.

Rosie, "a daughter of the Digs," is finishing off a glass of whisky. "She is a sturdy, well-shaped girl of 20, pretty and pert in manner. She is wearing a cream blouse, with an obviously suggestive glad neck; a grey tweed dress, brown stockings and shoes. The blouse and most of the dress are hidden by a black shawl. She has no hat, and in her hair is jauntily set a cheap, glittering, jewelled ornament."

It's a dull night with Rosie, with the men "all in a holy mood." "You'd think they were th' glorious company of the saints an' th' noble army of martyrs thrampin' through the streets of Paradise," says Rosie. "They're all thinkin' o' higher things than a girl's garthers. . . ."

On the platform outside the window a man is beginning to speak. "It is a glorious thing to see arms in the hands of Irishmen," he is saying. "We must accustom ourselves to the thought of arms, we must accustom ourselves to the sight of arms, we must accustom ourselves to the use of arms . . . Bloodshed is a cleansing and sanctifying thing, and the nation that regards it as the final horror has lost its manhood. . . . There are many things more horrible than bloodshed, and slavery is one of them!"

Peter and Fluther are in from the meeting, hot, excited and thirsty. Also excessively patriotic.

"Get the Dublin men goin'," splutters Fluther over his drink, "an' they'll go on full force for anything that's thryin' to bar them away from what they're wantin', where th' slim thinkin' counthry boyo ud limp away from th' first faintest touch of compromization!"

"Th' memory o' all the things that was done," echoes Peter, ordering two more halves of the Barman; "an' all th' things that was suffered be th' people, was boomin' in me brain. . . . Every nerve in me body was quiverin' to do somethin' desperate!"

"Jammed as I was in th' crowd," reports Fluther, "I listened to th' speeches pattherin' on th' people's head, like rain fallin' on th' corn; every derogatory thought went out o' me mind, an' I said to meself, 'You can die now, Fluther, for you've seen th' shadow-dhreams of th' past leppin' to life in th' bodies of livin' men that show, if we were without a titther o' courage for centuries, we're vice versa now!' Looka here. (*He stretches out his arm under* PETER's *face and rolls up his sleeve.*) The blood was BOILIN' in me veins!"

Again a speaker has mounted the platform outside the window. "Comrade Soldiers of the Irish Volunteers and of the Citizens' Army," his voice reaches the listeners, "we rejoice in this terrible war. The old heart of the earth needed to be warmed with the red wine of the battlefields. . . . Such august homage was never offered to God as this: the homage of millions of lives given gladly for love of country. And we must be ready to pour out the same red wine in the same glorious sacrifice, for without shedding of blood there is no redemption!"

Gulping the last of their drinks Peter and Fluther make for the door that they may miss nothing of the mounting excitement.

The Covey is in for a quiet drink, but Rosie Redmond is not of a mind to let him have it. She would join him, whether he be in a social mood or not. She manages finally to stir him into a declaration for the economic freedom all workers should be fighting for. But soon the liquor has put other ideas in Rosie's mind, and for these she finds no responsive thought in the Covey's mind. It's not love makin' he's thinkin' of, and he'll have none of a lassie of her kind.

Now Peter and Fluther are back, followed by Mrs. Gogan with a baby in her arms. They are all three excited, the men by their emotional reactions to the meeting as well as their drink, Mrs. Gogan by contemplations inspired by what she has seen.

"The Foresthers is a gorgeous dhress," she admits, admiring the proud Peter, "I don't think I've seen nicer, mind you, in a pantomime. . . . Th' loveliest part of th' dhress, I think, is th' osthrichess plume. . . . When yous are goin' along, an' I see them wavin' an' noddin' an' waggin', I seem to be lookin' at each of yous hangin' at th' end of a rope, your eyes bulgin' an' your legs twistin' an' jerkin' an' gaspin' for breath while yous are thryin' to die for Ireland!"

Which leads Peter to a defense of his own patriotism and

Fluther to an attack on Peter for certain ambiguous insinuations. They are all in a state of mind when the Covey and Bessie Burgess come in. They, too, are belligerent and covertly sneer at the group they find at the bar.

BESSIE (*speaking to the* COVEY, *but really at the other party*) —I can' for th' life o' me undherstand how they can call themselves Catholics, when they won't lift a finger to help poor little Catholic Belgium.

MRS. GOGAN (*raising her voice*)—What about poor little Catholic Ireland?

BESSIE (*over to* MRS. GOGAN)—You mind your own business, ma'am, an' stupify your foolishness be gettin' dhrunk.

PETER (*anxiously*)—Take no notice of her; pay no attention to her. She's just tormentin' herself towards havin' a row with somebody.

BESSIE—There's a storm of anger tossin' in me heart, thinkin' of all th' poor Tommies, an' with them me own son, dhrenched in water an' soaked in blood, gropin' their way to a shattherin' death, in a shower o' shells! Young men with th' sunny lust o' life beamin' in them, layin' down their white bodies, shredded into torn an' bloody pieces, on th' althar that God Himself has built for th' sacrifice of heroes!

MRS. GOGAN—Isn't it a nice thing to have to be listenin' to a lassie an' hangin' our heads in a dead silence, knowin' that some persons think more of a ball of malt than they do of th' blessed saints.

FLUTHER—Whisht: she's always dangerous an' derogatory when she's well oiled. Th' safest way to hindher her from havin' any enjoyment out of her spite, is to dip our thoughts into the fact of her bein' a female person that has moved out of th' sight of ordinary sensible people.

BESSIE—To look at some o' th' women that's knockin' about now, is a thing to make a body sigh . . . A woman on her own, dhrinkin' with a bevy o' men is hardly an example to her sex. . . . A woman dhrinkin' with a woman is one thing, an' a woman dhrinkin' with herself is still a woman—flappers may be put in another category altogether—but a middle-aged married woman makin' herself th' center of a circle of men is as a woman that is loud an' stubborn, whose feet abideth not in her own house.

THE COVEY (*to* BESSIE)—When I think of all th' problems in front of th' workers, it makes me sick to be lookin' at oul' codgers goin' about dhressed up little green-accoutered figures gone asthray out of a toyshop!

PETER—Gracious God, give me patience to be listenin' to that blasted young Covey proddin' at me from over at th' other end of th' shop!

MRS. GOGAN (*dipping her fingers in the whisky, and moistening with it the lips of her baby*)—Cissie Gogan's a woman livin' for nigh on twenty-five years in her own room, an' beyond biddin' th' time o' day to her neighbours, never yet as much as nodded her head in th' direction of other people's business, while she knows some as are never content unless they're standin' senthry over other people's doin's! (BESSIE *is about to reply when the tall dark figure is again silhouetted against the window, and the voice of the speaker is heard speaking passionately.*)

VOICE OF SPEAKER—The last sixteen months have been the most glorious in the history of Europe. Heroism has come back to the earth. War is a terrible thing, but war is not an evil thing. People in Ireland dread war because they do not know it. Ireland has not known the exhilaration of war for over a hundred years. When war comes to Ireland she must welcome it as she would welcome the Angel of God! (*The figure passes out of sight and hearing.*)

THE COVEY (*towards all present*)—Dope, dope. There's only one war worth havin': th' war for th' economic emancipation of th' proletariat.

BESSIE—They may crow away out o' them; but it ud be fitther for some o' them to mend their ways, an' cease from havin' scouts out watchin' for th' comin' of th' Saint Vincent de Paul man, for fear they'd be nailed lowerin' a pint of beer, mockin' th' man with an angel face, shinin' with th' glamour of deceit an' lies!

MRS. GOGAN—An' a certain lassie standin' stiff behind her own door with ears cocked listenin' to what's being said, stuffed till she's sthrained with envy of a neighbour thryin' for a few little things that may be got be hard sthrivin' to keep up to th' letther an' th' law, an' th' practices of th' Church!

PETER (*to* MRS. GOGAN)—If I was you, Mrs. Gogan, I'd parry her jabbin' remarks be a powerful silence that'll keep her tantalizin' words from penethratin' into your feelin's. It's always betther to leave these people to th' vengeance o' God!

BESSIE—Bessie Burgess doesn't put up to know much, never havin' a swaggerin' mind, thanks be to God, but goin' on packin' up knowledge accordin' to her conscience: precept upon precept, line upon line; here a little, an' there a little. But (*with a passionate swing of her shawl*), thanks be to Christ, she knows when she was got, where she was got, an' how she was got; while there's some she knows, decoratin' their finger with a well-polished weddin' ring, would be hard put to it if they were assed to show their weddin' lines!

MRS. GOGAN (*plunging out into the centre of the floor in a wild tempest of hysterical rage*)—Y' oul' rip of a blasted liar, me weddin' ring's been well earned be twenty years be th' side o' me husband, now takin' his rest in heaven, married to me be Father Dempsey, in th' Chapel o' Saint Jude's, in th' Christmas Week of eighteen hundred an' ninety-five; an' any kid, livin' or dead, that Jinnie Gogan's had since, was got between th' bordhers of th' Ten Commandments! . . . And that's more than some o' you can say that are kep' from th' dhread o' desthruction be a few drowsy virtues, that th' first whisper of temptation lulls into a sleep that'll know one sin from another only on th' day of their last anointin', an' that use th' innocent light o' th' shinin' stars to dip into th' sins of a night's diversion!

BESSIE (*jumping out to face MRS. GOGAN, and bringing the palms of her hands together in sharp claps to emphasize her remarks*)—Liar to you, too, ma'am, y' oul' hardened thresspasser on other people's good nature, wizenin' up your soul in th' arts o' dodgeries, till every dhrop of respectability in a female is dhried up in her, lookin' at your ready-made manœuverin' with th' menkind!

BARMAN—Here, there; here, there; speak asy there. No rowin' here, no rowin' here, now.

FLUTHER (*trying to calm MRS. GOGAN*)—Now, Jinnie, Jinnie, it's a derogatory thing to be smirchin' a night like this with a row; it's rompin' with th' feelings of hope we ought to be, instead o' being vice versa!

PETER (*trying to quiet BESSIE*)—I'm terrible dawny, Miss Burgess, an' a fight leaves me weak for a long time afterwards. . . . Please, Miss Burgess, before there's damage done, thry to have a little respect for yourself.

BESSIE (*with a push of her hand that sends PETER tottering to the end of the shop*)—G'way, you little sermonizing, little yella-faced, little consequential, little pudgy, little bum, you!

MRS. GOGAN (*screaming*)—Fluther, leggo! I'm not goin' to keep an unresistin' silence, an' her scattherin' her festherin' words in me face, stirrin' up every dhrop of decency in a respectable female, with her restless rally o' lies that would make a saint say his prayer backwards!

BESSIE (*shouting*)—Ah, everybody knows well that th' best charity that can be shown to you is to hide th' thruth as much as our thrue worship of God Almighty will allow us!

MRS. GOGAN (*frantically*)—Here, houl' th' kid, one o' yous; houl' th' kid for a minute! There's nothin' for it but to show this lassie a lesson or two. . . . (*To* PETER)—Here, houl' th' kid, you. (*Before* PETER *is aware of it, she places the infant in his arms to* BESSIE, *standing before her in a fighting attitude*)— Come on, now, me loyal lassie, dyin' with grief for little Catholic Belgium! When Jinnie Gogan's done with you, you'll have a little leisure lyin' down to think an' pray for your king an' counthry!

It is the Barman who separates the women before a blow is struck and gets them into the street, followed by a protesting Peter with Mrs. Gogan's baby, which she for the moment has forgotten.

The men are back at their drinking, with Rosie Redmond joining them whenever she has a chance to be included. And now it is Fluther and the Covey who are having a battle of words and terrible threats of extinction. And Rosie flying to the defense of the Fluther as of a new-found friend and likely prospect; and the Covey denouncing Rosie for the thing she is and refusing to take reprimandin' from a prostitute. Which calls forth the sting of Rosie's deepest, vilest wrath and puts the Covey in her books as a louse, no less.

Again the Barman is forced to dive into the center of hostilities and clear the floor of the lot of them, with Fluther flying manfully to the protection of Rosie and remaining gratefully with her when the others are gone.

The parade is over now, and the marchers are coming in. Here are Clitheroe, Captain Brennan and Lieutenant Langon of the Irish Volunteers. "Captain Brennan carries the banner of The Plough and the Stars and Lieutenant Langon a green, white and orange tri-color. They are emotionally excited. Their faces are flushed and their eyes sparkle; they speak rapidly, as if unaware of the meaning of what they said. They have been mesmerized by the fervency of the speeches."

CLITHEROE (*almost pantingly*)—Three glasses o' port! (*The* BARMAN *brings the drinks.*)

CAPT. BRENNAN—We won't have long to wait now.

LIEUT. LANGON—Th' time is rotten ripe for revolution.

CLITHEROE—You have a mother, Langon.

LIEUT. LANGON—Ireland is greater than a mother.

CAPT. BRENNAN—You have a wife, Clitheroe.

CLITHEROE—Ireland is greater than a wife.

LIEUT. LANGON—Th' time for Ireland's battle is now—th' place for Ireland's battle is here. (*The tall, dark figure again is silhouetted against the window. The three men pause and listen.*)

VOICE OF THE MAN—Our foes are strong, but strong as they are, they cannot undo the miracles of God, who ripens in the heart of young men the seeds sown by the young men of a former generation. They think they have pacified Ireland; think they have foreseen everything; think they have provided against everything; but the fools, the fools, the fools!—they have left us our Fenian dead, and, while Ireland holds these graves, Ireland, unfree, shall never be at peace!

CAPT. BRENNAN (*catching up The Plough and the Stars*)— Imprisonment for th' Independence of Ireland!

LIEUT. LANGON (*catching up the tri-colour*)—Wounds for th' Independence of Ireland!

CLITHEROE—Death for th' Independence of Ireland!

THE THREE (*together*)—So help us God! (*They drink. A bugle blows the Assembly. They hurry out. A pause. FLUTHER and ROSIE come out of the snug; ROSIE is linking FLUTHER, who is a little drunk. Both are in a merry mood.*)

ROSIE—Come on home, ower o' that, man. Are you afraid or what? Are you goin' to come home, or are you not?

FLUTHER—Of course I'm goin' home. What ud ail me that I wouldn't go?

ROSIE (*lovingly*)—Come on, then oul' sport.

OFFICER'S VOICE (*giving command outside*)—Irish Volunteers, by th' right, quick march!

ROSIE (*putting her arm around FLUTHER and singing*):

I once had a lover, a tailor, but he could do nothin' for me,
An' then I fell in with a sailor as strong an' as wild as th' sea.
We cuddled an' kissed with devotion, till th' night from th'
    mornin' had fled;
An' there, to our joy, a bright bouncing boy
Was dancin' a jig in th' bed!

Dancin' a jig in th' bed, an' bawlin' for butther an' bread.
An' there, to our joy, a bright bouncin' boy

Was dancin' a jig in th' bed!
(*They go out with their arms round each other.*)

CLITHEROE'S VOICE (*in command outside*)—Dublin Battalion
of the Irish Citizen Army, by th' right, quick march!
The curtain falls.

ACT III

Some months later, in front of the tenement house in which
the Clitheroes occupy the front parlor, Mrs. Gogan is helping her
daughter, Mollser, to a place in the sun at the side of the steps.
"The house is a long, gaunt, five-story tenement; its brick
front is chipped and scarred with age and neglect. . . . The door
lurches a little to one side, disjointed by the continual and reck-
less banging when it is being closed by most of the residents.
. . . At the left corner of the house runs a narrow lane, bisecting
the street and connecting it with another of the same kind. At
the corner of the lane is a street lamp."

Mollser Gogan has been ailing lately, but it is her mother's
opinion that she will be on the mend now as soon as she can
have a few weeks of sunshine. Especially if the shootin' will
stop and she can get some sleep.

There's excitement in the tenement. Nora Clitheroe's out looking for her husband and expecting to find him wounded and torn
any minute. And Fluther is chasin' around lookin' for Nora.

There's news of the fighting when the Covey and Peter get
home. They have seen at least a part of it first hand, but they
have no news of Clitheroe or Nora. Nor can they do anything
about it.

THE COVEY—We can do nothin'. You can't stick your nose
into O'Connell Street, an' Tyler's is on fire.

PETER—An' we seen th' Lancers—

THE COVEY (*interrupting*)—Throttin' along, heads in th' air;
spurs an' sabres jinglin' an' lances quiverin', an' lookin' as if they
were assin' themselves, "Where's these blighters, till we get a
prod at them," when there was a volley from th' Post Office that
stretched half o' them, an' sent the rest gallopin' away wondherin'
how far they'd have to go before they'd feel safe.

PETER (*rubbing his hands*)—"Damn it," says I to meself, "this
looks like business!"

THE COVEY—An' then out comes General Pearse an' his staff,

an' standin' in th' middle o' th' street, he reads th' Proclamation.

MRS. GOGAN—What Proclamation?

PETER—Declarin' an Irish Republic.

MRS. GOGAN—Go to God!

PETER—The gunboat *Helga's* shellin' Liberty Hall, an' I hear that people livin' on th' quays had to crawl on their bellies to Mass with th' bullets that were flyin' around from Boland's Mills.

MRS. GOGAN—God bless us, what's going to be th' end of it all!

BESSIE (*looking out of the top window*)—Maybe yous are satisfied now; maybe yous are satisfied now! Go on an' get guns if yous are men—Johnny get your gun, get your gun, get your gun! Yous are all nicely shanghaied now; th' boyo hasn't a sword on his thigh, now! Oh, yous are all nicely shanghaied now!

MRS. GOGAN (*warningly to* PETER *and the* COVEY)—S-s-sh, don't answer her. She's th' right oul' Orange bitch! She's been chantin' "Rule, Britannia" all th' morning.

PETER—I hope Fluther hasn't met with any accident, he's such a wild card.

THE COVEY—Fluther's well able to take care of himself.

MRS. GOGAN—God grant it; but last night I dreamt I seen gettin' carried into th' house a sthretcher with a figure lyin' on it, stiff an' still, dhressed in the habit of Saint Francis. An' then, I heard th' murmurs of a crowd no one could see saying th' litany for th' dead; an' then it got so dark that nothin' was seen but the white face of th' corpse, gleamin' like a white wather lily floatin' on the top of a dark lake. Then a tiny whisper thrickled into me ear, saying, "Isn't the face very like the face o' Fluther," an' then, with a thremblin' flutther, th' dead lips opened, an', although I couldn't hear, I knew they were saying, "Poor oul' Fluther, afther havin' handin' in his gun at last, his shakin' soul moored in th' place where th' wicked are at rest an' th' weary cease from throublin'."

PETER (*who has been putting on a pair of spectacles, and has been looking down the street*)—Here they are, be God, here they are; just afther turning the corner—Nora an' Fluther!

THE COVEY—She must be wounded or something—he seems to be carryin' her. (FLUTHER *and* NORA *enter.* FLUTHER *has his arm around her and is half leading, half carrying her in.*)

Nora is pale and dishevelled but she is not hurt. She has spent hours searching the streets and the outposts for her husband, despite the slurs of the patriots who insisted that she shamed her husband and the women of Ireland carryin' on so.

She is hysterical still and convinced her Jack will be killed, butchered as a sacrifice to the dead.

There are taunts from Bessie Burgess, leaning out her upper window, singing "Rule Britannia" and cursing the lot of them. "God'll have a bloody quick endin'," prophesies Miss Burgess. "Turning bitther into sweet an' sweet into bitther. . . . Stabbin' in th' back th' men that are dyin' in th' threnches for them! It's a bad thing for any one that thrys to jilt th' Ten Commandments, for judgments are prepared for scorners an' sthripes for th' back o' fools!"

They do what they can to quiet Nora, but with little success. She can think of nothing, vision nothing, but Jack Clitheroe shot down and mangled. She had roamed like a wild woman in search of him, and she is of no mind to listen to their pleas for patience.

FLUTHER (*to* NORA)—Nothin' derogatory'll happen to Mr. Clitheroe. You'll find, now, in th' finish up, it'll be vice versa.

NORA—Oh, I know that wherever he is, he's thinkin' of wantin' to be with me. I know he's longin' to be passin' his hand through me hair, to be caressin' me neck, to fondle me hand an' to feel me kisses clingin' to his mouth. . . . An' he stands wherever he is because he's brave? (*Vehemently.*) No, but because he's a coward, a coward, a coward!

MRS. GOGAN—Oh, they're not cowards anyway.

NORA (*with denunciatory anger*)—I tell you they're afraid to say they're afraid! . . . Oh, I saw it, I saw it, Mrs. Gogan. . . . At th' barricade in North King Street I saw fear glowin' in all their eyes. . . . An' in th' middle o' the sthreet was somethin' huddled up in a horrible tangled heap. . . . His face was jammed again' th' stones, an' his arm was twisted around his back. . . . An' every twist of his body was a cry against th' terrible thing that had happened to him . . . An' I saw they were afraid to look at it. . . . An' some o' them laughed at me, but th' laugh was a frightened one. . . . An' some o' them shouted at me, but the shout had in it th' shiver o' fear . . . I tell you they were afraid, afraid!

MRS. GOGAN (*leading her towards the house*)—Come on in, dear. If you'd been a little longer together, th' wrench asunder wouldn't have been so sharp.

NORA—Th' agony I'm in since he left me has thrust away every rough thing he done, an' every unkind word he spoke; only th' blossoms that grew out of our lives are before me now; shakin' their colours before me face, an' breathin' their sweet scent on every thought springin' up in me mind, till, sometimes, Mrs. Gogan, sometimes I think I'm goin' mad!

MRS. GOGAN—You'll be a lot better when you have a little lie down.

NORA (*turning towards* FLUTHER *as she is going in*)—I don't know what I'd have done, only for Fluther. I'd have been lyin' in th' streets, only for him. . . . (*As she goes in.*) They have dhriven away th' little happiness life had to spare for me. He has gone from me for ever, for ever . . . Oh, Jack, Jack, Jack!

They get her into the house as Bessie Burgess comes out, bringing a mug of milk to Mollser. She's off down the street with her head in the air, calling back her imprecations upon them for the trouble their sham-battle soldiers are causing her, "havin' to go an' ferret out a bit o' bread, God knows where!"

The men are getting themselves settled for a little quiet gambling when suddenly the boom of big guns fairly close at hand throws them into something of a panic. That's not playin' the game, declares Fluther. The idea of usin' the artillery on 'em!

Now the street begins to boil with excitement. Soon Bessie Burgess is back, heavy with loot and reporting that the people are breaking into the shops, "smashin' the windows, battherin' in th' doors an' whippen away everything!" With the Volunteers firing on them.

"I seen two men and a lassie pushin' a piano down the street," continues Bessie excitedly, "an' th' sweat rollin' off them thryin' to get it up on th' pavement; an' an oul' wan that must ha' been seventy lookin' as if she'd dhrop every minute with th' dint o' heart beatin', thryin' to pull a big double bed out of a broken shop window! I was goin' to wait till I dhressed meself from th' skin out."

Now Bessie has helped Mollser into the house and the Covey and Peter have gone to join the looters. Mrs. Gogan, too, is making a profitable trip of it by taking a baby carriage with her, but she is not quick enough for Bessie Burgess. Bessie has the same idea. Nor will either give up until finally they must either compromise and wheel the pram away together or miss the opportunity of "pickin' up anything shaken up or scatthered about in th' loose confusion of a general plundher!"

Soon the Covey is back shouldering a ten-stone sack of flour, with a ham on top of that. Now Mrs. Gogan and Bessie Burgess return with the loaded pram, filled with clothes and boots. "On the top of the boots and clothes is a fancy table, which Mrs.

Gogan is holding on with her left hand, while with her right hand she holds a chair on the top of her head."

"I don't remember ever havin' see such lovely pairs as them," Mrs. Gogan is saying, "with the pointed toes an' th' Cuban heels."

"They'll go grand with the dhresses we're after liftin'," agrees Miss Burgess. "When we've stitched a sthray bit o' silk to lift th' bodices up a little bit higher, so as to shake th' shame out o' them, an' make them fit for women that hasn't lost themselves in th' nakedness o' th' times."

Inside, Peter reports, Mollser Gogan seems about to faint and the Gogan infant is in convulsions. Mrs. Gogan has started in when the report of a rifle fired close at hand rings out and they all make a rush for the door, each trying to bar the other out.

A moment later Captain Brennan, supporting Lieutenant Langon, wounded, comes around the corner of the tenement. Their retreat is being covered by Commandant Clitheroe with his rifle at the ready. They've come for help for Langon.

Nora, rushing down the stairs, throws herself wildly in Clitheroe's arms. Nor will she let him go, even when he has returned her greeting with the enthusiasm she demands. He begs that she will not make a scene, and is eager to return to the help of his wounded comrade. But Nora still clings to him until Brennan demands that he quit his dallyin' and go for help for Langon.

CLITHEROE (*to* NORA)—I must go, I must go, Nora. I'm sorry we met at all. . . . It couldn't be helped—all other ways were blocked be th' British. . . . Let me go, can't you, Nora? D'ye want me to be unthrue to me comrades?

NORA—No, I won't let you go. . . . I want you to be thrue to me, Jack. . . . I'm your dearest comrade; I'm your thruest comrade. . . . They only want th' comfort of havin' you in the same danger as themselves. . . . Oh, Jack, I can't let you go!

CLITHEROE—You must, Nora, you must.

NORA—All last night at th' barricades I sought you, Jack. . . . I didn't think of th' danger—I could only think of you. . . . I asked for you everywhere. . . . Some o' them laughed. . . . I was pushed away, but I shoved back. . . . Some o' them even sthruck me . . . an' I screamed an' screamed your name!

CLITHEROE (*in fear her action would give him future shame*)— What possessed you to make a show of yourself, like that? . . . What way d'ye think I'll feel when I'm told my wife was bawlin' for me at th' barricades? What are you more than any other woman?

NORA—No more, maybe; but you are more to me than any
other man, Jack. . . . I didn't mean any harm, honestly, Jack.
. . . I couldn't help it. . . . I shouldn't have told you. . . . My
love for you made me mad with terror.

CLITHEROE (*angrily*)—They'll say now that I sent you out th'
way I'd have an excuse to bring you home. . . . Are you goin' to
turn all th' risks I'm takin' into a laugh?

LIEUT. LANGON—Let me lie down, let me lie down, Bill; th'
pain would be easier, maybe, lyin' down. . . . Oh, God, have
mercy on me!

CAPT. BRENNAN (*to* LANGON)—A few steps more, Jim, a few
steps more; thry to stick it for a few steps more.

LIEUT. LANGON—Oh, I can't, I can't, I can't!

CAPT. BRENNAN (*to* CLITHEROE)—Are you comin', man, or
are you goin' to make an arrangement for another honeymoon.
. . . If you want to act th' renegade say so, an' we'll be off!

BESSIE (*from above*)—Runnin' from th' Tommies—choke th'
chicken. Runnin' from th' Tommies—choke the chicken!

CLITHEROE (*savagely to* BRENNAN)—Damn you, man, who
wants to act th' renegade? (*To* NORA): Here, let go your hold;
let go, I say!

NORA (*clinging to* CLITHEROE, *and* *indicating* BRENNAN)—
Look, Jack, look at th' anger in his face; look at th' fear glintin'
in his eyes. . . . He, himself's afraid, afraid, afraid! . . . He
wants you to go th' way he'll have th' chance of death sthrikin'
you an' missin' him! Turn round an' look at him, Jack, look at
him, look at him! . . . His very soul is cold . . . shiverin' with
th' thought of what may happen to him. . . . It is his fear that
is thryin' to frighten you from recognisin' th' same fear that is in
your own heart!

CLITHEROE (*struggling to release himself from* NORA)—Damn
you, woman, will you let me go!

CAPT. BRENNAN (*fiercely, to* CLITHEROE)—Why are you beg-
gin' her to let you go? Are you afraid of her, or what? Break
her hold on you, man, or go up, an' sit on her lap! (CLITHEROE
trying roughly to break her hold.)

NORA (*imploringly*)—Oh, Jack . . . Jack . . . Jack!

LIEUT. LANGON (*agonizingly*)—Brennan, a priest; I'm dyin',
I think, I'm dyin'!

CLITHEROE (*to* NORA)—If you won't do it quietly, I'll have to
make you! (*To* BRENNAN): Here, hold this gun, you, for a
minute. (*He hands the gun to* BRENNAN.)

NORA (*pitifully*)—Please, Jack. . . . You're hurting me, Jack.

. . . Honestly. . . . Oh, you're hurting . . . me! . . . I won't, I won't, I won't. . . . Oh, Jack, I gave you everything you asked of me. . . . Don't fling me from you, now! (*He roughly loosens her grip, and pushes her away from him,* Nora *sinks to the ground and lies there. Weakly*)—Ah, Jack . . . Jack . . . Jack!

CLITHEROE (*taking the gun back from* BRENNAN)—Come on, come on!

From her upper window Bessie Burgess sees Nora lying in the street and comes down to her. She has carried her in the house when Fluther arrives, wild-eyed and roaring drunk. In his arms is an earthen half-gallon jar of whiskey, his pockets are stuffed with shirts, on his head he wears a woman's vivid blue hat, and in song he is assuring the neighborhood that Fluther is a jolly good fella, which no one can deny.

He bangs on the tenement door but it has been closed against him. He returns to his song, and then to his cursing, and then to his drinking. He is kicking at the door when Bessie Burgess comes out suddenly and grips him by the collar and drags him in.

"You bowsey," she warns him, "come in ower o' that. . . . I'll thrim you thricks o' dhrunken dancin' for you, an' none of us knowin' how soon we'll bump into a world we were never in before!"

Bessie is out again, followed by Mrs. Gogan. From inside the Clitheroes' flat a scream of pain from Nora rends the air. Some one must go for a doctor, and with Fluther drunk and Mollser ill, Bessie Burgess is the only one to go.

There are rifle shots that frighten her, but only for a minute. "She tightens her shawl around her as if it were a shield," and firmly and swiftly goes out.

"Oh, God, be Thou my help in time of trouble. And shelter me safely in the shadow of Thy wings!"

Her voice comes trailing back as she turns the corner of the building.

The curtain falls.

ACT IV

Several days later the body of Mollser Gogan lies in an oak coffin under the window of one of Bessie Burgess's attic rooms. Two lighted candles have been placed near by on a home-made stool. It is a small room, the sloping ceiling at back giving it a look of compressed confinement. In the furnishings there is "an unmistakable air of poverty bordering on destitution."

It is late afternoon. The dusk is gathering and the only light in the room comes from the candles and a smoldering fire in the fireplace. By this same light Fluther and the Covey are engaged in an unfinished card game, Fluther taking time out occasionally to peer cautiously out the window. Through the windows the distant sky shows the glare of burning buildings in the town.

As the game goes on there comes occasionally the putt-putt of machine-gun fire or the sharp crack of a sniper's rifle, varied by a lilting chant of "Red Cr . . . oss, Red Cr . . . oss!— Ambu . . . lance, Ambu . . . lance!"

In an inner room, from which her moaning can be heard from time to time, Nora Clitheroe raves in delirium for the return of her absent husband.

"Th' doctor thinks she'll never be the same," the Covey reports of Nora; "thinks she'll be a little touched here. (*He touches his forehead.*) She's ramblin' a lot; thinkin' she's out in th' counthry with Jack; or, gettin' his dinner ready for him before he comes home; or, yellin' for her kiddie. All that, though, might be th' chloroform she got. . . . I don't know what we'd have done only for oul' Bessie; up with her for th' past three nights, hand runnin'."

"I always knew there was never anything really derogatory wrong with poor oul' Bessie," Fluther agrees.

When the card players get too noisy Bessie Burgess hastens from the inner room to quiet them. She has just got Nora to sleep and she doesn't want her waked again.

Suddenly a pounding on the door below is followed by the sound of steps on the stairs. It is Captain Brennan, out of uniform and in a dusty and mud-spattered suit of civies, come to give to Mrs. Clitheroe her husband's last words. Jack Clitheroe has been killed in the fighting at the Imperial hotel.

"We fought till the place was in flames," Brennan wearily reports. "He was shot through th' arm, an' then through th' lung. . . . I could do nothin' for him—only watch his breath comin' an' goin' in quick, jerky gasps, an' a tiny sthream o' blood thricklin' out of his mouth, down over his lower lip. . . . I said a prayer for th' dyin', an' twined his rosary beads around his fingers. . . . Then I had to leave him to save myself. . . . (*He shows some holes in his coat.*) Look at th' way a machine-gun tore at me coat, as I belted out o' th' buildin' an' darted across th' sthreet for shelter. . . . An' then, I seen The Plough an' th' Stars fallin' like a shot as th' roof crashed in, an' where I'd left poor Jack was nothin' but a leppin' spout of flame!"

"Ay, you left him," sneers Bessie Burgess. "You twined his rosary beads around his fingers, an' then you run like a hare to get out o' danger!"

"I took me chance as well as him," Brennan offers in defense. "He took it like a man. His last whisper was to 'Tell Nora to be brave; that I'm ready to meet my God, an' that I'm proud to die for Ireland.' An' when our General heard it he said that 'Commandant Clitheroe's end was a gleam of glory.' Mrs. Clitheroe's grief will be a joy when she realizes that she has had a hero for a husband."

As he is talking Nora appears at the door. "She is clad only in her nightdress; her hair, uncared for for some days, is hanging in disorder over her shoulders."

Pathetically, monotonously, Nora calls to her Jack to come to her; directs him in the ways they shall walk, as they used to do in the country; begs him to be gentle with his kissing; cries out in terror at the thought of his leaving her; pleads piteously to be allowed to hold her baby!

With gentle insistence, Bessie manages to get Nora back to her room with a promise to sing to her. Presently the strains of the song float back to the men at their game.

> "Lead, kindly light, amid th' encircling gloom,
>   Lead Thou me on.
> The Night is dark an' I am far from home,
>   Lead Thou me on.
> Keep Thou my feet, I do not ask to see
> Th' distant scene—one step enough for me."

The Covey is for getting Brennan out, lest his presence bring the Tommies hoppin' in to find him. There is little chance he could get back safely, Brennan insists. Even as he talks there's a tramping on the stairs and Corporal Stoddart of the Wiltshires appears at the door in full war kit, rifle, bayonet and trench tools. The Corporal has come for the body of the dead woman, and will allow one other person to go out with it. That would be Mrs. Gogan, naturally, Bessie Burgess decides.

The Corporal is satisfied, and sympathetic as well. But 'e 'as to do 'is dooty! 'E's also a bit of a socialist, even though he has to admit to the Covey that he has never yet read Jenersky's "Thesis on the Origin, Development and Consolidation of th' Evolutionary Idea of the Proletariat."

Again the ping of the sniper's bullet, a cry of pain from a hit

Tommy somewhere in the street below and curses from the protesting Corporal.

"Gawd, when we gets the bloighter we'll give 'im the cold steel, we will. We'll jab the belly aht of 'im, we will!"

Mrs. Gogan, "a little proud of the importance of being directly connected with death," follows Mollser's coffin as it is carried out by the Covey, Fluther, Brennan and Peter. The Corporal stays behind to check up the premises to see if there are more men around. They all have to be rounded up.

"If I 'ad my woy, Oi'd make 'em all join hup, hand do their bit," the Corporal explains to Bessie. "But Oi suppowse they hand you are all Shinners."

"Bessie Burgess is no Shinner," shouts Bessie, dragging her outraged senses back from the sleep into which she was sinking; "and never had no thruck with anything spotted be th' fingers o' th' Fenians. But always made it her business to harness herself for Church whenever she knew that God Save the King was goin' to be sung at t'end of th' service; whose only son went to th' front in th' first contingent of the Dublin Fusiliers an' that's on his way home carryin' a shatthered arm that he got fightin' for His King an' counthry."

The volunteer pallbearers are up from below stairs and would go back to their card game but for the advice of Corporal Stoddart. There will be no time for cards, says he, seeing they are all to be rounded up and held for the night in a Protestan' church! Still, that might not be so bad, thinks Fluther. There couldn't be anything derogatory about playin' cards in a Protestan' church!

Sergeant Tinley, "pale, agitated and fiercely angry," is in to collect Corporal Stoddart and his accumulations. Another Tommy has just been shot and the Sergeant is for taking reprisal.

"Private Taylor; got 'it roight through the chest, 'e did; han 'owl in front hof 'im has 'ow you could put your fist through, hand arf 'e's back blown awoy! Dum dum bullets they're using. Gang hof Hassassins plotting at hus from behind roofs. That's not ploying the goime; why down't they come hinto the howpen hand foight fair!"

"Fight fair!" explodes Fluther, unable to stand the slight. "Fight fair! A few hundhred scrawls o' chaps with a couple o' guns an' Rosary beads, again' a hundhred thousand thrained men with horse, fut an' artillery . . . an' he wants us to fight fair! (To SERGEANT): D'ye want us to come out in our skins an' throw stones?"

The men are gone and Bessie Burgess has fallen into a deep

sleep in the chair by the fire. At the door appears Nora, still in
her nightdress. She is vaguely mystified by the room, but goes
quietly to the fire, stirs it, puts the kettle on and begins to lay
the table for tea. It's a strange room, but she must not forget
Jack's tea.

She is humming, now—the old song—

"The violets were scenting th' woods, Nora,
    Displaying their charms to the bee,
When I first said I lov'd only you, Nora,
    An' you said you lov'd only me."

She is partly through the third verse when a burst of rifle and
machine-gun fire in the street disturbs her. She has rushed to the
window and is screaming wildly for Jack before Bessie awakens
and rushes to bring her back into the room. Nora struggles, refusing to leave the window. As Bessie forces her out of danger
two rifle shots ring out in quick succession.

"Bessie jerks her body convulsively, stands stiffly upright for a
moment, a look of agonized astonishment on her face. Then she
staggers forward, leaning heavily on the table with her hands."

BESSIE (*with an arrested scream of fear and pain*)—Merciful
God, I'm shot, I'm shot, I'm shot! . . . Th' life's pourin' out o'
me! (*To* NORA): I've got this through . . . through you . . .
through you, you bitch, you! . . . O God, have mercy on me!
. . . (*To* NORA): You wouldn't stop quiet, no you wouldn't, you
wouldn't, blast you! Look at what I'm afther gettin', look at
what I'm afther gettin'. . . . I'm bleedin' to death, an' no one's
here to stop th' flowin' blood! (*Calling.*) Mrs. Gogan, Mrs.
Gogan! Fluther, Fluther, for God's sake, somebody, a doctor, a
doctor! (*She staggers frightened towards the door, to seek for
aid, but, weakening half way across the room, she sinks to her
knees, and bending forward, supports herself with her hands resting on the floor.* NORA *is standing rigidly with her back to the
wall opposite, her trembling hands held out a little from the sides
of her body, her lips quivering, her breast heaving, staring wildly
at the figure of* BESSIE.)
NORA (*in a breathless whisper*)—Jack, I'm frightened. . . .
I'm frightened, Jack. . . . Oh, Jack, where are you!
BESSIE (*moaningly*)—This is what's afther comin' on me for
nursin' you day and night. . . . I was a fool, a fool, a fool! Get
me a dhrink o' wather, you jade, will you? There's a fire burnin'

in me blood! (*Pleadingly.*) Nora, Nora, dear, for God's sake, run out and get Mrs. Gogan, or Fluther, or somebody bring a doctor, quick, quick, quick! (*As* NORA *does not stir.*) Blast you, stir yourself, before I'm gone!

NORA—Oh, Jack, Jack, where are you!

BESSIE (*in a whispered moan*)—Jesus Christ, me sight's goin'! It's all dark, dark! Nora, hold me hand! (BESSIE's *body lists over and she sinks into a prostrate position on the floor.*) I'm dyin', I'm dyin'. . . . I feel it. . . . Oh, God, oh, God! (*She feebly sings*):

> I do believe, I will believe
> That Jesus died for me!
> That on th' cross He shed His blood,
> From sin to set me free. . . .
>
> I do believe . . . I will believe
> Jesus died . . . me;
> 'th cross He shed . . . blood,
> From sin . . . free.

(*She ceases singing, and lies stretched out, still and very rigid. A pause. Then* MRS. GOGAN *runs hastily in.*)

MRS. GOGAN (*quivering with fright*)—Blessed be God, what's afther happenin'? (*To* NORA): What's wrong, child, what's wrong? (*She sees* BESSIE, *runs to her and bends over the body.*) Bessie, Bessie! (*She shakes her body.*) Miss Burgess, Miss Burgess! (*She feels* BESSIE's *forehead.*) My God, she's as cold as death. They're afther murdherin' th' poor inoffensive woman! (SERGEANT TINLEY *and* CORPORAL STODDART *enter agitatedly, their rifles at the ready.*)

SERGEANT TINLEY (*excitedly*)—This is the 'ouse. That's the window!

NORA (*pressing back against the wall*)—Hide it, hide it; cover it up, cover it up!

SERGEANT TINLEY (*going over to the body*)—'Ere, what's this? Who's this? (*Looking at* BESSIE.) Ow Gawd, we've plugged one of the women of the 'ouse.

CORPORAL STODDART—Whoy the 'ell did she gow to the window! Is she dead?

SERGEANT TINLEY—Ow, dead as bedamned. Well, we couldn't afford to toike any chawnces.

NORA (*screaming*)—Hide it, hide it; don't let me see it! Take me away, take me away, Mrs. Gogan. (MRS. GOGAN *runs into room, left, and runs out again with a sheet which she spreads over the body of* BESSIE.)

MRS. GOGAN (*as she spread the sheet*)—Oh, God help her, th' poor woman, she's stiffenin' out as hard as she can! Her face has written on it th' shock o' sudden agony, an' her hands is whitenin' into th' smooth shininess of wax.

NORA (*whimperingly*)—Take me away; take me away; don't leave me here to be lookin' an' lookin' at it!

MRS. GOGAN (*going over to* NORA, *and putting her arm around her*)—Come on with me, dear, an' you can doss in poor Mollser's bed, till we gather some neighbors to come an' give th' last friendly touches to Bessie in th' lonely layin' of her out. (MRS. GOGAN *and* NORA *go slowly out.*)

CORPORAL STODDART (*who has been looking around, to* SERGEANT TINLEY)—Tea there, Sergeant. Wot abaht a cup of scald?

SERGEANT TINLEY—Pour it hout, Stoddart, pour it hout. Oi could scoff hanything just naow. (CORPORAL STODDART *pours out two cups of tea, and the two soldiers begin to drink. In the distance is heard a bitter burst of rifle and machine-gun fire, interspersed with the boom, boom of artillery. The glare in the sky seen through the window flares into a fuller and deeper red.*) There gows the general attack on the Powst Office.

VOICES IN A DISTANT STREET—Ambu . . . lance, Ambu . . . lance! Red Cro . . . ss, Red Cro . . . ss! (*The voices of soldiers at a barricade outside the house are heard singing*):

> They were summoned from the 'illside,
> They were called in from the glen,
> And the country found 'em ready
> At the stirring call for men.
> Let no tears add to their 'ardship,
> As the soldiers pass along,
> And although our 'eart is breaking,
> Make it sing this cheery song.

SERGEANT TINLEY *and* CORPORAL STODDART (*joining in the chorus, as they sip tea.*)

> Keep the 'owme fires burning,
> While your 'earts are yearning;
> Though your lads are far away
> They dream of 'owme;

There's a silver loining
Through the dark cloud shoining,
Turn the dark cloud inside out,
Till the boys come 'owme!

The curtain falls.

THE PLAYS AND THEIR AUTHORS

"Strange Interlude." Drama in nine acts by Eugene O'Neill. Copyright, 1927, by the author. Copyright and published, 1928, by Boni & Liveright, New York.

Eugene O'Neill's frequent appearance in these volumes makes any extended biographical reference to his work unnecessary. Five of his previous plays, "Beyond the Horizon," "Anna Christie," "Emperor Jones," "Desire Under the Elms" and "The Great God Brown" have been included among the best plays of their respective seasons. The son of James O'Neill, famed American actor, Eugene, whose birthplace is usually given as Provincetown, Mass., was, it transpires, really born in New York City, and christened Eugene Gladstone. His first stage work was done for and in association with the Provincetown Players. He worked indirectly one year with the Actors' Theatre.

"The Royal Family." A comedy in three acts by George Kaufman and Edna Ferber. Copyright, 1927, by the authors. Copyright and published, 1928, by Doubleday, Doran & Co., New York.

These collaborators previously appeared in "The Best Plays" series in the issue covering the season of 1924-25, when they were represented by the comedy "Minick," adapted for the stage from Miss Ferber's short story, called "Old Man Minick." Miss Ferber is best known as a novelist, though her stage connections, represented this year by the enormously successful musical comedy version of her "Show Boat" as well as "The Royal Family," are constantly broadening. She was born in Kalamazoo, Mich., and worked several years as a newspaper reporter.

Mr. Kaufman, an old-timer as a "Best Play" contributor, has been previously represented by "Dulcy," "Merton of the Movies," "Beggar on Horseback" and "The Butter and Egg Man," the first three written with Marc Connelly and the last one alone. He was born in Pittsburg, Pa., and drifted into playwriting from newspaper work, in which he is still actively engaged as dramatic editor of the *New York Times*.

"Burlesque." Drama by George Manker Watters and Arthur Hopkins. Copyright, 1927, by the authors. Copyright and published, 1928, by Doubleday, Doran & Co., New York.

George Manker Watters, born in Rochester, N. Y., in 1891 took to show business naturally. His father was a grand opera and concert singer. At the tender age of four young George sang Irish songs at the St. Patrick's day celebration in Des Moines. In his sophomore year at St. Louis University he left school to become the manager of a vaudeville troupe in Chicago. A year later he staged a musical comedy of which Lon Chaney was the comedian. He was manager of the Princess Theatre in Des Moines for seven years. Then he went into pictures, writing scenarios. Among these was "The Naked Truth" which he tried for two years to exploit and then sold cheap. It made huge profits for its new owners. After that he managed stock companies in Dallas, Houston and Birmingham. He packed his wife and two children into a motor car in 1924 and came to New York; lived on a farm near Ossining, and spent eight months looking for a job in the city. Finally was made house manager of the Criterion, later the Central and finally the Astor. Wrote "Burlesque," sold it to L. Lawrence Weber who took it to Arthur Hopkins. Hopkins tried to get some one to rewrite parts of it, and finally decided to do the job himself. Of recent years Watters has been again working with pictures in Hollywood.

Arthur Hopkins has confined his theatrical activities principally to management, after a start as a broker in and producer of vaudeville sketches. He wrote a one-act play called "Moonshine" for the Lambs' gambol some years ago. He was born in Cleveland, O., in 1878. He has managed all three Barrymores at different times and has produced many fine plays, including "Redemption," "The Jest," O'Neill's "Anna Christie" and "The Hairy Ape." Mrs. Hopkins was Eva O'Brien, an Australian actress. Their home is in Great Neck, L. I.

"Coquette." Drama by George Abbott and Ann Bridgers. Copyright, 1926, by the authors. Copyright and published, 1928, by Longmans, Green & Co., New York, London and Toronto.

George Abbott was part author of "Broadway" and also part author of "The Fall Guy," both of which plays have been published in previous volumes of this series. As has been previously reported, he has served the stage creditably as actor and stage director, as well as author. He was born in Hamburg, N. Y., graduated from Rochester University, and studied playwriting at Harvard.

Ann Bridgers, who provided the skeleton story from which Mr. Abbott constructed the play "Coquette," is a Southern girl, born in Raleigh, N. C. She was an understudy when she and Mr. Abbott were touring with "Dulcy." Together they wrote a one-act play and later this longer play, which was first called "Norma." Jed Harris, the producer, suggested the "Coquette" title and held the play for a year, until Helen Hayes was available to play the name part.

"Behold the Bridegroom." Drama in three acts by George Kelly. Copyright, 1927-28, by the author. Copyright and published, 1928, by Little, Brown & Co., Boston, Mass.

Three of the Kelly plays, "The Show-off," "Craig's Wife" and "Daisy Mayme," have been selected with the best plays of their respective seasons and included in former volumes. Mr. Kelly's record is therefore well known to this public. He was born in Philadelphia, wrote many vaudeville sketches and played in some of them before he tried writing longer plays.

"Porgy." Drama in three acts by Du Bose and Dorothy Heyward. Copyright, 1925, by George H. Doran Co., as a short story. Copyright, 1927, by Du Bose and Dorothy Heyward.

Du Bose Heyward, some time insurance man as well as poet and novelist of Charleston, S. C., was sufficiently far-sighted to marry a playwright. She was, and is, Dorothy Hartzell Kuhns. For her Mr. Heyward wrote the novel, "Porgy," and for him, we may reasonably assume, Mrs. Heyward turned the story into this play, which became an outstanding success of the theatre season of which this book is a record. Mr. Heyward has for many years been a frequent contributor to the better magazines, is the author of "Skylines and Horizons," was the organizer and secretary of the Poetry society of Charleston, is a member of the Poetry society of America and of the Macdowell colony. The Heywards' home is in Charleston.

"Paris Bound." Comedy in three acts by Philip Barry. Copyright, 1927, by the author.

Philip Barry, after graduating from Yale in 1918 and studying playwriting at Harvard the following year, won a Harvard play prize with "You and I" and, with that play, made his way into this series of published "Best Plays." He was elected again with "The Youngest" the following year. His third appearance is with "Paris Bound" this year. He was born in Rochester, N. Y., and tried to be happy as a writer of advertising copy after leaving college.

"Escape." Drama in nine episodes by John Galsworthy. Copyright, 1926, by the author. Copyright and published, 1927, by Charles Scribner's Sons, New York.

Previous appearances as a writer of fine plays were made by Mr. Galsworthy in this volume covering the season of 1920-21, when he was represented by "The Skin Game," and that of 1922-23 when his "Loyalties" was a success of the year. As is generally known, this author gave up the law to write novels. After some success as a novelist he tried playwriting and won a quick artistic success but a somewhat delayed popular and commercial success in that field. He has a long list of sterling character dramas to his credit. The rumor was spread that he had said he would write no more for the stage after he had finished "Escape." But happily this statement was later denied. Mr. Galsworthy was born in Coombe, England.

"The Racket." Drama in three acts by Bartlett Cormack. Copyright, 1927-28, by the author. Copyright and published, 1928, by Samuel French, Ltd., New York.

Bartlett Cormack was born in Indiana and went to school in Chicago, being graduated finally from the University of Chicago, with honors and a Phi Beta Kappa pin. He wrote a couple of college shows and took to newspaper reporting when he went to work, being employed for some time on the *Chicago American.* While he was in college he devoted some time to the Little theatre group directed by Maurice Browne. In addition to "The Racket" Cormack has also adapted Joseph Hergesheimer's novel "Tampico" and has recently been working on "The Canary Murder."

"The Plough and the Stars." Drama by Sean O'Casey. Copyright, 1925, by the author. Copyright and published, 1926, by the Macmillan Co., New York.

Sean O'Casey was born and brought up in a tenement on the north side of Dublin, where Dublin life has been described as being most native. For years he worked as an unskilled laborer. He was at different times a dock hand, a hod-carrier and a stone breaker on the roads. At fourteen he taught himself to read. At thirty-nine he won the Hawthorndon prize "for the best work of imaginative literature produced by a writer under forty." This was for his second play, "Juno and the Paycock," which won a London success. His first play, "The Shadow of a Gunman," was produced at the Abbey Theatre in Dublin in 1923. He is now in his early forties and is generally accredited with being the literary successor of John Millington Synge. He has brought to the stage the huddled life of the city as Synge did that of the Irish countryside.

PLAYS PRODUCED IN NEW YORK

June 15, 1927—June 15, 1928

(Plays marked with asterisk were still playing June 15, 1928)

BOTTOMLAND

(21 performances)

A musical comedy in three acts. Music and book by Clarence Williams. Produced by Clarence Williams, Inc., at the Princess Theatre, New York, June 27, 1927.

Cast of characters—

May Mandy Lee	Eva Taylor
At the Piano	Clarence Williams
Mammy Lee	Sara Martin
Pappy Lee	James A. Lilliard
Jimmy	Louis Cole
Tough Tilly	Katherine Henderson
Joshua	Slim Henderson
The Dumb Waiter	John Mason
Henry Henpeck	Charles Doyle
Shiftless Sam	"Nuggie" Johnson
Skinny	Raymond Campbell
Rastus	Edward Farrow
Sally	Olive Otiz
Mammy Chloe	Willie Porter
Kid Slick	Emanuel Weston
Policeman Doolittle	Edwin Tonde
Specialty	Craddock and Shadney

Acts I and III.—1—Bottomland. 2—A Country Road. 3—A Barbecue Restaurant. Act II.—A Street in New York. 2—A Cabaret in Harlem.

May Mandy Lee wants to get away from the bottom lands where she was bo'n and go no'th, like Sally done. Her pappy and her mammy let her go, but she finds Sally singin' in a cabaret and rather fond of her gin. Disillusioned May Mandy goes back home to Bottomland.

PADLOCKS OF 1927

(95 performances)

A musical revue in two acts. Sketches by Paul Gerard Smith and Ballard Macdonald; lyrics by Billy Rose; music by Lee

David, Jesse Greer and Henry H. Tobias. Produced by Duo Art Productions, Inc., at the Shubert Theatre, New York, July 5, 1927.

Principals engaged—

Texas Guinan	Harry Jans
Lillian Roth	Harold Whalen
Helen Shipman	Carl D. Francis
Drina Beach	Jay C. Flippen
Francis Healy	A. S. Byron
Virginia Smith	Walter Burke
Laura Wilkinson	Dave Mallen
Rosemary Ryder	Don Fiser
Mary Titus	George Raft
Eleanor Smith	Ojeda and Inbert
Mae Burke	Romancers quartet
Hedwig Langer	Phelps sisters
Irene Faery	

Staged by W. J. Wilson.

MADAME X

(22 performances)

A play in a prologue and three acts, adapted from the French of Alexandre Bisson by John Raphael. Produced by Murray Phillips at the Earl Carroll Theatre, New York, July 6, 1927.

Cast of characters—

Rosie	Mabel Montgomery
Dr. Chennel	Donald Campbell
Floriot	Charles Waldron
Jacqueline	Carroll McComas
Noel	Reginald Goode
La Rocque	Douglas Wood
Victor	Arthur C. Morris
Perrisard	G. A. Forbes
Merivel	Percy Hemus
Marie	Miriam Stuart
Helene	Betty Lawrence
Raymond Floriot	Rex Cherryman
Clerk of the Court	James Coyle
President of the Court	Wilfred Lucas
Fontaine	Edward Jones
Valmorin	Edd Russell
Foreman of the Jury	John Brewster

Prologue—The Library of Floriot's Home in Passy. Act I.—Room in a Hotel in Bordeaux. Act II.—Raymond's Home in Bordeaux. Act III.—The Court of Assizes.

Jacqueline, suffering the misfortunes following hard upon a false step, is denied the love of her son, and the comfort of his father's support. Drifting from riches to rags and worse, she is finally arrested and brought to court and is there defended by a youthful lawyer, Raymond Floriot, who never suspects the woman at the bar to be his mother.

AFRICANA

(72 performances)

A musical revue in two parts. Music and lyrics by Donald Heyward. Produced by Earl Dancer at the Daly Theatre, New York, July 11, 1927.

Principals engaged—

Billy Mills	Margaret Beckett
Henry Winifred	Baby Goins
Mike Riely	Louis Douglas
Paul Bass	Edna Barr
Al Winkins	Taskiana Four
Ed Pugh	Eddie and Sunny
Bobby Goins	

Staged by Louis Douglas.

RANG TANG

(119 performances)

A musical revue in two acts. Book by Kaj Gynt; lyrics by Jo Trent. Produced by Messrs. Walker and Kavanaugh at the Royale Theatre, New York, July 12, 1927.

Principals engaged—

F. E. Miller	Evelyn Preer
A. Lyles	Josephine Jackson
Daniel Haynes	Lillian Westmoreland
Zaidee Jackson	May Barnes
James Strange	Lavinia Mack
Josephine Hall	Crawford Jackson
Marie Mahood	Edward Thompson
Inez Draw	Jo Willis
Le'etta Revells	Byron Jones
George Battles	Gilbert Holland

Staged by Charles Davis and Miller and Lyles.

KISS ME

(32 performances)

A musical comedy, adapted by Derick Wulff and Max Simon; lyrics by Derick Wulff; music by Winthrop Cortelyou. Produced by J. J. Levinson at the Lyric Theatre, New York, July 18, 1927.

Cast of characters—

Billings	William Sellery
Denise	Marjorie Peterson

```
Tom Warren....................................Ralph Whitehead
Eugene Moreaux..............................Charles Lawrence
A Clerk.......................................Eddie Russell, Jr.
Paul Travers..................................Frederic Santley
Doris Durant Dodo............................Desiree Ellinger
Prince Hussein Dschahangie Mirza..............Joseph Macauley
Gendarme.....................................Eddie Russell, Jr.
Talazada......................................Enid Romany
     Acts I and III.—Travers' Studio in Paris.  Act II.—In the Shah's
Harem.
     Staged by Edward Elsner.
```

Tom Warren, an American portrait painter, is commissioned by Prince Hussein of Persia to paint a portrait of his favorite wife. Tom, being a bachelor, is obliged to contract a marriage of convenience with his secretary, Doris Dodo, in order to enter the harem where the prince keeps his wives. His agreement never to presume upon his marriage rights piques Doris into wearing her most seductive pajamas.

THE MATING SEASON
(24 performances)

A farce in three acts by William A. Grew. Produced by Lew Cantor, in association with Dave Chasen, at the Selwyn Theatre, New York, July 18, 1927.

Cast of characters—

```
Jack Stratford.................................William A. Grew
Okay.......................................Edw. T. Colebrook
Betty Stratford................................Lillian Walker
Cliff Stratford...............................Kenneth Manion
Violet LaVere.................................Gladys Feldman
Marion Crawford..............................Gwendolyn Pates
Cyrus Stratford...............................Walter Poulter
Martha Stratford................................Ethel Martin
James Augustus Bellamy...........................Jack Coyle
Pompeia..........................................By Herself
     Acts I and II.—Hotel Cottage, Atlantic City.  Act III.—Bedroom
of Jack Stratford's Cottage.
     Staged by William A. Grew.
```

Jack Stratford, pursuing his sister-in-law, is himself pursued by his wife's aunt. As a result Jack's bedroom is simply crowded with amorous ladies wearing passionate pajamas at 12 midnight.

THE MANHATTERS
(68 performances)

A musical revue in two acts. Music by Alfred Nathan and lyrics by George S. Oppenheimer; sketches by Aline Erlanger and

George S. Oppenheimer. Produced by The Manhatters Company at the Selwyn Theatre, New York, August 3, 1927.

Principals engaged—

James Norris
Jacques Cartier
Burke Boyce
Edward Hale
Geo. Francis Brown
William Johnstone
Raymond Knight
Lehman Byck
 Staged by Dave Bennett.

Eleanor Shaler
Sally Bates
Doris Vinton
Dorothy Chard
Katherine Renwik
Mabel Zoeckler
Mary Marsh
Aida Ward

ALLEZ-OOP

(120 performances)

A musical revue in two acts. Sketches by J. P. McEvoy; music by Charig and Richard Myers; lyrics by Leo Robin. Produced by Carl Hemmer at the Earl Carroll Theatre, New York, August 2, 1927.

Principals engaged—

Victor Moore
Charles Butterworth
Lon Haskell
Bobby Watson
Sydney Reynolds
Valodia Vestoff
Herman and Seamon
Cliff O'Rourke
Edgar Gardiner
Alan Moran
Walter Feldkamp
 Staged by Carl Hemmer.

Esther Howard
Evelyn Bennett
Madeleine Fairbanks
Joyce Booth
Wanda Valle
George Sisters
Joan Karr
Dra Lea
Gladys Yates
Catherine Crandall
Lillian Burke

TENTH AVENUE

(88 performances)

A melodrama in three acts, by John McGowan and Lloyd Griscom. Produced by the Lexington Productions, Inc., at the Eltinge Theatre, New York, August 15, 1927.

Cast of characters—

Benny Hewitt....................................John A. Butler
Curly Neff.....................................Frank McHugh
Carl Fink......................................Gregory Ratoff
Lyla Mason.....................................Edna Hibbard
Guy Peters.....................................Frank Morgan
Elzy Everetts..................................William Boyd
Paddy McGurn...................................Hal Wolf

```
Ed Burton.......................................Purnell B. Pratt
A Policeman.........................................Jack Curtis
    Acts I, II and III.—A Rooming House in West 38th Street, New
York City.
```

Lyla Mason, keeping a boarding house in West 38th Street, has a habit of mothering crooks and inducing them to go straight. Among her boys she loves Guy Peters, a reformed card man, most, but feels that Elzy Everetts, whom she has known from old Tenth Avenue days, needs her. Learning that Lyla needs rent money both Guy and Elzy go out to get it for her. Guy wins it at poker and Elzy shoots another crook and takes it away from him. The police round up both boys, but at the finish Elzy starts for the chair and Guy wins the landlady.

BABIES A LA CARTE

(24 performances)

A farcical comedy in three acts, by Seaman Lewis. Produced by S. L. Simpson at Wallack's Theatre, New York, August 15, 1927.

Cast of characters—

```
Jim Kidder........................................Alfred Cross
John Lawson.......................................Leonard Lord
Nettie..........................................Mildred Southwick
Bettie...........................................Harriet Rempell
Mr. I. P. Berry....................................Robert Lowe
Mr. M. T. Dial...................................Stanley James
    Acts I and III.—Drawing Room of the Kidder Home. Act II.—A
New York Law Office.
    Staged by Francis Fraunie.
```

Nettie and Bettie, heirs under an uncle's will which leaves a lot of money to the first baby born to either, enter a race for the fortune. Bettie, being married, has a slight advantage, but Nettie hurriedly overcomes that handicap. Babies are born within twenty-five minutes of each other, one in New York and the other in Chicago. The lawyers make an issue of daylight saving and then a new will is discovered specifying the heir must be a boy. There is only one.

ZIEGFELD FOLLIES

(167 performances)

A musical revue in two acts. Lyrics by Irving Berlin; sketches by Harold Atteridge and Eddie Cantor. Produced by Erlanger and Ziegfeld at the New Amsterdam Theatre, New York, August 16, 1927.

Principals engaged—

Eddie Cantor	Claire Luce
Andrew Tombes	Frances Upton
Phil Ryley	Ruth Etting
Harry McNaughton	Lora Foster
Leo Bill	Irene Delroy
Franklyn Bauer	Brox Sisters
Dan Healy	Jean Audree
William H. Power	Muriel Finley
Paul Chezzi	Helen Brown
Ross Hines	Desha
Fairchild and Rainger	Peggy Chamberlin
The Ingenues	Albertina Rasche Girls

Staged by Florenz Ziegfeld, Sammy Lee and Zeke Colvan.

A LA CARTE

(45 performances)

A musical revue in two acts. Sketches by George Kelly; music and lyrics by Herman Hupfeld, Louis Alter, Norma Gregg, Paul Lanin and Creamer and Johnson. Produced by Rosalie Stewart at the Martin Beck Theatre, August 17, 1927.

Principals engaged—

Charles Irwin	Helen Lowell
William Holbrook	Harriet Hoctor
Jay Velie	Rose King
Little Billy	Bobbe Arnst
Chick York	Marian Hamilton
Billy Bradford	Giersdorf sisters, Elvira,
Roy Fant	Irene and Ray
Vernon Wallace	Myrtle Hayes
Frank Rowan	Maude Powers
Kotchetovski	Cynthia Farr
Fred Bishop	Frances Stein
Joseph McKenzie	Margaret Schilling

Staged by George Kelly.

WHAT THE DOCTOR ORDERED

(20 performances)

A farce in three acts, by Cæsar Dunn. Produced at the Ritz Theatre, New York, August 18, 1927.

Cast of characters—

Cuthbert St. Clair, Ph.D.	Herbert Yost
Daphne	Ruth Abbott

Mrs. Hortense Smiley.............................Eva Condon
Thomas Foster, M.D...........................Hale Hamilton
Fifi...Galina Kopernak
Will Scott.....................................Frank Allworth
Judy Rock..Dedette Lee
Office Nurse.......................................Eden Gray
Bell Hop......................................Joseph Johnson
House Detective...................................A. O. Huan
Bathing Girls.................Berenice Dewey, Katherine Bogart
Wife......................................Mrs. Gene Hughes
Husband...Carye Gillen
Hotel Clerk....................................Victor Killian
      Act I.—Doctor Foster's Office in New York City. Acts II and
III.—Sunnycrest Inn, Sunnycrest, Florida.
      Staged by John Cromwell.

Daphne St. Clair complains that Cuthbert, her husband, is a
better philosopher than he is a man around home. Dr. Foster
decides that Cuthbert needs rest, change and general stimulation
of the nervous system. The doctor orders Cuthbert to Florida,
and sees to it that his contacts are feminine and exciting. Following the doctor's orders Cuthbert becomes greatly interested in the
lady occupying the adjoining hotel room, and the doctor never
suspects until the last act that this lady is his own wife.

FOOTLIGHTS

(43 performances)

A musical comedy in two acts, by Roland Oliver. Produced by
The Tom Cat, Inc., at the Lyric Theatre, New York, August 19,
1927.

Cast of characters—

Oscar Jennings.....................................Le Roi Operti
Roy Royal..Jack Coyle
Jacob Perlstein.......................................Louis Sorin
Sam..Jack Wilson
George Weston.................................J. Kent Thurber
Meyer Schmidt.....................................Harry Denny
Violet Wilding.....................................Ruth Wheeler
Elsie Quinn..................................Lorraine Sherwood
Hazel Deane......................................Ellalee Ruby
Billy Bamper.....................................George Sweet
Tom...Edward Shaw
Lola La Verne ....Frances Walker
Fawn Rosey......................................Lulu Thorne
Cleo Patrick.....................................Nathalie Segal
Rachel Murphy....................................Vilma Walden
Jeannie Grinkle................................Lenore Laurence
Maisie Buckman....................................Anne Page
Patsie Cohen.....................................Rita Krivett
Weenie De La Tour.................................June Martin
Marigold Murphy....................................Tiah Devitt
Estelle Flannigan.............................Catherine Dixon
Cutie Fischbaum................................Evelyn Warcoux
Silvya Wimple..................................Evelyn Eldridge

Trilbie Jenkins...................................Judy Gilmore
Eileen Olsen......................................Lily Burton
Billie McIntyre...................................Doris Babb
Gloria Lyttle.....................................Mae Cathcart
Mugsie Mulligan...........................Dorothy Livingston
Lucia Baccigaloupi...............................Harriett Dixon
    Acts I and II.—Stage of the Folly Theatre.
Staged by Bunny Weldon.

George Weston, a boy from upstate, is hooked by Jacob Perlstein, a producer of Broadway, and a burlesque queen named
Violet. He loses $20,000 in a bad show but finds Hazel Deane,
also a fledgling in the show business, and goes back to Auburn.

BLOOD MONEY

(64 performances)

A melodrama in three acts, by George Middleton (from a story
by H. H. Van Loan). Produced by Mrs. Henry B. Harris at the
Hudson Theatre, New York, August 22, 1927.

Cast of characters—

Nellie McKenna...................................Kate McComb
Julia Jones.......................................Phyllis Povah
James Bolton......................................Thomas Mitchell
Captain Harry Dark..............................Reginald Barlow
Ned Timmins.......................................Robert Brister
Mary Jefferson....................................Beatrice Nichols
Tom Jefferson....................................Malcolm Duncan
Wu Fang...Harold De Becker
Smith...Lawrence Cecil
Passenger...John D. Seymour
    Act I.—The Late Senator Bolton's Study. Acts II and III.—On
Board the Yacht Gloria.
Staged by Ira Hards.

Julia Jones, Senator Bolton's secretary, finding $100,000 in
bills in the senator's desk after the senator is dead, fights off the
crooks who try to take it away from her and escapes with it
aboard the Bolton yacht, where she finds both the Bolton sons,
James and his brother, a drug addict. Julia seeks to keep the
money hidden for fear its disclosure will blacken the senator's
name. In the end it is proved to be money the senator was sending to the lady crook to buy off her interest in his weaker son.

HER FIRST AFFAIRE

(136 performances)

A comedy in three acts by Merrill Rogers. Produced by Gustav
Blum at the Bayes Theatre, New York, August 22, 1927.

Cast of characters—

Carey Maxon.....................................Stanley Logan
Hildegarde Maxon.............................Aline MacMahon
Vivian Leiter....................................Ethel Wilson
Ann Hood..Grace Voss
Brian Cutler....................................Anderson Lawler
      Acts I, II and III.—The Living Room of the Maxons' Summer
Place in Connecticut.
      Directed by Gustav Blum.

Ann Hood, eager for the full test of life at 20, is convinced she must have an affair or two before she will be ready to settle down to marriage. She picks on Carey Maxon, free-thinking novelist, and boldly confesses her intentions to Mrs. Maxon. Mrs. Maxon, knowing Carey, leaves him alone with Ann, who immediately assumes a negligee costume and a provocative manner without result. The adventure serves, however, to excite Brian Cutler to action, and he elopes with Ann.

SUCH IS LIFE

(21 performances)

A play in three acts by Peter Glenny and Marie Armstrong Hecht. Produced by the Messrs. Shubert at the Morosco Theatre, New York, August 31, 1927.

Cast of characters—

Agatha Sterling...............................Kathleen Robinson
Noel Gignon...................................Ralph Sprague
Jemima Sterling...............................Ethel Remey
Dr. Charles Gignon............................William Jeffrey
Barbara Sterling..............................Sydney Shields
Tiny Sterling.................................Marie Carroll
Mrs. Deffingwell..............................Ethel Martin
Florabella Burton.............................Ernestine Gaines
Expressman....................................M. Bundoon
Adam Gignon...................................Omar Le Gant
Noel Gignon (The Boy).........................Joseph Donohue
Noel Gignon, Jr. ....Hardie Albright
      Acts I, II and III.—Living Room of the Sterlings.
      Directed by Clarke Silvernail.

Barbara, Agatha, Jemima and Tiny Sterling are restless maidens living together and getting on each other's nerves. All four of them are in love with Noel Gignon, a handsome but unprincipled artist they undertake to mother. Noel marries Barbara secretly, and then takes up with Agatha, running away with her to Paris. Within the year both girls present him with sons. Agatha, to avoid exposure, agrees to bring both boys up as her own. Later she leaves Noel, returns home, and for twenty years Barbara,

as his aunt, rears her own son. When Noel demands that his wife
and sons return to him Barbara rebels, confesses and threatens his
arrest on a charge of bigamy unless he clear out and leave her
and her son alone.

* BURLESQUE

(338 performances)

A comedy in three acts by George Manker Watters and Arthur
Hopkins. Produced by Arthur Hopkins at the Plymouth Theatre,
New York, September 1, 1927.

Cast of characters—

Bonny	Barbara Stanwyck
Jimmy	Paul Porter
Skid	Hal Skelly
Lefty	Charles D. Brown
A Fireman	Jack B. Shea
Mazie	Eileen Wilson
Gussie	Pauline Dee
Sylvia Marco	Ruth Holden
Bozo	Mitty DeVere
Harvey Howell	Ralph Theadore
Jerry Evans	Oscar Levant
A Waiter	Wilkie Dodsworth
Stage Carpenter	Joseph Burton
Scotty	Jack B. Shea
Jack	Wilkie Dodsworth

Act I.—A Dressing Room in a Mid-West Burlesque Theatre. Act
II.—Drawing Room of a New York Hotel Suite. Act III.—Bare
Stage of the Star Theatre, Paterson. 2—The Opening Performance.
Staged by Arthur Hopkins.

See page 122.

PICKWICK

(72 performances)

A comedy in three acts by Cosmo Hamilton and Frank C.
Reilly. Based upon "The Pickwick Papers" by Charles Dickens.
Produced by Frank C. Reilly at the Empire Theatre, New York,
September 5, 1927.

Cast of characters—

Coach Guard	Sol Solomon
Housekeeper	Ruby Hallier
Organ Grinder	John A. Regan
Betsy	Alice Southern
Sam Weller	Charles McNaughton

Nathaniel Winkle, Esq........................Ralph Bunker
Augustus Snodgrass, Esq.......................MacKenzie Ward
Tracy Tupman, Esq.............................Harry Plimmer
Waiter.......................................Marshall Hale
Miss Emily Wardle............................Elaine Temple
Mr. Bob Sawyer...............................Basil Hanbury
Miss Arabella Allen..........................Sheelagh Hayes
Mr. Ben Allen................................Guido Alexander
Miss Isabella Wardle..........................Jill Willis
Mr. Trundle..................................Malcolm Duffield
Mr. Wardle...................................Walter Edwin
Tony Weller..................................Bruce Winston
Miss Rachael Wardle..........................Olga Katzin
Mr. Perker...................................John Rogers
Mary...Marie Paxton
Joe..Maxime Pomada
Cabman.......................................Fred Monti
Samuel Pickwick, Esq.........................John Cumberland
The 'Ead 'Ostler at the White Hart...........Edward Garbett
Stable-Boy...................................Tom McKay
Mr. Alfred Jingle............................Hugh Miller
The Elderly Gallant..........................Claude Gouraud
Link-Boy.....................................Sol Solomon
The Lady in the Sedan Chair..................Maureen Dillon
Chairbearers.......................Henry Waters, Arthur Hains
Mrs. Martha Bardell..........................Katherine Stewart
Martin.......................................Claude Gouraud
Gamekeeper's Boy.............................Maureen Dillon
Carol Singers................................Dickens Trio
Butler.......................................Albert Somers
First Housemaid..............................Alice Southern
Second Housemaid.............................Josephine Dunn
Old Mrs. Wardle..............................Maureen Dillon
Jackson......................................Basil Hanbury
Mrs. Cluppins................................Ruby Hallier
Mrs. Sanders.................................Pauline Porter
Mr. Dodson...................................Fred Monti
Sergeant Buzfuz..............................Bruce Winston
Mr. Skimpin..................................Edward Jephson
Sergeant Snubbin.............................Frank Andrews
Mr. Phunky...................................Marshall Hale
The Gentleman in Black.......................Basil Hanbury
Clerk of the Court...........................Claude Gouraud
First Usher..................................Guido Alexander
Second Usher.................................Malcolm Duffield
Mr. Justice Stareleigh.......................Sol Solomon
A Poor Debtor................................George Spelvin
His Granddaughter............................Maureen Dillon
Roker..John A. Regan

Act I.—The White Hart Inn, London. Act II.—Mr. Pickwick's
Living Room at Mrs. Bardell's. 2—Shooting Party at Dingley Dell.
3—Manor Farm, Dingley Dell. Act III.—A Courtroom in Guildhall.
2—Fleet Prison, London. 3—Manor Farm, Dingley Dell.
Directed by Campbell Gullan.

Episodes from "Pickwick Papers" starting with the arrival of
Pickwick, Tupman, Snodgrass and Winkle at the White Hart
Inn; the meeting with Alfred Jingle; the frustrated elopement of
Rachael; the engagement of young Sam Weller; the misunder-
standing of Mrs. Bardell; the shooting party at Wardle's; the
suit for breach of promise; the trial and the Buzfuz charge; the
commitment to Fleet Street gaol; the release and wedding of
Emily and Snodgrass at Dingley Dell.

MISTER ROMEO

(16 performances)

A play in three acts by Harry Wagstaff Gribble and Wallace A. Manheimer. Produced by Murray Phillips at Wallack's Theatre, New York, September 5, 1927.

Cast of characters—

Maisie Clark	Jane Merredith
Helen Hughes	Sheila Trent
Jack Wainwright	Frank W. Hilliard
Babe Pierson	Isabelle Lowe
Buck Edwards	G. Pat Collins
Carleton Hazleton	J. C. Nugent
Ethel Trundle	Thais Lawton
Rose DuFrayne	Aileen Grenier
Ralph Shelton	Joseph Baird
Harry Wilkins	Sherrold Page
Maybelle	Julie Chandler
Bobbie	Sarah Gabler
Loretta	Eleanor Livingston

Acts I, II and III.—The Home of Babe and Maisie, Uptown New York.

Directed by Edward Eliscu.

Henry Trundle, posing as an author in search of Bohemian atmosphere, becomes Carleton Hazelton when he visits Babe Pierson of the burlesque stage. Henry's wife, discovering what is going on, conspires with Babe and Maisie to help her cure Henry. Maisie strips his pocketbook, and Babe lures him on until drama threatens in the person of Babe's true lover, a burlesque manager.

IN ABRAHAM'S BOSOM

(88 performances)

A play in seven scenes by Paul Green. Revived by the Provincetown Playhouse at the Provincetown Theatre, September 6, 1927.

Cast of characters—

Bud Gaskins	Stanley Greene
Lije Hunneycutt	Thomas Mosley
Puny Avery	James Dunmore
Abraham McCranie	Frank Wilson
Colonel McCranie	L. Rufus Hill
Lonnie McCranie	George Denny
Goldie McAllister	Rose McClendon
Muh Mack	Abbie Mitchell
Douglass McCranie	R. J. Huey
Eddie Williams	Melvin Greene

Lanie Horton...............................Armithine Lattimer
Neilly McNeill...............................Stanley Greene
  Scene 1—The Turpentine Woods of Eastern North Carolina, the Summer of 1885. 2, 5 and 7—Abraham McCranie's Cabin. 3—The School House. 4—A House in Durham. 6—On a Road.
  Staged by Jasper Deeter.

See "Plays of 1926-27."

* GOOD NEWS

(332 performances)

A musical comedy in two acts by Laurence Schwab and B. G. DeSylva; lyrics by B. G. DeSylva and Lew Brown; music by Ray Henderson. Produced by Laurence Schwab and Frank Mandel at the 46th Street Theatre, New York, September 6, 1927.

Cast of characters—

Tom Marlowe...............................John Price Jones
"Beef" Saunders...................................John Grant
Bobby Randall...Gus Shy
Bill Johnson...............................Edwin Redding
"Pooch" Kearney...................................John Sheehan
Charles Kenyon...........................Edward Emery
Patricia Bingham...........................Shirley Vernon
Constance Lane...................................Mary Lawlor
Babe O'Day...Inez Courtney
Sylvester...Don Tomkins
Windy...Wally Coyle
Slats...Jack Kennedy
Millie...Ruth Mayon
Flo...Zelma O'Neal
The Band Leader...............................George Olsen
The College Band...........................George Olsen's Music
The Glee Club Trio.......................{ Bob Rice / Fran Frey / Bob Borger
  Acts I and II.—Tait College, a Co-educational Institution in a Small Town.
  Staged by Edgar MacGregor.

Tom Marlowe, captain of the football team at Tait college, has flunked his astronomy and is barred from the big game with Colton. He tutors strenuously with Connie Lane the night before the exams and skins through. He plays, makes a long run, fumbles the ball and the game is saved by Bobby Randall. Tom returns to singing love duets with Connie, who for a while misunderstood his advances, thinking him engaged to another.

WOMEN GO ON FOREVER

(117 performances)

A play in three acts by Daniel N. Rubin. Produced by William A. Brady, Jr., and Dwight Deere Wiman, in association with John Cromwell, at the Forrest Theatre, New York, September 7, 1927.

Cast of characters—

Minnie	Elizabeth Taylor
Mary	Edna Thrower
Billy	Sam Wren
Pearl	Constance McKay
Mrs. Daisy Bowman	Mary Boland
Mr. Givner	Francis Pierlot
Dr. Bevin	Willard Foster
Jake	Morgan Wallace
Pete	Osgood Perkins
Harry	Douglass Montgomery
Louie	Edwin Kasper
Daly	David Landau
Hulbert	Myron Paulson
Mabel	Mary Law
Eddie	James Cagney
Sven	Hans Sandquist

Acts I, II and III.—Hallway Living Room at Daisy Bowman's Rooming House.

Staged by John Cromwell.

Daisy Bowman, running a cheap boarding house in a northern city, fights fate, her boarders and her passions for thirty-six hours. During that time she sees her lover, Jake, killed by her blind son Harry; shields Harry from the police, only to learn that he has been seduced by Minnie, whose unattractive spinsterhood his blindness prevents his appraising; saves Mabel, drunk, from the attack of Pete by getting Pete neatly murdered, and nurses Mrs. Givner, second floor back, through the birth of her firstborn.

YELLOW SANDS

(25 performances)

A comedy in three acts by Eden and Adelaide Phillpotts. Produced by Sir Barry Jackson at the Fulton Theatre, New York, September 10, 1927.

Cast of characters—

Richard Varwell	Reginald Bach
Emma Major	Eileen Beldon
Arthur Varwell	Jack Livesey
Joe Varwell	Lester Matthews
Thomas Major	Wilson Colman

Lydia Blake...Joyce Moore
Mary Varwell...Winnie Tempest
Jenifer Varwell..Madge Burbage
Minnie Masters...Nellie Sheffield
Nelly Masters..Florence Barnes
Mr. Baslow...Arthur Claremont
    Act I.—The Beach at Yellow Sands. Acts II and III.—Miss Varwell's Parlour.
    Staged by H. K. Ayliff.

Jenifer Varwell, 80, about to make her will, is variously approached and coddled by her next of kin. Two of her prospective heirs are Joe and Arthur Varwell, Arthur smart and sophisticated, Joe dull and bolshevist. After Jenifer passes the will is read. Those who expected most get the least, and Joe, who expected nothing, gets the most. Helped by his philosophic but otherwise shiftless uncle, Richard Varwell, Joe is able to accept the money and still square his conscience with his radical principles.

REVELRY

(48 performances)

A play in three acts by Maurine Watkins, from the novel by Samuel Hopkins Adams. Produced by Robert Milton at the Masque Theatre, New York, September 12, 1927.

Cast of characters—

Willis Markham...Berton Churchill
Dan Lurcock..George MacFarlane
Andy Gandy...William B. Mack
Charlie Madrigal.......................................James Crane
Duke Forrest...Harry Bannister
Tim Fosgate..Frederick Burton
Jeff Sims..Jefferson de Angelis
Frothingham..Charles Ellis
First Guard..David Munroe
Second Guard...Lionel Bevans
Edith Westervelt.......................................Eleanor Woodruff
Gladys Hartley...Rose Hobart
Bonnie Forrest...Adele Klaer
Zoe Farley...Irene Homer
    Prologue—Scene 1—The Crows' Nest. 2—Edith's Apartment. Act I.—Cabinet Room at the Executive Mansion. Act II.—Hotel Room of Duke Forrest. 2—Crows' Nest. Act III.—Scene 1—Cabinet Room at the Executive Mansion. 2—The Crows' Nest. The action takes place in Washington, D. C., in the Day Beyond Our Own Day.
    Staged by Robert Milton.

Willis Markham, some time president of the United States, is popular with "the boys," led by Dan Lurcock, big political boss. Willis plays poker and liquors with them at the "Crows' Nest." One night, seeking to escape the boys and also his secret service guards, the president is caught up an alley and held as a possible burglar by Edith Westervelt, widow. Thereafter he is, partly through her, made aware of the grafting crowd his supposed friends represent and, exposure threatening, kills himself.

BABY CYCLONE

(184 performances)

A farce in three acts, by George Cohan. Produced by George Cohan at the Henry Miller Theatre, New York, September 12, 1927.

Cast of characters—

Evans	Joseph Holickey
Crandall	Agnes Gildea
Jessie Hurley	Nan Sunderland
Joseph Meadows	Grant Mitchell
Dr. Hearn	John T. Doyle
Gene Hurley	Spencer Tracy
Lydia Webster	Natalie Moorehead
Cassidy	Charles F. McCarthy
Kellog	Joseph Allen
Robert Webster	William Morris
Mrs. Robert Webster	Georgia Caine
Edwards	Oliver Putnam
Maid	Doris Freeman
McCracken	Barlowe Borland

Act I.—Joseph Meadows' Home in New York. Act II.—At the Hurleys. Act III.—At the Websters.

Staged by Sam Forrest.

Mrs. Hurley owns a Pekinese. Mr. Hurley, who hates the Peke because Mrs. Hurley talks baby talk to it, takes it out and sells it to a lady on Fifth Avenue. Mrs. Hurley, hearing the news, screams, a passing Mr. Meadows interferes, Mr. Hurley pokes Mr. Meadows in the eye, Mr. Meadows threatens to have the law on Mr. Hurley and takes Mrs. Hurley home for her protection. Mr. Hurley follows, explains about the Peke, Mr. Meadows understands and all is well until Mr. Meadows' fiancée walks in with the dog. She is the lady who bought it from Mr. Hurley. Both women demand the dog and it requires another act and a half to settle rights of ownership.

MY MARYLAND

(312 performances)

A musical romance in three acts. Book and lyrics by Dorothy Donnelly; music by Sigmund Romberg. Produced by the Messrs.

Shubert at the Jolson Theatre, New York, September 12, 1927.

Cast of characters—

Sue Royce	Berta Donn
Laura Royce	Margaret Merle
Mammy Lou	Mattie Keene
Edgar Strong	Rollin Grimes, Jr.
Sally Negly	Joan Ruth
Barbara Frietchie	Evelyn Herbert
Jack Negly	Warren Hull
Dr. Hal Boyd	Edwin Delbridge
Zeke Bramble	George Rosene
Colonel Negly	Louis Casavant
Arthur Frietchie	James Meighan
Captain Trumbull	Nathaniel Wagner
Mr. Frietchie	Fuller Mellish
Sergt. Perkins	George V. Dill
Mrs. Hunter	Marion Ballou
Fred Gelwex	Wallace Mattice
Tim Green	Arthur Cunningham
General Stonewall Jackson	James Ellis

Act I.—A Street in Frederick, Maryland. Act II.—The Minister's
House in Hagerstown. Act III.—The Frietchie House in Frederick.
The Period is 1862.
Staged by J. J. Shubert.

A version of the "Barbara Frietchie" legend taken from Clyde
Fitch's play of the same title. Barbara is a young, blonde daughter of the South who protects her Northern lover, Capt. Trumbull,
and is in turn protected by Gen. Stonewall Jackson.

HALF A WIDOW

(8 performances)

A musical play in three acts. Book and lyrics by Harry B.
Smith and Frank Dupree; music by Shep Camp. Produced by
Wally Gluck at the Waldorf Theatre, New York, September 12,
1927.

Cast of characters—

Babette	Gertrude Lang
Captain Bob Everett	Halfred Young
Izzy Preiss	Benny Rubin
Nita	Julia Kelety
Captain Wagner	Robert C. Cloy
Edith Proctor	Frances Halliday
Lieutenant Turner	Geoffrey O'Hara
Jean Marie Alphonse Bettincourt	Paul Doucet
Pierre Lafarge	Albert Froom
Gyp, the Dip	Lew Christy
Stubbs	Lewis Newman
Brannigan	Ralph D. Sanford
June Love	Beryl Halley
Antoinette	Vivian Martin
Murphy	Harry Donaghy
Tony	Daniel Da Silva

Red...Henry Jockin
Scotty..Edgar Welch
Orderly..George Rogers
    Acts I and III.—Refreshment Garden of the Maison Lafarge.
Act II.—Scenes 1 and 5, Interior Red Cross Canteen. 2—Communi-
cation Trench Near the Front. 3—Front Line Trench at Château-
Thierry. 4—No Man's Land.
    Staged by Lawrence Marston and Edwin T. Emery.

Bob Everett, rich, generous and in love with Babette, marries her the night before his outfit moves up to the front in France, leaves her all his wealth and expects her, as his widow, to marry her French sweetheart. But Bob fails to die, and that leaves Babette wedded but neither wife nor widow. The situation is adjusted at the play's end.

THE WILD MAN OF BORNEO

(15 performances)

A comedy in three acts by Marc Connelly and Herman J. Man-kiewicz. Produced by Philip Goodman at the Bijou Theatre, New York, September 13, 1927.

Cast of characters—

Erma...Sarah Enright
Ed Le Mott..Harold Elliott
Francine Diamond.....................................Anna Thomas
Mrs. Diamond.......................................Lotta Linthicum
Mrs. Marshall.....................................Josephine Hull
J. Daniel Thompson................................George Hassell
Mary..Marguerite Churchill
Birdo..Spencer Charters
Doc Smalley......................................Edward F. Nanary
Ferderber..Charles Moran
Population Harry...................................Royal C. Stout
Marvelous Morton...Ajax
Murdock...Murray Alper
Attendant...Frank Butler
First Policeman.......................................Jess Barrett
Second Policeman...............................James P. Houston
    Acts I, II and III.—A Room at Mrs. Marshall's and the Hall of
Living Wonders.
    Staged by Marc Connelly.

J. Daniel Thompson becomes suddenly aware of a grown daughter he has not seen in fifteen years, tries to make good with her by telling her he is a great and prosperous actor when in reality he has never been anything but a cheap medicine show faker. In New York he convinces his daughter and his fellow boarders that he is Mansfield's understudy in "Cyrano de Bergerac," but they discover him instead made up as the Wild Man of Borneo in a Fourteenth Street museum and his pathetic exposure follows.

TEN PER CENT
(23 performances)

A comedy in three acts by Eugene Davis. Produced by Thomas Jackson and H. S. Kraft at the George M. Cohan Theatre, New York, September 13, 1927.

Cast of characters—

Pearl	Myra Hampton
Roy Tracey	Albert Hackett
James Depew	John Williams
Henry Fuller	Roger Allen
George Moss	Walter Plimmer, Jr.
Lucy Kane	Florence Arden
Rudolf Schwartz	Robert Leonard
Martha Black	Patricia Calvert
Doris Rankin	Nancy Sheridan
Frederick Merton	Frank Dae
The Character Man	Edward O'Connor
The Leading Man	Walter Ferrell
The Character Lady	Violet Barney
"At Liberty"	Clifton Self

Acts I, II and III.—In the Office of Moss & Tracey, Theatrical Agents.

Staged by Thomas Jackson.

George Moss of Moss and Tracey, booking agents, in love with Doris Rankin, is forced to play up professionally to Martha Black, whose father, Rudolf Schwartz, is ready to back her as the star of "Love's Torrents." George nearly loses Doris, the show is nearly a terrible failure and the comedy is not over until nearly 11 o'clock.

THE TRIUMPHANT BACHELOR
(12 performances)

A play in three acts by Owen Davis. Produced by David Burton at the Biltmore Theatre, New York, September 15, 1927.

Cast of characters—

Bob Farley	Ray Walburn
Lydia Farley	Mona Kingsley
Ben Brittan	Richard Sterling
Barbara Brittan	Anne Morrison
Jessie Emery	Dorothy Libaire
David Emery	Harold Hendee
Mrs. Calvert	Olive May
Flora Calvert	Mildred MacLeod
Jack Sylvester	Robert Ames
Mildred Spence	Elsie Lawson
Servant at the Farleys'	Chas. Ashley

```
Butler  at  the  Calverts'..........................George  Roberts
Maid  at  Mrs.  Calvert's...........................Dorothy  Tree
     Act  I.—At  the  Farleys'.   Acts  II  and  III.—At  the  Calverts'.
     Staged  by  David  Burton.
```

Jack Sylvester, an experienced sheik, bets three of his married pals that no one of their wives trusts her husband. The bet is made and Jack slips three prepared love notes into the three dinner jackets of the would-be suspected men. The wives find the notes and three explosions follow. Even the truth will not prevail and it takes two hours to convince the women that they are wrong.

MIKADO

(105 performances)

An opera in two acts. Words by W. S. Gilbert; music by Arthur Sullivan. Produced by Winthrop Ames at the Royale Theatre, New York, September 17, 1927.

Cast of characters—

```
The  Mikado  of  Japan............................John  Barclay
Nanki-Poo........................................William  Williams
Ko-Ko............................................Fred  Wright
Pooh-Bah.........................................William  C.  Gordon
Pish-Tush........................................J.  Humbird  Duffey
Yum-Yum..........................................Lois  Bennett
Pitti-Sing.......................................Suissabell  Sterling
Peep-Bo..........................................Bettina  Hall
Katisha..........................................Vera  Ross
The  Mikado's  Umbrella-Bearer...................George  C.  Lehrian
The  Mikado's  Sword-Bearer......................Paula  Langlen
     Act  I.—Ko-Ko's  Garden  in  Titipu.   Act  II.—Courtyard  of  Ko-Ko's
Official  Residence.
     Staged  by  Winthrop  Ames.
```

A restoration of the popular Gilbert-Sullivan classic to its original Savoy Theatre form.

FOUR WALLS

(144 performances)

A play in three acts, by Dana Burnet and George Abbott. Produced by John Golden at the John Golden Theatre, New York, September 19, 1927.

Cast of characters—

```
Bertha...........................................Bella  Finkle
Mrs.  Horowitz...................................Clara  Langsner
```

Mrs. Clampman	Josephine Wehn
Mendel	Jacob Frank
Benny Horowitz	Muni Wisenfrend
The Monk	Averell Harris
Lefty	William Pawley
Herman	Charles Wagenheim
Jake	George Wright, Jr.
Nick	Lee Strassberg
Marty	William Cox
Paul	Lionel Dante
Sullivan	Edward Keane
Frieda	Jeanne Greene
Sammy	Edwin Philips
Tom	James C. Lane
Sally	Eloise Keeler
Lizzie	Suzanne Browne
Gertie	Gertrude Manfred
Stella	Olga Nova
Rose	Evelyn Platt
Looey	Jay Lindsey
Sid	Sanford Meisner
First Musician	William Smith
Second Musician	Peter Du Conge
Third Musician	George Nicols
Fourth Musician	Steve Jones

Act I.—The Horowitz Flat. Act II.—2—Tom's Café. 3—The Roof. Act III.—The Flat.

Staged by George Abbott.

Benny Horowitz, leader of the gas house gang, is home from Sing Sing after having done a five-year stretch. In place of being bitter he has convinced himself that it is not stone and steel cells that make a man a prisoner, but the shackles he forges on himself. He comes out of prison determined to remain free not only in body but in spirit as well. He will never again belong to any gang, or any woman, or any habit he cannot master. Gradually the old forces begin to hedge him in, and he is guilty of an accidental killing. Rather than lie himself out of it he gives himself up.

*THE TRIAL OF MARY DUGAN

(310 performances)

A melodrama in three acts, by Bayard Veiller. Produced by A. H. Woods at the National Theatre, New York, September 19, 1927.

Cast of characters—

Judge Nash	John Ravold
District Attorney Galway	Arthur Hohl
Italian Lawyer	Jasper Mangione
Pauline Agguerro	Marie Santas
Dr. Welcome	Dean Raymond
Stenographer of the Court	Lewis McMichael

Edward West.....................................Cyril Keightley
James Madison..Oscar Polk
Police Inspector Hunt..........................Robert Cummings
Police Captain Price..............................John Sharkey
Mrs. Kate Burton...................................Julia Ralph
Dagmar Lorne.....................................Leona Maricle
Mary Dugan.......................................Ann Harding
Farne Arthur.....................................Anna Kostant
Mary Harris......................................Dennie Moore
Jimmy...Rex Cherryman
Mrs. Edgar Rice.................................Merle Maddern
Patrick Kearney....................................Edwin Jones
Harry Jones.......................................Louis Heydt
Marie Ducort...................................Madame Burani
Henry Plaisted.................................Charles Edwards
Assistant District Attorney.....................Barton MacLane
Clerk of the Court.................................Jack Sayer
                                              John Dougherty
Court Attendants.............................. Robert Williams
                                              Robert Beggs
        Staged by A. H. Van Buren.

Mary Dugan, professionally known as Mona Tree of the "Follies," has been found staring stupidly at the dead body of Edgar
Rice, the man with whom she has most recently been living. Her
clothes are blood smeared and her finger prints are on the dagger
with which Rice has been killed. At her trial, with the evidence
all against her, her young brother, Jimmy, arrives from California.
Being a lawyer Jimmy objects to the way in which Mary's attorney is conducting her case, the attorney resigns and Jimmy
takes it over. Then he learns for the first time of his sister's
mode of life and the sacrifices she has made to pay for his education. He defends her passionately and twists the state's own
witnesses into an admission of guilt.

ENCHANTED ISLE

(32 performances)

A musical play in three acts. Book, lyrics and music by Ida
Hoyt Chamberlain. Produced by the American Allied Arts, Inc.,
at the Lyric Theatre, New York, September 19, 1927.

Cast of characters—

Mrs. Stewart Haverhill-Smith....................Madeleine Grey
Count Romeo De Spagino.......................George E. Mack
Stewart Haverhill-Smith..........................Basil Ruysdael
Bill Capps.......................................Hansford Wilson
Maria...Marga Waldron
Enoch...Harry Hermsen
Yen Sing..Martin Wolfson
Bob Sherill..Greek Evans
Julianne Sanderleigh..............................Kathryn Reece
Angela...Thera Dawn
Bella..Lucile Reece
Captain Yacht.....................................Philip Snyder

John P. Stone..J. Paul Callan
    Act I.—Bob Sherill's Ranch-house in Southern California. Act
II.—Living Room, Bob Sherill's Summer Home. Act III.—Deck of
Haverhill-Smith's Yacht.
    Staged by Oscar Eagle.

The true love of Bob Sherill, rough but honest forest ranger, and Maria Whozis, society girl of the East, is threatened by the machinations of a foreign count and intriguing natives, but it all ends happily on board the Haverhill-Smith yacht in the last act.

LOVERS AND ENEMIES

(2 performances)

A tragi-comedy in five acts, by Artzybashell; translated by Madame Strindberg. Produced by the Grand Street Follies Company at the Little Theatre, New York, September 20, 22, 27, 29, 1927.

Cast of characters—

Nicolai Ivanovich..............................Leo N. Bulgakov
Olga...Eva Condon
Valentina.....................................Esther Mitchell
Peter..Marc Loebell
Pavel..Albert Carroll
Irina...Joanna Roos
Serge Karnovich.................................John F. Roche
Valeria.......................................Paula Trueman
Lieutenant Zankowsky...........................Otto Hulicius
Dasha...Lily Lubell
    Acts I, III and V.—Veranda in Nicolai Ivanovich's Country Home.
Acts II and IV.—The Sitting Room.
    Staged by Agnes Morgan.

An illustration of a cynical scientist's contention that true happiness in love is impossible; that, in fact, lovers and enemies are much the same. Thus, passion-fired Irina leaves Pavel, her dreaming musician husband; Peter, tempted almost beyond his strength by Valeria, manages to remain true to Valentina, and Nicolai and Olga, many years married, come to realize that neither has ever really understood the other but that both are helplessly bound by bonds of sentiment.

THE COMMAND TO LOVE

(247 performances)

A comedy in three acts, by Rudolph Lothar and Fritz Gottwald. Adapted by Herman Bernstein and Brian Marlow. Produced by William A. Brady, Jr., and Dwight Deere Wiman, in association with John Tuerk, at the Longacre Theatre, New York, September 20, 1927.

Cast of characters—

Don Pedro Munaterra	Thomas Louden
The French Ambassador to Spain	Henry Stephenson
Marie-Anne	Violet Kemble Cooper
A Lackey	Walter Colligan
Gaston, Marquis du Saint-Lac	Basil Rathbone
Emile Ardillot	Anthony Kemble Cooper
Don Tomas Martinez	Percy Hemus
Manuela	Mary Nash
The Spanish War Minister	Ferdinand Gottschalk
The French Foreign Minister	David Glassford

Acts I and III.—A Room in the French Embassy. Act II.—The Attaché's Rooms.
The Place is Madrid.
Staged by Lester Lonergan.

Gaston, with a reputation as the most successful of the modern Don Juans, is drafted as an attaché of the French embassy at the court of Spain. His unofficial duties include such social contacts with the influential ladies of the court as will help his country. Gaston, however, being true to his ambassador's wife, refuses to flirt until the ambassador practically orders him to do so. Then he reluctantly but successfully acknowledges the advances of Manuela, wife of the Spanish war minister, and thus helps along the signing of a treaty the war minister previously had opposed.

CREOLES

(28 performances)

A comedy drama in three acts, by Samuel Shipman and Kenneth Perkins. Produced by Richard Herndon at the Klaw Theatre, New York, September 22, 1927.

Cast of characters—

Monsieur Daudet	Gene Mason
Madame Fourmet	Pauline March
Madame La Grange	Rita Vale
Mlle. Germaine	Kay Titus
Mlle. Collette	Palma Rita
Mlle. Du Bois	Mabel Williams
Mlle. Garlet	Elizabeth Darling
Mlle. Dupont	Jean Neville
Mlle. Duane	Sonia Rasova
Monsieur Goulet	William Murray
Monsieur Raffael	David Sager
Monsieur Fougart	Jean Loubet
Monsieur André	William Parke, Jr.
Señor Martinez	Raoul DeLeon

```
Bess...............................................Bessie Allison
Christopher...................................Richard N. Gregg
Eve................................................Eva Franklin
Sue...............................................Susie Franklin
Mose..............................................William Jones
Rastus...........................................Nelson Turner
Golondrina....................................Natacha Rambova
Monsieur Merluche...............................George Nash
El Gato.........................................Allan Dinehart
Madame Hyacinthe...........................Princess Matchabelli
José...............................................Jay Mondaye
Allasandro........................................Neil Burgess
Pere Alphonse..................................Redfield Clarke
Jacinta...........................................Helen Chandler
Pierre...............................................Sol Padrone
Jules...........................................Edward Ferguson
     Acts I, II and III.—The Hyacinthe Mansion.  New Orleans, 1850.
     Staged by Benrimo.
```

Madame Hyacinthe, forced to mortgage Hyacinthe mansion to
Monsieur Merluche, thinks to marry her innocent Jacinto, just returned from convent, to Monsieur Merluche and thus solve a
family and financial problem.   But Jacinto, romantically in love
with El Gato, pirate, refuses to marry Merluche, and to make her
escape sure pleads with El Gato to make her his mistress.   El
Gato he is bad fellow but not that bad, so Jacinto hides in his
room.   After which Merluche casts her off and El Gato makes
marriage with her.

THE LETTER

(104 performances)

A play in three acts by W. Somerset Maugham.   Produced by
Messmore Kendall at the Morosco Theatre, New York, September 26, 1927.

Cast of characters—

```
Leslie Crosbie.................................Katharine Cornell
Geoffrey Hammond.............................Burton McEvilly
Head-Boy............................................M. Wada
John Withers.......................................John Buckler
Robert Crosbie.....................................J. W. Austin
Howard Joyce......................................Allan Jeayes
Ong Chi Seng....................................James Vincent
A Sikh Sergeant of Police...........................B. Landon
Mrs. Parker....................................Mary Scott Seton
Chung Hi...........................................Sam Kim
A Chinese Woman...........................Lady Chong Goe
Mrs. Joyce...................................Eva Leonard-Boyne
     Act I.—The Drawing Room of the Crosbies' Bungalow.  Act II.—
A Room in the Gaol at Singapore.  Act III.—A Room in the Chinese
Quarter at Singapore; 2—The Drawing Room.
     Staged by Guthrie McClintic.
```

Leslie Crosbie, shooting Geoffrey Hammond full of bullets,
swears he had attacked her and she killed him in self-defense.

Her story holds until the appearance of a letter she had written Hammond demanding that he visit her the night of the murder. Leslie then confesses she killed Hammond in rage because he had thrown her over for a Chinese woman. The letter is kept out of the trial and she is cleared.

MANHATTAN MARY

(264 performances)

A musical comedy in two acts; book, lyrics and music by B. G. DeSylva, Lew Brown, Ray Henderson, Wm. K. Wells and George White. Produced by George White at the Apollo Theatre, New York, September 26, 1927.

Cast of characters—

Sam Katz	Lou Holtz
Policeman	James Scott
R. C. ("Arcy") Blair	Paul Stanton
Helen King	Amy Revere
A Society Bud	Suzanne Fleming
Police Sergeant	Harry Oldridge
Mary Brennan	Ona Munson
"Ma" Brennan	Dorothy Walters
Jimmy Moore	Paul Frawley
Al	Sam Ledner
Bob Sterling	Harland Dixon
Diana Day	Mary Farley
Tiny Forsythe	Suzanne Fleming
Fritzie DeVere	Doree Leslie
Viola Fay	Mae Clark
Show Girl	Adele Smith
A Dramatic Actress	Vada Alexander
Embassy Boys	Messrs. Goff, Kerr and Barth
McCarthy Sisters	Themselves
Crickets	Ed Wynn
Micky	Victor Munro
"Two-Gun" Terry	James Scott
George White	Himself
Ruth Beverly	Suzanne Fleming
M. Max Duval	Marcel Rousseau
Scott Sisters	Themselves
Newsboy	Ray Hunt
His Honor, the Mayor of New York City	Harry Oldridge

Act I.—Scene 1—Broadway. 2—Barrow Street, Greenwich Village. 3—Stage Manager's Office. 4—Stage of Apollo Theatre. 5—Five-Step Curtain. 6—Mother Brennan's Lunch Room. 7—A Tree in the Park. 8—"400" Club. 9—A Secluded Spot. 10—Memories. 11—"Scandals" Dress Rehearsal, Apollo Theatre. Act II.—Scene 1 —Barrow Street. 2—A News Stand. 3—Folies Bergere, Paris. 4—Huber's Museum. 5—The Meeting Place. 6—Roof Garden. Staged by George White.

Mary Brennan, Ma Brennan's daughter, has to go to work when Ma's Greenwich Village restaurant fails because Ma has invested her money in bonds sold by that rascal Sam Katz. Crickets, a waiter in the restaurant, helps Mary get a job in

George White's "Scandals," she is the hit of the show and everything's joyous at the finale.

MERRY MALONES

(192 performances, 16 performances return engagement)

A musical comedy in two acts, by George M. Cohan. Produced by George M. Cohan at Erlanger's Theatre, New York, September 26, 1927.

Cast of characters—

Announceress	Jane Manners
Martin	Leo Henning
Carlysle	David London
Mrs. Van Buren	Ina Hayward
Annabelle	Marjorie Lane
Mr. Westcott	Robinson Newbold
Gloria Westcott	Mary Jane
Joe Thompson	Alan Edwards
Joe Westcott	Alan Edwards
Molly Malone	Polly Walker
Tony Howard	Frank Otto
Kennedy	Frank Masters
Capt. of Police	Mercer Templeton
Capt. of Police	James Templeton
Delia Malone	Dorothy Whitmore
John Malone	George M. Cohan
Helen Malone	Sarah Edwards
Annie	Patsy Ball
Charlie Malone	Charles Finin
Tom	Richard Barry
Jenkins	Harry Rose
Mr. Rosinsky	Nat S. Jerome
Mrs. Rosinsky	Angela Jacobs

Act I.—Scene 1—Westcott Home. 2—A Drug Store in the Bronx. 3—John Malone's Home. 4—The Bronx Express. 5—The Stage Door. 6—The Ball Room of the Van Buren Home. Act II.—Scene 1—A Street in the Bronx. 2—Westcott's Office. 3—The Pathway to the "Rose Garden." 4—The "Rose Garden" of the Westcott Home.

Staged by Edward Royce.

Joe Westcott, of the rich Westcotts, loves Molly Malone of the Bronx Malones so much that he is willing to give up a hundred million dollars and be a soda water clerk just to sing duets with her. But Molly will have nothing to do with so rich a fellow, so Joe has to get himself disinherited. He succeeds in doing this but Papa Westcott fools him. He takes the money away from Joe and gives it to Molly.

SHANNONS OF BROADWAY

(288 performances)

A comedy in three acts by James Gleason. Produced by Crosby Gaige and Earle Boothe at the Martin Beck Theatre, New York, September 26, 1927.

Cast of characters—

Pa Swanzey	George Farren
Charley Dill	George Spelvin
Hez Davis	Guy Nichols
Vance Atkins	Leo Lindhard
Bert Savage	Thomas Joyce
Minerva Harper	Helen Mehrmann
An Actor	Phil Sheridan
His Wife	Daphne Wilson
Oscar	Jos. Raymond
"Chuck" Bradford	Frank Hearn
Emma Shannon	Lucile Webster
Mickey Shannon	James Gleason
Ma Swanzey	Louise Crolius
Theresa Sutton	Suzanne Sheldon
Charles Bradford, Sr.	Percy Moore
Newt Eddy	Charles Brokate
Annie Todd	Daphne Wilson
"Shorty" Jones	Eddie Heron
Eddie Allen	Harry Tyler
Alice Allen	Gladys Crolius
Tom	Willard Keeler
Bill	G. B. Stayman
Jake	Matthew Zentner
Pat	Clarence Doench
A Departing Guest	Phil Sheridan
Mr. Albee	Bertram Millar

Acts I, II and III.—Office of the "Swanzey House" in Sutton, New England.

Staged by Paul Dickey.

Emma and Mickey Shannon, small-time vaudeville troupers, are stranded in Sutton, New England. Stopping in Pa Swanzey's inn to get warm, they discover the village skinflint is about to throw Swanzey into the street and take over the hotel. The Shannons decide to buy in and try the hotel business. They help to settle many of the town's minor problems and then go back to show business.

SPEAK EASY

(57 performances)

A melodrama in three acts by Edward Knoblock and George Rosener. Produced by William B. Friedlander at the Mansfield Theatre, New York, September 26, 1927.

Cast of characters—

Rita...Adelaide Rondelle
Paul Martin...................................Donald Campbell
Daisy...Beatrice Lee
Old Annie.....................................Marie Pettes
"Fuzzy" Arnold................................Leo G. Carroll
Teddy...Kate-Pier Roemer
Willy Boy.....................................Leopold Badia
"Min" Denton..................................Anne Shoemaker
"Junkie" Joe..................................John Crone
Alice Woods...................................Dorothy Hall
"Cannon" Costello.............................Arthur R. Vinton
Jack Vickery..................................Edward Woods
Virginia Arnold...............................Ruthelma Stevens
    Acts I, II and III—"Min" Denton's Apartment—a Speakeasy in
"Hell's Kitchen."

Alice Woods, an innocent from the country, finds herself in Min's place, hard by Hell's Kitchen. She is threatened by Cannon Costello, a fearfully tough fellow, and rescued by her Princeton boy friend.

JIMMIE'S WOMEN

(216 performances)

A comedy in three acts by Myron C. Fagan. Produced by B. J. Witbeck at the Biltmore Theatre, New York, September 26, 1927.

Cast of characters—

Billy Wells...................................William Wayne
Thomas..Sam Parks
Algernon Simpson..............................Junior Cook
Teddie Kane...................................Lucia Laska
Jimmie Turner.................................Robert Williams
Robert Fowler.................................Roy Gordon
Dr. Richard Turner............................Felix Krembs
Samuel Kane...................................Charles Abbe
Mrs. Samuel Kane..............................Beatrice Terry
Florence Standish.............................Minna Gombel
Maid..Frances Horine
Mrs. Reginald Van Alstyne.....................Helene Mitchell
    Acts I and II.—Home of Dr. Richard Turner, Greenwich, Conn.
Act III.—Jimmie's Bedroom.
    Staged by Myron C. Fagan.

Jimmie Turner, in love with Gypsy Adair, actress, is liable to lose his father's money unless he accepts the family dictum that he shall marry his cousin, Teddie Kane, who is already in love with another. To turn Teddie's interests to Jimmie his uncles import a flirt to make her jealous. The flirt turns out to be Gypsy Adair and also Jimmie's secretly married wife.

THE GARDEN OF EDEN

(23 performances)

A comedy in three acts by Avery Hopwood, from the German of Rudolph Bernauer and Rudolph Oesterreicher. Produced by Arch Selwyn at the Selwyn Theatre, New York, September 27, 1927.

Cast of characters—

Adele	Barbara Barondess
Diane	June Leslie
Cleo	Betsy Jane Southgate
Rosa	Alison Skipworth
Revard	Stapleton Kent
Toni Lebrun	Miriam Hopkins
A Call Boy	Daniel Wolf
Durand	Harlan Briggs
Madame Rimsky	Camilla Dalberg
Henri Glessing	C. Stafford Dickens
Count de Mauban	Gordon Ash
Baron Laperau	A. G. Andrews
Count de L'Esterel	T. Wigney Percyval
Richard Lamont	Douglass Montgomery
Maitre d'Hotel	Alfred A. Hesse
Professor Rossio	Ignacio Martinetti
Aunt Matilde	Doris Rankin
Uncle Herbert	Ivan F. Simpson
Prince Miguel de Santa Rocca	Russ Whytal
Servant of the Prince	Walter Geer

Act I.—Dressing Room of the "Palais de Paris." Act II.—Lounge Room in the Hotel Eden, Monte Carlo. Act III.—Room in a Boarding-house in Paris.
Staged by Edwin H. Knopf.

Toni Lebrun is a dancer in an obscure Paris cabaret where terrible things happen. Rosa, the charwoman of the place, is in reality a baroness down on her luck. Every year Rosa takes her savings and spends them all on one grand splurge on the Riviera. After Toni has been attacked by Henri Gissing, Rosa takes her with her to the Riviera. There she meets and loves Richard Lamont, who wants to marry her. Everything is set for the wedding, with Toni all dressed up in the Lamont finery. Gissing turns up, but agrees to keep still if Toni will share her favors with him. Toni refuses, confesses all, and when Richard is not prompt in forgiveness, strips her wedding dress from her back and walks out of the Eden hotel in her step-in. Later, in Paris, she agrees to marry Richard's royal ancestor, Prince de Santa Rocco, who is 75, very rich and eager to be revenged upon his snobbish relatives.

BLACK VELVET

(15 performances)

A play in three acts by Willard Robertson. Produced by M. J. Nicholas at the Liberty Theatre, New York, September 27, 1927.

Cast of characters—

General John William Darr..........................Arthur Byron
Sampson...Jimmie Rosen
Patricia Harper...................................Leona Hogarth
Cleo..Nadea Hall
Alice Darr..Kate Byron
John William Darr, 3rd..............................Nelan Jaap
The Peddler.......................................Louis La Bey
Mr. Harper......................................Frank Sylvester
Joe Lancaster....................................Peter Bentley
Calhoun Darr.....................................Joseph Green
Yeller Richmond................................Leonard Doyle
Charles Ware..................................Parker Fennelly
Smith...Charles Slattery
     Acts I, II and III.—In the Rose Arbour of the Darr Plantation in the "Yellow Pine" Belt of the South.
     Staged by Willard Robertson.

Gen. J. W. Darr, 84-year-old Southerner, still has his pride and his sense of Dixie justice. When his overseer kills a labor agent come from the North to recruit black labor the general approves. When a mulatto, full of coke, strikes the general's grandson in the face and is lynched the general agrees that that is what might be expected. But when he learns that his grandson, engaged to a Northern belle, has been flirting in the canebrush with a yellow lady his family pride wells up and he is ready to kill the boy. Would have killed him if he had not dropped dead.

THE UNINVITED GUEST

(7 performances)

A drama in three acts by Bernard J. McOwen. Produced by L. M. Simmons, Inc., at the Belmont Theatre, New York, September 27, 1927.

Cast of characters—

Johanna Jackson..................................Peg Entwistle
T. Jefferson White..............................John Carmody
Matty Jackson................................Helen Strickland
Alfred Jackson...................................Elmer Grandin
Horace Bascom..................................Robert Conness
Hanna White......................................Mabel Colcord

James Malcolm.................................Walter Davis
    Acts I, II and III.—Living Room of Alfred Jackson's Home, a
Farm House in the Ramapo Mountains, New York State.

Johanna Jackson, young wife of a flinty 70-year-old husband, has a child by the local minister to satisfy her overpowering maternal urge. Her husband and his aged sister turn upon Johanna, the child dies and Johanna kills the minister when he tries to take advantage of her in violation of his promise to stay away.

MURRAY HILL

(28 performances)

A farce in three acts by Leslie Howard. Produced by the Messrs. Shubert at the Bijou Theatre, New York, September 29, 1927.

Cast of characters—

Van...Harry Lillford
Mrs. Cass.......................................Alice May Tuck
May Tweedie.....................................Florence Edney
Elizabeth Tweedie...................................Gaby Fay
George Appleway..................................John Brewer
Amelia Tweedie...............................Genevieve Tobin
Worthington Smythe...............................Glenn Anders
Wrigley...Leslie Howard
    Acts I, II and III.—In the Morning Room of the Tweedie House
in the Murray Hill District of New York.

Wrigley, being a youthful stranger in New York, gazes deeply into the eyes of Amelia Tweedie during a traffic jam. On love adventure bent thereafter he manages to get into the Tweedie house on Murray Hill by bribing a deputy mortician who is to officiate at a will reading. Once in, he is called upon to impersonate a drunken nephew of the Tweedies, which he does successfully. Falling more deeply in love with Amelia he is, in the end, obliged to confess all and is forgiven.

THE HOUSE OF WOMEN

(40 performances)

A play in three acts by Louis Bromfield. Dramatized from his novel, "The Green Bay Tree." Produced by Arthur Hopkins at the Maxine Elliott Theatre, New York, October 3, 1927.

Cast of characters—

Hattie Tolliver...............................Roberta Bellinger
Julia Shane.......................................Nance O'Neil

Irene Shane..Helen Freeman
Lily Shane..Elsie Ferguson
Henry Bascom......................................Walter Abel
Sarah...Julia Jackson
Arthur Morven....................................Curtis Cooksey
          Acts I, II and III.—In the Shane Drawing Room.
          Staged by Arthur Hopkins.

Julia Shane is living with her daughters, Irene and Lily, in the big Shane house upon which the mills and factories have encroached. Lily, being restless and rebellious, has a child by the young governor of the state but refuses frankly to marry him. Irene, who loves the governor, is so shocked by Lily's adventure that she joins the Catholic church as a protective measure. Years later Lily ventures a second time into love competition with Irene, taking Arthur Marven, a strong young Laborite, away from her sister. The mother, Julia, grown old and philosophical, dies.

AN ENEMY OF THE PEOPLE

(127 performances)

A play in five acts by Henrik Ibsen. Produced by Walter Hampden at Hampden's Theatre, New York, October 3, 1927.

Cast of characters—

Doctor Thomas Stockmann......................Walter Hampden
Mrs. Stockmann....................................Mabel Moore
Petra..Marie Adels
Eilif..Leroy Wade
Morten...George Offerman, Jr.
Peter Stockmann..........................C. Norman Hammond
Morten Kül..W. H. Sams
Hovstad...Dallas Anderson
Billing...Stanley Howlett
Horster..Ernest Rowan
Aslaksen..Cecil Yapp
Mr. Vik...Hart Jenks
A Drunken Man....................................P. J. Kelly
          Acts I and II.—Dr. Stockmann's Sitting-room. Act III.—The
          Editor's Room of the *People's Messenger*. Act IV.—A Room in
          Captain Horster's House. Act V.—Dr. Stockmann's Study. The
          Action Passes in a Town on the South Coast of Norway.
          Staged by Walter Hampden.

Dr. Thomas Stockmann, physician in charge of the baths at a small Norwegian watering place, discovers that the waters are polluted. Promptly preparing a report, he urges his brother, the burgomaster, and other village officials to close the baths at once and clear up the source of supply. The radicals and liberals rally to him until it is discovered the loss to the town the closing of the baths would entail. Then they all turn on the doctor as an enemy of the people. He is left fighting determinedly but utterly disgusted with the "compact majority" that, he is convinced, is always wrong.

SIDEWALKS OF NEW YORK

(112 performances)

A musical comedy; book, lyrics and music by Eddie Dowling and Jimmy Hanley. Produced by Charles Dillingham at the Knickerbocker Theatre, New York, October 3, 1927.

Cast of characters—

August Brewster	Frank Kingdon
Dorothy Brewster	Linda
Mrs. Brewster	Winifred Harris
Hon. Percival Short	Carl Francis
Perkins	T. F. Thomas
Sergeant Daley	Fiske O'Hara
Mrs. O'Brien	Elizabeth Murray
Mickey O'Brien	Dick Keene
Whitey	Chas. Gale
Izzy	Alex Calm
Monk	Lester Hope
Fingers	Geo. Byrne
Goofy	Will Ahern
Muggsy	Henry Dowling
Miss Brown	Carolyn Nolte
Miss Smith	Woodey Lee Wilson
Gertie	Ray Dooley
Parker	Cecil Owen
The Governor	Harry Short
Mamie	Ruby Keeler
Gladys	Gladys Ahern
Willie	William Ahearn
Buckley	Sam Morton
Abe Cohen	Chas. Dale
Moe Zimmermann	Joe Smith
A Policeman	Emil Cote
Three Old Timers	Jim Thornton / Josephine Sabel / Barney Fagan
Ruby	Ruby Keeler
Carrie	Carolyn Nolte
Dolly	Woodey Lee Wilson
Organ Grinder	Edward Maurelli

Staged by Edgar MacGregor.

Gertie is a waif in an orphan asylum. Mickey O'Brien, half orphan, is her pal. August Brewster, millionaire philanthropist, offers a $25,000 prize for the best model tenement housing plan. Mickey draws a plan Gertie sees in her dreams and wins the prize. Brewster also adopts him as a boy of talent. Gertie is desolated, but manages to escape the orphanage and follow Mickey to a happy ending.

YES, YES, YVETTE

(40 performances)

A musical comedy in three acts; book by James Montgomery and William Cary Duncan, based on a story by Frederick S. Isham; lyrics by Irving Cæsar; music by Philip Charig and Ben Jerome. Produced by H. H. Frazee at the Sam H. Harris Theatre, New York, October 3, 1927.

Cast of characters—

Ethel Clark	Brenda Bond
Dick Donnelly	Roland Woodruff
Mr. Van Dusen	Joseph Herbert
S. M. Ralston	Charles Winninger
Mrs. Ralston	Virginia Howell
Yvette Ralston	Jeanette MacDonald
Bishop Doran	Arnold Lucy
Robert Bennett	Jack Whiting
Mabel Terry	Helene Lynd
Sabel Terry	Dorothy Waterman
J. P. Clark	Frederick B. Manatt

Act I.—Drawing-Room of Ralston's Winter Home. Act II.—On Board Ralston's Yacht, Lake Worth. Act III.—Garden of Ralston's Home. The Action is on Washington's Birthday at Palm Beach, Florida.

Staged by H. H. Frazee.

Robert Bennett wagers $30,000 that he can tell the truth, and nothing else but, for twenty-four hours. He wins the bet, but not until he has all but lost his sweetheart, ruined his prospective father-in-law and his own business chances.

ROMANCIN' ROUND

(24 performances)

A dramatic comedy in three acts by Conrad Westervelt. Produced by L. Lawrence Weber at the Little Theatre, New York, October 3, 1927.

Cast of characters—

"Bill" Torlini	Misha Ferenzo
Sally Orton	Beatrice Blinn
Gunner's Mate James Dade, U.S.N.	Theodore Westman
Quartermaster Henry Conboy, U.S.N.	Ralph Morgan
George Spelvin	Francis Herbert
Neena Dobson	Helen MacKellar
Lieut. Commander Ralph Hanscomb, U.S.N.	Fleming Ward
Donald Hillton	C. T. Davis
Lieut. "Bud" Monarhan, U.S.N.	Charles Ritchie

Phillip Dobson.....................................Matt Hanley
Bluejackets.................................. ⎰ Frank Reyman
                                             ⎨ Guy Lorenz
                                             ⎱ Michael Markham
A Stenographer....................................Lucille Keating
      Acts I and II.—"Bill" Torlini's Café. Act III.—Ward Room of a
U. S. Naval Destroyer.
      Staged by C. T. Davis.

Neena Dobson, escaping a rotten father and working out her own salvation in a coffee and sandwich café near the Brooklyn navy yard, is swept off her feet by the casual but effective love-making of Henry Conboy. Having been sold to a Park Avenue millionaire by her father, Conboy tries to protect Neena, is involved in a murder possibility when the rich man dies during an argument, and is finally freed at a court martial.

HIDDEN

(79 performances)

A play in three acts by William Hurlbut. Produced by David Belasco at the Lyceum Theatre, New York, October 4, 1927.

Cast of characters—

Nick Faring......................................Philip Merivale
Ellen Faring.......................................Mary Morris
Violet Cadence.....................................Beth Merrill
Kate Du Plessis................................Marjorie Gateson
Mary...Mary Wall
      Acts I, II and III.—In the Faring House in New York City.
      Staged by David Belasco.

Violet Cadence, living with her sister and brother-in-law, Nick and Ellen Faring, is so desperately in love with Nick that she is unconsciously driven to force Ellen to leave Nick. Later she recognizes her hidden passion, induces Nick to submit to her love and then confesses to Ellen. When the Farings are reunited Violet kills herself.

DRACULA

(261 performances)

A play in three acts. Dramatized by Hamilton Deane and John Balderston from Bram Stoker's novel, "Dracula." Produced by

Horace Liveright at the Fulton Theatre, New York, October 5, 1927.

Cast of characters—

Wells	Nedda Harrigan
Jonathan Harker	Terrence Neill
Dr. Seward	Herbert Bunston
Abraham vanHelsing	Edward Van Sloan
R. M. Renfield	Bernard Jukes
Butterworth	Alfred Frith
Lucy Harker	Dorothy Peterson
Count Dracula	Bela Lugosi

Act I.—Library in Dr. Seward's Sanatorium, at Purley. Act II.—Lucy's Boudoir. Act III.—A Vault.

Staged by Ira Hards.

Lucy Harker, daughter of the physician in charge of a sanatorium near London, is mysteriously anemic. Dr. vanHelsing, a specialist in obscure diseases, suspects a vampire which, according to legend, is an ugly soul that, grave-bound by day, roams the earth at night and sustains its earthly life by sucking the blood of approachable victims. Instituting a search, vanHelsing uncovers Count Dracula as such a vampire and, finding the grave, drives a stake through the heart of the corpse from which he comes.

JACOB SLOVAK

(21 performances)

A play in three acts by Mercedes de Acosta. Produced by Joseph P. Bickerton, Jr., at the Greenwich Village Theatre, New York, October 5, 1927.

Cast of characters—

Josiah Flint	Arthur Hughes
Rev. Ezra Hale	Wyrley Birch
Samuel Jones	Jerome Collamore
Theophilus Brent	Leslie Hunt
Sarah Flint	Beatrice Moreland
Lola Flint	June De Witt
Myra Flint	Miriam Doyle
Jacob Slovak	José Ruben
Kitty	Nancy Baker
Hezekiah Brent	Richard Abbott

Acts I and III.—Parlor-Dining Room of Josiah Flint. Act II.—The Room of Jacob Slovak Over the Store. A Small Town in New England.

Staged by James Light.

Jacob Slovak, a sensitive Pole with a musician's soul, is clerking in an upstate grocery store and being persecuted by the bigoted neighbors. Myra Flint, his boss's daughter, defends him and, though she does not love him, invites his seductive attentions. She would not marry him, however, even as the father of her child, and turns to her own Hezekiah Brent to make an honest woman of her.

MY PRINCESS

(20 performances)

An operetta in two acts, based on a play by Edward Sheldon and Dorothy Donnelly; adaptation and lyrics by Dorothy Donnelly; music by Sigmund Romberg. Produced by Alfred E. Aarons at the Shubert Theatre, New York, October 6, 1927.

Cast of characters—

Faxon	Leo Stark
Mrs. Johnson	Marie Stoddard
Darwin P. Johnson	Donald Meek
Augustus Tonks	Robert Woolsey
Minnie Johnson (Mimosa)	Hope Hampton
Maud Satterlee	Evelyn Darville
Polly Carter	Miriam Wootton
Guiseppe Ciccolini (Chick)	Leonard Ceeley
Mrs. Cruger Ten Eyck	Audrey Maple
Lord Barchester	Vernon Kelso
Peter Loomis	Robert F. Ford
Mitchell	Granville Bates
The Ambassador	Luis Alberni
Palchi	James Moore
Mamma Pompilia	Phyllis Newkirk
Richotto	John Emerson Haynes
Street Singer	Frank Pandolphi

Act I.—Scene 1—Garden of the Johnson Country Home, Long Island. 2—A Room in the Johnson Residence, New York. 3—Reception Hall. Act II.—Scene 1—A Block Party, Cherry Street, New York. 2—Chick's Room in a Tenement. 3—The Consul General's Residence, Washington Square, New York.

Minnie Johnson, trying to break into New York society with papa's oil money, hires an organ-grinding Italian to pose as a prince and her fiancé. Guiseppe is tractable until after the wedding, when he grabs up his heiress and takes her to live in Little Italy. Here Minnie learns to love him in spite of everything and then discovers that he really is a prince.

HIGH GEAR

(20 performances)

A comedy in three acts by Larry E. Johnson. Produced at Wallack Theatre, New York, October 6, 1927.

Cast of characters—

Stella	Edith Gordon
Sylvia Allen	Olga Krolow
Mary Marshall	Shirley Booth
Harvey P. Marshall	William Shelley
Limpy Lanigan	Royal C. Stout
Uncle Elmer	Erman Seavey
Florence Ainslee	Peggy Shannon
Dr. Gerald Niles (Jerry)	Cecil W. Secrest
Officer Shea	Martin Malloy

Acts I, II and III.—The Dining Room of the Marshalls in a Suburb of New York.

Staged by Roy Walling.

Mary Marshall, faced with the problem of deceiving a rich uncle as to the identity of her husband, drafts a second husband from the neighborhood, makes her own husband act as butler and whips up various complications involving a burglar, a policeman and an amorous housemaid.

* PORGY

(217 performances; return engagement 14)

A play in four acts by Dorothy and Du Bose Heyward. Produced by the Theatre Guild at the Guild Theatre, New York, October 10, 1927.

Cast of characters—

Maria	Georgette Harvey
Jake	Wesley Hill
Lily	Dorothy Paul
Mingo	Richard Huey
Annie	Ella Madison
Sporting Life	Percy Verwayne
Serena	Rose MacClendon
Robbins	Lloyd Gray
Jim	Peter Clark
Clara	Marie Young
Peter	Hayes Pryor
Porgy	Frank Wilson
Crown	Jack Carter
Crown's Bess	Evelyn Ellis
A Detective	Stanley de Wolfe
Two Policemen	Hugh Rennie, Maurice McRae
Undertaker	Leigh Whipper
Scipio	Melville Greene
Simon Frazier	A. B. Comathiere
Nelson	G. Edward Brown
Alan Archdale	Edward Fielding
The Crab Man	Leigh Whipper
The Coroner	Garrett Minturn

Acts I, II, III and IV.—In a Charleston, S. C., tenement neighborhood known as Catfish Row, and in a palmetto jungle near by.

Staged by Rouben Hamoulian.

See page 212.

SYNTHETIC SIN

(24 performances)

A play by Frederic and Fanny Hatton. Produced at the 49th Street Theatre, New York, October 10, 1927.

Cast of characters—

Sheila Kelly	Peggy Allenby
Stephen Anthony	Geoffrey Harwood
Cassie	Valarie Valaire
Stage Doorman	Joe Smith
Betty Fairfax	Dorothy Burgess
Brandy Mullane	Ryder Keane
Tad Thompson	Deen Cole
Charlie	Lloyd Sabian
Peter Delardis	Louis D'Arclay
Don Sharon	Alan Birmingham
Marie Duvall	Helene Sinnott
Jim	Harold Chase
Harry	Claude E. Archer
Tim Kelly	Edward Butler

Prologue—A Dressing Room in a Theatre at Easton, Pa. Acts I, II and III.—An Apartment on the West Side, New York.
Staged by Franklyn Underwood.

Betty Fairfax of the South wants to be an actress and goes to New York to try. Following her first failure the playwright tells her she can never hope to act until she has had experience; until she has sinned and suffered, as it were. He offers to help, but Betty prefers to gather experience in her own way. With her faithful maid she rents a room in a "dump," meets many queer people, is nearly seduced by a dope peddler and happily saved by an author seeking atmosphere.

CHAUVE-SOURIS

(80 performances)

An entertainment in nineteen sketches from the Bat Theatre of Moscow. Produced by F. Ray Comstock and Morris Gest at the Cosmopolitan Theatre, New York, October 10, 1927.

Titles of sketches—

Russian Matrimonial Rites	The Abduction from the Seraglio
The Pastrycook's Wife	The Nightingale
A Russian Barcarolle	The Passing Band
Love Waxes . . . and Wanes	Romanesque
The Calvary	La Traviata

The Shooting Gallery	An Eighteenth Century Fan
Grotesque Espagnol	Where Is Our Meyer,
Returning from the War	Where's Himalaya?
Russian Folk Songs	Sarcasm
Love in the Ranks	Round the Hay-Wain

5 O'CLOCK GIRL

(280 performances)

A musical comedy in two acts; book by Guy Bolton and Fred Thompson; music and lyrics by Bert Kalmar and Harry Ruby. Produced by Philip Goodman at the 44th Street Theatre, New York, October 10, 1927.

Cast of characters—

Madame Rosalie	Vahrah Verba
Elsie	Vera Trett
Jane	Brownie Walsh
Maisie	Biddy Wilkenson
Ronnie Webb	Danny Dare
Dorothy	Lola deLille
Ethel	Gloria Gilbert
Marie	Frances Thress
Roy	Al Shaw
Oswald	Sam Lee
Policeman	Carl Judd
Susan Snow	Pert Kelton
Hudgins	Louis John Bartels
Patricia Brown	Mary Eaton
Photographer	Jack Hughes
Gerald Brooks	Oscar Shaw
Mollie	Marian Bonnell
Eugene	Mary Phillips
Priscilla	Marjorie Phillips
Cora Wainwright	Allys Dwyer
Jasper Cobb	Frank McNellis
Jules	Michael Barroy
Billy	Billy Walsh
Footman	Chester Bennett

Act I.—Scene 1—A Block Party Near Beekman Place, New York. 2—On the Telephone. 3—A Room in Gerry's Roof Garden Apartment. 4—The Snow Flake Cleaner's Shop. 5—The Kit Kat Club. Act II.—Scene 1—Outside the Field and Stream Hotel, Southampton, L. I. 2—Cleaner's. 3—Ronnie's Roof Garden Apartment. 4—Eavesdropping on the Telephone. 5—Outside the Church.
Staged by Philip Goodman.

Patricia Brown, working in a cleaner's shop, carries on a telephone flirtation with an unknown young man whom she calls up at 5 o'clock every afternoon. Borrowing fine dresses from the cleaners, she meets him finally, loves him and is happy. At which moment her deception is discovered and all seems lost. But is it? You know very well it isn't.

THE 19TH HOLE

(119 performances)

A play in three acts by Frank Craven. Produced by A. L. Erlanger at the Geo. M. Cohan Theatre, New York, October 11, 1927.

Cast of characters—

George Gill	Homer Barton
Mrs. Chase ("Emmy")	Mary Kennedy
Vernon Chase	Frank Craven
Mrs. Everett	Marion Abbott
Nedda Everett	Kitty Kelly
The Postman	Charles MacDonald
"Mac"	Roy Cochrane
Caddy	Harold Grau
Tom Everett	Howard Sidney
Halliday	Walter Downing
Ben	Beecher Zebbs
Sam Bloomer	Harry Lewellyn
Col. Hammer	Robert Wayne
Walter Trumbull	Barry Walsh
Prof. Albert Bancroft	John Harwood
Mrs. Col. Hammer	Adora Andrews

Act I.—Scene 1—Living Room at the Chases. 2—Practice Tee at the Harmony Golf Club. 3—Men's Locker Room in the Harmony Golf Club. Act II.—At the Chases. Act III.—Scene 1—The First Tee. 2—Chases' Hall.

Staged by Sam Forrest.

Vernon Chase, highbrow author, moves for the summer to a cottage near a golf course. Investigating the game academically, he becomes an addict. Soon he is neglecting his work and irritating his wife. Then he becomes involved in a club scandal, is forced into an important match which he loses on the 19th hole and is threatened with the loss of his membership. Apologies, explanations and peace follow.

WHITE LIGHTS

(31 performances)

A musical comedy in two acts by Paul Gerard Smith and Leo Donnelly; lyrics by Al Dubin and Dolf Singer; music by J. Fred Coots. Produced by James La Penna at the Ritz Theatre, New York, October 11, 1927.

Cast of characters—

Flossie Finch	Rosalie Claire
Danny Miles	Sam Ash

```
Jimmy.............................................Jimmie Steiger
Jean Paige........................................Gertrude Lang
Syd Burke.........................................Leo Donnelly
Toodles...........................................Florence Parker
Teddy Harlow......................................Tammany Young
Billy Winslow.....................................Robert Lynn
Head Waiter.......................................James Barbour
Mercedes..........................................Dorothy Deeder
Mazie.............................................Molly O'Doherty
William Parson....................................James S. Barrett
Mr. Higgins.......................................J. Harry Jenkins
A Maid............................................Edna Skodak
'The Villain".....................................Frank Leslie
Johnny............................................Leonard Scott
George............................................James Howkins
Gordon & King.....................................Gordon & King
       Act I.—At "The Monastery."  Act II.—In a Broadway Theatre.
```

A romance of the theatre filled with conspiring and ambitious actors and a villainous manager or two.

JUST FANCY

(79 performances)

A musical play founded on a play by A. E. Thomas; book by Joseph Santley and Gertrude Purcell; lyrics by Leo Robin; music by Joseph Meyer and Philip Charig. Produced by Joseph Santley at the Casino Theatre, New York, October 11, 1927.

Cast of characters—

```
                          NOW
Griggs............................................George Harcourt
Jimmy.............................................Archie Thomson
Helen.............................................Peggy O'Neill
Jill..............................................Thelmo Edwards
Bobby Vanderpoel..................................Charles Baron
Harold............................................Jack Bauer
Jonsey............................................Frank Sills
Gloria............................................Frances Nevins
Aunt Linda Lee....................................Mrs. Thomas Whiffen
His Royal Highness................................Joseph Santley
Harvey Warren.....................................Harry Kendall

                         THEN
Flora.............................................Peggy O'Neill
Linda Lee Stafford................................Ivy Sawyer
Jane Stafford.....................................Berenice Ackerman
Kay...............................................Thelma Edwards
Geraldine de Peyster..............................Kathryne Burnside
Mrs. Kingsley Stafford............................Peggy Whiffen
Hannibal..........................................Edward Cutler
Sir Calverton Shipley.............................Eric Blore
Jack Warren.......................................John Hundley
Edward Chester....................................Joseph Santley
Hon. Philander J. Wood............................George Harcourt
First Alderman....................................George Spelvin
Second Alderman...................................Willard Charles Fry
Third Alderman....................................Allan Greene
Charlie Van Bibber................................Raymond Hitchcock
```

Lola..Gertrude Lemmon
Chiquita..Mlle. Marguerite
A Gentlemanly Highwayman....................Willard Charles Fry
The Marquis of Karnaby........................H. Reeves-Smith
    Staged by Joseph Santley.

In this adaptation of the comedy "Just Suppose" a prologue is
added in which years ago a former Prince of Wales visited America and fell in love with an American girl whom he later was
forced to give up. As the story is begun by Aunt Linda Lee,
the little old lady whose adventure it was, the scene is blacked
out and the original romance is acted.

THE SPRINGBOARD

(37 performances)

A comedy in three acts by Alice Duer Miller. Produced by
Charles L. Wagner at the Mansfield Theatre, New York, October
12, 1927.

Cast of characters—

Ellen...Mary Marble
Rhoda Brice...................................Elizabeth Risdon
Mary McVittey.................................Madge Kennedy
George Bayard.................................Walter Connolly
Dr. Neal..John Maroney
Victor Hazen.................................Sidney Blackmer
Mrs. Flemming.................................Jane Houston
Mrs. Hazen..................................Adelaide Prince
Secretary.....................................Thaddeus Gray
    Acts I and II.—A Studio Apartment in New York.   Act III.—
The Law Office of George Bayard.
    Staged by T. Daniel Frawley.

Mary McVittey, booked to sail for Europe to study art, is held
in New York by Victor Hazen, a personable youth by whom she
is fascinated at the first meeting. For a year or more after they
are married they live happily, but finally Victor's habit of using
matrimony merely as a springboard from which to leap to other
and more amorous adventures causes Mary to leave him. Victor,
however, refuses to be left. He even acquires typhoid fever and
comes to Mary to be looked after, and she just has to take him
back.

THE MATRIMONIAL BED

(13 performances)

A play in three acts, adapted from the French of T. Mirande and Mouesy-Eon by Seymour Hicks. Produced by A. H. Woods at the Ambassador Theatre, New York, October 12, 1927.

Cast of characters—

A Workman	John Hendricks
Marianne	Winifred Kingston
Corinne	May Vokes
Juliette Corton	Lee Patrick
Sylvaine Jaimet	Vivian Oakland
Gustave Corton	Kenneth Hill
Auguste Chabbonais	Lennox Pawle
Doctor Baudin	Clay Clements
Adolph Noblet	John T. Murray
The Nurse	Amy Dennis
Suzanne Trebel	Kay Strozzi
Gendarme	Fred Sutton

Acts I, II and III.—In Cortons' Apartment in Paris.
Staged by Bertram Harrison.

Adolph Noblet, sauce manufacturer and victim of amnesia, turns up as a hairdresser at the home of Juliette Corton, his former wife. He finds her married again and admits that he, too, is married. Follows an active and comic dispute as to which husband, the old or new, will occupy Juliette's bed the evening of the play.

SKIN DEEP

(8 performances)

A comedy in three acts by Lynn Starling. Produced by M. J. Nicholas at the Liberty Theatre, New York, October 17, 1927.

Cast of characters—

Carl Beman	Sam Wren
Parrish Weston	Reginald Owen
Julia Weston	Chrystal Herne
Mrs. Fanny Matthews	Spring Byington
Aline Corliss	Frances Goodrich
Carrie	Betty Barlow
Corinne Marvel	Marian Warring-Manley
Olivie	Ilse Bloede
Pietro Martini	Guido Nadzo
Joe Zamadi	Ivan Servais
Jasper Dooley	Charles W. Adams

Acts I, II and III.—A Room in Julia Weston's Home on the Outskirts of San Diego.
Staged by Bertram Harrison.

Julia Weston realizes that her husband, Parrish, after seven years of married life is endangered by the return of an old-time sweetheart, Corinne Marvel. In place of registering jealousy and excluding Corinne from her home circle, Julia invites her to come visiting and literally turns Parrish over to her. Within a week Parrish is cured and happy to return to Julia.

OUT OF THE NIGHT

(56 performances)

A mystery comedy in three acts by Harold Hutchinson and Margery Williams. Produced by the Night Producing Co., Inc., at the Lyric Theatre, New York, October 17, 1927.

Cast of characters—

Tom Holland	James Spottswood
Ichabod Blivens	Spencer Charters
Dr. Sarah Walters	Vessie Farrell
Kathryn Smith	Mary Loane
Zelna	Jack Motte
Captain Monahan	Kenneth Loane
Frederick Ayer	Fred E. Strong
Jim Boyle	Carroll Ashburn
Robert Hartwell	Albert Tavernier
Lenita Lenare	Diantha Pattison

Acts I, II and III.—At "Sunny Crest"—Hartwell's Summer Home in Maine.

Robert Hartwell is murdered in his hunting lodge in Maine. There is reason to suspect the entire cast, but late in the evening it is proved that Lenita Lenare, Uncle Robert's second and dissatisfied wife, did the deed because the old gentleman refused to show her where he kept his money.

INTERFERENCE

(224 performances)

A play in three acts by Roland Pertwee and Harold Dearden. Produced by Gilbert Miller at the Empire Theatre, New York, October 18, 1927.

Cast of characters—

Douglas Helder	John Williams
Al Lavery	Philip Tonge
Joseph Craghurst	F. H. Day
Childers	Arthur Lewis
Sir John Marlay, M.D.	Arthur Wontner
Barbara Marlay	Elsie Landford
Faith Marlay	Phœbe Foster
Philip Voaze	A. E. Matthews

Deborah Kane.................................Kathlene MacDonell
Mrs. Barme...Ethel Griffies
Fred...Alfred Ayre
P. C. Cleaver..Colin Hunter
Chief Inspector Haines............................Charles Dalton
Doctor Puttock....................................Horace Sinclair
Mrs. Florence Rooke..............................Winifred Fraser
Detective Sergeant Bourne...........................Oscar Stirling
    SYNOPSIS: Acts I and III.—Sir John Marlay's Consulting Room.
Act II.—Living Room in Deborah Kane's Flat.
    Staged by Campbell Gullan.

Sir John Marlay, eminent London physician, discovers that his
young wife is being blackmailed. Her first husband has turned
up alive when he was supposed to have been killed in the war.
Sir John, deeply in love with Lady Marlay, visits the blackmailer,
a woman named Deborah Kane, with the intention of calling her
off. On a second visit he finds Deborah dead and, fearing his
wife has had a hand in the killing, seeks to establish evidence of
suicide. The suspicious police end by suspecting Sir John, but it
is the returned husband himself who has done the killing and he
is ready to sacrifice himself by confessing.

THE GOOD HOPE

(49 performances)

A drama in four acts by Herman Heijermans, translated from
the Dutch by Lilian Saunders and Caroline Heijermans-Houwink.
Produced by the Civic Repertory Theatre at the Civic Repertory
Theatre, New York, October 18, 1927.

Cast of characters—

Clementine.................................Josephine Hutchinson
Cobus..J. Sayre Crawley
Daantje...Robert Ross
Jelle...John Eldridge
Berend ....Charles McCarthy
Kniertje...Alma Kruger
Jo..Eva Le Gallienne
Clemens Bos......................................Egon Brecher
Geert...Donald Cameron
Marietje.................................Beatrice de Neergaard
Simon.......................................J. Edward Bromberg
Saart...Margaret Love
Mees...Alan Campbell
First Coastguard..............................Harold Moulton
Second Coastguard........................Walter Tupper Jones
Truus...Leona Roberts
Kaps..Harry Sothern
Mathilde..Mary Ward
    Acts I, II and III.—Kniertje's Cottage. Act IV.—Offices of
Clemens Bos.

Clemens Bos, unscrupulous ship owner of Holland, sends his
fishing boat, the Good Hope, to the herring beds when he knows

her hull is rotten. Drafted in her crew are the two sons of the
widow Kniertje, Gaert, bolshevistic and recently thrown out of
the navy, and Berend, younger and cursed with a whimpering fear
of the sea. His mother drives Berend aboard and is conscience
stricken when the boat goes down. Bos fights down the rising
tide of public wrath and subscribes to the fund for the sailors'
survivors.

THE IVORY DOOR

(310 performances)

A play in three acts by A. A. Milne. Produced by Charles
Hopkins at the Charles Hopkins Theatre, New York, October 18,
1927.

Cast of characters—

PROLOGUE

King Hilary	Henry Hull
Prince Perivale	David Vivian
Brand	A. P. Kaye

THE PLAY

King Perivale	Henry Hull
Brand	A. P. Kaye
Anna	Louise Closser Hale
Thora	Helen Chandler
The Chancellor	Ernest Lawford
Jessica	Margaret Gaillard
Anton	John Pote
Old Beppo	Donald Meek
Simeon	William Boren
Count Rollo	Trevor Bland
The Mummer	Edward Nannery
Titus, Soldier of the Guard	Earl McDonald
Carlo, Soldier of the Guard	Trevor Bland
Bruno, Captain of the Guard	Edward Rigby
Princess Lilia	Linda Watkins

A GLIMPSE INTO THE FUTURE

The King	Henry Hull
The Prince	Lawrence Bevans

Acts I, II and III.—At the King's Castle.
Staged by Charles Hopkins.

King Perivale having all his life heard the legend of the ivory
door—that no one who has walked through it has returned alive—
determines before he marries the lovely Princess Lilia to investi-
gate for himself. He must know the truth. Through the door
he goes and, as he suspected, comes out at the end of a dusty
passage. But when he comes back to the castle gates neither the
guard nor any of his intimates of the palace know him. They
insist the devil has bewitched him and made him look like the

king. Only Princess Lilia recognizes him, and to prove her loyalty she, too, walks through the ivory door. Then the people deny them both. So they walk back through the door together and let the people get them another king.

WEATHER CLEAR—TRACK FAST

(63 performances)

A play in three acts by Willard Mack. Produced by Willard Mack at the Hudson Theatre, New York, October 18, 1927.

Cast of characters—

Two Time Kelly	Charles Hill
Chicken Man	Joe Buck
Baltimore Sleeper	Jim Bubbles
Biddy Francis	Tommy Meade
Dick Rotherrock	Frank Lyon
Fern Wilson	Walda Mansfield
Gladiola Jennings	Gertrude Walker
Silent Johnson	William Courtleigh
Johnny Coreleson	Clark Marshall
Alex Cerinac	Joseph Sweeney
Joe McGinn	Joe Laurie, Jr.
Mrs. Upshaw	Florence Earle
Mary Marlo	Janet McLeay
Monte Gilmay	Richard Cubitt
Cy Treadwell	Herbert Ashton

Acts I, II and III.—In and Around Havre de Grace, Maryland Race Track, During the Spring Meetings.
Staged by Willard Mack.

Joe McGinn, one-time popular jockey, is hoping to win enough on one race to quit the track, marry Mary Marlo and buy a newsstand. Silent Johnson, old-time owner, has been saving his best horse, Dr. Patrick, for just the right spot and decides to start him at the Havre de Grace meet. Joe, Johnson's friend, bets his last red on Dr. Patrick, and then Alex Cerinac, villain and horse poisoner, bribes the Johnson jockey to throw the race. Dr. Patrick doesn't win, but Johnson forces Cerinac to stake Joe to the newsstand.

LOVE IN THE TROPICS

(15 performances)

A comedy drama in three acts by Corning White. Produced by Clark Ross at Daly's Theatre, New York, October 18, 1927.

Cast of characters—

Mendoza	Benedict MacQuarrie
Ahola	Lao Nan

Slinkins..Frank Horton
Isabella..Gilda Kreegan
Helen Blanton...Isabel Baring
Hugh Blanton.......................................E. J. Blunkall
Dick Gray...Walter N. Greaza
Wing..Allen Atwell
Wambo..Effingham Pinto
Natto ....Kemii
Lieut. Seymour.....................................Prentice Abbot
    Acts I, II and III.—On the Porch of a Plantation House in the
Philippines.
    Staged by Cyril Raymond.

Hugh Blanton is jealous of his wife Helen, who is loved desperately but honorably by his plantation foreman, Dick Grey, and
pursued by Mendoza, a Spaniard. Blanton dismisses Dick and
when he is later stabbed by Mendoza Dick is accused, but later
cleared.

THE BELT

(29 performances)

A play in three acts by Paul Sifton. Music composed and directed by Heaton Vorse. Produced at the New Playwrights Theatre, New York, October 19, 1927.

Cast of characters—

Flora Thompson......................................Jane Barry
Nancy Thompson....................................Gail De Hart
Jim Thompson....................................Ross Matthews
Bunner...Franchot Tone
Aaronson......................................Benjamin Osipow
The Old Man.....................................George N. Price
Sam..Willard Williams
Bill Vance....................................Lawrence Bolton
George...Herbert Bergman
Frank...Murray Franklin
Fred...Herman Bandes
Harry...Edward Franz
Jack..Edward Buckman
Steve...Benjamin Osipow
A Foreman.......................................Parker Totten
Tracy..Moss Fleisig
Carlson......................................Charles P. Thompson
Jacobson.......................................Irwin Swerdlow
Hendricks......................................Lionel Ferrend
A Police Captain..................................Parker Totten
    Acts I and II.—The Living Room of Jim Thompson's Home. Act
III.—The Belt.
    Staged by Edward Massey.

Jim Thompson, overworked in the automobile factory of the
Old Man in Detroit, sees red when his wife Flora takes up with
a wealthy lover and his daughter is ruined by Bill Vance. He
demands that Vance marry the girl. Vance stirs the Old Man's
factory workers to revolt and they wreck the plant. The revolt
is suppressed and Vance arrested.

THE LOVE CALL

(88 performances)

A musical play in three acts; music by Sigmund Romberg; book by Edward Locke; lyrics by Harry B. Smith. Produced by the Messrs. Shubert in Association with L. Lawrence Weber at the Majestic Theatre, New York, October 24, 1927.

Cast of characters—

Sam Wong	Carlos Mejia
Joe	Frank Erwin
Tim	John L. King
Mike	Bradley F. Lane
Slim Carter	Shep Camp
Lena Keller	Jane Egbert
Tony Mustano	Joseph Macauley
Estrella-Canby-Bonham	Roberta Beatty
Colonel Bonham	William T. Carleton
Henry Canby	W. L. Thorne
Reginald Pargester	Barry Lupino
Doctor Fenlon	Charles Lawrence
Miss McCullagh	Violet Carlson
Mrs. Canby	Alice Fischer
Bonita Canby	Berna Deane
White Horse	William Balfour
Captain Hodgman	John Rutherford
Sergeant Keller	Richard Lee
Lieutenant Denton	John Barker
Red Crow	Frederick Kaufman
Black Hawk	Stanley Jessup
Fiesta Dancers	Veloz and Volanda
Manuel	Frank King

Act I.—The Canby Ranch, Aravaipa Valley, Arizona. Act II.—Colonel Bonham's Quarters at Fort Apache, Arizona. Act III.—The Del Ario Rancho. Time of Play—1869.
Staged by J. C. Huffman.

Musical version of Augustus Thomas's "Arizona" in which Henry Canby, Arizona rancher, is threatened by the Indians stirred to the massacre urge by the renegade Hodgman. Brave Lieutenant Denton gets through the Indian lines and brings the regulars to the rescue of the beleaguered ranchhouse.

IF

(27 performances)

A play in four acts by Lord Dunsany; music by Edmond Rickett. Produced by the Actor-Managers (in association with Sidney Ross) at the Little Theatre, New York, October 25, 1927.

Cast of characters—

Bert	Harry Green
Bill	Charles Cardon
John Beal	Walter Kingsford
Mary Beal	Alice Moffat
Liza	Paula Trueman
Ali	Albert Carroll
Miralda Clement	Margot Lester
The Man in the Corner	Vincent Mallory
Daoud	Albert Carroll
Archie Beal	Harry Green
Ben Hussein	Otto Hulett
Hafiz el Alcolahn	Marc Loebell
Bazzalol	Doe Doe Green
Thoothoobaba	Walter Crumbley
Omar	George Heller
The Sitharpi Player	Marietta Bitter
The Fluboe Player	Beatrice Oliver
Sheik of the Bishareens	Otto Hulett

Bishareens:

The Faithful One	Harvey Cripps
The Suspicious One	John Rynne
The Craven One	Leslie Mahlon
The Leader	Francis Ward

Guests:

A Chinese Notable	Brewster Board
A Lady of Fashion	Nan Marriott-Watson
A Persian Prince	John Ralph Geddis
A Beauty of Burma	Alma Rochford
A Persian Pundit	Vincent Mallory
A Turkish Emissary	Charles Cardon
The Dancer with the Scimitar	J. Blake Scott
The Dancer with the Tymbals	Lily Lubell

Act I.—Scene 1 and 3—A Small Railway Station Near London. 2—John Beal's Suburban Home, "The Acacias." Act IV.—4—A Second-Class Railway Carriage. Act II.—John's Tent in Al Shaldomir. Act III.—1 and 3—The Palace of Al Shaldomir. 2—A Small Street.

Staged by Agnes Morgan.

John Beal has for ten years smarted under the memory of a railway guard's rudeness in making him miss a train. A visiting Yogi gives him a wishing crystal that permits him to recover ten years of his life and see what would have happened if he had caught the train. He would, he learns, have met a girl on the train who would have taken him into Persia to help her collect an inheritance. There he would have ruled a kingdom and a harem and escaped just in time to save his head. Then he wakes up and is satisfied with life as he has found it.

THE TAMING OF THE SHREW

(175 performances)

A comedy in two parts by William Shakespeare. Produced by the Garrick Players at the Garrick Theatre, New York, October 25, 1927.

Cast of characters—

INDUCTION

A Lord	Berresford Lovett
Christopher Sly	C. H. Croker-King
Hostess	Engel Sumner
Page	Teddy Jones
Huntsman	Thomas Donnelly
Valet	Robert Vivian
A Guest	Elda Frankau

Scene—A Country Estate in England.

THE PLAY

Lucentio	Leslie Barrie
Tranio	Reginald Bach
Baptista Minola	Fothringham Lysons
Gremio	Maurice Cass
Hortensio	Gerald Hamer
Katherina Minola	Mary Ellis
Bianca Minola	Betty Linley
Biondelio	John McGovern
Petruchio	Basil Sydney
Grumio	Junius Matthews
Servant to Baptista	Mylom Merriam
Widow	Margaret George
Curtis	Maria Ouspenskaya
Nathanial	Walter Speakman
Gregory	Richard Skinner
Tailor	Seldon Bennett
Pedant	Robert Vivian
Vincentio	Thomas Donnelly
Officer	John Turner
Bridesmaids	Elda Frankau Emily Graham Dorothy Folk

Part I.—In Padua. Part II.—At Petruchio's Country Home; a Public Road; and in Padua.
Staged by H. K. Ayliff.

The Shakespearean comedy in modern dress with Katherine in sports clothes and Petruchio in striped sweater and derby hat. The forced wedding journey is taken in a trick flivver.

THE WASP'S NEST

(31 performances)

A mystery comedy in three acts, by Adelaide Matthews and Martha Stanley. Produced by Clarke Painter, Inc., at Wallack's Theatre, New York, October 25, 1927.

Cast of characters—

Reid Carson	Richard Gordon
Hank	Frank McCormack
Mrs. Neely McDowell	Gertrude Fowler
Ben Hickman	James Boshell
Lillie	Gertrude Clemens
Lafe Curtis	Albert Hyde
Henry Fifield	Albert Phillips
Myrtle	Rose Mary King
Nancy Merrivale	Dorothea Chard

Roger McDowell.......................................Frank Beaston
Steve Nelson..Victor Shipley
Mrs. Emmeline Jessup...........................Louise Sydmeth
    The Scene is in the Entrance Hall of the Old McDowell Mansion
deep in the woods outside of Elliston, Virginia.
Staged by Frank McCormack.

ESCAPE

(173 performances)

A play in nine episodes, by John Galsworthy. Produced by
Winthrop Ames at the Booth Theatre, New York, October 26,
1927.

Cast of characters—

Matt Denant......................................Leslie Howard
The Girl of the Town..........................Henrietta Goodwin
The Plain Clothes Man..........................Edgar B. Kent
The Policeman...................................A. B. I. Imeson
The Other Policeman............................F. Cecil Butler
The Fellow Convict.............................Lawrence Hanray
The Warder.....................................A. B. I. Imeson
The Other Warder...............................Edgar B. Kent
The Shingled Lady.............................Frieda Inescort
The Maid.......................................Cyrena Smith
The Old Gentleman.............................Lawrence Hanray
The Shopkeeper.................................J. P. Wilson
His Wife......................................Lily Kerr
His Sister....................................Ruth Vivian
The Captain..................................St. Clair Bayfield
The Man in Plus Fours.........................Alan Trotter
His Wife......................................Viva Tattersall
The Dartmoor Constable........................Edgar B. Kent
The Laborer..................................St. Clair Bayfield
The Other Laborer.............................F. Cecil Butler
The Farmer...................................Lawrence Hanray
The Little Girl...............................Geraldine Kay
Miss Dora....................................Renee Macready
Miss Grace...................................Lois Heatherley
The Parson...................................Austin Trevor
The Bellringer...............................Alan Trotter
    Prologue—London: Hyde Park. Episode I.—The Prison Farm,
Dartmoor. II.—The Moor in a Fog. III.—Bedroom in an Inn on
the Moor. IV.—An Open Space by the River. V.—The High Moor.
VI.—In the Valley. VII.—A Gravel Pit on the Moor. VIII.—A
Cottage of Gentility. IX.—The Vestry of a Village Church.
Staged by Winthrop Ames.

See page 286.

THE MULBERRY BUSH

(29 performances)

A comedy in three acts by Edward Knoblock. Produced by
Charles Dillingham and A. H. Woods at the Republic Theatre,
New York, October 26, 1927.

Cast of characters—

Anne Lancaster.....................................Isobel Elsom
Edgar Worth.....................................Edwin Nicander
Sylvia Bainbridge..............................Claudette Colbert
Judge...Stanley Harrison
Harry Bainbridge....................................James Rennie
Natalie Dunsmore.....................................Ruth Lyons
    Acts I and III.—Living Room of Anne Lancaster's Villa. Act
II.—Anne's Bedroom.
    Staged by Clifford Brooke.

Harry and Sylvia Bainbridge, three months before their divorce is made absolute, find themselves guests in the home of Anne Lancaster, who hopes to marry Bainbridge when he is free. Discovering that Bainbridge has other plans Anne determines to block his divorce. She locks the Bainbridges in a bedroom for the night, knowing that under the English law this will be accepted as proof of a reconciliation.

IMMORAL ISABELLA?

(60 performances)

A satirical comedy in three acts by Lawton Campbell. Produced by Chamberlain Brown at the Bijou Theatre, New York, October 27, 1927.

Cast of characters—

Talavera, Bishop of Avila.........................Eugene Powers
Ferdinand, King of Aragon.......................Reginald Mason
Beatrice, Marchioness of Moya....................Patricia Barclay
Roderigo..Edward Rose
Isabella, Queen of Castile.........................Frances Starr
Christopher Columbus............................Julius McVicker
A Moor...Gordon Mullen
A Bishop..Joseph Burke
Jester...Irwin Emmer
Indian Brave.......................................Sam Hassan
Indian Women....................Dorothy Paule, Blanche Collins
Lords and Ladies of the Court, Guards, Pages, etc.: Christine Hunter, Sally Matthews, Evelyn Frost, Hilma Moss, Marion Barnett, Dorothy Swick, Mary Hill, Marjorie King, Marie Todd, Raymond Jones, Zola, Zaphir, Willie Trost, Carl Parks, James Lansing, Howard Allen.
    Acts I, II and III.—Isabella's Private Council Chamber in the Alhambra, Granada.
    Staged by Mabel Brownell.

A modern satire in which Isabella is shown to have had amorous designs upon Columbus when she pawned her jewels to finance his voyage of discovery. When Columbus returns to Spain and seeks to resume his affair with Isabella Ferdinand sends him on the second voyage to get rid of him.

BEHOLD THIS DREAMER

(56 performances)

A paradox in five scenes from the novel by Fulton Oursler. Dramatized by Fulton Oursler and Aubrey Kennedy. Produced by George C. Tyler at the Cort Theatre, New York, October 31, 1927.

Cast of characters—

Clara Turner	Patricia O'Hearn
Charley Turner	Glenn Hunter
Mr. Harris	William Lorenz
Constance	Leonore Sorsby
John Strickler	Dodson Mitchell
Piggles	J. J. Hyland
Melodie	Sylvia Field
Dr. Ephraim Tanneyday, M.D.	Thomas A. Wise
Harold Blessings, One by One	Edward Donnelly
D. D. D.	James Seeley

Scenes 1 and 4.—The Home of Charley Turner. 2 and 3.—A Cottage on the Pikesville Road. 5.—Arcady.

Staged by Frederick Stanhope.

Charley Turner, a sensitive youth, married to a shrewish small town girl, amuses himself plaguing her and her family with his dreams of being an artist. His father-in-law, thinking him a little crazy, has him committed to a sanatorium. In the sanatorium Charley paints a picture that wins a $5,000 prize, takes the money and returns home to capitalize his fame. Again he can't stand the family and runs back to the sanatorium, realizing that in a mad world an insane asylum is the only place a sane man can live in peace.

THE ARABIAN

(32 performances)

A melodrama in three acts by Gordon Kean. Produced by Barbour-Conrad & Bryant at the Eltinge Theatre, New York, October 31, 1927.

Cast of characters—

Waiter	Richard Ranier
Colonel Gordon	Barry Whitcomb
Captain Fenway	Hugh Huntley
Major Cromwell	Paul McGrath
Diane	Ellis Baker
Abd el Rey	Walker Whiteside

Hassenen..J. Irving White
Sharik.......................................John J. Burns, Jr.
Ta Urt...Michael Rale
Yezic...Edward Colebrook
Jarrida..Franc Hale
Myrza.......................................Lorayne Carpenter
Amrah.. Maude Allan
Nitah......................................Camelia Campbell
Bacca..Carl Vose
    Act I.—Corner of a Roof Top Café in Cairo. Acts II and III.—
Interior of Abd el Rey's Tent in the Desert.
    Staged by Rollo Lloyd.

Abd el Rey, an Arabian with an English education, hates England because of society's treatment of his English wife. Returned to the desert he guides an English regiment into the trap of a desert bandit and, preceding them there, is about to order their massacre when he discovers the English girl who pleads for them is his own daughter.

INK

(15 performances)

A satirical melodrama in three acts by Dana Watterson Greeley. Produced by Charles L. Wagner at the Biltmore Theatre, New York, November 1, 1927.

Cast of characters—

Hester Trevelyan...................................Clara Blandick
Hal Somerset ....Robert Hyman
Jack Davis.......................................John H. Dilson
Franklin W. Jerome.............................Charles Richman
Clarence Jerome ....Dwight Frye
Henrietta Scott..................................Isabel Randolph
Robert Buchanan..............................William Harrigan
Mrs. Jerome.................................Sue MacManamy
Jim Reynolds.................................. Brandon Evans
"Bull" Taggart....................................Leo Kennedy
Jeanne Keenan.......................................Kay Strozzi
Office Boy.......................................Carlyle Moore
    Acts I, II and III.—The Office of the Managing Editor of the
"Chronicle."
    Staged by T. Daniel Frawley.

Franklin Jerome, made publisher of the newspaper his rich wife owns, becomes involved in a scandal with an actress, who leaves him drunk and asleep in her bed while she goes riding with a bootlegger. Their car kills a woman and a child. The crusading managing editor of the paper, ignorant of the publisher's association with the actress, prints the story. Exposure of the publisher threatens but he is saved by the flight of the bootlegger.

TAKE MY ADVICE

(39 performances)

A comedy by Elliott. Produced by William Caryl at the Belmont Theatre, New York, November 1, 1927.

Cast of characters—

Bud Weaver.....................................Raymond Guion
Ann Weaver.......................................Vivian Tobin
Jim Thayer.......................................Ray Walburn
Kerry Van Kind....................................Herbert Yost
John Weaver....................................Lawrence Grattan
Mrs. Weaver.......................................Lucia Moore
Bradley Clement..................................Ralph Morgan
Marella Scott......................................Mary Stills
      Acts I, II and III.—The Living Room of Mr. and Mrs. Weaver's
Suburban Home.

Prof. Bradley Clement, dropping in unexpectedly upon the Weaver household, saves Bud from an actress, and Ann, his sister, from a fake dramatic school and Mrs. Weaver from an oil-stock salesman. As a reward he wins the right to love and support Ann the rest of her life.

JOHN

(11 performances)

A play in five scenes by Philip Barry. Produced by The Actors' Theatre, Inc., at the Klaw Theatre, New York, November 2, 1927.

Cast of characters—

Nathaniel.......................................William Adams
Aaron Hanan......................................Ralph Roeder
Old Man...Luther J. Adler
Simon...Marshall Vincent
Andrew..Lawrence Leslie
Dan...Benjamin Hoogland
John..Jacob Ben-Ami
James...Richard Nichols
Ethan..Ben Smith
Herodias......................................Constance Collier
Antipas..George Graham
First Guard.....................................Gordon Gunniss
Second Guard.....................................Gordon McRae
John Zebedee......................................James Todd
Salome..Anna Duncan
A Dancing Master..................................Harry Redding
Joel...Donald Lee
Pete ....Albert West

A Prison Official.................................George White
    Scenes 1 and 2—The Tent, Near Jericho. 3—The Tent, Near
Ænon. 4—The Living-Hall at Machærus. 5—The Guard Hall at
Machærus.
    Staged by Guthrie McClintic.

The time is the year 30, when John was encamped near Jericho, waiting wonderingly and impatiently for the coming of Jesus, whom he had baptized and recognized as holy. Jesus sets up a rival camp and, preaching the gospel of peace and humility, takes the crowds away from John. Still John will not listen to the temptings of Herodias, who would place him in command of her armies to oppose Jesus. He is imprisoned and later beheaded.

* A CONNECTICUT YANKEE

(266 performances)

A musical adaptation of Mark Twain's story in two acts. Book by Herbert Fields; music by Richard Rodgers; lyrics by Lorenz Hart. Produced by Lew Fields and Lyle D. Andrews at the Vanderbilt Theatre, New York, November 3, 1927.

Cast of characters—

IN THE PROLOGUE

Albert Kay.......................................Gordon Burby
Gerald Lake......................................Jack Thompson
Marvin...William Norris
Martin...William Gaxton
Arthur Pendragos.................................Paul Everton
Fay Morgan.......................................Nana Bryant
Alice Carter.....................................Constance Carpenter
Lawrence Lake....................................William Roselle

IN THE PLAY

Sir Kay the Seneschal............................Gordon Burby
The Yankee.......................................William Gaxton
The Demoiselle Alisande La Carteloise............Constance Carpenter
King Arthur of Britain...........................Paul Everton
Sir Launcelot of the Lake........................William Roselle
Sir Galahad......................................Jack Thompson
Merlin...William Norris
Maid Angela......................................Dorothy Roy
Mistress Evelyn La Belle-Ans.....................June Cochrane
Queen Morgan Le Fay..............................Nana Bryant
Queen Guinevere..................................Celeste Dueth
Sir Bors...G. Douglas Evans
Sir Sagramor.....................................John Morton
Sir Tristan......................................Chester Bree
    Prologue—Grand Ball Room of a Hotel in Hartford, Conn. Act
I.—Scene 1—On the Road to Camelot. 2—Courtyard of the Castle
of King Arthur. Act II.—Scene 1—A Corridor of the Royal Fac-
tory. 2—On the Road from Camelot. 3—The Palace of Queen Mor-
gan Le Fay. Epilogue—The Gardens of the Hotel in Hartford.
    Staged by Alexander Leftwich.

A musical version of Mark Twain's "A Yankee at King Arthur's Court," generously jazzed, in which Martin, flirting with

his true love, Alice Carter, at his bachelor supper, is struck over
the head with a champagne bottle by his bride-to-be, Fay Morgan. As a result of the blow he dreams that he is at King Arthur's court where he brings about a modern industrial revolution.

THE WICKED AGE

(19 performances)

A comedy drama in three acts by Anton Scibilia. Produced by
Anton Scibilia at Daly's Theatre, New York, November 4, 1927.

Cast of characters—

Aunt Elizabeth	Emily Francis
Ruth Carson	Doris Haslett
Peggy McShane	Peggy Doran
Willie Weller	Hassell Brooks
Gloria Carson	Ruth Hunter
Robert Carson	Hal Clarendon
John Ferguson	Francis Reynolds
Warren Hathaway	Carroll Daly
The Count	Robert Bentley
Mrs. Martha Carson	Augusta Perry
Evelyn ("Babe") Carson	Mae West
Bob Miles	David Newell
Al Smalley	Hub White
Tom Hathaway	William Langdon
Jack Stratford	Raymond Jarno
Ray Dempster	Harry W. Williams
George Smith	Harold Leonard
Lou Ginsberg	Harry W. Carter
Gladys Blake	Louise Kirtland
Nell Brown	Ethel Maynard
Norma Faire	Wilva Davis
Polly Acker	Phœbe Otis
Annie Lawrence	Billy LeSuer
Mack Hadden	Hal Findlay
Bert Astor	Arthur Boran
Stephany Joy	Veritza Winter
Chauffeur	Pete Segreto
Jazzbo Williams	Mike Jackson
Henry Lee	Thomas Morris
Jeannette	Georgia Clark
Dick Adams	Harry W. Williams
Henry Arthur	Harold Leonard

Act I.—Episodes 1 and 2—The Home of Robert Carson, Bridge-
town, N. J. Act II.—Moonlight Park. Act III.—"Babe" Carson's
Apartment in New York City.
Staged by Edward Elsner.

Evelyn (Babe) Carson, a plump flapper of Bridgetown, N. J.,
brings her gin-toting roadhouse friends to her home and, in the
absence of her guardian, stages such an orgy as befits the younger
degeneration. Carson unexpectedly returns and orders Babe not
to darken his doorstep again. Two weeks later Babe wins the
local bathing beauty contest and makes thousands of dollars
endorsing kidney and liver ads.

THE FANATICS
(16 performances)

A play in three acts by Miles Malleson. Produced by A. H. Woods at the 49th Street Theatre, New York, November 7, 1927.

Cast of characters—

Mr. Freeman	Paul Gill
Mrs. Freeman	Nellie Malcolm
John	Richard Bird
Gwen	Joan MacLean
Colin Mackensie	George Barraud
Frances Sewell	Rose Hobart
Margaret Heal	Ann Andrews
Toby	Anita Kerry
Rosie	Eileen Beldon

Acts I, II and III.—Mr. Freeman's House Near Lancaster Gate, London.

Staged by Leon M. Lion.

John Freeman, disillusioned by the war, is for changing the world, particularly in the matter of its marriage customs. Two people should not marry for good and all until they know their love is right. He not only preaches this to the world but to his chaste and chilly sweetheart. And when she will have none of such experiments he takes unto himself a mistress, is found out by his family and would have been disciplined if he had not left home. John's sister, Gwen, also adopts his theories and goes to live with her sweetheart previous to marrying him.

THE STAIRS
(8 performances)

A drama in three acts by Rosso Di San Secondo, adapted by Dario Forza. Produced by Throckmorton, Light & Rockmore at the Bijou Theatre, New York, November 7, 1927.

Cast of characters—

First Maid	Mary True
Second Maid	Madeline King
Janitor	Lance Burritt
Gianfranchi	Granville Bates
Manuel Barritos	Luis Alberni
Third Maid	Patricia Barron
Mrs. Demetti	Claire Townshend
First Scholar	Jack Horner
Second Scholar	Lister Hayward
Mrs. Cordella	Eleanor Wesselhoeft

The Porter......................................Sointu Syrjala
A Doctor......................................James Malaidy
Terpi......................................Lester Lonergan
Bank Clerk......................................Russel Wright
Nina......................................Nadea Hall
Motorcyclist......................................Joseph Baird
First Poor Relation......................................Martin Wolfson
Second Poor Relation......................................Moss Fleisig
Vitalbi......................................James F. Kelly
Martha Vitalbi......................................Ethel Cunningham
Concettina Vitalbi......................................Aura Hoffman
Richard Vitalbi......................................Joe Colgan
Clothilde......................................Dorothy Sands
Carengo......................................Goldwin Patten
Sbrani......................................Clarence Derwent
Commissary of Police......................................Joseph Baird
Act I.—Landing in an Apartment House. Acts II and III.—Living
Room of Mrs. Inez Lodoletti's Apartment. Place—Any Busy City.
Staged by James Light.

Clothilde, neglected by her husband, Terpi, ran away with an
Argentine dancer, Manuel Barritos. Years later Terpi found her
in a café and, under threat of harming her daughter, forced her to
live in one of his apartments as a prostitute by way of revenge.
She kills herself in the end.

* COQUETTE

(253 performances)

A play in three acts by George Abbott and Ann Preston
Bridgers. Produced by Jed Harris at the Maxine Elliott Theatre,
New York, November 8, 1927.

Cast of characters—

Jimmie Besant......................................Andrew Lawlor, Jr.
Dr. Besant......................................Charles Waldron
Norma Besant......................................Helen Hayes
Stanley Wentworth......................................G. Albert Smith
Betty Lee Reynolds......................................Una Merkle
Mr. Wentworth......................................Frederick Burton
Julia......................................Abbie Mitchell
Michael Jeffery......................................Elliot Cabot
Joe Reynolds......................................Gaylord Pendleton
Ethel Thompkins......................................Phyllis Tyler
Ed Forsythe......................................Frank Dae
Acts I, II and III.—A Small Town in the South, in the Living
Room of Dr. Besant's Home.
Staged by George Abbott.

See page 146.

AND SO TO BED

(189 performances)

A comedy in three acts by James B. Fagan, being a sequel to
the diary of Samuel Pepys. Produced by James B. Fagan under

the direction of Lee Shubert at the Shubert Theatre, New York, November 9, 1927.

Cast of characters—

Sue	Moon Carroll
Boy to Pepys	Emlyn Williams
Samuel Pepys	Wallace Eddinger
Doll	Roberta Brown
Mrs. Knight	Mary Grey
A Watchman	Carfax Turl
Julia	Mary Newnham Davis
Pelling	A Henderson Storie
Pelham Humfrey	Glen Byam-Shaw
W. Cæsar	Luigi Salvatore Calbi
Mrs. Pierce	Beryl Freeman
Mrs. Knepp	Mary Robson
Mrs. Pepys	Yvonne Arnaud
Lettice	Gemma Fagan
Prodgers	Gyles Isham
Charles II	Charles Bryant

Acts I and III.—A Room in Pepys' House in Seething Lane, London. Act II.—Mrs. Knight's Lodging in Gray's Inn Fields.
Staged by James B. Fagan.

The day after he laid down the diary he had kept so faithfully for nine years Samuel Pepys assisted in the rescue of the attractive Mistress Knight from the attack of a cutpurse. Calling upon the lady later to receive her thanks Samuel's visit is interrupted, first by the King and then by the jealous Mrs. Pepys. Hiding in a chest Samuel is forced to listen to the King make love to Mrs. Pepys, and later is at some pains to explain his own presence at Mistress Knight's.

NIGHTSTICK

(52 performances; 32 return engagements)

A melodrama in three acts, by John Wray, the Nugents and Elaine Sterne Carrington. Produced by Crosby Gaige at the Selwyn Theatre, New York, November 10, 1927.

Cast of characters—

Pete Manning	Charles Kennedy
Mary Manning	Judith Lowry
Joan Manning	Lee Patrick
Tommy Glennon	Thomas Mitchell
Danny McGann	Raymond Hackett
Daisy Thomas	Kathryn Givney
Buck Backman	Harry Stubbs
Charles "Chick" Williams	John Wray
Jack Trask	William Tennyson
Soft Malone	Edgar Nelson
Toots	Edna White
Nita	Velma Forrest
Blake	Victor Kilian
Ed Brown	Harry R. Irving

Act I.—Dining Room of Pete Manning's Home, Tenth Avenue, New York. Act II.—Scene 1—Detectives' Room, Station House. 2—Room in Buck Backman's Place in the Forties. Act III.—A Cabin in the Catskills.
Staged by Crosby Gaige.

Joan Manning, a policeman's daughter, is suspicious of all the men hunters. To prove her faith in "Chick" Williams' promise to reform she marries him when he gets out of prison, breaking her engagement to her detective sweetheart, Tommy Glennon. Glennon keeps after Williams and finally fastens a second murder on him, capturing him in an Adirondack cabin.

SPELLBOUND

(24 performances)

A play in three acts by Frank Vosper. Produced by George C. Tyler at the Earl Carroll Theatre, New York, November 14, 1927.

Cast of characters—

Mrs. Underwood	Elizabeth Patterson
Harold Carter	Campbell Gullen
Mr. Underwood	O. P. Heggie
Ethel	Pauline Lord
Ivy Underwood	Cecile Dixon
Dickie Miles	Charles Courtneidge
Rowlie Bateson	Donn Cook
Mrs. Bateson	Alison Skipworth
A Neighbor	Edward Broadley
First Wardress	Grace Mills
Second Wardress	Gladys Hopetown
Third Wardress	Gene Magnus
The Warden	Richard Bowler

SYNOPSIS: Act I.—The Underwoods' Parlour. Acts II and III.—The Carters' Sitting Room.
Staged by O. P. Heggie.

Ethel Underwood, highly imaginative and very unhappy at home, marries Harold Carter to escape her shrewish mother and because Carter promises her a trip to India. Carter fails to keep his promise, and goads Ethel to a deep hatred. She, without the courage to avenge her own wrongs, leads her young boarder, Rowlie Bateson, on to murder Carter. Ethel and Bateson both go to the gallows.

THE MARQUISE

(80 performances)

A play in three acts by Noel Coward. Produced by Kenneth MacGowan and Sidney Ross at the Biltmore Theatre, New York, November 14, 1927.

Cast of characters—

The Compte, Raoul De Vriaac................Arthur Byron
Adrienne..Madge Evans
Jacques Rijar................................Theodore St. John
Esteban, El Duce De Santaguano................Reginald Owen
Miguel...Rex O'Malley
Father Clement...............................Harry Lillford
The Marquise, Eloise De Kestournel................Billie Burke
Alice..Dorothy Tree
Hubert..William Kershaw
    Acts I, II and III.—In the Château De Vriaac, a Few Hours from
Paris, During an Autumn in the Eighteenth Century.
    Staged by David Burton.

Eloise De Kestournel comes back to the home of her former protector, the Compte De Vriaac, hoping to see the daughter she had borne him eighteen years before. She finds the girl, Adrienne, about to marry Miguel, who also happens to be a son of the marquise and therefore Adrienne's half brother. Eloise's confession and explanation save the situation and the Compte De Vriaac, his old love reawakened, makes an honest woman of her.

NEW YORK

(8 performances)

A melodrama in three acts, by Samuel Ruskin Golding. Produced by Isaiah Leebove at the Mansfield Theatre, New York, November 14, 1927.

Cast of characters—

Mary Conway.................................Viola Fortescue
George Conway.............................John M. Sullivan
Madeline Conway...............................Ruth Shepley
Sanchez..George Probert
Mrs. Herbert Van Elton.........................Ruth Mason
O'Brien..George Lewis
"Lefty" Jackson................................Henry Ashby
Alma Lavelle...................................Mabel Acker
Herbert Van Elton.........................Geo. Drury Hart
Edmund Crane..............................George MacQuarrie
Neil Kent...................................John D. Seymour
Christine...............................Marguerite Osborne
    Act I.—Scene 1—Living Room at the Conways. 2—Police Headquarters. 3—A Bedroom in a West 50th Street Flat. Acts II and III.—Living Room in Madeline's Apartment, Cathedral Towers, New York.
    Staged by Paul Dickey.

An attempt to justify the good heart and honest intentions of a kept woman.

IOLANTHE

(11 performances)

An operetta; words by W. S. Gilbert; music by Arthur Sullivan. Revived by Winthrop Ames at the Royale Theatre, New York, November 14, 1927.

Cast of characters—

Lord Chancellor......................................Fred Wright
Earl of Mountararat..................................John Barclay
Earl Tolloller...................................J. Humbird Duffey
Private Willis................................William C. Gordon
Strephon...William Williams
The Train-Bearer.............................George C. Lehrian
Queen of the Fairies.................................Vera Ross
Iolanthe...Bettina Hall
Celia...Virginia Fox
Leila..Suissabell Sterling
Fleta...Paula Langlen
Phyllis...Lois Bennett
    Staged by Winthrop Ames.

First revived by Winthrop Ames the season of 1925-26. Added to repertory each year since.

ARTISTS AND MODELS

(151 performances)

A musical revue in two acts; music by Harry Akst and Maurie Rubens; lyrics by Benny Davis; additional lyrics by J. Keirn Brennan, Jack Osterman and Ted Lewis. Produced by the Messrs. Shubert at the Winter Garden Theatre, New York, November 15, 1927.

Principals engaged—

Florence Moore   Ted Lewis
Nayan Pearce   Jack Osterman
Catherine Gallimore   Jack Pearl
Gladys Wheaton   Jack Squires
Marietta O'Brien   Jan Oyra
Margie Evans   John McDowell
Eleanor Brooks   Eddie Chester
Lucille Arnold   Harry O'Neal
Veloz and Yolanda   William Davis
King and King   Walter Johnson
Jscherey and Hully   Chauncey Parsons
    Staged by J. C. Huffman.

TIA JUANA

(7 performances)

A melodrama in three acts by Chester DeVonde and Kilbourn Gordon. Produced by Kilbourn Gordon at the Bijou Theatre, New York, November 15, 1927.

Cast of characters—

Sprutt	Frederic Burt
Juata	Mabel Colcord
Maxwell	Paul Wilson
Chief	Harry D. Southard
Flop	Clyde Dilson
Skeleton	Willard S. Robertson
Measles	Walter Horton
Marcelle D'Arcy	Edna Bennett
Evetta	Jeannette Fox-Lee
Bill Knapp	Paul Wright
Fayette	Carolyn Ferriday
Dick Stone	Harold Elliott
Emilio	Emilio A. Bonsilau
Hortez	Salvatore Casenza
Sancho	John Somme
Fragone	Tino Sibello
An Officer	George Amesbury
Judge Stone	Charles Hammond

Acts I, II and III.—In Sprutt's Place, Tia Juana, Mexico.
Staged by the authors.

Sprutt, out of San Quentin prison, seeks to revenge himself upon Judge Stone, who sentenced him, by luring the judge's son, Dick, and Dick's sweetheart, Fayette, into Tia Juana. There, when Dick refuses to help smuggle Chinese across the border, Sprutt frames a charge of murder against him. Bill Knapp, whose bride Sprutt tried to steal, finally does for Sprutt.

THE KING CAN DO NO WRONG

(13 performances)

A melodrama in three acts by F. S. Merlin. Produced by James W. Elliott at the Masque Theatre, New York, November 16, 1927.

Cast of characters—

Princess Maria	Jean Hartryce
Casper	Leonard Doyle
José	Kenneth Manion
Baron Almeria	Felix Krembs
Baron Reus	Lionel Atwill
General Moro	Edwin Mordant
Dr. López	Leigh Lovel
Manuel	Edward Forbes
Prince Ferdinand	Guy Phillips

```
Alfred Langdon.....................................Alfred Frith
Richard Barton Ware.............................Larry Fletcher
Baroness Almeria.................................Leona Hogarth
Pedro.............................................Albert Froom
His Majesty, the King..........................Edward De Tisne
Kitty Ware........................................Ellen Dorr
```
Act I.—A Corridor in the Summer Palace. 2—Prince Ferdinand's
Apartments. Acts II and III.—The Prince's Apartments.
Staged by the author.

The Crown Prince of a mythical South American kingdom having been murdered the Baron Reus, chief of the secret service, is set on the trail of the murderer. He is violently opposed by the Baron Almeria who is in sympathy with the crown's enemies and whose wife Baron Reus has always loved. Revolution springs from the investigation, the country goes republican, Reus is elected president, Almeria is killed and his widow marries the people's choice.

MIDSUMMER NIGHT'S DREAM

(23 performances)

Comedy by William Shakespeare. Produced by Max Reinhardt (direction Gilbert Miller) at the Century Theatre, New York, November 17, 1927.

Cast of characters—

```
Theseus, Duke of Athens.........................Paul Hartmann
Hippolyta, Queen of the Amazons.................Dagny Servaes
Philostrate.....................................Dietrich Jenke
Egeus...........................................Othmar Biegler
Hermia...........................................Maria Solveg
Lysander.........................................Hans Thimig
Demetrius.....................................Hermann Thimig
Helena........................................Rosamond Pinchot
Quince (Squenz).................................Arnold Korff
Snug (Schnock).........................Eduard Von Winterstein
Bottom (Zettel)................................Otto Wallburg
Flute (Flaut)....................................Hans Moser
Snout (Schnauz).................................Ernst Matray
Starveling (Schlucker)..........................Erich Schilling
First Fairy.......................................Tilly Losch
Sprite .......................................Harald Kreutzberg
Puck..........................................Wladimir Sokoloff
Oberon, King of the Fairies....................Alexander Moissi
Titania, Queen of the Fairies.....................Lili Darvas
```

CHARACTERS IN THE INTERLUDE
```
Prologue.........................................Arnold Korff
Lion.....................................Eduard Von Winterstein
Pyramus.........................................Otto Wallburg
Thisbe...........................................Hans Moser
Wall............................................Ernst Matray
Moonshine......................................Erich Schilling
A Clown.....................................Harald Kreutzberg
```
Act I.—Scene 1—The Palace of Theseus. 2—A Room in Quince's House. 3—A Wood Near Athens. Act II.—The Wood Near Athens. Act III.—Palace of Theseus.

"Midsummer Night's Dream" was given in its German version, including an accompaniment of the Mendelssohn score. During the Reinhardt engagement the plays presented included the Von Hofmannstahl version of the old English morality, "Everyman," with Alexander Moissi in the name part; George Beuchner's "Danton's Tod," with Paul Hartmann as Danton; Frantisek Langer's "Peripherie"; Goldoni's "Servant of Two Masters," and Tolstoi's "He Is to Blame for Everything," as a double bill.

MUCH ADO ABOUT NOTHING

(22 performances)

A comedy by William Shakespeare in three acts. Produced by the American Laboratory Theatre, New York, November 18, 1927.

Cast of characters—
```
Don Pedro, Prince of Arragon.....................Robert Gordon
Don John.......................................Herbert Gellendre
Claudio............................................Francis Burk
Benedick.......................................George Macready
Leonato..........................................Joaquin Souther
Balthasar.........................................Grover Burgess
Conrade............................................Harold Hecht
Borachio..........................................Donald Hartman
Friar Francis.....................................Robert Parsons
Dogberry..........................................Thomas Hayes
Verges.............................................Lester Ford
A Sexton..........................................Greely Curtis
Hero............................................Martha Johnson
Beatrice.........................................Blanch Tancock
Margaret.........................................Frances Simpson
Ursula............................................Frances Wilson
Watches.............Katherine Squire and Mariane F. Wetzel
   Action Takes Place in Messina.
   Staged by Richard Boleslavsky.
```
The first revival of the Laboratory Theatre's season.

THE DOCTOR'S DILEMMA

(115 performances)

A play in five acts by Bernard Shaw. Produced by the Theatre Guild at the Guild Theatre, New York, November 21, 1927.

Cast of characters—
```
Redpenny.........................................Charles Romano
Emmy..............................................Helen Westley
Sir Colenso Ridgeon..............................Baliol Holloway
Dr. Schutzmacher................................Morris Carnovsky
```

```
Sir Patrick Cullen...............................Dudley Digges
Mr. Cutler Walpole............................ Earle Larimore
Sir Ralph Bloomfield Bonington.....................Ernest Cossart
Dr. Blenkinsop...................................Henry Travers
Jennifer Dubedat...............................Lynn Fontanne
Louis Dubedat....................................Alfred Lunt
Minnie Tinwell.................................Phyllis Connard
Newspaper Man..................................... Philip Leigh
Secretary........................................Charles Romano
A Waiter........................................Edward Hartford
```
　　Act I.—Sir Colenso Ridgeon's Consulting Room, London.　Act II.
—Terrace at the Star and Garter, Richmond.　Acts III and IV.—
Dubedat's Studio.　Act V.—In a Bond Street Picture Gallery.
Staged by Dudley Digges.

Sir Colenso Ridgeon, eminent British surgeon, has been knighted for his discovery of a tuberculosis serum. His hospital wards are full, his staff overworked when Jennifer Dubedat pleads with him to accept her artist husband, Louis, as a patient. Ridgeon, interested in Dubedat's work and also in Mrs. Dubedat, hesitates. Later faced with the choice of helping either the artist genius, who is utterly a waster morally, or his old classmate, Blenkinsop, Sir Colenso turns Dubedat over to an unskillful associate. The artist dies and Sir Colenso inherits the widow's utter contempt.

THE RACKET

(119 performances)

A play in three acts by Bartlett Cormack. Produced by Alexander McKaig at the Ambassador Theatre, New York, November 22, 1927.

Cast of characters—

```
Sergeant Sullivan.....................................Mal Kelly
Pratt...........................................Willard Robertson
Miller.........................................Hugh O'Connell
Lieutenant Gill....................................Harry English
Detective Sergeant Delaney.....................Fred Irving Lewis
Patrolman Johnson...........................G. Pat Collins
Assistant State's Attorney Welch...............Romaine Callender
Turck.............................................Harry McCoy
Captain McQuigg..................................John Cromwell
Dave Ames........................................Norman Foster
Joe.............................................Edward Eliscu
Irene Hayes.....................................Marion Coakley
Clark...............................................Jack Clifford
Alderman Kublacek...............................Louis Frohoff
Sam Meyer.........................................Ralph Adams
An Unidentified Man........................Edward G. Robinson
A Patrolman...................................Charles O'Connor
Another Patrolman.............................. Mike Flanagan
Glick......... ....................................Charles Peyton
Sergeant Schmidt................................C. E. Smith
```
　　Acts I, II and III.—An Outlying Chicago Police Station in Early November.

See page 313.

* FUNNY FACE

(236 performances)

A musical comedy in two acts; book by Fred Thompson and Paul Gerard Smith; music by George Gershwin; lyrics by Ira Gershwin. Produced by Alex A. Aaronns and Vinton Freedley at the Alvin Theatre, New York, November 22, 1927.

Cast of characters—

Dora	Betty Compton
June	Gertrude McDonald
"Frankie"	Adele Astaire
Jimmy Reeve	Fred Astaire
"Dugsie" Gibbs	William Kent
Chester	Earl Hampton
Herbert	Victor Moore
Peter Thurston	Allen Kearns
Sergeant of Police	Ted MacLean
Hotel Clerk	Edwin Hodge
Porter	Walter Munroe
Bell Hop	Dorothy Jordon
Ritz Quartette	

Act I.—Scenes 1 and 3—Living Room of Jimmy Reeve's House. 2—Outside Peter Thurston's House. Act II.—Scene 1—The Canoe Inn, Lake Wapatog, N. J. 2—A Suite at the Paymore, Atlantic City. 3—The Ward Room. 4—The Two Million Dollar Pier.

A singing and dancing romp in which "Frankie" induces Peter Thurston to help her steal back the pearls her guardian, Jimmy Reeve, has hidden from her. Dugsie and Herbert, comic burglars, are also after the pearls.

TAKE THE AIR

(206 performances)

A musical comedy in two acts; book and lyrics by Anne Caldwell and Gene Buck; airs by Dave Stamper. Produced by Gene Buck at the Waldorf Theatre, New York, November 22, 1927.

Cast of characters—

"Mink"	Al Ochs
"Monte"	Hugh Bennett
Gloria	Geneva Mitchell
Marguerite	Audrey Berry
"Happy" Hokum	Will Mahoney
"Goldie"	Rose King
Lieutenant Sullivan	Bud Pearson
Lieutenant Berg	Jack Pearson
Sergeant Mooney	Chick York
Broncho Liz	Kitty O'Connor
Lieutenant Dale	Walter Scott Kolk
Captain Haliday	Greek Evans
"Red," the Mule Skinner	Wm. F. Donahue

Lillian ("Baby") Bond............................Dorothy Dilley
Señor José..Maurice Lupue
Señorita Carmela Cortez................................Trini
Wing..Simeon Karavaeff
Sing Song...Gladys Keck
Nagasaki...Kikobi Murai
    Prologue—A Railroad Station Platform Somewhere on the Texas-Mexican Border. Act I.—Scene 1—The Kennels. 2—Rickenbacker Field, U. S. Army Aviation Border Patrol. 3—Office at Headquarters. 4—Inside a Hangar. Act II.—Scene 1—A Ranch House Courtyard. 2—A Road in the Texas Desert. 3—A Fête on the Estate of Oliver Bond, Sands Point, Long Island.
    Staged by Alexander Leftwich and Gene Buck.

Señorita Cortez, flying over from Spain, lands at a field in Texas where Happy Hokum, a stranded hoofer, is making love to Lillian Bond and Captain Haliday is out after the border smugglers. Thence to a garden party on Long Island.

PEOPLE DON'T DO SUCH THINGS

(13 performances)

A comedy in three acts by Lyon Mearson and Edgar M. Schoenberg. Produced by A. L. Jones and Morris Green at the 48th Street Theatre, New York, November 23, 1927.

Cast of characters—

Bartlett..Ernest Stallard
Jeffrey Osborne...............................Lynne Overman
Ted Converse.....................................Stanley Logan
Viola..Millicent Hanley
Elaine Osborne....................................Isobel Elsom
Hobbs...William Sellery
Dolly Converse....................................Elsie Lawson
    Acts I, II and III.—In the East Seventies, in New York City.

Jeffrey Osborne, caught by Elaine, his wife, while he is entertaining Viola, his mistress, is divorced by Elaine and marries Viola. A year later Viola is the wife and Elaine the mistress, and to solve this problem Jeffrey proposes that all three live together. The plan works for a time, or until Jeffrey turns to Dolly Converse for comfort. All three women leave him finally and he is studying his list of addresses at curtain time.

PIRATES OF PENZANCE

(10 performances)

A musical play with words by W. S. Gilbert; music by Arthur S. Sullivan. Revived by Winthrop Ames at the Royale Theatre, New York, November 24, 1927.

Cast of characters—

Richard..John Barclay
Samuel...J. Humbird Duffey
Frederic...William Williams
Major-General Stanley................................Fred Wright
His Orderly......................................George C. Lehrian
Edward...William C. Gordon
Doctor of Divinity...............................George C. Lehrian
Mabel..Lois Bennett
Kate..Suissabell Sterling
Edith..Virginia Fox
Isabel..Bettina Hall
Maud...Paula Langlen
Ruth..Vera Ross
    Staged by Winthrop Ames.

Last year's production added to Winthrop Ames' repertoire of
Gilbert and Sullivan revivals.

THE PLOUGH AND THE STARS

(32 performances)

A play in four acts by Sean O'Casey. Produced by George C.
Tyler at the Hudson Theatre, New York, November 28, 1927.

Cast of characters—

Fluther Good.......................................Arthur Sinclair
Peter Flynn..J. A. O'Rourke
Mrs. Gogan...Maire O'Neill
The Covey..Sydney Morgan
Nora Clitheroe....................................Shelah Richards
Bessie Burgess..Sara Allgood
Jack Clitheroe.......................................Michael Scott
Capt. Brennan....................................Harry Hutchinson
Mollser..Margaret O'Farrell
A Bartender...E. J. Kennedy
Rosie Redmond.......................................Cathleen Drago
The Figure in the Window..............................Joseph French
Lieut. Langon...Tony Quinn
Corporal Stoddart.....................................Edwin Ellis
Sergeant Tinney......................................Joseph French
    Act I.—The Living Room of the Clitheroe Flat in a Dublin Tene-
ment. Act II.—A Public House. Act III.—The Street Outside the
Clitheroe Tenement. Act IV.—The Room of Bessie Burgess.
    Staged by Arthur Sinclair.

See page 350.

2 × 2 = 5

(16 performances)

A comedy in four acts by Gustav Wied; translated from the
Danish by Ernest Boyd and Holger Koppel. Produced at the
Civic Repertory Theatre, New York, November 28, 1927.

Cast of characters—

Thomas Hamann.....................................Paul Leyssac
Maria...Margaret Love
Esther Abel..Ruth Wilton
Frederick Hamann.................................John Eldridge
Mathias Hamann.................................Sayre Crawley
Paul Abel..Harry Sothern
Gerhard Konik...................................Egon Brecher
Lena.......................................Beatrice de Neergaard
The Widow Truelsen........................Leona Roberts
Othella Lustig............................Josephine Hutchinson
Mrs. Kluver....................................Alma Kruger
The Lawyer...............................J. Edward Bromberg
Torgensen................................J. Edward Bromberg
The Prison-Clergyman..........................Harold Moulton
Siverts..Robert F. Ross
A Policeman...............................Walter Tupper Jones
A Prisoner..................................Charles McCarthy
Dora..Oahlee Hubbard
Two Prisoners....................Arthur Donnell, John Hilbert
    Act I.—The Apartment of Paul and Esther Abel. Acts II and IV.
—Paul Abel's Bachelor Apartment and Study. Act III.—A Single
Cell in the Jail.
    The Action Takes Place in Copenhagen.
    Staged by Egon Brecher.

The futuristic and somewhat obscure adventures of Paul Abel, a radical novelist, exposing his efforts to get along with his wife, to get himself into jail and finally to readjust the world nearer to his heart's desire.

DELMAR'S REVELS

(112 performances)

A revue in twenty-four exhibits; sketches by William K. Wells; lyrics by Billy Rose and Ballard MacDonald; music by Jimmy Monaco, Jesse Greer and Lester Lee. Produced by Samuel Baerwitz and Harry Delmar at the Shubert Theatre, New York, November 28, 1927.

Principals engaged—

Frank Fay
Hugh Cameron
Dick Lancaster
Glen Dale
Bert Lahr
William Gaston
Artie Leeming
Trado Twins
Ivan Triesault
    Staged by Harry Delmar.

Winnie Lightner
Helen Eby Rock
Patsy Kelly
Dorothea James
Janne Hackett
E. Mercedes
Carolyn Nolte
Patterson sisters
Chester Hale Dancers

STORM CENTER

(29 performances)

A farce comedy in three acts by Jessie Hein Ernst and Max Simon. Produced by the Personality Players (Inc.) at the Klaw Theatre, New York, November 30, 1927.

Cast of characters—

Lena	Maude Eburne
Grace Todd	Betty Lawrence
Theodore Todd	Russell Mack
Julia	Dorothy Tierney
Shultz	Hans Hansen
The Sheik	Arthur Lee
Ivory	Marshall Hale
New Man	William Howard
Peter Mitchell	John Daly Murphy
Professor Henry Johnson	Stuart Fox
A Painter	Cliff Heckinger
A Varnisher	Fred Bradbury
Freeman	John A Regan
Hodge	Franklin Waite
Roberts	Robert Brister

Acts I, II and III.—The Todds' Apartment in New York City.

The Theodore Todds have a day of experiences moving out to their new home in Storm Center, L. I., which they have purchased from a scheming uncle. They suffer suburban ills galore and then outwit uncle and sell for $90,000.

CENTURIES

(39 performances)

A play in three acts by Em Jo Basshe. Produced by the New Playwrights at the New Playwrights Theatre, New York, November 29, 1927.

Cast of characters—

Chave	Cecile Lifter
Gitel	Sylvia Feningston
Yankel	Franchot Tone
An Old Immigrant	Edward Robbin
The Rabbi	Lawrence Bolton
Aaron	Irwin Swerdlow
Zwi	Edward Franz
Chono	Samuel Schneider
The Shames	Herman Bandes
Uncle Chiam	Edwin Clare
Berel	Max Leavitt
Motke	Felix Jacoves
David	Albert Gilman
Vladislav	Lionel Ferrend
Flossie	Jane Barry

Yoshke..Herbert Bergman
Louis..Murray Franklin
Elke...Ellen Bartlett
Old Clothes Man..................................Nelson Frank
Reuben...Peter Brocco
Young Man..Edwin Clare
Young Woman.....................................Miriam Gumble
The Boss...Irwin Swerdlow
The Girl...Mona Lewis
The Mother.......................................Mary Doerr
The Daughter....................................Sheba Strunsky
Girl Striker.....................................Marion Johnson
Police Captain..................................Felix Jacoves
First Woman.....................................Marta Proudfoot
Second Woman....................................Mona Lewis
Third Woman.....................................Sheba Strunsky
Fourth Woman....................................Gladys Wess
Fifth Woman.....................................Miriam Gumble
    The scene is laid in a tenement house.
    Staged by the author.

Episodes from the lives of immigrant Jews in their pilgrimage
from the deep east side to the more prosperous Bronx in New
York.

GOLDEN DAWN

(184 performances)

A music drama in two acts by Otto Harbach and Oscar Hammerstein, 2nd; music by Emmerich Kalman and Herbert Stothart.
Produced by Arthur Hammerstein at Hammerstein's Theatre,
New York, November 30, 1927.

Cast of characters—

Dago...Carlo Benetti
Anzac..Archie Leach
Pigeon...Len Mence
Mooda...Marguerita Sylva
Hasmali..Kumar Goshal
Captain Eric......................................Reginald Pasch
Sister Hedwig.....................................Paula Ayers
Shep Keyes..Robert Chisholm
Steve Allen.......................................Paul Gregory
Blink Jones.......................................Gil Squires
Sir Alfred Hammersley.............................Olin Howland
Dawn..Louise Hunter
Johanna...Nydia d'Arnell
Colonel Judson....................................W. Messenger Bellis
Ann Milford.......................................Barbara Newberry
Dr. Milford.......................................Henry Pemberton
An Old Man of Africa..............................Robert Paton Gibbs
A Witch Dancer....................................Jacques Cartier
A Dancing Girl....................................Kohana
Mombassa Moll.....................................Hazel Drury
    Act I.—Scene 1—Mooda's Canteen Near a Prison Camp in German
East Africa. 2—The Temple Cave. 3—The Jungle. 4—The Prisoners' Stockade. 5—The Tree of Mulunghu. Act II.—Scene 1—The
Canteen. 2—The Old Stockade. 3—Geng Lee's Joint in Mombassa.
4—The Temple Cave. 5—The Gate to the Mission. 6—The Golden
Dawn.
    Staged by Dave Bennett and Reginald Hammerstein.

Dawn, supposedly a young and beautiful native, is brought up by her native nurse, Mooda, to believe she is the destined princess of an African tribe. Along comes Steve Allen, war prisoner of Germany, to make love to Dawn and unfit her for the princess job. Shep Keyes, a big black, seeks to keep Dawn in the tribe, but Steve finds a way.

FALLEN ANGELS

(36 performances)

A comedy in three acts by Noel Coward. Produced by The Actors' Theatre, Inc., at the 49th Street Theatre, New York, December 1, 1927.

Cast of characters—

Julia Sterroll	Fay Bainter
Frederick Sterroll	Gordon Ash
Jane Banbury	Estelle Winwood
William Banbury	Gerald Hamer
Maurice Duclos	Luis Alberni
Saunders	Eileen Beldon

Acts I, II and III.—In the Sterrolls' Flat.
Staged by Guthrie McClintic.

Julia Sterroll and Jane Banbury, before they married, happened at different times to have had love affairs with the same dashing Frenchman, Maurice Duclos. Five years after marriage, when they are dully content with their prosaic husbands, they hear Maurice is visiting England. Excitedly they prepare to receive him while their husbands are golfing. While they wait for the tardy lover, they drink and as they drink they become squiffy, then angry, and finally quarrelsome.

ELECTRA

(12 performances)

Tragedy of Sophocles. Revived by Margaret Anglin at the Gallo Theatre, New York, December 1, 1927.

Cast of characters—

Torch Boys	Herbert Barr, Paul Heller
Guardian	Clarence Derwent
Orestes	Ralph Roeder
Pylades	Howard Phillips
Leader of the Chorus	Dorothy Scott

Chorus of Argive Maidens—Ruth Chandler, Marjorie Hamilton, Grace

Lynn, Betty Beeman, Grace Fisher, Doris Dagmar, Elizabeth
Zachary, Bonnie Hawthorne, Marjorie Moffett, Margaret Strathey,
Xenia de Plessen, Juana Nelson, Joan Williams, Sally Sanford
Electra...Margaret Anglin
Chrysothemis.................................... Elwyn Harvey
Attendants........Mercedes Desmore, Cynthia Blake, Henriette Kay
Clytemnestra....................................Antoinette Perry
Attendants—Dorothy Zommer, Faire Terry, Dolores Terry, Marie
Ware, Leah Rose, Jean Hawthorne
Palace Attendants—William Barto, Hall Taggart, Sidney Hart, Julian
Ruben, Harry Hart
Ægisthos..Ian Maclaren
The Scene Is Laid Before the Royal Palace at Mycenæ.
Staged by Miss Anglin.

OUT OF THE SEA

(16 performances)

A play in four acts by Don Marquis. Produced by George C.
Tyler at the Eltinge Theatre, New York, December 5, 1927.

Cast of characters—

John Marstin.......................................Rollo Peters
Arthur Logris......................................Claude Rain
Mrs. Hockin.................................Octavia Kenmore
Coastguard Dunstan........................Thomas Coffin Cooke
Timbury..O. P. Heggie
Mark Tregesal.....................................Lyn Harding
Physician.......................................Guy Cunningham
Isobel Tregesal.................................Beatrix Thomson
First Fisherman................................Richard Simson
Second Fisherman................................William Burnett
Hockin..Reginald Barlow
Acts I, II, III and IV.—The Southwest Coast of Cornwall, Near
Land's End—Overlooking the Sea Where the Land of Lynnesse Sank
in the Year 1089.
Staged by Walter Hampden.

John Marstin, American poet visiting the Cornish coast, meets
and loves Isobel Tregesal, the unhappy wife of Mark Tregesal, a
brute of a man who has sworn to master her and make her love
him. Marstin and Isobel, helped by all the good people of the
story, seek to elope and are frustrated by Tregesal. Isobel stabs
her husband. Realizing there is no happiness for her with Marstin she goes back to the sea and is drowned.

BRASS BUTTONS

(8 performances)

A drama in three acts by John Hunter Booth. Produced by
Lew Cantor, Inc., at the Bijou Theatre, New York, December 5,
1927.

Cast of characters—

Minnie Schultz..Ada Ayres
Herman Schultz.......................................Lee Kohlmar
Mrs. Flynn..Beryl Mercer
Dan Flynn..Frank Shannon
Rosie Moore.....................................Muriel Kirkland
Father Sullivan....................................John T. Dwyer
Dr. McNulty.......................................Edward Finley
Kid Dickson..Gerald Kent
Miss Sabine Trumbell...........................Edith M. Shayne
    Acts I, II and III.—In the Living Room of the Flynns, Three
Flights Over Schultz's Delicatessen Store, New York.
    Staged by Victor Morley.

Patrolman Dan Flynn proves he's one of the finest by rescuing Rosie Moore, ex-ashcan foundling but more recently a despondent cafeteria cashier, from a watery grave. Rosie has a baby in the same act and even though Kid Dickson, a handsome pugilist, gets a sock on the jaw from copper Dan, he will not own up to its paternity. Neither will the author nor Rosie tell. But Dan makes Rosie an honest gal by marrying her.

HAPPY

(80 performances)

A musical comedy in three acts; book by Vincent Lawrence and McElbert Moore; lyrics by Earle Crooker and McElbert Moore; music by Frank Grey. Produced by Murray Phillips at the Earl Carroll Theatre, New York, December 5, 1927.

Cast of characters—

Bill Wentworth......................................John Kane
Teddy...Gene Collins
Tommy...Bill Brown
Marion Brooker..................................Virginia Smith
Siggy Sigler..Percy Helton
Jack Gaynor...Fred Santley
Edith Dale.......................................Shirley Sherman
Lorelei Lynn..............................Madeleine Fairbanks
Grace..Lucile Reece
Milly..Rosa Lee
President Dale..................................Joseph Clayton
Lewis Pollock...................................Donald Campbell
Harry...Bob Nelson
Mr. Bennett....................................Willard Dashiell
Marjorie..Alice Cochran
Helen...Ann Cochran
Blanche...Betty Rourke
Butler..George Fredericks
    Acts I, II and III.—At Hadley College, Hadley, Mass., and at
Sigler's Home at Southampton, L. I.
    Staged by Walter Brooks.

Siggy Sigler, inheriting a sausage fortune, must show a bank balance of $100,000 within a given time. He just makes it, after various lyrical interruptions by his college mates.

THE BANSHEE

(48 performances)

A melodramatic mystery farce in three acts by W. D. Hepenstall and Ralph Cullinan. Produced by Banshee Incorporated at Daly's Theatre, New York, December 5, 1927.

Cast of characters—

Peter Adair	Joseph Brennan
Mrs. Grimes	Kitty Collins
Tom Scott	Barry Macollum
Yuru	Richard Whorf
Joan Walker	Lillian Walker
Tiberious Lamb	Dan Kelly
Dr. Neville Lacey	Herbert Ranson
Blanche Lamb	Marion Kerby
Hazel Orphen	Dana Desboro
Clem Durward	Edmund George
Dr. Morrison	Conway Wingfield
Sheriff Abner Heckenshell	Edward Favor
Jim Sprague	Michael Rice
Walter Payne	Frank Peters

Acts I, II and III.—The Living Room of Peter Adair's Home at Blackridge, New York.

Staged by Charles J. Mulligan.

Peter Adair is murdered. His murder is laid to one of those "banshees" that used to roam Ireland and warn the folks of imminent disaster. Not being able to uncover a banshee the cast in general is suspected until the crime is laid at the feet of an Indian boy servant.

JEDERMANN

(Everyman)

(14 performances)

English morality as rewritten by Hugo von Hofmannstahl; music by Einar Nilson. Produced by Max Reinhardt under the direction of Gilbert Miller at the Century Theatre, New York, December 7, 1927.

Cast of characters—

Messenger	Hans Thimig
The Voice of the Lord	Paul Hartmann
Death	Wladimir Sokoloff
Everyman (Jedermann)	Alexander Moissi
Steward (Vogt)	Harald Kreutzberg
Cook	Ernst Matray
Fellowship (Gutergesell)	Hermann Thimig
Poor Neighbor	Hans Moser
Debtor	Eduard von Winterstein

Debtor's Wife............................Johanna Terwin Moissi
Everyman's Mother...............................Hedwig Pauly
Lechery...Dagny Servaes
Chorister..Hans Thimig
Ladies.................................{ Elizabeth Alexandrowa
                                       { Rosamond Pinchot
                                       { Tilly Losch
Male Guests..............................{ Othmar Biegler
                                         { Erich Schilling
Fat Cousin.....................................Otto Wallburg
Lean Cousin.......................................Hans Moser
Retainer.......................................Erich Schilling
Mammon..Arnold Korff
Good-Deeds....................................Maria Solveg
Faith...Lili Darvas
Retainer of Everyman's Mother....................Othmar Biegler

The Devil..................................{ Wladimir Sokoloff
                                           { Ernst Matray

In the German version the somber English morality becomes a
spectacle drama with an elaborate banquet scene, at which Death
appears to lay a clammy hand over the heart of the gaily cele-
brating Everyman. Thereafter Everyman suffers partial physical
collapse, is strengthened by Faith, encouraged by Good Deeds
and escorted finally toward the portals of heaven through descent
into the grave.

BROKEN WINGS

(17 performances)

(Con las Alas Rotas)

Drama in three acts by Emilio Berisso. Presented by Camilla
Quiroga, Argentinian star, at the Manhattan Opera House, New
York, December 8, 1927.

Cast of characters—

Nelly...Camila Quiroga
Fanny Dover.....................................Carmen Olivet
La Institutriz....................................Consuelo Abbad
Rita..Myrtha D'Arlys
Carmen.......................................Carmen Ganduglia
Julieta..Niña N. N.
Julián Valmar....................................Gerardo Blanco
Roberto Cladel.................................Florindo Ferrario
Linares...Juan Porta
Cladel...José Olarra
Osvaldo Melvil...................................Angel Reyes
            Staged by Hector C. Quiroga.

Nelly Valmar, having had an affair with one Linares before she
married Dr. Valmar, is urged by Linares to resume their old relations. If she refuses Linares threatens to send the doctor certain
correspondence. Nelly refuses, her friend Cladel tries to get the

letters from Linares, but they reach the doctor who promptly leaves Nelly. Seven years later Nelly, her home broken, her child taken from her, is in the depths and Valmar has taken to drink. During the same engagement Mme. Quiroga and her company played Cuitino's "La Fuerza Ciega," Moock's "La Serpiente," Novion's "Bendita Seas," Gardel's "Los Mirasoles," Aquino's "Una Mujer Desconocida."

TRIGGER

(47 performances)

A play in three acts by Lula Vollmer, author of "Sun-Up." Produced by Richard Herndon at the Little Theatre, New York, December 6, 1927.

Cast of characters—

John Stafford	Walter Connolly
George Fleetwood	Minor Watson
Bill Grayson	Louis Mason
West Fry	Milton McGovern
Trigger Hicks	Claiborne Foster
Eleanor Stafford	Natalie Schafer
Etta Dawson	Sara Haden
Jake Hawkins	John Taylor
Rus Cleaver	Rupert Brae
Sam	Sonny Collins
Granny Raines	Elinor Retsof
Mother	Catherine Gray
Zedrach	Zeddie

Acts I and II.—Engineers' Camp. Act III.—Trigger's Cabin.
Staged by George Cukor.

Trigger is the name given a spirited young woman, daughter of a drunkard, who takes in washing and prays for the health of the community in the Carolina mountains. She achieves some local reputation as a faith healer, which arouses the suspicions of the natives that she may also be some sort of witch. Two civil engineers, John Stafford and George Fleetwood, become interested in Trigger. Stafford hopes to seduce her, but Fleetwood honorably saves her and there is a promise he may marry her later.

AT THE GATE OF THE KINGDOM

(17 performances)

A play in four acts by Knut Hamsun. Produced by The American Laboratory Theatre, at the American Laboratory Theatre, New York, December 8, 1927.

Cast of characters—

Ivar Kareno.....................................Grover Burgess
Elina Kareno.....................................Florence House
Ingeborg...Elizabeth Tyler
Endre Bondesen...............................Robert H. Gordon
Carsten Jerven, Dr. of Philosophy.................Joaquin Souther
Nathalia Hovind..............................Katharine Squire
Professor Gylling............................Herbert V. Gellendre
A Taxidermist......................................Greely Curtis
A Sheriff.......................................Howard Buchanan
  Acts I, II and III.—Kareno's Living Room.
  Staged by Richard Boleslavsky.

JUNO AND THE PAYCOCK

(40 performances)

A play in three acts by Sean O'Casey. Produced by the Irish
Players at the Gallo Theatre, New York, December 19, 1927.

Cast of characters—

"Captain" Jack Boyle.............................Arthur Sinclair
Juno Boyle..Sara Allgood
Johnny Boyle.................................Harry Hutchinson
Mary Boyle...Ria Mooney
"Joxer" Daly....................................Sydney Morgan
Mrs. Masie Madigan..............................Maire O'Neill
"Needle" Nugent.................................J. A. O'Rourke
Mrs. Tancred.....................................Cathleen Drago
Jerry Devine.....................................Michael Scott
Charlie Bentham................................E. J. Kennedy
An Irregular Mobilizer.............................Tony Quinn
Second Irregular Mobilizer..........................George Dillon
A Coal-block Vendor................................Edwin Ellis
A Sewing Machine Man............................Joseph French
Furniture Removal Men......................{ William O'Connell
                                           { Frank Donovan
Two Neighbors............................{ Margaret O'Farrell
                                         { Shelah Richards
  Acts I, II and III.—The Living Room Apartment of a Two Room
Tenancy of the Boyle Family in a Tenement House in Dublin.

Captain Jack Boyle, shiftless and imaginative, struts like a
paycock in the eyes of Juno, his wife. Tragedy comes upon the
Boyles after they think they have inherited a sum of money and
spend it before they get it. But the "Captain" goes philosoph-
ically along with his liquor and his pals. ("Best Plays of
1925-26.")

LOS ANGELES

(16 performances)

A comedy in five scenes by Max Marcin and Donald Ogden
Stewart. Produced by George M. Cohan at the Hudson Theatre,
New York, December 19, 1927.

Cast of characters—

Mrs. Canfield	Jane Oaker
Mrs. Jones	Alison Skipworth
Cynthia Nelson	Martha Manners
Ethel Grierson	Frances Dale
Mr. Pirrano	Jack LaRue
Nita	Thelma Pritchard
Mark G. Livermore	Neil Pratt
Joe Britt	Frank Ford
Miss Harrison	Helen Vinson
Eddie Trafford	Alan Brooks
Mamie Prentice	Mary Robinson
Lucius Towne	G. Davison Clark
Hobart Towne	Harold Vermilyea
Pearl Wiley	Rosalie O'Reilly
Tom Ellery	W. W. Shuttleworth
Butler	Daniel Wolf
Mr. Rosebud	Louis Sorin

Scenes 1 and 5—Ladies' Retiring Room at the Club Pierrot, New York City. 2 and 4—Office of the President of the Superb Pictures Corporation, Hollywood, California. 3—Reception Hall in the Home of Eddie Trafford.

Staged by Sam Forrest.

Ethel Grierson, a gold-digger in New York, goes to Hollywood hoping to involve a big movie manager or actor in a scandal and then collect. She is engaged to get a favorite comedian of the screen into trouble, does so with some success, but finds she loves him. Then she involves her employer's son also, plays scandal against scandal, and saves the play's ending.

PLAYING THE GAME

(8 performances)

A comedy-drama in three acts by Bruce Reynolds. Produced by Pendennis Productions, Inc., at the Ritz Theatre, New York, December 19, 1927.

Cast of characters—

Mrs. Loring	Louise Mackintosh
Barnes	Harry Neville
Mrs. Briggs	Caroline Newcomb
Jack Winthrop	Byron Hatfield
Helen	Mary Charles
Margaret	Virginia Morgan
Louise Loring	Donna Padeloup
Gerald Graham	Martin Burton
Reverend Stanley	James G. Morton
Gurvey	Aubrey Beattie
Rose Donohue	Irene Homer
Madge	Joan Blair
Handsome	A. J. Herbert
Malone	Louis Larimore
Greene	Edward A. Curry

Act I.—A Living Room. Act II.—Another Living Room. Act III.—A Roadhouse.

Staged by Arthur Hurley.

DANTON'S TOD

(15 performances)

Max Reinhardt's Production of the tragedy by Georg Buchner, in two acts. Presented by Gilbert Miller at the Century Theatre New York, December 20, 1927.

Cast of characters—

A Lady	Maria Solveg
A Gentleman	Robert Viera
Another Gentleman	Harald Kreutzberg
Another Lady	Tilly Losch
A Third Gentleman	Erich Hellsen
A Fourth Gentleman	Erich Schilling
A Fifth Gentleman	Othmar Biegler
A Third Lady	Hedwig Pauly
A Fourth Lady	Edel Blank
Danton	Paul Hartmann
Julie	Dagny Servaes
A Fifth Lady	Laura Schaffer
Herault-Sechelles	Hermann Thimig
A Sixth Gentleman	Heins Nachmann
Lacroix	Otto Wallburg
A Grisette	Elizabeth Alexandrowa
Another Grisette	Annie Korff
Lucile	Lili Darvas
Philippeau	Erich Mann
Camille Desmoulins	Hans Thimig
Simon	Hans Moser
His Wife	Johanna Terwin-Moissi
A Citizen	Othmar Biegler
Another Citizen	Otto Wallburg
A Third Citizen	Ernst Matray
A Fourth Citizen	John Feistel
A Young Man	Erich Schilling
An Old Woman	Hedwig Pauly
Robespierre	Wladimir Sokoloff
A Deputy from Lyon	Hermann Thimig
Legendre	Eduard von Winterstein
Collot D'Herbois	Othmar Biegler
The President of the Club of Jacobins	John Gerard
Marion	Rosamond Pinchot
St. Just	Arnold Korff
The President of the National Convention	Con MacSunday
Hermann	John Feistel
Deputies	Erich Mann / Eugene Vass / Max Frank / Walter Thierfelder / Willie Trosh / William Beyer
An Officer	Arthur Laubert

Acts I, II and III.—In Paris During the Revolution.

The tragedy of Danton's fall before the merciless and fanatical attacks of Robespierre in the French revolution, showing his arrest, trial before the revolutionary tribunal, condemnation and execution.

SPRING SONG

(13 performances)

A play in four acts by Virginia Farmer. Produced by Gustav Blum at the Bayes Theatre, New York, December 20, 1927.

Cast of characters—

Oscar Schoenvogel...................................Leo Bulgakov
Walker Pendleton..............................Lewis Leverett
Nellie Lee Bell...............................Marienne Francks
Caterina Corwin.................................Ethel Wilson
    Acts I, II and III.—Dining Room in Walker Pendleton's House in
Redville, a Small Town in the South. Act IV.—Walker Pendleton's
Studio in New York.
    Staged by Gustav Blum.

Caterina Corwin, prima donna, finds Walker Pendleton, young and ambitious sculptor, in a small town and offers him tuition and a tour of Europe in exchange for his love. Walker refuses and marries his small-town girl. Two years later he is disillusioned, is given a second chance, goes to live with Caterina and becomes famous. Then he wants his wife back and Caterina lets him fetch her. It is really as a mother that she loves Walker most.

THE LOVE NEST

(23 performances)

A comedy in three acts by Robert Emmet Sherwood, based on Ring Lardner's story of that name. Produced by the Actor-Managers, Inc. (in association with Sidney Ross), at the Comedy Theatre, New York, December 22, 1927.

Cast of characters—

Slim Carey.......................................Albert Carroll
Pete...John Francis Roche
An Extra..Brewster Board
A Stage Hand..................................Vincent Mallory
A Voice...George Hoag
Bernie..John Rynne
Violinist.......................................Julius Goldman
Mae Jennings....................................Geraldine Wall
Property Man.....................................George Heller
Lou Gregg.......................................Clyde Fillmore
Mercer..Otto Hulett
Francis Deane....................................Marc Loebell
Miss Jacobs..Lily Lubell
Tobin..George Hoag
Maureen Milton..................................Paula Trueman
Celia Gregg..June Walker
Forbes...G. G. Thorpe
    Act I.—The Stage of the Gregg Unit in the World-Famous-Schip-
stein Studio at Hollywood. Act II.—The Patio of the Gregg Home
in Beverly Hills. Act III.—Lou Gregg's Study.

Celia, married to the great picture director, Lou Gregg, bears him three children and stands his overbearing ego as long as possible. Then she fills up on bourbon whisky and tells a movie picture interviewer exactly what she thinks of Lou, picture people, Hollywood, "the game," and all the rest of it. Gregg is fearfully upset, but makes the best of it and goes back to the lot. Celia takes the nurse, the children and a sympathetic butler to New York.

CASTE

(11 performances)

A play in three acts by Cosmo Hamilton. Produced by Joe Weber at the Mansfield Theatre, New York, December 23, 1927.

Cast of characters—

Augustus Brownlow	Philip Bamshaw
Reginald Walter Willett	T. Wigney Percyval
Col. Erskine Dalbeatie Farquhar, Late Canadian Highlanders	Reginald Mason
Lillian Shepreth	Vera Neilson
Denham	Gordon Richards
Edmond Gamlingay	John Astley
Helen Farquhar	Winifred Kingston
Anthony Northrup	Anderson Lawyer
Lord Warminster	Halliwell Hobbes
Lady Warminster	Nancie B. Marsland
Jean Farquhar	Vivian Martin
La Duchess De Bercy	Hilda Spong
Max Lorbenstein	Horace Braham
Mrs. Otto Saab	Jean Shelby
Albert	Michel De Polo
Jacob J. Lorbenstein	Albert Bruning

Acts I, II and III.—Fiesole, Italy; Paris and New York City.
Staged by Campbell Gullan.

Jean Farquhar, modern daughter of an old Knickerbocker family, meeting Max Lorbenstein, genius son of a most successful and very proud Jewish family, agrees that they should marry. Jean's parents are reconciled to the idea, but Max's father remains obdurate until his heart is softened by a message from his dead wife.

WHAT DO WE KNOW?

(35 performances)

A play in three acts by Olga Petrova. Produced by W. Herbert Adams at Wallack's Theatre, New York, December 23, 1927.

Cast of characters—

Samuel Lovejoy	John C. Carlyle
Susan Western	Josephine Morse

Sara Peabody.....................................Lillian Kemble
Ephraim Swiggles.............................Maxwell Sholes
Pearl du Barrie...............................Wilma Thompson
Ina Baliefska.......................................Helen Blair
Ben Pederson...Jack Leslie
Kasha...Olga Petrova
Lyons Johns..................................Carlton Brickert
Morgan Western................................Bradley Page
Ernestine Fox................................Suzanne Bennett
Myra Winslow................................Gladys Feldman
Billy...Jack Root
Ah Sing..Hoi Poi Kee
Olivia Herford...............................Wilma Thompson
Philip Herford..................................Chester Erskine
Mrs. Wills......................................Mabel Wright
Mr. Potter..Jack Root
Luther Martin..................................John C. Carlyle
Swami Vyasa Sidhenta..........................Maxwell Sholes
  Act I.—A Room in the House of Morgan Western. Act II.—
Studio of Lyons Johns. Act III.—A Room in Ina's House.

Kasha, married to the president of the Purity League and unhappy, flees his bed and board and takes up with Lyons Johns,
an attractive free soul of Greenwich Village. Her husband trails
after, both lover and husband are killed by lightning and Kasha
seeks contact with them through the medium of a spiritual séance.
It is her lover's shade she greets as she dies in her place at the
séance.

SISTERS

(9 performances)

A comedy in three acts by John Willard. Produced by the
Messrs. Shubert at the Klaw Theatre, New York, December 24,
1927.

Cast of characters—

Gwendolyn....................................Roberta Arnold
Pete..Arthur Aylsworth
Dick...Leonard Doyle
Ann..Irene Purcell
Larry...Wilfred Lytell
Mary...Millicent Hanley
Malcom......................................C. W. Van Voorhis
  Acts I and III.—Gwendolyn's Flat in Upper New York City. Act
II.—Mary's Apartment on Park Avenue.
  Staged by John Willard.

Ann has one sister, Gwen, married to Pete and unhappily poor
but respectable, and a second sister, Mary, who is living in sin
in Park Avenue. Each sister wants her to escape the particular
kind of unhappiness she has suffered. Ann's two suitors, one rich
and married, the other poor and a rotter, fight it out for her with
the rich fellow having the advantage.

BEHOLD THE BRIDEGROOM

(88 performances)

A play in three acts by George Kelly. Produced by Rosalie Stewart at the Cort Theatre, New York, December 26, 1927.

Cast of characters—

Antoinette Lyle	Judith Anderson
Edwards	Kenneth Lawton
Sheppard	Mary Gildea
Mrs. Eleanor Ridgway	Mary Servoss
Spencer Train	John Marston
Constance Peyton	Jean Dixon
Gehring Fitler	Lester Vail
Mary McGrath	Virginia Russell
Robert Lyle	Thurston Hall
Doctor Huntington	Carl Hamilton
Doctor Loebell	Clarence Bellair
Nurse	Marion Evenson

Acts I, II and III.—The Estate of Robert Lyle at Shadow Brook, Just Beyond the City Line.
Staged by George Kelly.

See page 174.

BLESS YOU, SISTER

(24 performances)

A play in three acts by John Meehan and Robert Riskin. Produced by A. E. and R. R. Riskin at the Forrest Theatre, New York, December 26, 1927.

Cast of characters—

Rev. Robert MacDonald	George Alison
Sandy MacDonald	Mildred MacLeod
Mary MacDonald	Alice Brady
Freddy Gribble	Robert Ames
Senator Gribble	George Lessey
Timothy Bradley	Charles Bickford
Esther Lewis	Dorothy Estabrook
Tony Nazarro	Eugene Donovan
Daisy	Eloise Keeler
Miss Hyde	Marie Ilka
Miss Quigley	Marjorie Dalton
George Hunter	Denis Gurney
Choir Leader	Olivia Martin
The Choir	Anne Elliott Bertha Rodgers Anton Teero Clark Bremer Edwin Marshall Edwin Rogers

Act I.—The Study and Living Room of Rev. MacDonald's Residence in Bridgewater. Act II.—Tabernacle Tents of Mary Mac-Donald's "On the Road."
Staged by John Meehan and George Abbott.

Mary MacDonald, embittered when her father, a small-town churchman, is relieved of his pulpit because he is not peppy enough to suit the modern spirit, goes in for making a business of soul saving with a go-getter Bible salesman. As a revivalist she is a great success, but tires of her hypocrisies and wants to marry her small-town sweetheart. Her business partner in the religious racket is also in love with her, which complicates but does not entirely spoil everything.

VENUS

(8 performances)

A comedy in three acts by Rachel Crothers. Produced by Carl Reed at the Masque Theatre, New York, December 26, 1927.

Cast of characters—

```
Virgie Gibbs.....................................Cecilia Loftus
Mason...........................................Charles Hampden
Dr. Dickie Wakely.................................Arnold Lucy
Herbert Beveridge................................Tyrone Power
Agnes Beveridge................................Patricia Collinge
Diana Gibbs....................................Katharine Francis
Ross Hurst.....................................Edward Crandall
    Acts I and III.—The Roof of Virgie Gibbs' House in New York.
Act II.—Living Room of Virgie's House.
    Staged by Rachel Crothers.
```

About the time the airplane becomes so common that everybody has a landing station on top of his apartment building there appears a professor with pills guaranteed to give a finer feminine quality to men and a stronger, more vigorous character to women. He feeds them to a party of experimenters and the results are fairly disastrous. Timid Agnes becomes a roaring, blustering person and big, overbearing Herbert minces and simpers. After which everybody flies, or is ready to fly away to Venus.

CELEBRITY

(24 performances)

A comedy in three acts by Willard Keefe. Produced by Herman Shumlin and Paul Streger at the Lyceum Theatre, New York, December 26, 1927.

Cast of characters—

```
Clem............................................Claude Cooper
Lonny O'Neil....................................Hale Norcross
Vera O'Neil.....................................Irene Hubbard
```

Josie Shaw.....................................Constance McKay
Barry Regan......................................Gavin Gordon
"Circus" Snyder...................................Crane Wilbur
Solly Gold.....................................Maurice Freeman
Dorothy Childs.................................Nancy Sheridan
Mrs. Hemingway............................Mabel Montgomery
Sebastien...Harry M. Cooke
Miss Vincent..Rose Keane
Mr. Collings.......................................Philip Wood
Miss Christgau.............................Margaret Armstrong
    Act I.—The Suburban Home of Lonny O'Neil, Outside New York.
Acts II and III.—Barry Regan's Suite in a Broadway Hotel.
    Staged by Edward Goodman.

Circus Snyder, capitalizing the fight racket, raises his protégé, Barry Regan, to be not only a great prizefighter but a gentleman and a littérateur. All for the good of the game and the gate. Barry goes through, but there are moments when he all but turns on Circus and exposes the whole racket, from fixed publicity to fixed fights.

PARADISE

(8 performances)

A play in three acts by William Hurlbut. Produced by Robert Milton at the 48th Street Theatre, New York, December 26, 1927.

Cast of characters—

Cassie Thesinger.................................Minnie Dupree
Margaret, Mrs. Elder.........................Elizabeth Patterson
Ella, Mrs. Springer................................Selena Royle
Adelaide, Mrs. Carlson............................Eloise Stream
Henry Elder.......................................Edward Poland
Mr. Thompson..................................Edward H. Robins
Winnie Elder.......................................Lillian Foster
Dr. Achilles Swain...............................Warren William
Harry Elder..Tom Brown
Norma Archer.......................................Helen Flint
Bert Heaney.......................................Arling Alcine
    Acts I, II and III.—The Front Room in the Elder Family's House
in a Village in Eastern Ohio.
    Staged by Robert Milton.

Winnie Elder, youthful spinster, jealous of her married sisters, goes to New York, invents herself a husband and then announces his death. To make the story hold she sends home not only a picture of the handsome boy she married, but buys a corpse and ships that back as proof that she is a perfectly good widow. Her morbid Aunt Cassie opens the coffin, however, and Winnie's trick is exposed. After which she finds happiness in the arms of the young doctor she has been long in love with.

IT IS TO LAUGH

(32 performances)

A comedy-drama in three acts by Fannie Hurst. Produced by Barbour, Crimmins & Bryant at the Eltinge Theatre, New York, December 26, 1927.

Cast of characters—

Spike Hennessey	Edward Butler
Eddie Lenzer	Frank Beaston
Birdie Goldfish	Edna Hibbard
Mrs. Julius Goldfish	Mme. Bella Gudinsky
Mr. Julius Goldfish	Irving Honigman
Maid	Jean Bryant
Mrs. Rabinovitch	Sonia Radina
Mr. Rabinovitch	Meyer Seltzer
Eulalie Goldfish	Muriel Reid
Mr. Morris Goldfish	John Davidson
Mrs. Morris Goldfish	Sonia Evanof
French Governess	Mona Bracken
Miss Binney	Lois Arnold
Doctor	Harry W. Pemberton

Act I.—Living Room of Eddie Lenzer's Apartment in the Bronx. Acts II and III.—Living Room of the Goldfish Apartment on the Upper West Side.
Staged by Rollo Lloyd.

Morris Goldfish, making money, insists on moving his old father and mother from Division Street to an expensive West End Avenue apartment wherein they are comically unhappy and protesting. Birdie, the Goldfish sister, rebels, marries a crook, sticks by him while he is in jail, welcomes and reforms him when he gets out and finally successfully forces him upon her snobbish brother. Everything lovely except for the death of Papa Goldfish.

L'AIGLON

(8 performances)

Rostand's drama in three acts; translated by Louis N. Parker. Produced by John D. Williams (by arrangement with Charles Frohman, Inc.), at the Cosmopolitan Theatre, New York, December 26, 1927.

Cast of characters—

L'Aiglon, the Duke of Reichstadt	Michael Strange
Flambeau	George Marion
Prince Metternich	William Courtleigh
Francis, Emperor of Austria	Hubert Wilke
Count Prokesch	Richard Nicholls
Baron Friederich von Gentz	Clifford Walker
French Attaché at Vienna	Edwin Jerome

The Tailor...Harold West
Count Dietrichstein...............................Perry Norman
Baron von Oberhaus............................Douglas Garden
Marmont.......................................James M. Sullivan
Count Sedlinsky...................................David Sager
Marquis of Bombelles.......................Benedict MacQuarrie
Tiburtius De Lozet...............................Robert Farrell
Lord Cowley...................................Raymond Arthur
Dr. Malfatti.....................................Charles Peyton
General Hartman................................Henry Stillman
Captain Foresti..............................Gordon McCracken
An Austrian Sergeant..............................John Hanley
Montenegro.....................................Antonio Salerno
Empress Maria Louisa.............................Effie Shannon
Archduchess Sophia............................Catherine Proctor
Theresa De Lozet.............................Madeline Delmar
The Countess Camerata.........................Gertrude Davis
Fanny Elssler................................Marjorie Vonnegut
Scarampi...Eva Benton
    Act I.—Maria Louisa's Villa at Baden. Act II.—The Palace at
Schonbrunn ("The Lacquered Room"). Act III.—Scene 1—The
Fête. 2—The Battlefield of Wagram. 3—The Duke's Bedchamber
at Schonbrunn.
    Staged by John D. Williams.

The Louis N. Parker version of the Rostand drama carries the
young Eaglet hopefully but futilely to the battlefield of Wagram,
and his death at Schonbrunn.

*EXCESS BAGGAGE

(198 performances)

A comedy in three acts by John McGowan. Produced by Barbour, Crimmins & Bryant at the Ritz Theatre, New York, December 26, 1927.

Cast of characters—

Jimmy Dunn....................................Frank McHugh
Sarah Benton.......................................Maud Blair
Jack Merrill.....................................Nace Bonville
Bob...Vladimir Dubinsky
Charlie..Charles Dalton
Bill...Merald Tollefsen
Frank Arnold....................................John H. Dilson
Mabel Ford.....................................Suzanne Willa
Marvin......................................Lawrence O'Sullivan
Eddie Kane.......................................Eric Dressler
Betty Ford...Doris Eaton
Elsa McCoy.....................................Miriam Hopkins
Herbert Crammon..................................Boyd Marshall
Val D'Errico.....................................Herbert Clark
Al Kent..Frank Horton
George McCarthy..................................Mort Downey
Joe DeLeon.......................................William Boula
Harry Hart...Denton Vane
Rita Rydell....................................Frances Goodrich
Dad...Howard Morgan
Band.."The Admirals"
    Act I.—Within a Small Time Vaudeville Theatre in Los Angeles.
Act II.—Scene 1—The N.V.A. Club, New York City. 2—Elsa Mc-
Coy's Park Avenue Apartment. Act III.—In and Around the Pal-
ace Theatre, New York.
    Staged by Melville Burke.

Eddie Kane and Elsa McCoy are a juggling team in small time vaudeville, Eddie being the act and Elsa the decoration. "Excess baggage" is all she is, insists Elsa. Then she gets a chance to go into pictures on her own and Eddie does not want her to go. Can't work without her, he thinks. But she goes and Eddie quits juggling. Lives on Elsa until his pride sends him back to make a try at the old act. The first night he falls as he makes his "slide for life," and Elsa, in the audience, sees him. After which they reach an understanding.

WHITE EAGLE

(48 performances)

A musical play in four episodes; based on Edwin Milton Royle's "The Squaw Man"; book and lyrics by Brian Hooker and W. H. Post; music by Rudolf Friml. Produced by Russell Janney at the Casino Theatre, New York, December 26, 1927.

Cast of characters—

The Sun Watcher	Ralph Moana
The Medicine Man of the Utes	John Mealey
Tabywana	Chas. E. Galagher
Silverwing	Marion Keeler
The Indian Dancer	Aysa Kaz
The English Dancers	Paula Lind, Helen Grenelle
Lady Mabel	Blanche Fleming
Lady Mary	Roberta Curry
Lieut. Henry George	Carlton Neville
Lieut. Alex. McGrath	Arthur Kellar
Capt. James Wynnegate	Allan Prior
Captain Leslie	Jock McGraw
Sir John Applegate	Lawrence D'Orsay
The Dowager Lady Kerhill	Isabelle O'Madigan
Countess of Kerhill	Hazel Glen
Earl of Kerhill	Fred Tiden
Mr. Chiswick	Ernest Ehler
Malcolm Petrie	Horace Pollock
Bates	Walter Cross
Sadie	Kay Hawley
Lily	Paula Lind
Nick	George Shields
Bud Hardy	Charles Henderson
Big Bill	Mark Smith
Happy	Jay Fassett
Gloomy	Earl Mayne
Andy	Royal Cutter
Thunder Face	Michael Evans
Pete	Leon Cunningham
Punk	Marius Rogati
Cash Hawkins	Forrest Huff
Little Hal	Master Albert Shaw

Staged by Richard Boleslavsky.

"The Squaw Man" story with tunes. Captain James Wynne-gate, assuming the guilt of his brother, the Earl of Kerhill, who has stolen regimental funds, flees to America, becomes Jim Carson, rancher, marries Silverwing, Indian princess, and then learns that he has succeeded to the Kerhill title. Silverwing kills herself so as not to stand in Jim's way and that of her son.

MONGOLIA

(48 performances)

A romance in three acts by Conrad Westervelt. Produced by George H. Brennan at the Greenwich Village Theatre, New York, December 26, 1927.

Cast of characters—

Captain Peter Smiridoff	Harry Nelson
Major Mulay Pasha	Boyd Agin
Mrs. Kate Haverstraw	Kate McComb
Stefan Oronoff	Warren McCollum
Dr. Oliver Shaw, D.D., M.D.	Fred House
General Alexieff Oronoff	Frederic Burt
Ivan Koronsky	W. J. Paul
Marion Robards	Mildred Florence
Frank Robards	Thomas Carrigan
Lilly Boggs	Belle Greene
Prissy Mullins	Phyllis Harding
The Living Buddha	Joseph Lawrence
Colonel Domsky	Burr Caruth
Anton	George Frederic
Vassili	Jerome Jordan

Lamas, Russian Soldiers, Mongolian Servants, etc.
Acts I and III.—General Oronoff's Headquarters in Urga, Mongolia. Act II.—Private Shrine of the Living Buddha.
Staged by Edwin R. Wolfe.

General Oronoff, in command of the Russian white army in Northern China in 1919, has charge of the last of the Romanoffs, a boy of five. Wishing to get him safely through to Paris in the company of an American couple, he tests the reliability of the pair by making desperate love to the wife and subjecting the husband to various unpleasant experiences.

RESTLESS WOMEN

(24 performances)

A comedy-drama in three acts, by Sydney Stone. Produced by Anna Held, Jr., at the Morosco Theatre, New York, December 26, 1927.

Cast of characters—

Betty Fawcett	Leila Frost
Fred Hascall	Robert Crozier

Alice Fawcett.. Mary Young
Arthur van Werne..................................Eric Kalkhurst
Sonia Jamieson....................................Marie Churchill
Ethel Jamieson.....................................Madeline Grey
Ned Jamieson.......................................Alfred Kappeler
Wilma Fawcett... Elsie Hitz
John Fawcett.......................................Wilfred Lucas
    Act I.—Living Hall in the Fawcett Home in Westchester. Acts
II and III.—Wilma's Studio in New York City.
    Staged by Warren Lawrence.

Alice Fawcett, come upon dangerous years, decides to romance
a bit with a younger and handsomer man than her husband. Her
daughter Betty, however, being flung into the breach, proceeds
not only to take mamma's boy away from her but to keep him
as well.

* SHOW BOAT

(197 performances)

A musical comedy adapted from Edna Ferber's novel of the
same name; book and lyrics by Oscar Hammerstein II; music by
Jerome Kern. Produced by Florenz Ziegfeld at the Ziegfeld Theatre, New York, December 27, 1927.

Cast of characters—

Windy..Allan Campbell
Steve...Charles Ellis
Pete..Bert Chapman
Queeny...Aunt Jemima
Parthy Ann Hawks.............................Edna May Oliver
Cap'n Andy................................... Charles Winninger
Ellie...Eva Puck
Frank...Sammy White
Rubber Face.................................Francis X. Mahoney
Julie..Helen Morgan
Gaylor Ravenal..................................Howard Marsh
Vallon...Thomas Gunn
Magnolia...Norma Terris
Joe..Jules Bledsoe
Faro Dealer..Jack Wynn
Gambler...Phil Sheridan
Backwoodsman.......................................Jack Daley
Jeb...Jack Wynn
La Belle Fatima.................................Dorothy Denese
Old Sport.. Bert Chapman
Landlady..Annie Hart
Ethel.. Estelle Floyd
Sister...Annette Harding
Mother Superior.............................Mildred Scewenke
Kim (child).......................................Eleanor Shaw
Kim (as young woman)...........................Norma Terris
Jake...Robert Faricy
Jim...Jack Daley
Man with Guitar..................................Ted Daniels
Charlie.......................................J. Lewis Johnson
Lottie.. Tana Kamp
Dolly..Dagmar Oakland
Old Lady on Levee................................Laura Clairon
    Staged by Florenz Ziegfeld, Sammy Lee, Zeke Cohan.

On the Cotton Blossom show boat Cap'n Andy and Parthy Ann Hawks have some difficulty bringing up their pretty daughter Magnolia, who not only turns actress but finally runs away and marries her handsome, irresponsible leading man, Gaylord Ravenal. The Ravenals suffer many trying experiences, but come through finally to success and happiness, thanks largely to the talents of Magnolia's daughter, Kim.

* PARIS BOUND

(197 performances)

A comedy in three acts by Philip Barry. Produced by Arthur Hopkins at the Music Box Theatre, New York, December 27, 1927.

Cast of characters—

Mary Hutton	Madge Kennedy
Jim Hutton	Donn Cook
Nora Cope	Ellen Southbrook
Helen White	Martha Mayo
Fanny Shippan	Hope Williams
James Hutton	Gilbert Emery
Richard Parrish	Donald Macdonald
Peter Cope	Edwin Nicander
Noel Farley	Mary Murray
Julie	Marie Bruce

Act I.—The Upstairs Sitting-Room of a House in the Country near New York. Acts II and III.—The Music-Room on the Top Floor of a House in Uptown New York—Near the East River.
Staged by Arthur Hopkins.

See page 254.

* THE ROYAL FAMILY

(196 performances)

A comedy in three acts by George S. Kaufman and Edna Ferber. Produced by Jed Harris at the Selwyn Theatre, New York, December 28, 1927.

Cast of characters—

Della	Josephine Williams
Jo	Royal C. Stout
Hall Boy	Wally Stuart
McDermott	Murray Alper
Herbert Dean	Orlando Daly
Kitty Dean	Catharine Calhoun-Doucet
Gwen	Sylvia Field
Perry Stewart	Roger Pryor
Fanny Cavendish	Haidee Wright
Oscar Wolfe	Jefferson De Angelis

```
Julie Cavendish..................................Ann Andrews
Anthony Cavendish................................Otto Kruger
Another Hall Boy...............................Lester Nielson
Chauffeur......................................Frank Vollmer
Gilbert Marshall................................Joseph King
Gunga.........................................Hubert Courtney
Miss Peake......................................Phyllis Rose
     Acts I, II and III.—In the Duplex Apartment of the Cavendishes,
in the East Fifties, New York.
     Staged by David Burton.
```

See page 78.

THE PRISONER

(37 performances)

A play in two acts by Emil Bernhard; translated by Alexander Berkman. Produced by the Provincetown Players at the Provincetown Theatre, New York, December 28, 1927.

Cast of characters—

```
Michael Abrastov..............................Reginald Goode
Anna Petrovna..................................Pauline Moore
Popov.........................................William Challee
General Kamishansky....... .................Reginald Carrington
Boris Tverskoy............. ...................Harold Johnsrud
Irene Polosova.................................Hilda Vaughn
The Maid.......................................Cynthia Blake
A Jew..........................................Jacob Sandler
The Doctor.....................................Goldwin Patten
     Acts I, II and III.—In a Siberian Prison Shortly Before the Revo-
lution of 1917.
     Staged by James Light.
```

LOVELY LADY

(164 performances)

A musical comedy in two acts, based on the French play "Déjeuner de Soleil"; book by Gladys Unger and Cyrus Wood; lyrics by Cyrus Wood; music by Dave Stamper and Harold Levey. Produced by the Messrs. Shubert at the Sam H. Harris Theatre, New York, December 29, 1927.

Cast of characters—

```
Jacques........................................Adrian Rosley
François.......................................Jules Epailly
A Decoy......................................Franklin J. Dix
A Decoy........................................Maryan Lynn
Lord Islington................................Frank Greene
Toe Dancer....................................Mary Dunckley
Paul De Morlaix................................Guy Robertson
Max...........................................Wesley Pierce
Aline Beaumont.................................Doris Patston
Waiter.........................................Dick Kennedy
Louis Farrell..................................Jack Sheehan
```

```
Monsieur Watteau...............................William  Holden
Folly Watteau..................................Edna  Leedom
Parthenia......................................Eloise  Bennett
Page...........................................Mae  Russell
Lisette........................................Hazel  Harris
Yvonne.........................................Dorothy  Jarrett
Yvette.........................................Margaret  Liste
Claudette......................................Miriam  Crosby
Desiree........................................Louise  Barrett
Celeste........................................Ruth  Gordon
Marcelle.......................................Mary  Dunckley
Gendarme.......................................Anthony  Sterling
```

Act I.—The Room Rendezvous of the "Royale Hotel," on the Island of Caprice, Off the Coast of France. Act II.—Scene 1—Boudoir, Suite 210. 2—Screen Room of the "Royale Hotel." Staged by J. C. Huffman.

Folly Watteau, forced by necessity and the playwrights to appear to be a married woman, borrows the tenorious and handsome Paul de Morlaix, serving as a "decoy," or paid guest, at the Hotel Royale. Next morning they innocently have breakfast in bed and do a good deal of singing about it.

PERIPHERIE

(8 performances)

A drama in two acts, produced by Max Reinhardt. Presented by Gilbert Miller at the Cosmopolitan Theatre, New York, January 2, 1928.

Cast of characters—

```
Anna...........................................Dagny  Servaes
Franzi.........................................Hermann  Thimig
A Shoemaker....................................Erich  Schilling
Barborka.......................................Paul  Hartmann
Toni...........................................Hans  Thimig
A Barkeeper....................................Arthur  Laubert
A Gentleman....................................Arnold  Korff
Policemen......................................{ Othmar  Biegler
                                               { Erich  Schilling
A Judge........................................Wladimir  Sokoloff
Manager of a Night Club........................Otto  Wallburg
Waiter.........................................Erich  Schilling
A Young Man....................................Harald  Kreutzberg
Police Inspector...............................Hans  Moser
```

Acts I, II and III.—In the Outskirts of Prague. Staged by Max Reinhardt.

"Servant of Two Masters" and "He is to Blame" also produced January 9, and "Der Lebende Leichman" January 23.

RED DUST

(8 performances)

A play in three acts by Wilson Collison. Produced by Hugo W. Romberg at Daly's Theatre, New York, January 2, 1928.

Cast of characters—

McHorg..Leo Curley
Lucien Fourville................................Curtis Cooksey
Maurice Chauvenet.......................Lenore Meyrick-Sorsby
André Chauvenet.............................Jerome Collamore
Jacques Guidon..................................Leonard Mudie
VanTene..Sydney Shields
Hoi...Reo Suga
Acts I, II and III.—The Living Room of Lucien Fourville's Bungalow on a Rubber Plantation in French Indo-China.
Staged by Ira Hards.

Excitement on a rubber plantation in French Indo-China, during which Jacques Guidon, being bad, whips Van Tene, who wants to be good and is shot for his pains. After which Lucien Fourville, foreman, is taken by Van Tene, being won away from another lady he thought he preferred.

OH, KAY!

(16 performances)

A musical comedy in two acts; book by Guy Bolton and P. G. Wodehouse; music by George Gershwin; lyrics by Ira Gershwin. Produced by Alex. A. Aarons & Vinton Freedley (in association with the Messrs. Shubert) at the Century Theatre, New York, January 2, 1928.

Cast of characters—

Phyllis Ruxton...................................Edith Cardell
Dolly Ruxton....................................Marion Cardell
The Duke...Chas. Brown
Larry Potter.......................................Fred Harper
Tom Powers....................................Allen McKenzie
Shorty McGee.................................John E. Young
Constance Appleton............................Beatrice Swanson
Jimmie Winter.................................Frank Crumit
Kay...Julia Sanderson
Revenue Officer Jansen............................Shep Camp
Molly Morse......................................Norma Byrne
Mae...Helen Arden
Peggy..May Wynn
Judge Appleton...............................Frank Gardiner
Acts I, II and III.—Jimmy's House, Beachampton, Long Island.
Staged by Harry Howell.

See "Best Plays, 1926-27."

SHE'S MY BABY

(71 performances)

A musical farce comedy in two acts; book by Bert Kalmar and Harry Ruby; music by Richard Rodgers; lyrics by Lorenz Hart. Produced by C. B. Dillingham at the Globe Theatre, New York, January 3, 1928.

Cast of characters—

Pearl	Pearl Eaton
Phyllis	Phyllis Rae
The Dance Director	Nick Long, Jr.
The Stage Manager	William McCarthy
Joan	Joan Clement
Meadows	William Frawley
The Nightingale Quartette	Evelyn Sayers Loretta Sayers Jessie Payne Doreen Glover
Josie	Ula Sharon
Polly	Irene Dunne
Bob Martin	Jack Whiting
Tilly	Beatrice Lillie
Clyde Parker	Clifton Webb
Mr. Hemingway	Frank Doane

Act I.—Scene 1—The Stage. 2—Mr. Martin's House, Greenwich.
Act II.—Mr. Martin's House. 2—The Stage Door. 3—Sutton Place.

Staged by Edward Royce.

The one in which Bob has to pretend to be married and the father of an heir in order to induce Uncle Hemingway to loan him $200,000 by the middle of the second act. Tilly, the maid, is commandeered as the wife and the infant is stolen from the janitor, or somebody.

MARCO MILLIONS

(92 performances)

A play by Eugene O'Neill. Produced by The Theatre Guild at the Guild Theatre, New York, January 9, 1928.

Cast of characters—

Christian Traveller	Philip Leigh
Magian Traveller	Mark Schweid
Buddhist Traveller	Charles Romano
A Mahometan	Robert Barrat
A Corporal	Albert Van Dekker
Kukachin	Margalo Gillmore
Marco Polo	Alfred Lunt
Donata	Natalie Browning
Tedaldo	Morris Carnovsky
Nicolo	Henry Travers
Maffeo	Ernest Cossart
A Dominican Monk	Albert Van Dekker
A Knight Crusader	George Cotton
A Papal Courier	Sanford Meisner
One Ali Brother	Mark Schweid
Older Ali Brother	H. H. McCollum
The Prostitute	Mary Blair
A Dervish	John Henry
An Indian Snake Charmer	John Henry
A Buddhist Priest	Philip Leigh
A Tartar Minstrel	William Edmonson
Emissary from Kublai	Albert Van Dekker
Kublai, the Great Kaan	Baliol Holloway
Chu-Yin	Dudley Digges
Boatswain	H. H. McCollum

Ghazan, Kaan of Persia.........................Morris Carnovsky
General Bayan.....................................Robert Barrat
Messenger from Persia...........................Charles Romano
Paulo Loredano....................................Philip Leigh
A Confucian Priest................................Mark Schweid
A Moslem Priest..................................H. H. McCollum
A Buddhist Priest...............................Charles Romano
A Tartar Chronicler...............................Philip Leigh
    Scenes in Venice, at the Court of Kublai Kaan and at Various
Stopping Places Between.
    Staged by Rouben Mamoulian.

Marco Polo, coming to man's estate in his late teens, is taken by his father, Nicolo, and his uncle, Maffeo, on a business trip to the court of Kublai Kaan. There he meets the Princess Kukachin, who falls desperately in love with him. Later Marco is commissioned by Kublai Kaan to escort the Princess into Persia. He accomplishes the assignment, remaining coldly impervious to the little lady's advances. She dies of love and Marco returns to Venice to marry Donata, his childhood's passion.

* ROSALIE

(181 performances)

A musical comedy in two acts; book by William Anthony McGuire and Guy Bolton; lyrics by P. G. Wodehouse and Ira Gershwin; music by George Gershwin and Sigmund Romberg. Produced by Florenz Ziegfeld at the New Amsterdam Theatre, New York, January 10, 1928.

Cast of characters—

Captain Carl Rabisco............................Halford Young
Michael O'Brien..................................Clarence Oliver
Mary O'Brien......................................Bobbe Arnst
Prince Rabisco.....................................A. P. Kaye
His Royal Highness King Cyril.....................Frank Morgan
Her Royal Highness Queen.........................Margaret Dale
Rosita..Claudia Dell
Marcia...Gladys Glad
Alla..Jeanne Audree
Xenia...Hazel Forbes
Maritza...Yvonne Grey
Sister Angelica.................................Katherine Burke
Bill Delroy..Jack Donahue
Lieut. Richard Fay, U. S. A. ....Oliver McLennan
Princess Rosalie.................................Marilyn Miller
Marinna...Antonina Lalaew
Steward...Charles Gotthold
Corps Lieutenant...................................Jack Bruns
Superintendent of West Point....................Charles Gotthold
Captain Banner.....................................Clay Clement
The Ex-King of Portugal..........................Charles Davis
The Ex-King of Bulgaria.......................Clarence De Silva
The Ex-King of Prussia............................Henri Jackin
The Ex-King of Greece..............................Mark Shull
The Ex-King of Bavaria..........................Harry Donaghy

The Ex-Sultan of Turkey..........................Edgar Welch
Eight Estelle Liebling Singers
Staged by Florenz Ziegfeld, Seymour Felix and William A. Mc-
Guire.

Rosalie, being the susceptible princess of Romanza, falls in love with Lieut. Richard Fay of West Point, and he, being obliging as well as baritone, flies the ocean, à la Lindbergh, to be near her. Later, when the royal family of Romanza tours the United States, Lieutenant Fay is appointed leader of a guard of honor. There are complications, lyrical and dramatic, but the abdication of Rosalie's comic king father permits a happy solution to the romance.

DIVERSION

(62 performances)

A play in three acts by John Van Druten. Produced by Adolph Klauber at the 49th Street Theatre, New York, January 11, 1928.

Cast of characters—

Ida Ballinger.....................................Elsie Wagstaff
Muriel Hayward....................................Rose Hobart
Parker..Morton Lucas
Owen Hayward......................................Leo G. Carroll
Wyn Hayward.......................................Richard Bird
Sir Charles Hayward...............................Guy Standing
Rayetta Muir......................................Cathleen Nesbitt
Miss Bunting......................................Eleanor Daniels
Mabs Kellet.......................................Nan Marriott-Watson
Tony Roscoe.......................................Harry Green
Lena..Ruby Hallier
Acts I, II and III.—Sitting Room in Sir Charles Hayward's House in Harley Street, London, and Rayetta Muir's Flat in Mayfair.
Staged by Jane Cowl.

Wyn Hayward, vacationing on Lake Como, meets the popular actress, Rayetta Muir. At Bellagio they spend the week-end together, deeply in love. Returned to London, Rayetta goes back to her stage work and her other lovers and Wyn, humiliated and wildly jealous, strangles her. Certain of arrest and conviction, he appeals to his physician father, Sir Charles, for a poison to take him out of life, which the father, after a struggle, gives him.

COCK ROBIN

(100 performances)

A comedy-drama by Philip Barry and Elmer Rice. Produced by Guthrie McClintic at the 48th Street Theatre, New York, January 12, 1928.

Cast of characters—

George McAuliffe	Edward Ellis
Julian Cleveland	Moffat Johnston
Richard Lane	Richard Stevenson
Hancock Robinson	Henry D. Southard
John Jessup	James Todd
Alice Montgomery	Beatrice Herford
Carlotta Maxwell	Muriel Kirkland
Clarke Torrance	Howard Freeman
Henry Briggs	Jo Milward
Dr. Edgar Grace	Wright Kramer
Maria Scott	Beulah Bondi
Helen Maxwell	Desmond Kelley

Acts I, II and III.—The Interior of an English Grog-Shop of the Eighteenth Century.

Staged by Guthrie McClintic.

Hancock Robinson is the least popular member of a Little Theatre group which is giving its annual performance for the benefit of the local hospital. In a duel scene Hancock is shot with a property revolver into which some one has slipped a loaded cartridge. At the same time he is mysteriously stabbed in the back. Nearly everybody, except the dramatic critics, is suspected. After a two-act search it transpires the professional coach did the job to avenge Robinson's mistreatment of a young girl.

A FREE SOUL

(100 performances)

A play in four acts by Willard Mack, from the novel by Adela Rogers St. John. Produced by William A. Brady at the Playhouse, New York, January 12, 1928.

Cast of characters—

Mrs. Deborah Ashe	Adelaide Prince
Mrs. Dorothea Joliffe	Jane Houston
Grace Carling	Ann Winston
Ramsay Joliffe	George Christie
Dean	Joseph Kennedy
Dwight Sutro	George Baxter
Jan Ashe	Kay Johnson
Stephen Ashe	Lester Lonergan
Bill Wilfong	James H. Bell
Abe Sloan	John Daly Murphy
Gwennie Wilfong	Ellen Dorr
Ace Wilfong	Melvin Douglas
Hooper	William E. Barry
Big Mack	Charles F. Lewis
A Gambler	Lou Turner
Fresno Kelly	John Irwin
Nelson	Edward F. Roseman
Carroll	Hugh Lester
Mullaly	John Costello
Red	Walter E. Powers
Jack	Lou Turner
Patrolman	Charles Stanley

```
Another Officer...............................Spencer Stoddart
Judge Beasley....................................George Christie
Nolan, District Attorney......................Frank McGlynn, Jr.
Clerk of the Court...............................George Benson
Foreman of Jury.................................Joseph Kennedy
Mullins...............................................John Morris
Bailiff..............................................E. J. Barrett
```
Act I.—The Drawing Room of Mrs. Ashe, San Francisco. Act II.—The Office of Ace Wilfong. Act III.—The Living Room of Mr. and Mrs. Ace Wilfong. Act IV.—Scene 1—A Corridor. 2—The Court Room.

Staged by George Cukor.

Jan Ashe is free-souled and strong-willed. To prove it she jilts Dwight Sutro, socially important, and marries Ace Wilfong, gambler, after her father has broken his promise never to drink again. After which Ace, suspecting Sutro of pleasuring himself at Jan's expense, shoots and kills him. In court he is given his freedom by a jury in response to the pleading of Jan's father.

THE INTERNATIONAL

(27 performances)

A musical play by John Howard Lawson. Music by Edward A. Ziman. Produced by the New Playwrights at the New Playwright Theatre, New York, January 12, 1928.

Cast of characters—

```
Simeon Silas Fitch............................George N. Price
Edward Elliot Spunk..........................Herbert T. Bergman
Ethel.............................................Miriam Gumble
David Fitch......................................Franchot Tone
T. Jerome Henley................................Ross Matthews
Karneski.........................................George Tobias
Alise................................................Jane Barry
Rubeloff, Soviet Commissar.....................Eduard Franz
The Grand Lama................................Lawrence Bolton
Tim Garritty....................................Felix Jacoves
Madam Miau....................................Ruth Chorpenning
Gussie.............................................Hazel Mason
Monsieur Fouchard, of the French Ministry........Lawrence Bolton
General Fitzmaurice, of the British Army............Lionel Ferrend
Benjamin Krumb.................................Ross Matthews
```
Staged by John Howard Lawson.

Simeon Fitch and Edward Spunk, two of Wall Street's meanest millionaires, start a revolt of capitalism's victims by certain dirty work in the oil fields of Thibet. The revolt spreads to Moscow, Paris and New York, many thousands of innocent workers are mowed down by machine-gun bullets and capitalism is still triumphant at the end.

THE FIRST STONE

(3 performances)

A play in three acts by Walter Ferris; based on a story by Mary Heaton Vorse. Produced by the Civic Repertory Theatre, at the Civic Repertory Theatre, New York, January 16, 1928.

Cast of characters—

John Peri	Egon Brecher
Sarah Peri	Eva Le Gallienne
Anita Peri	Josephine Hutchinson
Victor Peri	Charles McCarthy
Bernard Ives	Donald Cameron
Dave	Walter Tupper Jones
Minnie Barton	Alma Kruger
Mrs. Bascomb	Leona Roberts
Mrs. Allen	Margaret Love
Fred Bliss	Harry Sothern

Acts I, II and III.—The Peri Home on Cape Cod.
Staged by Miss Le Gallienne.

Sarah Peri, a young Cape Codder, married a Portuguese who, after their children were grown, took a job trucking. After that he was away from home weeks at a time, and Sarah, being still attractive, and in love with life, got to walking out with a village sheik. The children try to protect her, but John, the husband, finds her out and casts her off. She goes back to her mother for a time, until she can clear her thought. Then she returns home, draws her children to her and defies her husband to do his worst. John, knowing he is whipped, makes the best of his defeat.

THE MERCHANT OF VENICE

(64 performances)

A comedy in five acts by William Shakespeare. Revived by Winthrop Ames at the Broadhurst Theatre, New York, January 16, 1928.

Cast of characters—

The Duke of Venice	George Graham
The Prince of Morocco	David Leonard
Antonio	Leonard Willey
Bassanio	Murray Kennell
Salanio	Hardie Albright
Salarino	Sydney Booth
Gratiano	Hugh Miller
Lorenzo	Guido Nadzo
Shylock	George Arliss
Tubal	Henry Morrell

```
Launcelot Gobbo................................... Romney Brent
Old Gobbo..........................................Henry Morrell
Stephano............................................Alan Willey
Balthasar.........................................Lewis A. Sealy
Portia............................................. Peggy Wood
Nerissa..........................................Spring Byington
Jessica............................................. Hope Cary
    Acts I, II and III.—At Venice, and at Belmont, the Seat of Por-
tia on the Continent.
    Staged by Winthrop Ames.
```

The version prepared by Winthrop Ames for Mr. Arliss's use cuts the text to essential scenes and is played with a single intermission after Bassanio's casket scene.

THE SILVER BOX

(23 performances)

A comedy in three acts by John Galsworthy. Revived by Henry Baron at the Morosco Theatre, New York, January 17, 1928.

Cast of characters—

```
John Barthwick, M.P. ...........................Halliwell Hobbes
Mrs. Barthwick............................... Louise Mackintosh
Jack Barthwick.................................... Martin Walker
Roper.........................................J. Malcolm Dunn
Mrs. Jones........................................Isobel Elsom
Marlow...........................................Gerald Rogers
Wheeler.......................................... Mary Forbes
Jones............................................. James Dale
Mrs. Seddon...................................... Florence Guise
Snow........................................... Arthur Stenning
A Police Magistrate............................Charles Hampden
An Unknown Lady.............................. Sheelagh Hayes
Two Little Girls............................. { Elizabeth Wragge
                                             { Eddie Wragge
Livens.............................................Lance Burritt
A Relieving Officer.............................. Charles Cardom
A Magistrate's Clerk............................. Isidore Marcid
    Acts I and II.—Scene 1—Rockingham Gate. John Barthwick's
Dining Room. Act II.—Scene 1—The Jones' Lodgings, Merthyr
Street. Act III.—A London Police Court.
    Staged by Laurence Hanray.
```

Jones, helping young Jack Barthwick, son of John Barthwick, M.P., home the night he could not navigate, remains to drink the sleeping man's liquor and finally to take from the table a silver cigarette box. The theft is charged to Jones' wife, a servant in the Barthwick house, and the case brings all parties to court. Barthwick, drunk, has taken a street girl's purse as a joke; Jones, drunk, has taken the silver box at Barthwick's maudlin suggestion. But Barthwick is freed by the cleverness of his rich father's lawyer and Jones is sent to the workhouse.

MIRRORS

(13 performances)

A play in three acts by Milton Herbert Gropper. Produced by Albert Lewis at the Forrest Theatre, New York, January 18, 1928.

Cast of characters—

Gilbert Norton	Hale Hamilton
Mrs. Norton	Marie Nordstrom
Joan Norton	Patricia Barclay
Phillips	Gerald Phillips
Mary Norton	Sylvia Sidney
Mrs. Trask	Lea Penman
Jack Trask	Richard Sterling
Phyllis Langdon	Dorothea Chard
William Slater	Jack Maclennan
Calvin Trask	Raymond Guion
Howard Brook	Bruce Evans
Fabia Carroll	Joan Brown
Richard Allen	Alan Purling
Donald Dean	Franklyn Fox
Roger King	Albert Hackett

Acts I, II and III.—In the Suburban Home of the Nortons. Staged by Albert Lewis.

The Gilbert Nortons have fallen easily into the ways of their community's fast set and are given to wild parties and a free exchange of wife for wife and man for man. To keep up with their parents the younger Nortons, Joan and Mary, invite in the girls and boys and Joan organizes what she calls a "blind necking" party. Mary, being younger, rebels at the promiscuousness of her sister, thus attracts the attention of the boys and is soon able to snare herself a banker's son without sacrificing her honor. The elder Nortons, momentarily sobered by the turn of events, then take another drink and go back to their party.

THE PATRIOT

(12 performances)

A drama in eight scenes; adapted from the German of Alfred Neumann by Ashley Dukes. Produced by Gilbert Miller at the Majestic Theatre, New York, January 19, 1928.

Cast of characters—

Count Peter Alexeievitch Pahlen	Leslie Faber
Ivan	Bernard Savage
Anna, Baroness Ostermann	Madge Titheradge
Count Nikita Petrovitch Panin	Austin Trevor

(By Courtesy of Winthrop Ames)

Major Muravieff.................................... Frank Elliott
Count Stroganoff.............................. Clarence Derwent
A Staff Captain................................... Forbes Dawson
Stepan.. Frank Shannon
Paul I, Tsar of Russia............................. Lyn Harding
A Corporal... Henry Berger
Grand Duke Alexander............................. John Gielgud
The English Doctor............................... Henry Carvill
Count Valerian Zuboff............................. Lumsden Hare
Prince Platon Zuboff.............................. John Parrish
General Talyzin............................. Reginald Carrington

Officers, Sentries, Servants

Acts I, II and III.—In the Mikhailovsky Palace.

Staged by Gilbert Miller.

The decline and fall of Tsar Paul I of Russia, as a result of the conspiracy of Count Peter Pahlen to force the abdication of Paul and the ascension of the Grand Duke Alexander. Into the conspiracy Pahlen draws his mistress, the Countess Anna, whom he forces to become the mistress of the king that she may act as a spy. Following Paul's death Pahlen arranges his own death and that of the guard who did the actual killing that their souls' account may be squared.

A DISTANT DRUM

(11 performances)

A play in three acts by Vincent Lawrence. Produced by William Harris, Jr., at the Hudson Theatre, New York, January 20, 1928.

Cast of characters—

Agnes.. Margery Card
Paul Fox....................................... Harold Elliott
Lynn Wilson.................................... Mary Newcomb
George Wilson.................................. Felix Krembs
Edith Reed.................................... Katherine Wilson
John Milburn................................... Louis Calhern
Carl Franken................................... Robert Thorne

Acts I and II.—A Room in Wilson's Apartment. Act III.—A Room in Milburn's Apartment.

Staged by William Harris, Jr.

John Milburn is utterly and confessedly a cad. He cheats at cards and lives on the donations of rich women. At the moment his mistress is Lynn Wilson, who loves him desperately. Her friend is Edith Reed. As soon as Milburn learns that Miss Reed is worth millions he schemes to ditch Mrs. Wilson and marry her friend. The plan is first halted by George Wilson's discovery of his wife's affair and later by his decision, while drunk, to shoot and kill the wrecker of his home. Which he does. Just in time to prevent an elopement of Milburn and Edith.

CARRY ON

(8 performances)

A play in three acts by Owen Davis. Produced by Carl Reed at the Masque Theatre, New York, January 23, 1928.

Cast of characters—

The Marston Family:

Horace	Berton Churchill
Ellen	Beatrice Terry
Aunt Mary	Elizabeth Patterson
Walter	Ben Smith
Alice	Flora Sheffield
Jerry	Owen Davis, Jr.

Those Outside the Family:

Paul Jewett	Fleming Ward
John Bartlett	Joseph Bell
Benjamin Robie	Edward H. Loeffler
Jim Durk	Robert Kelly
Wanda Durk	Irene Homer
Martha	Lizzie McCall
Lena	Joan Sudlow

Act I.—The Old Marston Mansion, North Broadway, Yonkers.
Acts II and III.—South Broadway.
Staged by Clifford Brooke.

Horace Marston, head of the Marstons of Yonkers, for over a hundred years engaged in the woolen mills business, sells out to a syndicate which throws the Marston mills into bankruptcy. With stanch New England honor Marston insists the debts must be paid, whether the Marstons are legally responsible or not. Pompously he holds to the decision until, in their desperation, his daughter seeks comfort in the arms of a married man, his oldest son turns thief in order to marry a mill girl, and his wife and old Aunt Mary suffer greatly from poverty and anguish of soul. Finally the wife herself steals enough securities to send the youngest son back to college and Marston is properly crushed.

WE NEVER LEARN

(24 performances)

A play in three acts by Daisy Wolf. Produced by William B. Friedlander at the Eltinge Theatre, New York, January 23, 1928.

Cast of characters—

Katy	Sheila Trent
Helen Bruce	Elisabeth Risdon
Constance Bruce	Wanda Perry
Isabelle Warren	Mabel Kroman
James Bruce	Charles Trowbridge

```
Jack Warren..................................Robert Lynn
Robert Kenyon................................Alfred Cross
Laura Deane.............................Estelle Winwood
David Willard...............................Austin Fairman
Drew......................................Charles La Torre
Weldon Deane..............................Brandon Evans
Romero Royce................................Richard Terry
George Barlow..................................Claude Main
```
    Acts I and III.—Living Room of James Bruce's Home in a Mid-
Western City. Act II.—A Room in Willard's Bachelor Apartment.
Staged by William B. Friedlander.

James Bruce, criminal attorney and married, has a mistress.
Dave Willard, cad, attempts to force himself upon the mistress
and Bruce shoots him. Romero Royce is charged with the murder, and Bruce engaged to defend him. He succeeds in getting a
verdict for the boy, but loses his wife, who, through the trial,
learns all.

THE QUEEN'S HUSBAND

(125 performances)

A play in three acts by Robert Emmet Sherwood. Produced
by William A. Brady, Jr., and Dwight Deere Wiman at the Playhouse, New York, January 25, 1928.

Cast of characters—

```
Frederick Granton................................Gyles Isham
Phipps........................................Edward Rigby
Lord Birten..............................Wallace Widdecombe
Petley.......................................James H. Morrison
Princess Anne.............................Katherine Alexander
Queen Martha..................................Gladys Hanson
Lady-in-Waiting.............................Marguerite Taylor
Another Lady-in-Waiting.........................Helen Cromwell
General Northrup.............................Reginald Barlow
King Eric VIII.................................Roland Young
Major Blent...................................William Boren
Sergeant.........................................John M. James
Dr. Fellman....................................Arthur Hughes
Prince William.................................Dwight Frye
Laker.......................................Benedict MacQuarrie
```
    Acts I, II and III.—An Island Kingdom in the North Sea. The
Scene Is in the King's Private Office in the Royal Palace.
Staged by John Cromwell.

Queen Martha, being the dominating influence in the royal
palace of an island kingdom in the North Sea, takes a trip to
America hoping to effect a loan. While she is away King Eric
VIII manages "to give the royal prerogatives a little much-
needed exercise." Faced with a revolution the king sits hard
upon the premier, who would be dictator, and finally arranges a
compromise satisfactory to both laborites and communists. He

also makes possible the runaway marriage of his daughter and his secretary, to save the princess from having to marry a royal worm from an adjoining kingdom.

57 BOWERY

(28 performances)

A comedy in three acts by Edward Locke. Produced by C. William Morganstern at Wallack's Theatre, New York, January 26, 1928.

Cast of characters—

David Schiller	Hyman Adler
Manny Schiller	John D. Seymour
Martha Schiller	Joan Blair
Olga Petrokoff	Renee Rush
Jake Rosenberg	Saul Z. Martell
Edward Rafferty	Harold Healy
Edward Van Clive	Robert Brister
John Southwood	Wilbur DeRouge
Mary Clapperton	Ann Reader
Mrs. Tewksbury Saint John	Eeda Von Buelow
Terry	Jonathan Hole
Mangold	Charles London
McNally	Robert Blake
Pearson	Alfred L. Regali

Acts I and III.—Schiller's Pawn Shop. Act II.—The Uptown Place. Place—New York City.

Staged by Edward Elsner.

David Schiller, honest pawnbroker, gets in with a bad gang when his son, Manny, brings him the trade of the crafty society crook, Edward Van Clive. David is arrested as a fence and seems to be on his way prisonward when a friendly detective saves him by extracting a confession from Van Clive.

THE MYSTERY MAN

(100 performances)

A melodrama in three acts by Morris Ankrum and Vincent Duffey. Produced by Gustav Blum at the Bayes Theatre, New York, January 26, 1928.

Cast of characters—

Robert Wheeler	Weldon Heyburn
Jerome Tuttle	Robert Farrell
Inspector Harrison	George Lessey
Detective Clancy	Allen Nagle
Ross	John O. Hewitt
Alice Prince	Gail De Hart

Togo..Reo Suga
Philip Jones.......................................Allyn Joslyn
Dr. Osborn.....................................Cameron Clemens
Dixon...Oscar Hewes
Yogo..Sizuo Kawata
Anson...Roger De Koven
Mr. Prince.....................................Willard Dashiell
Evelyn Wells..................................Marjorie Dalton
        Acts I, II and III.—The Living Room of Robert Wheeler's Apart-
ment, Park Avenue, New York City.
        Staged by Gustav Blum.

Robert Wheeler, coming home late and tight, discovers a
strange man dead on his davenport. He calls the police and the
investigation following involves every one—from Wheeler's best
friend, Jerome Tuttle, to his fiancée, Alice Prince. Finally it is
proved that the dead man was shot by the real mother of Alice,
who had been serving her all these years as maid. The dead man
was Alice's father and had threatened exposure.

SO AM I

(27 performances)

A comedy in three acts by C. M. Selling; from the Italian by
Camillo Scolari. Produced by Schiffer and Shifrin at the Comedy
Theatre, New York, January 27, 1928.

Cast of characters—

First and Third Acts

Elena Stiradi.......................................Betty Linley
Paolina..Louise Carter
Giovanni Stiradi...............................Walter Kingsford
Roberto..Vernon Steele

Second Act

Francesca..Betty Linley
Peppina..Louise Carter
Sebastino......................................Walter Kingsford
Gino...Vernon Steele
        Acts I and III.—Library of Stiradi's Home in Southern Europe.
        Act II.—An Interlude. "Francesca and Her Lover." (As Envisioned
by Elena.) Living Room of Sebastino's House in Perugia, Italy,
1350 A.D.
        Staged by Marion Gering.

In Italy Elena, young and beautiful and just from a convent,
is married to the rich and older Signor Stiradi. Elena is an obe-
dient wife but she prefers to sleep alone in the alcove of the cold
castle because it reminds her of the convent. Signor Stiradi
thinks to make certain architectural changes in the castle and
thus inspire Elena's interest in her home and a different sleeping
arrangement. He engages a handsome young architect who intro-

duces the young wife to a tale from Boccaccio. As she reads it she envisions the story and it forms the second act of the play. After which she knows what to do. She throws the architect out of the alcove and welcomes her husband home.

* STRANGE INTERLUDE

(112 performances)

A play in nine acts by Eugene O'Neill. Produced by the Theatre Guild at the John Golden Theatre, New York, January 30, 1928.

Cast of characters—

Charles Marsden .... Tom Powers
Professor Leeds .... Philip Leigh
Nina Leeds .... Lynn Fontanne
Sam Evans .... Earle Larimore
Edmund Darrell .... Glenn Anders
Mrs. Amos Evans .... Helen Westley
Gordon Evans, as a Boy .... Charles Walters
Madeline Arnold .... Ethel Westley
Gordon Evans, as a Man .... John J. Burns
    Acts I, II and IV.—Library, Leeds' Home in a Small University Town of New England. Act III.—Dining Room of the Evans' Homestead in Northern New York. Acts V and VI.—Sitting Room of Small House at the Seashore. Act VII.—Sitting Room of the Evans' Apartment on Park Avenue. Act VIII.—Section of Afterdeck of the Evans' Cruiser. Act IX.—A Terrace on the Evans' Estate on Long Island.
    Staged by Philip Moeller.

See page 28.

THE OPTIMISTS

(24 performances)

A musical play in two parts; music by Melville Gideon; sketches and lyrics by Clifford Grey, Greatrex Newman and Austin Melford. Produced by Melville Gideon at the Casino de Paris, New York, January 30, 1928.

The principals—

Melville Gideon	Luella Gear
George Hassell	Sally Starr
Bobby Watson	Flora Le Breton
Fred Hillebrand	Evelyn de la Tour
Richard Bold	Eleanor Powell

Staged by Melville Gideon.

SALVATION

(31 performances)

A play in three acts by Sidney Howard and Charles MacArthur. Produced by Arthur Hopkins at the Empire Theatre, New York, January 31, 1928.

Cast of characters—

Mrs. Jones	Helen Ware
Whittaker	Osgood Perkins
Brady	George MacFarlane
Bethany	Pauline Lord
Virgie	Emma Wise
Victor	Donald Gallaher
First Man	Thomas Meegan
First Woman	Bernice Richmond
Second Man	James Mulady
Second Woman	Marjorie Main
Third Woman	Maud Sinclair
Warner Putnam	Elmer Cornell
Mrs. Putnam	Emily Boileau
Mrs. Albertson	Mary Hubbard
Waiter	Edward Broadley
A Porter	George Colan
Another Porter	Stephen Irving
The Detroit Free Press	Geo. Cassellberry
Photographer	Geo. Colan
Chicago News	Bernice Richmond
Chicago Tribune	Jean Rich
Chicago Herald & Examiner	Jarvis Kerr

Act I.—The Sitting Room of a Chicago Hotel. Act II.—Bethany's Bungalow on an Island in a Wisconsin Lake. Act III.—Behind the Auditorium of the Bethany Tabernacle in Chicago.
Staged by Arthur Hopkins.

Bethany Jones, saved at the age of twelve, becomes a popular and profitable revivalist under the shrewdly dishonest guidance of her mother and an ex-circus man named Brady. Bethany also falls in love with Victor, the tenor in her choir, a shifty young man also with an eye to her value as an investment. Bethany and Victor are secretly married, hide away for a honeymoon, are charged with scandalous behavior and routed out by Bethany's exploiters. For the first time the girl realizes what religion means to all of them, including Victor, and after one final rehabilitation meeting she walks out on the family.

THE MADCAP

(103 performances)

A musical comedy in three acts; adapted from the French of Regis Gignoux and Jacques Thery by Gertrude Purcell and Gladys Unger; lyrics by Clifford Grey; music by Maurice Rubens.

Produced by the Messrs. Shubert at the Royale Theatre, New York, January 31, 1928.

Cast of characters—

Petunia...Marie Dayne
Helene...Lillian Lane
Claire Valmont....................................Ethel Intropidi
Lord Clarence Steeple..........................Sydney Greenstreet
Lady Mary Steeple...............................Ethel Morrison
Hon. Harry Steeple...............................Harry Puck
Chibi...Mitzi
Emmeline Hawley...............................Marcella Swanson
Cuthbert Custard.................................Charley Sylber
James..Pat Clayton
Sir Bertram Hawley..............................Arthur Treacher
Footman..Clifford Smith
    Act I.—Claire Valmont's Villa on the Outskirts of Deauville. Act II.—Lord Steeple's House in Deauville. Act III.—Claire Valmont's Garden.
    Staged by Duane Nelson.

Chibi, at twenty, pretends to be twelve, wears rompers and curls, so her mother will not appear to be as old as she is. Mamma, having been run over by Lord Clarence Steeple's automobile, wants to marry Lord Clarence. But she has told him she is only twenty-nine, and here is this bouncing daughter to account for.

LA GRINGA

(13 performances)

A play in three acts by Tom Cushing. Produced by Hamilton MacFadden at the Little Theatre, New York, February 1, 1928.

Cast of characters—

Soror Felicidad...................................Arline Francis
Madre Superior...................................Isabel Irving
Pedro..William Lovejoy
Captain Aaron Bowditch.......................George Nash
Carlota D'Astradente............................Claudette Colbert
Sarah Bowditch...................................Clara Blandick
Belle Spinney......................................Eva Condon
Charity..Marie Haynes
Bertha Beales......................................Cecil Kern
Mrs. Nott...Jessie Graham
Captain Jabez Spinney...........................Frank Sylvester
Dr. Caleb Sprague................................Paul Wright
    Act I.—The Convent of Santa Ginevra at La Rincona in Mexico. Act II.—The Bowditch House on County Street, New Bedford, Mass. Act III.—Caleb Sprague's Study.
    Staged by Hamilton MacFadden.

Carlota D'Astradente, orphan, is at school in a Mexican convent when the roving Capt'n Bowditch, hearing her father has left her a fortune in Spain, induces her to run away and marry him.

The captain leaves Carlota with his puritan sister, Sarah, while he goes to Spain for the money. He finds no money and returns to learn that Carlota is in love with Caleb Sprague. He casts Carlota off. Sprague wants to marry her, but she fears she will ruin his school position and goes back to her Mexican convent.

ATLAS AND EVA

(24 performances)

A comedy in three acts by Harry Delf. Produced by Harry Delf at the Mansfield Theatre, New York, February 6, 1928.

Cast of characters—

Pop	George Marion
Ma	Helen Lowell
Herbie	Tom Brown
Nebblepredders { Aunt Emma	Lotta Linthicum
Cousin Bessie	Sara Floyd
Eva	Leona Hogarth
Elmer	Harry Delf
Josie	Dorothea Chard
Al Sprocket	Donald Dillaway
Mrs. McGorky	Clara Thropp
Bill Donahue	Charles Hanna
Dr. Parker	Arthur C. Morris
Mr. Mullen	Herbert Fortier
A Gatekeeper	A. C. Henderson

Acts I and II.—The Nebblepredders' Parlor. Act III.—Elmer's Bedroom.

Staged by Ira Hards.

Elmer Nebblepredder, floorwalker, carries the burdens of all his family on his own frail shoulders. This brings him to a state of physical collapse. Then his wife, Eva, turns on the family and announces that they will have to get along without Elmer's support. Elmer suffers a lapse of consciousness during which he sees himself at St. Peter's gate and learns that worriers are not wanted even in heaven. When he comes back he calls for a taxi and an Atlantic City time table. He and Eva are going to step out.

MRS. DANE'S DEFENSE

(16 performances)

A play in four acts by Henry Arthur Jones. Produced by the Chamberlain Brown Cosmopolitan Artists at the Cosmopolitan Theatre, New York, February 6, 1928.

Cast of characters—

Mrs. Bulsom-Porter............................Alison Skipworth
Mr. Bulsom-Porter............................Conway Wingfield
Mr. James Risby...................................Stanley Logan
Mrs. Dane...Violet Heming
Lionel Carteret...................................Horace Braham
Sir Daniel Carteret..............................Robert Warwick
Lady Eastney.......................................Julia Hoyt
Janet Colquhoun..................................Vivian Martin
Canon Bonsey......................................J. H. Brewer
Adams...Robert Linden
Mr. Fendick......................................George Alison
Wilson...Edgar Henning
    Acts I, II and III.—At Sunningwater, About Twenty-five Miles
from London.
    Staged by Clifford Brooke and Mabel Brownell.

Lionel Carteret falls desperately in love with Mrs. Dane, about
whom there is some gossip. Mrs. Dane defends herself by deny-
ing everything, but Sir Daniel Carteret, Lionel's foster father,
finally breaks down her defenses and she stands exposed as a
woman with a past. She and Lionel are convinced that no woman
who has committed this sin of sins can successfully recover her
old position in society, so they give up their marriage.

MEEK MOSE

(24 performances)

A comedy-drama in three acts by Frank Wilson. Produced by
Lester A. Walton at the Princess Theatre, New York, February
6, 1928.

Cast of characters—

Ezra...Arthur Ray
Nathan..J. Lawrence Criner
Josephine..Laura Bowman
Penolia...Ruth Ellis
Mose..Charles H. Moore
Claribel..Ruth Carl
Enos Green.....................................Sidney Kirkpatrick
Madam Jones....................................Olyve P. Hopkins
Miss Minnie.......................................Susie Sutton
Dave Roberts....................................Richard Gregg
Cole Turner.....................................Alston Burleigh
Dr. Slaughter...................................Thomas Moseley
Prof. A. P. ....J. (Onion) Jeffry
Stanley Brown.....................................Joe Chapman
Policeman.......................................William Edwards
Dr. Strickland.................................Oliver Sanderson
Mr. Harmon......................................George MacEntee
    Acts I, II and III.—Mose Johnson's Home in Mexia, Texas.
    Staged by George MacEntee.

Mose is the pacifistic leader of the church-going brethren in
his community. When the white people want to move the colored

folk to a low and damp section of town Mose counsels them to accept the order without protest. When disease and death follow his former supporters turn on old Mose, but he gets out with a happy ending when oil is also discovered on the property.

* THE SILENT HOUSE

(149 performances)

A melodrama in four acts by John G. Brandon and George Pickett. Produced by Lee Shubert at the Morosco Theatre, New York, February 7, 1928.

Cast of characters—

```
Benson.......................................Charles McNaughton
Ho-Fang........................................Clarke Silvernail
Mateo..........................................James MacDonald
T'Mala...........................................Helen Chandler
Philip Barty...............................Gerald Oliver Smith
George Winsford.................................Allan Dinehart
Dr. Chan-Fu........................................Howard Lang
Hwang..............................................Bryan Lycan
Jacob Herrington..................................Wyrley Birch
Señor Leon Peroda................................Luis Alberni
    Acts I, II and IV.—The Morning Room of Richard Winsford's
House on Barnes Common, London, Known as "The Silent House."
Act III.—The Chinese Room of the Red House, Barnes.
    Staged by C. W. Hunt.
```

George Winsford's uncle, living mysteriously in a silent house in England, dies and leaves a will. The will provides that George shall inherit the house and also a fortune in bonds if he will live a certain time in the house and find the bonds, which are secretly hidden. George agrees, falls in love with T'Mala, a visitor from next door, is pursued by a sinister Dr. Chan-Fu, protected by an amiable body-servant, Ho-Fang, and finally made master of a happy ending, including the fortune.

SUNNY DAYS

(101 performances)

A musical comedy in three acts; book and lyrics by Clifford Grey and William Cary Duncan from the French of Hennequin and Veber; music by Jean Schwartz. Produced by Hassard Short at the Imperial Theatre, New York, February 8, 1928.

Cast of characters—

```
Victor Duval.................................Maurice Holland
Nanine......................................Marjorie Finley
```

```
Babette............................................Peggy Cornell
Georgette..................................Evangeline Raleigh
Lulu.............................................Maxine Carson
Robert...........................................Sid Hawkins
Angele Larue....................................Rosalie Claire
Rudolph Max.......................................Billy B. Van
Ginette Bertin............................Jeanette MacDonald
Maurice Vane....................................Lynne Overman
Leon Dorsay.....................................Frank McIntyre
Paul Morel.........................................Carl Randall
A Thief...........................................Harry Gordon
Bergeot..............................................Bob Lively
Mircourt..........................................Donald Black
Countess D'Exmore................................Claire Hooper
Premier Dancer.................................Charlotte Ayres
Madame Dorsay...................................Audrey Maple
```

Act I.—Shop of "Victor Duval et Cie," Florist, Rue de la Paix, Paris. Act II.—The Gardens of Leon Dorsay's Château, Fontaine-bleau. Act III.—Reception Room in Leon Dorsay's Château. Staged by Hassard Short.

Leon Dorsay, banker, has been playing around with Ginette Bertin and now wants to quit and return to his wife. Ginette makes little fuss, having also made other plans. But there are temporary complications when the banker discovers on his return home that Ginette's plans included being adopted by Mme. Dorsay, who wants to do good and raise a family.

* RAIN OR SHINE

(146 performances)

A musical play in two acts; book by James Gleason and Maurice Marks; lyrics by Jack Yellen; music by Milton Ager and Owen Murphy. Produced by A. L. Jones and Morris Green at the Geo. M. Cohan Theatre, New York, February 9, 1928.

Cast of characters—

```
Amos K. Shrewsberry.............................Tom Howard
Katie..............................................Ethel Norris
Harry..........................................Edgar Gardner
Frankie Schultz (The Princess de Chimay)............Helen Lynd
Zelda..............................................Rita Garcia
Jesse Dalton........................................Joe Lyons
Mary Wheeler....................................Nancy Welford
Jack Wayne.........................................Warren Hull
Rosie..............................................Rosie Moran
"Smiley" Johnson.....................................Joe Cook
The Policeman.....................................Walter Pharr
The Mother.......................................Dimples Riede
The Child........................................Marian Herson
The Ticket Seller...............................James Gregory
Smiley's Protégé..................................Dave Chasen
Grocko.........................................Vernon Jacobson
The Head Waiter...................................Dave Chasen
The Barker..........................................Joe Lyons
Folte..........................................William V. Powers
The Acrobat........................................Paul Brack
Mrs. Patricia Conway..............................Janet Velie
```

Grace Forsythe..............................Devah Worrell
Lord Gwinnie Llandidrodd Wells, R.A.F. ....Ernest Lambert
   Acts I, II and III.—In and Near Higginstown, R. I., During the
Visit of the Wheeler Shows.
Staged by Alexander Leftwich.

Wheeler of the Wheeler shows dies and leaves his circus to his daughter Mary. "Smiley" Johnson, a trusted executive, seeks to run it for her. Jesse Dalton tries to get it away from her. Mary falls in love with Jack Wayne, a roustabout who turns out to be an heir. The chief performer strikes and "Smiley" gives most of the show himself, after which Marry marries the roustabout.

PARISIANA

(28 performances)

A musical revue in two acts, by Vincent Valentini. Produced by the Associated Artists, Inc., at the Edyth Totten Theatre, New York, February 9, 1928.

Principals engaged—

Neil Fletcher	Olive May
Melvin Stokes	Kathleen Terry
Billy Bann	Mildred Skinner
Horace Kola	Peggy Heavens
George Laird	Beth Miller
Carol Lynne	Maria Racelle
Ilya Racelle	Thomas sisters
	Dorothy Morrison

Staged by Vincent Valentini.

SHANGHAI GESTURE

(16 performances)

A play in four acts by John Colton. Produced by A. H. Woods at the Century Theatre, New York, February 13, 1928.

Cast of characters—

Cæsar Hawkins............................C. Haviland Chappell
Lin Chi...Conrad Cantzen
Prince Oshima..................................C. Henry Gordon
Poppy...Mary Fowler
Mother Goddam.................................Florence Reed
Ching Chang Mary................................Louie Emery
Ni Pau..Georgia Decker
Ex-Envoy Mandarin Koo Lot Foo..................Langdon Bruce
Sir Guy Charteris................................Percy Waram
Sir John Blessington............................Henry Warwick
Lady Blessington ....Maym Kelso

M. Le Comte De Michot...........................Charles Mather
Mme. La Comtesse De Michot.......................Eunice Lyle
Mrs. Dudley Gregory.............................Gladys Heaney
Dudley Gregory..................................Frank Hotaling
Don Querebro d'Achuna............................J. Carrol Nash
Donna Querebro d'Achuna.................... Margarita Orlova
Apprentice Mice...............................
{ Beatrice Bayard
{ Helen Ray
} Ruth Weeker
(Bobby Lee

Acts I, II and III.—In the Home of Mother Goddam, Shanghai, China.
Staged by Guthrie McClintic.

See "The Best Plays of 1925-26."

THESE MODERN WOMEN

(24 performances)

A comedy in three acts by Lawrence Langner. Produced by Kenneth MacGowan and Robert Rockmore at the Eltinge Theatre, New York, February 13, 1928.

Cast of characters—

Harold Haynes...................................Minor Watson
Bobby..Norman Williams
Marie Louise................................. Camilla Dalberg
Miss Agnew................................... Catherine Haydon
Annabelle Marvin..................................... Helen Flint
Richard Cornwall..................................Alan Mowbray
Roberta Watson Coakley..........................Chrystal Herne
Acts I, II and III.—In the Study of Harold Haynes.
Staged by Rouben Mamoulian.

Roberta Watson Coakley, wife of Harold Haynes, the novelist, comes to believe, after nine years of matrimony, that both husbands and wives are entitled to an occasional affair in order that they may recapture something of the romantic love thrill of their youth. She takes an English writer for her own experiment and suggests that her husband make love to his pretty secretary. Husband obliges and likes the secretary so much that he decides to divorce Roberta and marry her, taking his young son with him.

QUICKSAND

(16 performances)

A play in three acts by Warren F. Lawrence. Produced by Anna Held, Jr., at the Masque Theatre, New York, February 13, 1928.

Cast of characters—

Mary Spencer	Anne Forrest
Mrs. Morse	Lois Arnold
Doctor Shaw	Seth Arnold
Chuey	Allan Atwell
Robert Clayton	Robert Ames
	(By arrangement with Dwight Deere Wiman)
John Austen	Frank Andrews
Parker	J. F. Robertson
Roger Spencer	C. W. Van Voorhis
Tony Angelo	Herbert Lindholm
Doctor Williams	Fred McGuirk
Policeman	Fred Raymond
Roberts	Stanley Andrews
Jane Baker	Betty Utmore

Act I.—Scene 1—Room in Mrs. Morse's Lodging House. 2—Vestibule, Robert Clayton's Apartment. Act II.—Scene 1 and Act III.—Ante-Room in Courthouse. 2—Living Room, Robert Clayton's Apartment.

Staged by Warren F. Lawrence.

Robert Clayton defends Roger Spencer, accused of murder, and secures an acquittal. Clayton also falls in love with Mrs. Spencer, only to learn after the trial that it was the Spencers who had been instrumental in sending his brother to the chair years before. Mrs. Spencer, however, is eventually absolved and Clayton manages the salvation of his own soul.

THE CLUTCHING CLAW

(23 performances)

A play in three acts by Ralph Thomas Kettering. Produced by Barbour and Bryant at the Forrest Theatre, New York, February 14, 1928.

Cast of characters—

John Thornton	Alex McLeod
Patrolman Cairnes	Charles Slattery
Mrs. Midgely	Minnie Dupree
Patricia Thornton	Georgia Lee Hall
Carlos	Bruce Leon
Captain Connelly	Robert Middlemass
Agnes Hayden	Dulcy Cooper
Jerry Hayden	Percy Hilton
Gordon	Ralph Morgan
Johannis Berlau	Duncan Penwarden

Acts I, II and III.—The Study of Thornton Manor, Outside of New York.

Staged by Rollo Lloyd.

John Thornton is murdered at the rise of the curtain and the search for his murderer, combined with a narcotic gang's efforts to throw the searchers off the scent, inspires the visits of ghosts and several minor killings.

HOT PAN

(19 performances)

A play in three acts by Michael Swift. Produced by the Provincetown Players at the Provincetown Theatre, New York, February 15, 1928.

Cast of characters—

Don Armidio Herrera	Eduard Franz
Lopo	Bennett Kilpack
Luz la Mar	Barbara Bulgakov
Ophir Bullgore	Warren Colston
Elam Hallow	Charles P. Thompson
Galen Hudgkins	Harold Johnson
Anthony Maloney	Maxwell Sholes
Simon Tales	Farrell S. Sheridan
Guy Flaunce	Harold Johnsrud
Josiah Snerp	James F. Kelly
John Farthinger	Goldwin Patten
Fortune Greatacre	James J. Martin
Len Dilloughby	Sven Dahl
Alonzo Goodball	Michael Lucy
Andrew Inche	Harold Johnson
"Buttonhole" Cloves	Charles Ashton
Seth Hawley	John Battle
Ringo Rollacher	L. Rufus Hill
"Barefoot" Finnegan	Michael Gray
Jonathan Mindmender	Charles Stepanek
"Cargo" Casey	William Challee
Reverend Frost	Harold McGee
Fanny Glowmoss	Ruth Chorpenning
Roderigo	Charles Stepanek
Guzman	Charles Ashton
A Man	Charles Stepanek

Acts I, II and III.—The Central Room of the Rancho Herrera During the California Gold Rush.
Staged by James Light.

Don Armidio Herrera and his beautiful mistress, Luz la Mar, are turned out of their ranch house during the gold rush days of '49 to make room for a gambling house and saloon. Gold is discovered under the parlor floor and the consequent battle for its possession results in a murder a minute. Anatole France's "Penguin Island" furnishes the thematic inspiration.

SPRING 3100

(29 performances)

A dream play in two acts, by Argyll Campbell and Willard Mack; adapted by Joseph H. Graham. Produced by Geo. L. Miller (in association with Maurice Wakeman) at the Little Theatre, New York, February 15, 1928.

Cast of characters—

Mike Callahan	Owen Martin
James Nolan	Edward Jephson
"Spark"	Tammany Young
"High Brow" Kreegan	"Vic" McLaughlin
Timmy Brownson	Mortie Fogel
Larry O'Day	Jack McKee
Penelope Leland	Lynn Eswood
Harold Storey	Corbet Morris
R. J. Storey	Joseph Kilgour
Josephine Douglas	Mariposa Hayes
Jack Cohen	J. Moy Bennett
Kelly	John M. Washburn
Madge	Maude Brooks
Nina	Eda Moulton

Act I.—Scene 1—The Employees' Entrance, Madison Square Garden. 2—A Glimpse of the Ring, Madison Square Garden. 3—Josephine's and Penny's Apartment on West 48th Street. Act II.—The Storey Apartment.

Staged by Joseph H. Graham.

Larry O'Day, prizefighter, falls in love with Josephine Douglas, society girl. His manager, Mike Callahan, bawls him out for wanting to marry the girl and predicts that if he does and gives up the ring he will go from bad to worse until the police pick him up and his phone number will be Spring 3100, police headquarters. Smarting under the tongue lashing Larry goes into his last fight, is knocked down for the count, dreams everything his manager has predicted and then jumps up and gets a draw.

HOBOKEN BLUES

(35 performances)

A fantasy in three acts by Michael Gold. Produced by the New Playwrights at the New Playwrights Theatre, New York, February 17, 1928.

Cast of characters—

Sally Pickens—Banjo Angel	Hazel Mason
Reverend Rosewater	George N. Price
Mr. Butler	Herbert T. Bergman
Oswald	Montague Ash
Chill McGregor	Lawrence Bolton
Henry Wineglass	Albert Gilman
Amelia Wineglass	Jane Barry
Conductor	Jack Robinson
Mike	Philip Epstein
Lil Joe	Mona Lewis
Sam Pickens	George Bratt
Barney	Ross Mathews
Kid Mumbo	Murray Franklin
Hank Spivey	Thomas Kilmartin
Granny Pickens	Mary Doerr
Daddy Jake	Paul Morton
Honey Lou	Sheba Strunsky
A Singer	Jane Barry

```
A Dancer......................................Jack Robinson
A Bum..........................................Ross Matthews
Hoboken Policemen........................{ Murray Franklin
                                         { Thomas Kilmartin
Doctor.........................................Paul Morton
Nurse..........................................Edith Frisbee
Leo............................................Philip Epstein
Em.............................................Mona Lewis
Jo.............................................Montague Ash
                                         { Isobel Jones
Harlemites.................................{ Jack Robinson
                                         { Albert Gilman
Fordist........................................Edith Frisbee
Policeman......................................Paul Morton
Joe McGregor...................................Thomas Kilmartin
Press Agent....................................Murray Franklin
A Jazz Dancer..................................Harold Boardley
     Act I.—Harlem.  Act II.—Hoboken.  Act III.—Harlem.
     Staged by Edward Massey.
```

A Greenwich Village futuristic revue with a super-amateur cast.

OUR BETTERS

(128 performances)

A comedy in three acts by W. Somerset Maugham. Revived by Messmore Kendall, in association with Gilbert Miller, at the Henry Miller Theatre, New York, February 20, 1928.

Cast of characters—

```
Elizabeth Saunders.............................Madge Evans
Pole...........................................Harry Lillford
Lady George Grayston (Pearl)...................Ina Claire
Fleming Harvey.................................Edward Crandall
Thornton Clay..................................Reginald Bach
Duchesse De Surennes...........................Constance Collier
Gibert Paxton..................................Hugh Sinclair
Principessa Della Cercola......................Lilian Kemble Cooper
Lord Bleane....................................Martin Walker
Arthur Fenwick.................................Frederick Truesdell
First Footman..................................Gordon McRae
Second Footman.................................Harry Joyner
Ernest.........................................Louis D'Arclay
     Act I.—Drawing Room at Lady Grayston's House in Grosvenor
     Street, Mayfair.   Acts II and III.—Morning Room at Feathers
     Nevil, the Graystons' Country Place.
     Staged by Reginald Bach.
```

Lady George Grayston (née Pearl Saunders of New York), having purchased herself a title in England and bought herself a place in English society, seeks to do as much for her younger sister, Elizabeth. But not only is Lady Grayston's set of English rotters and American expatriates of frail morals disgusting to Elizabeth, but Lady George is also caught in a scandalous affair with Gilbert Paxton, who is really the property of the Duchesse de Surennes. After this Elizabeth decides to return to her obscure but honest American sweetheart, Fleming Harvey.

WHISPERING FRIENDS

(112 performances)

A farce in two acts by George M. Cohan. Produced by Mr. Cohan at the Hudson Theatre, New York, February 20, 1928.

Cast of characters—

Daly	Walter Edwin
Natalie	Edith Gresham
Al Wheeler	Chester Morris
Doris Crawford	Elsie Lawson
Emily Sanford	Anne Shoemaker
Joe Sanford	William Harrigan

Acts I, II and III Occur at the Sanfords' in New York City.
Staged by Sam Forrest.

Joe and Emily Sanford, back from their honeymoon, have their best friends, Al Wheeler and Doris Crawford, in for dinner. Joe, suggests Doris to Al, married Emily for her money. No, insists Al, Emily took Joe as a convenience so she could go on flirting on the side. To prove their respective points Doris and Al decide to put Joe and Emily to the test. As a result everybody gets mad at everybody else and serious consequences threaten. But only threaten.

SHERLOCK HOLMES

(16 performances)

A play in five acts by William Gillette. Revived by the Chamberlain Brown Cosmopolitan Artists at the Cosmopolitan Theatre, New York, February 20, 1928.

Cast of characters—

Madge Larrabee	Julia Hoyt
Forman	Philip Heege
Jim Larrabee	Fred L. Tiden
Terese	Fritzi Scheff
Mrs. Faulkner	Jennie A. Eustace
Sid Prince	Horace Braham
Alice Faulkner	Vivian Martin
Sherlock Holmes	Robert Warwick
Dr. Moriarty	Frank Keenan
John	Robert Linden
Bassick	Conway Wingfield
Billy	Raymond Guion
Dr. Watson	Stanley Logan
Leary	John Littell
McTague	Ralph Vincent
Craigin	Edward Rose
Parsons	Edgar Henning

Sir Edward Leighton................................George Alison
Count Von Stalberg..................................J. H. Brewer
      Act I.—Drawing Room at the Larrabees. Act II.—Professor Mo-
riarty's Underground Office. Act III.—Sherlock Holmes' Apartments in Baker Street. Act IV.—The Stopney Gas Chamber. Act
V.—Dr. Watson's Consulting Room, Kensington.
      Staged by Clifford Brooke.

The favorite detective's effort to save Miss Faulkner from the
machinations of the Moriarity gang is again crowned with success.

MAYA

(15 performances)

A play in prologue, nine scenes and epilogue, by Simon Gan-
tillon; translated by Ernest Boyd. Produced by the Actor-
Managers, Inc., at the Comedy Theatre, New York, February 21,
1928.

Cast of characters—

—PROLOGUE—

The Sailor..Otto Hulett
The Girl..Aline MacMahon

—THE PLAY—

Bella...Aline MacMahon
Celeste... Helen Tilden
Phonsine.. Mary Robson
Ida...Louise Lorimer
Albert..George Heller
Fifine..Sylvia Feningston
A Laundress....................................... Shirley Gale
A Fruit Vender....................................Josephine Wehn
A Dockyard Laborer................................Otto Hulett
"Mama".. Florence Gerald
Valentin..George Heller
His Companion.....................................John Rynne
The Italian.......................................Marc Loebell
The Norwegian.....................................Otto Hulett
Ernest..William Shelley
The Painter.......................................John Parrish
Hermance.. Paula Trueman
The Cockney.......................................Harold de Becker
Victor.. William Shelley
Sidi, the Arab....................................Marc Loebell
The Wharf Hand....................................Otto Hulett
The East Indian...................................Harold de Becker
Man from a Jazz Band..............................Marc Loebell
The Guitarist..................................... Sven Von Hallberg
      Nine Scenes in Bella's Room on a Street Leading to the Harbor
of Marseilles, the Mediterranean Seaport.
      Staged by Agnes Morgan.

The symbolical biography of a Marseilles prostitute who represents to each of her callers no more than the confidante, comforter, illusion or ideal his soul hunger demands. Her author sees
her as "a mythical personage, apparition and illusion, vender of

pleasure and purveyor of dreams." To others she is no more than a pathetic soul cast by fate into the ugly environment of the cheaper flesh marts.

SH, THE OCTOPUS

(47 performances)

A comedy mystery play in three acts by Ralph Murphy and Donald Gallaher. Produced by Donald Gallaher and J. M. Welch, for M. & G. Amusements, Inc., at the Royale Theatre, New York, February 21, 1928.

Cast of characters—

Mr. Dempsey	Clifford Dempsey
Mr. Kelly	Harry Kelly
Vesta Vernoff	Beatrice Allen
Three Mysterious Figures	James B. Linhart John Jones Luigi Balestro
Mr. Cobb	Ignacio Martinetti
Paul Morgan	Gavin Gordon
Captain Hook	Francis M. Verdi
Polly	Adele Windsor
Nanny	Lynne Clarke
A Stranger	Bernard J. McOwen

Prologue—Somewhere on Long Island. Acts I and III.—A Deserted Light House. Act II.—Down Below.

Staged by Donald Gallaher.

Mr. Dempsey and Mr. Kelly, detectives, on the way back from a Long Island assignment, are held up by a flat tire. Mr. Kelly takes to gin for comfort, a woman comes out of the night yelling for help, the detectives follow her to an abandoned lighthouse where murder is frequent and worse crimes threatened. After which Mr. Kelly wakes up.

ROPE

(31 performances)

A drama in three acts by David Wallace and T. S. Stribling, based upon Mr. Stribling's novel, "Teeftallow." Produced by James W. Elliott at the Biltmore Theatre, New York, February 22, 1928.

Cast of characters—

Willie Purvis	Alan Goode
Tim Fraley	Bryant Sells

```
John..........................................James H. Dunmore
Zed Parrum...................................Willard Robertson
Old Man Tolbert...............................J. K. Applebee
Pearlie Tolbert.............................Betty Lee Morton
Stinker Smith.................................Kenneth Dana
Mrs. Roxie Biggers........................Elizabeth Patterson
Miss Lydia Scovell.........................Caroline Newcomb
Abner Teeftallow...............................Ben Smith
Nessie Sutton..................................Mary Carroll
Henry Ditmas...................................Crane Wilbur
Rev. Tobe Blackman...........................Leslie Hunt
Railroad Jones..............................Ralph Cummings
Buck Nailer..................................Anthony Blair
Sheriff Bascom.................................Cliff Self
Peck Bradley...............................Herbert Heywood
```

Acts I, II and III Occur Back of the Scovell House and Baxter's Store in Irontown, Tenn., a Village of 800 Souls.

Staged by Frank Merlin.

In Irontown, a Tennessee village of 800 souls, the Rev. Blackman is holding a tent revival and Henry Ditmas, engineer, is building a railroad. Abner Teeftallow, one of the town's garage gang of bad boys, is working for Ditmas and eluding the soul-savers of the revival crowd. Both Abner and Ditmas are in love with Nessie Sutton, the village milliner. One of Abner's friends is killed, Abner organizes the whitecaps to lynch him, Ditmas tries to stop the lynching and Nessie finally manages to keep Abner away from the hanging by submitting to his passion. Abner and Nessie are married and Ditmas goes back to liquor.

DR. KNOCK

(23 performances)

A satirical comedy in three acts by Jules Romain; translated by Harley Granville-Barker. Produced by The American Laboratory Theatre at the American Laboratory Theatre, New York, February 27, 1928.

Cast of characters—

```
Jean...........................................Harold Hecht
Doctor Parpalaid...........................Herbert V. Gellendré
Doctor Knock.................................Robert H. Gordon
Madame Parpalaid.............................Florence House
A Nurse.......................................Mary Martin
Mousquet.......................................Tom Hayes
The Town Crier................................Francis Burk
Bernard.....................................Donald Hartman
Madame Pons..................................Anne Schmidt
A Farmer's Wife.............................Erna Obermeier
A Country Fellow.........................William D. Post, Jr.
Another Country Fellow....................Francis Fergusson
Madame Remy.................................Frances Wilson
```

Act I.—The Road to St. Maurice.   Act II.—The Doctor's Office.

Act III.—The Front Hall of the Hotel.

Staged by Richard Boleslavsky.

Dr. Knock, a sharper, takes over the practice of a legitimate medico in a small town in France, promptly and successfully votes practically the entire population on the sick list and collects fees for the prescriptions he writes from an exhaustless memory of many patent medicine recipes.

THE SPIDER
(16 performances)

A melodrama in three acts by Fulton Oursler and Lowell Brentano. Produced by Albert Lewis and Sam H. Harris at the Century Theatre, New York, February 27, 1928.

Cast of characters—

The Manager	Wm. E. Morris
The Man	Donald Mackenzie
The Girl	Eleanor Griffith
The Sergeant	John F. Morrissey
The Doctor	Arthur Stuart Hull
Bill	John Burkell
Dick	Anton Ascher
Mrs. Wimbleton	Priscilla Knowles
The Reporter	Frederick Smith
The House Leader	Ralph Stone
The Captain	Thomas Findlay
Officer Simpson	J. Howard
Officer Burke	J. Romer
Officer Shayne	Will Warner
Officer Casey	J. Gordon
Officer Dougherty	D. J. Flanagan
Officer Jones	W. Plunkett
Officer Thornton	Jack Morgan
The Electrician	Jack Bennett
Alexander	Paul Nugent
Tommy	H. Yano
Estelle	Germaine Giroux
Chatrand, The Great	John Halliday

Acts I, II and III.—During a Performance at the Tivoli Vaudeville Theatre.

Staged by Albert Lewis.

See "The Best Plays of 1926-27."

THE WRECKER
(40 performances)

A mystery melodrama in three acts by Arnold Ridley and Bernard Merivale. Produced by Guy Bates Post (by arrangement with E. J. Carroll and Harry I. Cohen) at the Cort Theatre, New York, February 27, 1928.

Cast of characters—

Gladys Elliot..Phyllis Harding
Milly Knight..Sara Haden
Noah Twemblett..............................Alfred Hemming
Mary Shelton...Elsie Wagstaff
Roger Doyle...Jack Leslie
Joshua Barney.....................................Clifford Walker
Inspector Ratchett.....................................Pacie Ripple
Sir Gervaise Bartlett.............................Douglas Garden
A Secretary...Frank Arundel
Lady Beryl Metchley..........................Annabella Murray
Chester Kyle...Roland Hogue
The Man..George Bowman
Alf..Lyman Watts
Horace Skeet...............................John M. Troughton
Haines..Tracy Graham
John Smith...Carlton Rivers
      Acts I and III.—General Office of the Great Trunk Railway, Eng-
land. Act II.—Scene 1—Library of Roger's House in Marylebone
Square. 2—Interior of a Switch Tower.
      Staged by Guy Bates Post.

Some sly fellow has been managing to wreck all the fastest and
finest trains in England. He not only wrecks them, but boasts of
the time and place the wrecking is to be done. Many are suspected but not until late in the evening is the real villain uncovered. He is none other than the old chief himself, made mad by
the constant noise of the trains and his inability to keep them
running on time.

KEEP SHUFFLIN'

(104 performances)

A musical comedy in two acts; book by Flourney Miller and
Aubrey Lyles; music by Jimmy Johnson, "Fats" Waller and
Clarence Todd; lyrics by Henry Creamer and Andy Razaf. Produced by Con Conrad, Inc., at Daly's Theatre, New York, February 27, 1928.

Cast of characters—

Boss...Jerry Mills
Henry...George Battles
Brother Jones......................................John Gregg
Mose...John Vigal
Walter.......................................Clarence Robinson
Scrappy...Byron Jones
Evelyn..Evelyn Keyes
Honey...Honey Brown
Alice...Jean Starr
Mrs. Jenkins...................................Margaret Lee
Steve Jenkins................................Flourney Miller
Sam Peck...Aubrey Lyles
Ruth..Josephine Hall
Maude...Maude Russell
Yarbo...Billie Yarbough
Hazel...Hazel Sheppard

```
Grit..............................................Gretta Anderson
Marie.................................................... Marie Dove
Bill................................................Gilbert Holland
Joseph ......................................... Herman Listerino
```

IN ORCHESTRA

```
On the White Keys..............................."Fats" Waller
On the Black Keys.................................Jimmy Johnson
Behind the Bugle.......................................Jabbo Smith
    Acts I, II and III.—In and Near Jimtown.
    Staged by Con Conrad.
```

The continuing adventures of Steve Jenkins and Sam Peck, whose ambition it is to keep on living without working. This time they plan to blow up a bank in the interests of the "Equal Got" League, thereby releasing a lot of lazy capital loafing in the vaults.

* THE BACHELOR FATHER

(125 performances)

A comedy in three acts by Edward Childs Carpenter. Produced by David Belasco at the Belasco Theatre, New York, February 28, 1928.

Cast of characters—

```
Larkin............................................George Riddell
Francis Keating, M.D...........................David Glassford
Sir Basil Winterton, V.C., K.C.B., K.C.G.M., K.W.,
                                                  C. Aubrey Smith
John Ashley......................................... Geoffrey Kerr
Kate Trent......................................... Viola Roache
Geoffrey Trent..................................... Rex O'Malley
Bianca Credaro ................................ Harriett Lorraine
Maria Credaro........................................ Adriana Dori
Antoinette ("Tony") Flagg ........................ June Walker
Dick Berney................................... Howard Bouton
Jennie.................................... Maryland Jarbeau
Hortense.......................................... Kitty Gray
Roberts ...................................... Thomas Reynolds
    Act I.—Scene 1—Living Room in Rooksfold House, Sir Basil Win-
terton's Home in Surrey, England.   2—Corner of a Room in Kate
Trent's House, Manchester, England.   3—Balcony of Bianca Cre-
daro's House, Florence, Italy.   4—Front Door and Steps of Tony
Flagg's Lodging House, New York.   Acts II and III.—Rooksfold
House.
    Staged by David Belasco.
```

Sir Basil Winterton, having had his affairs as a young man, comes upon the lonesome days of his sixties when he decides to call in and do what he can to help the illegitimate progeny he has been supporting for many years. His solicitor rounds up a boy Geoffrey in rural England, a girl Maria in Florence, and a girl Tony in New York. They are taken to Rooksfold house, Sir Basil's estate, and there agree to give the old gentleman a chance to act like a father. In no time Sir Basil is happy and the children content. Then come partings and problems.

MARRIAGE ON APPROVAL

(12 performances)

A drama in three acts by Michael Kallesser. Produced by the author at Wallack's Theatre, New York, March 1, 1928.

Cast of characters—

Mrs. Morley	Lou Ripley
Willard Keane	Larry Fletcher
Marie Tobin	Phyllis Povah
Mrs. Miller	Carrie Weller
Henry Wippen	Lawrence Leslie

Acts I, II and III.—Home of Larry Fletcher.

Willard Keane and Marie Tobin agree on trial marriage for a year. Within that time Keane, feeling the shackles, gets away to South America. Thinking herself deserted Marie takes up with Henry Wippen, who turns out a rotter. Willard returns, shoots Wippen, forgives Marie and goes to jail. (A rewritten version of "Trial Marriage," produced January 31, 1927.)

IMPROVISATIONS IN JUNE

(14 performances)

A comedy in three acts by Max Mohr; translated by Susanne Behn and Cecil Lewis. Produced by the Civic Repertory Theatre at the Civic Repertory Theatre, New York, March 5, 1928.

Cast of characters—

Majordomo	Paul Leyssac
First Servant	Harold Moulton
Second Servant	Walter Tupper Jones
Third Servant	Neil Cornell
Elkin, Secretary to Samuel Mill	J. Edward Bromberg
Varley, Physician to Samuel Mill	Sayre Crawley
Tompkinov	Donald Cameron
Princess Orloff	Eva Le Gallienne
Adam Zappe, Improvisator	Egon Brecher
Olga	Josephine Hutchinson
Samuel Mill	Walter Beck
Ian Mill	John Eldridge
First Officer	Walter Tupper Jones
Second Officer	Neil Cornell

Acts I, II and III.—Entrance Hall of the Castle Orloff on a Lake Near Salzburg.
Staged by Miss Le Gallienne.

A bloated American plutocrat takes over a Salzburg castle and seeks to buy happiness for his melancholy son. But all his gold buys him nothing but the contempt of his neighbors, while the proud princess of the castle, rather than be contaminated by the gold, arranges to have herself shot by a faithful retainer.

THE CHERRY ORCHARD

(5 performances)

A comedy in four acts by Anton Tchekov; translated by George Calderon. Produced by James B. Fagan at the Bijou Theatre, New York, March 5, 1928.

Cast of characters—

Dunyasha	Mary Newnham Davis
Lopakhin	Edwin Maxwell
Ephikhodof	A. Henderson Storie
Firs	Edward Rigby
Anya	Gemma Fagan
Madame Ranevsky	Mary Grey
Leonid Gayef	James B. Fagan
Barbara	Esther Mitchell
Charlotte	Ethel Griffies
Simeonof-Pishtshik	Gyles Isham
Yasha	Charles Courtneidge
Peter Trophimof	Glen Byam Shaw
Tramp	Lowden Adams

Acts I, II and III.—On Madame Ranevsky's Property in Russia. Staged by James B. Fagan.

Mme. Ranevsky, back from Paris, discovers her estates threatened with sale for debt. Trusting in the divine providence that should protect the aristocracy she permits affairs to take their course and the family is finally ejected, the property going at auction to the son of a peasant who formerly was a vassal to the Ranevsky family.

WITHIN THE LAW

(16 performances)

A play in four acts by Bayard Veiller. Revived by the Chamberlain Brown Cosmopolitan Artists at the Cosmopolitan Theatre, New York, March 5, 1928.

Cast of characters—

Sarah	Julia Hoyt
Smithson	Edward Rose
Richard Gilder	Charles Ray
Edward Gilder	Conway Wingfield
George Demarest	Fred L. Tiden
Helen Morris	Peggy Allenby

```
Detective Sergeant Cassidy.........................Philip Heege
Mary Turner.......................................Violet Heming
Aggie Lynch....................................Claudette Colbert
Joe Garson......................................Robert Warwick
Fannie.........................................Margaret Luerssen
William Irwin....................................George Alison
Eddie Griggs......................................Stanley Logan
Police Inspector Burke............................Frank Shannon
Thomas............................................Robert Linden
Chicago Red......................................James T. Ford
Tom Dacey........................................Ralph Vincent
Williams.........................................Edgar Henning
Thompson..........................................George Hoag
Dan................................................J. H. Brewer
```
Act I.—Private Office of Edward Gilder. Act II.—Mary Turner's Apartment. Act III.—Edward Gilder's Library. Act IV.—Inspector Burke's Office.

Staged by Clifford Brooke and Mabel Brownell.

Mary Turner, unjustly accused of theft from her employer, Edward Gilder of the Emporium, is sent to prison for three years at Gilder's insistence. Out of prison Mary plans an elaborate campaign of revenge, including the commission of various crimes kept scrupulously within the law. Finally she will be thoroughly revenged upon Gilder by marrying his son. Mary's gang, against her orders, plan to rob the Gilder home, are caught and Mary is only saved by the sacrifice of Joe Garson, who confesses the murder of a stool pigeon killed in the raid. After which Mary confesses her love for Richard Gilder.

HER UNBORN CHILD

(47 performances)

A play in three acts by Howard McKent Barnes and Grace Hayward; revised by Melville Burke. Produced by the Majestic Productions, Inc., at the Eltinge Theatre, New York, March 5, 1928.

Cast of characters—

```
"Pegs" Kennedy................................Margaret Byers
Stewart Kennedy...............................Elisha Cook, Jr.
Mrs. Kennedy...................................Effie Shannon
Elizabeth Gilbert..............................Pauline Drake
Doris Kennedy...................................Ivy Mertons
Miss Conover....................................Lea Penman
Jack Conover..................................Theodore Hecht
Dr. Remington................................William Corbett
```
Acts I, II and III.—At the Home of the Kennedys in a midwestern City.

Staged by Melville Burke.

Doris Kennedy finds herself in trouble as a result of a roadhouse adventure with Jack Conover, whom she expected to marry.

Facing her problem Doris considers an abortion, which an honest doctor refuses to perform. She also refuses to marry the deceiving Jack when he has a change of heart and wishes to make her an honest woman. The family stands by Doris and she and Jack marry in the end.

THE GREAT NECKER

(39 performances)

A comedy in three acts by Elmer Harris. Produced by Chamberlain Brown at the Ambassador Theatre, New York, March 6, 1928.

Cast of characters—

Workmen	{ Charles A. Baker
	{ Frank Milan
Madame Estelle	Marjorie Gateson
James	Sidney Paxton
Arthur Pomroy	Taylor Holmes
Adolph Cohen	James B. Carson
Sam	Kenneth Curtis
Oscar Squibbs	Ray Walburn
Mrs. Hawthorne	Blanche Ring
Pansy Hawthorne	Irene Purcell
Teddy Ferguson	Hal Thompson
Nina Squibbs	Zola Talma
Hawkins	Gordon Wescott

Acts I and II.—Drawing Room, Pomroy's Town House, Park Avenue, New York. Act III.—Garden, Madame Estelle's Country Place, Long Island.

Staged by J. Fred Butler.

Backing the films, Arthur Pomroy seeks to influence the judgment of Mrs. Hawthorne of the censor board. He does not get very far with this lady but he does better with her daughter Pansy, an overwise virgin representing the younger generation. Put in his place finally by Miss Hawthorne the investigating Arthur turns to the widow Estelle, who has been waiting somewhat impatiently to be turned to.

THE FURIES

(45 performances)

A play in three acts by Zoe Akins. Produced by John Tuerk at the Shubert Theatre, New York, March 7, 1928.

Cast of characters—

Harvey Bell Smith	John Cumberland
Bennett	Ernest Stallard

Dr. Paul Hemmingway..............................Ian Maclaren
Owen MacDonald...........................Frederick Worlock
Caroline Lee............................Greta Kemble Cooper
Fern Andrews...................................Estelle Winwood
Oliver Bedloe...A. E. Anson
Fifi Sands.................................... Laurette Taylor
Alan Sands...Alan Campbell
District Attorney..............................Alfred Kappeler
Hayes.......................................Clarence Handyside
Theresa...................................... Maurine O'Moor
Bradley.. Ross Herts
Otis...John Parrish
Bedloe's Man...............................Charles Henderson
    Act I.—Harvey Bell Smith's Apartment, New York City. Act II.
—The Sands' Home on Fifth Avenue. Act III.—Oliver Bedloe's
Apartment.
    Staged by George Cukor.

Fifi Sands, emboldened by an extra glass of champagne, tells
her husband what she really thinks of him and also of her plan
to divorce him and marry Owen MacDonald. That night Mr.
Sands is found dead. Fifi is included with the suspects questioned
by the district attorney. It develops two men are in love with
her, the MacDonald she expects to marry and Oliver Bedloe, her
husband's attorney. Locked in Bedloe's apartment forty-two
stories from the ground Fifi finally discovers that MacDonald is
a cad and Bedloe crazy. Bedloe confesses the murder and jumps
out the window to his death. Fifi is providentially rescued.

NAPOLEON

(11 performances)

A play in three acts by B. Harrison Orkow. Produced by
James W. Elliott at the Empire Theatre, New York, March 8,
1928.

Cast of characters—

Joan...Marie Paxton
Landlord.......................................Herbert Ashton
Napoleon.. Lionel Atwill
Sergeant of Guard................................D. J. Hamilton
Rostand...Eugene Donovan
Letizia...Thais Lawton
Gourgaud.....................................Herbert Standing
Countess Walewska................................Selena Royle
Marshal Ney.....................................Barry Whitcomb
General Bertrand.............................Beresford Lovett
General Gaulaincourt............................Charles White
Fouche...Albert Bruning
Pauline.......................................Margaret Mower
Lackey..Lionel Bevans
Lucien...Robert Bentley
Lafayette.......................................Charles Angelo
Constant.......................................J. Malcom Dunn
Meneval...Paul Doucet

Henri...D. J. Hamilton
Captain Maitland................................Eugene Donovan
Rustam...Robert Bentley
Santini...Charles Angelo
Dr. O'Meara....................................J. Malcom Dunn
Sir Hudson Lowe................................Beresford Lovett
    Acts I and III.—Scene 1—Room of an Inn on the Road to Paris,
1815. Act II.—Ante-Room in the Elysee Palace. Scene 2—St.
Helena.
    Staged by Robert Milton and Frank Merlin.

Sketchy episodes from the life of the emperor, beginning with
the escape from Elba and ending in his death on St. Helena.

12,000

(64 performances)

A play in three acts by Bruno Frank; adapted by William A.
Drake. Produced by Garrick Players at the Garrick Theatre,
New York, March 12, 1928.

Cast of characters—

Piderit...Basil Sydney
The Elder Brother..............................Leonard Mudie
The Younger Brother...........................John McGovern
Treysa...Robert Vivian
Faucitt..Walter Kingsford
His Serene Highness, the Prince of ———.......C. H. Croker-King
The Baroness of Spangenburg....................Mary Ellis
A Colonel......................................Lumsden Hare
    Acts I, II and III.—A Summer Pavilion in the Gardens of a Ger-
man Ducal Palace at the Time of the American Revolution.
    Staged by Basil Sydney.

Piderit, a secretary employed by his Hessian Highness, conspires to defeat the sale and shipment of 12,000 Hessian farmers
sold to the British for use in the war against America. Piderit
arouses the sympathy and gains the aid of the Baroness Spangenburg, favorite to His Highness, and is himself saved, when his
conspiracy is uncovered, by Frederick the Great.

YOURS TRULY

(16 performances)

A musical play in two acts; book by Clyde North; lyrics by
Anne Caldwell; music by Raymond Hubbell. Presented by Gene
Buck at the Century Theatre, New York, March 12, 1928.

Cast of characters—

Shuffling Bill..................................Irving Fisher
Joey Ling......................................Jack Stanley

```
Mac..................................................John Kearney
Phil...............................................Jean Kirkland
Diana..........................................Elizabeth Duray
J. P. Stillwell..............................Theodore Babcock
Truly.............................................Leon Errol
Bonzolino.........................................Vic Casmore
Ruth............................................Lotta Fanning
Scats.............................................Vera Meyers
Mary Stillwell...................................Evelyn Hoey
Bandit...........................................Jean Kirkland
Dinty Moore.......................................Tom Waters
Chang..........................................Forrest Yarnall
A Bowery Rose.....................................Eunice Hall
Tillie Dupont.................................Valerie Raemore
Minnie Fletcher..................................Eve Johnston
Cynthia Jones..................................Inez Van Horn
Abe Levy........................................Earl Van Horn
Paquita.......................................Marguerite Marano
Chinese Girls....................................{ Peggy Frawley
                                                 { Dolly Pross
Flower Girl.......................................Gladys Lake
Victor..........................................Jean Kirkland
Miss Longstreet...............................Diane Du Verne
Miss Newbury......................................Eunice Hall
Miss Stuyvesant..................................Edith Babson
Miss Hemingway...............................Virginia Hawkins
Miss Glendening...................................Gladys Lake
Miss Butterfield.................................Eve Johnston
Miss Buckminster................................Queenie French
Miss Fairweather..............................Valerie Raemere
Miss Northcliffe.............................Betty MacDonald
Miss Matteson...................................Lucille Rich
Miss Tillinghast................................Lotta Fanning
Miss Southworth.................................Olive Manlet
```

Act I.—Mission Square, New York City. Act II.—Scene 1—A Garden on the Estate of J. P. Stillwell. 2—Street Back of Dinty Moore's. 3—Interior of the "Mission." 4—Underneath Dinty Moore's. 5—Chang's "Open Door Night Club."
Staged by Gene Buck.

See "Best Plays of 1926-27."

* THE THREE MUSKETEERS

(109 performances)

An operatic version in two acts adapted from the famous story by Alexandre Dumas; written by William Anthony McGuire; music by Rudolph Friml; lyrics by P. G. Wodehouse and Clifford Grey. Produced by Florenz Ziegfeld at the Lyric Theatre, New York, March 13, 1928.

Cast of characters—

```
Jussac......................................Robert D. Burns
Comte De La Rochefort..........................Louis Hector
Innkeeper...................................Harrison Brockbank
Zoe...........................................Naomi Johnson
Lady De Winter.............................Vivienne Osborne
Porthos.......................................Detmar Poppen
Athos......................................Douglass R. Dumbrille
Aramis........................................Joseph Macaulay
```

Constance Bonacieux...............................Vivienne Segal
Planchet..Lester Allen
D'Artagnan...Dennis King
The Duke of Buckingham...........................John Clarke
Anne, Queen of France............................Yvonne D'Arle
M. De Treville.......................................John Kline
Cardinal Richelieu................................Reginald Owen
Louis XIII.....................................Clarence Derwent
Brother Joseph..................................William Kershaw
Première Danseuse of the Court...................Harriet Hoctor
Aubergiste..Catherine Hayes
The Bo'sun....................................Richard Thornton
Patrick..Raymond O'Brien
Cardinal's Guards........................... Andy Jochim
                                             Randolph Leyman
King's Attendant......................................G. Moore
    Act I.—Scene 1—Inn of the Jolly Miller. 2—Lane Leading to
Rue du Colombier. 3—Courtyard in Rue du Colombier Outside the
Convent of Carmier. 4—Cardinal Richelieu's Chambers in the Pal-
ace of the King. 5—The Garden of the Tuileries. Act II.—Scene 1
—An Inn at the Port of Calais. 2—Duke of Buckingham's Palace,
England. 3—The Shrine. 4—Before the Inn of the Jolly Miller.
5—Milady's Bedchamber. 6—Cabinet of the Queen. 7—The Ball-
room of the Hotel De Ville.
    Staged by William Anthony McGuire.

Here are Athos, Porthos, Aramis and young D'Artagnan adventuring to music. D'Artagnan arrives in Paris, makes friends
with the king's guards and pretty Constance Bonacieux, becomes
a Musketeer, undertakes the journey to London to recover the
queen's jewels from the Duke of Buckingham and is back in time
to avert a court scandal at the king's ball.

KILLERS

(23 performances)

A play in four acts by Louis E. Bisch and Howard Merling.
Produced by the Contemporary Theatre, Inc., at the 49th Street
Theatre, New York, March 13, 1928.

Cast of characters—

ACT I—THE JADE ROOM

Billy..Charles Dingle
Babe...Earle Mayne
Fanny...Beatrice Nichols
Geoggory Palmer....................................Albert Berg
Helen Harrington..................................Cynthia Blake
Pete...Harold Vermilyea
Grace Palmer...................................Ethlynne Bradford
Flynn...Jethro Warner
Arthur Harrington.............................George Clarkson

ACT II—CRIMINAL COURT

Fisk..Harry Clarens
James...Harvey Hays
Vandergriff....................................William B. Calhoun
Todd...H. R. Chase
Mittlefinger..Paul Rek

Phillpots...................................Conway Washburne
Wheterall.....................................Donald Thompson
Blake...Pennington Young
Watts.?......................................Joseph Prosser
Calepino..Charles Seel
Stearns..Frank A. Howson
Conners..A. S. Byron

ACT III—THE TIER

Carey..George Saunders
Abrams...Mel Tyler
Williams...Alan Allyn
Slant..George J. Williams
McMahon...Victor Shipley
Keeper Joe......................................Harry Johnson
Warden...Jerry Ryan

ACT IV—ON THE RIVER

Griggs...Bernard Sobel
Warden...Jethro Warner
Jim..Albert Berg
Doctor Jackson.................................Hallam Bosworth
Father Dunn....................................Frank A. Howson
George...Ernest Howard
    Staged by Howard Merling.

Helen Harrington, invading a night club in search of her husband and the woman he is favoring at the moment, hires gunmen
to slay her rival. When the shooting occurs it comes mysteriously
from an unsuspected direction, but the gunmen are convicted on
circumstantial evidence by a tired jury. There is a jailbreak
which nets another innocent crook for the chair, and the belated
revealment of Mrs. Harrington herself as the real killer.

THE BUZZARD

(13 performances)

A play in three acts by Courtenay Savage. Produced by Knox
Winslow, Inc., at the Broadhurst Theatre, New York, March 14,
1928.

Cast of characters—

John Collier....................................Eugene Powers
Ike Saunders.................................Lawrence O'Sullivan
Mrs. Burns......................................Clara Blandick
Tommy McGee....................................Billy Quinn
Susie Sunshine..................................Dorothy Cox
Avis Morrow.....................................Leona Hogarth
Frederick Turner................................Leonard Doyle
Richard Collier.................................Robert Lynn
Arthur Lyon.....................................Clyde Fillmore
Coogan...Harry Jenkins
Virginia Wells..................................Velerie Dade
Harry Keene.....................................Percy Kilbride
    Acts I, II and III.—The Library of John Collier in Chesterton, a
Small New England City.
    Staged by Melville Burke.

John Collier, district attorney and newspaper proprietor as well, is killed mysteriously by some one carrying a gun equipped with a Maxim silencer. So many people have reason to hate Collier the suspects are many and the search for the guilty person prolonged. A mistreated mother's protection of her son figures prominently in the dénouement.

KING HENRY V

(44 performances)

A play in five acts by William Shakespeare. Produced by Walter Hampden at Hampden's Theatre, New York, March 15, 1928.

Cast of characters—

Chorus	Mabel Moore
King Henry	Walter Hampden
Duke of Gloucester	Jan Lindermann
Duke of Bedford	Robert C. Schnitzer
Duke of Exeter	William Sauter
Archbishop of Canterbury	Stanley Howlett
Bishop of Ely	Edwin Cushman
Earl of Westmoreland	Gage Bennett
Earl of Cambridge	Howard Claney
Lord Scroop	Charles Wright
Sir Thomas Grey	Jack Gilchrist
Sir Thomas Erpingham	Ben Probst
Earl of Salisbury	Jack Gilchrist
Duke of York	Joseph Latham
Earl of Warwick	Randolph Carleton
An English Herald	Murray Darcy
Bardolph	Thomas Gomez
Nym	Gordon Hart
Pistol	C. Norman Hammond
Mistress Quickly	Caroline Meade
Boy	Edwin Phillips
Gower	Stanley Howlett
Fluellen	Cecil Yapp
Macmorris	P. J. Kelly
Court	Charles Wright
Williams	Ernest Rowan
Bates	P. J. Kelly
Charles VI, of France	W. H. Sams
The Dauphin	Dallas Anderson
The Constable	Reynolds Evans
Duke of Orleans	Howard Claney
Duke of Bourbon	Gordon Hart
Lord Rambures	Franklin Salisbury
Duke of Burgundy	Ernest Rowan
Montjoy	Louis Polan
A French Soldier	Thomas Gomez
A French Attendant	Joseph Latham
Governor of Harfleur	Franklin Salisbury
Princess Katherine	Marie Adels
Alice	Andrée Corday
Queen Isabel	Caroline Meade

Staged by Claude Bragdon.

VEILS

(4 performances)

A musical play in twelve episodes by Irving Kaye Davis; musical score by Donald Heywood. Produced by A. A. Snyder at the Forrest Theatre, New York, March 13, 1928.

Cast of characters—

The Reverend Mother Superior	Hilda Spong
Sister Agnes	Charlotte Granville
His Grace the Archbishop	Grant Stewart
Mrs. Angela Lumis	Frances Underwood
Mr. Robert Sloan	Warren William
Nan	Elsa Shelley
Mrs. Annie Hughes	Julia Ralph
Father Francis	Alan Floud
Sister Mary	Elsa Shelley
Sister Veronica	Mary Moore
Sister Gertrude	Helen Steele
Sister Louise	Ann Sherman
Sister Theresa	Florence Foxhall
Jim	Arthur R. Vinton
Col. Gerard Owens	Alex Loghe
Patricia Kent	Mimi Helmuth
Julien Macklin	Chris Holt
Oscar Van Wyck	Henry Crosby
Clifford Sturgis	Arthur Wellington
A Butler	Frank B. Miller
A Detective	Donald Page
Jake	Alan Winterburn
Mike Brady	Geo. Rogers
Lil	Helen O'Donnell
A Bum	John Mackley
Mag	Florence Pendleton
Nell Baxter	Mary Tabor
Rosa	Irene Winston
Birdie	Charlotte Wilkins
Flossie	Grace Allen
Jane	Alice Manny
Mamie	Agatha Lowry
Gladice	Nancy Chalmers
Prison Guard	J. Manley

Staged by Edward Elsner.

Nan and Mary are twin sisters. Mary is a nun in a convent and Nan a prostitute on the streets. Then Mary runs away from the convent and marries the artist who has been painting her in the chapel, while Nan, out of jail after serving time to shield her lover, renounces the world and takes the veil.

THE MERRY WIVES OF WINDSOR

(24 performances)

A farcical comedy in five acts by William Shakespeare. Produced by Harrison Grey Fiske at the Knickerbocker Theatre, New York, March 19, 1928.

Cast of characters—

Sir John Falstaff	Otis Skinner
Master Fenton	Geoffrey Wardwell
Robert Shallow	Owen Meech
Abraham Slender	France Bendtsen
Francis Ford	Lawrence H. Cecil
George Page	Henry Mowbray
Sir Hugh Evans	Hannam Clark
Doctor Caius	Rodolpho Badaloni
Host of the Garter Inn	William C. Masson
Bardolph	Tracy Barrow
Pistol	Will Geer
Nym	Horace Cooper
Cricket	Mary Walsh
Bede	Ella Houghton
Robin	Virginia Smith
Peter Simple	Burford Hampden
John Rugby	George Le Soir
Mistress Ford	Henrietta Crosman
Mistress Page	Mrs. Fiske
Anne Page	Elaine Temple
Mistress Quickly	Eleanor Gordon
Robert	Boyd Zook
John	Rene Roberti

The Five-Act Version with Scenes in and Around Windsor, the Garter Inn and Windsor Park. Act V.—Scene 1—In Windsor Park. 2—Herne's Oak in the Park.

Staged by Harrison Grey Fiske.

THE BEHAVIOR OF MRS. CRANE

(23 performances)

A play in three acts by Harry Segall. Produced by Eugene W. Parsons at Erlanger's Theatre, New York, March 20, 1928.

Cast of characters—

Harley	Stapleton Kent
Edith Hayes	Kathryn Givney
Cicely Prentiss	Phyllis Joyce
Doris Crane	Margaret Lawrence
Myra Spaulding	Isobel Elsom
Elliott Crane	Charles Trowbridge
Lord Winchmore	George Thorpe
Luis Garcia	Walter Connolly
Victor Follansby	L'Estrange Millman
Bruce King	John Marston

Acts I, II and III.—In the Crane Country Home Near New York City.

Staged by Bertram Harrison.

Doris Crane, knowing her husband has fallen in love with Myra Spaulding, summons the two before her and tells them that she is perfectly willing to give Mr. Crane a divorce so they can marry— but not, however, until they find her another acceptable husband. Both Miss Spaulding and Mr. Crane submit candidates, and Mrs. Crane accepts one of them, a handsome young fellow named Bruce King. Then Myra decides she, too, had rather have Bruce than Mr. Crane. But she doesn't get him. Mrs. Crane holds them to their agreement.

HEDDA GABLER

(15 performances)

A drama in four acts by Henrik Ibsen; revised translation by Julie Le Gallienne and Paul Leyssac. Produced by the Civic Repertory Theatre at the Civic Repertory Theatre, New York, March 26, 1928.

Cast of characters—

Miss Juliana Tesman	Alma Kruger
Berta	Leona Roberts
George Tesman	Paul Leyssac
Hedda Tesman	Eva Le Gallienne
Mrs. Elvstead	Josephine Hutchinson
Judge Brack	Sayre Crawley
Eilert Lovborg	Donald Cameron

Acts I, II and III.—Drawing Room of Tesman's Villa, in the West End of Christiania.

Staged by Miss Le Gallienne.

Hedda Gabler, married to George Tesman, home from her wedding journey, grows restless and depressed under the pressure of many disappointments. Embittered by the seeming success of Thea Elvstead in helping to mold the career of Eilert Lovborg, a former suitor for her favors, Hedda in jealous rage burns the manuscript of a book Lovborg has written and Thea has copied for him. Following Lovborg's death by his own hand, Hedda also shoots herself.

DIVORCE A LA CARTE

(8 performances)

A satirical farce in three acts by Samuel Ruskin Golding. Produced by The Drama Associates, Inc., at the Biltmore Theatre, New York, March 26, 1928.

Cast of characters—

Celeste	Sheelagh Hayes
Smythe	Charles D. Pitt
Patrick McAvoy	Albert Cross
Grace Horton	Kathleen Lowry
Chapman Pell	Geoffrey Harwood
Leslie Maitland	Hale Hamilton
Cyrilla Maitland	Regina Wallace
Janet Furniss McCook	Diantha Pattison
Philo Buller	George Drury Hart

Acts I, II and III.—The Living Hall of the Maitlands in New York City.

Staged by Samuel Ruskin Golding.

Cyrilla Maitland drinks too much and her husband, Leslie, golfs too much, so they quarrel and agree upon a Mexican divorce. As neither wants to go to Mexico a friend, Chapman Pell, agrees to impersonate Leslie and bring back the papers, which he does. Then Cyrilla marries Pell and Leslie marries a flapper. Before any particular damage can be done, however, discovery is made that the divorce is phony and the Maitlands still married.

THE SCARLET FOX

(79 performances)

A play in three acts by Willard Mack. Produced by James W. Elliott at the Masque Theatre, New York, March 27, 1928.

Cast of characters—

Henry Smithers	Victor R. Beecroft
Jenkins	Orville O. Harris
Eric Hammersley (R.C.M.P.)	Arthur Wellesley
Michael Devlin (R.C.M.P.)	Willard Mack
John Christansen (R C.M.P.)	Hans Sandquist
Novak	Victor Esker
Ling Foo Loo	Sam Lee
Harry Spatz	Joseph Sweeney
"Swede" Cora	Marie Chambers
Kathlyn McGuire	Katherine Wilson
Martha	Alice Moe
Trixie	Helen Handin
Cherry	Betty Brenska
Bessie	Beatrice Banyard
Tommy McGuire	Clark Marshall

Acts I, II and III.—The Small Town of Drumheller, Alberta, Seventy Miles Northeast of Calgary. The Story Is Borrowed Intact from the Royal Mounted Records of Drumheller's Last Coal Strike. Staged by Willard Mack.

Sergeant Michael Devlin, of the Royal Mounted, on patrol in Drumheller, has his attention called to the dead body of a mine boss lying in an alley back of Harry Spatz's hat store and just below "Swede" Cora's scarlet parlors. Letting the local constabulary think he suspects striking miners, the Sergeant stages an investigation in Cora's place and eventually traps Spatz, her lover, as the murderer and likewise a trafficker in dope.

THE BEGGAR'S OPERA

(36 performances)

A musical play in three acts by John Gay. New settings of the airs and additional music by Frederic Austin. Revived by J. C. Duff, in association with A. L. Jones and Morris Green at the 48th Street Theatre, New York, March 28, 1928.

Cast of characters—

Peachum..Charles Magrath
Lockit..Norman Williams
Macheath..George Baker
Filch...Alfred Heather
The Beggar......................................George Gregson
Mrs. Peachum....................................Lena Maitland
Polly Peachum...................................Sylvia Nelis
Lucy Lockit.....................................Celia Turrill
Diana Trapes....................................Julie Meo
Mrs. Coaxer.....................................Marjorie Chard
Dolly Trull.....................................Beatrice Morson
Mrs. Vixen......................................Vera Hurst
Betty Doxy......................................Julia Meo
Jenny Diver.....................................Alison Ramsay
Mrs. Slammekin..................................Audrey Mildmay
Molly Brazen....................................Zaidee White
Suky Tawdry.....................................Julie Cornelius
  Act I.—Peachum's House.   Act II.—Scene 1—A Tavern, Near
Newgate. 2—Newgate. Act II.—Scene 1—A Gaming House. 2—
Newgate. 3—The Condemn'd Hold. Period—1728.

John Gay's eighteenth-century ballad opera.   First revived in
New York December 27, 1920.

MARCH HARES
(19 performances)

A satire in three acts by Harry Wagstaff Gribble.   Revived by
Charles L. Wagner at the Little Theatre, New York, April 2,
1928.

Cast of characters—

Ethel...Natalie Schafer
Mrs. Janet Rodney...............................Josephine Hull
Edgar Fuller....................................Bruce Evans
Geoffrey Wareham................................Richard Bird
Oliver..Francis Compton
Janet Rodney....................................Vivian Tobin
Claudia Kitts...................................Dorothy Stickney
The Cook..Margaret Hinton
Mr. Brown.......................................Ryder Keane
  Acts I, II and III.—The House of Mrs. and Miss Rodney, Near
New York City.
  Staged by Daniel Frawley.

See "Best Plays of 1921-22."

MARTINE
(16 performances)

A drama in five scenes by Jean-Jacques Bernard; translated by
Helen Grayson.   Produced by The American Laboratory Theatre
company at the American Laboratory Theatre, New York, April
4, 1928.

Cast of characters—

Martine Gévin	Ruth Nelson
Julien Mervan	Frank Burk
Madame Mervan	Frances Williams
Alfred Murieux	Herbert V. Gellendre
Jeanne	Mary Steichen Martin

Scenes 1 and 3—On the Road to Frandchin. 2 and 4—Madame Mervan's Living Room. Alfred Murieux' House.
Staged by Richard Boleslavsky.

Martine, a pretty French peasant girl, meets Julien Mervan, back from the wars, when he visits his grandmother in the country. It is spring and Julien likes Martine. Then his smarter Paris sweetheart comes to claim him and he forgets his peasant friend. Disillusioned and unhappy, Martine marries her peasant lover and dolefully takes up her life as a farm drudge.

* VOLPONE

(46 performances)

A sardonic farce based on Ben Jonson's famous comedy, by Stefan Zweig; translated by Ruth Langner. Produced by The Theatre Guild at the Guild Theatre, New York, April 9, 1928.

Cast of characters—

Mosca	Alfred Lunt
First Groom	Louis Veda
Second Groom	Mark Schweid
Volpone	Dudley Digges
Slave to Volpone	John Henry
Voltore	Philip Leigh
Corvino	Ernest Cossart
Corbaccio	Henry Travers
Canina	Helen Westley
Colomba	Margalo Gillmore
Maid to Colomba	Mary Bell
Corbaccio's Servant	John C. Davis
Leone	McKay Morris
Captain of the Sbirri	Albert Van Dekker
Judge	Morris Carnovsky
Clerk of the Court	Sanford Meisner
Court Attendants	Vincent Sherman / John C. Davis

Acts I, II and III.—Venice at the Time of the Renaissance.
Staged by Philip Moeller.

Volpone, a miserly money lender with a passion for getting the better of equally avaricious intimates, lets report be spread that he is dying and about to make his will. Each of the prospective heirs seeks to gain the sick man's favor by offering gifts. One, Corbaccio, is even induced to send over his young wife as a comforter. But when Volpone would possess himself of the wife he gets into trouble, is arrested for attempted rape, haled into court and eventually stripped of his fortune and his citizenship.

* GREENWICH VILLAGE FOLLIES

(78 performances)

A musical revue in two acts; sketches by Harold Atteridge; music by Ray Perkins and Maurie Rubens; lyrics by Max and Nathaniel Lief. Produced by The Bohemians, Inc., at the Winter Garden, New York, April 9, 1928.

Principals engaged—

Dr. Rockwell	Grace La Rue
Harold Whalen	Florence Misgen
Harry Jans	Evelyn Law
Bobby Watson	Grace Brinkley
Benny Fields	Laura Lee
Eddie Shubert	Blossom Seeley
Walter Armin	Lola Raine
Billy McLeod	Sheila Barrett
Carlos and Valeria	Annie Pritchard
Ralph Reader girls	Chester Hale girls

Staged by J. C. Huffman, Chester Hale and Ralph Reader.

* DIAMOND LIL

(78 performances)

A drama in three acts by Mae West; suggested by Mark Linder. Produced by Jack Linder at the Royale Theatre, New York, April 9, 1928.

Cast of characters—

Diamond Lil	Mae West
Capt. Cummings	Curtis Cooksey
Chick Clark	Herbert Duffy
Gus Jordon	J. Merrill Holmes
Dan Flynn	Ernest Anderson
Rita Christinia	Raffælla Ottiano
Jim	Mark Linder
Kane	Jack Cheatham
Juarez	Jack La Rue
Sally	Lois Jesson
Jacobson	Louis Nusbaum
Frances	Marion Day
Kitty	Mary Martin
Flo	Helen Vincent
Mary Ryan	Thelma Lawrence
Mike	Joseph A. Barrett
Pete the Duke	Ramald Savery
Bill	Jack Howard
Frank Kelly	David Hugbes

Maggie..Patsy Klein
   Acts I and III.—Jordon's Dance Hall in Chatham Square—Thirty
Years Ago.   Act II.—Diamond Lil's Room Above the Dance Hall.
   Staged by Miss West.

Lil lives with Gus Jordon, who runs a Bowery dance hall (1898) and does a little white slaving on the side. Falling for Captain Cummings of the Salvation Army, she unwittingly helps him break up the white slave trade and then discovers he is a captain of police. Which doesn't disappoint her much. She was tired of Jordon anyway.

THE OUTSIDER

(56 performances)

A play in three acts by Dorothy Brandon. Revived by Lionel Atwill at the Ambassador Theatre, New York, April 9, 1928.

Cast of characters—

Mr. Frederick Ladd, F.R.C.S. ....Wallace Erskine
Sir Montague Tollemache, F.R.C.S. ....Beresford Lovett
Mr. Vincent Helmore, F.R.C.S. ....Gilbert Douglas
Sir Nathan Israel, F.R.C.S. ....Charles Angele
Mr. Jasper Sturdee, M.S. ....Albert Bruning
Lalage Sturdee......................................Isobel Elsom
Madame Klost .... Fernanda Eliscu
Anton Ragatzy....................................Lionel Atwill
Pritchard .... Jessamine Newcombe
Basil Owen .... Vernon Kelso
   Act I.—The Honorary Staff Room at St. Martha's Hospital, S. E.
Act II.—Lalage's Sitting Room.   Act III.—Lalage's Flat.
   Staged by Lionel Atwill.

See "Best Plays of 1923-24."

THE PLAY'S THE THING

(24 performances)

A comedy in three acts by Ferenc Molnar; adapted by P. G. Wodehouse. Presented by Gilbert Miller at the Empire Theatre, New York, April 9, 1928.

Cast of characters—

Mansky...Hubert Druce
Sandor Turai.....................................Holbrook Blinn
Albert Adam..Gavin Muir
Johann Dwornitschek..............................Ralph Nairn
Almady..Harry Mestayer
Ilona Szabo.......................................Selena Royle

```
Mell................................................Claude Allister
Lackeys..........................................{ Stephen Kendal
                                                 { Kirby Hawkes
```
The Characters Are the Guests of a Wealthy Count in His Castle
on the Italian Riviera.
Staged by Holbrook Blinn.

See "Best Plays of 1926-27."

SATURDAY'S CHILDREN

(16 performances)

A comedy in three acts by Maxwell Anderson. Presented by
The Actors' Theatre, Inc., Guthrie McClintic, Director, at the
Forrest Theatre, New York, April 9, 1928.

Cast of characters—

```
Florrie Sands...................................Ruth Hammond
Willie Sands....................................Richard Barbee
Mrs. Halevy...............................Grace Roth Henderson
Bobby..........................................Ruth Gordon
Mr. Halevy.....................................Frederick Perry
Rims O'Neil...................................Humphrey Bogart
Mrs. Gorlik....................................Anne Tonetti
```
Act I.—The Dining Room of the Halevy's Apartment. Act II.—
The Kitchen-Dining Room of Mr. and Mrs. O'Neil. Act III.—
Small Room in Mrs. Gorlik's Boarding House, New York.
Staged by Guthrie McClintic.

See "Best Plays of 1926-27."

COUNTESS MARITZA

(16 performances)

A musical revue in three acts; book and lyrics from the original
of Julius Brammer and Alfred Grunwald by Harry B. Smith;
music by Emmerich Kalman. Produced by The Messrs. Lee &
J. J. Shubert at the Century Theatre, New York, April 9, 1928.

Cast of characters—

```
Bela Torek....................................Louis E. Miller
Nepomuk.......................................Robert Roltner
Count Tassilo Endrody..........................Leonard Ceeley
Tscheko........................................Hugh Chilvers
Lazlo..........................................Arthur Geary
Manja..........................................Odette Myrtil
Stefan........................................Clarence Tolman
Servant........................................Jules Waldeck
Zingo.........................................James C. Morton
Countess Maritza...............................Gladys Baxter
Lisa.........................................Marjorie Peterson
Prince Populescu...............................Robert Greig
```

First Officer.......................................Robert Roltner
Baron Koloman Szupan.............................George Dobbs
Freda...Mitzi Kish
Princess Bozena Klopensheim...................Alexandra Dagmar
    Prologue—Grand Salon in the Château of Count Tassilo Endrody.
Act I.—Garden of Countess Maritza's Château. Acts II and III.—
Drawing Room.
Staged by J. C. Huffman.

See "Best Plays of 1926-27."

BOTTLED

(62 performances)

A comedy in three acts by Anne Collins and Alice Timoney.
Produced by Herman Gantvoort at the Booth Theatre, New York,
April 10, 1928.

Cast of characters—

Ashton McMullin............................William H. Gerald
Tuttle Cobb....................................Halliam Bosworth
Jo McMullin......................................Nellie Callahan
Mary Lou Alexander............................Mildred McCoy
Randy Logan....................................John M. James
Trimble Rice...Al Roberts
Ellen McMullin....................................Maud Durand
Bulger..Walter Robinson
    Acts I, II and III.—The Living Room of the McMullin Home.
Staged by Herman Gantvoort.

Mary Lou, having come of age, three McMullin heirs expect to
divide considerable money. At the reading of the will they discover that all they inherit is the McMullin distillery. There are
warehouses stocked with rare old bourbon for which there is no
legal market. Old Ellen McMullin, grandmother, refuses to
make any other disposition of the property. The heirs try to
sneak several cases out of warehouse No. 1 and sell them to New
York millionaires for $20 a bottle, but are caught. So is grand-
mother, who, it transpires, has been bootlegging the contents of
warehouse No. 3. As a compromise she gives the heirs $75,000
of her profits.

A LADY FOR A NIGHT

(8 performances)

A mystery comedy in three acts by Hutcheson Boyd. Produced by Chamberlain Brown at the 49th Street Theatre, New
York, April 16, 1928.

Cast of characters—

Jim Dexter......................................Warren Ashe
Lucy Dexter....................................Dorothy Hall
Bobby..Percy Helton
Edith Morris...................................Betty Lawrence
Miss Wimple....................................Helen Lowell
Aunt Abbie Patterson...........................Mabel Montgomery
Clarisse.......................................Esther Howard
Anthony Wing...................................Frank Allworth
Snod Tanner....................................Robert Barrat
Emma...Gladys Feldman
Alf Weyland....................................Edward Rose
Henry Thomas...................................Mark Haight
Mary Nester....................................Alden Gay
Hennesey.......................................Joseph Thayer
Reynolds.......................................Harry O. Studds
  Acts I, II and III.—Living Room, Dexter Bungalow, Staten Island.
Staged by John Meehan.

The Dexters of Staten Island, facing a servant problem, try
out Jim Dexter's idea of taking a girl named Clarisse from the
ribbon counter of a department store. Clarisse is a flirt and
slightly goofy, causing much incoherent comedy until it is explained that Mrs. Dexter has dreamed the whole thing while Jim
was out to the employment agencies scaring up help.

FORBIDDEN ROADS

(16 performances)

A play in three acts; adapted from José Lopez Pinillos' "El
Caudal de los Hijos," by Roland Oliver. Produced by Walter O.
Lindsey, in association with James E. Kenney at the Liberty The-
atre, New York, April 16, 1928.

Cast of characters—

Orosia...Genevieve Williams
Gaspar Gomez...................................Richard Farrell
Don Augustin Zarate............................Robert Bentley
Javier...Richard Nicholls
Isabel...Judith Vosselli
Marta..Maxine Calvert
Rodrigo..Alan Birmingham
  Acts I, II and III.—Occur in a Little Spanish Village.
Staged by Henry Stillman.

Caspar Gomez might, with cause, kill his wife after he discovers her affair with an older lover. He refrains to save the
honor of his son. Fifteen years later the son is also restrained
from killing his wife and again for the sake of their son. Thus
the vicious drama circle.

THE BREAKS

(8 performances)

A comedy in three acts by J. C. and Elliott Nugent. Produced by Richard Herndon at the Klaw Theatre, New York, April 16, 1928.

Cast of characters—

Amy	Sylvia Sidney
Hank Dolf	Claude Cooper
Jim Dolf	Elliott Nugent
Jed Willis	J. C. Nugent
Amos Strett	Harry Blakemore
"Belch" Atkins	Conrad Cantzen
Landis	Frederic Burt
Manson	Malcolm Williams
Jane	Helen Carew
Badger	Edward H. Loeffler

Acts I, II and III.—Jed Willis' Cabin.
Staged by J. C. Nugent and Alan Dinehart.

Jed Willis, a small-minded, dominating cotton farmer in Texas, hates women but is willing to force marriage upon his nineteen-year-old housekeeper in order that she may bear him an heir to certain entailed estates. If he should die without issue the property goes to a hated cousin, the irresponsible Jim Dolf, with whom the little housekeeper is really in love. Jed has his way until, in a scuffle with Dolf, he is injured and the doctors tell him he will never have issue. The young folks elope and Jed shoots himself.

HIM

(27 performances)

A play in three acts by E. E. Cummings. Produced by the Provincetown Playhouse at the Provincetown Theatre, New York, April 18, 1928.

Cast of characters—

ACT I

Me	Erin O'Brien-Moore
Him	William S. Johnstone
The Doctor	Lawrence Bolton
First Weird	Della Mounts
Second Weird	Sara Floyd
Third Weird	Virginia Rose

ACT II.—SCENE 2

First Drunk	Stanley Zipser
Second Drunk	George Bratt
Third Drunk (the Doctor)	Lawrence Bolton

Virgo..Louise Bradley
Porter...Hemsley Winfield

SCENE 3

Soap-box Orator (the Doctor).....................Lawrence Bolton

SCENE 4

Will...Philip Frank
Bill..Jack Daniels
Intruder (the Doctor)...........................Lawrence Bolton

SCENE 5

Female Black Figure............................Goldye Steiner
Male Black Figure..............................Hemsley Winfield
Personage (the Doctor)...........................Lawrence Bolton
Frankie...Christine Cooper

SCENE 6

Plainclothesman (the Doctor).....................Lawrence Bolton
An Englishman...................................George Bratt
A Cop...Lionel J. Stander

SCENE 7

First Passenger (the Doctor)...................Lawrence Bolton
Second Passenger...........................Herbert T. Bergman

SCENE 8

First Centurion................................... Morton Russell
Second Centurion................................Philip Frank
Ethiopian.................................. Hemsley Winfield
First Fairy....................................Lionel J. Stander
Second Fairy.......................................George Bratt
Third Fairy.......................................Stanley Zipser
Fourth Fairy....................................Herbert T. Bergman
Mussolini (the Doctor)...........................Lawrence Bolton
A Fascist.......................................Henry Rosenberg
Messenger....................................Leo Francis Ruttle

SCENE 9

Interlocutor (Him)...........................William S. Johnstone
A Gentleman (the Doctor).......................Lawrence Bolton
First Shape.......................................Louise Bradley
Second Shape.......................................Stanley Zipser
Woman..Virginia Dale
Old Woman.......................................Virginia Rose
Third Shape.......................................Jack Daniels
A Whore...Alice Swanson
Fourth Shape.......................................George Bratt
Mother with a Child............................Edith Frisbie
A Policeman.................................Arthur William Row

ACT III.—SCENE 3

Headwaiter...George Bratt
Waiter.......................................Arthur William Row
A Fairly Young Woman...........................Virginia Dale
An Older Woman..............................Ruth Chorpenning
Elderly Woman..............................Christine Cooper
A Youthful Woman..............................Marion Johnson
Chasseur....................................Leo Francis Ruttle
Vestiare...Louise Bradley
A Blonde Gonzesse.................................Evelyn Hill
A Whore...Ora Laddon

SCENE 4

A Barker (the Doctor)...........................Lawrence Bolton
Nine-foot Giant.................................George Spelvin
Queen of Serpents.................................Edith Frisbie
Human Needle.....................................Heaton Vorse
Missing Link.....................................Henry Rosenberg
Tattooed Man.................................Morton Russell

```
Six Hundred Pounds of Passionate Pulchritude.........Mary Jones
King of Borneo..................................Hemsley Winfield
Eighteen-Inch Lady..............................⎰ Madeleine Ray
                                                ⎱ Virginia Dale
    Crowds, Cripples, Beggars, Black Figures, Jazz Dancers, Shapes
    Act I.—Scene 1—Picture. 2—Room. 3—Picture. 4—Room.
5—Picture. Act II.—Scene 1—The Stage. 2—Lawn. 3—Street
Corner. 4—Office. 5—Semicircular Piece of Depth. 6—Fifth Ave-
nue. 7—Liner. 8—Old Howard's Conception of a Roman Villa.
9—The Stage. Act III.—Scene 1—Room. 2—Picture. 3—Le Père
Tranquille. 4—Picture. 5—Room. 6—Semicircular Piece of Depth.
7—Room.
    Staged by James Light.
```

Twenty episodes about nothing in particular and everything in general, variously illuminated by dialogue between "Him" and his lady, "Me."

BOX SEATS

(28 performances)

A play in three acts by Edward Massey. Produced by Gordon M. Leland at the Little Theatre, New York, April 19, 1928.

Cast of characters—

```
Hazel Lawrence.....................................Joan Storm
Jim Larkin....................................Frederick B. Manatt
Myrtle Dugan.......................................Jane Barry
Noah Lawrence.................................George N. Price
Dolly..........................................Patricia Barclay
Doc Blake....................................George W. Barbier
Mrs. Slocum.................................Elizabeth Patterson
Duke..........................................Joaquin Souther
Alf.............................................Millard Mitchell
Monty Slocum...................................Paul Guilfoyle
Joe Stanwood..................................Harold Elliott
Martha.........................................Edna Thrower
Piano Player................................Henry G. Hoffschmidt
Saxophone Player..................................Ted Sutherland
    Act I.—Scenes 1 and 2—Jim Larkin's Flat, Detroit. Act II.—
Scenes 1 and 2—Behind the Scenes. Act III.—A Room in a New
York Hotel.
    Staged by Edward Massey.
```

Hazel Lawrence, having deserted an unlovely husband and a baby in the far west, takes to living with rich men in Detroit. One day her brother-in-law brings her the baby, now twelve, and the information that her husband is dead. Hazel decides to rear the child Dolly and to keep her pure. Hazel saves her from one young dope fiend by confessing her own affair with him. Later, when they are both in "The Follies," she schemes to marry Dolly to rich Joe Stanwood and succeeds.

KIDDING KIDDERS

(8 performances)

A satirical farce in three acts by Stephen Champlin; based on a story by Frederic S. Isham. Produced by Hilmas Productions, Inc., at the Bijou Theatre, New York, April 23, 1928.

Cast of characters—

```
Denby Kidder.........................................Neil Pratt
Vivian Macy........................................Estelle Jayne
Chief Moran........................................Edwin Walter
Policeman...........................................Jack Klendon
William Sherwood..............................Walter Jay Wilson
Betty Kidder.....................................Grace Valentine
Teddy Horton...............................Raymond Van Sickle
Detective Carrol...................................John Ferguson
Ames...............................................Tom McElhany
Anne Thorne........................................Ruth Thomas
Maggie..............................................Lida Kane
Farrand Truxton....................................Jesse LeRoy
     Prologue—Scene 1—Vivian Macy's Studio.  2—District Attorney's
Office.  Acts I, II and III.—The Home of the Kidders.
     Staged by Frank McCormack.
```

Denby Kidder calls on his wife's best friend, Vivian Macy, when he is a little tight and tries to induce her to be companionate. Vivian, flourishing a revolver, indicates that if necessary she can protect herself. Denby tries to take the gun from her, there is a report and Denby faints. The police come, call it a murder, and take Vivian away. Before they get back Denby recovers and goes home. Thereafter Betty Kidder, in seeking to free Vivian on bail, stages another silly murder to convince the district attorney how foolish a thing is circumstantial evidence.

* THE SKULL

(62 performances)

A mystery play in three acts by Bernard J. McOwen and Harry E. Humphrey. Produced by Lew Cantor at the Forrest Theatre, New York, April 23, 1928.

Cast of characters—

```
Anna Mason.........................................Carola Parson
Mary Harris........................................Camilla Crume
Dorothy Merrill...................................Winifred Barry
Prof. Vorheese...................................C. W. Van Voorhis
Dr. Steve Tolman.....................................Allan Davis
Bob Demarest.......................................Sydney Riggs
Jerry Brownell......................................Harry Nelson
Capt. Vernon Allenby.........................Reginald Carrington
```

Harry Alsing.................................Harold De Becker
    Acts I, II and III.—An Old Deserted Church—It Has Not Been
Used for Services in Years—Located on a Deserted Country Road
Near Greenwich, Conn.
    Staged by Victor Morley.

Steve Tolman, international jewel thief, has lost his jewels. Posing as a detective, he seeks to recover them. The search takes him mostly to a haunted church full of everything from slamming doors to ghosts, but mostly full of a professor of psychic phenomenon, Professor Vorheese.

THE GOLDEN AGE

(6 performances)

A play in three acts by Lester Lonergan and Charlton Andrews. Produced by John Tuerk at the Longacre Theatre, New York, April 24, 1928.

Cast of characters—

Margaret Barnes....................................Selene Johnson
Golden Voice.....................................Diantha Pattison
Little Cliff......................................Warren McCullom
Clifford Barnes.....................................David Landau
Chief Silver Cloud................................George Marion
Elmer Barnes..John Anthony
Peggy Barnes..Leila Frost
The Stranger.....................................Warren William
The Pilot..Walton Butterfield
The Mechanician....................................Donald Gallaher
    Acts I and II.—The Interior of a Cabin in the Enchanted Land,
Utah. Act III.—Among the Rocks at the Edge of the Grand Canyon.
    Staged by Lester Lonergan.

The Clifford Barnses live for fifty years out of touch with civilization at the edge of the Grand Canyon in Utah. One day a Stranger Man comes along and is allowed to join in with them. In time Stranger Man is betrothed to the youngest of the Barnses, Peggy of the third generation. Then a mailplane crashes and the aviators reveal Stranger Man as a fugitive from the army. Stranger Man has a tragic story, tells it and goes away, leaving one of the young airmen to console Peggy.

THE WALTZ OF THE DOGS

(35 performances)

A play in four acts by Leon Andreyev; translated by Herman Bernstein. Produced by Celia Avramo at the 48th Street Theatre, New York, May 7, 1928 (Cherry Lane Playhouse, April 25 to May 5, 1928).

Cast of characters—

Carl Tile	Rudolph Lovinger
Henry Tile	Harold Johnsrud
Alexandrov, nicknamed Feklusha	Jules Artfield
Andrey Tizenhausen	Edward England
Dmitry Yermolayev	Douglas B. Krantzor
Ivan	Samuel Baron
Elizabeth	Sylvia Hoffman
Happy Jennie	Antoinette Crawford

Acts I, II and III (Scene 2) and IV.—Apartment of Henry Tile, Petrograd. Act II.—Scene 1—The Bank of One of the Petrograd Canals.

Staged by Celia Avramo.

Henry Tile, disappointed in love and disillusioned with the world, seeks release in the milder dissipations, groping feverishly for explanations to the mysteries of life. Not finding either relief or understanding he kills himself.

* PRESENT ARMS

(57 performances)

A musical comedy in two acts; book by Herbert Fields; music by Richard Rodgers; lyrics by Lorenz Hart. Produced by Lew Fields at Lew Fields' Mansfield Theatre, New York, April 26, 1928.

Cast of characters—

McKabe	Jock McGraw
Frank Derryberry	Franker Wood
Chick Evans	Charles King
McKenna	Fuller Mellish, Jr.
Gadget	Robert Spencer
Douglas Atwell	Busby Berkeley
Capt. Wiggins	Richard Lane
Edna Stevens	Joyce Barbour
Fay	Rachel Chester
Lady Delphine	Flora Le Breton
Luana	Alma Ross
Lord Oliver Witherspoon	Sydney Smith
Herr Ludwig Von Richter	Anthony Knilling
Maria	Florence Hunter
Hortense Mossback	Gaile Beverley
Daisy	Demaris Dore
Minerva	Aline Green
Karl	Alexander Lewis
Elsa	Frances Hess
Moulika	Alma Ross

Act I.—Spring. Scene 1—The Barracks of the Marine Base at Pearl Harbor, Hawaii. 2—Within the Quarters. 3—Sir Oliver's Home, Honolulu. Act II.—Scene 1—Promenade Deck of Edna's Yacht. 2—A Raft at Sea. 3—Deserted Island Off Mani. 4—Delphine's Room in Honolulu. 5—Aboard the Transport St. Mihiel Bound for Kohala. 6—The Dock at Kohala.

Staged by Alexander Leftwich.

Chick Evans is a hard-boiled hick from Brooklyn, but a likable leatherneck withal. Stationed with the Marines in the Hawaiian islands he stirs up a flirtation with Lady Delphine, blonde daughter of a peer, telling her he is a captain. Dismissed for his deception, recalled for his bravery in a yacht wreck, Chick is finally loved for himself alone and his love songs.

* HERE'S HOWE

(54 performances)

A musical comedy in two acts; book by Fred Thompson and Paul Gerard Smith; music by Roger Wolfe Kahn and Joseph Meyer; lyrics by Irving Cæsar. Produced by Alex. A. Aarons and Vinton Freedley at the Broadhurst Theatre, New York, May 1, 1928.

Cast of characters—

Cora Bibby	Peggy Chamberlin
Mr. Petrie	Ross Himes
Edwin Treadwell	Arthur Hartley
Toni Treadwell	Helen Carrington
Sir Basil Carraway	Eric Blore
Joyce Baxter	Irene Delroy
Billy Howe	Allen Kearns
Dan Dabney	Ben Bernie
Toplis	William Frawley
Mary	June O'Dea
Polly	Mary Horan
Pelham	"Fuzzy" Knight
Claudette Pernier	Colette D'Arville
Wilbur	Dillon Ober

Act I.—Scene 1—Rest Room of the Community Hall of the Treadwell Motors Co., Inc. 2—The Barber Shop. 3—Outside Edwin Treadwell's Gardens. 4—The Gardens of Edwin Treadwell's House. Act II.—Scene 1—Lounge Room of the Track Club, Havana. 2—Gardens of the Club. 3—Private Suite at the Sevilla-Biltmore Hotel. 4—Boston Post Road.

Billy Howe is a smart young mechanic in the Treadwell Auto factory, and Joyce Baxter is the prettiest of the stenographers. Some day they hope to marry and buy a tearoom and filling station on the Boston Post Road. Then Treadwell discovers Joyce and offers her a trip around the world as his secretary. Joyce doesn't want to leave Billy but Billy makes the sacrifice. Later they meet in Havana, where Billy is a rich gambler. Finally they are poor again and happy and the filling station looms large.

* THE HAPPY HUSBAND

(46 performances)

A comedy in three acts by Harrison Owen. Produced by Gilbert Miller at the Empire Theatre, New York, May 7, 1928.

Cast of characters—

Arthur Tolhurst	George Thorpe
Bill Rendell	Lawrence Grossmith
Frank K. Pratt	Walter Connolly
Dot Rendell	Billie Burke
"Sosso" Stephens	Mackenzie Ward
Sylvia Fullerton	Nancy Ryan
Harvey Townsend	A. E. Matthews
Consuelo Pratt	Ilka Chase
Stella Tolhurst	Irene Browne
Ada	Alice Moffat
Burglar	John Williams

Acts I, II and III.—The Hall of the Tolhursts' Country House. Staged by A. E. Matthews.

Dot Rendell is disappointed that her chuckle-headed husband, Bill, never suspects her of even so much as a mild flirtation with another man. When Harvey Townsend, a notorious philanderer, is caught by a burglar in the south room with a lady, and every woman in the house, except Dot, including the maids, is suspected of being Harvey's companion, Mrs. Rendell boastfully declares her own guilt. But her husband will not believe her even when she confesses. She manages finally to arouse Rendell's jealousy and is satisfied.

LITTLE THEATRE TOURNAMENT

(7 performances)

Conducted by Walter Hartwig, in coöperation with the Manhattan Little Theatre Club, Inc., for the David Belasco Trophy, at The Frolic Theatre, New York, the week of May 7, 1928.

MONDAY EVENING, MAY 7

Ye Curtaine Players of Manhattan in "Carnival," by Arthur Fribourg.
The Cast—

The Duke of Mantua	Richard A. Zinn
The Duchess of Mantua	Lois K. Fribourg
Jacopo, Their Son	Edward Bendhem
Velata, His Sister	Helen T. Morse
Beppo, Servant to the Duke	Arnold S. Miller
Barbara, Another Servant	Audrey M. Miller
Sir James Crighton, Tutor to Jacopo	Nathan L. Fribourg
Glos, His Servant	Ben Grauer
A Clown	Emil W. Bloch
A Reveler	Janice Adelsberg

A Reveler .... Ruth Butler
Masked Man... Johnson Gray
Scene—The Courtyard of the Home of the Duke of Mantua.
Directed by Marjory D. Zinn.

The Mansfield Players of Manhattan in "Wine of Life," by Amy L.
Weber.
The Cast—
Phenicia, Cook and Washerwoman.................. Juanita Stewart
Impy.. David Mindlin
Pete.................⎫   ⎧........ Basil Leather
Shorty..............⎪   ⎪........ Alvin Stern
Teddy...............⎬.....his gang......⎨..... Ronald Leather
Ked.................⎭   ⎩... Frederick Luhnow
Mrs. Morrow, a War Widow and Mother.......... Louise Mansfield
Harvey Powers, an Insurance Collector.......... C. Ruphert Ardsley
Richard Morrow, Shell-shocked Son............. Herbert Strickland
John Morrow, College Graduate.................... H. N. Parsons

The Manhattan College Players of Manhattan in "The Outcast," by
August Strindberg.
The Cast—
Mr. X, an Archeologist............................. Robert Walsh
Mr. Y, a Traveller from America.................... Leo Garvey
Directed by John Kanaley.

The Association Players Stock Company of the Y.M.H.A., Manhat-
tan, in "The Dance Below," by Hudson Strode and Larry Hornthal.
The Cast—
John Bates.. Pat Feil
Paul Knox.. Saul Trochman
Agnes........ .... Eve Lynn
Scene—A Living Room in Hell—Late Afternoon.
Directed by Myron E. Sattler.

TUESDAY EVENING, MAY 8

The Dramatic Union of Our Lady of Lourdes of Manhattan, in
"Wedding Presents," by John W. Rogers, Jr.
The Cast—
Raymond Oliver............................... Edward F. Finney
Mary Morrow, His Fiancée........................ Virginia Warder
Mrs. Morrow, Mary's Mother..................... Gladys Ruton
Judge Morrow, Mary's Father..................... John C. Hiro
Octavia Wrenn, a Cousin of Mrs. Morrow............ Mabel Burke
Scene—The Back Parlor of the Morrow Home.
Directed by Gertrude Wainwright.

The Thalian Players of the Bronx Y.M.H.A., the Bronx, in "The
Valiant," by Holworthy Hall and Robert Middlemass.
The Cast—
Warden Holt, About 60......................... Emanuel Weider
Father Daly, the Prison Chaplain.................. Samuel Roland
James Dyke, the Prisoner........................... John H. Brown
Josephine Paris, the Girl........................... Elise Maillard
Dan, a Jailer..................................... Charles D'Yuro
Scene—The Warden's Office in the State's Prison at Wethersfield,
Conn., About Half-past Eleven.
Directed by Philip Gross.

The Krigwa Players Little Negro Theatre, Associated with The
Workers Drama League, of Manhattan, in "Aftermath," by Mary
Burrill.
The Cast—
Mam Sue... Marion King
John Thornton, A.E.F. .... Siegie Bell
Millie, John's Sister.............................. Helen McIntosh
Lonnie, John's Brother............................. James Brown
Mrs. Hawkins, a Neighbor........................ Margaret Foster

Rev. Luke Moseby.............................Charles Burroughs
Scene—The Thornton Cabin in South Carolina.

The Center Players of Temple Ansche Chesed of Manhattan in
"Jubilee," by Herman Heijermans.
The Cast—
The Director......................................Irving Davidson
Warden...Joseph Kehoe
Number One Hundred Thirteen.....................Harold Levey
His Daughter..Irene Cohn
Number Seven..Allen Seigel
Number Two Hundred Fifteen........................Al. Luloff
Number Eighty-three.............................Jerome Kanner
His Mother..Dorothy Herbst
Number Sixty-seven.............................Raymond Miller
Directed by Henry Howard.

WEDNESDAY EVENING, MAY 9

The Jackson Heights Players of Jackson Heights, N. Y., in "Prison
Bars," by Carl Bixby.
The Cast—
Sir Gaston, Counselor to King Richard...............O. J. Gude, Jr.
Lady Edithe, His Wife.............................Octavia Hicks
Sir Harold..Carl Bixby
Richard Cœur de Lion...........................Horace Canning
Scene—A Chamber in Sir Gaston's Home.

The Brookside Open Air Theatre, of Mount Kisco, New York, in "A
Tale Retold," by Martia Leonard.
The Cast—
Adam......................................Robert Hugh Hamilton
Eve..Jane King
Lilith..Gertrude Connell
Scene—The Garden of Eden.

The Community Players of Mount Vernon, New York, in "Little
Italy," by Horace B. Fry.
The Cast—
Fabio Rinaldo, an Italian Baker of Forty..........George Pendleton
Michele, an Itinerant Singer of Twenty-five.......Wolfango Cribari
Guila, Fabio's Wife, a Nervous, Hard-working Woman of Twenty-two
.... Florence Aitken Tompkins
Goija Pinaldi, a Girl of Eight Years, Step-daughter of Guila........
....Adele Ritchie
Scene—The Italian Quarter on the East Side of New York City.
Directed by Holland Hudson.

The Maskers of the Y.M.H.A., of Elizabeth, N. J., in "Where the
Cross Is Made," by Eugene O'Neill.
The Cast—
Nat Bartlett..................................... Daniel Wagner
Doctor Higgins...............................Joseph M. Feinberg
Sue Bartlett....................................Florence L. Levy
Capt. Isaiah Bartlett...........................Samuel J. Marantz
Scene—Captain Bartlett's "Cabin" at the Top of His House Situated
on a High Point of Land on the California Coast.
Directed by Sara Shakow.

THURSDAY EVENING, MAY 10

The Players' Club of Columbus, Ohio, in "Trifles," by Susan Glaspell.
The Cast—
George Henderson, County Attorney..................Edwin Judy
Henry Peters, a Sheriff......................Ferd P. Schoedinger
Lewis Hale, a Neighboring Farmer................Phil S. Bradford
Mrs. Peters..............................Gladys Hamilton Mohler
Mrs. Hale..................................Agnes Jeffrey Shedd

Scene—A Kitchen.
Directed by Stokes McCune.

The Blackfriars of Agnes Scott College, Decatur, Georgia, in "Pink and Patches," by Margaret Bland.
The Cast—
Texie Hollifield, a Mountain Girl................Elizabeth McCallie
Rexie Hollifield, Her Twin Brother...............Frances Freeborn
Mrs. Hollifield, Their Mother.........................Louisa Duls
Mrs. Allen, the "Summer Lady" from the Hotel........Sara Carter
Scene—The Side Yard of the Hollifields' Mountain Cabin Near Little Switzerland, North Carolina.
Directed by Frances K. Gooch.

The Ardrossan and Saltcoats Players of Ardrossan, Scotland, in "The Old Lady Shows Her Medals," by Sir James M. Barrie.
The Cast—
Mrs. Dowey, a Charwoman........................Isabel Jamieson
Mrs. Mickleham, a Charwoman...................Nora Huntingford
Mrs. Tully, a Charwoman...........................Nettie Taylor
Mrs. Huggerty, a Charwoman......................May Hamilton
Mr. Wilkinson, a Clergyman..................Harold L. Wightman
Private Kenneth Dowey (Black Watch)...............Jack Lambert
Scene—The Home of Mrs. Dowey in a London Basement During the War.
Directed by James T. Woodburn.

The Community Theatre of Poughkeepsie, New York, in "The White Peacock," by Priscilla Flowers.
The Cast—
Harlequin, a Youth of Bergamo................Theodore H. Moller
His Mother....................................Elizabeth Haggerty
His Father...................................Raymond Baumbusch
Bettina..Pauline Girard
Flaminia..................................Sylvia Decker Crauer
Scaramouche..............................Philip M. Kerridge, Jr.
Old Doctor Gratiano, Pantaloon.....................M. A. Couper
Columbine, his daughter............................Bonnie Dow
Pierrot, His Apprentice.........................William Clinton
Flavio..Richard O'Donnell
His Servant......................................William Clock
Directed by Antoinette Swan.

FRIDAY EVENING, MAY 11

The Birmingham Little Theatre of Birmingham, Alabama, in "'Lijah," by Edgar Valentine Smith.
The Cast—
Judge Holmstead............................William T. Warren
First Stranger....................................J. N. Yates, Jr.
Second Stranger....................................H. G. Mann
'Bama...Martha Ordway
Scene—Living Room at Home Acres.
Directed by Bernard Szold.

The Town Theatre of Savannah, Georgia, in "Hero Worship," by Frances Hargis.
The Cast—
"Robby" Robbins, a Civil War Veteran..............Ole Burroughs
Mrs. Robbins.....................................Lucy McIntire
Sam Robbins, Their Orphaned Grandson..............John Mercer
Sally Mitchell, Their Daughter....................Augusta Lynah
Scene—Kingston, Georgia, a Small Town About Sixty Miles from Atlanta.

The Memphis Little Theatre of Memphis, Tennessee, in "The Dreamy Kid," by Eugene O'Neill.
The Cast—
Mammy Saunders..................................Martha Frost
Abe, Her Grandson............................Clifford Penland

Ceely Ann..................................Ethel Sivley Moore
Irene...Allison Davant
Scene—Mammy Saunders' Bedroom in a House Just Off Carmine Street, New York.
Directed by Alexander Wyckoff.

The Manhattan Theatre of Manhattan, Kansas, in "The Other Room," by Frances Witherspoon.
The Cast—
Annie Darr.......................................Renna Raeburn
Rev. Graham......................................Miles Heberer
Matthew Darr.......................................Paul Pfeutze
Bob Anderson....................................James Maxwell
Scene—The Living Room at the Darrs' in a Small Eastern Town.
Directed by Miles Heberer.

At the conclusion of the tournament prizes were awarded the Androssan and Saltcoats Players of Androssan, Scotland; The Thalian Players of the Bronx Y.M.H.A.; the Town Theatre of Savannah, Ga., and the Blackfriars of Agnes Scott College, Decatur, Ga. The Belasco trophy was awarded the Androssan Players for their performance of Sir James Barrie's "The Old Lady Shows Her Medals."

THE HIGH HATTERS

(12 performances)

A farce comedy in three acts by Louis Sobol. Produced by Louis Isquith, Inc., at the Klaw Theatre, New York, May 10, 1928.

Cast of characters—
Bim...Gilbert Douglas
Cookie.......................................Thomas H. Manning
Doctor Pendragon Quarrie............................John Robb
Miss Jellison..............................Josephine MacNicol
Ellen Quarrie..............................Marguerite McNulty
The Lady in Red...........................Marie Louise Walker
The Lady in Black..............................Juanita Hansen
Dick Halloway..............................Robert Montgomery
Chief of Police Halloran...............Robert Webb Lawrence
The Man in Brown................................Willard Hall
Hank, the Chauffeur...............................Billy Stone
Carabelli......................................Walter Pearson
Prologue—Dressing Room of a Vaudeville Theatre, Tarrytown, N. Y. Acts I, II and III.—Dr. Quarrie's Sanitarium for Psychoneurotics, Near Tarrytown, N. Y.
Staged by Ralph Murphy.

Bim and Cookie, crooks, scheme admission to a sanitarium as patients. From this point of vantage they rob the neighboring rich folk, but several of their fellow patients turn out to be planted secret-service operators and they are caught.

* BLACKBIRDS OF 1928

(43 performances)

A musical revue in prologue and two parts; lyrics by Dorothy Fields; music by Jimmy McHugh. Produced by Lew Leslie at the Liberty Theatre, New York, May 9, 1928.

Principals engaged—

Adelaide Hall	Bill Robinson
Aida Ward	Tim Moore
Ruth Johnson	Crawford Jackson
Marjorie Hubbard	Blue McAllister
Eloise Uggams	Lloyd Mitchell
Billie Cortez	George Cooper
Mamie Savoy	Mantan Moreland
Elizabeth Welch	Harry Lucas
Baby Banks	Willard McLean
Philip Patterson	Earl Tucker
Staged by Lew Leslie.	

THE FATHER

(8 performances)

A play in three acts by August Strindberg (Robert Whittier's Version). Produced by Robert Whittier (by arrangement with Richard Herndon) at the Belmont Theatre, New York, May 11, 1928.

Cast of characters—

The Captain	Robert Whittier
The Pastor	Albert Reed
Sjord	Edward Broadley
Nojd	Edward E. Hale
Laura	Florence Johns
The Doctor	Robert Le Sueur
Margaret	Kate Mayhew
Bertha	Peggy Keenan

Acts I, II and III Take Place in the Captain's Quarters Adjoining the Barracks.

Staged by Allan Dinehart.

A wife deliberately deludes her husband into the belief that he is not the father of his much-loved daughter. Insanity develops and the husband is finally tricked into a straitjacket by his old nurse. Death solves his problem.

SHE STOOPS TO CONQUER

(16 performances)

A revival of Oliver Goldsmith's play in five acts, prologue by David Garrick. Produced by George C. Thler at Erlanger's Theatre, New York, May 14, 1928.

Cast of characters—

Sir Charles Marlow	Lawrance D'Orsay
Young Marlow	Wilfrid Seagram
Jeremy	George Tawde
Squire Hardcastle	Lyn Harding
Mrs. Hardcastle	Mrs. Leslie Carter
Kate Hardcastle	Fay Bainter
Tony Lumpkin	Glenn Hunter
Maid to Miss Hardcastle	Marie Carroll
Diggory	O. P. Heggie
George Hastings	Horace Braham
Constance Neville	Patricia Collinge
Stingo	Thos. Coffin Cooke
Jack Slang	George Tawde
Mat Muggins	John D. Saymour
Tim Twist	Harold Thomas
Aminadab	William Lorenz
A Bar Maid	Suzanne Lawrance

Acts I, II, III, IV and V.—A Room in Mr. Hardcastle's House, in an Ale-house, and the Back of the Garden at Mr. Hardcastle's. Staged by William Seymour.

IN LOVE WITH LOVE

(8 performances)

A play in three acts by Vincent Lawrence. Produced by Joseph E. Shea at the Cosmopolitan Theatre, New York, May 14, 1928.

Cast of characters—

Robert Metcalf	Percy Helton
Ann Jordan	Miriam Meehan
Mr. Jordan	Marshall Vincent
Julia	Flavia Arcara
Frank Oakes	Philip Tonge
Miriam Sears	Margaret Borough
Robert Gardner	Brandon Tynan

Acts I, II and III.—Mr. Jordan's Home. Staged by Mr. Shea.

See "Best Plays of 1923-24."

ANNA

(31 performances)

A play in three acts by Rudolph Lothar; adapted by Herman Bernstein and Brian Marlow. Produced by Samuel Samach at the Lyceum Theatre, New York, May 15, 1928.

Cast of characters—

Anna Plumer	Judith Anderson
Olga Metz	Jean Dixon
Model	Diane Brook
Peter Torrelli	Lou Tellegen
Freddie	Harold Vermilyea
Plumer	J. Malcom Dunn
Otto Marbach	Ben Johnson
Kohnlein	Cecil Owen

Acts I, II and III.—The Studio of Peter Torrelli.
Place—A City in Europe.
Staged by Edgar J. MacGregor.

Anna Plumer, in love with Peter Torrelli, sculptor, smuggles herself into his studio as a model. She knows that Torrelli has sworn not to know her because she is the daughter of his rich patron. Anna wagers Torrelli that he will hold the rich girl he claims to despise in his arms within a month—and he does. Which fixes everything.

* GET ME IN THE MOVIES

(30 performances)

A farce comedy in three acts by Charlton Andrews and Philip Dunning. Produced by Laura D. Wilck at the Earl Carroll Theatre, New York, May 21, 1928.

Cast of characters—

Jim Jackson	Pat Ahearn
Miss Starbuck	Doris Rich
Dorothy Gray	Mildred Van Dorn
Cicely Arno	Gwendolyn Hathaway
Mrs. Pringle	Evelyn Carter Carrington
Mrs. Calkins	Clara Thropp
Johnny Loring	Sterling Holloway
Secretary	Paul Ker
Benjamin Roth	Alan Devitt
Count Henrico Mardones	Lenore Sorsby
Dolores Calkins	Courtney White
Tony Baduro	Sheila Trent
Queenie Quaint	Helen Baxter
Fame Dawson	Charles Hanna
Sergeant Smith	

Acts I, II and III.—Johnny Loring's Apartment in Hollywood.
Staged by Ralph Murphy.

Johnny Loring of Sheboygan, Mich., wins a prize for a pure scenario and goes to Hollywood to capitalize. He is given a big publicity reception after being mistaken for a nobody. Thereafter he is besieged by vamps, soubrettes and other ladies who are eager to make any sacrifice to get in the movies. For the love of his Sheboygan sweetheart Johnny fights off temptation and emerges mussed but triumphantly pure.

* SKIDDING

(30 performances)

A comedy in three acts by Aurania Rouverol. Produced by Hyman Adler and Marion Gering, Inc., at the Bijou Theatre, New York, May 21, 1928.

Cast of characters—

Aunt Milly	Louise Carter
Andy	Charles Eaton
Mrs. Hardy	Clara Blandick
Judge James Hardy	Carleton Macy
Grandpa Hardy	Burr Caruth
Estelle Hardy Campbell	Isabel Dawn
Marion Hardy	Marguerite Churchill
Wayne Trenton, III	Walter Abel
Mr. Stubbins	Thomas V. Morrison
Myra Hardy Wilcox	Joan Madison

Acts I, II and III.—The Living Room of Judge Hardy in a Certain Town in Idaho.
Staged by Marion Gering.

Marion Hardy, daughter of a judge in a small Idaho town, returns from school in the East engaged to a young New Yorker. Being wilful and bent upon a career, Marion is turned away from matrimony by the spectacle presented by her slaving married sisters. She goes into politics, quarrels with her fiancé (who believes woman's place is in the home) and helps elect her father to office. Then she gives in to matrimony.

DORIAN GRAY

(16 performances)

A play in prologue and three acts by David Thorne (based on Oscar Wilde's story, "The Picture of Dorian Gray"). Produced by The Oscaria Theatre Corporation at Chanin's Biltmore Theatre, New York, May 21, 1928.

Cast of characters—

IN THE PROLOGUE

Satan..Wallis Clark
Seraph.. Burton Mallory
Voice of God.....................................Lionel Adams

IN THE PLAY

Lord Henry Wotton................................Wallis Clark
Basil Hallward...................................Lionel Adams
André...................................... K. Andrew Fernando
Dorian Gray...................................... Howard Cull
Lord George Fermor..............................Ray L. Royce
Duchess of Harley...............................Helen Holmes
Alan Campbell..................................Burton Mallory
Sibyl Vane......................................Adele Ronson
Mazie Kent...................................Ruth Chorpenning
James Vane......................................Will Marsh
Parker...Raoul De Leon
Prologue—In Heaven. Act I.—Basil Hallward's Studio, London.
Act II and Act III, Scene 2—Dorian Gray's Home. Act III.—
Scene 1—An Opium Den.
Staged by Augustus Thorne.

The soul of Dorian Gray is analytically dissected in heaven by
Satan, Seraph and Voice of God. On earth Dorian's fatal beauty
involves him in many scandals leading to the suicide of his sweetheart, the murder of his best friend and finally his own murder at
the hands of his sweetheart's brother.

*THE ROAD TO ROME

(30 performances)

A comedy in three acts by Robert Emmet Sherwood. Presented by William A. Brady, Jr., and Dwight Deere Wiman at
the Playhouse, New York, May 21, 1928.

Cast of characters—

Varius.. Fairfax Burgher
Meta...Joyce Carey
Fabia...Jessie Ralph
Fabius..Richie Ling
Amytis... Jane Cowl
Scipio... Charles Brokaw
Cato...Ben Lackland
Drusus..................................... William R. Randall
Sertorius... Lionel Hogarth
Tibullus..Alfred Webster
Sergeant.......................................John T. McNulty
Corporal .... Lewis Martin
First Guard....................................Clement O'Loghlen
Second Guard......................................Ben Lackland
Third Guard....................................Walter A. Kinsella
Fourth Guard..............................Laurence W. Adams
Fifth Guard....................................... Daniel Coxe
Thotmes...Lionel Hogarth
Hasdrubel.. Hale Norcross
Maherbal...Alfred Webster
Carthalo...George Tobias
Mago .... Barry Jones

Hannibal...Guy Standing
Bala...Gert Pouncy
    Act I.—A Courtyard in the House of Fabius Maximus at Rome;
Acts II and III.—Hannibal's Headquarters in a Temple About Three
Miles East of Rome.
    Staged by Lester Lonergan.

See "Best Plays of 1926-27."

* GRAND ST. FOLLIES

(22 performances)

A musical revue in nineteen acts; book and lyrics by Agnes
Morgan; music by Max Ewing, Lily Hyland and Serge Walter.
Produced by the Actor-Managers, Inc., at the Booth Theatre,
New York, May 28, 1928.

Principals engaged—

Albert Carroll	Dorothy Sands
Marc Loebell	Vera Allen
James Cagney	Paula Trueman
Otto Hulett	Joanna Roos
Harold Minjer	Lily Lubell
George Bratt	Mae Noble
Hal Brogan	Mary Williams
George Hoaz	Frances Cowles
Richard Ford	Edla Frankau
Blake Scott	Laura Emond
George Heller	Jean Crittenden
Milton Leroy	Ruth McConkie
Michael McCormick	John Rynee
Harold Hecht	

Staged by Agnes Morgan.

* DIPLOMACY

(22 performances)

An English version of a play in four acts by Victorien Sardou.
Revived by George C. Tyler at Erlanger's Theatre, New York,
May 28, 1928.

Cast of characters—

Markham...Tyrone Power
Mion..Georgette Cohan
Henry Beauclerc...............................William Faversham
Madame La Marquise De Rio-Zares.................Cecilia Loftus
Michael Orloff.....................................Jacob Ben-Ami
Captain Julian Beauclerc..........................Rollo Peters
Algie Fairfax.....................................Antony Holles
Lady Henry Fairfax............................Margaret Anglin
Dora..Frances Starr
Comtesse Zicka..................................Helen Gahagan
Baron Stein.....................................Charles Coburn

Antoine.......................................Georges Renavent
Sheppard......................................Guy Cunningham
    Act I.—Apartment in a Hotel in Monte Carlo. Acts II and III.—
Henry Beauclerc's Rooms in Champs Elysées. Act IV.—British Embassy, Paris.
    Staged by Campbell Gullan.

An English version of Victorien Sardou's "Dora," used by Gerald Du Maurier in which the diplomat, Henry Beauclerc, fastens the stolen papers on the Comtesse Zicka through the scent of the perfume she affects, and thus saves his brother Julian.

THE BEAUX STRATAGEM

(8 performances)

A revival of a play in four acts by George Farquhar, prologue by Edgar Lee Masters. Produced by The Players at Hampden's Theatre, New York, June 4, 1928.

Cast of characters—

Boniface, Landlord of the Inn.................Raymond Hitchcock
Aimwell.......................................Wilfrid Seagram
Archer..Fred Eric
Cherry..Dorothy Stickney
Scrub...James T. Powers
Gipsey..Ruth Hammond
Dorinda.......................................Helen Menken
Mrs. Sullen...................................Fay Bainter
Sullen..Lyn Harding
Gibbet..William Courtleigh
Foigard.......................................John Daly Murphy
Count Bellair.................................John Westley
A Countrywoman................................Kate Mayhew
Lady Bountiful................................Henrietta Crosman
Hounslow......................................Paul A. Curtis
Gagshot.......................................Herbert Ranson
Sir Charles Freeman...........................O. P. Heggie
A Countryman..................................Owen Meech
Servants in the Inn...........................{ Josephine Hull
                                         { F. H. Day
Soldiers—Reinald Werrenrath, William Gustafson, James Stanley, Robert I. Aitken, Joseph Cummings Chase, Ray Vir Den, Thomas Chalmers, Ernest Hunter, William B. Taylor, Edwin T. Emery, John C. King, Raymond Thayer.
Travellers—Patterson McNutt, Eric Pape, Jack O'Donnell, Loren Stout, Brian Hooker, Frederic Dorr Steele, Harry Grant Dart, T. C. Pakenham, Thompson Sweeny, George B. Fife, Pamela Hooker, Judith Vosselli, Essie Mercedes.
Epilogue by David Belasco.
    Acts I, II, III and IV.—At the Inn, at Lady Bountiful's and in Mrs. Sullen's Bedroom.
    Staged by Howard Lindsay.

Aimwell and Archer, adventuring gentlemen more or less in disguise, invade an inn, make love to the unhappy Mrs. Sullen and her sister Dorinda and are exposed to their final advantage.

* THE CYCLONE LOVER

(13 performances)

A comedy in three acts by Fred Ballard and Charles A. Bickford. Produced by W. Herbert Adams and Roy Walling at the Frolic Theatre, New York, June 5, 1928.

Cast of characters—

John Black	Thomas McLarnie
Katherine	Suzanne Bennett
James Lacey	Harold Wolfe
Bob White	Harold Elliott
Betty Black	Emily Graham
Judge Fish	John C. Brownell
Tony Mariochetti	Theodore Hecht
Pansy Fish	Eugenia Woodward
Maggie	Beatrice Loring
Harry	Al Roberts
Captain O'Dell	William Crimans

Act I.—Scene 1—John Black's Office, New York. 2—Home of Judge Fish. Acts II and III.—A Yacht.
Staged by Al Roberts and Roy Walling.

Bob White, timid with women, undertakes to place an insurance policy with Lloyds guaranteeing John Black that his daughter Betty will not marry Tony Mariochetti, an alleged artist. White, falling desperately in love with Betty, becomes cyclonic in his love making, abducts Betty to keep her from Mariochetti, and after many adventures wins her love.

* MARRIED—AND HOW!

(1 performance)

A comedy in three acts by Ray Hodgdon. Produced by Phil Bush at the Little Theatre, New York, June 14, 1928.

Cast of characters—

Joe Graham	Jerry Devine
Vie Tracy	Peggy Allenby
Elevator Man	Albert Berg
Flo Ballinger	Dulcie Cooper
Phil Ballinger	Robert Bentley
Jim Carroll	George Le Guere
John Ballinger	Walter Jones
Doctor Lewis	Robert Le Sueur
Doctor Stewart	Joseph Baird
Nurse Durkin	Ethelynn Bradford

Acts I, II and III.—The Ballingers' Living Room in an Apartment in the West Forties.
Staged by Priestly Morrison.

Phil Ballinger, following a party, marries Flo of the chorus, gives the wedding party a wild week at Atlantic City, returns to New York to find himself disinherited and broke. Flo is for making a fuss to get even with her father-in-law, Phil wants to get a job and make good. Phil is knocked down by a car driven by Flo's younger brother and the care of him brings Flo and Phil together and softens the anger of the father-in-law.

STATISTICAL SUMMARY

(Last Season Plays Which Ended Runs After June 15, 1927)

Plays	Number Performances
Abie's Irish Rose	2,318
Baby Mine	12
Barker, The	221
Broadway	603
Caponssachi	269
Circus Princess, The	192
Constant Wife, The	295
Countess Maritza	318
Crime	186
Desert Song, The	471
George White's Scandals	424
Gertie	248
Grand Street Follies	148
Her Cardboard Lover	152
Hit the Deck	352
Honeymoon Lane	364
In Abraham's Bosom	200
Kempy	46
Ladder, The	640
Lombardi, Ltd.	24
Merry-go-Round	136
Mr. Pim	72

Plays	Number Performances
Mystery Ship	120
Ned McCobb's Daughter	156
Night in Spain, A	222
Oh, Ernest	56
Oh, Kay	256
(return engagement 16 performances)	
Peggy Ann	333
Play's the Thing, The	326
Queen High	378
Road to Rome, The	392
(return engagement 32 performances)	
Rio Rita	494
Saturday's Children	310
Second Man, The	178
Spider, The	319
Squall, The	444
Talk About Girls	13
Thief, The	83
Tommy	232
Triple Crossed	52
2 Girls Wanted	320
Very Wise Virgin, A	20
Woman in Bronze, The	30
Wooden Kimono	209

The number of performances played by each attraction during the season of 1927-28 is given with the record of production.

PLAYS THAT HAVE RUN OVER 500 PERFORMANCES ON BROADWAY

To June 15, 1928

Plays	Number Performances	Plays	Number Performances
Abie's Irish Rose	2,532	Student Prince	608
Lightnin'	1,291	Broadway	603
The Bat	867	Adonis	603
The First Year	760	Kiki	600
Seventh Heaven	704	Blossom Time	592
Peg o' My Heart	692	The Show-off	571
East Is West	680	Sally	570
Irene	670	The Music Master	540
A Trip to Chinatown	657	The Boomerang	522
Rain	648	Sunny	517
The Ladder	640	The Vagabond King	511
Is Zat So	618	Shuffle Along	504

WHERE AND WHEN THEY WERE BORN

Abarbanell, Lina............Berlin 1880
Abbott, George ....Forestville, N. Y.........1895
Adams, Maude ....Salt Lake City, Utah 1872
Adelaide, La Petite ....Cohoes, N. Y. 1890
Allen, Viola ....Huntsville, Ala. 1869
Ames, Robert ....Hartford, Conn. 1893
Ames, Winthrop ....North Easton, Mass. 1871
Andrews, Ann ....Los Angeles, Cal. 1895
Anglin, Margaret ....Ottawa, Canada 1876
Anson, A. E. ....England 1879
Arbuckle, Maclyn ....San Antonio, Texas 1866
Arliss, George ....London, England 1868
Arthur, Julia ....Hamilton, Ont. 1869
Astaire, Adele ....Omaha, Neb. 1900
Astaire, Fred ....Omaha, Neb. 1899
Atwell, Roy.................Syracuse, N. Y. 1880
Atwill, Lionel ....London, England 1885

Bacon, Frank ....California 1864
Bainter, Fay ....Los Angeles, Cal. 1892
Barbee, Richard ....Lafayette, Ind. 1887
Barrie, James Matthew ......Kirriemuir, N. B. 1860
Barrymore, Ethel ....Philadelphia, Pa. 1879
Barrymore, John ....Philadelphia, Pa. 1882
Barrymore, Lionel ....London, England 1878
Bates, Blanche ....Portland, Ore. 1873
Bayes, Nora ....Milwaukee, Wis. 1880
Beban, George ....San Francisco, Cal. 1873
Beckley, Beatrice ....Roedean, England 1885
Best, Edna ....England 1901
Beecher, Janet ....Chicago, Ill. 1884
Belasco, David ....San Francisco, Cal. 1862
Ben-Ami, Jacob ....Minsk, Russia 1890
Bennett, Richard ....Cass County, Ind. 1873
Bennett, Wilda ....Asbury Park, N. J. 1894
Benrimo, J. Harry ....San Francisco, Cal. 1874

Dolly, Rosy ....Hungary 1892
Dolly, Jennie ....Hungary 1892
Donnelly, Dorothy Agnes .....New York 1880
Doro, Marie ....Duncannon, Pa. 1882
D'Orsay, Lawrence...........England 1860
Dressler, Marie ....Cobourg, Canada 1869
Drew, John ....Philadelphia, Pa. 1853
Drew, Louise ....New York 1884
Druce, Herbert ....England 1870
Duncan, Isadora ....San Francisco, Cal. 1880
Duncan, Augustin ....San Francisco, Cal. 1873
Dunn, Emma ....England 1875
Dupree, Minnie ....San Francisco, Cal. 1875
Duse, Eleanora ....Vigerano, Italy 1859

Eagels, Jeanne ....Kansas City, Mo. 1894
Eames, Clare ....Hartford, Conn. 1896
Eddinger, Wallace ....New York 1881
Edeson, Robert ....Baltimore, Md. 1868
Eldridge, Florence ....Brooklyn, N. Y. 1901
Ellis, Mary ....New York 1900
Elliston, Grace ....Wheeling, W. Va. 1881
Ellinger, Desirée ....Manchester, Vt. 1895
Elliott, Gertrude ....Rockland, Me. 1874
Elliott, Maxine ....Rockland, Me. 1871
Elliott, William ....Boston, Mass. 1885
Ellsler, Effie ....Philadelphia, Pa. 1898
Eltinge, Julian ....Boston, Mass. 1883
Emerson, John ....Sandusky, Ohio 1874
Errol, Leon ....Sydney, Australia 1881
Ewell, Lois ....Memphis, Tenn. 1885

Fairbanks, Douglas...........Denver, Colo. 1883
Farnum, Dustin ....Hampton Beach, N. H. ...1874
Farnum, William ....Boston, Mass. 1876
Farrar, Geraldine ....Melrose, Mass. 1883
Faversham, William ....Warwickshire, England ...1868
Fealy, Maude ....Memphis, Tenn. 1883
Fenwick, Irene ....Chicago, Ill. 1887
Ferguson, Elsie ....New York 1883
Fields, Lewis ....New York 1867
Findlay, Ruth ....New York 1897
Fischer, Alice ....Indiana 1869

Fisher, Lola .... Chicago, Ill. 1892
Fiske, Minnie Maddern .... New Orleans, La. 1867
Fontanne, Lynn .... London, England 1892
Forbes, Robertson, Sir J. ..... London, England 1853
Foy, Edward Fitzgerald .... New York 1854
Frederick, Pauline .... Boston, Mass. 1884
Friganza, Trixie .... Cincinnati, Ohio 1870
Frohman, Daniel .... Sandusky, Ohio 1850
Fulton, Maude .... St. Louis, Mo. 1883

Garden, Mary .... Scotland 1876
Gaythorne, Pamela .... England 1882
George, Grace .... New York 1879
Gillette, William .... Hartford, Conn. 1856
Gillmore, Frank .... New York 1884
Gillmore, Margalo .... England 1901
Glaser, Lulu .... Allegheny, Pa. 1874
Gleason, James .... New York 1885
Glendinning, Ernest .... Ulverston, England 1884
Gottschalk, Ferdinand .... London, England 1869
Grey, Jane .... Middlebury, Vt. 1883
Grey, Katherine .... San Francisco, Cal. 1873

Hackett, James K. .... Wolf Island, Ont. 1869
Haines, Robert T. .... Muncie, Ind. 1870
Hale, Louise Closser .... Chicago, Ill. 1872
Hall, Laura Nelson .... Philadelphia, Pa. 1876
Hamilton, Hale .... Topeka, Kansas 1880
Hampden, Walter .... Brooklyn, N. Y. 1879
Harding, Lyn .... Newport, England 1867
Harris, Sam H. .... New York 1872
Hawtrey, Charles .... Eton, England 1858
Hayes, Helen .... Washington, D. C. 1900
Hazzard, John E. .... New York 1881
Hedman, Martha .... Sweden 1888
Heggie, O. P. .... Australia 1879
Heming, Violet .... Leeds, England 1893
Herbert, Evelyn .... Brooklyn, N. Y. 1900
Herbert, Victor .... Dublin, Ireland 1859
Herne, Chrystal .... Dorchester, Mass. 1883
Hilliard, Robert .... New York 1857
Hitchcock, Raymond .... Auburn, N. Y. 1870
Hodge, William .... Albion, N. Y. 1874

Starr, Frances .... Oneonta, N. Y. 1886
Stevens, Emily .... New York 1882
Stone, Fred .... Denver, Colo. 1873
Sydney, Basil .... London 1894

Taliaferro, Edith .... New York 1892
Taliaferro, Mabel .... New York 1887
Tanguay, Eva .... Middletown, Conn. 1878
Taylor, Laurette .... New York 1884
Tell, Alma .... New York 1892
Tell, Olive .... New York 1894
Terry, Ellen .... Coventry, England 1848
Thomas, Augustus........... St. Louis, Mo. 1859
Thomas, John Charles .... Baltimore, Md. 1887
Tinney, Frank .... Philadelphia, Pa. 1878
Tobin, Genevieve .... New York 1901
Tobin, Vivian .... New York 1903
Toler, Sidney .... Warrensburg, Mo. 1874
Trevor, Norman .... Calcutta 1877
Treux, Ernest .... Denver, Colo. 1890
Tynan, Brandon .... Dublin, Ireland 1879

Ulric, Lenore .... New Ulm, Minn. 1897

Valentine, Grace .... Indianapolis, Ind. 1892
Varesi, Gilda .... Milan, Italy 1887
Victor, Josephine .... Hungary 1891

Wainwright, Marie .... Philadelphia, Pa. 1853
Walker, June .... New York 1904
Walker, Charlotte........... Galveston, Texas 1878
Warfield, David .... San Francisco, Cal. 1866
Warwick, Robert .... Sacramento, Cal. 1878
Ware, Helen .... San Francisco, Cal. 1877
Weber, Joseph .... New York 1867
Welford, Dallas .... Liverpool, England 1874
Westley, Helen .... Brooklyn, N. Y. 1879
Westman, Nydia .... White Plains, N. Y. 1906
Whiffen, Mrs. Thomas .... London, England 1845
Whiteside, Walker .... Logansport, Ind. 1869
Wilson, Francis............. Philadelphia, Pa. 1854
Winant, Forrest .... New York 1888
Winwood, Estelle .... England 1883

NECROLOGY

June 15, 1927—June 15, 1928

John Drew, actor, 73. For fifty-four years a leader in the American theatre; began with his mother's company in Philadelphia when he was 20; joined Augustin Daly in New York in 1875; played with Edwin Booth and in support of Fanny Davenport and with his brother-in-law, Maurice Barrymore, for a few seasons, and then returned to Daly, where he stayed until 1892. Became a star under Charles Frohman's direction and was a reigning favorite until 1915. Was with all-star revival of "Trelawny of the Wells" at the time of his death. Born Philadelphia, Pa.; died San Francisco, Cal., July 9, 1927.

Gregory Kelly, actor, 36. Gained prominence as a player of juvenile rôles, particularly in the Booth Tarkington comedies, "Seventeen" and "Clarence." Later featured in "The Butter and Egg Man." Played with Stuart Walker's Portmanteau Theatre and headed a local stock company with his wife, Ruth Gordon, in Indianapolis. Born New York; died New York, July 9, 1927.

Florence Roberts, actress, 56. Was prominent as leading woman of her husband's (Lewis Morrison's) company and well known in western stock companies for many years. A cousin of Theodore Roberts. Died Hollywood, Cal., July 17, 1927.

June Mathis, actress and scenario writer, 35. Had played in vaudeville and in several comedies before she turned to her scenario work, in which she was unusually successful, the writing of "The Four Horsemen of the Apocalypse" and the engagement of Rudolph Valentino to play the lead being two of her achievements. Died in the 48th Street Theatre, New York, during a performance of "The Squall," July 26, 1927.

Elita Proctor Otis, actress, 76. Starred for many years in such plays as "Oliver Twist," "The Sporting Duchess," and "The Two Orphans," afterward taking to vaudeville. Died Pelham, N. Y., August 13, 1927.

Delyle, Alda, prima donna, 33. Sang with the Ziegfeld "Follies" and the George White "Scandals." Died Chicago, August 27, 1927.

Amelia Bingham, actress, 58. For many years a prominent leading woman in American companies. Began with McKee Rankin on the Pacific coast; played in New York first in 1893 in "The Struggle for Life." In 1900 became manageress of the Bijou Theatre in New York and was successful as a producer for several years, notably with Clyde Fitch's "The Climbers." Played many engagements in western stock companies and was known to vaudeville for her "Big Moments from Great Plays." Born Hicksville, Ohio, 1869; died New York, September 1, 1927.

Arthur Deagon, comedian, 56. Prominent in George Ade's comedies and had played in many musical comedy hits, including "Rose Marie" and the "Follies." Was playing in "The Merry Malones" at the time of his death. Born Kilmarnock, Scotland; died Boston, Mass., September 4, 1927.

Johnny Ray, comedian, 68. Famed for years as an Irish character comedian, and starred with his wife, Emma, in "A Hot Old Time." Later went into pictures to do the "Bringing Up Father" series. Born Wales, family name Matthews; died Los Angeles, September 4, 1927.

Isadora Duncan, dancer, 49. Gained fame as the creator of interpretative dancing in the American theatre and later in England. Restored the Greek dances to the stage, both as interpreter and teacher. Born San Francisco, died in an automobile accident in Paris, September 14, 1927.

G. P. Huntley, comedian, 59. Known for his "silly-ass" English types in America musical comedies as well as numerous importations. Born Ireland; died London, September 21, 1927.

Tom Lewis, comedian, 63. Went on stage as a boy, known in minstrels, made his first comedy hit in Cohan's "Little Johnnie Jones." Born St. John, N. B.; died New York, October 19, 1927.

Florence Mills, colored comedienne, 29. One of the first and long the most popular comedienne of her race. Played in "Shuffle Along," "From Dixie to Broadway" and "The Blackbirds." Died New York, November 1, 1927.

Valli Valli, comedienne, 45. Sang in many American musical comedies, notably "The Merry Widow." Born Berlin; educated in London; died London, November 4, 1927.

Frank Bush, monologist, 71. For 54 years a prominent teller of

Irish and Jewish stories in vaudeville. Died Mt. Vernon, N. Y., November 14, 1927.

Henry W. Savage, manager, 68. Formerly a successful realtor in Boston, Mr. Savage took over the Castle Square Opera House when a client made a failure of it. Remaining in the theatrical business he produced many plays, notably the George Ade comedies, starting with "The Sultan of Sulu." He was the producer of "The Merry Widow," and made the first production of "Parsifal" in English. He was the organizer of the grand opera company that gave opera in English. Born New Durham, N. H.; died Boston, Mass., November 29, 1927.

Edward Rosenbaum, Sr., manager, 72. For many years prominent in directing the tours of the Ziegfeld "Follies." Died New York, December, 1927.

Charles Dickson, comedian, 67. Played in support of Robson and Crane, and was a member of the Lyceum Theatre stock company. Starred in "Incog." Later did some writing, being part author of "Three Twins." Born New York, family name Doblin; died New York, December 11, 1927.

Eva Randolph, actress, 64. Had played with Warfield in "The Auctioneer" and in support of E. H. Sothern. Died New York, December 27, 1927.

Theodore Westman, juvenile, 24. Played with his father, mother and sisters in vaudeville. Wrote "Solid Ivory." Died New York, November 22, 1927.

Dorothy Donnelly, actress and playwright, 48. For many years prominent as leading woman, particularly in the Bernard Shaw repertoire revived by Arnold Daly. Late years devoted to playwriting, with the books of many operettas to her credit, including those of "Blossom Time," "The Student Prince" and "My Maryland." Died New York, January 3, 1928.

Emily Stevens, actress, 46. Played her first engagements in the company of Mrs. Fiske, her aunt. Of late years won success as Hedda Gabler and played in "The Second Man" with the Theatre Guild. Died New York, January 2, 1928.

Charles Harbury, actor, 85. Many years with the Frohman companies. Played with David Warfield in 1923. Died Astors' Home, Staten Island, January 6, 1928.

Ralph Sipperley, actor, 38. As a comedian was featured in George Cohan's "A Prince There Was" and "The Fall Guy." Died Bangor, Me., January, 1928.

Guy Nichols, actor, 65. Played in support of leading stars for 50 years. Last engagement with "The Shannons of Broadway." Died Hempstead, N. Y., January 23, 1928.

Wallace McCutcheon, actor, 47. Came to prominence as a dancer, played numerous comedy rôles, achieved fame and a major's commission in the war; tried pictures. Died Los Angeles, Cal., January 27, 1928.

Forest Winant, actor, 36. Played juvenile and light comedy rôles. Died Alameda, Cal., January 30, 1928.

Eddie Foy, comedian, 71. Spent 57 years on the stage, a good part of that time as a featured performer, and later as a star of musical comedy. Last years devoted to vaudeville, with and without his seven children as partners. Died Kansas City, Mo., February 16, 1928.

William H. Crane, actor, 83. Began, at the age of 19, with the Holman opera company. Achieved prominence as a comedian which resulted in his joining with Stuart Robson for a series of comedy successes including "The Henrietta." Later, as an independent star, was widely popular in "The Senator" and "David Harum." Retired ten years ago. Born Leicester, Mass.; died Hollywood, Cal., March 7, 1928.

Nora Bayes, comedienne, 48. From obscure beginnings rose to a position of high artistic and salary prominence as a singer of popular songs. On the stage about 30 years. Co-starred with Jack Norworth for many seasons. Born Milwaukee, Wis.; died New York, March 19, 1928.

Tom Wise, actor, 63. Gained prominence as a comedian in support of many old-time stars, later a star on his own account, notably with Douglas Fairbanks in "The Gentleman from Mississippi." Played Falstaff successfully in a revival of "The Merry Wives of Windsor." Born England; died New York, March 21, 1928.

Richard Claude Carton, playwright, 75. Famed as one of that successful trio of English dramatists, including Arthur Wing Pinero and Henry Arthur Jones. The author of a hundred plays, including "Lord and Lady Algy," "Liberty Hall," "The Squire of Dames," etc. Died London, March 31, 1928.

Georgia O'Ramey, comedienne, 42. Well known in musical comedy productions, her last engagement of importance being in "No, No, Nanette." Born Mansfield, Ohio; died New Haven, Conn., April 2, 1928.

Lydia Dickson, comedienne, 40. Played many character comedy

rôles, attracting attention first in Hoyt's "A Texas Steer."
Recently played in "The Old Soak" and "Chicago." Died
Los Angeles, April 2, 1928.

Frank Currier, actor, 71. Played in support of most of the old-
time stars, including Booth, Modjeska, Maude Adams. Last
nine years in pictures. Died Hollywood, Cal, April 22, 1928.

Johnny Dooley, comedian, 41. Popular comedian and acrobatic
dancer; in vaudeville for years with his brothers, William
and Gordon, and his second wife, Yvette Rugel. Later featured in Ziegfeld and Shubert revues. Rehearsing with Carroll "Vanities" when stricken. Born Glasgow, Scotland,
family name Dool; died Yonkers, N. Y., June 7, 1928.

INDEX OF AUTHORS

INDEX OF PLAYS AND CASTS